McGRAW-HILL

LANGUAGE ARTS TODAY

Great literature is an inspiration. Katherine Paterson's *The Great Gilly Hopkins* inspired artist Don Daily to create the illustration on the cover of your book. The story begins on page 192. We hope that you enjoy the story and the illustration!

SENIOR AUTHORS

ANN McCALLUM   WILLIAM STRONG   TINA THOBURN

Literature Consultant   Joan Glazer

McGraw-Hill School Division

New York   Farmington

ACKNOWLEDGMENTS

The publisher gratefully acknowledges permission to reprint the following copyrighted material:

"The Enormous Egg" is excerpted from *The Enormous Egg* by Oliver Butterworth. Copyright © 1956 by Oliver Butterworth; Copyright © renewed 1984 by Oliver Butterworth. By permission of Little, Brown and Company and Sidgwick & Jackson Ltd., London.

"The Great Gilly Hopkins" from *The Great Gilly Hopkins* by Katherine Paterson. (Thomas Y. Crowell). Copyright © 1978 by Katherine Paterson. Reprinted by permission of Harper & Row, Publishers, Inc.

"Japanese Houses" excerpted from *Shelters: From Tepee to Igloo* by Harvey Weiss (Thomas Y. Crowell). Copyright © 1988 by Harvey Weiss. Reprinted by permission of Harper & Row, Publishers, Inc.

"Lucy Looks Into a Wardrobe" from *The Lion, the Witch and the Wardrobe* by C. S. Lewis. Copyright © C. S. Lewis Pte Ltd. 1950. Published by William Collins Sons & Co Ltd. and used with their permission.

"Maggie Marmelstein for President" from *Maggie Marmelstein for President* by Marjorie Weinman Sharmat. Copyright © 1975 by Marjorie Weinman Sharmat. Reprinted and recorded by permission of Harper & Row, Publishers, Inc.

"Project Turtle" from *Turtle Watch* by George Ancona. Copyright ©1987 by George Ancona. Used by permission of the author.

"Zeely" is excerpted from *Zeely* by Virginia Hamilton. Copyright © 1967 by Virginia Hamilton. Reprinted with the permission of Macmillan Publishing Company. Reprinted also and recorded by permission of McIntosh and Otis, Inc.

Poems, Brief Quotations, and Excerpts

"They're Tearing Down a Town" by Jed Strunk from *The Saturday Evening Post*, 1974. © 1974 The Curtis Publishing Co. Reprinted by permission.

Excerpt from "Surprises" by Jean Conder Soule is used by permission of the author.

Haiku by Gaki and by Kyorai from *Birds, Frogs, and Moonlight* translated by Sylvia Cassedy and Kunihiro Suetake. Reprinted by permission of Sylvia Cassedy.

"Hog-Calling Competition" by Morris Bishop from *Spilt Milk* (G. P. Putnam's Sons). Copyright © 1936, 1964 Alison Kingsbury Bishop. Originally in *The New Yorker*. Used by permission.

Excerpt from "National Book Award Acceptance Speech" by Katherine Paterson. Copyright © 1979 by Katherine Paterson. Reprinted by permission of the author.

Excerpt from "The Door" from *Selected Poems* by Miroslav Holub, translated by Ian Milner and George Theiner (Penguin Modern European Poets, 1967). Copyright © Miroslav Holub, 1967, translation copyright © Penguin Books, 1967. Reprinted by permission of the publisher.

"Sea Shell" from *The Complete Poetical Works of Amy Lowell*. Copyright © 1955 by Houghton Mifflin Company. Copyright © 1983 renewed by Houghton Mifflin Company, Brinton P. Roberts, Esquire, and G. D'Andelot Belin, Esquire. Reprinted by permission of Houghton Mifflin Company.

"Seal" from *Laughing Time, Nonsense Poems* by William Jay Smith. Published by Delacorte Press, 1980. Copyright © 1955, 1980 by William Jay Smith. Reprinted by permission of William Jay Smith.

Excerpt from "The Elephant" in *Laughing Time: Nonsense Poems* by William Jay Smith, published by Delacorte Press, 1980. Copyright © 1955, 1957, 1980 by William Jay Smith. Reprinted by permission of William Jay Smith.

Brief quotation from Oliver Butterworth from *Fourth Book of Junior Authors & Illustrators*, edited by Doris de Montreville and Elizabeth D. Crawford. (Bronx, NY: HW Wilson, 1978) All rights reserved. Reprinted by permission of the publisher.

Haiku by Sho-u from *Cricket Songs*, Japanese haiku translated by Harry Behn. Copyright © 1964 by Harry Behn. All rights reserved. Reprinted by permission of Marian Reiner.

(Acknowledgments continued on page 553.)

Cover Design: Barnett-Brandt Design
Cover Illustration: Don Daily

McGraw-Hill School Division

A Division of The McGraw-Hill Companies

McGraw-Hill School Division
1221 Avenue of the Americas
New York, New York 10020

Printed in the United States of America

ISBN 0-02-244303-7

5 6 7 8 006/046 02 01 00 99

Classic Edition

McGRAW-HILL

LANGUAGE ARTS TODAY

C O N T E N T S

THEME: *SURPRISES*

AWARD WINNING
SELECTION

THEME: *PATTERNS*

Language Study

Writing

THEME: *PRIZES*

AWARD WINNING
SELECTION

THEME: *IMAGES*

AWARD WINNING
SELECTION

THEME: *VIEWS*

THEME: *ADVENTURES*

AWARD WINNING
SELECTION

THEME: *INVESTIGATIONS*

AWARD WINNING
SELECTION

WRITER'S REFERENCE

Sentences

- A **sentence** is a group of words that tells a complete thought.

- A **statement** is a sentence that tells something.
  It ends with a **period**.
  The Pacific Ocean is the world's largest ocean.

- A **question** is a sentence that asks something.
  It ends with a **question mark**.
  How many oceans are there?

- A **command** tells or asks someone to do something.
  It ends with a **period**.
  Count them.

- An exclamation shows strong feeling.
  It ends with an **exclamation mark**.
  I know the answer!

Write each group of words that is a sentence.

1. The Atlantic Ocean is the next largest ocean.
2. The largest body of water.
3. North of Antarctica.
4. The Indian Ocean is smaller than the Atlantic.

Write each sentence. Circle the sentences that are statements. Underline the sentences that are questions.

5. What are small bodies of salt water called?
6. They are seas.
7. The Mediterranean Sea is between Africa and Europe.

Write each command or exclamation. Add the correct end punctuation.

8. Find Italy on a map
9. Look for it by the Mediterranean Sea
10. Wow, how small it looks

Sentence Parts

- The **complete subject** includes all the words in the subject.
- The **simple subject** is the main word in the complete subject.
- The **complete predicate** includes all the words in the predicate.
- The **simple predicate** is the main word in the complete predicate.

complete subject complete predicate

The <u>bands</u> in parades <u>march</u> to a special
   ↓   ↓ kind of music.

 simple subject   simple predicate

Write each sentence. Draw a line between the complete subject and the complete predicate.

1. My brother marches with his band.
2. The parade will be on the Fourth of July
3. The band's route takes them down Main Street.
4. The long parade ends on Elm Street.

Write the complete subject of each sentence. Draw a line under the simple subject.

5. Many marches were written by John Philip Sousa.
6. He composed our most popular march tunes.
7. Almost all parades play at least one of his marches.
8. Every American has heard his *The Stars and Stripes Forever*.

Write the complete predicate of each sentence. Draw a line under the simple predicate.

9. My brother plays the tuba.
10. He practices his music every day.
11. I prefer the drums.
12. Our poor parents need ear plugs.

Nouns

- A **noun** is a word that names a person, place, or thing.
  The <u>engineer</u> made a new <u>plow</u>. It was used on <u>farms</u>.

↓	↓	↓
person	thing	place

- A **common noun** names any person, place, or thing. → **farm**

- A **proper noun** names a special person, place, or thing. → **Clover Valley Farm**

- A **possessive noun** shows who or what owns something.

- Add an **apostrophe** and an **s** to a singular noun to make it possessive. → **Josh's** hat

- Add an **apostrophe** to make most plural nouns possessive. → the **cows'** barn

- Add an apostrophe and an **s** to plural nouns that don't end in **s**. → **men's   deer's**

Write each sentence. Underline the nouns. Then write **person**, **place**, or **thing**.

1. A combine is a machine that harvests wheat on farms.
2. Then workers bring the grain to elevators in towns.

Write each noun. Write **common** or **proper** next to each noun.
3. corn   **4.** Kansas City   **5.** country   **6.** merchant

Write each sentence with the possessive form of the singular noun in parentheses.

7. (Iowa) main crop is corn.
8. That (state) climate is perfect for growing corn.

Write the plural possessive form of each phrase.

9. prices of the crops
10. chores of the children

Action Verbs

- An **action verb** is a word that expresses action.
  walk, **dance**, **jump**

- The **tense** of a verb tells whether an action takes place in the past, present, or future.

- A verb in the **present tense** tells what happens now.
  I **walk** to school.

- A verb in the **past tense** tells what has happened.
  I **walked** about six blocks.

- A verb in the **future tense** tells what will happen.
  I **will walk** again tomorrow.

- **Irregular verbs** are verbs that do not add **ed** to form the past tense.

  I **sing** today.   I **sang** yesterday.   I had **sung** before.

Write each sentence. Draw one line under the complete predicate. Circle each action verb.

1. Jeremy exercises daily.
2. He plays ball with his sister.
3. His family has joined a gym.
4. I go to karate class.

Write each sentence. Then write **past**, **present**, or **future** to show the tense of each underlined verb.

5. Mrs. Raffay teaches gymnastics.
6. She studied physical education in college.
7. I will take her class next year.
8. Ana took her class last year.
9. She will continue in gymnastics.
10. Ana enjoys the exercise.

Linking Verbs

- A **linking verb** connects the subject of a sentence to a noun or adjective in the predicate.

  The dog **seems** hungry.   My bike **was** there.

- A linking verb does not express action.

- The verb be changes in the present tense and in the past tense to agree with the subject.

  Present   Tom **is** my cousin.   They **are** my cousins.

  Past   Sheila **was** happy.   We **were** happy.

Write each sentence. Underline each verb. Then write **action verb** or **linking verb**.

1. We are happy about the family reunion.
2. Uncle Ray invited everyone to his house.
3. Uncle Ray and Aunt Sara live in Seattle.
4. My cousin Elise is their daughter.
5. Elise and I were best friends as children.

Write each sentence. Choose the correct linking verb in parentheses to complete each sentence.

6. The Sandozes (was, were) the first to arrive.
7. Dom Sandoz (is, are) my favorite cousin.
8. He (was, were) at the last reunion, too.
9. Baseball (is, are) an interest we share.
10. Chess and mystery stories (is, are) our other favorites.
11. We (is, are) happy to see our cousins.
12. We (was, were) very tired that day.

Adjectives

- An **adjective** is a word that describes a noun.
  A squall is a **small** storm.

- Add **er** or **more** with an adjective to compare two nouns.
  A squall is **smaller** than a hurricane.
  Hurricanes are **more dangerous** than squalls.

- Add **est** or **most** to an adjective to compare more than two nouns.
  That was the **biggest** hurricane of all.
  It was the **most powerful** one I've seen.

Write each sentence. Underline each adjective.

1. Two twisters hit the quiet town.
2. First, there were big winds and dark clouds.
3. The little town was lucky.
4. Some tall trees and one car were damaged.

Write the correct form of each underlined adjective.

5. A blizzard is <u>powerful</u> than a normal snowstorm.
6. Last winter was the <u>cold</u> in many years.
7. One storm was the <u>strange</u> I have ever seen.
8. The snow was <u>heavy</u> than usual.
9. Is a typhoon <u>powerful</u> than a hurricane?
10. Are twisters <u>common</u> than other storms?
11. A twister is <u>frequent</u> of all in the Midwest.
12. A typhoon is <u>common</u> in Asia.

Pronouns

- A **pronoun** is a word that takes the place of one or more nouns.

- A **subject pronoun** is used as the subject of a sentence.
  The Aztecs lived in Mexico.
  They lived in Mexico.

- An **object pronoun** is used after a verb or words such as *for, at, of, with,* and *to.*
  The Aztecs founded Mexico City.
  The Aztecs founded **it**.

- A **possessive pronoun** shows *who* or *what* owns something.
  The Aztecs' city is now Mexico's capital.
  Their city is now Mexico's capital.

Write the sentences. Underline each pronoun. Label it **subject** or **object**.

1. We are studying the Aztecs.
2. The class read stories about them.
3. They built a magnificent city.
4. You would like reading about the Aztecs, too.
5. I made an Aztec diorama with Cindy.
6. We built little temples and palaces.
7. The award for best diorama went to us.
8. The class decided to give it to the library.

Write each sentence. Use a possessive pronoun in place of the underlined word or words.

9. The Aztecs had conquered the Toltecs' kingdom.
10. They cleared the area's forests for farming.
11. Carlos's report tells about that.
12. Justin and I family wants to visit Mexico City.

Adverbs

- An **adverb** is a word that tells more about a verb.
- Add **er** or use **more** when two actions are compared.
- Add **est** or use **most** when more than two actions are compared.

Write the sentence. Draw one line under the adverb. Draw two lines under the verb it describes.

1. My best friend moved away.
2. I slowly made new friends.
3. I still miss Jeff terribly.
4. I will never have another friend like Jeff.

Use the correct form of the adverb in parentheses ( ) to complete each sentence.

5. I write (frequently) to Jeff than to anyone else.
6. E-mail sends ideas (quickly) than letters.
7. Jeff sends photographs (often) than I do.
8. My sister enjoys Jeff's letters (eagerly) than I do.
9. His letters interest her (deeply) than mine.
10. I read the letters (easily) now than before.

UNIT

Sentences

In Unit 1 you will learn about sentences. There are many kinds of sentences. Some sentences ask questions, and some sentences express strong feeling. All sentences help you to communicate with others.

Discuss Read the poem on the opposite page. The poet uses poetry to communicate with others. What does the poem communicate to you?

Creative Expression The theme of this unit is *Surprises*. What surprises have you received lately? Write a few sentences to tell about a surprise. You may want to illustrate your sentences. Write your sentences in your journal.

THEME: *SURPRISES*

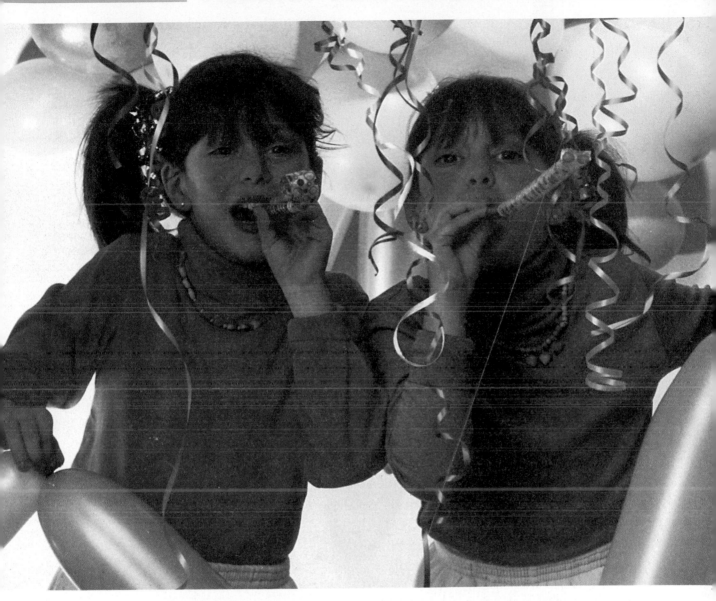

**Surprises are round
Or long and tallish.
Surprises are square
Or flat and smallish.**

**Surprises are wrapped
With paper and bow,
And hidden in closets
Where secrets won't show.**

—Jean Conder Soule, from "Surprises"

1 WHAT IS A SENTENCE?

A sentence is a group of words that expresses a complete thought.

A sentence states an idea. A sentence is complete if it can stand alone and make sense. Every sentence begins with a capital letter and ends with a punctuation mark.

Sentences
We planned Diane's birthday party. Sabrina and Peter made the decorations.

Not Sentences
Served fruit and snacks. Sabrina and others.

We play / a new record.

Guided Practice

Tell which groups of words are sentences and which are not sentences.

Example: A lovely dress.   *not a sentence*

1. Made streamers for the party.
2. Barbara brought flowers.
3. Kept a secret.
4. Miguel found an interesting gift.
5. The records on the record player.

 THINK

■ How can I decide if a group of words is a sentence?

REMEMBER

- A **sentence** is a group of words that expresses a complete thought.
- A sentence begins with a capital letter and ends with a punctuation mark.

More Practice

A. Write each group of words. Next to each group write **sentence** or **not a sentence.**

Example: a lonely morning.   *not a sentence*

6. Diane was sad.
7. No one wished her a happy birthday.
8. She did not know about the party.
9. The surprise party was a secret.
10. Started at seven o'clock.
11. Carlos, Roberta, Michele, and Diane's father.
12. Looked for the perfect gift.
13. Gave money for the gift.
14. Alan took the money to the pet store.
15. He bought a wonderful gift for Diane.

B. Add words to each fragment to make it complete.

Example: An interesting pet.
        I have an interesting pet.

16. Never saw one with white fur.
17. Would not hold it in his hand.
18. Always loved animals.
19. Punched holes in a box for the pet.
20. The most wonderful birthday.

Extra Practice, page 28

WRITING APPLICATION A Description

Write a paragraph that describes the best party you ever went to or imagined. What did you eat? What music was played? Who was there? Have a partner underline any group of words that does not express a complete thought.

2 FOUR KINDS OF SENTENCES

There are four kinds of sentences: **declarative, interrogative, imperative,** and **exclamatory.** The chart below lists each type and gives an example.

Begin every sentence with a capital letter. Notice the punctuation mark that ends each kind of sentence. Study the chart below.

Declarative Sentence

Purpose: makes a statement
Example: I am tired of winter.
End Punctuation: period (.)

Imperative Sentence

Purpose: tells or asks someone to do something
Examples: Wear your scarf. Please stay home.
End Punctuation: period (.)

Interrogative Sentence

Purpose: asks a question
Example: Is it snowing?
End Punctuation: question mark (?)

Exclamatory Sentence

Purpose: expresses strong feeling
Example: That poor cat looks frozen!
End Punctuation: exclamation mark (!)

Guided Practice

Identify each sentence as **declarative, interrogative, imperative,** or **exclamatory.**

Example: Are you cold?   *interrogative*

1. How deep the snow is!
2. Where are my warm gloves?
3. Please wear your snowshoes.
4. We did not expect snow in May.
5. Are the telephones working?

 THINK

■ How can I decide if a sentence is declarative, interrogative, imperative, or exclamatory?

GRAMMAR: Four Kinds of Sentences

REMEMBER

- The four types of sentences are **declarative, interrogative, imperative,** and **exclamatory.**
- Sentences end with a **period,** a **question mark,** or an **exclamation mark.**

More Practice

A. Write each sentence. Then write whether each sentence is **declarative, interrogative, imperative,** or **exclamatory.**

Example: Do snowstorms scare you?
　　　　　interrogative

6. Turn on the radio.
7. Is there news about the hurricane?
8. The weather reporter made a big mistake!
9. She predicted sunshine for today.
10. Are schools closed because of the storm?
11. How heavy the rainfall is!
12. Make sure the windows are closed.

B. Write each sentence. Add the correct end punctuation.

Example: The floor is soaked　　*The floor is soaked!*

13. Have you seen a tornado before
14. How dark the sky looks
15. Is the basement the safest place in the house
16. Yes, we will wait downstairs in the playroom
17. The weather reporter says the tornado is near
18. Where do animals hide during a tornado
19. Pets stay indoors
20. Birds and squirrels hide in the trees

Extra Practice, page 29

WRITING APPLICATION A Comic Strip

Draw a comic strip that shows how people prepare for a big storm. Under each picture in your comic strip, write a sentence that describes what you have drawn. Have a partner identify each type of sentence in your comic strip.

COOPERATIVE
LEARNING

3 COMPLETE SUBJECTS AND COMPLETE PREDICATES

Every sentence has two main parts, the subject and the predicate. Both the subject and the predicate can be one word or more than one word.

The **complete subject** of a sentence includes all the words that tell whom or what the sentence is about. The **complete predicate** of a sentence includes all the words that tell what the subject does or is.

The children hear strange noises.
The boys and girls are curious.

Guided Practice

Tell the complete subject and the complete predicate in each sentence.

Example: The quiet house became filled with noises.
The quiet house   complete subject
became filled with noises.   complete predicate

1. Louie heard the noises first.
2. Harry and Brenda heard them, too.
3. The sounds came from upstairs.
4. The children called Uncle Sydney.
5. Uncle Sydney brought a flashlight.

 THINK

■ How can I find the complete subject and the complete predicate in a sentence?

REMEMBER

- The **complete subject** of a sentence includes all the words that tell whom or what the sentence is about.
- The **complete predicate** of a sentence includes all the words that tell what the subject does or is.

More Practice

A. Write each sentence. Draw one line under the complete subject. Draw two lines under the complete predicate.

Example: <u>Mysterious noises</u> <u><u>disturb the family</u></u>.

6. Celia and Rosa went up to the attic.
7. Strange noises came from that room.
8. The attic was dusty.
9. The light was dim.
10. Uncle Sydney seemed puzzled.
11. The night sounds remained a mystery.
12. Uncle Sydney and the children went downstairs.
13. The scratching noises started again during dinner.

B. Add a complete subject or a complete predicate to each group of words. Write the new sentence.

Example: joined the search
The children joined the search.

14. left their meal on the table
15. Uncle Sydney and the children
16. looked carefully around the attic
17. heard a tiny, scratching sound in the corner
18. looked beneath a pile of old magazines
19. saw a furry tail
20. a mother squirrel and two babies

Extra Practice, page 30

WRITING APPLICATION A Story

Write a story about mysterious sounds or shadows. Have a partner draw one line under each complete subject and two lines under each complete predicate.

COOPERATIVE
LEARNING

4 SIMPLE SUBJECTS

The complete subject of a sentence includes all the words that tell whom or what the sentence is about. Within the complete subject you can find the simple subject. The **simple subject** is the main word or words in the complete subject.

A mysterious **envelope** lay on the table.

Mary Ann was surprised.

Sometimes, the simple subject is the same as the complete subject.

Mary Ann thought about the problem.

Guided Practice

Tell which word or words make up the simple subject.

Example: The surprise confused Mary Ann.
surprise

1. Mary Ann showed her mother the envelope.
2. Her mother noticed the address.
3. The envelope had only Mary Ann's name on it.
4. Who sent Mary Ann five dollars?
5. The girl was puzzled by the mysterious gift.

 THINK

■ How can I decide which word or words make up the simple subject?

REMEMBER

- The **simple subject** is the main word or words in the complete subject.
- The **simple subject** can be the same as the complete subject.

More Practice

A. The complete subject is underlined in each sentence. Write the simple subject.

Example: <u>The letter</u> raises questions.   *letter*

6. <u>Mary Ann's birthday</u> was months away.
7. <u>The letter</u> came from her town.
8. <u>Her mother</u> thought about the mystery.
9. <u>The envelope</u> gave no clue about the sender.
10. <u>Mary Ann</u> put it into her drawer.
11. <u>She</u> asked her friends many questions.
12. <u>Nobody</u> had the right answer.
13. <u>Mary Ann</u> thought about the envelope all day.

B. Write each sentence. Add a simple subject to each group of words.

Example: had a plan   *Mother had a plan.*

14. _____ finally asked her neighbors.
15. _____ had an idea.
16. "_____ shoveled snow for Mrs. Jefferson, Mary Ann."
17. "Maybe _____ sent the money."
18. _____ asked Mrs. Jefferson about the envelope.
19. _____ smiled kindly at Mary Ann.
20. _____ had a secret.

Extra Practice, page 31

WRITING APPLICATION A Map

Make a map that shows the way to a hidden treasure chest. Write a paragraph about how your friend will use the map to find the treasure. Ask a partner to draw one line under the simple subject in each of your sentences.

5 SIMPLE PREDICATES

The complete predicate of a sentence includes all the words that tell what the subject does or is. The **simple predicate** is the main word or words in the complete predicate. The simple predicate is also called the **verb**. Read the sentences below. Notice the words in dark type.

Jeanne **looked** through the window.
A boy **was** at the front door.
He **wore** a red jacket.
Jeanne **thought** for a moment.

Jeanne opened the door.

Guided Practice

The complete predicate is underlined in each sentence. Tell which word or words make up the simple predicate.

Example: Jeanne <u>wondered about him.</u>   *wondered*

1. Jeanne <u>walked to the door.</u>
2. The little boy <u>ran to the corner.</u>
3. He <u>waited by the tree.</u>
4. Jeanne <u>remembered his face.</u>
5. The boy <u>stood silently by the tree.</u>

 THINK

■ How can I find the simple predicate in a sentence?

REMEMBER

- The **simple predicate** is the main word or words in the complete predicate.
- The simple predicate is also called the verb.

More Practice

A. The complete predicate in each sentence is underlined. Write the simple predicate.

Example: Jeanne <u>felt curious</u>.   *felt*

6. Jeanne and the boy <u>went to the same school</u>.
7. The boy <u>spoke only with pencil and paper</u>.
8. Jeanne <u>brought a pencil and notebook from the house</u>.
9. The boy <u>wrote a message on the paper</u>.
10. The message <u>was the boy's name and phone number</u>.
11. Jeanne <u>understood the boy's problem</u>.
12. She <u>took Paul into her house</u>.
13. She <u>called the boy's mother</u>.

B. Write each sentence. Add a simple predicate to complete each sentence.

Example: Jean and Paul _____ a snack.   *ate*

14. Paul _____ a deck of cards from his pocket.
15. He _____ Jeanne a magic trick with the cards.
16. Jeanne _____ magic tricks.
17. Jeanne _____ her paint set from a drawer.
18. Paul _____ a picture.
19. He _____ something on a piece of paper.
20. The message _____ Jeanne for the visit.

Extra Practice, page 32

WRITING APPLICATION A Paragraph

Think about a time you met a new friend. Write a paragraph telling about the meeting. Include any details that will help the reader to understand what made the event fun or unusual. Exchange paragraphs with a classmate. Underline the simple predicates.

6 COMPOUND SUBJECTS AND COMPOUND PREDICATES

Your sentences can be about more than one person, thing, or action. A sentence with a **compound subject** has two or more simple subjects with the same predicate. The simple subjects are joined by *and* or *or*.

A sentence with a **compound predicate** has two or more simple predicates with the same subject. The predicates can also be joined by *and* or *or*. Some sentences have both a compound subject and a compound predicate.

> **JoJo** and **Merry** are birds. They **chirp** and **sing**.
> **Selina** and **Tomas watched** and **laughed**.

Guided Practice

Tell whether each sentence has a compound subject, a compound predicate, or both.

Example: Selina and Thomas look for the birds.
compound subject

1. The blue parakeet hops or flies around the cage.
2. The green parakeet eats and sleeps on the perch.
3. The children stand and watch the birds.
4. Selina and Tomas bought and named the birds.
5. Jojo and Merry chirped all afternoon.

 THINK

- How can I tell if a sentence has a compound subject, a compound predicate, or both?

REMEMBER

- A **compound subject** has two or more simple subjects with the same predicate.
- A **compound predicate** is two or more simple predicates with the same subject.

More Practice

A. Write each sentence. Draw a line under the word that connects the simple subjects or the simple predicates.

Example: Mom <u>and</u> Dad wait with the children.

  6. Tomas stops and notices something in the cage.
  7. Tomas or Selina checks the box each day.
  8. JoJo watches and guards an egg.
  9. The children and Mom go to the pet store.
10. The clerk welcomes and shows them some supplies.
11. The children look and choose a special box for the egg.
12. JoJo and Merry like the nesting box.
13. Mom and Dad buy a book about parakeets.

B. Write each sentence. Draw one line under the compound subject. Draw two lines under the compound predicate.

Example: <u>Boys and girls</u> ask about the birds.
              Selina <u>sketches and photographs</u> the birds.

14. JoJo or Merry sits on the eggs.
15. Mom chooses and buys food for the parakeets.
16. Selina and Tomas tell their classmates about the eggs.
17. Friends visit and see the birds.
18. The children watch and protect the birds.
19. Parakeets develop and hatch in three weeks.
20. Sheryl and Greg each want a baby parakeet.

Extra Practice, page 33

WRITING APPLICATION A Caption

Draw or find a picture that shows a group of baby animals. Write a caption describing the animals. Label each compound subject and compound predicate.

7 COMPOUND SENTENCES

Sentences can also be compound. A **compound sentence** contains two sentences joined by a comma and the words *and*, *or*, or *but*. You can form compound sentences by joining two or more sentences that contain similar ideas. Each sentence that makes up the compound sentence has a subject and a predicate of its own.

My friends enjoy the movies, **and** I like movies, too.
I like all movies, **but** James prefers Westerns.
June reads reviews, **or** she asks other people for their opinions.

Pay one admission <u>and</u> see the next feature for free.

Guided Practice

Tell which sentences are compound sentences.

Example: My friends chose a movie, and I met them at one o'clock.   *compound sentence*

1. Everybody met at the school, and we were ready for the movie.
2. *Master of the World* sounded like an adventure movie.
3. I bought tickets, and June bought snacks.
4. James sat in the front, but we sat farther back.
5. We can sit near the aisle, or we can sit in the middle of the row.

 THINK

■ How can I recognize a compound sentence?

REMEMBER

■ A **compound sentence** contains two sentences joined by a comma and *and*, *or,* or *but*.

More Practice

Write each compound sentence. Add the correct punctuation. Label correct sentences *correct*.

Example: I like old movies, <u>and</u> Carol likes them, too.

6. The lights dimmed and the audience became quiet.

7. The beginning was too boring and the music was too loud.

8. Maurice and Carol were bored by the movie.

9. Maurice was disappointed and Carol was restless.

10. Ten minutes passed and I liked the story less and less.

11. We did not expect this kind of movie.

12. The movie title had sounded exciting but this was not an adventure story.

13. The movie was about a scientist.

14. We could wait outside in the cold or we could stay inside and watch the movie.

15. The movie started slowly but it became more exciting.

16. Carol watched the movie eagerly, now.

17. The scientist began a dangerous experiment and the movie took a surprising turn.

18. The audience was completely silent.

19. The movie seemed short but it was more than two hours long.

20. It was a thrilling movie and I hope for a sequel.

Extra Practice, page 34

WRITING APPLICATION A Movie Review

Write a review, or summary, of a movie you have seen recently. In your review, explain what happens in the movie. Exchange papers with a classmate. Underline the compound sentences in each other's reviews.

8 CORRECTING SENTENCE FRAGMENTS

A sentence has a subject and a predicate, and it expresses a complete thought. Sometimes a group of words may look like a sentence but is actually a sentence fragment. A **sentence fragment** is a group of words that does not express a complete thought. You must add words or phrases to sentence fragments to form complete sentences.

Sentences

Jennifer and I planned a surprise.
We thought about the surprise all week.

Sentence Fragments

As a present for our mother.
Made a shopping list.

Guided Practice

Tell which groups of words are sentences and which are sentence fragments.

Example: Looked through a cookbook.   *sentence fragment*
I found a simple recipe.   *sentence*

1. Sat at the kitchen table.
2. Jennifer watched me gather the ingredients.
3. I put the utensils on the counter.
4. Studied the recipe.
5. To the store for ingredients.

 THINK

■ How can I decide if a group of words is a sentence fragment?

REMEMBER

- A **sentence fragment** is a group of words that does not express a complete thought.
- You must add words or phrases to sentence fragments to form complete sentences.

More Practice

Decide which group of words in each pair is a sentence fragment. Add words to make the fragment a complete sentence. Write the new sentence. Label each complete sentence *sentence*.

Example: Took the list.   *Jennifer took the list.*

6. Gone for a long time.
7. Jennifer often takes a long time at the store.
8. Reads the labels carefully.
9. I cleaned up the house.
10. Made the beds and washed the dishes.
11. Still had time for more work.
12. The floor needed.
13. I used the buffing machine.
14. Came into the kitchen.
15. She had bought the wrong kind of flour.
16. No time for another shopping trip.
17. I was not angry at her.
18. We can surprise our mother another time.
19. Mother came home.
20. Really pleased and happy.

Extra Practice, page 35

WRITING APPLICATION A Recipe

Write a recipe or set of instructions for preparing a dish. In your recipe, include the ingredients needed to make this dish. Then tell your reader what to do with each ingredient. Exchange recipes with a classmate. Underline any sentence fragments in each other's recipes.

9 MECHANICS: Capitalizing and Punctuating Sentences

Sometimes writers combine sentences to form run-on sentences instead of compound sentences. A **run-on sentence** joins together two or more sentences that should be written separately. You can correct a run-on sentence by dividing it into separate sentences. You can also fix a run-on sentence by making it into a compound sentence.

> North America was unexplored in the early 1800s, no one had traveled from coast to coast.

> North America was unexplored in the early 1800s. No one had traveled from coast to coast.

> North America was unexplored in the early 1800s, and no one had traveled from coast to coast.

Which of the sentences above is a run-on? Which is a compound sentence? Which sentences have been correctly punctuated and capitalized?

Guided Practice

Tell which sentences are run-on sentences.

Example: Most people lived in the eastern part of the country it was safe territory.   *run-on*

1. People were curious about the wild country, and they dreamed of adventure.
2. The Rocky Mountains were dangerous people needed a clear path to the West.
3. In 1803, America bought the Louisiana Purchase the new territory was huge.
4. The addition of this new land doubled the size of the United States.
5. There were no roads in the new land, and the country was mostly forest.

 THINK

- How can I recognize and correct run-on sentences?

REMEMBER

■ You can rewrite a **run-on sentence** as separate sentences or as a compound sentence.

More Practice

Correct the run-on sentences by separating them into two sentences or by forming a compound sentence. Write each new sentence. Label each correct sentence *correct*.

Example: The explorers drew maps they made careful studies. *The explorers drew maps, and they made careful studies.*

6. Meriwether Lewis led an expedition through the new territory.
7. Lewis needed a partner, and he hired William Clark.
8. They looked for a path to the West they searched for a waterway to the Pacific Ocean.
9. They started their expedition in 1804, and they traveled for three years.
10. They had a Native American guide her name was Sacajawea.
11. Everyone waited for news the expedition took three years.
12. Sacajawea led them through the Rockies she was a knowledgeable guide.
13. On the return trip, Lewis and Clark separated they traveled two different rivers.
14. The expedition showed the size of the country, everyone was surprised.
15. It was a country of many natural resources it was bountiful.

Extra Practice, Practice Plus, pages 36–38

WRITING APPLICATION An Explanation

Imagine that you are about to set out on an expedition or a trip to a strange land. Write a paragraph explaining how you will prepare for your expedition. Have a partner check for any run-on sentences.

10 VOCABULARY BUILDING: Using Context Clues

The words that you already know can help you to figure out the meaning of new words. The familiar words in a sentence are the **context**, or setting, for a word that you do not recognize. Which words in the sentence below give clues about the meaning of the word *wilted*?

It did not rain, so the flowers *wilted* and became limp.

The word *limp* describes what happened to the flowers when *it did not rain*. These words are **context clues** that help you guess the meaning of *wilted*.

Guided Practice

Use the context clues in each sentence to tell the meaning of the underlined words.

Example: Our country cousins live on a farm and love <u>rural</u> life.   *Clues: country, farm*

1. Since we grew up in the city, we only knew <u>urban</u> life.
2. Most campers did not say anything, but Mary was quite <u>vocal</u>.
3. She dug with her <u>trowel</u> because a shovel was too big.
4. She watched the farmer shear wool from the sheep and pile the soft <u>fleeces</u> on the ground.
5. Tod was <u>cautious</u> in the woods because he knew hikers must be careful.

THINK

■ How can I use context clues to figure out the meaning of unfamiliar words?

REMEMBER

■ **Context clues** are familiar words that help you understand the meaning of unknown words in a sentence.

More Practice

Write each sentence. Draw a line under each familiar word that helps you to define the underlined word in each sentence.

Example: The thick <u>foliage</u> of the woods gave us shade.
    woods, shade

6. The trail was <u>concealed</u> by the leaves and branches that covered it.
7. We found only a <u>narrow</u> path instead of the wide trail marked on the map.
8. We heard a loud crash, and the tent <u>swayed</u> and shook.
9. A huge <u>limb</u> from the tree fell between the other branches.
10. We saw two deer, a <u>fawn</u> and its mother.
11. Sharp rocks and poison ivy are two <u>hazards</u> of hiking in the woods.
12. Although his voice was <u>gruff</u>, the ranger was a kind person.
13. Nora was usually happy, but she felt <u>forlorn</u> when we left her alone.
14. Our team finally <u>defeated</u> the other team after losing to them all season.
15. I can smell the soup because its <u>aroma</u> is reaching us from the forest.

Extra Practice, page 39

WRITING APPLICATION A Letter

Write a letter to a friend describing an event that you enjoyed. Use a dictionary to find some unfamiliar words to use in your letter. Give context clues in your sentences so that others can understand any difficult words. Exchange letters with a classmate. Use context clues to guess the meaning of any unfamiliar words in each other's letters.

GRAMMAR
—AND
WRITING
CONNECTION

Combining Sentences

In your writing, you can show that the ideas in two separate sentences are related. You can show the relationship between the sentences by using a comma and the word *and* to join or connect the sentences.

The circus is in town. We will see it.
The circus is in town, **and** we will see it.

You can also use *but* or *or* to show a relationship between the sentences.

Dad usually works on the weekends, **but** he has the day off today.
Are we going by bus, **or** will Mom drive the car?

Working Together

COOPERATIVE LEARNING

With your classmates, discuss how to join sentences with *and*, *but*, or *or*. Look at each pair of sentences. Then tell how you would join them to make a single sentence.

Example Dad wore a new tie.
He looked handsome.
Dad wore a new tie,
and he looked handsome.

1. Sally put on her new dress.
   I shined my shoes.
2. We were ready five minutes later.
   It took Mom an hour to get a baby-sitter.
3. Can we leave now?
   Should we wait?

Revising Sentences

Tommy wrote the following sentences in his journal about his family's trip to the circus. Help Tommy revise his notes by joining each pair of sentences. Use a comma and *and*, *but*, or *or* to show the connection between the ideas.

4. It was a beautiful day.
   The sky was clear.
5. Are we going into the big tent?
   Will we go to the sideshow first?
6. There was a huge crowd today.
   The tent had enough room for everyone.
7. At first Sally was startled by the clowns.
   She was soon laughing with everyone else.
8. The acrobats were graceful.
   Their act was thrilling.
9. The elephants were the biggest animals in the circus.
   The lions were scarier.
10. The circus was exciting.
    The trip brought the family closer together.

Think about some of the other surprises you read about in this unit. Brainstorm to choose a surprise you would like to write about. Write a story. Be sure to include a description of the setting and the characters. When you revise, look for any pairs of sentences that you can combine.

UNIT CHECKUP

LESSON 1

What Is a Sentence? (page 2) Write each group of words. Next to each group write **sentence** or **not a sentence**.

1. Stood in line for the bus.
2. Steve, Sam, and Mary.
3. They waited for an hour.
4. I was impatient.
5. Realized it was Saturday!

LESSON 2

Four Kinds of Sentences (page 4) Write each sentence. Add the correct end punctuation.

6. Who is at the door
7. Open the door
8. I am so surprised
9. My oldest friend has arrived
10. Did you receive my letter

LESSONS 3-5

Subjects and Predicates (pages 6–11) Write each sentence. Draw a line between the complete subject and the complete predicate. Then, draw one line under the simple subject and two lines under the simple predicate.

11. Our school expected another defeat.
12. The team lost every game last year.
13. This year was a good year.
14. We had a secret weapon.
15. Our star player saved the day.

LESSON 6

Compound Subjects and Compound Predicates (page 12) Write each sentence. Draw one line under the compound subject. Draw two lines under the compound predicate.

16. Yolanda and Wally made a collage.
17. They painted and added photos.
18. We begged and pleaded for a peek.
19. Howard and I have made collages.
20. The collage shows and tells a story.

LESSON 7

Compound Sentences (page 14) Write each sentence. Write **simple** or **compound** next to each.

21. The light will not work, and the room is dark.
22. I called the repair crew, but they were gone.
23. The bulb is new and is not broken.
24. We are impatient, or we would have looked more carefully.
25. The plug is out and lying on the floor!

LESSON 8

Correcting Sentence Fragments (page 16) Write each group of words. Write **sentence** or **fragment** next to each group.

26. My friend Sara.
27. I have a big umbrella.
28. With this umbrella.
29. Sara was surprised.
30. Even though it rained.
31. Sara likes the rain.

LESSON 9

Mechanics: Capitalizing and Punctuating Sentences (page 18) Correct and rewrite the run-on sentences.

32. The king was proud he never smiled.
33. No one smiled at him they were scared of his anger.
34. Fran wanted to tell a joke she was afraid of the king.
35. We saw the king sit down on his throne it broke into pieces.
36. We were silent soon the king actually laughed.

LESSON 10

Vocabulary Building: Using Context Clues (page 20) Write the correct definition of each underlined word.

37. I used binoculars to see things that were far away.
    a. special lenses for seeing long distances
    b. walking shoes   c. large umbrella
38. Janice spotted a heron with its wings folded.
    a. type of snake   b. small water plant   c. bird
39. I saw some toxic plants and stayed far away from them.
    a. leafy   b. poisonous   c. beautiful

Writing Application: Complete Sentences (pages 2–19) The following paragraph contains 6 errors. Rewrite the paragraph correctly.

40.–45.
    My visit to Aunt Jane's house. It was more fun this year than last my little cousin was finally old enough for games. Like softball and volleyball. Summer is pretty in Massachusetts the trees are shady. Cool weather, too. Lovely time.

WORD VOLLEYS

Think of an interesting or funny subject for a sentence. Have a partner complete the sentence with a predicate. Then, let your partner begin a sentence with the same subject, while you supply the predicate. Form a compound sentence.

Pantomime Play this game in a small group. Take turns performing a simple action. For example, one person could pretend to make a campfire. The others should each write a complete sentence that describes what the person is doing. One person might write, "You are having trouble making a fire." Another might write, "You are building a fire with sticks and branches."

SENTENCE SALAD

Try this game with a group of classmates. Each student will write a sentence on a large sheet of paper.

The cook

Then, cut the paper so that one half contains the subject and one half contains the predicate.

ate lunch.

Put all the pieces of paper in a pile. Take turns choosing slips from the pile until everyone has a whole sentence that makes sense.

Paul and Ned

WORD DETECTIVES

Play this game with a small group. Find three unfamiliar words in your dictionary. Write each word on a separate slip of paper. Next to the word, draw a picture showing something that would help a person to guess the meaning of the word. Exchange slips with the other players. The first player to guess the meaning of all the words wins.

★★★ MEET THE PRESS ★★★

Did you ever watch a journalist interview someone? Try this activity with a partner. Write three questions that you could ask your partner. Write his or her answers in your notebook. Then, add the correct punctuation and capitalization to your recorded interview. When you have finished, let your partner interview you.

EXTRA PRACTICE

Three levels of practice
What Is a Sentence? (page 2)

LEVEL
A. Write each group of words. Next to each group write **sentence** or **not a sentence**.

1. We spent the gloomy morning alone.
2. The rain fell heavily.
3. Jim, Peter, and David.
4. A loud knock at the door.
5. Uncle Harry stood in the doorway.
6. Had not warned us of his visit.
7. Felt so happy!
8. Uncle Harry had a mysterious box.
9. Had holes in the top.

LEVEL
B. Write each group of words. Then, add words to each group to make a complete thought. Write the new sentence.

10. Opened the box.
11. Inside the box.
12. Gave a kitten to each of us.
13. My favorite one.
14. Played with us.
15. Forgot about the rainy day.
16. None of us.
17. Always makes us happy.

LEVEL
C. For each pair, write the group of words that is a sentence. Then, add words to the other group to make a complete thought.

18. Then, Uncle Harry went outside. To his car.
19. He came back to the house. Carried a big green sack.
20. We screamed and jumped with surprise. Excited by the surprise.
21. Made us sit down. Jim put his hand over his mouth.
22. A moment later. The bag moved!
23. We were amazed at first. All four of us.
24. Opened the bag. There was a puppy inside.
25. Mother came home later. Decided we could keep the pets.

Three levels of practice
Four Kinds of Sentences (page 4)

LEVEL A. Write each sentence. Next to each, write **declarative, interrogative, imperative,** or **exclamatory**.

1. Mr. and Mrs. Sanchez woke up suddenly.
2. What is that sound?
3. Go downstairs and look.
4. The basement is flooded!
5. Please do not shout.
6. Where did the water come from?
7. There is a leak somewhere.
8. Call the plumber.
9. Here is his telephone number.

LEVEL B. Write each sentence. Add the correct end punctuation.

10. When will the plumber come
11. He will be here soon
12. It is so cold down here
13. Turn off the faucet in the sink
14. Is that where the flood started
15. Help me move these boxes out of the water
16. What a terrible surprise this is
17. Do you hear the doorbell

LEVEL C. Change each declarative sentence into an imperative sentence. Change each exclamatory sentence into an interrogative sentence. Write the new sentences and add the correct end punctuation.

18. You can turn off the faucet.
19. You can see where all the water ran out!
20. The basement is completely ruined!
21. The plumber is here!
22. Let us go down to the basement.
23. You could ask him if he needs a flashlight.
24. This is a terrible mess!
25. We will need more than a mop!

EXTRA PRACTICE

Three levels of practice
Complete Subjects and Complete Predicates (page 6)

LEVEL
A. Write each sentence. Draw one line under the complete subject. Draw two lines under the complete predicate.

1. Mona and I saw a funny play.
2. The play is about a detective.
3. He owns a very smart dog.
4. His dog helps him solve mysteries.
5. The man and his dog make a good team.
6. The front doorbell rang three times.
7. A woman rushed into the room.
8. Someone had stolen her necklace!
9. The detective had a new job.

LEVEL
B. Add a complete subject or a complete predicate to each group of words. Write the new sentence.

10. Played the detective.
11. Broke into sobs.
12. About her necklace.
13. Was an interesting stage set.
14. Her cats Daisy, Tab, and Louie.
15. Acted guilty.
16. The whole third act.
17. Gathered all the clues.

LEVEL
C. Match each subject with a predicate. Write a complete sentence.

Subjects	Predicates
18. My friends and I	were covered with red velvet.
19. The main actors	was surprising.
20. The play	guessed the ending.
21. The theater seats	were very professional.
22. The ending of the play	discussed the play.
23. Nobody	was the detective's helper.
24. The best actor	concerned a strange crime.
25. The young assistant	solved the crime by himself.

EXTRA PRACTICE

Three levels of practice
Simple Subjects (page 8)

LEVEL A. The complete subject is underlined. Write the simple subject.

1. The children looked in the attic.
2. The windows were broken.
3. The wooden floor was full of splinters.
4. The whole attic smelled dusty.
5. The two youngsters had a plan.
6. Their father kept an old trunk there.
7. The wooden trunk was covered with cobwebs.
8. Curious Jules wondered about the trunk.
9. Annie thought of pirates and lost treasure.

LEVEL B. Write each sentence. Draw a line under the simple subject.

10. The dark room was dangerous.
11. Annie found a flashlight.
12. Her brother discovered a key.
13. The children both looked at the trunk.
14. Jules handed the key to Annie.
15. His sister held the key for a moment.
16. The old trunk probably contained treasure.
17. The attic was dark and mysterious.

LEVEL C. Add a simple subject to each group of words. Write the new sentence.

18. The _____ seemed more exciting than ever.
19. _____ walked toward it.
20. The _____ opened the trunk together.
21. The brass _____ fit the lock.
22. The heavy _____ swung open suddenly.
23. Many old _____ were inside the trunk!
24. _____ laughed and laughed.
25. _____ told their father about their discovery.

EXTRA PRACTICE

Three levels of practice

Simple Predicates (page 10)

LEVEL A. The complete predicate is underlined. Write the simple predicate.

1. The boys <u>planned an interesting trip.</u>
2. Stanley and Burt <u>visited a museum.</u>
3. The two friends <u>looked at a map of the city.</u>
4. They <u>chose a museum in their neighborhood.</u>
5. The museum <u>had many fascinating exhibits.</u>
6. Burt <u>requested a map of the exhibits.</u>
7. Stanley <u>bought a book about dinosaurs.</u>
8. Each room <u>held exhibits of plants, rocks, or animals.</u>
9. The museum <u>was very famous.</u>

LEVEL B. Write the simple predicate in each sentence.

10. The boys found the dinosaur exhibit.
11. Stanley heard a noise.
12. The noise came from a skeleton of a dinosaur.
13. The dinosaur made strange sounds.
14. Burt looked closely at the dinosaur.
15. He laughed suddenly.
16. The sounds were the clicks of someone's camera.
17. A man photographed the huge skeletons.

LEVEL C. Add a simple predicate to each group of words. Write the new sentence.

18. The boys _____ an interesting room.
19. It _____ many rows of old rocks.
20. A card near the rocks _____ "Fossils."
21. Fossils _____ animal traces left in rock.
22. Stanley _____ at the fossils again and again.
23. The boys _____ that exhibit.
24. The museum _____ at five o'clock.
25. Stanley and Burt _____ until closing time.

EXTRA PRACTICE

Three levels of practice
Compound Subjects and Compound Predicates (page 12)

LEVEL A. Write each underlined group of words. Then write **compound subject** or **compound predicate** after each group of words.

1. <u>Saturday and Sunday</u> were boring days.
2. <u>Susan and I</u> miss our old friend Bonnie.
3. Her family <u>packed and moved</u> away.
4. <u>Tuesday and Wednesday</u> passed.
5. <u>My sister and brother</u> asked about Bonnie.
6. <u>The house and yard</u> were empty.
7. I <u>wait and hope</u> for a letter soon.
8. <u>Aunt Paula and Uncle Edward</u> must know Bonnie's address.
9. I <u>call and ask</u> them for any news.

LEVEL B. Write each sentence. Draw one line under each compound subject. Draw two lines under each compound predicate.

10. Susan and I received a letter from Bonnie.
11. Friends and neighbors heard about Bonnie's new home.
12. We dressed and ran to school.
13. Richard and Jenny showed each other post cards from Bonnie.
14. Her phone number and address were both on the cards.
15. My classmates talked and laughed during recess.
16. The teacher and students were all excited.
17. Everyone knew and liked Bonnie.

LEVEL C. Write the compound subject or the compound predicate in each sentence. Then write the joining word in each sentence.

18. The teacher smiled and welcomed the whole class.
19. She and a student had a secret.
20. Susan giggled and whispered to me.
21. The boys and girls got a surprise.
22. Bonnie and her friends were together again.
23. Bonnie grinned and waved at her classmates.
24. The teacher and the class voted for a celebration.
25. A party or picnic was an excellent idea.

GRAMMAR

Three levels of practice
Compound Sentences (page 14)

LEVEL A. Write each sentence. Then write whether the sentence is a **simple sentence** or a **compound sentence**.

1. I read a good book this week.
2. The librarian recommended it, and I took it home.
3. Annie liked the book, too, and she told Joe about it.
4. The story was funny and full of surprises.
5. I waited until the weekend and read all morning.
6. On Saturdays I often read, or I visit my friends.
7. I read until Saturday night, and I could not stop!
8. The hero was a cat named Max, but he was just like a person.
9. He lived in the country, and he had many friends.

LEVEL B. Draw a line under the word that joins the two separate sentences in each compound sentence. Add the correct punctuation.

10. The book was funny and it was exciting.
11. The cat needed excitement or he became bored.
12. He was brave and he was also intelligent.
13. Max had adventures but he always escaped.
14. One day Max found a path and he faced a decision.
15. The cat could go to the right or he could go to the left.
16. He chose the left path and he admired the scenery.
17. Everything seemed safe but danger was ahead.

LEVEL C. Add a sentence to each one below to make a compound sentence. Write the new compound sentence.

18. A strange animal appeared.
19. He had a huge, square head.
20. Max could run.
21. Max approached the enemy.
22. He looked closely at the animal.
23. The animal had a problem.
24. A bag was stuck on his head.
25. Max almost laughed out loud.

EXTRA PRACTICE

Three levels of practice
Correcting Sentence Fragments (page 16)

LEVEL A. Write each group of words. Write **sentence** or **sentence fragment** next to each.

1. One sunny morning.
2. Dreams of treasure.
3. Lenore walked through the park.
4. On the ground near the swings.
5. She saw a golden object.
6. It was shiny.
7. Wondered what it was.
8. Could it be gold?
9. An exciting idea.

LEVEL B. Join each group of words to make a complete sentence. Write the new sentence.

10. Without stopping, the girl. Ran all the way home.
11. Maybe it was worth. A hundred dollars.
12. As she ran. She thought about her new wealth.
13. Perhaps she could. Spend it on a new bike.
14. A hundred dollars. Was a wonderful discovery.
15. Now she had money. For presents.
16. A number of ideas. Popped into Lenore's mind.
17. In her pocket. Was the golden treasure.

LEVEL C. Add words to these fragments to make them complete sentences. Write the new sentences.

18. Reached the front door.
19. Her brother and sister.
20. As she explained her discovery.
21. Held her breath.
22. Showed them her treasure.
23. Laughed and laughed at her.
24. When she showed them the chocolate wrapped in gold paper.
25. Laughed with the others.

EXTRA PRACTICE

Three levels of practice
Mechanics: Capitalizing and Punctuating Sentences (page 18)

LEVEL A. Write **correct** or **run-on** after each word group.

1. Dr. Porter lived in his laboratory.
2. He had a special project it took all his time.
3. The scientist worked every day he worked hard and long.
4. He was uncertain about his new project.
5. The chemicals he mixed were new they were not tested yet.
6. What could happen?
7. The experiment might succeed it could fail.
8. Dr. Porter dreamed of success he longed for fame.
9. He continued with his experiment.

LEVEL B. Correct the punctuation and capitalization in each sentence. Write the new sentence.

10. dr. Porter sat and worried about his work.
11. he mixed two red chemicals.
12. the mixture was red but he wanted something purple.
13. it was not the correct result and he threw out the chemicals and started over.
14. he mixed two blue chemicals and made a dark powder.
15. the scientist became angry.
16. he was frustrated by his mistakes.
17. his experiment was important to him.

LEVEL C. Correct the run-on sentences. Write the new sentence.

18. The scientist yelled he was very upset.
19. He made one last attempt he began again.
20. Purple stuff suddenly filled the tube it smelled sweet.
21. It was a fabulous new invention it was a success.
22. Maybe it was a new food maybe it was a type of fuel.
23. He smelled the mixture it was grape jelly.
24. Dr. Porter made a sandwich he ate every bit of it.
25. He is famous now and his invention is delicious.

PRACTICE + PLUS

Three levels of additional practice for a difficult skill
Mechanics: Capitalizing and Punctuating Sentences (page 18)

LEVEL
A. Read each sentence. Write **correct** or **run-on** for each.

1. Bill plays the guitar he also plays the drums.
2. His best friend plays the piano.
3. They know twenty songs they write songs, too.
4. Bill and Robin play rock music and jazz.
5. Audiences love them they are wonderful.
6. Their band played ten times last week.
7. We listened to the band they played for hours.
8. They played fast songs I danced all evening.
9. I like funny songs and serious ones, too.
10. Horace can sing and dance well he is talented.
11. Debby is also a good dancer she is graceful.
12. We can watch the show or dance again.
13. The orchestra plays tonight the ballet performs tomorrow I like them both.
14. Darnell plays the violin and the cello.
15. I like classical music it is beautiful and it is restful.
16. We rehearse every afternoon the music is difficult we also rehearse on weekends.
17. The orchestra still needs an oboe player we could also use another flute player.
18. The conductor is here and ready for the rehearsal.

LEVEL
B. Rewrite each run-on sentence as two correct sentences or one compound sentence.

19. The morning was cool the sun shone brightly.
20. Patricia had no plans she felt restless.
21. Her mother suggested some ideas Patricia did not like any of them.
22. She called a friend the friend was not at home.
23. Patricia sat on the steps the cement was too hot.
24. The neighborhood was deserted the girl saw no one.
25. Patricia walked to the end of the block she noticed a sign.

GRAMMAR

26. The sign was on a tree it said, "Help Wanted."
27. Patricia read the words they gave her a new idea.
28. A neighbor had a dog the dog needed a bath.
29. Patricia ran home she found a pencil and notepad.
30. She ran to the corner again the sign was still there.
31. She copied down the phone number she also wrote the address.
32. Patricia's mother met her on the steps Patricia told her about the job.
33. Her mother liked the idea Patricia could wash the dog.
34. They went inside together her mother dialed the number.

LEVEL C. Rewrite each run-on sentence correctly.

35. Mrs. Blake was happy her spaniel needed a bath now someone was available for the job.
36. Patricia and her mother met Mrs. Blake the woman had a broken arm she needed help with her dog.
37. The spaniel's name was Jinx Jinx was a funny dog.
38. Patricia patted the dog Jinx licked Patricia's hand.
39. Mrs. Blake got a bucket she also brought some soap.
40. Patricia and Jinx went to the garden Patricia put Jinx into a special tub.
41. She used the garden hose water filled the tub Jinx barked happily.
42. Patricia soaped the dog's fur the shampoo made thick suds.
43. She used warm water the dog enjoyed it.
44. Patricia rinsed the soap away Mrs. Blake and Patricia's mother watched the whole bath.
45. Jinx jumped from the tub he shook the water from his ears.
46. Patricia brushed his wet fur the dog stood calmly the sun quickly dried his fur.
47. Mrs. Blake brought a tray of sandwiches to the patio everyone ate a sandwich Jinx had one also.
48. Mrs. Blake paid the girl five dollars she thanked Patricia and offered her another job.
49. Jinx needed a dog walker Patricia was delighted she liked Jinx.
50. Everyone was happy Mrs. Blake had a helper Patricia and her mother had a new friend.

EXTRA PRACTICE

Three levels of practice
Vocabulary Building: Using Context Clues (page 20)

LEVEL A. Write a definition for each underlined word. Draw a line under the familiar words that you used as context clues.

1. The composer <u>startled</u> the listeners with surprising music.
2. At first the tune was <u>soothing</u>, soft, and gentle.
3. He <u>deceived</u> us by tricking us with this quiet beginning.
4. The instruments <u>blared</u> loud notes at the end.
5. Anyone who <u>dozed</u> was awakened suddenly.

LEVEL B. Write each sentence. Use context clues to select the correct definition of the underlined word. Write the correct definition.

6. The band played <u>popular</u> pieces, so we heard our favorite songs.

   a. unpleasant   b. well-liked   c. lively

7. The crowd was <u>enthusiastic</u> and loved every song the band played.

   a. angry   b. strongly responsive   c. loud

8. Last time, the music was awful, but this time, it was <u>superb</u>.

   a. terrible   b. musical   c. excellent

9. I <u>appreciated</u> the concert, but Bill hated it.

   a. disliked   b. enjoyed   c. learned

10. The concert included Jan's favorite song, one that he <u>adored</u>.

    a. hated   b. wrote   c. loved

LEVEL C. Write each sentence. Use context clues to help you guess the meaning of the underlined words. Write a definition for the word.

11. If I could select tonight's concert, I would <u>opt</u> for a rock band.
12. At the last classical concert I was bored, and I do not think this one will <u>delight</u> me.
13. I expected something dull, so I was <u>astonished</u> by the exciting music.
14. The conductor <u>beamed</u>, and the audience smiled back at him.
15. Before, I thought that nothing could <u>alter</u> my opinion of classical music, but this concert has given me different ideas.

UNIT

2

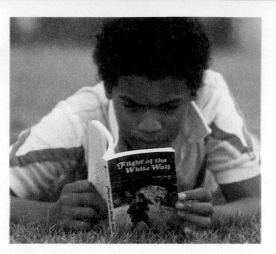

Writing Personal Narratives

Read the quotation and look at the picture on the opposite page. Oliver Butterworth wrote the story that you will read in this unit. How does Oliver Butterworth feel about writing?

When you write a personal narrative, you will want your audience to understand the way you felt about an event that was important to you.

Focus A personal narrative tells about something that happened in your life.

What event would you like to write about? On the following pages you will find a story that tells of a momentous event in one person's life. You will see some photographs, too. You can use both the story and the photographs to find ideas for writing.

THEME: *SURPRISES*

Sometimes I think I might pinch myself and wake up and find that I just dreamed about writing books. It seems too good to be true.

—Oliver Butterworth

AWARD
WINNING
SELECTION

Did you ever have a surprise that was too exciting to enjoy alone? How did you share the experience with other people?

In this story, a boy named Nate and his family discover that their ordinary hen has hatched the surprise of the century.

As you read the selection, look for the specific details that the author uses to describe the amazing event.

from THE ENORMOUS EGG

by Oliver Butterworth

I just went over to the nest and put a little grain down for that poor old hen, and started to turn away, when I realized all at once that something had changed. The hen wasn't sitting on the nest any more. She was walking back and forth with a kind of wild look in her eye, and every time she came near the nest she gave a little hop and fluttered away again. I bent down to look in the nest, and—wow! There was something in there, and it was alive! It was moving around.

I thought at first that it was a rat or something that had busted the egg and eaten it. But after I got a good look I could see that it wasn't any rat. It was about the size of a squirrel, but it didn't have any hair, and its head—well, I couldn't believe my eyes when I saw it. It didn't look like anything I'd ever seen before. It had three little knobs sticking out of its head and a sort of collar up over its neck. It was a lizardy-looking critter, and it kept moving its thick tail slowly back and forth in the nest. The poor hen was looking pretty upset. I guess she hadn't expected anything like this, and neither had I.

I just stood there for a minute, I was so surprised all I could do was look. Then I started yelling, and lit out across the yard as fast as I could go. When I busted into

The first paragraph introduces the main idea of the selection and prepares you for the details in the narrative.

Notice the author's use of details to help you "see" the strange animal in the hen's nest.

the kitchen Mom was so startled that she dropped a saucepan in the sink. Pop came running down the stairs with lather over one side of his face and a razor in his hand, and Cynthia was right behind.

"For goodness' sakes!" Mom said. "What's the matter with you?"

"It's alive!" I shouted. "It's alive! And it moves around, and it wiggles its tail and has horns and it looks like a lizard, and it doesn't have any fur, and the hen's running round and round and doesn't know what to do about it, and—"

"Hold on there, Nate," Pop said. "You look as if you'd seen a ghost. What's all the excitement about?"

I was so out of breath that I couldn't talk for a while. "It's the egg," I said. "It's hatched!"

"What!" Pop shouted. "It did? Why didn't you say so?" And he ran out the door and down the steps, still holding on to his razor. I grabbed Mom's hand and pulled her along, and Cynthia was just ahead of us. She'd forgotten to put on her shoes, and Mom was saying, "All this excitement over an egg. My goodness!"

When we all got out to the nest, Pop was leaning over, looking hard at it. Mom was still saying, "Why we should all come running out here only half dressed, just to see an egg that hatched out—I can't see anything in there, it's too dark. Walt, why don't you bring it out here so we can look at it, whatever it is?"

Pop was still leaning over staring at the thing in the nest. All he said was, "By jing!" under his breath, sort of. By that time Cynthia had squeezed in beside Pop. She took one good look and then let out a screech that you could have heard way down to the post office. That started the hen off, and she began squawking and flapping around in circles, and Ezekiel started crowing, and the goat started bleating. There was an awful lot of commotion, and everybody was talking at the same time and nobody could hear anything.

When it quieted down a little, Pop said, "Nate, you better run into the house and call Dr. Ziemer. He wanted to be told first thing. Remember, he's at the MacPhersons' place."

D r. Ziemer arrived while we were still staring at the thing in the nest. He jumped out of his car and came running out to us in the back yard. He was wearing a red bathrobe over his pajamas, and he looked pretty excited.

He ran up to the nest and looked in. His eyes opened up wide and he knelt down on the ground and stared and stared and stared. After a long while he said softly, "That's it. By George, that's just what it is." Then he stared for another long time and finally he shook his head and said, "It can't be true, but there it is."

He got up off his knees and looked at us. His eyes were just sparkling, he was so excited. He put his hand on my shoulder, and I could feel he was quivering. "An amazing thing's happened," he said, in a kind of whisper. "I don't know how to account for it. It must be some sort of freak biological mixup that might happen once in a thousand years."

The writer tells about the surprise clearly by narrating each event in the order in which it happened.

"But what is it?" I asked.

Dr. Ziemer turned and pointed a trembling finger at the nest. "Believe it or not, you people have hatched out a dinosaur."

We just looked at him.

"Sounds incredible, I know," he said, "and I can't explain it, but there it is. I've seen too many Triceratops skulls to be mistaken about this one."

"But—but how could it be a dinosaur?" Pop asked.

"Goodness gracious!" Mom spluttered. "And right here in our back yard. It doesn't seem hardly right. And on a Sunday, too."

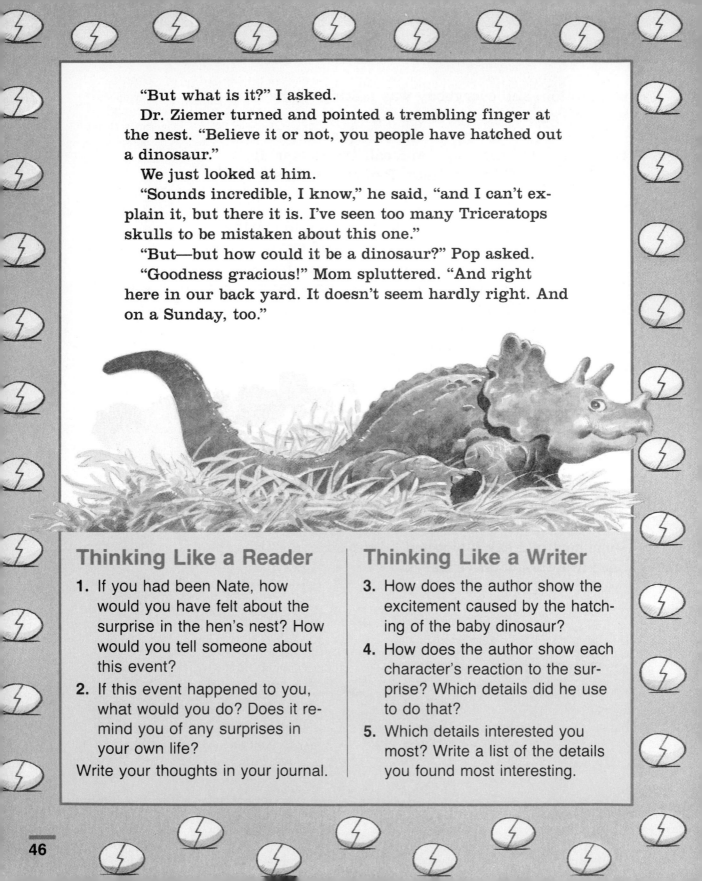

Thinking Like a Reader

1. If you had been Nate, how would you have felt about the surprise in the hen's nest? How would you tell someone about this event?

2. If this event happened to you, what would you do? Does it remind you of any surprises in your own life?

Write your thoughts in your journal.

Thinking Like a Writer

3. How does the author show the excitement caused by the hatching of the baby dinosaur?

4. How does the author show each character's reaction to the surprise? Which details did he use to do that?

5. Which details interested you most? Write a list of the details you found most interesting.

Responding to
LITERATURE

Brainstorm

Vocabulary

In "The Enormous Egg," Nate uses words like "screech," "commotion," and "excitement" to show how the characters respond to the arrival of the dinosaur. Think of an exciting event that has happened to you. What words might describe the surprise? In your journal write any words or phrases that come to mind. Begin to create a personal vocabulary list.

Talk It Over

Talk About a Surprise

Nate is amazed to find a dinosaur in the hen's nest where he expected to find an unhatched egg or a baby chick. Imagine that you have just experienced a surprise. Talk about the surprise with a partner. Tell him or her what happened, using as many clear details as possible. Ask your partner if your description needs more details in order to be precise. Then, let your partner tell you about a surprise while you listen carefully.

Quick Write *Write a Letter*

You have been thinking about surprises and how people respond to them. Think about a surprise that you have experienced. Write a brief letter to a friend that describes the surprise. For example, you might write to a friend to share your surprise at a sudden bad storm.

Keep your letter in your folder.

Dear Karla,
I know it's the middle of May, but we just had the biggest snowstorm of the year. Mother was getting ready to plant tomatoes when she heard about the storm on the radio. The

Idea Corner

Things That Surprised Me

You have already thought about some surprises that you might want to share. Take time to record some of them in your journal. You may write down words or phrases, topics for writing, or even drawings that illustrate events that have happened to you.

PICTURES

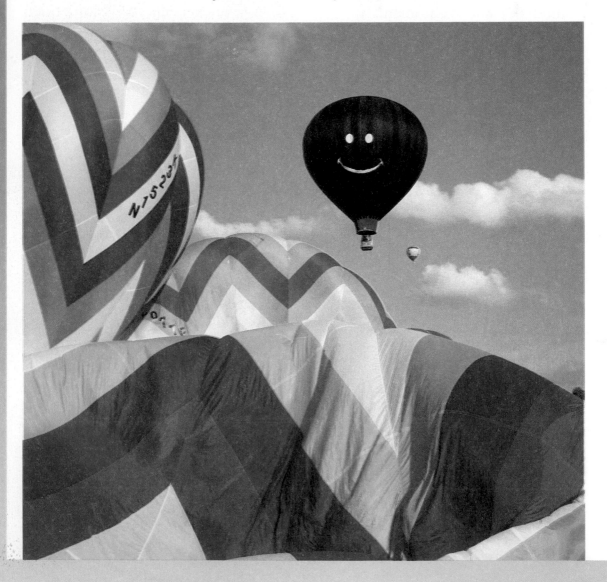

SEEING LIKE A WRITER

Finding Ideas for Writing
Look at the pictures. Think about what you see.
What ideas for narrative writing do the pictures give you?
Write your ideas in your journal.

1 GROUP WRITING: A Personal Narrative

COOPERATIVE
LEARNING

In a personal narrative, your purpose is to share an event with your readers. How can you help your audience to experience the event?

- Main-Idea Sentence
- Supporting Details
- Time Order

As you write, think about your **purpose** or reason for writing a personal narrative. You may be writing to entertain your reader or to communicate a particular idea. Your readers, or **audience**, may be other students, friends, a teacher, or someone whom you have never met.

Main-Idea Sentence

Read the paragraph below. Notice how the first sentence prepares you for what follows.

> <u>Before our camping trip, we prepared for every possibility except one.</u> On Monday, Mary packed the maps and compass. Then she reminded Rufus to bring the first-aid kit. On Thursday, Sue bought extra water containers, and we packed enough food for a whole army. The only thing for which we were not prepared was rain.

The first sentence in the paragraph is the **main-idea sentence.** It states the main, or overall, idea of the paragraph and catches the reader's attention.

Guided Practice: Main-Idea Sentence

Imagine that you and your friends have made plans to take a trip together. Work with your class to write a main-idea sentence for a narrative about the unexpected events that happened during your trip.

Supporting Details

Details support the main idea in a personal narrative. They give more information about the event or situation. Each detail sentence further develops the main idea and helps the reader to understand the narrative.

Time Order

In a personal narrative, the sentences that support the main idea often appear in **time order**, the order or sequence in which events occur.

Look at the paragraph about the camping trip. Notice the sentences that support the main idea.

- Which words in these sentences show time order?
- What other words could you use to show the order of events?

Read the paragraph again, replacing each of the time-order words or phrases with a time-order word from the following list.

after, always, before, finally, first, last, later, meanwhile, now, soon, then

Do the time-order words you have chosen make the sequence of events clear?

Guided Practice: Charting Supporting Details

Your class has written a main-idea sentence for a personal narrative. With your class, make a chart like the one that follows. Fill in the chart with details that tell about the experience.

Example: My camping trip was filled with unexpected events.

saw a bear
fell into a creek
lost my knapsack
decided to give up camping

Putting a Personal Narrative Together

With your class, you have written a main-idea sentence for a narrative. You have charted supporting details and used time-order words.

Think about your main-idea sentence. Then, look at your chart of supporting details. You will need to decide which details best support the main idea of your narrative. Which supporting details will you include? What details might you add to your narrative?

Here is one student's personal narrative. The student used the main-idea sentence and some of the details you have already seen to write her own paragraph. She ordered her sentences carefully to make her narrative clear. As you read the paragraph, look for the time-order words that show the sequence of events.

> My camping trip was filled with unexpected events. First, the weather turned overcast and rainy. Then, there were unexpected animals. Raccoons and bears ate our food. They knocked over the garbage pails, too. Finally, Joey had an accident. He fell into the little creek on the campgrounds and got completely soaked. In the future, we have to prepare more carefully.

Guided Practice: Writing a Personal Narrative

Use the main-idea sentence you wrote with your class to write a personal narrative. Write three or four detail sentences that support the main idea. Include some supporting details from your chart. Use time-order words to arrange the sentences in a logical order.

Exchange paragraphs with a classmate. Underline the detail sentences in each other's narratives. Ask your partner which detail sentences helped him or her to understand your narrative. Then, ask your partner if more details are needed to make your meaning clear.

Checklist: Narrative Writing

When you write a personal narrative, you will want to keep some points in mind. You can use the checklist below to remind you to include these points.

Make a copy of the completed checklist. You can add other points to it to help you write. Keep a copy of it in your writing folder. You can use it when you write your personal narrative.

CHECKLIST

✔Purpose and audience   ✔Supporting details

■ _____   ■ _____

■ _____   ■ _____

✔Main idea _____   ✔Time-order words _____

■ _____   ■ _____

■ _____   ■ _____

2 THINKING AND WRITING: Main Idea and Details

You have learned that writing a personal narrative is one way to share an experience with a reader. In a narrative you tell your reader about an event or events. You help the reader to understand what happened by selecting and ordering details carefully.

Every narrative begins with a main, or an overall, idea. The detail sentences in the narrative support the main idea by giving more information about the event. Look at this page from a writer's journal. This writer is preparing to write a personal narrative about a short trip on a ferryboat. On the page, details are listed.

> *My first trip on the ferryboat was the most exciting part of summer vacation.*
>
> *Mother's dog, Willie, got lost in the engine room.*
>
> *The trip took three hours.*
>
> *My little sister Carmen wandered away.*
>
> *Carmen's birthday is tomorrow.*

Thinking Like a Writer

■ Which details support this writer's main idea?

Not all of the details in the writer's journal add to the main idea of the narrative. For instance, the sentence about Carmen's birthday does not give more information about the ferryboat trip.

THINKING APPLICATION Choosing Supporting Details

COOPERATIVE
LEARNING

Each of the writers below is planning to write a personal narrative. Help each one to decide which detail sentences support his or her main idea. Write the details to include on a separate piece of paper. You may work with a group of students to discuss your ideas. Share the reasons for your choices with your classmates.

1. Lisa's personal narrative will tell about the exciting day on which she first saw her newborn twin sisters. Which details should she include? What might she add?

    My favorite baby-sitter read to me.

    Mom came home with twins!

    I like to read aloud.

    Dad brought Mom and the babies home.

2. Brian's personal narrative will tell about his first night at camp. Which details should he include? What might he add?

    The bunkhouse was warm and stuffy.

    Strange noises kept me awake.

    I grew up in the city.

    Dad promised us a puppy in the fall.

3. Gabriella's personal narrative will tell about the day she learned to play baseball. Which details should she include? What might she add?

    I watched other players hit the ball.

    I felt eager to try, too.

    I already knew how to play tennis.

    I hit a home run that day.

4. Mel's personal narrative will tell about his visit to a bakery. Which details should he include? What might he add?

    The air smelled delicious.

    The bakers rolled out trays of dough.

    I tasted a piece of fresh bread.

    Bread at the supermarket is already sliced.

3 INDEPENDENT WRITING: A Personal Narrative

Prewrite: Step 1

You have learned some important ideas about narration. Now you are ready to choose your own topic for writing. Louis, a student in the fifth grade, decided his **audience** would be other students. He chose a topic in this way.

Choosing a Topic

1. First, Louis wrote a list of events that might interest other students.
2. Next, he thought about narrating each event.
3. Last, he selected the event he thought would make the most interesting narrative.

working in my father's store
my little brother
learning to ski
raising turtles

Louis decided to write about learning to ski. He narrowed his topic to the first time he skied. His **purpose** was to show what his first day on the ski slopes was like.

Louis made a **cluster** that helped him to explore ideas for writing. Louis's cluster looked like this.

Exploring Ideas: Clustering Strategy

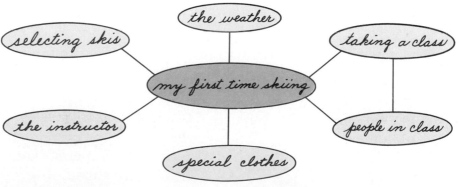

the weather
selecting skis
taking a class
my first time skiing
the instructor
people in class
special clothes

Before beginning to write, Louis tried to remember as many details as he could about that day. He wanted to give a clear account of the event. Louis also added some more details to his cluster.

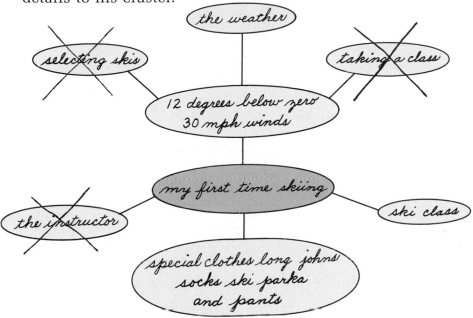

Thinking Like a Writer

- What did Louis add?
- What did he cross out?
- Why do you think he decided to leave out certain details?

Think of an experience that you would like to share. Use **Pictures** or your journal for ideas. Follow these steps.

- Make a list of events or experiences.
- Choose one that you would like to share.
- Narrow the topic if it is too broad.
- Decide on the main idea of your personal narrative.
- Think about your purpose and audience.

Make a cluster. Remember, you can add to or take away from the cluster at any time.

Write a First Draft: Step 2

Louis has decided which details to include in his personal narrative. He used a planning checklist. Louis is ready to write his first draft.

Louis's First Draft

> First because it was really cold. I put on two pairs of long johns and socks. The wind howled and it blue really hard. Then I put on my ski parka and ski pants. When I went outside I could hardly walk. My ski class hadn't prepared me for this. The wind blue me into a snowdrift. Later I heard the temperature was 12 degrees below zero with 30 mile-an-hour winds.

While Louis was writing his first draft, he did not worry about errors. He wanted to put all of his ideas down on paper.

Planning Checklist
- Remember purpose and audience.
- State a main idea.
- Use supporting details.
- Use time-order words.

YOUR TURN

Write your first draft. As you prepare to write, ask yourself these questions.

- What is my main idea? How can I best explain it?
- Which details would my audience want to know?

TIME-OUT You might want to take some time out before you revise. That way you will be able to revise your writing with a fresh eye.

Revise: Step 3

After Louis finished his first draft, he read it over to himself. He decided to share his narrative with his classmate Fernando. Fernando had some suggestions for improving the narrative.

Louis reviewed his planning checklist. He saw that he had forgotten an important point. He checked it off so that he would remember it when he revised. Louis now has a checklist to use as he revises.

Louis made some changes to his personal narrative. Notice that he did not correct small errors. He knew he could correct them later.

The revisions Louis made changed his paragraph. Turn the page. Read Louis's revised paragraph.

Revising Checklist
- ■ Remember purpose and audience.
- ✔ ■ State a main idea.
- ■ Use supporting details.
- ■ Use time-order words.

Louis's Revised Draft

My first day skiing, I thought I was prepared for everything. First because it was really cold. I put on two pairs of long johns and socks. The wind howled and it blue really hard. Then I put on my ski parka and ski pants. When I went outside I could hardly walk. My ski class hadn't prepared me for this. The wind blue me into a snowdrift. Later I heard the temperature was 12 degrees below zero with 30 mile-an-hour winds.

Thinking Like a Writer

WISE
WORD
CHOICE

- Which sentence did Louis add? How does adding the sentence improve the paragraph?
- Which sentences did Louis put in a different order? Do you think the changes improve the paragraph?

YOUR TURN

Read your first draft. Make a checklist. Ask yourself these questions.

- Is my main idea clear?
- Do my supporting details develop the main idea?
- Have I used time-order words correctly?

If you wish, ask a friend to read your narrative and make suggestions. Then revise your paragraph.

Proofread: Step 4

Louis knew that his work was not complete until he proofread his paragraph. He used a proofreading checklist while he proofread.

Louis's Proofread Draft

My first day skiing, I thought I was prepared for everything. First, because it was really cold, I put on two pairs of long johns and socks. The wind howled and it ~~blue~~ *blew* really hard. Then I put on my ski parka and ski pants. When I went outside I could hardly walk. My ski class hadn't prepared me for this. The wind ~~blue~~ *blew* me into a snowdrift. Later I heard the temperature was 12 degrees

YOUR TURN

Proofreading Practice

Use the paragraph below to practice your proofreading skills. Find the errors. Write the paragraph correctly on a separate piece of paper.

I thought I new everything about Ronnie. He was my age and he had two sisters. Because he was knew at skool. He didn't have a lot of friends. He was smart. He liked to study. The girls liked him because he was really nice to them. When I finally met his parents, they were French. Ronnie talked to them in perfect French, and translated for me!

Proofreading Checklist
- Did I indent my paragraph?
- Did I spell all words correctly?
- What punctuation errors do I need to correct?
- What capitalization errors do I need to correct?

Applying Your Proofreading Skills

Use your checklist to proofread your personal narrative. Review **The Grammar Connection** and **The Mechanics Connection**, too. Use the proofreading marks to mark changes.

THE GRAMMAR CONNECTION

Remember these rules about sentences.

- A sentence expresses a complete thought.
- A sentence contains both a subject and a predicate.

  Must guard against frostbite. *not a sentence*
  Skiers must guard against frostbite. *sentence*

Check your narrative. Have you used complete sentences?

THE MECHANICS CONNECTION

Remember these rules about punctuating sentences.

- A sentence begins with a capital letter and ends with a period, an exclamation mark, or a question mark.
- To join two or more sentences, use a comma and a joining word.

  Tomorrow we will ski**, and** we will ride the chair lift.

Check your narrative paragraph. Have you used the correct punctuation to combine your sentences?

Proofreading Marks
¶ Indent
∧ Add
⌿ Take out
≡ Make a capital letter
／ Make a small letter

THE WRITING PROCESS: Proofreading

Publish: Step 5

Louis shared his personal narrative by having it published in the school newspaper. He copied his work neatly and sent it to the editor. The editor printed Louis's paragraph in the sports section. Several students wanted to know if Louis actually managed to ski during that freezing day.

YOUR TURN

Make a final copy of your narrative paragraph. Think of a way to share your work. Some ideas are listed in the **Sharing Suggestions** box below.

SHARING SUGGESTIONS

Create a notebook of personal narratives. Ask others for their work.	Read your work aloud to the class. Invite questions from your listeners.	Mail your work to a friend in another city. Ask him or her to respond to your narrative.

SPEAKING AND LISTENING: Having a Class Discussion

You have just written a narrative about an event that happened to you. You told your ideas and experiences to readers. In a good conversation, you speak *and* listen to others. You can learn a great deal by listening to someone's ideas, and you can also share some of your own knowledge.

In a class discussion, students take turns offering ideas and responding to them. Every class discussion has a specific purpose. Often, the purpose of a discussion is to share information about a topic.

Suppose your class has been given a social studies project. The assignment is to prepare for a group discussion about what makes your school's neighborhood special. Each student thinks about or researches one interesting or unusual thing about the neighborhood. Each student records some main points and details on a note card to prepare for the class discussion. Look at this note card.

Notes on What the Neighborhood Looks Like

1. *has a beautiful park planned 100 years ago*

2. *has many wide streets shaded by tall trees*

3. *is located in a part of the city in which there are many old houses*

4. *school stands on a hill and has a nice view of the river*

Notice that this student's main idea appears in the title at the top of the note card. How do the details add to the main idea that she will bring up in the class discussion?

When you prepare for a class discussion, it will help you to keep your **purpose** and **audience** in mind. These speaking guidelines will help you to focus your talk.

SPEAKING GUIDELINES: A Class Discussion

1. Remember your **purpose** and **audience**.
2. Make a note card. Practice speaking in class, using the note card as a memory aid.
3. Tell the main idea. Add supporting details. Use time-order words.
4. Look at your classmates as you speak.
5. Speak clearly when it is your turn.

- How do I prepare to join in a class discussion about a specific topic?
- How can I use details to support the main idea I wish to contribute to a class discussion?

SPEAKING APPLICATION A Class Discussion

Work with your class to decide on an interesting topic for a class discussion. Think about the main idea you would like to contribute to the discussion. List some points that support and develop this main idea. Prepare a note card with the specific information that you will use in the discussion. Use the speaking guidelines to help you prepare. Your classmates will be using the following guidelines as they listen to your ideas.

LISTENING GUIDELINES: A Class Discussion

1. Listen for each speaker's main idea.
2. Listen for the supporting details.
3. Listen for the logical order of details.

5 WRITER'S RESOURCES: Finding Words in a Dictionary

You have learned that choosing precise words helps you to share your experiences. When you wrote a personal narrative, you were careful to select just the exact details you needed. Using a dictionary correctly allows you to find and spell many additional words you can use in your writing.

You use a dictionary to look up the correct spelling and meaning of a word. Words appear in a dictionary in **alphabetical order**. The first letter of a word determines whether it can be found in the **front**, **middle**, or **back** of the dictionary. Each word in dark type is an **entry word**. The entry word is the basic form of the word, without endings such as *ed*, *ing*, *s*, *er*, and *est*.

On the top of each page of the dictionary, there are two **guide words**. The guide word on the left is the first word on the page. The guide word on the right is the last word on the page. The entry words on each page fall alphabetically between the two guide words. Look at the dictionary entry below. What are the guide words that appear above the first entry word?

---

mesquite/metaphor

mes·quite (mes kēt′) *n.* a small thorny tree or shrub that grows in desert regions from the southwestern United States to Chile, bearing small flowers and slender seed pods containing beans used as feed for livestock.

mess (mes) *n., pl.* **mess·es. 1.** an untidy, disorderly, or dirty state or condition: *The closet is a mess.* **2.** a person or thing that is in such a state or condition: *The room was a mess after the party.* **3.** an unpleasant, difficult, or confusing situation: *to make a mess of one's life.* **4.** an untidy or confused mass or collection; jumble: *a mess of newspapers on the floor.* **5.** an indefinite amount: *to catch a mess of fish.* **6.a.** a group of people who take meals together regularly, especially in the army or navy. **b.** the meal eaten by such a group. **c.** the place where such a meal is eaten; mess hall. —*v.i.* **1.** to interfere or tamper: *Don't mess with my typewriter.* **2.** to take one's meals in a mess hall.

mes·sage (mes′ij) *n.* **1.** a communication sent from one person or group to another. **2.** a formal or official communication: *the president's message to Congress.* **3.** the point of view or idea meant to be communicated: *The movie's message was that crime doesn't pay.*

Practice

A. Look at these guide words. Which of the words listed below appear on the page of the dictionary that has these guide words at the top? Write the words on a separate piece of paper.

1. fiesta/ figure

   a. fire   d. fig

   b. fifth   e. fib

   c. figure   f. film

2. hibachi/high frequency

   a. hibernate   d. height

   b. highchair   e. hide

   c. hiccup   f. highlight

B. Read each definition for the word *buckle*. On a separate piece of paper, write three different sentences in which you use *buckle* correctly.

> **buck·le** (buk′əl) *n.* **1.** a clasp used to fasten together two loose ends, such as the ends of a belt or strap. **2.** something that resembles this, such as an ornament on a shoe. **3.** a bend or sag in a surface: *a buckle in the counter top.* —*v.,* **buck·led, buck·ling.** —*v.t.* **1.** to fasten with a buckle. **2.** to cause (something) to sag or bend, especially from strain or heat. —*v.i.* **1.** to be fastened or joined by a buckle. **2.** to sag or bend: *A beam supporting the roof buckled.*

WRITING APPLICATION A Narrative

Choose two words from the list below. Look up the meaning of each word. Write the definitions on a separate piece of paper. Then write a narrative paragraph in which you use both words correctly. Exchange paragraphs with a group of classmates. Read each other's paragraphs and check for the correct use of each word.

horizon	gauge	taut
standard	permit	zone
mode	legend	fund

6 WRITER'S RESOURCES: Using a Dictionary

When you see an unfamiliar word, use a dictionary to learn its meaning. Often, there is more than one definition of a word in the dictionary. You use the **context**, or setting, of the word to select the correct dictionary definition.

Here is a dictionary entry for the word *transfer*.

trans·fer (*v.*, trans fûr′, trans′fər; *n.*, trans′fər) *v.*, **trans·ferred, trans·fer·ring.** —*v.t.* **1.** to move or remove from one person, place, or the like, to another: *to transfer money from one pocket to another.* **2.** to give or sell the title or possession of to another: *to transfer property from parents to children.* **3.** to convey (a drawing, design, pattern, or the like) from one surface to another. —*v.i.* **1.** to transfer oneself: *to transfer to a new school.* **2.** to be transferred: *The office will transfer to new quarters.* **3.** to switch from one bus, train, airplane, or the like, to another, usually with little or no extra charge: *to transfer at Chicago.* —*n.* **1.** the act of transferring or the state of being transferred: *the transfer of property by a will.* **2.** something that is transferred, especially a drawing, design, pattern, or the like, moved from one surface to another. **3.** a ticket allowing a passenger to continue a journey on another vehicle, usually with little or no extra charge. **4.** the place or means of transferring. —**trans·fer′ a·ble,** *adj.*

Many words can be used as more than one part of speech. If you look closely at the dictionary entry for the word *transfer*, you will notice a small letter *v.* or *n.* before some of the definitions. This letter tells you whether the word is defined as a verb or as a noun in the definition and example sentences. The word *transfer* can be used as either a verb or a noun. Notice that the pronunciation of *transfer* depends upon whether it is used as a noun or as a verb.

After each entry word, you will find a phonetic respelling of the word, which also shows how many syllables the word contains. The pronunciation key at the bottom of the dictionary page tells you how to pronounce the word.

at; āpe; fär; câre; end; mē; it; īce; pîerce; hot; ōld; sông, fôrk; oil; out; up; ūse; rüle; pùll, tûrn, chin; sing; shop; thin; this; hw in white; zh in treasure. The symbol ə stands for the unstressed vowel sound heard in about, taken, pencil, lemon, and circus.

Practice

A. Choose one word from the following list. Look up the word in your dictionary. Copy the first and second definitions of the word. Write one sentence for each definition. Be sure that you have used the word in its correct context, or setting.

parade   rugged   hurdle   common

B. Look back at the definitions for the entry word *transfer* on page 68. Figure out the meaning of the word in each of the sentences below. Write the number of the correct definition and whether it is a noun or a verb. Write the two phonetic respellings of the last syllable. Then, write three sentences in which you use the word *transfer*.

a. Please transfer your bicycle to the bicycle rack outside.

b. Do we transfer to a different bus at Elm Street?

c. I will transfer to a jazz dance class next term.

d. Did the bus driver give you a transfer?

e. The artist made a transfer of his drawing.

WRITING APPLICATION A Paragraph

Look up the word *history* in your dictionary. Write a paragraph in which you use *history* in two separate sentences. See if you can use the word differently in each sentence. Exchange paragraphs with a classmate. Ask your partner to tell you what the word means in the two different sentences. If you wish, you can illustrate each of your sentences with a sketch or painting.

Writing About Social Studies

When you think of social studies, you may think of history. What we call history is often a record of facts and dates. Sometimes history is recorded as personal narratives like those you wrote with your class and on your own.

The building of a road through your town is a historical fact. The fact might be recorded in the town hall. You could write a letter describing the road and how it changed the way you live. Your letter would become a part of history, too.

ACTIVITIES

Imagine a Highway   Imagine that a highway was built right through the middle of your town or city. Your home has been separated from your school and the stores in the neighborhood. Write a paragraph describing how you would go to school and the stores to shop.

Write a Family History   What types of experiences has your family had? Where were your parents and your grandparents born and raised? Write a narrative that includes information about your family's life over the years. You may need to interview some of your relatives to find out some facts.

Look at the Scene   Look at the picture on the opposite page. Think about how you would feel if you were in this picture. Write a narrative based on what you think the picture tells you about life in that place at that particular moment. What would you see and hear? Would you be frightened? Use your imagination to add exciting details to your narrative.

Respond to Literature   The following personal narrative is taken from the book *My Prairie Year, Based on the Diary of Elenore Plaisted*. Elenore's experiences on the prairie in 1889 were different from her life in Maine. Read the following narrative in which the author and her family protect themselves from a tornado. Then, write a narrative about an incident you found exciting, such as a storm, a sudden change in the weather, or another incident. You might also choose to write a summary of the narrative below. If so, you can mention specific details that helped you to picture the tornado.

Tornado!

At sunset, after one of these scorching days, great clouds began to gather, all reddish brown and orange and flame-colored. They came so close you felt you could touch them, and they were rolling and boiling, but we felt no wind. Suddenly there was a draft of cold air and off in the distance, a snakey black cloud was rushing toward us. The men came running in from the fields shouting, "Tornado!" The oxen were turned loose, and we all crowded into the cellar. As we crouched in that dark, quiet place, the sky seemed to tear loose, as if a freight train were passing right over us. When we came out everything was silent and dripping wet, and the house still stood.

UNIT CHECKUP

LESSON 1

Group Writing: A Personal Narrative (page 50) Read the following paragraph. On a separate sheet of paper, write a sentence that tells the main idea of the paragraph.

First, Leon started yelling. Then, Marcy froze in her tracks. Finally, Dad picked up the little garter snake with a stick and put it in the bushes.

LESSON 2

Thinking: Main Idea and Details (page 54) Imagine that you are going to write a narrative about why you decided to learn photography. Which of the following details would you include?

1. want to have pictures of family and friends
2. start a scrapbook
3. started a stamp collection last year
4. an expensive hobby

LESSON 3

Writing a Personal Narrative (page 56) Imagine that you have traveled through time and landed in another century. Write a personal narrative in which you describe what life is like in this other time. Tell your reader how life in the past or future is different from life in the twentieth century.

LESSON 4

Speaking and Listening: A Class Discussion (page 64) Imagine that your class will discuss adopting a classroom pet. Prepare a note card with some ideas for the discussion.

LESSONS 5-6

Writer's Resources: The Dictionary (pages 66-68) Look at the guide words. Which of the entry words listed below will you find on this page of the dictionary?

mantle/march

1. map
2. marigold
3. maple
4. miller
5. nine
6. marble

THEME PROJECT   *ART EXHIBIT*

You have been reading and writing about surprises, the unusual or unexpected events that make life exciting. In your personal narrative, you shared your experience and feelings with readers. You have created a personal narrative that may have surprised your audience, too!

Writing a personal narrative is one way to share a surprise. You can also share a surprise by creating a picture and letting your audience study it.

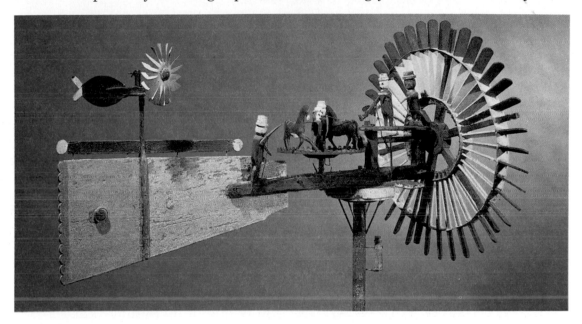

Think of an object that might surprise or seem mysterious to your classmates.

- Draw or paint a picture of this special object.
- Hang your drawing or painting where your classmates can see it clearly. Have the other students make guesses about the mystery item in the picture.
- Make a museum show by hanging these pictures around the classroom.
- With your class write a brochure, or booklet, that describes each artwork in the museum show.

UNIT

3

Nouns

In this unit you will learn about nouns. Nouns name people, places, things, and ideas. Think of how many times you use nouns in your writing.

Discuss Read the poem on the opposite page. What different things are mentioned in the poem?

Creative Expression The theme of this unit is *Patterns*. Look at the poem again. What kinds of patterns might the rain make on the grass? What other kinds of patterns do you know? Draw a picture that shows a pattern. You might want to draw a quilt pattern or the pattern the clouds make in the sky. Write your ideas in your journal.

*Rain went sweeping on
in the twilight, spilling moons
on every grass blade.*

—Sho-u

WHAT IS A NOUN?

A noun is a word that names a person, place, thing, or idea.

Nouns are the words that you use to tell others about the persons, places, things, or ideas that are important to you. A noun can be a single word or two or more words used together.

	Nouns	
Persons	lawyer woman student	Michael Jackson singer plumber
Places	state island country	Texas valley park
Things	bicycle book tree	quilt sewing machine table
Ideas	happiness goodness sadness	courage liberty truth

Guided Practice

Tell which words are nouns.

Example: A quilt is a special kind of blanket. *quilt blanket*

1. Quilts are difficult to make.
2. Sometimes people work together.
3. Choose pretty fabric for the quilt.
4. Many patterns can be made.
5. Look for diagrams in a book.

 THINK

- How do I know if a word is a noun?

REMEMBER

- A **noun** is a word that names a person, place, thing, or idea.
- A **noun** can be more than one word.

More Practice

A. Write each sentence. Draw a line under each noun.

Example: The <u>quilt</u> in my <u>room</u> is very old.

6. People can sew a quilt by hand.
7. Now sewing machines can be used, too.
8. Quilts are made in this way.
9. Stitch two pieces of fabric together.
10. Place stuffing between the layers of fabric.
11. Use soft materials.
12. Feathers are a good choice.
13. Goose down is also an excellent material.

B. Write each sentence. Draw a line under each noun. Then write whether the noun names a **person, place, thing,** or **idea.**

Example: Read these <u>instructions</u> carefully. *thing*

14. Next, sew the layers together.
15. A person needs patience for this craft.
16. Some quilts are made from scraps.
17. Patchwork quilts are popular with many people.
18. The scraps are sewn together in a pattern.
19. Squares and circles are common designs.
20. A sewing room is a busy place.

Extra Practice, page 100

COOPERATIVE
LEARNING

WRITING APPLICATION A Description

Write a description of an object in your home or classroom that is interesting. Describe what the object looks like and why it is interesting. If you like, illustrate your description with a drawing of the object. Exchange descriptions with a group of classmates. Look for nouns in each other's writing.

2 SINGULAR NOUNS AND PLURAL NOUNS

A **singular noun** names one person, place, thing, or idea. A **plural noun** names more than one person, place, thing, or idea.

Many plural nouns are formed by adding *s* to the singular form of the noun. The spelling of some nouns changes when they become plural.

SINGULAR: The *town* looks sleepy, but the *city* looks lively.

PLURAL: The *towns* look sleepy, but the *cities* look lively.

How to Form Plural Nouns		
Singular	**Plural**	**Examples**
most nouns	Add *s*	student—students
nouns that end in *s, x, ch, zz* or *sh*	Add *es*	guess—guesses box—boxes branch—branches bush—bushes buzz—buzzes
nouns that end with a vowel and *y*	Add *s*	toy—toys day—days
nouns that end with a consonant and *y*	Change *y* to *i* and add *es*	country—countries body—bodies

Guided Practice

Tell the plural form of each noun.

Example: story *stories*

1. girl

2. wrench

3. ray

4. puppy

one wrench—$5

two wrenches—$9

 THINK

■ How do I decide whether a noun is singular or plural?

REMEMBER

- A **singular noun** names one person, place, thing, or idea.
- A **plural noun** names more than person, place, thing, or idea.

More Practice

A. Write each noun. Then, write its plural form.

Example: peach *peaches*

5. band

6. dish

7. berry

8. chorus

9. box

10. singer

11. choir

12. chimney

13. lunch

14. bus

B. Write the plural form of each underlined noun.

Example: The <u>singer</u> sang beautifully. *singers*

15. The <u>song</u> had the best <u>verse</u>.

16. The <u>composer</u> repeated the <u>line</u> several times.

17. My <u>friend</u> sang in the <u>concert</u>.

18. The <u>ditty</u> told of life on the <u>ranch</u>.

19. The <u>cowboy</u> had lost the fastest <u>horse</u>.

20. He follows the <u>animal</u> through the scratchy <u>bush</u>.

21. The <u>stallion</u> roamed the <u>county</u> in Montana.

22. The <u>searcher</u> traveled the <u>range</u>.

23. The <u>cloud</u> in the <u>sky</u> wept for him.

24. The <u>rain</u> made the <u>grass</u> muddy.

25. The <u>cowboy</u> sang about the missing <u>pony</u>.

Extra Practice, page 101

WRITING APPLICATION A Caption

Draw a picture that shows what your favorite song is about. Write a summary of the song as a caption for your drawing. Exchange work with a classmate. Look for singular and plural nouns in each other's captions.

3 MORE PLURAL NOUNS

You can form the plural of many nouns by adding *s* or *es*. There are special rules for forming the plural of some nouns.

Special Endings for Plural Nouns		
Noun	**Noun**	**Examples**
Nouns that end in *f* or *fe*	Change the *f* to v and add *es* to some nouns. Add *s* to other nouns.	wife—wives calf—calves bluff—bluffs
Nouns that end with a vowel *and o*	Add *s*.	stereo—stereos video—videos
Nouns that end with a consonant and *o*	Add *s* or *es*.	silo—silos hero—heroes
Nouns that have special plural forms		tooth—teeth foot—feet man—men woman—women
Nouns that have the same forms in singular and plural		deer—deer sheep—sheep

Guided Practice

Tell the plural form of each noun.

Example: calf *calves*

1. potato
2. rodeo
3. half
4. wolf
5. knife

 THINK

■ How can I remember to form the plural of special nouns correctly?

REMEMBER

■ The plural forms of certain nouns are made by following special rules.

More Practice

A. Write each noun. Then write its plural form. You can use a dictionary to check your spelling.

Example: batch *batches*

6. trout
7. alto
8. reef
9. deer
10. tooth
11. man
12. radio
13. bluff
14. pinto
15. studio

B. Write each sentence. Complete the sentences with the correct plural form of each noun in parentheses.

Example: People sit on _____ of grass. (patch) *patches*

16. _____ and adults enjoy games. (Child)
17. Three _____ and three boys form a team. (man)
18. Two _____ play water polo. (woman)
19. A family brought their _____ so they can play musical chairs. (radio)
20. These soccer players can run as fast as _____. (deer)
21. The players' voices created _____. (echo)
22. Boys and girls fish for _____ in a pool. (trout)
23. _____ cover the water. (Leaf)
24. A baseball flew over the _____. (roof)
25. Some girls imitate cowgirls in the _____. (rodeo)

Extra Practice, page 102

WRITING APPLICATION A Set of Rules

Write a set of rules for playing your favorite game. Tell how the game is played and how the score is kept. Exchange rules with a classmate. Find the singular and plural nouns in each other's set of rules.

COMMON NOUNS AND PROPER NOUNS

You know that a noun is a naming word. A **common noun** names any person, place, thing, or idea. A **proper noun** names a particular person, place, thing, or idea. Proper nouns begin with a capital letter.

Common Nouns	Proper Nouns	Common Nouns	Proper Nouns
building	Sears Tower	river	Mississippi River
holiday	Veterans Day	day	Friday
month	October	lake	Lake Charles
state	Nebraska	city	Chicago
bridge	Oakland Bay Bridge	mountain	Mt. Mansfield
author	Mark Twain	continent	Africa

Guided Practice

Tell which nouns are **common nouns** and which are **proper nouns.**

Example: The water in Lake Superior is bright blue in this photograph.
water   common   Lake Superior proper
photograph common

1. Students can make a design with photographs.
2. Magazines such as *Life* or *Newsweek* have many illustrations.
3. Cut the pictures out with scissors.
4. Look for photographs of Paris, London, or Rome.
5. Chris found a painting of the Eiffel Tower in one issue.

 THINK

■ How can I decide if a word is a common noun or proper noun?

REMEMBER

- A **common noun** is a noun that names any person, place, thing, or idea.
- A **proper noun** is a noun that names a particular person, place or thing.

More Practice

A. Write the nouns below. Capitalize the proper nouns.

Example: country—spain—capital   *Spain*

6. author—toni morrison—edgar allan poe
7. the persian gulf—caribbean sea—lake
8. texas—state—county
9. the lincoln tunnel—the golden gate bridge—road
10. the declaration of independence—paper—document
11. stonington—bakersfield—town
12. africa—australia—continent

B. Write each sentence. Draw one line under each common noun. Draw two lines under each proper noun.

Example: The <u>teacher</u> assigns a <u>project</u> on <u>Tuesday</u>.

13. Materials for artwork are everywhere.
14. Some artists use macaroni, string, photographs, and paint.
15. Objects for a design can come from a particular place.
16. Jaime made a picture of things from the Mojave Desert.
17. The picture showed cactus, pebbles, dried flowers, and insects.
18. Frances made a poster about big cities in the United States.
19. The poster showed photos of Seattle, Chicago, and Dallas.
20. José made a poster about lakes and rivers in America.

Extra Practice, page 103

WRITING APPLICATION A Set of Directions

Write a set of directions for creating an artwork from things found outdoors. Exchange your set of directions with a classmate. Identify the common and proper nouns in each other's work.

SINGULAR POSSESSIVE NOUNS

One of the ways you can use nouns in your sentences is to show ownership. A noun that shows ownership is called a **possessive noun.**

Singular Possessive Nouns
The **cat's** whiskers are long.
The **girl's** paintbrush is dry.
The **dog's** paws are wet.

Form the possessive of a singular noun by adding an apostrophe (') and *s* ('s) to the noun.

the home of Mr. Stein   **Mr. Stein's** home
the land of the farmer   **the farmer's** land
the hobbies of the student   **the student's** hobbies

c a t ' s   w h i s k e r s

Guided Practice

Tell the possessive form of each singular noun.

Example: farm *farm's*

1. Nell
2. painter
3. child

4. clerk
5. horse

THINK

■ How do I decide if a word is a singular possessive noun?

REMEMBER

- A **singular possessive noun** shows that one person, place, or thing owns something.
- Form the possessive of a singular noun by adding an apostrophe (') and *s*.

More Practice

A. Write the singular possessive form of each noun.

Example: eagle *eagle's*

6. president

7. artist

8. driver

9. baker

10. man

11. sculptor

12. gardener

13. lion

B. Write each sentence. Change the words in parentheses to include the singular possessive form of the underlined noun.

Example: (The studio of the <u>artist</u>) is cheerful.
　　　　　The artist's studio is cheerful.

14. (The sculptures of <u>Jenny Grove</u>) are wonderful.

15. (The lions of <u>Jenny</u>) are majestic.

16. (The birds of the <u>sculptor</u>) are graceful.

17. (The work of the <u>artist</u>) delights people.

18. There is always a visitor in (the studio of <u>Jenny</u>).

19. (The friend of my <u>father</u>) bought a seal and a dove.

20. (The wings of the <u>dove</u>) are opened wide.

Extra Practice, page 104

WRITING APPLICATION An Explanation

Design a sculpture that you might make out of wood, clay, or metal. Then write a paragraph that explains your sculpture. You could include details about how it will be made, how big it will be, and the materials from which it will be made. Exchange your work with a classmate. Look for possessive nouns in each other's writing.

PLURAL POSSESSIVE NOUNS

A plural noun that shows ownership is called a **plural possessive noun.** When a plural noun ends in s, the possessive is formed by adding *only* an apostrophe (') after the s.

The dresses of the girls hang on the rack.
The **girls'** dresses hang on the rack.

The tools of the gardeners are new.
The **gardeners'** tools are new.

When a plural noun *does not* end in s, the possessive is formed by adding an apostrophe (') and s.

The clothes of the children are colorful.
The **children's** clothes are colorful.

CHILDREN'S CLOTHES

Guided Practice

Tell the plural possessive form of each noun.

Example: sheep *sheep's*

1. men
2. workers
3. adults
4. women
5. boys

 THINK

■ How do I decide if a word is a plural possessive noun?

REMEMBER

- Form the possessive of a plural noun that ends in *s* by adding an apostrophe (') after the *s*.
- Form the possessive of a plural noun that does not end in *s* by adding an apostrophe (') and *s*.

More Practice

A. Write the plural form of each noun. Then write the plural possessive form of the noun.

Example: goose *geese geese's*

6. child
7. doctor
8. lawyer
9. farmer
10. engineer
11. kitten
12. horse
13. mother

B. Write each sentence. Change the words in parentheses to the plural possessive form.

Example: (The return of the birds) signals the new season.
   The birds' return signals the new season.

14. (The gardens belonging to the neighbors) are beautiful.
15. (The children of the gardeners) help with the work.
16. Every spring (the work of the gardeners) begins.
17. (The goal of the people) is the improvement of the area.
18. (The job of the young children) is done after school.
19. Vegetable seeds are planted in (the gardens of the neighbors).
20. (The labor of the workers) will be rewarded.

Extra Practice, page 105

WRITING APPLICATION A Description

Imagine that you and your friends have entered a garden contest. You each enter a special flower, vegetable, or fruit. Write a paragraph in which you use possessive nouns to describe what each person's flower, vegetable, or fruit looks like. Show your description to a classmate. Circle the possessive nouns in each other's descriptions.

7 USING POSSESSIVE NOUNS

You often use nouns to show ownership. If you are not sure how to form the possessive of a particular noun, review these rules. You may need to use your dictionary to check the spelling of certain plural nouns.

Study the chart below.

> The gloves of the **men** protect their hands.
> The **men's** gloves protect their hands.
>
> The gymnasium of the **children** gets a new floor.
> The **children's** gymnasium gets a new floor.

Singular Possessive Nouns

Add an apostrophe (') and an *s* to a singular noun to form the possessive. *Mom'**s** pies   Charles'**s** comb*

Plural Possessive Nouns Ending with *s*

Add an apostrophe (') to a plural noun ending with *s* to form the possessive. *boys' gymnasium   teachers' meeting*

Plural Possessive Nouns Not Ending with *s*

Add an apostrophe (') and an *s* to a plural noun not ending with *s*. *children'**s** desks   women'**s** rights*

Guided Practice

Tell the possessive noun in each sentence.

Example: The principal's project teaches the students good safety rules. *principal's*

1. The children listen to Mrs. Denkar's speech.
2. The woman's words are important.
3. She has the students' attention.
4. The children's safety is important.
5. The speaker is the principal's guest.
6. Mr. Isaac's ideas about safety are good.

?! THINK

■ How do I form a possessive noun?

REMEMBER

- Form the possessive of singular nouns and plural nouns that do not end in *s* by adding an apostrophe (') and an *s*.
- Form the possessive of plural nouns that end with *s* by adding an apostrophe (').

More Practice

A. Write each sentence. Underline the possessive noun.

Example: The <u>teachers'</u> words were heard.

7. He told students about the fire warden's drills.
8. Mr. Issac praised the fifth graders' safety habits.
9. Mrs. Denkar sees Cindy's raised hand.
10. Cindy is this year's crossing guard.
11. She needs people's cooperation.
12. Parents' help is very important.
13. Children's safety involves everyone.

B. Write each sentence. Change each underlined phrase to include a possessive noun.

Example: <u>The remarks of the chief</u> are intelligent.
        The chief's remarks are intelligent.

14. <u>The safety habits of the students</u> should be perfect.
15. The students listen to <u>the opinions of adults</u>.
16. <u>The comments of the visitors</u> are helpful.
17. <u>The hands of many pupils</u> are raised now.
18. <u>The work of the hall monitors</u> improves safety in our school.
19. The principal reminds students to use <u>the office of the nurse</u>.
20. <u>The goals of the assembly</u> have been met.

Extra Practice, Practice Plus, pages 106–107

WRITING APPLICATION A Poster

Make a poster that shows good safety habits. Write clear captions that explain your drawings. Have a classmate check your poster for possessive nouns.

8 MECHANICS: Abbreviations

An **abbreviation** is the shortened form of a word. Most abbreviations begin with a capital letter and end with a period. Abbreviations are often used in addresses, lists, and titles.

Initials are also a kind of abbreviation. Initials can be used instead of a whole name. Initials are capitalized and are followed by a period.

Some Common Abbreviations and Initials			
Addresses	Avenue–Ave.	Drive–Dr.	Street–St.
Titles	Doctor–Dr.	Senior–Sr.	Junior–Jr.
States	Ohio–OH	New Mexico–NM	Rhode Island–RI
Time and Initials	before noon–A.M.	after noon–P.M.	Joseph Peter Gordon–J.P. Gordon
Businesses	Company–Co.	Corporation–Corp.	Incorporated–Inc.
Days	Monday–Mon.	Thursday–Thurs.	Sunday–Sun.
Months	November–Nov.	April–Apr.	August–Aug.

Guided Practice

Tell the abbreviation or initial for each underlined word.

Example: Davis and Davis, <u>Incorporated</u> *Inc.*

1. Lakeville, <u>Ohio</u>
2. Four o'clock in the <u>afternoon</u>
3. Seven o'clock in the <u>morning</u>
4. 421 Bryant <u>Avenue</u>
5. <u>Doris Jane</u> Bailey

 THINK

■ How do I decide when to use an abbreviation?

REMEMBER

- An **abbreviation** is a shortened form of a word. Most abbreviations are capitalized and end with a period.
- An **initial** is the first letter of a name. Initials are capitalized and are followed by a period.

More Practice

A. Write the correct abbreviation for the following words. Be sure to use correct punctuation.

Example: Sunday Sun.

6. Doctor
7. Company
8. Drive
9. New Mexico
10. before noon
11. Street
12. Avenue
13. April

B. Write each group of words. Abbreviate the underlined word or words in each group.

Example: Sam Dugan, <u>Junior</u> Jr.

14. Paul <u>James</u> Tyler
15. 129 Ocean <u>Road</u>
16. <u>Doctor</u> Bonson
17. <u>November</u> 1, 1951
18. <u>Monday</u>, April 15
19. Jamestown Railway <u>Company</u>
20. Dogwalkers, <u>Incorporated</u>

Extra Practice, page 108

COOPERATIVE LEARNING

WRITING APPLICATION A Telegraph Message

Write a telegraph message to a friend about the opening of an art show. In your message, be sure to include the date, time, place, and the name of the artist. Abbreviate words to save space in your message. When you have finished, exchange messages with two classmates. Check to see that all abbreviations are spelled and punctuated correctly in each other's work.

9 VOCABULARY BUILDING:
Compound Words

A **compound word** is a word made from two or more words joined together. You can often tell the meaning of a compound word from the two separate words in the compound. You can also use your dictionary to look up the definition of a compound word.

Many compound words are written as one word.

basket + ball = basketball   news + paper = newspaper

Some compound words are written as two words.

brain wave   fairy tale   fire engine   peanut butter

basket

ball

Guided Practice

Tell the compound word that can be made from each pair. Then tell the meaning of the new word.

Example: mail box   *mailbox*   *a box where mail is put*

1. door   bell
2. board   walk
3. dog   house
4. vault   pole
5. note   book

THINK

■ How can I decide if a word is a compound word?

REMEMBER

■ A **compound word** is made from two or more words.

More Practice

A. Write each sentence. Draw a line under the compound word in each sentence.

Example: This fish comes from a <u>fishpond</u>.

6. Marty has three fish in a fish tank.
7. He bought the fish at a pet shop.
8. He put them into the water with a fishnet.
9. Marty bought a model lighthouse for the tank.
10. His fish need warm saltwater.
11. The plastic top on the tank works as a safeguard.
12. It keeps Marty's house cat away from the fish.
13. The cat thinks the fish are playthings.

B. Match the words in Column A and Column B to form compound words. Look up any words that you do not know in the dictionary.

Example: fire place *fireplace*

	Column A	Column B
14.	river	hook
15.	board	car
16.	bell	bar
17.	fish	bank
18.	box	card
19.	salad	bath
20.	bird	fruit

Extra Practice, page 109

WRITING APPLICATION A Description

Imagine a new type of animal. Write a description of the imaginary animal. Exchange papers with a classmate. Circle any compound words in each other's writing.

GRAMMAR —AND WRITING CONNECTION

Combining Sentences

When you revise your writing, you may want to combine two sentences that contain related information. When words in two sentences are repeated, the sentences may often be combined into one by using *and* or *or*.

Separate: Will our team be *victorious*?
Will our team be *defeated*?

Combined: Will our team be *victorious or defeated*?

Look at the example sentences above. Notice that the two separate sentences share the subject *team*. When the sentences are combined, none of the meaning is lost.

Working Together

COOPERATIVE LEARNING

Discuss each pair of sentences with your classmates. Then tell how you would combine them to make a single sentence.

Example: **In tennis,** players earn points.
In racquetball, players earn points.
In tennis and racquetball, players earn points.

1. In football, players score goals.
   In hockey, players score goals.
2. Our uniforms are colorful.
   Our uniforms are attractive.
3. Will East be the winner?
   Will West be the winner?

Revising Sentences

Andrew wrote these sentences as captions for a comic strip about his favorite sport. Help Andrew to improve the sentences in his caption. Rewrite these pairs of sentences by combining them.

4. Referees enforce the rules in sports.
   Umpires enforce the rules in sports.
5. The quarterback is strong.
   The quarterback is fast.
6. Will Sal be on our team?
   Will Vic be on our team?
7. The coach can choose Marty.
   The coach can choose Ben.
8. Is Saturday's game out of town?
   Is Saturday's game at home?
9. Did number forty catch the pass?
   Did number forty fumble the pass?
10. I enjoyed last year's games.
    I enjoyed this year's games even more.
11. Did you try out for the team?
    Did you change your mind?
12. The fans cheered for hours.
    The fans waved bright pennants.

WRITER AT WORK

Below is the beginning of Dale's letter describing a game of hide-and-seek at a picnic. Help Dale to improve her letter by combining sentences where possible. Add sentences of your own to complete the letter.

Dear Cathy,

I wish you had been at our picnic. José wishes you had been there, too. The boys in our class played hide-and-seek. The girls in our class played hide-and-seek. The woods were dark. The woods were scary. I enjoyed the suspense. The other students enjoyed the suspense.

UNIT CHECKUP

LESSON 1

What Is a Noun? (pages 76–77) Write each sentence. Draw a line under each noun.

1. Two groups can sing a song.
2. Singers start at different places in the song.
3. This song is called a round.
4. The parts make a beautiful sound.
5. The end comes when the last group finishes.

LESSONS 2-3

Singular Nouns and Plural Nouns (pages 78–81) Write each noun. Then write its plural form.

6. mouse
7. fox
8. survey
9. bunch
10. video

LESSON 4

Common and Proper Nouns (pages 82–83) Write each noun. Next to each noun write **common** or **proper**.

11. Susan takes the bus to school.
12. Her route follows the river.
13. The driver turns left on Elm Street.
14. The bus stops at Pine Road and Oak Street.
15. Martin walks to school from his house on Ohio Road.

LESSONS 5-6

Singular and Plural Possessive Nouns (pages 84–87) Write each sentence. Change the underlined group of words to include a possessive noun.

16. Marjorie brought a picture of the cats to school.
17. The ears of one cat are white.
18. The family of Marjorie found a cat in an alley.
19. The cat belonging to Marjorie will soon have kittens.
20. The wish of the children is to have one of the kittens.

LESSON 7

Using Possessive Nouns (pages 88–89) Write each sentence. Change the underlined group of words to include a possessive noun.

21. The book that belongs to Wayne has many pictures.
22. They show the work of a scientist.
23. The experiments of Dr. Wong are important.
24. I like the explanations of the doctors.
25. The research of the scientists is fascinating.

LESSON 8

Mechanics: Abbreviations (pages 90–91) Write the abbreviation or initials for each underlined group of words.

26. September 8, 1978
27. Doctor Gray
28. Perry James, Senior
29. 57 Kiley Drive
30. Gretchen Lewis Brown

LESSON 9

Vocabulary Building: Compound Words (pages 92–93) Match the words (Columns A and B; C and D) to form compound words. Look up any words that you do not know in the dictionary.

Column A	Column B	Column C	Column D
31. cracker	walk	36. rain	boat
32. ice	nut	37. tree	air
33. bag	skate	38. life	door
34. side	hand	39. plane	bow
35. ground	play	40. mat	house

41.-50.

Writing Application: Noun Usage (pages 76–88) The following paragraph contains 10 errors with nouns. Rewrite the paragraph correctly.

I really like interesting autoes. i want a Car of my own. My sister brenda drives me place sometimes. Brendas car is nice. It is a blue convertibles. Her friends car is not as comfortable. She bought it Sep. 20 of last year. She keeps it parked on oak Road.

WORD SAFARI

Play this game in a small group. One person chooses a noun from the list below. Then, he or she will begin a story with a sentence using that noun. The next player will continue the story with a sentence that uses one of the other nouns. Take turns until all the nouns have been used.

elephant	jungle	trail
gasoline	water	food truck
game warden		hunter

WORD BLENDS

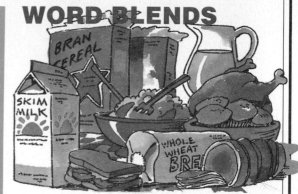

You have learned that compound words are made by joining two or more words. Another type of word is made by blending parts of two words together.

breakfast + lunch = brunch
smoke + fog = smog
motor + hotel = motel

Make up some new words of your own. Pick two words and use parts of each to make the new word. Have a classmate guess the meaning of your words.

WORD-WICH

Any number of people can play this game. The first player says a word. The second player turns the word into a compound word. The next player takes the second part of the compound and makes it the first part of a new compound. Keep going until you run out of words.

Concrete Poems

Seal

See how he dives
From the rocks with a zoom!
See how he darts
Through his watery room
Past crabs and eels
And green seaweed,
Past fluffs of sandy
Minnow feed!
See how he swims
With a swerve and a twist,
A flip of the flipper,
A flick of the wrist!
Quicksilver-quick,
Softer than spray,
Down he plunges
And sweeps away;
Before you can think,
Before you can utter
Words like "Dill pickle"
Or "Apple butter,"
Back up he swims
Past Sting Ray and Shark,
Out with a zoom,
A whoop, a bark;
Before you can say
Whatever you wish,
He plops at your side
With a mouthful of fish!

—William Jay Smith

TRY IT OUT!

The poem "Seal" is a concrete poem. It suggests the shape of a swimming seal.
Think of something that you would like to describe. Write a concrete poem about
this subject.

EXTRA PRACTICE

Three levels of practice

What Is a Noun? (page 76)

A. Write each sentence. Write **person, place, thing,** or **idea** above each underlined noun.

1. Summer is a wonderful season.
2. My sister goes to the country for vacation.
3. Sylvia throws a rock into the still lake.
4. A small wave races across the surface.
5. The stone makes ripples.
6. Sunlight makes the water sparkle.
7. Many people enjoy the scenery.
8. I prefer the beach to the mountains.
9. My holiday begins next month.

B. Write each sentence. Draw a line under each noun.

10. Wind blows across the hot sand.
11. The sands of the desert are in constant motion.
12. A small tornado hovers in the distance.
13. A man rides a mule over a dune.
14. In a day the dune will be much smaller.
15. More sandy mounds will form.
16. The land looks different each morning.
17. Only cactuses grow on this dry earth.

C. Complete each sentence with a noun from the list below. After the noun write **person, place, thing,** or **idea.**

shore   excitement   wave   seal   people   sound   sun   boat

18. At the beach huge waves crash onto the _____.
19. Children express their _____ with shouts.
20. The waves break with a thunderous _____.
21. A _____ swims in the surf.
22. Each _____ breaks and then falls.
23. _____ watch the changing patterns of the ocean.
24. The _____ makes everyone squint.
25. I can barely see the _____ in the distance.

EXTRA PRACTICE

Three levels of practice

Singular Nouns and Plural Nouns (page 78)

LEVEL A. Write each sentence. Draw a line under the plural nouns.

1. Many animals have special markings.
2. Certain creatures are almost invisible.
3. Some bears are white and blend in with the snow.
4. Many jungle animals are green.
5. They can hide easily in leafy trees.
6. The deserts of the world contain many brown rodents.
7. Garter snakes look like sticks.
8. People sometimes wear special outfits that blend into the background.
9. Safari clothes are usually in shades of green and brown.

LEVEL B. Write each noun. Then write its plural form.

10. plain
11. brush
12. ax
13. bay
14. watch
15. dress
16. bounty
17. buzz
18. country

LEVEL C. Write the plural form of each underlined noun.

19. The <u>lobster</u> looks just like the <u>rock</u> behind it.
20. A brown <u>bird</u> is invisible in a winter <u>bush</u>.
21. A <u>leopard</u> blends easily into its <u>setting</u>.
22. The <u>lizard</u> is famous for its <u>change</u> of color.
23. The <u>seahorse</u> also changes <u>color</u> and hides from its <u>enemy</u>.
24. A <u>butterfly</u> can look like a <u>flower</u>.
25. The <u>insect</u> looks just like a <u>twig</u>.

EXTRA PRACTICE

Three levels of practice

More Plural Nouns (page 80)

LEVEL
A. Draw a line under the plural noun in each sentence.

1. Interesting sounds fill the hall.
2. Three radios play the same music.
3. Four videos show different movies.
4. Two sopranos sing a song.
5. Twenty feet dance across the floor.
6. Fifty echoes are heard.
7. The movie studios are hard at work.
8. The director suggests changes in the music.
9. The composer writes more songs for the movie.

LEVEL
B. Write each noun. Then write its plural form.

10. piano
11. fish
12. moose
13. solo
14. man
15. hero
16. horse
17. branch

LEVEL
C. Write each sentence. Complete each sentence with the correct plural form of the noun in parentheses.

18. Three _____ were born in the barn this year. (calf)
19. _____ build their nests in the hayloft. (Mouse)
20. Two _____ hold grain. (silo)
21. _____ graze in the pasture. (Sheep)
22. Ten _____ float on the pond. (goose)
23. _____ are kept in the cellar. (Potato)
24. _____ roam the woods. (Deer)
25. Owls perch on the _____ of the house and barn. (roof)

GRAMMAR

EXTRA PRACTICE

Three levels of practice

Common Nouns and Proper Nouns (page 82)

LEVEL A. Write the nouns below. Capitalize the proper nouns.

1. marie curie — scientist — person
2. river — hudson river — stream
3. atlantic ocean — water — sea
4. oakdale — town — place
5. thanksgiving — holiday — feast
6. city — rome — capital
7. volcano — mount saint helens — mountain
8. mark twain — man — author
9. statue — statue of liberty — tower

LEVEL B. Write each sentence. Draw one line under each common noun and two lines under each proper noun.

10. Washington, D.C. is the capital of the United States.
11. There are many monuments in this city.
12. People visit the Lincoln Memorial every year.
13. Tourists always enjoy the Washington Monument.
14. Perhaps the most beautiful monument is the Jefferson Memorial.
15. The Smithsonian is a wonderful museum.
16. Many people admire the White House.
17. Students visit the Library of Congress.

LEVEL C. Write the nouns in each sentence. Next to each noun write **common** or **proper**. Capitalize the proper nouns.

18. All countries have famous monuments and buildings.
19. In paris, france, there are the eiffel tower and the louvre museum.
20. The sphinx and the tomb of king tut are in egypt.
21. The taj mahal is a famous memorial in india.
22. The ruins of the city of troy lie in turkey.
23. Ancient buildings such as the colosseum are in rome, italy.
24. The parthenon is in greece.
25. The kremlin is a famous building in moscow, russia.

GRAMMAR

Three levels of practice

Singular Possessive Nouns (page 84)

LEVEL A. Each sentence contains an underlined singular possessive noun. Write each sentence. Draw two lines under the word that names what is owned.

1. The doctor's office is crowded.
2. The designer's pattern is simple.
3. The architect's blueprints are complex.
4. The builder's plans are on the table.
5. The musician's cello is in a black case.
6. The girl's report is excellent.
7. The man's ideas are interesting.
8. The student's questions are intelligent.
9. The teacher's lecture is fascinating.

LEVEL B. Write each noun. Then write its singular possessive form.

10. lawyer
11. nurse
12. author
13. plumber
14. sailor
15. pilot
16. painter
17. dancer

LEVEL C. Write each sentence. Change the words in parentheses to include a singular possessive noun.

18. (The mitt of the catcher) is made of leather.
19. (The ship of the captain) is off course.
20. (The script of the actor) is long.
21. (The tools of the electrician) are handy.
22. (The briefcase of the judge) is full.
23. (The truck of the farmer) is loaded with potatoes.
24. (The mane of the horse) is braided with ribbons.
25. (The slippers of the dancer) are pink.

EXTRA PRACTICE

Three levels of practice

Plural Possessive Nouns (page 86)

LEVEL A. Write the possessive form of each plural noun.

1. gardeners

2. mice

3. leaves

4. neighbors

5. geese

6. heroes

7. bushes

8. dogs

9. trout

LEVEL B. Write the plural form of each noun. Then write its plural possessive form.

10. soldier

11. inventor

12. wife

13. officer

14. sculptor

15. child

16. grandfather

17. actor

LEVEL C. Rewrite each phrase to include a plural possessive noun.

18. the paints of artists

19. the bicycles of the boys

20. the tools of the workers

21. the dresses of women

22. the letters from the children

23. the smiles of the aunts

24. the speed of the runners

25. the applause of the people

EXTRA PRACTICE

Three levels of practice

Using Possessive Nouns (page 88)

Write each sentence. Underline the possessive noun.

1. Tom's new telescope is fun.
2. We study stars in Mrs. Williams's class.
3. The children's books explain constellations.
4. The ancient Greeks' legends about stars are fascinating.
5. The three stars show Orion's belt.
6. Tomorrow we will stargaze from our neighbor's roof.
7. Mr. Anderson's building is many stories high.
8. I borrowed my cousin's telescope.
9. Our friend's telescope is too weak.

Write each sentence. Change each underlined phrase to include the possessive noun.

10. The picture of the boy was unusual.
11. The life of the artist is hard.
12. The work of the weavers was beautiful.
13. They used the picture by the painter as a pattern.
14. Jim explained the job of the dyer.
15. The colors of the dyers must match the original art.
16. The knowledge of the historians is helpful.
17. The delight of the viewers makes the work worthwhile.

Write and complete each sentence with a possessive noun.

18. The _____ visit to the park was fun.
19. The _____ favorite part was the playground.
20. _____ dog ran through the grassy field.
21. Molly held the _____ leash.
22. The _____ friend brought his dog, too.
23. A sudden shower soaked the _____ clothes.
24. The _____ paws were muddy and wet.
25. The rain did not spoil the _____ pleasure.

PRACTICE + PLUS

Three levels of additional practice for a difficult skill

Using Possessive Nouns (page 88)

LEVEL A. Write each sentence. Change the underlined group of words to include a possessive noun.

1. The farm of my aunt is in Nebraska.
2. The school of my cousins is in a nearby town.
3. The truck of my uncle takes them to school.
4. The sister of my mother plants corn and wheat.
5. The husband of my aunt is a farmer, too.
6. The produce of my relatives is sold throughout the country.
7. The work of Aunt Maggie is very hard.
8. The hours of a farmer are long.
9. The day of the farmer begins at dawn.

LEVEL B. Rewrite each sentence using a possessive noun.

10. The apartment of Uncle Brad is in the city.
11. The day of my uncle is spent at an office.
12. The wife of Uncle Brad works in the city, too.
13. The brother of my father is a lawyer.
14. The daughter of Uncle Brad goes to my school.
15. The name of my cousin is Celia.
16. The favorite subject of Celia is history.
17. Many of the books belonging to Celia are about history.

LEVEL C. Write a sentence for each of the possessive nouns below.

18. brother's
19. friend's
20. parent's
21. cat's
22. speaker's
23. visitor's
24. doctor's
25. artist's

GRAMMAR

Three levels of practice

Mechanics: Abbreviations (page 90)

LEVEL A. Write the word for which each abbreviation stands.
  1. Mon.
  2. Dr.
  3. Blvd.
  4. Corp.
  5. Co.
  6. Ave.
  7. NM
  8. Sr.
  9. St.

LEVEL B. Write the correct abbreviation for each of the following words.
  10. Junior
  11. afternoon
  12. Friday
  13. November
  14. New Jersey
  15. before noon
  16. Road
  17. New York City

LEVEL C. Write each group of words. Complete each group with the correct abbreviation or initials for the word or words in parentheses.
  18. _____ 9, 1972 (September)
  19. Mayfair, _____ (Incorporated)
  20. _____, July twenty-third (Tuesday)
  21. _____ Griggs (John Paul)
  22. _____ Box 2221 (Post Office)
  23. Jennings and _____ (Company)
  24. San Diego, _____ (California)
  25. _____ 52 B (Apartment)

EXTRA PRACTICE

Three levels of practice

Vocabulary Building: Compound Words (page 92)

LEVEL
A. Write each sentence. Draw a line under the compound word in each sentence.

1. Only an expert tracker can follow a trail in grassland.
2. Footprints are very light.
3. Even a horseshoe may not leave much of a mark.
4. After a rainstorm, tracking is easier.
5. A muddy riverbank shows the tracks of an animal.
6. The dry streambed shows no marks at all.
7. At night, trackers can use a flashlight.
8. Torchlight can also reveal tracks.
9. Sunlight is the best light of all.

LEVEL
B. Make compound words by matching the nouns in the two columns.

10.	way	boat
11.	tug	path
12.	teller	knob
13.	suit	barrow
14.	house	story
15.	flower	case
16.	wheel	dog
17.	door	sun

LEVEL
C. Make compound words by matching the nouns in the two columns. Then, write the definition of each word.

18.	place	fish
19.	gold	market
20.	dog	shift
21.	holder	paint
22.	book	sheep
23.	gear	window
24.	pane	pot
25.	brush	picture

MAINTENANCE

UNIT 1: Sentences

Complete Subjects and Complete Predicates (p. 6)
Write each sentence. Draw one line under the complete subject. Draw two lines under the complete predicate.

1. The ducks swim on the pond.
2. A heron flies overhead.
3. The sun sparkles through the trees.
4. Many people enjoy the day.

Simple Subjects and Simple Predicates (p. 8, 10)
Write each sentence. Draw one line under the simple subject and two lines under the simple predicate.

5. The food is gone!
6. Perhaps the dog ate it.
7. I doubt that.
8. Roger saw a raccoon out here.

Compound Subjects and Compound Predicates (p. 12)
Write each sentence. Draw one line under each compound subject. Draw two lines under each compound predicate.

9. Pat and Jo went to the fair.
10. They rode and enjoyed the rides.
11. Jo won and kept a prize.

Compound Sentences (p. 14)
Write each sentence. Write **simple sentence** or **compound sentence** next to each.

12. The music is beautiful.
13. The band plays more, and the audience is pleased.
14. The concert ends, and it is time to go home.

Correcting Sentence Fragments (p. 16)
Rewrite each group of words to make a complete sentence.

15. Valerie plays the flute. But does not like the piano.
16. Some people can whistle and dance. At the same time.
17. The first time Henry painted. He liked it.

Vocabulary Building (p. 20)
Write the meaning of the underlined word in each sentence. Then, write the word or words you used as context clues.

18. The robber's accomplice aided him.
19. John felt blissful about the beautiful weather.

UNIT 3: Nouns

What Is a Noun? (p. 76) Write each sentence. Draw a line under each noun.

20. Many flowers grow in the garden.
21. Alexandra is growing corn and peas.
22. Frank shovels the soil.
23. Birds fly around and land in trees.

Singular Nouns and Plural Nouns (p. 78, 80) Write each noun. Then write its plural form.

24. deer
25. moose
26. dairy
27. wish
28. potato
29. box
30. boy
31. wife

Common Nouns and Proper Nouns

(p. 82) Write each sentence. Draw one line under each common noun. Draw two lines under each proper noun.

32. The pyramids are in Egypt.
33. The capital of Egypt is Cairo.
34. Tourists from every continent visit this country.
35. The pyramids were built long before Europeans came to North America.

Singular and Plural Possessive Nouns (p. 84, 86) Write each noun. Then write its singular and plural possessive forms.

36. lady
37. fox
38. prince
39. hound

Using Possessive Nouns

(p. 88) Write each sentence. Replace the words in parentheses with a phrase that includes a possessive noun.

40. (The bicycle belonging to Juan) is new.
41. (The father of Miriam) works at home.
42. (The names of the patients) are written in red on the list.

Mechanics: Abbreviations

(p. 90) Write the abbreviations or initials for each word.

43. Doctor
44. Road
45. Sunday
46. Paul Jerry Smyth

Vocabulary Building: Compound Words (p. 92) Match words in the columns to make compound words.

47. horse	light
48. drop	care
49. sun	shoe
50. free	dew

UNIT
4

Writing Instructions

Read the quotation and look at the picture on the opposite page. Ezra Jack Keats is a famous writer. You may have read some of his books. What creative activity is Ezra Jack Keats explaining? What sort of pattern did he see in his work?

Instructions are most helpful to people when they are clear and in step-by-step order. When you write instructions, you will want to be sure that your audience clearly understands them.

Focus Instructions present information about how to do something in a clear and orderly way.

What do you know how to do or create? What would you like to explain? In this unit you will find an article and some interesting photographs. You can use the article and the photographs to find ideas for writing.

THEME: *PATTERNS*

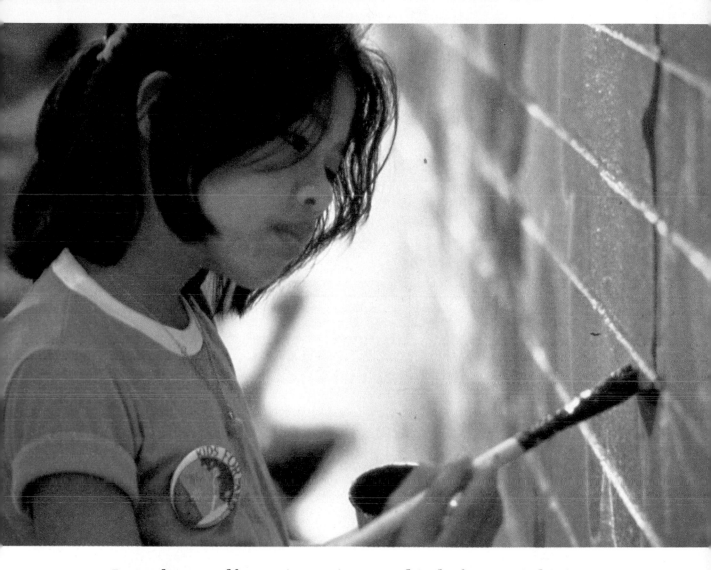

I taught myself to paint, using any kind of material I could find. Once, I covered a board with blue paint, then dipped my brush into the white and dabbed it onto the board, shook the brush a little and let it trail off. I stepped back and got the greatest thrill I can remember. I saw a little cloud floating across a blue sky.

—Ezra Jack Keats

Think about where you live. What is special about your home?

Traditional Japanese houses are different from those in the United States. Japanese homes are kept almost empty. A low table for eating is usually the only furniture in the room.

As you read the selection, notice that the author chooses details that make the subject easy to understand.

JAPANESE HOUSES

from *Shelters*   by Harvey Weiss

Japan is one of the world's most modern countries. It has large industrial centers and cities such as Tokyo, Osaka, and Yokohama, teeming with people, cars, and trucks. Japanese cities have all the advantages and problems found in large urban areas anywhere. There are steel and concrete skyscrapers, business buildings and apartment complexes jammed close together, and houses of all sorts.

But one kind of dwelling is typical of the warmer parts of Japan, although it is not as common as it once was. That is a small, light, airy family house built with simple, traditional materials. It is put together with enormous skill, delicacy, and attention to detail.

Many of these houses are built with movable walls. You won't find walls made of massive logs or the weighty solidity of an African adobe dwelling. The walls are lightweight wood frames covered with paper or a light wood lattice. These screen-like walls slide back and forth to open up a space or close it off. In winter the thin walls are sometimes replaced by heavier ones, or panels to protect against the cold, dry winds that blow in over the Sea of Japan from Siberia.

This kind of lightweight Japanese house is practical and works well in the particular climate where it is found. But there is another reason it is built this way. The Japanese are very aware of their history and cultural heritage. Where

Notice that the author introduces the topic sentence as the second sentence in paragraph 2. The topic sentence prepares you for the details that follow.

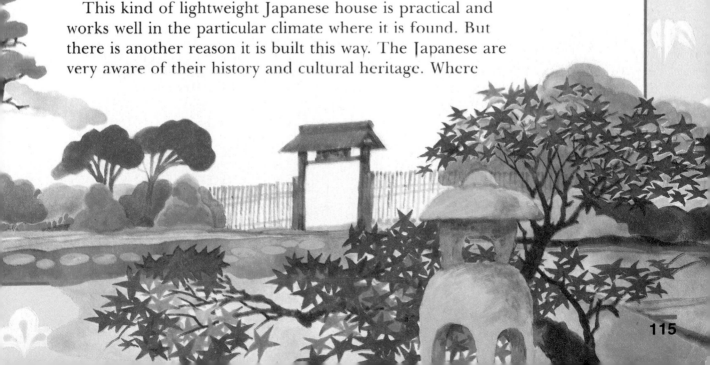

possible, they like to continue this heritage by building in the traditional manner.

The traditional Japanese house has very little furniture. In fact it looks quite bare to the foreign visitor. The reason is that its inhabitants sit on cushions on the floor. There are no chairs, benches, end tables, or sofas. Usually, the only furniture is a low table around which the family gathers to eat.

There are no beds. A mat or quilt on the floor is used for sleeping and put away during the day. Clothing, blankets, and other household materials are folded up and placed in storage areas set into the walls.

The floors are covered with grass mats. These are fairly fragile, and to protect them and keep them clean, visitors and family remove their shoes before entering the house.

To the Japanese, a house is more than a place to keep out of the weather or a place to store one's possessions. The house is considered a part of the natural world, like a field, or a mountain, or a forest. It is regarded with appreciation, care, and sensitivity. The house is an important part of the world, and something to be made as beautiful as possible. It is a work of art.

Thinking Like a Reader

1. Do you think you would enjoy living in a Japanese house? Why or why not? Record your ideas in your journal.
2. What are houses in your neighborhood like? How do they compare with Japanese houses?

Write your responses in your journal.

Thinking Like a Writer

3. What does the author explain about Japanese houses?
4. Which details does he use to explain his topic?
5. Which details do you find most interesting? Make a list of these details.

Write your responses in your journal.

BRAINSTORM *Vocabulary*

The author of "Japanese Houses" uses some nouns that may be new to you. Read the selection again and look for words that describe Japanese houses. In your journal write any nouns that come to mind. Begin to create a personal vocabulary list. You can use these words when you write an explanation.

Talk It Over
Explain Your Work

In the selection you read, the author explains how traditional Japanese houses are built. Think of something you have made. Explain to a partner how you did it. Tell what steps the task included. Then, listen as your partner tells you about something she or he made.

Example: "I made a diorama. I used a shoebox, thin cardboard, paint, and string. I cut figures of people and buildings out of the cardboard. Then, I painted each piece. Next, I glued the string to the back of each piece. I punched holes through one side of the shoebox and threaded the string through the holes so that the pieces hung down. I knotted each string. When I was finished, I had a scene of a city street with people."

Quick Write   *Write a Label*

When you buy a product, it often comes with a set of directions that tells you how to use it. Write a set of directions that includes clear instructions for making something. Here is an example:

Brownie Mix
1. Preheat oven to 350 degrees.
2. Place brownie mix in a large bowl.
3. Add half a cup of water.
4. Add one egg, then stir mixture.
5. Pour mixture into baking pan.
6. Bake for thirty minutes.

Keep your set of directions in your folder.

Idea Corner
Giving Explanations

You have already started to think about problems or tasks you could explain. How could you help your reader to understand and solve a problem? In your journal make some notes about the steps involved in solving a problem. Use these notes when you write an explanation.

PICTURES

SEEING LIKE A WRITER

Finding Ideas for Writing

Look at the photographs. What ideas
for writing instructions do the photographs give you?
Write your ideas in your journal.

PICTURES: Ideas for Explanatory Writing

1 GROUP WRITING: Instructions

COOPERATIVE LEARNING

The **purpose** of a written explanation is to provide clear, useful instructions about how to do something. An explanation states a problem (what is to be done) and then goes on to solve it (steps to follow). What makes an explanation easy for an audience to follow?

- Topic Sentence
- Transition Words
- Clear Details

Topic Sentence

Read the following set of instructions. Notice the underlined sentence.

How to Find a Book in the Library

Finding a book in the library is not difficult if you follow three main steps. First, recall the title of the book you want to find. Second, look for the title in the card catalog. The cards are in alphabetical order. Then, find the number on the card. The number tells you on which shelf the book can be found. After you know the number, find the correct shelf.

The underlined sentence is called the **topic sentence**. A topic sentence states the main idea of a paragraph. In an explanation, the topic sentence introduces what will be explained or what problem will be solved.

Guided Practice: Writing a Topic Sentence

With your class, choose a topic on which you all agree. Brainstorm ideas with your classmates. Then write a topic sentence that states the problem to be solved.

Example: Making wind chimes takes only a few simple materials.

Transition Words

Look back at the paragraph on page 120. Notice that the writer takes you from one step to the next by using words such as *first* and *second*. These words are called **transition words**. They show the *order* of steps to be followed.

The paragraph clearly shows how to find a book in the library. The instructions are simple and clear. Reread the paragraph.

- What other transition words does the writer use?
- How do these words make the instructions clear?

Guided Practice: Using Transition Words

Remember the problem you have chosen to solve in your explanation. Your instructions will tell your audience how to make something. With your classmates, discuss the steps needed to make this object. As a class, make a list of transition words like the one below.

first, second, third
now, next, then
later, last, finally

Clear Details

Each detail in a set of instructions must be clear. The reader has to be able to follow the writer's explanation. In the directions for finding a book in the library, the details tell the reader just what to do. Look back at the paragraph.

- Which details are given?
- Are the steps easy to understand?

Guided Practice: Listing Clear Details

Look at the list of transition words you made with your class. Which words would help you to order your details? Is there enough information in your explanation?

Make a list of details to include in your explanation. Work with your classmates to fill in any missing steps in your instructions.

Putting a Set of Instructions Together

With your classmates you have written a topic sentence for a paragraph that explains how to make something. You have listed some details and some transition words, too.

Think about your topic sentence. Then look at your list of details. Which details would your reader need to understand your instructions? Be sure to include those details. Cross out any details that do not help to make your explanation clear.

A student listed some steps that show how to make wind chimes. These are the steps he chose to include. Look at the details below.

could use glass, metal, or wood   need 6–8 pieces
  need larger piece of material   use medium-weight string

This student listed details that tell more about what materials are needed for a wind chime than about how to put the pieces together.

Guided Practice: Writing Instructions

Use your topic sentence and detail sentences to write a set of instructions. Include transition words to order the steps correctly. Choose words that tell the reader exactly what to do in each step of the instructions.

Share your instructions with a classmate. Ask your partner if he or she could make the object by following your instructions.

Checklist: Instructions

When you write a set of instructions, you will want to keep some points in mind. A checklist will remind you of the things you will want to include in your instructions.

Look at this checklist. Some points need to be added. Make a copy of the checklist and complete it. Keep a copy of it in your writing folder. You can use it when you write your instructions.

CHECKLIST

✔ Purpose and audience

✔ Topic sentence

✔ Transition words

✔ Clear details _____

_____

_____

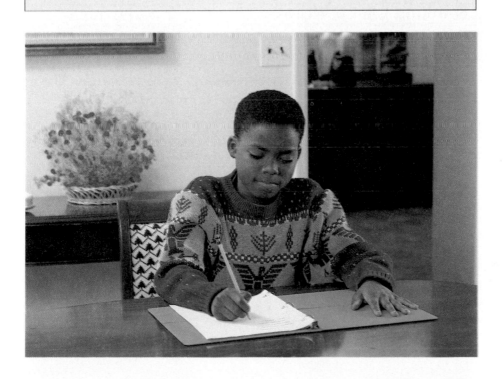

2 THINKING AND WRITING: Solving Problems

You know that when you write a set of instructions, you state a problem and then go on to solve it. The steps of your instructions must be clear.

Writers think carefully about the **purpose** of their explanations and state the problem in a topic sentence. Writers decide which details are important for the **audience** to know and arrange them in logical step-by-step order.

Look at this page from a student writer's journal.

Making Your Own Photo Album
heavy cardboard for covers
thick paper or thin cardboard
string or yarn and paste

Thinking Like a Writer

- Is there enough information here to show a reader how to make an album for photographs?

In your set of instructions, you will have to explain the problem to be solved and how to solve it.

Making your own photograph album is easy and requires only a few simple steps. You need two pieces of heavy cardboard, some sheets of light cardboard or heavy paper for the inside leaves, string or yarn, and paste. First, punch three holes on the left-hand side of each piece of cardboard or paper. Put as many sheets inside the covers as you want. Thread the string through the holes and tie it so that your album stays together. Apply paste to the backs of the photographs, and arrange them as you like.

THINKING APPLICATION Making Details Clear

COOPERATIVE
LEARNING

Each of the writers named below is planning to write a set of instructions. The instructions should be as precise as possible. Help each student to decide which details are clear. Write the details on a separate piece of paper. Do you think you could make the object by following the steps in each set of instructions? You may wish to discuss your thinking with other students. In your discussion, explain your choices to each other.

1. Linda's instructions will tell readers how to make a terrarium. Which details are clear? What details could be added?

   get glass or plastic tank   fill with grass or pebbles
   put in plants   small animals can live in
                                   terrarium.

2. Daryl's instructions will tell readers how to make a layer cake. Which details are clear? What details could be added?

   buy round or square   bake layers for 30 minutes
     cake pans   let cool before icing
   make batter and pour
     into pans

3. Terry's instructions will tell readers how to make a skateboard. Which details are clear? What details could be added?

   get a 12″ by 6″ piece of   could use wheels from
     wood   roller skates
   fasten wheels with   make sure board is
     screwdriver   balanced

4. Jill's instructions will tell readers how to make a window box for flowers. Which details are clear? Which details are unclear?

   wood or aluminum box   pack with soil
   small plants or flowers   place on window

3 INDEPENDENT WRITING: Instructions

Prewrite: Step 1

You have seen how writers put together instructions. Now you can write instructions of your own. Lily, a student your age, wanted to write instructions for the members of her cooking club. She chose a topic in this way.

Choosing a Topic

1. First, Lily thought of foods she liked.
2. Next, she started a list of foods she knew how to cook.
3. Last, she chose the recipe she thought she could explain the most clearly.

making a stew

making a tuna casserole

making chili

making corn bread

Lily decided to explain how to prepare chili. Once she had narrowed her topic, she was ready to explore her idea.

Exploring Ideas: Using a Flow Chart

Lily used a flow chart to organize the steps of her instructions. Notice her topic sentence.

This is how to make the world's best chili.

Chop onion, garlic

⬇

Add ground beef

⬇

Add beans and other ingredients

⬇

Brown onions and ground beef

Lily knew that the **purpose** of her writing was to explain how to make chili. She thought about the steps she would need to explain.

Before she actually wrote her instructions, Lily decided it was important to review each step carefully. She made some changes to her flow chart.

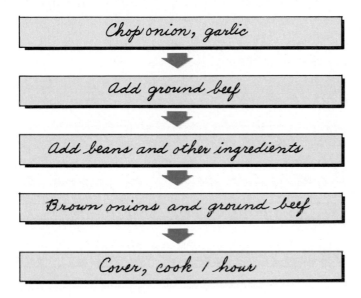

Chop onion, garlic

Add ground beef

Add beans and other ingredients

Brown onions and ground beef

Cover, cook 1 hour

Thinking Like a Writer
- What changes did Lily make to her flow chart?
- Do her changes make sense?

YOUR TURN

Think of something you have made that you would enjoy explaining. Use **Pictures** or your journal for ideas. Follow these steps.

- Write a list of things you know how to make.
- Choose one that you can easily explain.
- Narrow the topic if it is too broad.
- Think about your purpose and audience.

Make a flow chart. Remember, you can change the order of steps on the flow chart later.

Write a First Draft: Step 2

Lily knows what to include in her set of instructions. She has made a planning checklist. Lily is now ready to write her first draft.

Lily's First Draft

aunt bess's Chili

This is how to make aunt bess's chili, the World's best chili. Chop up one onion and two cloves of garlic. Add one to two pounds of ground beef. Add five cups of canned beans and two cups of canned tomatos. Add one teaspoon of salt and four tablespoons of chili powder. Stir and cook for about one hour until chili is brown.

As Lily wrote, she did not worry about errors. She wanted to put her ideas down on paper.

Planning Checklist
- Remember purpose and audience.
- Include a topic sentence.
- Use transition words.
- Choose clear details.

YOUR TURN

Write your first draft. As you prepare to write, ask yourself these questions.

- What will my audience need to know?
- How can I best explain my ideas?

TIME-OUT You might want to take some time out before you revise. That way you will be able to revise your writing with a fresh eye.

Revise: Step 3

After she finished her first draft, Lily read it over to herself. Then she shared her writing with her friend, David. She asked David to suggest ways she could improve her work.

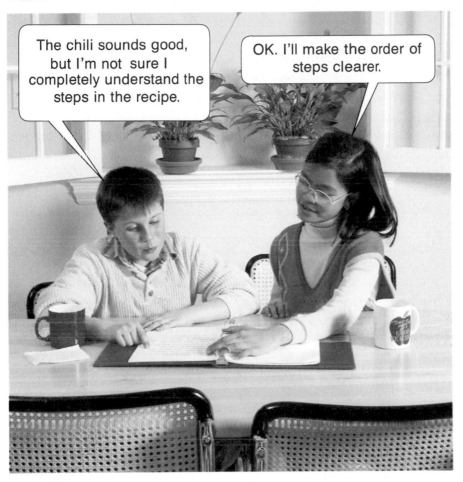

The chili sounds good, but I'm not sure I completely understand the steps in the recipe.

OK. I'll make the order of steps clearer.

Lily then looked at her planning checklist. She realized that she had forgotten one point. She checked it off so that she would remember it when she revised. Lily now has a checklist to use as she revises her instructions.

Lily made changes to her work. She did not correct small errors. She knew she could fix them later.

The revisions Lily made changed her set of instructions. Turn the page. Look at Lily's revised draft.

Revising Checklist
- ■ Remember purpose and audience.
- ■ Include a topic sentence.
- ✔■ Use transition words.
- ■ Choose clear details.

WRITING PROCESS

> aunt bess's Chili
>
> This is how to make aunt bess's chili, the World's
> ~First, melt two tablespoons of butter in a pan.~
> best chili. Chop up one onion and two cloves of
> ~Next,~ ~Then,~ ~After that,~ garlic. Add one to two pounds of ground beef. Add
> five cups of canned beans and two cups of canned
> tomatos; Add one teaspoon of salt and four
> ~Finally,~ ~all the ingredients~ tablespoons of chili powder. Stir and cook for
> about one hour until chili is brown. ~Aunt bess's chili serves six.~

Thinking Like a Writer

WISE
WORD
CHOICE

- Which words did Lily add? How did this make her instructions clearer?
- Which sentences did she combine? How does this improve her writing?
- Which sentences are new or changed? How does this revision help make the instructions clear?

YOUR TURN

Read your first draft. Ask yourself these questions.

- What is my topic sentence?
- What transition words have I included to show the order of the steps in my instructions?
- How can I make my details clearer?

If you wish, ask a friend to read your instructions and make suggestions. Then revise your set of instructions.

Proofreading: Step 4

Lily knew that her work was not complete until she proofread her instructions. She used a proofreading checklist while she proofread.

Part of Lily's Proofread Draft

aunt bess's Chili

This is how to make aunt bess's chili, the World's
best chili. Chop up one onion and two cloves of
~First, melt two tablespoons of butter in a pan.~
garlic. Add one to two pounds of ground beef. Add
Next,   Then,   After that,
five cups of canned beans and two cups of canned

tomatos, Add one teaspoon of salt and four

YOUR TURN

Proofreading Practice

Below is a paragraph that you can use to practice your proofreading skills. Find the errors. Write the paragraph correctly on a separate sheet of paper.

First remove all the furniture and rugs. Then spread a drop cloth over the floor Be sure it covers up to the walls. Wear a mask to protect you from the paint fume. Open the paint and stir it well. Next paint around the edges of the ceiling with a brush Then roll paint on the ceiling with a roller. After that, paint the four corners with a brush. Then roll paint on the wall finally, clean up and put back the furniture when the paint is dry.

Proofreading Checklist
- Did I indent at the beginning of each paragraph?
- Did I spell all words correctly?
- What punctuation errors do I need to correct?
- What capitalization errors do I need to correct?

Applying Your Proofreading Skills

Now proofread your set of instructions. Read your checklist again. Review **The Grammar Connection** and **The Mechanics Connection**, too. Use the proofreading marks to mark changes.

THE GRAMMAR CONNECTION

Remember these rules about nouns.

- Most nouns form the plural by adding *s*.
- Nouns ending in *s*, *x*, *ch*, or *sh* form the plural by adding *es*.
- Nouns ending with a vowel and *y* form the plural by adding *s*.
- Nouns ending with a consonant and *y* form the plural by changing the *y* to *i* and adding *es*.

    The gift**s** were under the tree.
    The tree branch**es** were decorated with tinsel.
    The boy**s** thought of their cousin**s** in other cit**ies**.

Check your work. Have you formed plural nouns correctly?

THE MECHANICS CONNECTION

Proper nouns are those that name a particular person, place, or thing. All proper nouns must be capitalized.

| river | → | Nile River | country | → | Egypt |
| mountain | → | Mt. Rainier | state | → | California |

Proofreading Marks

- ¶ Indent
- ∧ Add
- ℛ Take out
- ≡ Make a capital letter
- / Make a small letter

Publish: Step 5

Lily shared her instructions with her cooking club. She copied the instructions in her best handwriting and gave them to the members of the club. Several members of her cooking club made Aunt Bess's chili. They said it was easy to make and tasted delicious.

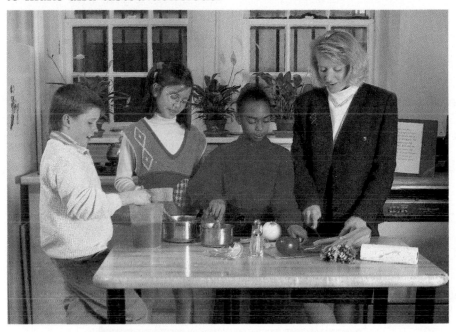

YOUR TURN

Make a final copy of your instructions. Write as neatly as you can. Think of a way to share your work. You might find some ideas in the **Sharing Suggestions** box below.

SHARING SUGGESTIONS

Create a how-to book that includes instructions for making various things.	Exchange instructions with a classmate. Try to make the thing described.	Read your instructions aloud to your class. Ask other students to tell you if the instructions are clear.

4 SPEAKING AND LISTENING: Giving Instructions

You have just written a set of instructions. Your instructions have shown readers how to make something. You included transition words and clear details in a logical order. Now you can use what you know about writing instructions to give a talk in which you explain to an audience how to make something.

First, you will want to make a flow chart for your explanation. The flow chart should include your topic and some details. Each detail in the flow chart should appear in the order in which you plan to discuss it.

Look at the flow chart below.

Making a Papier-Mâché Sculpture

sculpt an object from torn paper

⬇

tear strips of newspaper

⬇

find object to mold paper around

⬇

make a flour paste

⬇

layer paper and paste on form

⬇

let sculpture dry, then paint

Notice that the title at the top of the flow chart gives the topic or main idea of the student's explanation. How does the order of steps help you to understand the instructions?

Keep in mind that as the student explains each step to his classmates, he will use appropriate transition words. These words will help his classmates to understand the order of steps in the process.

When you give a talk, it will help you to keep your **purpose** and **audience** in mind. These speaking guidelines will help you to focus your explanation.

SPEAKING GUIDELINES: Giving Instructions

1. Remember your **purpose** and **audience**.
2. Make a flow chart. Practice using the flow chart.
3. Begin with a topic sentence.
4. Use transition words to show the order of details.
5. Look at your listeners and speak in a strong, clear voice.

- What is the purpose of my explanation?
- Do the instructions serve this purpose?

SPEAKING APPLICATION A Set Of Instructions

Think of something you know how to make. Prepare a flow chart to use as you organize the details of your explanation. Use the speaking guidelines to help you prepare. Your classmates will be using the following guidelines as they listen to your instructions.

LISTENING GUIDELINES: Instructions

1. Listen for the purpose of the explanation.
2. Listen for the logical order of the steps in the instructions.
3. Listen for clear details.

5 WRITER'S RESOURCES: The Thesaurus

In this unit you have prepared instructions explaining how to make several things. You have learned that it is important to find the precise words to explain your meaning in each step of your instructions.

A useful resource for the writer is a **thesaurus**. This is a book that contains lists of **synonyms**, words that mean almost the same thing as the word you have looked up. The thesaurus helps you to find words that say exactly what you mean.

Sample Entry
laugh, chuckle, giggle, guffaw, snicker
antonyms: *See* **cry**.

A list of **entry words** can be found in the thesaurus. Entry words are written in **dark type** and are listed in alphabetical order. The words listed after each entry word are synonyms. At the end of some entries is a list of **antonyms**, words that mean the opposite of the **entry word**. The number next to the entry word in the **index** of a thesaurus tells you where the word is listed in the book. Some thesauruses give the definition of the entry word and an example sentence.

Practice

A. Use the Thesaurus on page 507 to find synonyms for the following entry words. Make a list of these synonyms on a separate sheet of paper.

1. big
2. look
3. smile
4. nice
5. run
6. interesting
7. good
8. like
9. plain
10. neat
11. sad
12. strong
13. think
14. surprised
15. little
16. ready
17. shy
18. see
19. hard
20. many

sick (continued)
   unwell not feeling well. You should lie down if you are *unwell*.
   antonyms: well, healthy

small *See* little.

smart *adj.* intelligent; bright; having learned much. There are many *smart* students in her class.
   clever mentally sharp; quick-witted. He gave a *clever* answer.
   intelligent able to learn, understand, and reason. Dolphins seem to be *intelligent* animals.
   shrewd clever or sharp in practical matters. The woman's *shrewd* decisions have made her a success.
   wise able to know or judge what is right, good, or true, often describing a person with good sense rather than one who knows a lot of facts. In this folk tale, a boy is guided by a *wise* woman.
   antonym: stupid

smile *v.* to show a smile, in a happy or friendly way. Our neighbor *smiled* and waved.
   beam to smile joyfully. Dan *beamed* when he received the award.
   grin to smile broadly with great happiness or amusement. Walter *grinned* when he saw the picture.
   smirk to smile in a silly or self-satisfied way. Nina *smirked* foolishly.
   antonyms: frown, scowl

strange *adj.* differing from the usual or the ordinary. We heard a *strange* noise in the basement.
   odd not ordinary. Jo has an *odd* pet.
   weird strange or odd, in a frightening or mysterious way. Kids say the *weird* house is haunted. *See also* unusual.

strong *adj.* having great strength or physical power. It took four *strong* men to move the piano.
   muscular having well-developed muscles; strong. That shirt makes you look *muscular*.
   powerful having great strength, influence, or authority. Their new car has a *powerful* engine.
   antonym: weak

sure *adj.* firmly believing in something. I'm *sure* I'll have a good time once I get there.
   certain free from doubt; very sure. Roy was *certain* he had left the key on the counter.
   confident firmly trusting; sure of oneself or of another. Wendy is *confident* of winning the prize.
   definite positive or certain. They have not made any *definite* plans.
   antonyms: doubtful, unsure

surprised *adj.* feeling sudden wonder. He was *surprised* at how cold it was outside.
   amazed overwhelmed with wonder or surprise. Daria was *amazed*

518
Thesaurus for Writing

B. Choose two of the entry words from Practice A. Write a sentence for each word. Then, replace each entry word with a **synonym** from your list.

WRITING APPLICATION Sentences

Choose three words that you used in your set of instructions. Write these words on a separate sheet of paper. Look up each word in your Thesaurus. Then, write two synonyms for each word. Finally, use each synonym in a sentence. Keep your list of words in your writing folder. You can use it in **The Curriculum Connection** on page 138.

THE CURRICULUM CONNECTION

Writing About Art

You can read about art in books, magazines, and newspaper reviews. There are many ways to write about art. A writer may describe a particular work of art or explain how it was created. An artist may tell something about his or her life and work.

ACTIVITIES

Describe a Painting   Look at the illustration on the opposite page. Write an explanation of what you see happening in the picture. Which details in the picture make you think your explanation is a good one? Include these details in your writing so that your reader can "see" the picture.

Explain How to Make a Work of Art   What kinds of things have you made in art class or outside of school? Think of the steps needed to make a painting, a photograph, a drawing, or other artwork. Recall the order of the steps. Then write an explanation of how to make the artwork. Be sure to order your steps clearly.

Respond to Literature   The following explanation is taken from a book about drawing living things. The author believes it is important to understand how an animal or a plant moves. He says that an artist must watch animals in action before trying to capture them on paper.

After reading the explanation, try drawing a living animal or plant. After you finish your drawing, write a description of what you did in order to understand how to draw the animal or plant.

IN YOUR DRAWINGS OF ANIMALS, MAKE IT CLEAR THAT THEY ARE AWARE OF THE WORLD AROUND THEM...

...THROUGH THEIR SENSES OF SIGHT,

HEARING,

SMELL,

OR TOUCH.

From Drawing Life in Motion

Animals move freely. Many are conscious of where and why they move. Life is moving around them. They can sense it. Life is pulsing within them. They can hardly contain it. Even when standing still, animals move with breaths or blinks, always ready for action.

You can breathe life into your drawings of still animals by giving them a look of awareness or by poising some part of their bodies on the verge of, or at the end of, a move.

Animals can move from place to place by pushing or pulling on other things. An inchworm crawls by pushing against the ground with its hind end and then pulling on the ground with its front end.

A toad's muscular hind legs push against the ground with every hop. A lizard climbing up a boulder pulls on the rock with each clawed step.

The most effective way I know to draw animals in motion is to show them in the midst of pushing or pulling themselves along.

UNIT CHECKUP

LESSON

Group Writing: Instructions (page 120) On a separate sheet of paper, arrange the following details in an order that makes sense. Begin each sentence with a transition word that shows the order of steps.

How to Make a Collage

—Arrange materials on paper or cardboard.

—Paste down paper and other loose objects.

—Collect materials like paper, string, paint, and paste.

—Paint or draw on paper before pasting any objects.

LESSON

Thinking: Solving Problems (page 124) Help your reader solve the following problem. Next to each detail, write a complete sentence that explains a step in the instructions. Then write your sentences in a clear, orderly paragraph.

Making a Set of Flashcards

—index cards without lines

—words you want to remember

—magic marker

—purpose of set of flashcards

LESSON

Writing Instructions (page 126) Imagine that a classmate will visit you. Write a set of instructions that explains how to get to your home from the school. Put each step of your directions in a logical order.

LESSON

Speaking and Listening: Giving Directions (page 134) Imagine that you will give an oral report in which you tell your classmates how to do or make something. Make a flow chart that includes each step in the proper order.

LESSON
5

Writer's Resources: The Thesaurus (page 136) Choose four words. Look them up in your thesaurus. Then choose a synonym for each word. On a separate sheet of paper, write a sentence for each synonym.

THEME PROJECT *QUILT DESIGN*

You have been reading about patterns of many kinds. Patterns exist everywhere. In art, music, science, cooking, gardening—anywhere you look, you can find a pattern.

Think of some of the patterns you have seen. They may be small or large. Sometimes, a pattern is hard to see. Once you see it, though, it seems quite clear.

Collection of the Museum of American Folk Art;
Gift of David Pottinger.
1980.37.27

Quilt; Sunshine and Shadow,
Amish, Susan Beechy,
Topeka, Indiana.
Cotton.
1935-40
83″ × 70″

The quilt in this photograph has patterns or designs that you can see easily. Talk with your classmates about the patterns you find in the quilt. Think of the kinds of patterns you like.

- Draw a design for a quilt that you would like to make or own.
- Begin by brainstorming some ideas.
- After you have drawn or painted the design for your quilt, write an explanation of its pattern. What does it look like? Why did you choose this particular pattern?
- Share your quilt design and written explanation with your classmates. Look for the patterns in each other's quilt designs.

5

Verbs

In this unit you will learn about verbs. Some verbs express action, and others do not. Which verbs can you think of that do not express action?

Discuss Read the poem on the opposite page. What are the people doing? Which verb can you find that does not express action?

Creative Expression The theme of this unit is *Prizes*. What kinds of prizes do you know about? Draw a medal or a ribbon that might be given as a prize. Write a few words on your drawing to explain the prize. You may wish to put your drawing in your journal.

THEME: *PRIZES*

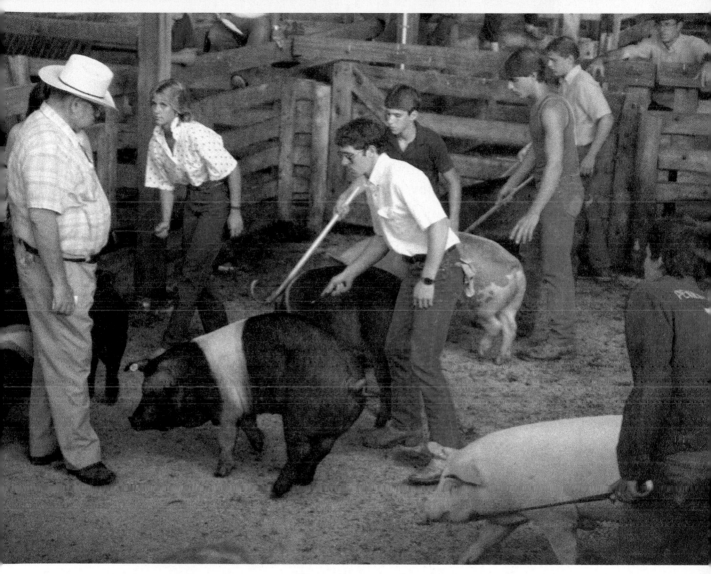

Hog-Calling Competition

*A bull-voiced young fellow of Pawling
Competes in the meets for hog-calling;
 The people applaud,
 And the judges are awed,
But the hogs find it simply appalling.*

—Morris Bishop

1 WHAT IS AN ACTION VERB?

An action verb is a word that expresses action.

Every sentence you write has two parts, a subject and a predicate. The main word in the predicate is often an **action verb.** The action verb tells what the subject of the sentence does or did. What kinds of actions are expressed in the sentences below?

> Sylvia **entered** the short story contest.
> Now many people **read** her story.
> We **enjoy** her tale about a leprechaun.

Verbs can also express action you cannot see.

> I **wonder** about the contest.
> Robin **hoped** for a prize.

Sylvia typed her story.

Guided Practice

Tell which word is the action verb in each sentence.

Example: The teacher discusses our stories.   *discusses*

1. We read the contest rules.
2. The judges outlined the rules.
3. Only fifth graders enter the contest.
4. We work on our stories all week.
5. Sylvia planned her story carefully.

 THINK

■ How can I recognize an action verb?

REMEMBER

- An **action verb** expresses action.
- An action verb tells what the subject of the sentence does or did.

More Practice

A. Write each sentence. Draw a line under the action verb in each sentence.

Example: The contest begins today.   *The contest <u>begins</u> today.*

  6. Sylvia writes in a diary.
  7. Her story comes from her diary.
  8. Details interest Sylvia.
  9. Past prize winners visited the state capital.
10. Sylvia hopes for a good prize.
11. Robin enters the contest, too.
12. He works slowly but carefully.

B. Write the sentences. Complete each sentence with an action verb.

Example: I _____ my story first.   *I finish my story first.*

13. Everyone _____ about his story.
14. No one _____ it except Robin.
15. Sylvia _____ about the contest.
16. Robin _____ eagerly.
17. We _____ for the judge's decision.
18. They _____ the winner on Friday.
19. The announcement _____ everybody.
20. Robin and Sylvia both _____ prizes.

Extra Practice, page 176

WRITING APPLICATION A List

Imagine that you must judge a short story contest. Write a list of the contest rules. Include your ideas about what makes a short story good. Read your work to a group of your classmates. Ask them to find the action verbs.

COOPERATIVE
LEARNING

2 VERBS WITH DIRECT OBJECTS

Often, a subject and a verb express a complete thought.

Subject	Verb
The dog	barked.
The sound	echoed.

Sometimes an action verb is followed by a direct object. A **direct object** is a noun or pronoun in the predicate that receives the action of the verb. A direct object answers the question *what?* or *whom?* after action verbs.

Elaine judges **dogs.**
She gives **prizes** to the winners.
Dogs love **her.**

The spaniel wants the prize.

Guided Practice

Tell the action verb and the direct object in each sentence.

Example: The pet owners follow the rules.
       follow   action verb   rules. direct object

1. We plan a dog show.
2. Each owner enters a dog.
3. Elaine judges our show.
4. George owns a spaniel.
5. The spaniel carries a bone.

 THINK

■ How can I recognize the direct object in a sentence?

REMEMBER

- A **direct object** receives the action of the verb.
- A direct object answers the question *what?* or *whom?* after action verbs.

More Practice

A. Write each sentence. Draw one line under the action verb and two lines under the direct object.

Example: The dogs wear tags.   *The dogs wear tags.*

6. A beagle shows her hunting skills.
7. Each owner wants the best prize.
8. Elaine brings dog biscuits.
9. The pets love the treats.
10. They all wag their tails.
11. The dogs obey the handlers.
12. They treat the dogs well.

B. Write each sentence. Complete each sentence with a direct object.

Example: The judges choose the _____.   *The judges choose the winners.*

13. We enter the _____.
14. Elaine pats a frightened _____.
15. Susan brushes a _____.
16. A collie chases a _____.
17. The judge announces the _____.
18. Ricky holds a _____.
19. A sheepdog wins the _____.
20. The audience applauds the _____.

Extra Practice, page 177

WRITING APPLICATION An Announcement

Write an announcement for a dog show. Include important information about the event. Have a classmate find the action verbs and direct objects in your work.

3 MAIN VERBS AND HELPING VERBS

You know that a simple predicate can be more than one word. Some sentences have a main verb and a helping verb. The **main verb** shows what the subject does or is. The **helping verb** helps the main verb to show an action in the sentence. By itself, a helping verb cannot show action.

The main verbs in the sentences below are in red. The helping verbs are in blue.

> Stan and Jan **are entering** the talent contest.
> I **can help** them rehearse.
> They **have created** a dance routine.
> They **will dance** together.

Study the chart below.

Common Helping Verbs					
am	are	were	shall	has	can
is	was	will	have	had	could

Guided Practice

Tell the main verb in each sentence. Then, tell the helping verb in each sentence.

Example: The dancers will perform soon.

perform   main verb   will   helping verb

1. Gerald is practicing for the contest.
2. He has danced in many talent shows.
3. He will perform some difficult dance steps.
4. We have started our rehearsals.
5. We can meet every afternoon.
6. Judson and I could use more practice.

 THINK

■ How can I recognize the main verb and the helping verb in a sentence?

REMEMBER

- The **main verb** shows what the subject does or is.
- The **helping verb** helps the main verb to show an action.

More Practice

A. Write each sentence. Draw one line under the helping verb. Draw two lines under the main verb.

Example: We are participating in the event.   *We <u>are</u> <u><u>participating</u></u> in the event.*

 7. We have met every day after school.
 8. Other students are planning their acts.
 9. Everybody is making fancy costumes.
10. Sandy has made a decision.
11. She shall enter the contest without a partner.
12. She is performing a solo act.

B. Write the sentences. Complete each sentence with a helping verb.

Example: My brother ____ coaching me.   *My brother is coaching me.*

13. We ____ practice very hard.
14. I ____ attend all the rehearsals.
15. Lucy ____ singing in her act.
16. My friends ____ come to the show.
17. The judges ____ make fair decisions.
18. We ____ planning a party after the contest.
19. We ____ invited many guests to the party.
20. We ____ waiting eagerly for that day.

Extra Practice, page 178

WRITING APPLICATION An Article

Imagine that you are writing for your school paper. Write a brief news article about a special event at the school. Have your classmates find the main verbs and the helping verbs in your article.

---

4 WHAT IS A LINKING VERB?

Some verbs do not show action. Verbs that do not show action are called linking verbs. A **linking verb** is a verb that links the subject of a sentence to a noun or an adjective in the predicate. The word that follows the linking verb names or describes the subject of the sentence. Many linking verbs are forms of the verb *to be.*

The state fair **is** a treat.

Some verbs can be either linking verbs or action verbs.

The fairgrounds **look** pretty. (linking verb)
You can **look** at the Ferris wheel. (action verb)

Common Linking Verbs			
am	was	seem	taste
is	were	appear	smell
are	will be	look	feel

The pie is delicious.

Guided Practice

Tell the linking verb in each sentence.

Example: The muffins smell good.
smell   linking verb

1. Mrs. Lowe's pies taste wonderful.
2. She is an excellent baker.
3. The cakes look beautiful.
4. They smell delicious.
5. The prizes are red and blue ribbons.

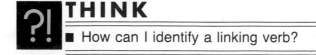

?! THINK

■ How can I identify a linking verb?

REMEMBER

- A **linking verb** links the subject of a sentence to a noun or an adjective in the predicate.
- The word that follows the linking verb names or describes the subject of the sentence.

More Practice

A. Write each sentence. Draw a line under the linking verb.

Example: The fairgrounds are crowded. *The fairgrounds are crowded.*

6. The animal shows are my favorite exhibits.
7. The farmers seem friendly.
8. The animals look healthy.
9. The judges are experts.
10. People are excited by the contests.
11. One judge is a farmer.
12. He appears knowledgeable about the animals.

B. Write each sentence. Draw one line under the linking verb. Draw two lines under the word that describes or names the subject.

Example: Hank is confident. *Hank is confident.*

13. Sheila seems quite skilled.
14. Her sewing appears perfect.
15. The dress is a blue ribbon winner.
16. Hans and Jody are relaxed, too.
17. They were contestants in last year's show.
18. That flower show looks interesting.
19. I am fond of flowers.
20. I will be a gardener one day.

Extra Practice, page 179

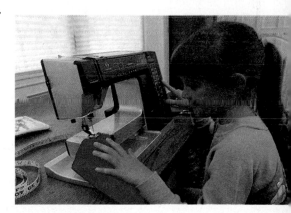

WRITING APPLICATION A Story

Imagine that you have just won first prize in a contest. Write a story about the events that took place during the contest. Have a classmate circle the linking verbs.

5 VERB CONTRACTIONS

When you speak, you sometimes use contractions. A contraction is a word made from two words. Contractions are often used in informal writing and conversation. They should not be used in formal reports or business letters. Sometimes you can combine a verb with the word *not* to form a **verb contraction.**

Use an apostrophe (') in place of the letter or letters that have been left out. Remember, *not* is a negative word and is not part of the verb phrase.

Contractions with Verbs Plus the Word *not*			
should not	shouldn't	would not	wouldn't
is not	isn't	cannot	can't
will not	won't	has not	hasn't
must not	mustn't	were not	weren't
was not	wasn't	are not	aren't
could not	couldn't	had not	hadn't
do not	don't	have not	haven't
does not	doesn't	has not	hasn't

Guided Practice

Tell the contraction of the underlined words.

Example: I could not decide upon a project. *couldn't*

1. Sylvia will not display her painting yet.
2. She does not feel ready.
3. I have not seen it.
4. She should not worry about her work.
5. We are not finished, either.

?! THINK

- How can I decide where to use an apostrophe in a contraction?

REMEMBER

- Contractions are formed from some verbs and the word *not*.
- Use an apostrophe (') to show the letter or letters that have been left out of the contraction.

More Practice

A. Write the word or words from which the contraction has been made.

Example: wouldn't   *would not*

6. mustn't
7. doesn't
8. aren't
9. haven't
10. don't

11. can't
12. isn't
13. won't
14. didn't
15. hadn't

B. Write each sentence, using a contraction of the underlined words.

Example: The students <u>are not</u> ready.   *The students aren't ready.*

16. The art show <u>was not</u> planned until last week.
17. There <u>is not</u> much time left!
18. Joe <u>will not</u> talk about his sculpture.
19. He <u>would not</u> explain his silence.
20. Mindy <u>cannot</u> stand secrets.
21. She <u>has not</u> hidden her pottery from viewers.
22. Many students <u>could not</u> stop for conversation all week.
23. Now we <u>are not</u> worried any longer.
24. The judges <u>were not</u> wrong about the artwork.
25. We <u>should not</u> forget to congratulate the winners.

Extra Practice, page 180

✏ WRITING APPLICATION An Advertisement

Write an advertisement for a contest. Your language can be informal, so feel free to use contractions. Have a partner look for the contractions in your work.

6 VERB TENSES

The verb you use in a sentence helps you to tell when something happens. The time expressed by a verb is called its **tense**. Verbs show time by changes in tense. The three main tenses are the **present, past,** and **future** tenses.

Present-tense verbs show something that is happening now.

Johanna always **wants** something different.

➡ Add *s* or *es* to a present-tense verb when a singular noun is its subject.

Past-tense verbs show action that has already happened.

Yesterday she **wanted** an Olympic medal.

➡ Add *ed* to the present tense of the verb to form the past tense of most verbs.

Future-tense verbs show something that has not yet happened.

Tomorrow Johanna **will want** something else.

➡ Add *shall* or *will* before the present tense of the verb to form the future tense.

Guided Practice

Tell whether the underlined verb is in the present, past, or future tense.

Example: I <u>ski</u> each winter.   *present tense*

1. The team <u>skied</u> downhill. past
2. Each team member <u>practices</u> daily. pres.
3. We <u>will watch</u> them ski. fut.
4. The best athletes <u>will receive</u> the prize. fut.
5. Our team <u>earned</u> the bronze medal. past

 THINK

■ How can I identify the **present, past,** and **future** tenses?

REMEMBER

■ The three main tenses are the **present, past,** and **future** tenses.

More Practice

A. Write **present, past,** or **future** after each underlined verb.

Example: We <u>watched</u> the whole show.   *past*

6. I <u>like</u> the figure skating.
7. Winners <u>will receive</u> medals.
8. Machines <u>scraped</u> the ice this morning.
9. A skater <u>twirled</u> on the ice.
10. The best athletes <u>will practice</u> for hours.
11. My favorite skater <u>races</u> today.
12. I <u>cheered</u> for Stacy yesterday.

B. Write each sentence. Complete each sentence with the correct tense of each verb in parentheses.

Example: The ball game _____ at four o'clock. (start) *The ball game starts at four o'clock.*

13. I _____ a baseball to school tomorrow. (carry)
14. Gretchen _____ me at the games last year. (watch)
15. Now, she _____ a chance, too. (want)
16. Last spring, I _____ softball. (play)
17. Later this year, I _____ for the team. (pitch)
18. This morning, the coach _____ a victory today. (promise)
19. Last time, the team _____ heavily. (score)
20. We _____ the other teams next fall. (defeat)

Extra Practice, page 181

WRITING APPLICATION A News Story

Imagine that you are a television reporter at an important event such as a track meet or game. Write a news story about the event and what makes it exciting. Exchange stories with a partner. Identify the verb tenses in each other's writing.

7

USING THE PRESENT AND PAST TENSES

A verb changes its form to agree, or work, with the subject to show its tense.

Rules for Forming the Present Tense				
1. Most verbs: Add *s*.			stop	stop**s**
			climb	climb**s**
2. Verbs ending in *s*, *ch*, *sh*, *x*, and *z*: Add *es*.	guess	guess**es**	fix	fix**es**
	catch	catch**es**	buzz	buzz**es**
	rush	rush**es**		
3. Verbs ending with a consonant and *y*: Change the *y* to *i* and add *es*.			fry	fr**ies**
			hurry	hurr**ies**
Rules for Forming the Past Tense				
1. Most verbs: Add *ed*. Verbs ending with *e*: Add *d*.			mend	mend**ed**
			free	free**d**
2. Verbs ending with a consonant and *y*: Change the *y* to *i* and add *ed*.			carry	carr**ied**
			bury	bur**ied**
3. Verbs ending with a single vowel and a consonant: Double the final consonant and add *ed*.			slip	slip**ped**
			fan	fan**ned**

Guided Practice

Tell the past tense of the underlined verb in each sentence.

Example: We <u>study</u> the campaign issues.   *studied*

fanned

1. We <u>vote</u> for a class president.
2. Students <u>elect</u> the person of their choice.
3. I <u>pick</u> the winner every time.
4. Sandra and I <u>support</u> Chris.
5. Chris <u>believes</u> in student government.

 THINK

How do I form the present and past tenses of most verbs?

REMEMBER

- Add *s* or *es* to form the present tense of singular verbs.
- Add *ed*, *d*, or *ied* to form the past tense of verbs.

More Practice

A. Write each sentence, using the past tense of the underlined verb.

Example: The teacher explains the rules.   *The teacher explained the rules.*

6. The class votes on Tuesday.
7. The students listen to the speeches.
8. The candidates rush around the halls.
9. They worry about their chances.
10. I plan a different speech for Chris.
11. My classmates discuss the issues.
12. Many problems need our attention.

B. Write each sentence. Use the correct form of the verb in parentheses.

Example: I _____ shorthand all week. (practice)   *I practiced shorthand all week.*

13. I _____ to school last Tuesday. (hurry)
14. The class _____ me as the spokesperson. (name)
15. I always _____ a pencil and notepad. (carry)
16. That way I _____ my ideas. (remember)
17. My speech _____ the candidates. (praise)
18. I _____ both the winner and the loser. (thank)
19. Everyone _____ when the election was over. (cheer)
20. The teacher _____ beverages and toasted the class. (pour)

Extra Practice, page 182

WRITING APPLICATION A Speech

Imagine that you have just finished your term as class president. Write a speech explaining what you have done to make school a better place. Check verb tenses.

SUBJECT-VERB AGREEMENT

A verb agrees with its subject in **number**. If the subject is singular, the verb must be singular. If the subject is plural, the verb must be plural.

Add *s* or *es* to the present-tense verb when the subject is a singular noun or *he*, *she*, or *it*.

    The winner **rushes** by us.   He **appears** happy.

Do not add *s* or *es* to the present-tense verb when the subject is a plural noun or *I*, *you*, *we*, or *they*.

    Morris and Cora **seem** excited.
    They **rush** into the room.

Notice that in the compound subject *Morris and Cora* the verb agrees with a plural subject.

Guided Practice

Tell which of the verbs in parentheses completes each sentence correctly.

Example: We (join, joins) the audience in the room. *join*

1. Bill (enter, enters) the spelling bee.
2. We (wish, wishes) him well.
3. He (tell, tells) us his plan.
4. He (study, studies) the dictionary every night.
5. Janet and I (spell, spells) well, too.

 THINK

■ How do I make the subject and the verb agree?

REMEMBER

■ In the present tense, the subject and verb must agree in number.

More Practice

A. Write each sentence, using the correct form of the verb in parentheses.

Example: We (prepare, prepares) for the spelling bee.   *We prepare for the spelling bee.*

6. The spelling bee (begin, begins) today.
7. The teachers (choose, chooses) the words.
8. Winners (receive, receives) a dictionary.
9. The words (seem, seems) difficult.
10. We all (learn, learns) quickly.
11. The contest (start, starts) in a minute.
12. I (read, reads) the rules first.

B. Write each sentence. Complete each sentence with the correct present-tense form of the verb in parentheses.

Example: Jo _____ the score. (check)   *Jo checks the score.*

13. My friends _____ the spelling bee. (watch)
14. Bonnie _____ the first word. (spell)
15. She _____ the next word. (miss)
16. We _____ the next hour in that room. (pass)
17. The judge _____ all the mistakes. (catch)
18. Many students _____ from the stage. (walk)
19. Bill _____ the spelling bee successfully. (finish)
20. The judge _____ the prize to him. (award)

Extra Practice, Practice Plus, pages 183–184

WRITING APPLICATION A Poster

Make a poster that gives information about a contest or another event that will take place at your school. Have a group of your classmates check for subject-verb agreement in your poster.

COOPERATIVE
LEARNING

USING *BE* AND *HAVE* CORRECTLY

9

Some verbs follow special rules to agree with their subjects. *Be* and *have* are two verbs that must change their form according to special rules in order to agree with their subjects.

Study the chart below to memorize the present and past tense forms of *be* and *have*.

Subject	Present	Past
I	am	was
you	are	were
he, she, it	is	was
we	are	were
they	are	were

Subject	Present	Past
I	have	had
you	have	had
he, she, it	has	had
we	have	had
they	have	had

Guided Practice

Tell which verb in parentheses agrees with the subject in each sentence.

Example: The garden club contest (is, are) fun.   *is*

1. First prize (is, are) a watering can.
2. I (is, am) a member of the club.
3. Jean (is, am) a member, too.
4. The club (has, have) regular meetings.
5. We (has, have) good prizes for the winners.

are watered

is watered

?! THINK

■ How do I decide which form of *be* and *have* to use in a sentence?

REMEMBER

- A verb and its subject must agree in number.
- The verbs *be* and *have* change in order to agree with their subjects.

More Practice

Complete each sentence, using the correct verb from the pair in parentheses.

Example: The contestants (is, are) excited.   *The contestants are excited.*

6. Paul's tulips _____ the prettiest in the neighborhood. (is, are)
7. Last year, he _____ a garden full of roses. (have, had)
8. Now, he _____ a new type of flower for the garden show. (have, has)
9. The tiger lilies _____ orange and black. (is, are)
10. Dana _____ a new member of the garden club. (is, are)
11. I _____ a friend of hers. (is, am)
12. We _____ all contestants in this year's show. (is, are)
13. Flowers and plants _____ the main entries in the contest. (is, are)
14. You _____ wonderful dahlias. (has, have)
15. My sister and I _____ begonias and violets. (has, have)
16. Jim _____ a great idea. (have, has)
17. He _____ a judge in the contest. (is, are)
18. The prizes _____ all perfect for gardeners. (is, are)
19. I _____ in charge of the prizes. (is, am)
20. Jim and I _____ many good prizes in mind. (has, have)

Extra Practice, page 185

WRITING APPLICATION A Description

Imagine that you are in charge of the prizes to be awarded to the winners of a contest. Decide what the contest and prizes should be. Write a description of the prizes. Ask a classmate to read your description. Have him or her check for subject-verb agreement.

USING IRREGULAR VERBS I

You form the past tense of **regular** verbs by adding *ed* to the verb. **Irregular** verbs are spelled differently in the past tense.

Irregular Verbs		
Present	**Past**	**Past with helping verbs**
see	saw	has, have, had seen
run	ran	has, have, had run
come	came	has, have, had come
go	went	has, have, had gone
give	gave	has, have, had given
eat	ate	has, have, had eaten
write	wrote	has, have, had written
drive	drove	has, have, had driven
ride	rode	has, have, had ridden
take	took	has, have, had taken
speak	spoke	has, have, had spoken
choose	chose	has, have, had chosen
fly	flew	has, have, had flown
draw	drew	has, have, had drawn

Guided Practice

Tell the past-tense form of the verb in parentheses.

Example: Aesop's animals (speak) like humans.   *spoke*

1. Aesop (write) about clever and foolish animals.
2. He (give) them names and ideas of their own.
3. Becky (choose) a book of funny animal fables.

 THINK

■ How do I form the past tense of an irregular verb?

REMEMBER

- Irregular verbs do not form the past tense by adding *ed*.
- The helping verbs *has*, *have*, and *had* are used with irregular verbs.

More Practice

A. Write each sentence. Write the past-tense form of the verb in parentheses.

Example: Last week, I (find) the book.   *found*

  4. The last story has (give) me an amusing idea.
  5. I have (write) a humorous fable, too.
  6. John and I (speak) about the fables.
  7. John (choose) his favorite fable.
  8. The animals (run) in a race.
  9. A bear (see) the entire race.
 10. Birds (fly) in the race.
 11. The race (take) almost an hour.
 12. Many animals (come) to the event.

B. Write each sentence. Write the correct past-tense form of the verb in parentheses.

Example: The race had (begin) already.   *begun*

 13. A bird has (fly) to the finish line.
 14. A flea had (ride) on his back.
 15. John and I have (speak) of this funny fable.
 16. We have (see) how the race ends.
 17. John has (draw) a picture of the lazy hare.
 18. The rabbit had (go) to sleep!
 19. The tortoise had (ran) the best race.
 20. Aesop had (choose) him as the winner.

Extra Practice, page 186

WRITING APPLICATION A Comic Strip

Draw a comic strip that shows a race between two animals. Write captions for your comic strip that explain your drawing.

USING IRREGULAR VERBS II

You know that irregular verbs do not form the past tense with *ed*. Remember these verb forms.

More Irregular Verbs		
Present	**Past**	**Past with helping verbs**
sing	sang	has, have, had sung
swim	swam	has, have, had swum
drink	drank	has, have, had drunk
do	did	has, have, had done
grow	grew	has, have, had grown
throw	threw	has, have, had thrown
know	knew	has, have, had known
wear	wore	has, have, had worn
bring	brought	has, have, had brought
teach	taught	has, have, had taught
say	said	has, have, had said
make	made	has, have, had made
sit	sat	has, have, had sat

Guided Practice

Tell the correct past-tense form of the verb in parentheses.

Example: Who (make) the award-winning movie?   *made*

1. The audience (sit) down in the theater.
2. Some of the stars (do), too.
3. An actor had (sing) the theme song already.
4. An excited director has (make) a speech.

 THINK

■ How can I decide which form of an irregular verb to use in a sentence?

REMEMBER

■ The helping verbs *has*, *have*, and *had* may be used with some past forms of irregular verbs.

More Practice

A. Write each sentence. Use the correct past-tense form of the verb in parentheses.

Example: We (grow) impatient.   *We grew impatient.*

5. He had (know) many famous actors for years.
6. A pop star (sing) another song.
7. The judges (sit) at a table.
8. A famous actor (make) the movie on the screen now.
9. Two sharks (swim) toward the beach.
10. The sunbathers (drink) refreshments.
11. The shark (swim) toward them.
12. We (grow) terribly frightened at this point.

B. Write each sentence. Use the correct past-tense form of the verb in parentheses.

Example: The actors have (wear) fancy clothes tonight. *The actors have worn fancy clothes tonight.*

13. One star has (say) something nice.
14. She has (do) her best for her family.
15. She had (know) many talented actors.
16. All the winners have (make) long speeches.
17. They have (do) this every year.
18. Lorraine had (know) all the movies on the show.
19. She has (bring) a list of movie titles.
20. The show has (teach) us about movies and stars.

Extra Practice, page 187

WRITING APPLICATION A Review

Write a review of a movie, book, or television program that you think deserves to win an award. Explain your reasons for recommending this book or entertainment. Circle past-tense forms of verbs in your work.

12 MECHANICS: Using the Comma

You have seen how commas are used to separate the sentences that form a compound sentence. Commas are also used to separate words in a series or list.

We brought poles, hooks, and hip boots.
Peter will bring sandwiches, juice, or milk.

These sentences contain words in a series. A series is a list of three or more items.

➡ Use a comma to separate each item in a list.

➡ Use the conjunction *and* or *or* before the last item in the list. The sentence below has only two items. This is not a series and does not need commas.

We brought poles and hooks.

Guided Practice

Tell where commas are needed in the following sentences.

Example: Sam Lily and Bob enter the fishing contest.
Sam, Lily, and Bob enter the fishing contest.

1. The fish are judged by size weight and beauty.
2. We can sign up on Monday Tuesday or Wednesday.
3. The fish are red blue green and silver.
4. Linda caught a bass and a trout.
5. We can fish from the boat the shore or the dock.

 THINK

■ How do I use commas to separate items in a series?

REMEMBER

■ Use commas to separate three or more items in a series.

More Practice

A. Write and correctly punctuate each sentence that contains a series. Underline the word that joins the items in each series.

Example: We wear hats gloves and sneakers. *We wear hats, gloves, and sneakers.*

6. We fish with hooks lines and sinkers.
7. I brought a fishing rod a bait box and extra hooks.
8. There are contests for adults and children.
9. Russell and Holly relax on the dock.
10. They eat sandwiches talk or read.
11. I caught three trout two sunfish and a crab.
12. Is that a starfish a sea urchin or a sea horse?

B. Write and punctuate each sentence correctly.

Example: Mom Dad and Sue stay on shore. *Mom, Dad, and Sue stay on shore.*

13. For bait we use worms bread or plastic flies.
14. Bob caught a fish threw it back and caught a bigger one.
15. We count our fish weigh them and bring them to the judges.
16. A red a blue and a gold ribbon are the prizes.
17. Bob Lily and Sam all won ribbons.
18. I reel in my line clean the rod and pack my gear.
19. We are hungry from the long day the fresh air and the excitement.
20. At home we scale clean and broil the fish.

Extra Practice, page 188

WRITING APPLICATION A Letter

Imagine that you have won a fishing contest. Write a letter to a friend describing the experience. With your partner, look at your writing to see if you have used commas correctly.

13 VOCABULARY BUILDING:
Homophones and Homographs

Homophones are words that sound alike but have different spellings and meanings.

> There were already **two** taco stands at the fair.
> Barney wanted **to** open a taco stand, **too.**

In these sentences *two*, *too*, and *to* are homophones. You must look at the **context** or overall meaning to tell which spelling is correct.

Homographs are words that are spelled the same but have different meanings and sometimes have different pronunciations.

> We hoped the **wĭnd** would not blow our stand down.
> Maurice wanted to **wīnd** up our awning.

In the first sentence, *wind* (wĭnd) names the movement of air. In the second sentence, *wind* (wīnd) is a verb that means "to roll up." You can tell the correct meaning of a homograph from its context.

Guided Practice

Use the context clues to select the correct homophone. Tell which word from the pair in parentheses completes each sentence correctly.

Example: (Our, Hour) taco recipe will win an award.   *Our*

1. Jeremy was (scene, seen) at the taco stand.
2. Our tacos are (maid, made) with secret ingredients.
3. Mouth (pain, pane) is caused by too much hot sauce.
4. The cook (ate, eight) another taco.
5. His special recipe was (great, grate).

 THINK

■ How can I recognize homophones and homographs?

REMEMBER

- **Homophones** are words that sound alike but have different spellings and meanings.
- **Homographs** are words that are spelled alike but have different meanings and sometimes different pronunciations.

More Practice

A. Write each sentence, using the correct homophone.

Example: Mary (peaks, <u>peeks</u>) into the saucepan.

6. George (red, read) a secret recipe.
7. George did not (right, write) the recipe for us.
8. He had to (by, buy) special peppers.
9. He (blew, blue) on the cooking fire.
10. He had entered the contest, (to, two, too).
11. His sauce simmered all (night, knight).
12. We could (hear, here) him at work.
13. We (sent, cent) Mary to George's stand.
14. George put (flower, flour) in his sauce.
15. Now we (no, know) the secret ingredient!

B. Write each sentence. Use your dictionary to write the correct definition of the underlined homograph.

Example: We <u>dove</u> into the crowd.   *plunged*

16. We <u>saw</u> the ingredients that went into the sauce.
17. His recipe was ours at <u>last</u>.
18. Jeremy and George clearly <u>lead</u> all competitors in the taco competition.
19. Jeremy will <u>record</u> the victory in his diary.
20. The judges called it a very <u>close</u> contest.

Extra Practice, page 189

WRITING APPLICATION A Billboard

COOPERATIVE
LEARNING

Imagine that you are going to open a booth at a fair. With a group of classmates, make a billboard or sign advertising the items for sale. Use some homophones and homographs in your writing.

GRAMMAR —AND WRITING CONNECTION

Keeping Verb Tenses Consistent

You know that verb tenses express time, or tell when something takes place. When you write, think about your choice of verb tenses. Does the action you are writing about take place in the present, the past, or the future? Once you can answer this question, you have decided on the right verb tense for your writing.

> We watched as our dog walked around the rink. Simba raised his head properly and waited quietly when the judge touched him. He stopped when the trainer gave him the command.

All of the verbs in the paragraph above show action that has already happened. The writer has used the past tense.

COOPERATIVE LEARNING

Working Together

With your classmates, discuss ways to keep verb tenses consistent. Look at the tense of each verb in the sentences below. Tell whether the verbs in each sentence are in the same tense or different tenses.

Example: Our dog was a winner, and he will know it. *different*

1. Simba circles the rink again and stood.
2. He is a champion, and we love him.
3. The judge recognizes and called each dog by name.

Revising Sentences

Marianna wrote these sentences about her summer vacation. Help her revise her work by changing the tense of the verb in the second sentence in each pair of sentences so that the verbs in the sentences are in the same tense. Write the new sentences on a separate piece of paper.

4. I have made my plans already.
   I arranged a visit to Europe.
5. I am excited about the trip.
   My parents were happy for me.
6. I will go to Switzerland soon.
   My plane left on June 30.
7. I will visit the Swiss Alps.
   I stay in a hotel on Lake Garda.
8. My aunt will meet me at the airport.
   She and my uncle also stay at the hotel.
9. I love my aunt's dog, Berry.
   He was a beautiful Saint Bernard.
10. Berry will compete in a dog show.
    He had won a prize for beauty and good behavior.

Where would you like to go on your summer vacation? Think of a place you would enjoy visiting. Write an itinerary or travel plan for your vacation.

Work with a classmate to revise your work. Ask him or her to help you check to see that you have used verb tenses properly. Change the tense of any verb that seems out of place in your itinerary.

UNIT CHECKUP

LESSONS **Action Verbs and Direct Objects** (pages 144–147) Write each sentence. Draw one line under the action verb in each sentence. Draw two lines under the direct object.

1. Joe's jump earns points.
2. The judge measures the distance.
3. Joe wins the event, to everyone's surprise.
4. He carries his trophy home proudly.

LESSON **Main Verbs and Helping Verbs** (page 148) Write each sentence. Complete each sentence with a helping verb.

5. We _____ enjoyed our holiday.
6. We _____ raced to the pool.
7. The sun _____ shone all day.
8. Bob _____ played water tag with Cindy.

LESSON **What Is a Linking Verb?** (page 150) Write each sentence. Draw one line under the linking verb. Draw two lines under the word that describes or names the subject.

9. I am ready for the test.
10. The test seems important to the class.
11. We all feel prepared for the questions.
12. The teacher looks happy.

LESSON 5 **Verb Contractions** (page 152) Write each sentence, using a contraction of the underlined words.

13. Hilary does not feel shy.
14. She will not forget her lines.
15. Acting is not hard for her.
16. She cannot wait for the first performance.

LESSONS **Using Verb Tenses** (pages 154–157) Write the correct tense of each verb below.

17. plan (future)
18. wrap (past)
19. placed (present)
20. dance (future)

LESSONS 8-9

Subject-Verb Agreement (pages 158–161) Write each sentence, using the correct present-tense form of the verb.

21. Jean _____ the bus would come. (wish)

22. She _____ at the bus stop on time this morning. (arrive)

23. An art show _____ at school today. (open)

24. The students _____ each other's best critics. (be)

LESSONS 10-11

Using Irregular Verbs (pages 162–165) Write each sentence. Complete each sentence with the correct tense of the verb.

25. The students (be) at a talent show at the moment.

26. We (see) the entire assembly now.

27. The last contestant (have) great talent.

28. The school has (grow) excited about the show.

LESSON 12

Mechanics: Using the Comma (page 166) Write each sentence, using correct punctuation.

29. We worked planned and practiced.

30. Performances took place on Friday Saturday and Sunday.

31. I invited my friends family and neighbors.

32. The audience applauded the actors the director and the writer.

LESSON 13

Vocabulary Building: Homophones (page 168) Write each sentence, using the correct homophone.

33. We (by, buy) a ticket for the raffle.

34. The tickets are (blew, blue) and red.

35. We (right, write) our addresses on the tickets.

36. We wait to see who (one, won).

37.–40.

Writing Application: Subject-Verb Agreement with Irregular Verbs (page 160) The following paragraph contains 4 errors with subject-verb agreement. Rewrite the paragraph correctly.

There is several main types of transportation. Cars moves slowly enough for a good view of the scenery. Trains rides along smoothly and comfortably. Airplane travel take passengers rapidly across long distances.

ENRICHMENT

ACTION TALES

Play this story game with a small group of class-mates. Together, make twenty small slips of paper. On each slip, write an action verb. Put the slips in a bag. The first player selects a verb and begins a story using the verb. The next player selects another verb and continues the story using the new verb. Keep playing until all of the verbs have been used.

Word Chameleons

Try this activity with a partner. The following words are used as both nouns and verbs. Select a word from the list and use it in a sentence as a noun. Your partner should then use the word in a sentence as a verb. You can use a dictionary to check the meaning of any word you do not know how to use.

frame	core	form
copy	beat	drive
exit	drink	fire
flip	howl	lace

ACTORS' WORKSHOP

Play this game with a small group. Have one member of the group act out an action verb. The other members of the group should try to guess the verb. The person who identifies the verb correctly takes the next turn.

TRICKY BUSINESS

You remember homophones, those tricky words that sound the same but have different spellings and meanings. Enter this contest with a partner. Time yourselves for five minutes. Within that time, see how many words that are homophones you can write down. Whoever has written the greatest number of correct homophones wins the contest.

FOUL

CHAIN LINKS

Play this game with a partner. Start a sentence that begins with a subject and a linking verb, like "I feel . . ." Your partner completes the sentence with a word that makes sense. Then, your partner starts a sentence with another subject and linking verb, and you complete the sentence. Keep going until you can't think of any more linking verbs.

I feel ?

GRAMMAR

Three levels of practice
What Is an Action Verb? (page 144)

LEVEL A. Write each sentence. Draw a line under the action verb in each sentence.

1. Three green frogs jump in this contest.
2. The first frog lands ten feet away.
3. The next frog passes him.
4. The longest jump earns the prize.
5. One frog wanders off the track.
6. Another frog sleeps in the sun.
7. Sleeping frogs never hop far.
8. The frogs learn their lesson.
9. The owners laugh at their pets.

LEVEL B. Write each sentence. Complete the sentence with an action verb.

10. I _____ my frog Jumper.
11. I _____ Jumper in a contest.
12. He _____ three feet down the track.
13. The judge _____ a prize.
14. Jumper _____ proudly at me.
15. Jumper _____ another leap.
16. He always _____ for me.
17. We all _____ him.

LEVEL C. Complete each sentence with an action verb.

18. I _____ a frog in a lake.
19. I _____ a nice home for my frog.
20. I _____ his home a terrarium.
21. I _____ plants, water, and sand in a glass box.
22. I _____ the top loosely.
23. My frog _____ his comfortable home.
24. I _____ some moss in the terrarium today.
25. He _____ around the terrarium all day.

EXTRA PRACTICE

Three levels of practice
Verbs with Direct Objects (page 146)

LEVEL A. Write each sentence. Draw a line under the action verb.

1. We planned a talent show.
2. Jan read poetry.
3. Andy played the flute beautifully.
4. Jeremy performed magic tricks for the crowd.
5. I memorized a song.
6. The audience judged our acts.
7. Our parents applauded our efforts.
8. Everyone really liked the show.
9. The acts certainly deserved attention.

LEVEL B. Write each sentence. Draw a line under the direct object of the action verb in each sentence.

10. Every student enjoyed the show.
11. Stanley's poem earned applause.
12. He crossed the stage slowly.
13. A judge displayed the trophy.
14. Stanley heard a cheer from his friends.
15. He received the award!
16. His sister threw roses at the stage.
17. Stanley hugged the trophy tightly.

LEVEL C. Write each sentence. Complete the sentence with an action verb that makes sense.

18. He _____ a smile to the crowd.
19. The audience _____ their hands loudly.
20. Stanley _____ a thank you speech.
21. He _____ the audience for their attention.
22. He _____ another poem about a football hero.
23. He _____ the stage happily.
24. I _____ a picture of Stanley.
25. He _____ the trophy above his head.

Three levels of practice
Main Verbs and Helping Verbs (page 148)

LEVEL A. Write each sentence. Draw one line under each helping verb and two lines under each main verb.

1. My family has entered a contest.
2. We have completed the forms.
3. My sister is waiting for an answer.
4. She is counting the days.
5. I have marked the calendar.
6. The date is circled in red ink.
7. We have planned the trip already.
8. My sister has picked the hotel.
9. We have selected our vacation wardrobe.

LEVEL B. Write each sentence. Complete each sentence with a helping verb.

10. We _____ waited long enough.
11. A letter _____ delivered to us.
12. The letter _____ promised us a trip.
13. We _____ traveling to Hawaii.
14. I _____ hoping for good weather.
15. My sister _____ purchased a bathing suit.
16. I _____ packed my camera.
17. We _____ traveling by airplane.

LEVEL C. Write each sentence. Complete each sentence with a main verb from the chart on this page. Use each verb only once.

18. We have _____ by plane before.
19. Now, we are _____ a tour.
20. I am _____ about my good luck.
21. We are _____ wonderful.
22. My sister has _____ her next trip already.
23. She has _____ of a trip to France.
24. We have _____ another contest.
25. My mother is _____ entry forms, too.

enjoying
planned
dreamed
thinking
entered
completing
feeling
journeyed

EXTRA PRACTICE

Three levels of practice
What Is a Linking Verb? (page 150)

LEVEL A. Write each sentence. Draw a line under the linking verb.

1. I am a runner.
2. I became an athlete last year.
3. My best friend is a runner, too.
4. The team seems ready at last.
5. We all feel excellent today.
6. You look prepared.
7. The track appears dry.
8. The sawdust smells sweet.
9. The race is difficult.

LEVEL B. Write each sentence. Complete the sentence with a linking verb from the list below.

are   became   look   was   is   feel   appears   seemed

10. The racetrack _____ endless to the runners.
11. You _____ very tired after the third lap.
12. The race _____ close to the viewers.
13. The team _____ confident.
14. We all _____ happy about the race.
15. The relay race _____ the most fun.
16. You _____ a wonderful teammate.

LEVEL C. Write each sentence. Complete the sentence with a linking verb.

17. The long jump _____ a challenge.
18. We _____ the best jumpers.
19. I _____ ready for the event.
20. George's jump _____ the longest.
21. He _____ the best athlete today.
22. Nelson _____ eager and fit.
23. His jump _____ spectacular.
24. I _____ a winner today, too.
25. We _____ proud of our team.

Three levels of practice
Verb Contractions (page 152)

LEVEL A. Write each sentence, using the correct contraction of the underlined words.

1. We <u>have not</u> seen the reptiles yet.
2. Peter <u>has not</u> seen any snakes before.
3. He <u>does not</u> fear most animals.
4. Snakes <u>are not</u> unfriendly.
5. Most snakes <u>cannot</u> hurt you.
6. They <u>will not</u> bite.
7. You <u>do not</u> know how pretty snakes are.
8. Peter <u>did not</u> hold the snake today.
9. There <u>are not</u> many snakes like this one.

LEVEL B. Write each sentence. Complete the sentence with a contraction.

10. Jean _____ seen a blue snake before.
11. I _____ tell you which snake won a prize.
12. It _____ the biggest one.
13. Anna _____ fear the reptiles.
14. She _____ wait for the turtle exhibit.
15. We _____ be late for this display.
16. The judges of the contest _____ wait.

LEVEL C. Change each sentence to include a contraction with the word *not*.

17. I can remember the path to the aquarium.
18. We should miss the turtles.
19. I would skip that part of the aquarium.
20. They are small reptiles.
21. The judges could pick just one winner.
22. One judge has made up his mind.
23. He should choose hastily.
24. The sea turtle has received a prize.
25. I can wait until the next contest.

EXTRA PRACTICE

Three levels of practice

Verb Tenses (page 154)

LEVEL
A. Write the tense of each underlined verb.

1. I <u>liked</u> the zoo better than the circus.
2. My friends <u>love</u> animals, too.
3. Boys and girls <u>will enjoy</u> the exhibits.
4. I <u>visit</u> the giraffes and the tigers.
5. Sue <u>admired</u> the elephants and the monkeys.
6. Cory <u>takes</u> some photographs of the animals.
7. The trained seal <u>will earn</u> our applause.
8. The zookeeper <u>tells</u> us about the tigers.
9. I <u>toss</u> bread to the ducks for awhile.

LEVEL
B. Write each sentence. Complete each sentence with the correct tense of each verb in parentheses.

10. The birds (gobble) the crumbs now.
11. The peacocks (parade) on the grass yesterday.
12. We (watch) the lions later.
13. First, we (want) our lunch.
14. Earlier, I (search) for a snack bar.
15. We (purchase) a sandwich already.
16. Soon, we (visit) the monkeys.

LEVEL
C. Change the underlined verb in each sentence to another verb in the same tense. Write the new sentence.

17. The monkeys <u>swing</u> on ropes.
18. These monkeys <u>show</u> talent.
19. Their tails <u>look</u> amazing.
20. We <u>will award</u> the monkeys prizes.
21. One monkey <u>performed</u> a double flip on the ropes.
22. The smallest monkey <u>climbed</u> a tree.
23. He <u>will learn</u> more monkey tricks.
24. I <u>liked</u> the monkey show the best.
25. You <u>applaud</u> the furry contestants with me.

Three levels of practice

Using the Present and Past Tenses (page 156)

LEVEL A. Write the present-tense verb in each sentence.

1. Our class plans an event.
2. The students arrange an art show for today.
3. I carry my painting to school.
4. Mary Louise brings her collage.
5. We choose our best work for the occasion.
6. Our artwork shows our talent.
7. We invite the other students.
8. We admire each other's exhibits.
9. Christina praises my winter landscape.

LEVEL B. Change each underlined verb to the past tense. Write the new sentence.

10. Mary Louise <u>applies</u> paper and paint to her collage.
11. I <u>use</u> watercolors in my painting.
12. Deirdre <u>works</u> with clay.
13. She <u>molds</u> beautiful sculptures of dancers.
14. Peter <u>sketches</u> with charcoal and chalk.
15. The judges <u>recognize</u> the talent of the students.
16. They <u>admire</u> all of the artwork.

LEVEL C. Change each underlined verb to the present tense. Write the new sentence.

17. Daniel's tapestry <u>glowed</u> with bright colors.
18. Gloria's portraits <u>proved</u> her talent.
19. Barbara's quilt <u>looked</u> wonderful.
20. The quilt <u>displayed</u> a circle pattern.
21. Bill's pottery <u>deserved</u> a blue ribbon.
22. The judges <u>whispered</u> to one another.
23. They <u>discussed</u> the artwork carefully.
24. They <u>handed</u> everyone an award.
25. Our exhibit <u>pleased</u> them.

EXTRA PRACTICE

Three levels of practice

Subject-Verb Agreement (page 158)

LEVEL A. Write each sentence, using the correct form of the verb.

  1. My class (plan, plans) an election.

  2. We (need, needs) a class president.

  3. Harold (run, runs) for the position.

  4. He (tell, tells) us his ideas.

  5. We (likes, like) his speech.

  6. Harold (talk, talks) to the class for an hour.

  7. We (vote, votes) on Tuesday of this week.

  8. Harold (leave, leaves) the room during the election.

  9. The teacher (show, shows) us the blank ballots.

LEVEL B. Write each sentence. Complete each sentence with the correct present-tense form of the verb in parentheses.

  10. We _____ slips of paper as ballots. (use)

  11. The other candidate _____ votes. (lose)

  12. Harold _____ my vote with his honesty. (earn)

  13. He _____ my respect. (command)

  14. I _____ in this election. (believe)

  15. Jake _____ the ballots from the class. (collect)

  16. The students _____ for the tally. (wait)

LEVEL C. Change each singular subject to a plural subject and each plural subject to a singular subject. Make sure the verb agrees with the new subject. Write the new sentences.

  17. The teacher runs the election.

  18. The candidates remain in the hall.

  19. Our classmates guess the outcome.

  20. The voters determine the result.

  21. The teacher counts the ballots.

  22. The elections are very exciting.

  23. The shout breaks the silence.

  24. The best candidates have succeeded!

  25. The student congratulates the winner.

PRACTICE + PLUS

Three levels of additional practice for a difficult skill
Subject-Verb Agreement (page 158)

(page 158)

LEVEL
A. Write each sentence, using the correct form of the verb.

1. Our class (plan, plans) a trip.
2. We (talk, talks) about our plan.
3. The teacher (help, helps) us with maps and information.
4. We (discuss, discusses) a field trip.
5. Julie (suggest, suggests) a visit to a lake.
6. She (remember, remembers) the perfect place.
7. We (agree, agrees) to the plan.
8. Our teacher (unfold, unfolds) a map of the countryside.
9. We (select, selects) a lake nearby.

LEVEL
B. Change each singular subject to a plural subject and each plural subject to a singular subject. Make sure the verb agrees with the new subject. Write the new sentences.

10. The teachers ride in front.
11. The bus reaches the lakeshore.
12. The lake looks cold and clear.
13. The duck paddles on the lake.
14. The children play on the grass.
15. The cloud forms in the sky.
16. The sky becomes dark for a few minutes.
17. The cloud disappears by noon.

LEVEL
C. Write each sentence. Complete the sentence with an action verb in the present tense. Be sure to use the correct form of the verb.

18. We all _____ to the dock.
19. Some men _____ from the end of the pier.
20. The fish _____ out of the water.
21. They _____ in the sunlight.
22. One man _____ a huge fish.
23. We _____ him for a while.
24. The teacher _____ us for lunch.
25. Everyone _____ the picnic.

EXTRA PRACTICE

Three levels of practice
Using *be* and *have* Correctly (page 160)

LEVEL
A. Write whether the subject and verb in each sentence are singular or plural.

1. Peter is a wonderful writer.
2. He has a summer job in Alaska.
3. His sisters have a letter from him.
4. The letter was an entry in a contest.
5. The judges are three teachers from Washington, D.C.
6. They have a special prize for him.
7. The prize is a trip to Spain.
8. Peter's friends are happy for him.
9. His parents have a camera for him.

LEVEL
B. Rewrite each incorrect sentence, using the correct form of the underlined verb. If the sentence is already correct, write **correct**.

10. Diane is ready for the canoe race.
11. She are an expert at this sport.
12. Her two pet turtles is with her.
13. One turtle is in the bottom of the canoe.
14. The other turtle are on the seat with her.
15. The turtles has a good time.
16. Both turtles have a love of water!

LEVEL
C. Write each sentence. Complete each sentence with the correct form of the verb in parentheses.

17. The turtles _____ from this lake. (be)
18. The race _____ started. (have)
19. The canoes _____ swift and light. (be)
20. The racers _____ a good audience. (have)
21. Diane _____ friends with her. (have)
22. The turtles _____ her allies. (be)
23. Diane and the turtles _____ the edge! (have)
24. She _____ strength and skill. (have)
25. Diane and the turtles _____ everyone's favorite racers. (be)

EXTRA PRACTICE

Three levels of practice
Using Irregular Verbs I (page 162)

A. Write each sentence. Write the past tense of the verb in parentheses.

1. The music awards (take) place tonight.
2. Jane and I (see) the awards.
3. We (make) a list of popular songs.
4. The host (introduce) the musicians.
5. Then (come) my favorite part.
6. The cameras (go) to the live acts.
7. The judges (give) an award for best album of the year.
8. The reporters (write) about the awards.
9. The big moment (come) at last.

B. Write each sentence. Write the correct past-tense form of the verb in parentheses.

10. The dancers have (fly) from the stage.
11. My favorite star has (draw) an envelope.
12. I had (choose) him as the winner.
13. The voters have (spoke).
14. The journalists have (take) many photographs.
15. The winners have (ride) in a victory parade.
16. The audience has (show) enthusiasm for the spectacle.

C. Change each underlined past-tense verb to its past form with a helping verb. Write the new sentence.

17. We <u>saw</u> the performance of the best song.
18. It <u>went</u> on for four minutes.
19. The song <u>won</u> an award.
20. The winners <u>showed</u> their awards to the audience.
21. The show <u>was</u> fun.
22. The winners <u>took</u> their awards home.
23. Jane and I <u>grew</u> tired at last.
24. We <u>left</u> the living room.
25. We <u>kept</u> a record of the winners in our journals.

EXTRA PRACTICE

Three levels of practice

Using Irregular Verbs II (page 164)

LEVEL A. Write each sentence. Write the past-tense of the verb in parentheses.

1. We (sing) at the picnic.
2. Lucy (swim) in the race.
3. She (drink) some cool lemonade.
4. We (do) many enjoyable things.
5. Kevin (draw) a picture of the scenery.
6. I (throw) a baseball to Roger.
7. You (know) some games, too.
8. We (fly) paper airplanes over the grass.
9. Jeremy (grow) tired of the sack race.

LEVEL B. Write each sentence. Write the correct past tense of the verb in parentheses.

10. We have (know) better games.
11. I had (wear) the sack all day.
12. Claudia has (teach) Sue the game.
13. Brett and Mike have (go) to the lake.
14. Now they have (swim) together.
15. They have (did) everything at the picnic.
16. We have (sing) songs, too.

LEVEL C. Change the underlined verb to the simple past-tense form of that verb. Write the new sentence.

17. We <u>have begun</u> another contest.
18. The students <u>had thought</u> of some prizes.
19. The adults <u>have brought</u> the prizes.
20. The children <u>have spoken</u> their thanks.
21. My sister <u>has made</u> a crown for the winner.
22. I <u>had thrown</u> the ball the farthest.
23. I <u>have worn</u> the crown for my sister.
24. We <u>had seen</u> the brilliant colors of the sunset.
25. We <u>have chosen</u> a wonderful spot for a picnic.

EXTRA PRACTICE

Three levels of practice
Mechanics: Using the Comma (page 166)

LEVEL A. Write each sentence. Add commas to separate items in a series. If the sentence does not need punctuation, write **correct** after it.

1. Jason sells seeds vegetables and fruit.
2. He works on Mondays Wednesdays Thursdays and Saturdays.
3. He can win prizes or more seeds.
4. The prizes include cameras toys and tents.
5. You can buy seeds for carrots and plums.
6. August September and October are the best months for this job.
7. People usually buy ten twenty or thirty packets of seeds.
8. Jason sold seeds for tomatoes pumpkins and squash today.
9. Jason sold seeds on wet days windy weekends and cold nights.

LEVEL B. Write each sentence. Add commas where they are needed. If the sentence does not need punctuation write **correct** after it.

10. He also paints furniture mows grass and baby-sits.
11. His seeds will grow into flowers fruits and vegetables.
12. His sales could be very big or very small.
13. The flower fruit and corn seeds sold fast.
14. Jason will win the camera two tents and a bike.
15. His friend won skates and a trip last year.
16. Jason waits and hopes for a prize.

LEVEL C. Write each sentence. Add commas where they are needed.

17. He will sell the seeds be the best salesman and win the prize.
18. Jason walks up the roads down each lane and into town.
19. Old seeds can age over time turn color in some cases and rot.
20. The rotten fruit or vegetable seeds must be thrown out.
21. He can buy more seeds sell them and apply for another prize.
22. Jason will knock on doors sell seeds and earn money.
23. His best customers are the gardener his teacher and the sheriff.
24. I admire his energy like his enthusiasm and hope he wins.
25. Next year I will work with Jason earn money and open a savings account.

EXTRA PRACTICE

Three levels of practice

Vocabulary Building: Homophones and Homographs (page 168)

LEVEL A. Write each sentence, using the correct homophone.

1. The teacher (red, read) us a fairy tale.
2. It was (by, buy) a Spanish writer.
3. A strange wind (blew, blue) through the villages.
4. Something was not (right, write) in the kingdom.
5. A noble (night, knight) came to the kingdom.
6. His (to, too, two) horses seemed uneasy.
7. After a (week, weak), he noticed the problem.
8. The people could (knot, not) breathe easily.
9. A bitter (scent, cent) filled the air.

LEVEL B. Write each sentence. Use your dictionary to write the correct definition of the underlined homograph.

10. A wise owl <u>saw</u> the problem in the kingdom.
11. There was a moldy object near the cow <u>pen</u>.
12. A giant crow had left a piece of cheese.
13. Everyone thought it was a lump of <u>lead</u>.
14. The age of the cheese set a <u>record</u>.
15. Another animal was <u>close</u> to the cheese.
16. When the <u>wind</u> blew, you could really smell that cheese.
17. You would soon <u>tire</u> of the odor.

LEVEL C. The underlined word in each sentence is wrong. Replace it with the correct homophone. Write the new sentence.

18. The farmers were very <u>pour</u>.
19. The knight will perform a <u>feet</u> to save them.
20. He will <u>higher</u> someone to take the cheese.
21. They will <u>so</u> it into a cloth bag.
22. I do <u>knot</u> know where they will take it.
23. Maybe a giant <u>bare</u> will carry away the cheese.
24. We will express <u>hour</u> thanks to the hero.
25. He could become the <u>knew</u> mayor of the town.

UNIT
6

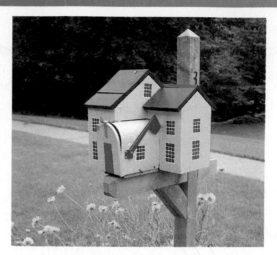

Writing Letters

Read the quotation and look at the picture on the opposite page. Why do you think it is sometimes easier to make a letter longer than shorter?

When you write a letter, your purpose and audience are very clear. You may want to write to a friend or to someone you do not know personally.

Focus A letter is a specific form of communication. There are different types of letters—friendly letters, business letters, and social notes, for example. Each type is written for a different purpose.

Is there someone to whom you would like to send a letter? What would you write? In this unit you will find the letters that one person wrote. You will find photographs, too. You can use both the letters and the photographs to find ideas for writing.

THEME: *PRIZES*

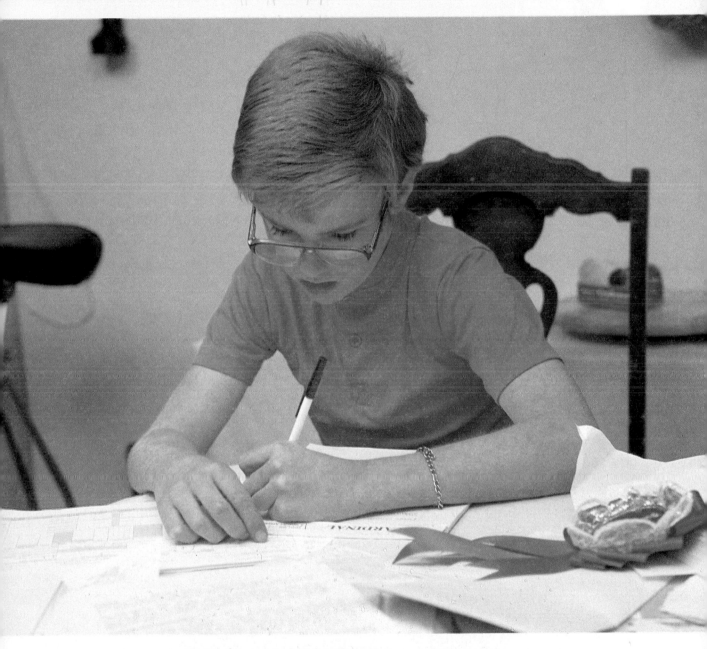

*I have made this letter longer because
I lack the time to make it shorter.*

—Blaise Pascal

Do you like to write and receive letters? To whom do you enjoy writing?

Gilly Hopkins has just moved to Virginia to live with her grandmother. In her letters, she compares her old home and school to her new ones.

As you read, notice how the author uses comparison and contrast to help you understand Gilly's feelings about her new home and friends.

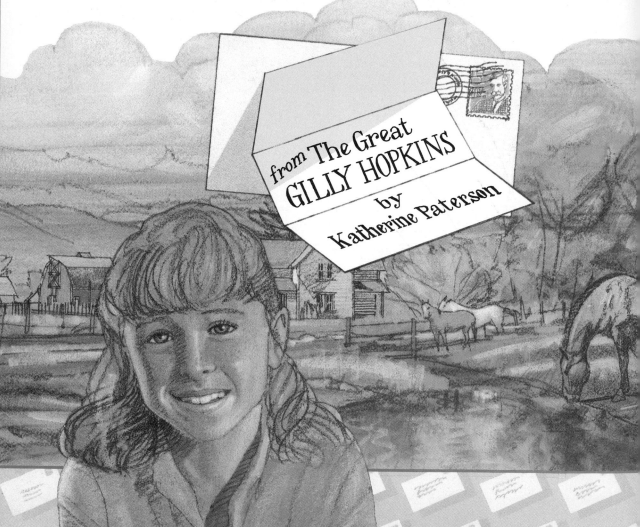

from The Great
GILLY HOPKINS
by
Katherine Paterson

P.O. Box 33
Jackson, Va.
December 5

Dear William Ernest,

Ha! I bet you thought I'd forget. But don't worry. I wouldn't forget you. I have just been so busy looking after the horses I have hardly had a minute to myself. I practically fall into bed I'm so worn out from all the work. Have you ever shoveled horse manure?

Just kidding. Actually, it is a lot of fun. We are getting six of the horses ready to race at the Charles Town track soon, so I have to help them train. I am sure one of them, named Clouds of Glory, is going to win. The prize is about a half a million dollars, so we will be even richer when he does. Not that we need the money, being millionaires and all.

How is school? I bet you zonked Miss McNair with all those new words you learned last month. You should keep in practice by reading out loud to Mr. Randolph.

Tell Trotter we have three maids and a cook, but the cook isn't half as good as she is, even though she uses lots of fancy ingredients. (Ha! Bet you knock Miss McNair over when you read her that word.)

Write soon.

Gilly

P.S. My grandmother told me to call her "Nonnie." Aren't rich people weird?

Thompson Park Elementary School
Thompson Park, Maryland
December 7

Dear Gilly,

If anyone had told me how much I would miss having you in my class, I'd never have believed it. I hope, however, that you are enjoying your new school and that the people there are enjoying you as well. You might like to know that when I send your records to Virginia, I do not plan to include any samples of your poetry.

You will be receiving soon some paperbacks that I'd been meaning to lend you, but now that you've left us, I want you to keep them as a souvenir of our days together in Harris 6.

I certainly won't forget you even if you never write, but it would be good to hear how you're getting along.

Best wishes,
Barbara Harris

Keep in mind that the type of closing a writer uses depends upon how formal the writer wishes to be.

December 10

Dear Gilly,

How are you? I am fine. I liked your letter. I liked your horses. Write me soon.

Love,
William Ernest Teague

P.S. Did you win the race?

P.O. Box 33
Jackson, Virginia
December 15

Dear Miss Harris,

The books by J. R. R. Tolkien came the day after your letter. Now I know who Galadriel was.* Do you think Frodo should keep trying to take back the magic ring? I think it would be better if he kept it and took charge of things himself. Do you know what I mean? Anyhow, thank you for the books. They are really exciting.

They help a lot because school is terrible. Nobody knows anything, including the teachers. I wish I was back in Harris 6.

Your former student,
Gilly Hopkins

P.S. It's OK if you want to call me Galadriel.

* The name of a beautiful queen in J.R.R. Tolkien's book, *The Hobbit.*

Thinking Like a Reader

1. Do you think Gilly likes her new home better than her old one? How did you decide on your answer?
2. Have you ever moved, changed schools, or made new friends? What do you remember most vividly about the experience?

Write your responses in your journal.

Thinking Like a Writer

3. How does the author let you know Gilly's feelings about her new home and school?
4. How do Gilly's letters show the things that are important to her?
5. If you wanted to compare or contrast a place you know well to an unfamiliar place, what details would you include?

Write some details in your journal.

LITERATURE

BRAINSTORM *Vocabulary*

In "The Great Gilly Hopkins," Gilly wants her friends to know about her new life. In her letters, she includes words and phrases such as *hardly had a minute to myself* and *practically fall into bed*. In your journal, write words and phrases that describe your life. Begin to create your own personal vocabulary lists. You can use these words and phrases as you write a letter of your own.

TALK IT OVER
Now and Then

Gilly misses her old school and friends, but she does seem excited about some things. Think about your life this year and your life last year. Play this game with a partner. Begin by telling about something that you like this year. Then let your partner tell about something that he or she likes. Next, tell something that you dislike about this year. Give your partner a chance to do this, too. Each person should have at least three turns.

QUICK WRITE
Write a Post Card

Imagine that you have just moved to a new town or city. Write a post card to a friend. Tell your friend at least two things that are alike or different about the old home and the new.

Dear Laura,
    I'm still busy unpacking, but I wanted to let you know that the move to Boston wasn't so bad, after all. My new room is much bigger than my old one, although it isn't as sunny in the morning. I have two new friends at school. They're really nice, but they aren't as funny as you and Beth!
    Write back soon.
                    Jan

IDEA CORNER *Alike, but Different*

You have already started to think about how things can be alike, yet different. In your journal write some ideas for topics that you might use in your letter. You might write topics such as "My Two Brothers," or "Two Different Vacations." You can choose from these topics when you write your letter.

PICTURES SEEING LIKE A WRITER

Finding Ideas for Writing
Look at the photographs.
What ideas for letter writing do the photographs give you?
Write your ideas in your journal.

COOPERATIVE
LEARNING

1 GROUP WRITING: A Business Letter

When you write a letter, you must consider your **purpose** and **audience.** You might write a thank-you letter for a gift you received or a friendly letter to a pen pal.

If your purpose is to relate information to an audience that you do not know, you would probably write a business letter. What do you need to know about a business letter?

- Correct Letter Form
- Purpose and Audience

Correct Letter Form

As you read the business letter below, notice that the six parts of the letter are labeled.

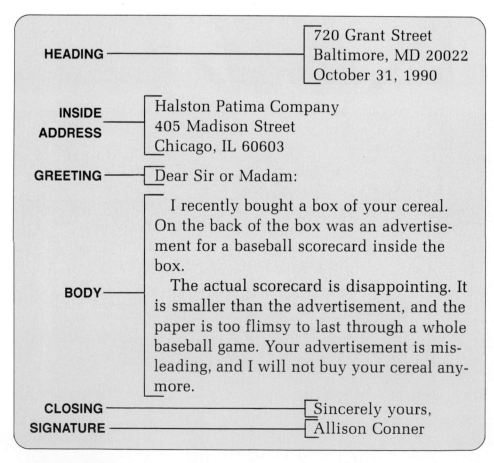

HEADING

720 Grant Street
Baltimore, MD 20022
October 31, 1990

INSIDE ADDRESS

Halston Patima Company
405 Madison Street
Chicago, IL 60603

GREETING Dear Sir or Madam:

BODY

I recently bought a box of your cereal. On the back of the box was an advertisement for a baseball scorecard inside the box.

The actual scorecard is disappointing. It is smaller than the advertisement, and the paper is too flimsy to last through a whole baseball game. Your advertisement is misleading, and I will not buy your cereal anymore.

CLOSING Sincerely yours,

SIGNATURE Allison Conner

- The HEADING is the writer's address and the date. The names of the street, city, state, and month all begin with a capital letter.
- The INSIDE ADDRESS shows to whom the letter is addressed. It includes the receiver's name and the full mailing address.
- The GREETING says "hello." It begins with a capital letter and ends with a colon.
- The BODY is the main part of the letter. It contains the writer's message.
- The CLOSING says "good-by." The first word of the closing begins with a capital letter. A comma follows the last word in the closing.
- The SIGNATURE tells who wrote the letter.

Purpose and Audience

As you know, you must consider your purpose or reason for writing to a particular person or organization. Often, a business letter is the correct form for a serious letter. You would write a business letter to a business, newspaper editor, city mayor, or to any type of organization. Since in each of these cases you would have an important purpose for writing, the language of your letter should be formal, or polite. (See page 521 for other letter forms.)

Guided Practice: Selecting a Purpose and Audience

As a class, read and discuss the list below. Then, decide the purpose of a business letter written to each of these people or organizations.

the sports editor of your local newspaper
the principal of your school
The National Council on Safety and Fitness
your state senator
NASA
a department store
a famous author
your local police department

Putting a Business Letter Together

With your class, you discussed the relationship between purpose and audience in a business letter. You studied the correct form of a business letter and learned what information to include in each part.

Look again at the letter of complaint to the cereal manufacturer. The body of the letter compares and contrasts the advertisement for the scorecard and the actual card inside the box. The clear organization of the letter as a comparison and contrast makes the information easy to follow.

When you write a letter, make sure you have organized your ideas so that the letter is clear and easy to understand. Notice that a business letter's envelope contains both the sender's and the receiver's addresses.

Allison Conner
720 Grant Street
Baltimore, MD 20022

Halston Patima Company
405 Madison Street
Chicago, IL 60603

Guided Practice: Writing a Letter

Decide how you want to organize your business letter. Make sure your paragraphs are clear. Do they state the purpose of your letter?

Share your letter with a classmate. Ask your partner if the purpose of your letter is clear.

Checklist: A Business Letter

When you write a letter, you should keep some points in mind. A checklist will help you to remember important points about writing a letter. Use the checklist to make sure you have included all of the parts of a letter and organized the letter properly.

Look at this checklist. Make a copy of the checklist and keep it in your writing folder. Add any points that will help you to write a good letter. You can use the checklist when you write a letter.

CHECKLIST

✔ Purpose and audience

✔ Correct letter form

  ■ Heading _____

  ■ Inside Address _____

■ Greeting _____

■ Body _____

■ Closing _____

■ Signature _____

2 THINKING AND WRITING: Comparing and Contrasting

When you **compare** two things, you show in what ways they are alike. When you **contrast** two things, you show how they are different from one another.

A writer organizes a comparison or a contrast by first noting whether two things, or subjects, have more similarities or differences.

The writer is comparing and contrasting dogs and cats. On the page, several points of comparison and contrast are listed.

Dogs	**Cats**
need to be walked outdoors	can stay indoors
good pets for families	good pets for families
need lots of space	happy in small spaces
bark and make noise	quiet animals
need a lot of attention	can be alone much of the time
can adopt one for free	can adopt one for free

Thinking Like a Writer

■ Do the notes of this writer show that cats and dogs have more similarities or more differences?

The writer will use her notes for a comparison and contrast paragraph on dogs and cats as pets. When you write to compare and contrast, remember to choose examples that clearly support your main idea.

THINKING APPLICATION Organizing Comparisons and Contrasts

COOPERATIVE
LEARNING

Jeffrey has made notes about two contests. Decide which information he should use in a letter that **compares** the two contests and in a letter that **contrasts** the contests.

You may wish to discuss your thinking with other students. In your discussions, explain your choices to each other.

Baking Contest
costs $5.00 to enter
for ages 10-14
$100.00 prize
takes place on Saturday
contestants bring
   ingredients
sign up by November 1

Spelling Contest
costs nothing to enter
for ages 10-14
$100.00 prize
takes place on Tuesday,
   Wednesday
contestants bring no
   materials
sign up by November 1

Kay has made notes about two art exhibits. Decide which information she should use in a letter that **compares** the two exhibits and in a letter that **contrasts** the exhibits.

Grace Hall Exhibit
paintings and sculptures
works by nineteenth-
   century artists
free admission for students
slide shows performed

Jennings Museum Exhibit
paintings and sculptures
works by twentieth-century
   artists
$6.00 admission fee
slide shows performed

Make two copies of the chart below on a separate piece of paper. Then list the information in each student's notes on the chart so that the examples are organized correctly.

Points of Comparison	Points of Contrast
_____	_____
_____	_____
_____	_____

3 INDEPENDENT WRITING: A Business Letter

Prewrite: Step 1

By this time, you know a great deal about writing letters. Now you can write a letter in which you compare and contrast. Rafael, a student in the fifth grade, wanted to write a letter to Carl Lewis, his hero.

Choosing a Topic

1. First, Rafael made a list of things to tell Lewis.
2. Next, he chose the topic that was most important to him.
3. Last, he decided upon the purpose of his letter.

> *Lewis compared to other runners*
>
> *Lewis's 1984 and 1988 Olympic victories*
>
> *Carl Lewis's success and mine*

Rafael liked his last idea best. Now that he had become a runner himself, he felt he had something in common with the great Olympic athlete. He narrowed his topic to include Carl Lewis's 1984 victory in the 100-yard dash and his own victory in his school's 100-yard dash.

Exploring Ideas: Charting Strategy

Rafael used a **chart** to organize his ideas. Here is Rafael's chart.

Carl Lewis's Victory	My Victory
100-yard dash, Olympics	100-yard dash, school
represented United States	represented my school
set record 9.9 s	won first place
won gold medal	set record 14.9 s

Before he began his letter, Rafael recalled his own experiences and remembered details about Carl Lewis's track record. He changed the order of one of the examples on his chart.

Carl Lewis's Victory	My Victory
100-yard dash, Olympics	100-yard dash, school
represented United States	represented my school
won gold medal	won first place
set record 9.9 s	set record 14.9 s

Thinking Like a Writer

- What change did Rafael make in the order of his examples?
- How did he organize his examples?
- How do these changes improve the organization of Rafael's letter?

YOUR TURN

JOURNAL

Think of some people to whom you would like to write a letter. Be sure that each of these people is an appropriate audience for a business letter. Remember, you would write a business letter to a person that you do not know well or to an organization. Use **Pictures** or your journal for ideas. Follow these steps.

- Make a list of possible topics for your letter.
- Select a person from your list as your audience.
- Decide upon the purpose of your letter.
- Narrow the topic if it is too broad.

Make a chart like the one Rafael made. Remember, you can add to or change the order of examples at any time.

Write a First Draft: Step 2

Rafael knows the correct form for his business letter. He has made a planning checklist. Rafael is now ready to write a first draft of his letter.

Part of Rafael's First Draft

Dear Mr. Lewis:

I know how you feels after a victory. We have both won 100-yard dashes. You represented the United States at the Olympics. I represented my school at the state track meet. We both won first place. I did not win a gold medil at my race, however. I only won a blue ribbon. My times was a lot slower than yours, too. You won in 9.9 seconds, but I won in 14.9 seconds.

As Rafael wrote, he did not worry about mistakes. He tried to get his ideas down on paper.

Planning Checklist
■ Remember purpose and audience.
■ Use correct letter form.
heading
inside address
greeting
body
closing
signature

YOUR TURN

Write a first draft of your letter. As you get ready to write, ask yourself these questions.

■ Is the purpose of my letter clear?
■ Have I included the six parts of a business letter?

TIME-OUT You might want to take some time out before you revise. That way you will be able to revise your writing with a fresh eye.

Revise: Step 3

After Rafael wrote his first draft, he read it to himself. Then he gave it to his friend Rebecca to read. He asked her to suggest some improvements.

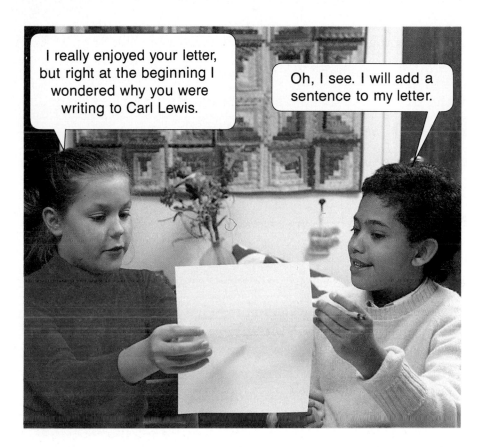

> I really enjoyed your letter, but right at the beginning I wondered why you were writing to Carl Lewis.

> Oh, I see. I will add a sentence to my letter.

Rafael looked at his planning checklist. He saw that he had forgotten one point. He had not explained the purpose of the letter soon enough. He checked it off so that he would remember it when he revised. Rafael now has a checklist to use as he revises his letter.

Rafael made changes to his letter. He did not correct small errors. He knew he could fix them later.

The revisions Rafael made changed his business letter. Turn the page. Look at Rafael's revised draft.

Revising Checklist
- ✔ ■ Remember purpose and audience.
- ■ Use correct letter form.
  heading
  inside address
  greeting
  body
  closing
  signature

Dear Mr. Lewis:

I admire you more than any other Olympic athlete in the world.
∧I know how you feels after a victory. We have both

won 100-yard dashes. *Just as* ∧You represented the United States

at the Olympics, I represented my school at the state

track meet. We both won first place. I did not win a

gold medil at my race, however. I only won a blue

ribbon. My times was a lot slower than yours, too. You

won in 9.9 seconds, but I won in 14.9 seconds.

Thinking Like a Writer

**WISE
WORD
CHOICE**

- What sentence did Rafael add to his letter? How does adding this sentence make the letter clearer?
- What sentences did he combine? How does combining them improve the writing?
- How did Rafael's changes improve the organization of his letter?

YOUR TURN

Read your first draft. Make a checklist. Ask yourself these questions.

- Are my points of comparison and contrast clear?
- Is the purpose of my letter clear?
- Have I remembered to include the six parts of a business letter?

If you wish, ask a friend to read your letter and make suggestions. Then revise your letter.

Proofread: Step 4

Rafael knew that he would not send his letter before he had proofread it. He used a proofreading checklist to help him proofread and correct his letter.

Part of Rafael's Proofread Draft

won 100–yard dashes. *Just as* You represented the United States

at the Olympics. I represented my school at the state

track meet. We both won first place. # I did not win a

gold *medal* ~~medil~~ at my race, however. I only won a blue

ribbon. My time*s* was a lot slower than yours, too. You

won in 9.9 seconds, but I won in 14.9 seconds.

YOUR TURN

Proofreading Practice

Below is a paragraph that you can use to practice your proofreading skills. Find the errors. Write the paragraph correctly on a separate sheet of paper.

> The National Baking Contest are very different from the local contest. We fly to the National contest but we take the bus to the local one. The prizes for a local victory is new baking dishes an oven and aprons but the prize for the National Contest is a new kitchen.

Proofreading Checklist
■ Did I indent my paragraph?
■ Did I spell all words correctly?
■ What punctuation errors do I need to correct?
■ What capitalization errors do I need to correct?

Applying Your Proofreading Skills

Now proofread your letter. Read your checklist one last time. Review **The Grammar Connection** and **The Mechanics Connection.** Use the proofreading marks to mark changes.

THE GRAMMAR CONNECTION

Remember these rules about subject-verb agreement.

- The verb must always agree with the subject in number.
- Singular verbs are used with singular subjects, and plural verbs are used with plural subjects.

> We **bring** a baseball bat to practice.
> Howard **brings** a catcher's mask.

Check your letter. Do the subjects and verbs agree?

Proofreading Marks

¶	Indent
∧	Add
ℐ	Take out
≡	Make a capital letter
/	Make a small letter

THE MECHANICS CONNECTION

Remember this rule about using commas in a series.

- Use commas to separate items in a series.
  > Miranda packed a towel, a swimsuit, and goggles.

Check your letter. Have you separated items in a series with commas?

Publish: Step 5

Rafael decided to send his letter to Carl Lewis in care of the Olympic Committee in Colorado. He made a clean copy of the letter and carefully addressed the envelope. He showed the final draft to his friends before he mailed it.

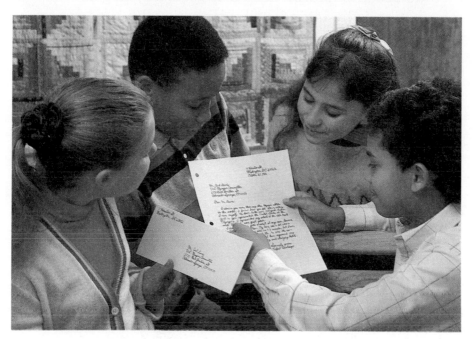

YOUR TURN

Make a final copy of your letter. Write as neatly as you can. Think of a way to share your work. Some ideas are given in the **Sharing Suggestions** box below.

SHARING SUGGESTIONS

| Mail the letter to the person to whom it is addressed. | Read the letter in class. Ask your classmates for their comments. | Exchange letters with a friend. Answer each other's letters. |

4 SPEAKING AND LISTENING: Conducting an Interview

When you write to compare or to contrast, you need to include specific information. One good way to get information is by interviewing someone who is an expert on your subject. You will want to ask questions that will help you to get the particular information you need.

First, consider the **purpose** of the interview. What do you wish to find out? Make a list of questions. Using a notebook for your questions and answers will help you to remember information.

Look at these questions from an interviewer's notebook.

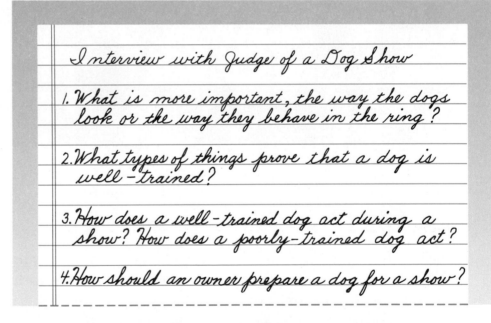

Interview with Judge of a Dog Show

1. What is more important, the way the dogs look or the way they behave in the ring?

2. What types of things prove that a dog is well-trained?

3. How does a well-trained dog act during a show? How does a poorly-trained dog act?

4. How should an owner prepare a dog for a show?

Notice that these questions are specific. They allow the person being interviewed to share his knowledge and give his opinions. Remember, during an interview you might want to change some of your questions. Listening closely to the responses of the person you are interviewing will help you to avoid asking for information that you have already been given.

When you conduct an interview, keep these speaking guidelines in mind. They will help you to focus your interview.

> **SPEAKING GUIDELINES:** An Interview
>
> 1. Remember that your **purpose** is to discover specific information about a topic from your **audience**.
> 2. Ask precise questions that let the other person form clear responses.
> 3. Use a notebook to record questions and answers. Practice asking the questions before the interview.
> 4. Give the person time to answer each question and to add any other information that comes to his or her mind.
> 5. Be polite, and thank the person you have interviewed.

■ How can I focus my questions so that they are clear and specific?

SPEAKING APPLICATION An Interview

Think of a topic that interests you. Choose a person who is an expert on this topic. Use the speaking guidelines to help you prepare. The person you interview will be using the following guidelines as he or she is interviewed.

> **LISTENING GUIDELINES:** An Interview
>
> 1. Listen carefully to each question.
> 2. Listen to discover what the interviewer wants to know.

5 WRITER'S RESOURCES: Using the Library

Libraries have many different kinds of material. They have novels, collections of short stories, reference books, newspapers, and magazines. You can borrow most of these resources.

The books that you cannot remove from the library are in the **reference** section. The books in this section include dictionaries, encyclopedias, atlases, and almanacs. The other books in the library are divided into two main sections, **fiction** and **nonfiction.**

Fiction books include novels, books of short stories, poetry, and drama. In the library, all fiction books are in one section and are arranged alphabetically by the author's last name. For example, if you were looking for *Stuart Little* by E.B. White, you would go to the fiction section and look for the authors whose last names begin with *W.*

Nonfiction books contain factual information. They are arranged by subject. When you are looking for a nonfiction book on a specific subject, you will find it with books under the general category. For example, if you wanted to find a book about roses, it would be with the books about plants.

You can find magazines, journals, and newspapers in the **periodicals** section of the library.

Practice

A. Make a list of five books you would like to read. After each title, write what type of book it is, for example, a novel, book of poetry, or nonfiction book.

B. Write each item below. Then write whether you would find it in the *reference*, *fiction*, *nonfiction*, or *periodicals* section of the library.

1. *Chicago Sun Times*, September 2, 1983
2. *Charlotte's Web*
3. *The Little Engine That Could*
4. a book about sculpture
5. A Spanish-English dictionary
6. *The Columbia Encyclopedia*
7. *Newsweek*, July 5, 1988
8. an almanac
9. a book about baseball rules
10. *San Francisco Chronicle*, May 9, 1990
11. *The New York Times*, November 21, 1990
12. a book on hunting dogs
13. an article about sewing
14. a thesaurus
15. *Sports Illustrated*, October 2, 1990
16. *The Complete Poems of Emily Dickinson*
17. *The Short Stories of Mark Twain*
18. a book about the space program
19. a book on nutrition
20. an atlas

WRITING APPLICATION Questions

Write questions for an interview with a librarian. Prepare several questions the librarian can answer about where and how a student can find books about health care. Make careful notes on the information the librarian gives you. You might wish to actually conduct an interview. If you do, you could record the results in writing or use a tape recorder.

6 WRITER'S RESOURCES: Using the Card Catalog

You have learned how to find a fiction book in the library when you know both the title and the author. If you know only the title of a book, you can find it listed in the **card catalog.**

The card catalog is a file of small drawers containing cards. Each card tells about a book that is in the library. These cards are arranged in alphabetical order. The drawers are marked with letters that tell you which part of the alphabet is covered in each drawer.

Every book in the library has an **author card** and a **title card.** The nonfiction books in the library have a third card called a **subject card.**

When you know the author of a book but not its title, you can find the book by looking in the card catalog under the author's name. If you know the title, you can find the book by locating the title card. If you do not have a particular book in mind but want a book about a certain subject, you will use the subject card file. For example, if you wanted a book about fish, you would look up *fish* alphabetically in the subject cards and find listings for all of the books about fish in the library.

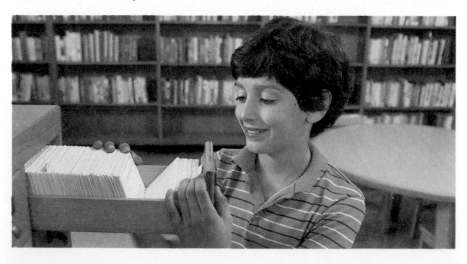

Here are some sample cards.

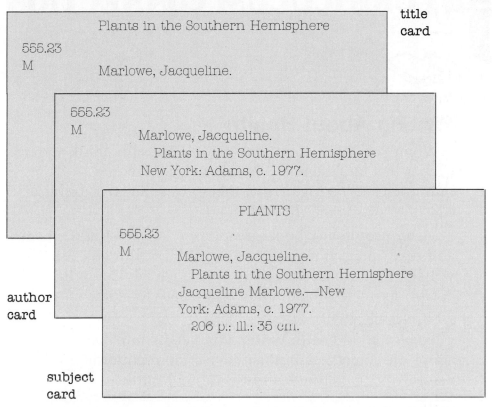

title
card

555.23
M

Plants in the Southern Hemisphere

Marlowe, Jacqueline.

555.23
M

Marlowe, Jacqueline.
    Plants in the Southern Hemisphere
New York: Adams, c. 1977.

PLANTS

555.23
M

    Marlowe, Jacqueline.
        Plants in the Southern Hemisphere
    Jacqueline Marlowe.—New
    York: Adams, c. 1977.
        206 p.: Ill.: 35 cm.

author
card

subject
card

The number on each of the cards in the upper left corner is called the **call number.** You use this number to find the book in the library. You will find this book about plants among other nonfiction books numbered between 500 and 599.

Notice that each of the three cards pictured here contains the same information. Remember, the card catalog system makes it easier to find a book when you are unsure about its title, author, or both.

WRITING APPLICATION A List

Use the subject portion of the card catalog to find books about sports and fitness. Write the names of five books you find listed there. Include the author's name and the call number.

Writing About Health

When you think about health, you probably think about proper diet and exercise. People today know the importance of taking care of themselves. Regular exercise can help you to feel fit and energetic.

Many people buy books about exercise. Most newspapers and many magazines carry columns by health and fitness writers. From these sources, you can get advice on the correct exercise program and equipment for someone of your age and body type.

To be a good health writer, you must know the facts about the subject. You must have accurate information before you give advice on fitness and health.

ACTIVITIES

Keep an Exercise Log   Keep a log or diary in which you record your exercise habits for an entire week. Write the date on each page and note every kind of exercise you do in one day and the amount of time you spend doing it. You might include brisk walking, biking, or sports. Write in the log each day for the whole week.

Design a Fitness Program   Now that you have recorded your physical activities for a week, you can think about what a good fitness plan might include. Choose a variety of sports and exercises to fit your needs, the weather, and the amount of time you can spend on an exercise program. Make a weekly calendar that shows which sports or activities you will perform. Remember, it is necessary to exercise at least three times a week in order to keep fit.

Respond to Literature The following paragraphs are from John Gaskin's book, *The Heart*. This book explains how the heart works. The excerpt below tells how the heart works differently in the heat and in the cold. After you read these paragraphs, write a letter to a friend in which you compare and contrast the way you feel on very hot and very cold days. You might also choose to compare and contrast another health topic, such as how you feel when you do two different types of exercises. Use the friendly letter model guide on page 521.

from The Heart

Whatever the temperature is around you, your body temperature needs to stay the same. Usually it is about 98.6 ° F, although it can go up or down a little during the day.

Your blood helps to keep your temperature at the right level. On a hot day, you need to lose heat. To cool the body down, the blood vessels near the skin open wider. This means that more blood comes to the surface and can lose its heat in the air. The extra blood makes the skin look redder than usual.

When you are cold, your skin often looks paler. The blood vessels near the skin close up a little so that heat can't escape into the air. The blood stays deep inside the body to keep you warm.

UNIT CHECKUP

LESSON 1

Group Writing: A Business Letter (page 200) Write this information in correct letter form. 2 Adams Ave. Staten Island, NY 10306 June 6, 1990 Ms. Paula Green Woodcraft, Inc. 34 Pierce Rd. Dublin, NH 03444 Dear Ms. Green: Please send a copy of your catalog to the above address. Thank you. Sincerely, Jane Dey

LESSON 2

Thinking: Comparing and Contrasting (page 204) Imagine that you are going to write a paragraph that *contrasts* two prizes. Look at the list below. Copy those items that you could use in your contrast paragraph.

First Prize	Second Prize
two-week trip to Bermuda	two-week trip to Bermuda
all expenses paid	$200 for expenses
deep-sea fishing trip	bicycle trip
first-class airfare	second-class airfare

LESSON 3

Writing a Business Letter (pages 206–213) Imagine that you have won a trip. The actual trip was different than the trip that was described to you. Write a letter to the company that sponsored the trip in which you contrast what you were promised with what you actually received.

LESSON 4

Speaking and Listening: An Interview (page 214) Suppose you have been asked to interview someone in your class for the school newspaper. Pick a person whom you would enjoy interviewing about a particular topic. Prepare five questions to ask this person during the interview.

LESSONS 5-6

Writer's Resources: The Library (pages 216, 218) Use the subject section of the card catalog to find titles of books about one of the following topics. Write the names of three books on a separate sheet of paper.

    dogs   Pulitzer Prize   Olympic Games   soccer   dance

THEME PROJECT PLANNING AN EVENT

People win prizes for many activities. Prizes are awarded at sporting events, dog shows, spelling bees, science fairs, county and state fairs, and even carnivals. These are only a few of the events at which prizes are given.

With your classmates, organize an event in which the whole class will take part.

- Begin by brainstorming for some ideas. You might plan a spelling or grammar bee, a poetry reading, an acting competition, or a "Beautify Our School" contest.
- Decide on the date, time, judges, and prizes for the event.

UNIT

Adjectives

In this unit you will learn about adjectives. Adjectives are words that describe, such as *spacious* and *amber*. Adjectives make your writing vivid and lively.

Discuss Read the words to the song on the opposite page. What images do you see?

Creative Expression The unit theme is *Images*. An image is a picture or a vision. How might you picture your area of the country? With a partner, write a description of your part of the country. You could write song lyrics or a poem. You might draw a picture, too. You might want to write your thoughts in your journal.

THEME: *IMAGES*

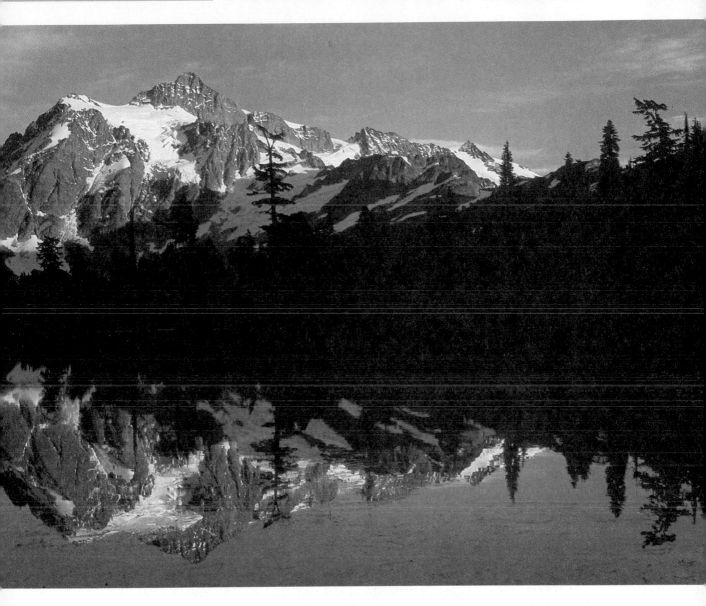

O beautiful for spacious skies,
For amber waves of grain,
For purple mountain majesties
Above the fruited plain!

—Katharine Lee Bates

1 WHAT IS AN ADJECTIVE?

An adjective is a word that describes a noun or a pronoun.

Adjectives tell *what kind* or *how many* about a noun or a pronoun. Adjectives may appear at the beginning, middle, or end of a sentence. Adjectives often come before the nouns they describe.

Vermont has **cold** winters. (what kind)

Some people enjoy winter. (how many)

Adjectives may also follow linking verbs.

The spring was **windy**.

The autumn is **beautiful**.

Two or more adjectives before a noun are usually separated by a comma.

Bright, clear weather arrives with spring.
Crisp, green buds unfold on trees.

A comma is not needed when one of the adjectives tells *how many*.

We had **three warm** days in March.
Several tiny birds come to our feeder.

Guided Practice

Tell which word in each sentence is an adjective. Then tell which noun the adjective describes.

Example: An owl perches on the icy branch. *icy   branch*

1. Snowy fields stretch to the woods.
2. The forest is still.
3. We were surprised by the sudden freeze.
4. A thin, clear frost covers the trees.
5. Two long icicles hang from a twig.

?! **THINK**

■ How can I decide if a word is an adjective?

REMEMBER

- An **adjective** describes a noun or pronoun.
- An adjective tells *what kind* or *how many* about a noun or pronoun.

More Practice

A. Write each sentence. Draw one line under each adjective that tells what kind or how many. Draw two lines under the noun that each adjective describes.

Example: We have several tall trees in our yard.

6. Summer weather is hot.
7. The cool autumn brings relief.
8. Bright, crisp leaves fall from the trees.
9. Nights become chilly.
10. Orange pumpkins grow in fields.
11. Some children wear costumes on Halloween.
12. Many animals prepare for winter.

B. Write each sentence. Complete the sentence with an adjective.

Example: The beach is a _____ place. *wonderful*

13. In July Ivan went to a _____ beach.
14. The sand was _____.
15. The _____ sun shone.
16. A _____ boat sailed on the water.
17. Ivan and his sister built a _____ sand castle.
18. They found _____ shells in the sand.
19. _____ waves rose and fell.
20. Ivan enjoyed the _____ summer.

Extra Practice, page 246

WRITING APPLICATION A Description

Write a description of your favorite season. Use words that give a clear, precise picture of the things you enjoy about the season. Circle the adjectives.

ADJECTIVES THAT COMPARE

Add *er* to most adjectives to compare two nouns or pronouns. Add *est* to most adjectives to compare more than two nouns or pronouns.

Spelling Adjectives That Compare	
Rule	**Example**
Most adjectives add *er* or *est*.	short, short**er**, short**est**
Adjectives that end with *e* drop the final *e* and add *er* or *est*.	true, tru**er**, tru**est**
Adjectives that end with a consonant and *y* change the *y* to *i* and add *er* or *est*.	happy, happ**ier**, happ**iest**
Adjectives with one syllable that end with a single vowel and a consonant double the final consonant and add *er* or *est*.	wet, wet**ter**, wet**test**

highest

higher

high

Guided Practice

Tell the correct comparing adjective.

Example: The _____ of the two boys wears a goblin mask. (taller, tallest)   *taller*

1. The _____ person at the party was James. (hungrier, hungriest)
2. My costume is _____ than yours. (warmer, warmest)
3. Gabe reminds us of the _____ soldier in the world. (braver, bravest)
4. The girl in the butterfly outfit has the _____ costume of all. (prettier, prettiest)
5. The parrot costume is _____ than mine. (brighter, brightest)

 THINK

■ How do I decide whether to add *er* or *est* to an adjective to make a comparison?

GRAMMAR

REMEMBER

- Add *er* to most adjectives to compare two nouns or pronouns.
- Add *est* to most adjectives to compare more than two nouns or pronouns.

More Practice

Write each sentence. Then complete the sentence with the correct form of the adjective in parentheses.

Example: The nights are (short) in autumn than in summer.   *shorter*

6. Your costume is made of (thin) material than mine.
7. Choose a (wide) piece of cardboard than that one for a shield.
8. You can paint a (bold) design than mine on your shield.
9. The (hot) lamp of all will dry paint in ten minutes.
10. Put the pumpkin on the (high) shelf of all.
11. Tom's jack-o'-lantern has the (angry) expression of all!
12. Martha's costume is (simple) than Jean's.
13. The costume party is (scary) than last year's.
14. Myra's costume is the (strange) of all.
15. She wears the (odd) hat I have ever seen.
16. Laura's costume is (snug) than mine.
17. The (funny) outfit of all belongs to Rico.
18. He is dressed as the (huge) pumpkin in the world.
19. Our door is (narrow) than his costume.
20. Next year he will wear a (small) outfit than that one.

Extra Practice, Practice Plus, pages 247, 248

WRITING APPLICATION A Set of Instructions

Design a costume that you might wear to a Halloween party or as a character in a play. Then write instructions about how to make this costume. Be sure to include details about the kind of materials needed for the costume. Circle all the adjectives of comparison.

3 COMPARING WITH *MORE* AND *MOST*

With some adjectives of two or more syllables, you add er or *est*. With others you use *more* and *most* to make adjective comparisons. Never use *more* or *most* with the er or *est* form of an adjective.

Use *more* to compare two nouns. Use *most* to compare more than two nouns.

Incorrect: Mt. Whitney is **more bigger** than Mt. Shasta.
Correct: Mt. Whitney is **bigger** than Mt. Shasta.
Incorrect: Mt. Whitney is the **most biggest** mountain in California.
Correct: Mt. Whitney is the **biggest** mountain in California.

Guided Practice

Tell which form of each adjective you would use to compare two nouns and more than two nouns.

Example: interesting   *more interesting*   *most interesting*

1. serious
2. plentiful
3. enjoyable
4. wonderful
5. astonishing

THINK

■ How do I decide when to use *more* and *most* to make comparisons?

REMEMBER

- Use *more* to form a comparison when two nouns are compared.
- Use *most* to form a comparison when more than two nouns are compared.

More Practice

A. Write the correct form of each adjective to compare two and more than two nouns.

Example: generous   *more generous*   *most generous*

6. frequent
7. imaginative
8. tender
9. careful
10. courageous
11. silent
12. helpful

B. Write each sentence. Use the correct form of the adjective in parentheses.

Example: The (glorious) landscapes in this country are found in the West.   *most glorious*

13. Arizona has (beautiful) scenery than my home state.
14. The Grand Canyon is the (amazing) place in the country.
15. It is one of the (spectacular) canyons in the world.
16. The Havasu Canyon is even (remote) than the Grand Canyon.
17. The Sonora Desert looks like the (rugged) land in the West.
18. The desert is (arid) than the White Mountains.
19. The (impressive) cactuses of all are the saguaros.
20. The desert has the (magnificent) air of any region.

Extra Practice, page 249

WRITING APPLICATION A Travel Guide

Write an entry for a travel guide. Describe an interesting place. Have a partner circle the adjectives that compare.

COOPERATIVE
LEARNING

4 COMPARING WITH *GOOD* AND *BAD*

The adjectives *good* and *bad* have special forms for comparing two and more than two nouns.

Our science class today was **good.**
Yesterday's class was **better**.
Last week's was the **best** class of the week.
Wendy had a **bad** day.
Her headache was even **worse** than the day before.
The **worst** part of her illness was the fever.

Guided Practice

Tell the correct form of *good* or *bad* in each sentence.

Example: I like science (best, better) than math. *better*

1. The teacher's lecture was (best, better) this week than last.
2. Wendy had the (worse, worst) feeling.
3. Her headache was (worse, worst) in the afternoon than in the morning.
4. I take the (better, best) notes in class.
5. I will give Wendy the (better, best) summary of the lecture.

 THINK

■ How can I decide which form of *good* or *bad* to use when making a comparison?

REMEMBER

- When comparing two nouns, use *better* or *worse*.
- When comparing more than two nouns, use *best* or *worst*.

More Practice

Write each sentence. Use the correct word from the pair in parentheses.

Example: Your results seem (better, best) than mine.
Your results seem better than mine.

6. Students get (better, best) results in the new laboratory than in the old one.
7. Lisa was judged to be the (best, better) scientist of all.
8. Sandra had the (worst, worse) time in the laboratory.
9. She likes lectures (best, better) than experiments.
10. Kim's experiments were (worst, worse) than Brian's.
11. Pietro got the (better, best) results in the class.
12. He thought his data was the (worse, worst) of all.
13. My projects this year are (better, best) than before.
14. Some disappointments are (worse, worst) than others.
15. Your new work is (better, best) than your old work.
16. Diane has the (worse, worst) suspicion.
17. Her results today are (worse, worst) than yesterday's.
18. Diane is a (better, best) scientist than some of us, though.
19. She may be the (better, best) researcher in the class.
20. In my (worse, worst) experiment last week, I forgot the formula.

Extra Practice, page 250

WRITING APPLICATION A Letter

Write a letter to a friend about one of your favorite subjects. In your letter, explain why this subject interests you. Try to use some forms of the adjectives *good* and *bad* in your writing. Exchange letters with a partner. Look for the words *good* and *bad* and their special forms in each other's letters.

GRAMMAR

5 USING ARTICLES AND DEMONSTRATIVE ADJECTIVES

Articles and **demonstrative adjectives** are two special kinds of adjectives that describe a noun or another adjective. *A*, *an*, and *the* are **articles.**

➡ Use *a* before a noun that begins with a consonant.
➡ Use *an* before a noun that begins with a vowel.

The refers to a specific person, place, or thing.

➡ Use *the* before a word beginning with either a vowel or a consonant.

A bird is nearby. **The** bird squawks. **An** ape roars.

This, *that*, *these*, and *those* are **demonstrative adjectives**. Demonstrative adjectives tell *which one*.

➡ Use *this* and *that* with singular nouns.
➡ Use *these* and *those* with plural nouns.

This camera needs film. **These** blankets are dirty.
That zebra runs fast. **Those** lions look majestic.

an elephant   the zebra   those lions   this bird

Guided Practice

Tell which word should be used in each sentence.

Example: Do you have (a, an) airplane ticket? *an*

1. (A, An) trip to Africa will be fun.
2. The scenery will make (a, an) nice photograph.
3. We are bringing (that, those) camera.

 THINK

■ How do I use articles and demonstrative adjectives?

REMEMBER

- *A* and *an* refer to any singular noun, and *the* refers to a specific noun.
- *This* and *these* refer to nouns that are nearby, and *that* and *those* refer to nouns that are farther away.

More Practice

A. Write each sentence, using the correct article from the pair in parentheses.

Example: We will leave in (<u>a</u>, an) moment.

4. Our photographs are in (a, an) envelope.
5. We need (a, an) roll of film, too.
6. (A, An) island across the river looks inviting.
7. (A, An) camera is in the truck.
8. (A, An) lion was in our camp last night.
9. (A, An) elephant drinks from the lake.
10. (A, An) jungle is hot and damp.
11. There is (a, an) leopard on the truck.
12. There is (a, an) antelope beside the tent.

B. Write each sentence. Complete each sentence with a correct demonstrative adjective.

Example Look at _____ photograph. *this*

13. Lonny has pictures of _____ elephant.
14. Is _____ elephant dangerous?
15. _____ country is spectacular.
16. I will have _____ memories always.
17. We will never forget _____ trip.
18. We have _____ photographs.
19. We keep _____ pictures in _____ book.
20. _____ animal looks friendly in _____ picture.

Extra Practice, page 251

WRITING APPLICATION A Caption

Write a caption describing a photograph or painting. Share your caption with a partner. Circle the articles and demonstrative adjectives in each other's captions.

6 MECHANICS: Capitalizing Proper Adjectives

You know that a proper noun names a particular person, place, or thing. A **proper adjective** is an adjective formed from a proper noun. A proper adjective begins with a capital letter.

Proper Noun	Proper Adjective
Spain	Spanish
Africa	African
Greece	Greek
North America	North American

Spanish moss

Guided Practice

Identify the proper adjective in each sentence.

Example: Alaskan winters can be extremely cold. *Alaskan*

1. The Siberian climate is also harsh.
2. Canadian air will make the temperature fall.
3. The cold makes us dream of Jamaican sunshine.
4. A Mexican vacation would be nice, too.
5. A Hawaiian holiday would bring relief.

 THINK

■ How can I decide if a word is a proper adjective?

REMEMBER

- A **proper adjective** is formed from a proper noun.
- A proper adjective begins with a capital letter.

More Practice

A. Write each sentence. Draw a line under the proper adjective. Be sure to write each proper adjective correctly.

Example: The _scottish_ moors are misty. Scottish

6. The greek islands are warm in the summer.
7. The arabian climate is very warm.
8. What have you heard about icelandic weather?
9. south american seasons are the opposite of ours.
10. I do not enjoy cold european winters.
11. It is always extremely hot in the north african deserts.
12. Wet and muggy weather comes with asian monsoons.

B. Complete each sentence with a proper adjective formed from the proper noun in parentheses. If necessary, you may use your dictionary for help.

Example: The _Swiss_ winters are glorious. (Switzerland)

13. The _____ climate is often damp. (England)
14. _____ winters are severe. (Russia)
15. _____ winds bring dust storms. (India)
16. The _____ outback is hot and sunny. (Australia)
17. The _____ mountains are snowy. (Tibet)
18. The _____ deserts are famous. (Egypt)
19. How hot is a _____ summer? (Turkey)
20. Are _____ seasons similar to ours? (Japan)

Extra Practice, page 252

WRITING APPLICATION A Comparison

COOPERATIVE LEARNING

Choose three different locations in the world. Using an almanac, compare the weather in each place in the same season. When you are finished, exchange papers with a group of classmates. Underline the proper adjectives in each other's work.

G
R
A
M
M
A
R

7 VOCABULARY BUILDING: Synonyms and Antonyms

You can introduce variety into your sentences by using synonyms and antonyms. A **synonym** is a word that has the same or almost the same meaning as another word.

The animals of the jungle are **strong**.

The animals of the jungle are **tough**.

The words *strong* and *tough* are synonyms.

A word may have more than one synonym. Notice these synonyms for the word **quiet: calm, peaceful, silent, still.**

Antonyms are words with opposite meanings.

The blades on my skates are **sharp**.
The blades on my skates are **dull**.

A word may also have more than one antonym. Quiet has the antonyms **loud** and **noisy**.

Some antonyms are made by adding the prefix *un* or *dis* to a word. *Un* and *dis* mean "no" or "not."

untrue = not true
unlikely = not likely

Guided Practice

Tell which pairs of words are synonyms and which are antonyms.

Example: gloomy–merry   *antonyms*

1. shiny–bright
2. clear–cloudy
3. unhappy–sad
4. strong–weak
5. careful–cautious

 THINK

- How do I decide whether words are synonyms or antonyms?

REMEMBER

- A **synonym** is a word that has the same or almost the same meaning as another word.
- **Antonyms** are words with opposite meanings.

More Practice

A. Write each sentence. Replace each underlined word with a synonym.

Example: I feel <u>cold</u>.   *I feel chilled.*

6. A freezing winter can make people <u>unhappy</u>.
7. Roads <u>glistening</u> with ice are dangerous.
8. Many people find winter weather <u>dreary</u>.
9. Other people enjoy the <u>chilly</u> air.
10. <u>Distant</u> mountains look beautiful in the snow.
11. <u>Beautiful</u> trees sparkle under the frost.
12. <u>Lively</u> children sled down hills.

B. Write each sentence. Replace each underlined word with an antonym.

Example: The park <u>bores</u> me.   *The park fascinates me.*

13. Rain forests are <u>dry</u> places.
14. Olympic National Park has a <u>small</u> rain forest.
15. The vegetation is very <u>sparse</u> there.
16. The woods are <u>empty</u> of animals.
17. <u>Tiny</u> ferns grow under the trees.
18. The area gets <u>low</u> levels of rainfall.
19. The <u>shallow</u> Pacific Ocean lies beyond the forest.
20. <u>Short</u> mountain peaks rise on the other side.

Extra Practice, page 253

WRITING APPLICATION A Weather Report

Write a weather report that describes the week's weather. Keep a record of any changes in the weather that occur from one day to another. Circle all of the adjectives in your work. Use the Thesaurus on page 507 to help you find synonyms or antonyms for these words.

GRAMMAR AND WRITING CONNECTION

Expanding Sentences

You know that adjectives can make your writing more colorful and precise. Compare these sentences.

Joanne wrote a poem about a forest.
Joanne wrote a poem about a **dark, dense** forest.

Notice that the adjectives *dark* and *dense* give the reader a clearer picture of the forest. Use adjectives in sentences to help your reader to see what you see. Read this sentence.

The cabin is near the lake.

Think of some adjectives that could describe the lake. Notice how this sentence can be expanded.

The **old** cabin is near the **blue** lake.
The **pleasant, old** cabin is near the **blue** lake.

COOPERATIVE
LEARNING

Working Together

With your classmates, discuss ways to make sentences more interesting and colorful by adding adjectives. Then, identify the adjectives used in the sentences below.

Example: A playful otter catches a silver fish.
playful, silver

1. Warm, bright sunlight sparkles through the trees.
2. Soft, cool breezes ruffle the leaves.
3. The gentle motion of the clear water is peaceful.
4. I watch the playful animals during the quiet, summer day.

Revising Sentences

Peggy has written these sentences about a peaceful scene in the countryside. Help her to expand her sentences by adding adjectives to each blank.

5. The _____ eagle soars over the trees.
6. Its _____ nest is on a _____ cliff.
7. A _____ fish dangles in the bird's _____ claws.
8. The _____ eaglets have a _____ appetite.
9. A _____ bear eats _____ berries.
10. Its _____ fur shines in the _____ sun.
11. _____ squirrels scurry in the grass.
12. Their _____ tails look like _____ brushes.
13. My _____ sister photographs the _____ scene.
14. We spread a _____ blanket on the ground.
15. The _____ food satisfies us.
16. _____ animals approach our blanket.
17. A _____ raccoon appears suddenly.
18. We feed the _____ creatures _____ scraps.
19. Later, we clean up the _____ area.
20. The _____ landscape grows dark at dusk.

Choose a place that you have been to, or imagine a place where you would like to be. Write a paragraph that describes the place. Use as many descriptive words as you can. Check to see that you have chosen precise adjectives.

UNIT CHECKUP

LESSON

What Is an Adjective? (page 226) Write each sentence. Draw one line under each adjective. Draw two lines under the noun that the adjective describes.

1. Our class gave a wonderful party yesterday.
2. We played festive music.
3. We decorated the room with bright balloons.
4. The food was delicious.
5. Some students performed a traditional dance.

LESSON

Adjectives That Compare (page 228) Complete each sentence with the correct form of the adjective in parentheses.

6. Your pack is (heavy) than mine.
7. The (safe) place for money is your pocket.
8. That tree is (large) than the oak tree.
9. Choose the (thick) branches for the fire.
10. The ground is (wet) today than it was yesterday.

LESSON

Comparing with *more* and *most* (page 230) Write each sentence. Use the correct form of the adjective in parentheses.

11. It was the (beautiful) place Gerry had ever seen.
12. The building was the (elegant) in town.
13. In the museum were the (incredible) paintings.
14. The (impressive) artwork was in the main gallery.
15. Gerry was (excited) than surprised.

LESSON

4

Comparing with *good* and *bad* (page 232) Write each sentence. Use the correct form of the adjective in parentheses.

16. The jazz concert was (good) than the pop concert.
17. The saxophone player was the (good) of all.
18. The (bad) part was the long intermission.
19. Our seats were (bad) than last time.
20. Bob's view was (good) than mine.

LESSON 5

Using Articles and Demonstrative Adjectives (page 234)
Write each sentence using the correct article or demonstrative adjective.

21. (An, A) play ended with a single actor on stage.
22. The actor held (a, an) orange in his hand.
23. (That, These) orange was important to the story.
24. I saw another play in (this, these) theater.
25. (These, This) actors were in the play.

LESSON 6

Mechanics: Capitalizing Proper Adjectives (page 236)
Write each sentence. Capitalize each proper adjective.

26. Many mexican buildings have red tile roofs.
27. Some spanish architecture uses brown adobe.
28. Many swiss houses have steep roofs.
29. Many english buildings are made of stone.
30. Modern african buildings are made of steel.

LESSON 7

Vocabulary Building: Synonyms and Antonyms (page 238)
Write each pair of words. Then write whether the words are synonyms or antonyms.

31. open–closed
32. huge–large
33. brilliant–bright
34. cool–scalding
35. loud–noisy

36. exciting–dull
37. special–ordinary
38. worse–better
39. peaceful–quiet
40. odd–weird

Writing Application: Adjective Usage (pages 226–236) The following paragraph contains 10 errors with adjectives. Rewrite the paragraph correctly.

41.-50.

We study spanish in school. Our teacher says I am the better student in the whole class. I study more harder than anyone. I have an good textbook with pictures. These one particular photograph is my favorite. It shows a old building with a garden. A smallest cat sits outside in the sunlight. Those cat looks like my cat at home. An woman in the photograph wears the big shawl I have ever seen.

ENRICHMENT

SYNONYM/ANTONYM HOTLINE

You can play this game with a small or large group. Form a circle. Say a word. The next person must say a word that is its synonym or antonym. Continue around the circle. You are out when you cannot think of a word. You can use a dictionary to settle any disagreements.

LANGUAGE STEW

Some English words come from other languages. *Kindergarten* (German) and *café* (French) are examples. Look at the definitions below. Think of the word that the definition describes. Then, add an adjective that tells more about the word.

—thin noodles with sauce
—a very popular string instrument
—a building for sports events

Write down noun and adjective pairs, such as *hungry bear*, on separate sheets of paper. Mix up the papers and pass them out. Then, silently act out the words on your paper. The other players must guess the words written on the piece of paper. The first player to guess the words takes the next turn.

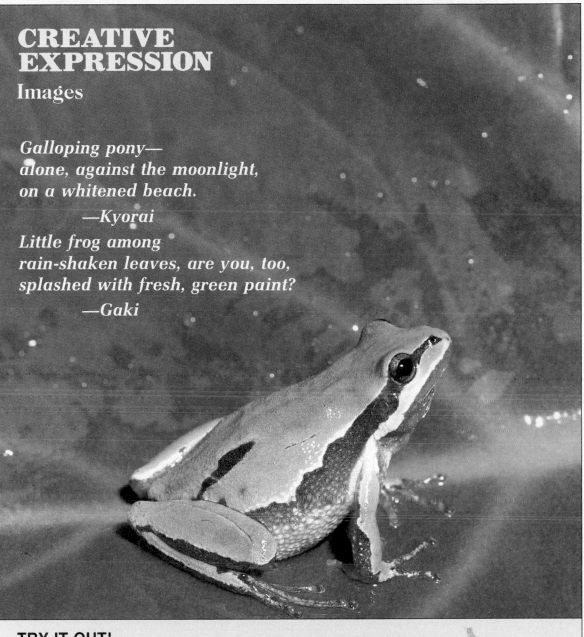

CREATIVE EXPRESSION
Images

Galloping pony—
alone, against the moonlight,
on a whitened beach.
—Kyorai

Little frog among
rain-shaken leaves, are you, too,
splashed with fresh, green paint?
—Gaki

TRY IT OUT!
A haiku has three lines and seventeen syllables. The first line has five syllables, the second line has seven syllables, and the third line has five syllables. Write a haiku. Choose vivid images.

EXTRA PRACTICE

Three levels of practice

What Is an Adjective? (page 226)

A. Write each sentence. Draw two lines under the adjective that describes each underlined noun.

1. Most cities contain tall <u>buildings</u>.
2. New York City has many <u>people</u>.
3. The busy <u>streets</u> attract visitors during daytime.
4. There are interesting <u>museums</u> in the city.
5. Speedy <u>subways</u> travel underground.
6. Yellow <u>taxicabs</u> take passengers around the city.
7. Blue <u>buses</u> provide comfortable <u>transportation</u>.
8. Athletic <u>tourists</u> can walk through the parks.
9. Curious <u>visitors</u> can take boat tours around Manhattan.

B. Write each sentence. Draw a line under each adjective. Write **what kind** or **how many** after each underlined adjective.

10. The old building has a wide courtyard.
11. A large family owns the beautiful house.
12. Three people stand in the doorway.
13. A young child runs into the courtyard.
14. He is stopped by two geese.
15. The noisy birds have scared him.
16. The hot sun beats down on the buildings.
17. A few people sit in the shade.

C. Write each sentence. Complete each sentence with an adjective.

18. Egypt has _____ pyramids.
19. They are _____ triangular buildings.
20. _____ pyramids are also found in Mexico.
21. The _____ jungle surrounds the pyramids.
22. It is a _____ climb to the top.
23. The view is _____.
24. A _____ king ordered the construction of the pyramids.
25. The workers struggled with the _____ task.

EXTRA PRACTICE

Three levels of practice

Adjectives That Compare (page 228)

A. Write each sentence. Draw a line under the adjective that compares in each sentence.

1. Ocean liners are speedier than sailing ships.
2. Tugboats are smaller than freighters.
3. Tugboats are the strongest boats for their size.
4. Super tankers are the biggest ships of all.
5. There are fewer passenger ships today than there were in the past.
6. Airplanes are faster than ships.
7. Our new car is quieter than our old one.
8. The ride was bumpier in the truck than in the automobile.
9. Transportation is better now than it was in the last century.

B. Write each adjective. Complete each sentence with the correct adjective from the pair in parentheses.

10. I am (busier, busiest) this year than I was last year.
11. I am a (faster, fastest) reader now than I was before.
12. I choose the (quieter, quietest) room in the house for my work.
13. The (sunnier, sunniest) spot in the room is perfect for my desk.
14. This chair is (softer, softest) than the other one.
15. I write my homework on the (cleaner, cleanest) paper of all.
16. My notes are (clearer, clearest) this week than they were last week.
17. I got the (higher, highest) grade of all on my last composition.

C. Write each sentence, using the correct form of the adjective.

18. This year's class picnic was (long) than last year's.
19. It took place on the (huge) field in the town.
20. Marty and Sonya chose the (shady) spot of all.
21. The food seemed (tasty) than our usual lunch.
22. My class is (friendly) than last year's class.
23. On the way home, Franny was the (sleepy) of all.
24. That day was the (happy) of the school year.
25. The picnic was the (good) event of all.

PRACTICE + PLUS

Three levels of additional practice for a difficult skill

Adjectives That Compare (page 228)

LEVEL
A. Write each sentence. Draw a line under the adjective that compares in each sentence.

1. Our dogs are swifter than greyhounds.
2. Tiger is bigger than Patches.
3. Patches is the fiercest dog in the neighborhood.
4. Tiger is the smarter of the two dogs.
5. My pets are cuter than the animals on television.
6. The spaniel is a better swimmer than the terrier.
7. My friend's retriever is bigger than our spaniel.
8. Our terrier has the loudest bark of all the dogs on the block.
9. The spaniel is the sweetest dog in the world.

LEVEL
B. Write each sentence. Complete each sentence with the correct adjective from the pair in parentheses.

10. That is the (funnier, funniest) movie of the year.
11. The hero is helped by the (small, smallest) mouse in the world.
12. The mouse is (nicer, nicest) than the hero's other friends.
13. The (harder, hardest) challenge for the hero comes at the end.
14. Our hero needs the (swifter, swiftest) messenger in the world.
15. The mouse delivers the message, and their friendship becomes even (stronger, strongest).
16. The mouse becomes the (speedier, speediest) messenger in town.
17. Next time, the two friends will be (wiser, wisest) than ever.

LEVEL
C. Write each sentence. Use the correct form of the adjective.

18. The meal was (heavy) than usual.
19. That was the (long) strand of spaghetti in the world.
20. My toast was (brown) than I like it.
21. The soup was (hot) than fire!
22. It was the (brief) meal imaginable.
23. I was (sorry) than ever about my appetite.
24. I ate (fast) than my friends.
25. I had the (bad) stomachache of all!

EXTRA PRACTICE

Three levels of practice

Comparing with *more* and *most* (page 230)

LEVEL A. Write each sentence. Draw a line under the adjective that compares in each sentence.

1. Mt. Everest is one of the most difficult mountains for explorers.
2. It has more severe weather than many other mountains.
3. The most strenuous part of the climb is near the top.
4. The lack of oxygen is even more dangerous than the slippery ice.
5. Explorers must use the most modern equipment of all.
6. Sherpa guides can carry the most remarkable loads.
7. One explorer was more eager than the others.
8. He became the most famous climber of all.
9. His journals are more exciting than many books.

LEVEL B. Write each sentence. Complete the sentence with the correct adjective from the pair in parentheses.

10. In this story, nature is _____ powerful than people. (more, most)
11. The _____ frightening event of all is a terrible storm. (more, most)
12. A girl struggles against the _____ alarming flood in history. (more, most)
13. She feels _____ tired by evening than she felt at dawn. (more, most)
14. The darkness is even _____ alarming than the flood. (more, most)
15. The story has the _____ unusual ending. (more, most)
16. The hero makes the _____ daring journey of her life. (more, most)
17. She respects nature's power _____ than she did before. (more, most)

LEVEL C. Write each sentence. Use the correct form of the adjective.

18. The Mona Lisa is one of the (beautiful) paintings in the world.
19. Van Gogh's paintings are even (colorful) than Picasso's.
20. Van Gogh's pictures are (striking) than many modern paintings.
21. To some people abstract art is the (exciting).
22. I like the (unusual) paintings best of all.
23. Other students prefer (realistic) art to abstract art.
24. My sister likes (startling) images than I do.
25. The (brilliant) painting in the museum is her favorite.

EXTRA PRACTICE

Three levels of practice

Comparing with *good* and *bad* (page 232)

LEVEL A. Write each sentence. Use the correct form of *good* or *bad*.

1. Our city has become one of the (better, best) in the country.
2. Most of the (worse, worst) problems have been solved.
3. Traffic is (better, best) than it was in past years.
4. The (worse, worst) pollution occurred ten years ago.
5. Unfortunately, the noise today is (worse, worst) than ever.
6. The planners will make the city even (better, best).
7. The (better, best) buildings in the city have received awards.
8. The (worse, worst) hazards of all have been corrected.
9. The city's (worse, worst) problem now is too many visitors!

LEVEL B. Write each sentence. Complete the sentence correctly.

10. The _____ movie of the year received many awards. (good)
11. The new movies are _____ than the old ones. (bad)
12. To others, movies have gotten _____ each year. (good)
13. Color movies may be _____ than black and white movies. (bad)
14. Both kinds of movies could be _____ than they are. (good)
15. The _____ movies of all often lose money for the producers. (bad)
16. My father is the _____ reviewer in the family. (good)
17. He avoids the _____ movies of all. (bad)

LEVEL C. Write each sentence. Choose the correct word in parentheses.

18. The weather today is _____ than it was yesterday. (worse, worst)
19. We were _____ prepared for the tornado than for the hurricane. (better, best)
20. We had the _____ storms of the year in March. (worse, worst)
21. The damage today is _____ than it was before. (worse, worst)
22. Our repair crews are _____ than most crews. (better, best)
23. The corn suffered the _____ damage of all. (worse, worst)
24. Our state has a _____ erosion problem than it had before. (worse, worst)
25. The _____ result of the storms is greater cooperation among the people in the state. (better, best)

EXTRA PRACTICE

Three levels of practice

Using Articles and Demonstrative Adjectives (page 234)

LEVEL A. Write each sentence, using the correct word in parentheses.

1. (A, An) apple tree stands on the hill.
2. (A, An) ripe apple hangs just out of reach.
3. A hungry boy wants (that, these) apple.
4. (A, The) branches of the tree tempt him.
5. The climb is (an, the) effort for the boy.
6. (Those, This) branches are rough and uncomfortable.
7. (This, These) time he succeeds in his attempt.
8. (The, This) apples are within his grasp.
9. Should he pick (this, those) one or that one?

LEVEL B. Write each sentence. Complete the sentence with the correct article or demonstrative adjective from the pair in parentheses.

10. _____ photograph is beautiful. (This, These)
11. Pat showed us _____ pictures yesterday. (that, those)
12. I want _____ one in my hand for myself. (this, that)
13. Choose _____ nice photograph from this pile. (a, an)
14. _____ picture in the pile shows the sea and sky. (A, An)
15. I love _____ two photographs of the sea gulls. (that, these)
16. Your picture of Janie is _____ excellent one. (a, an)
17. _____ main problem with my camera is a dirty lens! (The, A)

LEVEL C. Write each sentence. Complete the sentence with a correct article or demonstrative adjective.

18. We visited _____ foggy beach one hundred miles from here.
19. _____ beach was rough and rocky.
20. Can you imagine _____ scene?
21. _____ photograph looks like an old post card.
22. _____ pictures are more recent.
23. Remember _____ beach in Maine?
24. _____ sea gulls ate clams on the sand.
25. I took _____ photographs of them last summer.

GRAMMAR

Three levels of practice

Mechanics: Capitalizing Proper Adjectives (page 236)

LEVEL A. Write each sentence. Draw a line under each proper adjective.

1. Greek statues are beautiful.
2. Italian painters were masters.
3. Iranian rugs are among the finest in the world.
4. These Peruvian blankets are very beautiful.
5. We admire Swiss watches for their accuracy.
6. North American quilts are warm and colorful.
7. My grandmother had a pair of Russian boots.
8. She cooked delicious Hungarian dishes.
9. Your mother makes wonderful Swedish pancakes.

LEVEL B. Write each sentence. Capitalize the proper adjective in each sentence.

10. Mrs. Lanski served polish sausage.
11. Mr. Lal brought indian curry.
12. Did you try the ethiopian bread?
13. I loved the korean rice dishes.
14. Concha cooks south american specialties.
15. You will enjoy the english pudding.
16. Please pass me the german potato salad.
17. Kerry made some irish soda bread.

LEVEL C. Write each sentence. Change each proper noun to a proper adjective.

18. (Japan) food is Mark's favorite.
19. Sylvia likes (Mexico) food best.
20. Most people like (Italy) food.
21. (North Africa) food is quite spicy.
22. (France) food is rich and good.
23. New York City has many (China) restaurants.
24. There is a (Portugal) restaurant in my neighborhood.
25. The grocer sells salty (Greece) olives.

EXTRA PRACTICE

Three levels of practice

Vocabulary Building: Synonyms and Antonyms (page 238)

LEVEL A. Write each pair of words. Then write whether they are **synonyms** or **antonyms**.

1. small–little
2. frisky–calm
3. frosty–chilly
4. untidy–neat
5. firm–hard
6. brave–courageous
7. crowded–empty
8. wild–tame
9. finished–complete

LEVEL B. Write each sentence. Replace each underlined word with a synonym or antonym as shown in parentheses.

10. Lily's kitchen is a cheerful place. (synonym)
11. The shelves hold dull pottery. (antonym)
12. The teakettle is always cold. (antonym)
13. Lily's cookies taste wonderful. (synonym)
14. Her big puppy sits by the table. (antonym)
15. A pretty canary sings in her cage. (synonym)
16. Dark curtains frame the windows. (antonym)
17. A pleasant smell fills the air. (synonym)

LEVEL C. Write each sentence. Rewrite the sentence with a synonym or antonym from the list in the box.

18. Our living room is ugly. (antonym)
19. Few plants hang by the windows. (antonym)
20. Bright paintings decorate the walls. (synonym)
21. A thick carpet covers the floor. (synonym)
22. Visitors find the room pleasant. (synonym)
23. The sloppy room is my favorite. (antonym)
24. It is a restful spot. (synonym)
25. I feel restless in that room. (antonym)

many
relaxing
appealing
tidy
attractive
calm
lush
colorful

MAINTENANCE

UNIT 1: Sentences

Sentences and Sentence Fragments (pages 2, 16) Write whether each group of words is a **sentence** or a **sentence fragment**.

1. Why do giraffes have such long necks?
2. Can eat leaves from tall trees.
3. Small animals cannot reach the high branches.
4. A definite advantage.

Subjects and Predicates (pages 6–11) Draw a line between the complete subject and the complete predicate of each sentence. Draw one line under the simple subject. Draw two lines under the simple predicate.

5. Janice hurries to the post office.
6. She passes two friends on the way.
7. The busy girl has no time for conversation.

Compound Subjects and Compound Predicates (page 12) Write each sentence. Draw one line under each compound subject. Draw two lines under each compound predicate.

8. My friends and I went to the zoo today.
9. Joshua watched and enjoyed the seals.
10. The seals swam and jumped out of the water.

Compound Sentences (page 14) Write each sentence. Write **simple sentence** or **compound sentence** next to each.

11. My family went to the desert and camped there.
12. The days were hot, but the nights were cool.
13. The desert was dry, and it never rained.
14. We brought our own water and food.

Using Context Clues (page 20) Write the correct meaning of the underlined word in each sentence. Then write the word or words you used as context clues.

15. Miguel tried to <u>envision</u> what his new house would look like.
    a. see   b. hear
16. The metal parts of the house must be <u>welded</u> together.
    a. separated   b. joined

UNIT 3: Nouns

What Is a Noun? (pages 76, 82)
Write each sentence. Draw a line under each noun. Capitalize each proper noun.

17. The panama canal was built many years ago.
18. The canal connects the atlantic ocean and the pacific ocean.
19. The canal improves industry in the republic of panama.
20. What is a famous canal in the united states?
21. The erie canal is quite famous.

Plural Nouns (pages 78, 80)
Write the plural form of each underlined noun.

22. The policeman helps the <u>child</u>.
23. He shows the <u>girl</u> the correct bus.
24. The driver waits for the <u>person</u>.
25. He tears the ticket in <u>half</u>.
26. He helps the <u>passenger</u>.

Singular and Plural Possessive Nouns (pages 84–89) Write each sentence. Replace the words in parentheses with a phrase that includes a possessive noun.

27. (The home of Jamie) is in the city.
28. (The jobs of her parents) are interesting.
29. (The work of Jamie) is done after school.
30. (The work of students) can help the community.

Abbreviations (page 90) Write the correct abbreviation for each word.

31. April
32. afternoon
33. Road
34. Senior
35. Corporation

Compound Words (page 92)
Make compound words by matching the nouns in columns.

36. ball   guard
37. gang   clothes
38. life   beach
39. linc   plank
40. jump   way
41. drive   rope

UNIT 5: Verbs

Main Verbs and Helping Verbs (page 148) Write each sentence. Draw one line under the main verb. Draw two lines under the helping verb.

42. We are playing baseball.
43. Marjorie is hitting the ball.
44. The ball has hit the fence.
45. She has scored a run.

MAINTENANCE

Linking Verbs (page 150) Write each sentence. Draw one line under each linking verb. Draw two lines under the word or words in the predicate to which the subject is linked.

46. Brian is ready for the race.
47. Domingo is an excellent runner.
48. Anne is a gracious winner.
49. The crowd looks excited.
50. The day seems perfect.

Verb Contractions (page 152) Write the correct contraction for the underlined words.

51. Luis <u>has not</u> seen the mountains.
52. His parents <u>have not</u> traveled very often.
53. We <u>cannot</u> believe his luck!

54. He <u>would not</u> forget his camera.
55. I <u>did not</u> see photographs from the last trip.

Verb Tenses (page 154) Change each underlined verb to the tense shown in parentheses.

56. Johan and Jim <u>watch</u> the younger children. (past)
57. The children <u>played</u> quietly. (present)

58. Louisa and Freddy <u>eat</u> dinner soon. (future)
59. Their parents <u>come</u> home at last. (past)
60. The family always <u>ate</u> dinner together. (present)

Subject-Verb Agreement
(page 158) Write each sentence, using the correct present-tense form of the verb in parentheses.

61. Many birds (migrate, migrates) in the fall.
62. They (fly, flies) great distances.
63. Some birds (travel, travels) from Europe to Africa.
64. A bird (find, finds) the same place every year.
65. Naturalists (study, studies) the flight patterns of the birds.

Using Irregular Verbs (pages 162, 164) Write each sentence. Use the past-tense form of the verb in parentheses.

66. Alicia has (teach) music for many years.
67. She (go) to music school.
68. She (give) a concert last week.
69. I have (choose) the music for her recital.

UNIT 7: Adjectives

What Is an Adjective? (page 226) Write each sentence. Draw one line under each adjective. Draw two lines under the noun described by the adjective.

70. The blue heron lives in a marsh.

71. A small creek flows through our garden.

72. Tiny hummingbirds eat from the feeder.

Adjectives That Compare (page 228) Write each sentence. Complete the sentence with the correct form of the adjective.

73. Rhode Island is _____ than New Jersey. (small)

74. New York City is _____ than Scranton. (large)

75. The _____ mountain in the United States is Mt. McKinley in Alaska. (high)

Comparing with *more* and *most* (page 230) Write each sentence. Use the correct word in parentheses.

76. Teddy and Lena have the (more, most) wonderful books of all.

77. Some of the books have (more, most) illustrations than others.

78. The (more, most) beautiful book on the shelf has large color pictures.

Comparing with *good* and *bad* (page 232) Write each sentence using the correct word.

79. Juan liked the amusement park (best, better) than the beach.

80. The roller coaster ride was (worse, worst) than the Ferris wheel.

81. Kim liked the beach (better, best) than the park.

82. The (worse, worst) problem of all was the rain.

Using Articles and Demonstrative Adjectives (page 234) Write each sentence. Complete the sentence with the correct article or demonstrative adjective.

83. _____ record is better than that one. (This, That)

84. Steve has _____ excellent record collection. (a, an)

85. Linda has _____ record from 1950. (a, an)

86. _____ album is good. (Those, That)

Vocabulary Building: Synonyms and Antonyms (page 238) Match the synonyms or antonyms in the two columns. Label each pair **synonym** or **antonym**.

87. full   foolish
88. acquaintance pier
89. dock   empty
90. wise   friend

UNIT

8

The Granger Collection

Writing Descriptions

Read the quotation and look at the picture on the opposite page. The quotation was written by Virginia Hamilton, the author of a story you will read in this unit. How does a writer use words to make worlds?

When you describe something, you want your audience to see the same image, or picture, that you see. Using vivid adjectives will help your audience see what you see.

Focus Descriptive writing creates a clear and vivid picture of a person, place, or thing.

What would you like to describe? On the following pages you will find a story that contains vivid descriptions and some photographs of things you might like to describe. You can use the story and the photographs to find ideas for writing.

Words that make worlds are magic for me . . .
Oh, I am a believer in language and its magic
monarchy. To bind its boundless spell to me
is why I write.

—Virginia Hamilton

AWARD
WINNING
SELECTION

Have you ever been amazed or delighted by something you saw? How did you describe it to other people?

Geeder has imagined many wonderful things about Zeely, a person she admires. Finally, Geeder hears the real story of Zeely's life.

As you read the selection, look for the details that the author uses to help you see Zeely as Geeder sees her.

From

Zeely

BY VIRGINIA HAMILTON

eeder stood in amazement. Never had she seen Zeely dressed in such a way. She wore a length of varicolored silk wound around her delicate body and draped over her left shoulder. Around her head was a band of green silk, brilliant against her black hair. The long garment was beautiful and strange but the band around Zeely's hair was what held Geeder's attention. In her mind, she saw the picture of the Watutsi woman, the picture which right now she had hidden in her blouse. The Watutsi woman had worn such a headband.

"I'm glad you've come," Zeely said. Her voice was quiet, hardly above a whisper, and yet, it was perfectly clear. She smiled, adding, "Please follow me." She turned and led the way into the forest. Geeder, still unable to speak, followed.

Zeely plunged through stinging nettles. Often, she stamped them down for Geeder or stopped to hold a bramble aside. At such times, Geeder forced herself to look up at Zeely; always, when she did so, she felt awfully small.

"Your many beads are pretty," Zeely said suddenly. "You have a lot of clothes?" She spoke as if Geeder were someone she had known for years. But her voice was halting, the way a person might speak when he hadn't had anyone to talk to for a long, long time.

Geeder was so startled by Zeely's question, her mind went empty. "Why, I don't know!" she said at last. "I've a dress to go to a party. I've got clothes for school. Mother buys them every fall and Christmas." She felt ashamed that she hadn't worn long pants instead of shorts to her meeting with Zeely.

"A girl should have clothes," Zeely said.

"Miss Zeely, I think your dress is about the most pretty one I've ever seen," Geeder said, shyly.

Zeely touched the bodice of her robe with her long fingers. Geeder could tell she was pleased by the compliment.

"I've had it a long time," Zeely said. "Twice a year, I hang it in the sun so that the colors will catch and hold the light." Very delicately, she gathered the skirt and smoothed it evenly about her feet. The colors leaped and glowed.

Geeder didn't know why they had started talking about clothes. Since they had begun to speak, she was bursting to ask Zeely about herself.

"Miss Zeely, do you come from Tallahassee?" she blurted out. "I think somebody told me you came from there."

"No," said Zeely, "we come from far to the north, from Canada."

"Canada!" Geeder said. The thought that Zeely came from such a place excited her. "I've never been there," she said. "Was it cold?"

"Where we were, it was cold," Zeely said. "It snowed and there was not much summer."

"Did you have hogs there, too?" Geeder asked. She entwined her fingers, eager to talk.

"We always have hogs," Zeely said. "We sell the best. We eat the meat of those that are left." She looked away from Geeder. "It's by them that we live."

The way Zeely spoke about the hogs made Geeder feel she had said something wrong. She grew uneasy. "Well," she said, "I just thought it was maybe Tallahassee you came from. I remember someone told me that."

"The same someone who says I am a queen?" Zeely asked. Her eyes held to Geeder's.

Geeder's hands flew to her face. "I didn't mean anything bad!" she cried. "Miss Zeely? Here!" she fumbled in her blouse and her hand shook as she gave Zeely the photograph of the Watutsi woman.

Zeely looked at the photograph. She smiled, vaguely, as though she didn't know she smiled. Finally, she gave the picture back to Geeder. She sat stiff and still. She could have been carved out of the trees, so dark was she seated there. Then, the rigid mask of her face melted, as if it were made of wax. A smile parted her lips. From deep in her throat came a warm, sweet giggle. She threw back her head and laughed and laughed. It was to Geeder a delicious, soft sound.

Geeder was so happy, she began to laugh, too, and got up to sit next to Zeely. All at once, they were side by side, just the way Geeder had dreamed it.

Notice the author's use of descriptive details that paint a picture of Zeely.

"You are very much the way I was at your age." Zeely said.

"You were like *me*?" Geeder said. "Were you just like me?"

Zeely smiled. "I mean that because you found this picture, you were able to make up a good story about me. I once made up a story about myself, too."

"Miss Zeely!" Geeder said. "I wouldn't have told a soul if I hadn't found that picture. The picture is proof!"

Carefully, Zeely ran her long fingers over her robe. "My mother's people were Watutsi people out of Africa a long time ago," she said quietly.

"Just like the lady in the picture!" Geeder said.

"Yes," said Zeely, "and I believed that through my veins ran the blood of kings and queens! So it was that my mother came to make this robe for me," Zeely said. "I had asked her many questions about her people—I talked of nothing else for quite a while. She made this robe exactly like the ones they wore." Then she added, "I put it on today because wearing it, I can be more the way I was. You may touch it, if you like."

And very gently, Geeder touched it.

Thinking Like a Reader

1. If you wanted to describe a special person or thing, what details would you select? Write these details in your journal.

2. Which of your details best captures this person or thing? List the details.

Thinking Like a Writer

3. What images does the author use to show how Geeder pictures Zeely?

4. How do the details in the description help you to understand the characters? Write a response in your journal.

Brainstorm *Vocabulary*

In "Zeely," the author describes the scene in which Zeely and Geeder meet. She uses phrases such as "The rigid mask of her face" and "the colors leaped and glowed." Think of a person or place you know well. Write any images in your journal that come to mind. These can be words or phrases. Begin to create your personal vocabulary lists. These lists can help you when you write a description of your own of a person or place.

Talk It Over
Describe a Person

When Geeder sees Zeely in her robes and headband, she is reminded of the picture that she carries. Describe a famous person. What makes this person unusual or interesting? Think of some details. Tell a partner your description. Be sure to use clear, precise language. Then, ask your partner to guess who the person is.

Quick Write
Write an Advertisement

You have been thinking about people and places to describe. Write an advertisement for a place or product. Include details that show why the place or thing is special.

Vacation Home for Rent

Lovely four-room summer cottage in Ocean Cove, New Jersey. This neat home faces the beach. The house has a two-car garage and five acres of land. The cottage is available from July 1 – August 26.

Idea Corner
Interesting People or Places

You have already started to think about interesting people and places that you would like to describe. How could you help your reader to see a person or place as you do? In your journal make some notes about people or places you know. Use these notes when you write a description.

PICTURES

SEEING LIKE A WRITER

Finding Ideas for Writing

Look at the pictures. Think about what you see.
What ideas for descriptive writing do the pictures give you?
Write your ideas in your journal.

PICTURES: Ideas for Descriptive Writing

1 GROUP WRITING: A Description

COOPERATIVE
LEARNING

The **purpose** of a good description is to give the reader or **audience** a picture that is clear and vivid. What makes a picture clear and vivid?

- An Overall Impression
- Sensory Details
- Order of Details

An Overall Impression

Read the following paragraph. Notice the underlined sentence.

> <u>One huge, snow-capped peak rose high out of the surrounding landscape.</u> The base of the mountain joined the lower hills, which stretched as far as the eye could see. On the lower part of the mountain were larger trees, green bushes, and tall wildflowers. Scrubby trees and rough, granite boulders could be seen under the snow line. Clear, fresh water roared down from hundreds of places to streams and lakes far below. Sheer, vertical cliffs dropped thousands of feet.

The underlined sentence gives an **overall impression** or general idea of the mountain. Each detail adds to the overall impression of the scene. The description lets the reader "see" what the writer sees.

Guided Practice: Stating an Overall Impression

Work with your class to choose a place that you would like to describe. Discuss important things to include in a description. Think about the picture you wish to create. Together, write a sentence that gives a strong overall impression of that place.

Example: The old house looks worn out and tired.

Sensory Details

In a description, the writer includes many sensory details. These details appeal to a reader's five senses. **Sensory details** tell how things look, feel, taste, sound, or smell.

In the paragraph about the mountain, the sensory details help you to get an overall impression of a place. Look back at that paragraph.

- Which words help you to picture the mountain rising up from the surrounding landscape?
- Which details appeal to your sense of sight, feeling, taste, sound, or smell?

Guided Practice: Charting Sensory Details

Remember the place you have chosen to describe. Think of sensory details that describe that place. Copy the chart below. Write two or three details that appeal to each sense.

Overall Impression: The old house looks worn out and tired.

SIGHT	FEEL	TASTE	SOUND	SMELL
drab peeling paint	drafty clammy sticky	rusty water in pipes	creaks dripping faucets	dusty moldy stale

Order of Details

In a description of a place, the most logical order of details is one that maps out the picture for the reader. Each detail is arranged so that the reader is able to get a clear impression.

In the paragraph describing the mountain, the details are arranged from bottom to top. The writer has ordered the details so that a reader's eye would move from the base of the mountain up to its peaks. You can also choose to describe something from left to right, or from right to left.

Putting a Description Together

With your class, you have written a sentence that gives an overall impression of a place. You have also made a chart of sensory words or details that describe this place.

Look at your overall impression sentence and your chart of sensory words. Choose those that best fit the overall impression you wish to create.

Here are the sensory details one student selected to support the overall impression sentence that describes the old house.

The old house looked worn out and tired.

SIGHT	FEEL	TASTE	SOUND	SMELL
gloomy dark	cold clammy	rusty water in pipes	creaky dripping	stale musty

Guided Practice: Writing a Descriptive Paragraph

Write at least four detail sentences to add to your overall impression sentence. Include sensory words from your chart in these detail sentences. Remember to put your detail sentences in a logical order.

Share your description with a classmate. Ask your partner to suggest ways which will make your description clearer and more vivid.

COOPERATIVE LEARNING: Group Writing

Checklist: Descriptive Writing

When you write a descriptive paragraph, you will want to remember some points. A checklist will help to remind you of the things you will want to include in your descriptive paragraph.

Look at this checklist. You can add other points to it if you wish. Make a copy of the checklist and keep it in your writing folder. You can refer to it when you write your descriptive paragraph.

CHECKLIST

✔ Purpose and Audience	■ Taste _____
✔ Sensory Details	✔ Order of Details
■ Sight _____	_____
■ Sound _____	_____
■ Smell _____	_____
■ Feel _____	

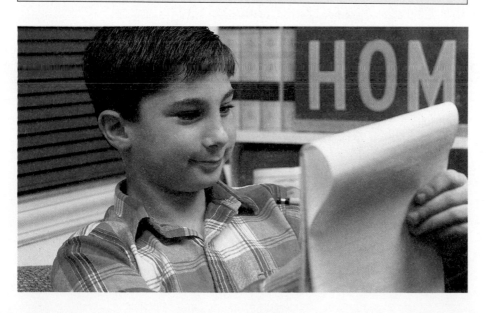

2 THINKING AND WRITING: Classifying Sensory Details

You have seen that good descriptive writing creates a clear picture for the reader. A description appeals to a reader's senses.

A writer classifies or groups sensory details that give an overall impression of a place. Details about sight, sound, smell, taste, and touch each belong to a separate group. The writer chooses certain details to fill in the picture for the reader. Look at this page from a writer's journal. The writer plans to write a description of her favorite Mexican restaurant. On the page, many details are listed.

close to my home

fresh corn tortillas

delicious, spicy enchiladas

dark and quiet inside

fast service

convenient parking lot

soft guitar music

flowers on table

Thinking Like a Writer

- Which details do you think are important to the overall impression?

The writer should select only the details that add important information about the restaurant to her description. She can leave out the details about the parking lot and the distance of the restaurant from her home.

When you write a description, you will have to select and classify details carefully, too.

THINKING APPLICATION Classifying Sensory Details

COOPERATIVE LEARNING

Each of the writers named below is planning to write a description. Help each writer to decide which details to include. On a separate piece of paper, list the sensory details that the student should include. You may wish to discuss your thinking with other students. In your discussions, explain your choices to each other.

1. Estelle's poem will describe a frightening thunderstorm. She wants to create an overall impression that the night is dramatic and scary. Which details should she include?

   deafening thunder   brilliant flashes of lightning
   heavy rain   a sea gull

2. Edward's paragraph will describe an angry elephant at the zoo. He wants to create an overall impression that the animal is wild and powerful. Which details should he include?

   loud, trumpeting call   stamping of huge feet
   pool of water in cage   thrashing, long trunk

3. Robin's letter will describe a pleasant summer day spent at a baseball stadium. He wants to create an overall impression of a lively, happy scene. Which details should he include?

   warm sunshine   green baseball field
   cheering fans   peanuts cost fifty cents

4. Katherine's paragraph will describe a neighborhood street fair. She wants to create an overall impression of a happy crowd in an entertaining place. Which details should she include?

   colorful booths on street   smell of barbecued food
   lively, loud music   street fair is free

3 INDEPENDENT WRITING: A Description

Prewrite: Step 1

You have learned a good deal about description. Now you can choose your own topic to describe. Janet, a student your age, wanted to write a description for her classmates. She chose a topic in this way.

Choosing a Topic

1. First, she made a list of people she admired.
2. Next, she thought about describing each person.
3. Last, she decided on the person she could best describe.

> *my grandfather*
> *Aunt Jane*
> *Eleanor Roosevelt*
> *a famous athlete*
> *my Girl Scout leader*
> *my teacher*

Janet decided that she would most like to describe someone she knew personally. She narrowed her topic to her grandfather, and she was ready to explore her idea.

Exploring Ideas: Charting Strategy

My Grandfather				
sight	sound	smell	feel	taste
white hair	snores	wood	rough	makes
blue eyes	tools	smoke	hands	maple
married				syrup
grandmother				
in 1935				

Janet thought she had some good ideas. She knew that her **purpose** was to describe her grandfather so that her **audience** could see him as she saw him.

Before she started to write, Janet recalled many details about her grandfather. She thought about the impression her grandfather made upon the people who knew him. Then, she changed some of the details on her chart.

My Grandfather

sight	sound	smell	feel	taste
white hair	snore	wood	rough	makes
glasses	tools	smoke	hands	maple
blue eyes	laugh		weathered	syrup
his dog			skin	

Thinking Like a Writer

- What did Janet add?
- What did she decide to leave out?
- How do these changes help to create an overall impression of her grandfather?

YOUR TURN

JOURNAL

Think of a person that you would like to describe. You might look at **Pictures** or your journal for ideas. Follow these steps.

- Make a list of people.
- Choose one whom you know well.
- Think of the overall impression this person makes.
- Think about your purpose and audience.

Make a chart of details. Remember, you can add or take away from the chart at any time.

Write a First Draft: Step 2

Janet knows what her description should include. She used a planning checklist.

Janet is now ready to write her first draft.

Janet's First Draft

> My grandfather is a carpenter. He has white hair, and his eyes are bluest than the sky. He smiles a lot. His big hands are rough. He wears baggy pants. He also has big work shoes. His english sheepdog, joe, goes with him everywhere. I hear the sound of his woodworking tools when I think of him.

While Janet was writing her first draft, she did not worry about errors. She wanted to put her ideas down on paper.

Planning Checklist
- Remember purpose and audience.
- Include an overall impression.
- Use sensory words or details.
- Use a logical order of details.

YOUR TURN

Write your first draft. As you prepare to write, ask yourself these questions.

- What will my audience want to know about my subject?
- How can I best express my overall impression?

TIME-OUT You might want to take some time out before you revise. That way you will be able to revise your writing with a fresh eye.

THE WRITING PROCESS: Writing a First Draft

Revise: Step 3

After she finished her first draft, Janet read it over to herself. She shared her writing with her classmate, Monica. She asked Monica to suggest ways to improve her work.

Janet then looked at her planning checklist. She noticed that she had forgotten an important point. She checked it off so that she would remember it. Janet now has a checklist to use as she revises.

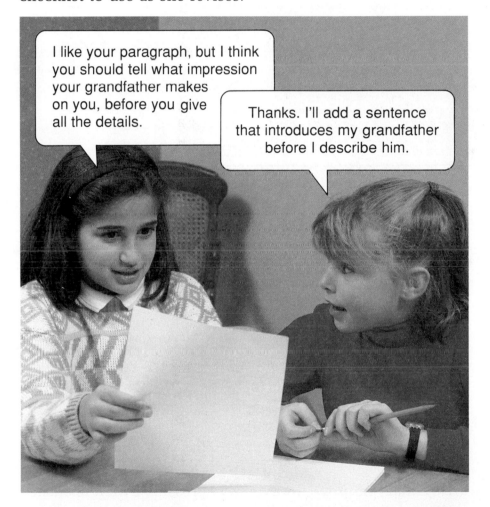

> I like your paragraph, but I think you should tell what impression your grandfather makes on you, before you give all the details.

> Thanks. I'll add a sentence that introduces my grandfather before I describe him.

Revising Checklist
- Remember purpose and audience.
- ✔ Include an overall impression.
- Use sensory details.
- Use a logical order of details.

Janet made changes to her paragraph. Notice that she did not correct small errors. She knew she could fix them later.

The revisions Janet made changed her paragraph. Turn the page. Look at Janet's revised paragraph.

is one of the most comfortable people to be around.

My grandfather is a carpenter. He has white hair, *He*

a wise face. and his eyes are bluest than the sky. He smiles *His cheeks wrinkle when*

feel a lot. His big hands are rough. He wears *when you shake them.*

and baggy pants. He also has big work shoes.

His english sheepdog, joe, goes with him

everywhere. I hear the sound of his

and smell wood shavings woodworking tools when I think of him.

Thinking Like a Writer

WISE
WORD
CHOICE

- Which sentence did Janet add?
- What sensory details did she add?
- Which sentences did she combine? How does combining sentences improve the paragraph?

YOUR TURN

Read your first draft. Make a checklist. Ask yourself these questions.

- How can I improve the overall impression I want to create?
- What details might I add to my description?
- How can I make the order of details more logical?

You may want to ask a classmate to read your paragraph and make suggestions. Then revise your paragraph.

THE WRITING PROCESS: Revising

WRITING PROCESS

Proofread: Step 4

Janet knew that her work would not be complete until she had proofread her paragraph. She used a proofreading checklist while she proofread.

Janet's Proofread Draft

> ⌗ _is one of the most comfortable people to be around._
> My grandfather ⌢is a carpenter. He has white hair,
> _a wise face._ ⌃He bluer _His cheeks wrinkle when_
> and ⌃his eyes are (bluest) than the sky. He smiles
> _feel_ _when you shake them._
> a lot. His big hands ⌃are ⌢rough. He wears
> _and_
> baggy pants. He also has ⌃big work shoes.
> His english sheepdog, joe, goes with him
> everywhere. I hear the sound of his
> _and smell wood shavings_
> woodworking tools ⌃when I think of him.

YOUR TURN

Proofreading Practice

Below is a paragraph that you can use to practice your proofreading skills. Find the errors. Write the paragraph correctly on a separate sheet of paper.

> My cats name is ex. Ex is short for exit. He is a large gray cat with gren eyes. his fur is thik and smooth. Ex's whiskers are long. At night he go outside and hunt for mice. He is the good hunter on my block. I like to watch him run threw tall grass.

Proofreading Checklist
- ■ Did I indent my paragraph?
- ■ Did I spell all words correctly?
- ■ What punctuation errors do I need to correct?
- ■ What capitalization errors do I need to correct?

Applying Your Proofreading Skills

Now proofread your description. Read your checklist again. Review **The Grammar Connection** and **The Mechanics Connection**. Use the proofreading marks to mark changes.

THE GRAMMAR CONNECTION

Remember these rules about adjectives.

■ Add *er* to most adjectives to compare two nouns.
   This car is **newer** than that car.
■ Add *est* to most adjectives to compare more than two nouns.
   The blue car is the **newest** car on the lot.
   Our house is the **oldest** one in town.

Check your descriptive paragraph. Be sure you have used adjectives of comparison correctly.

THE MECHANICS CONNECTION

Remember these rules about proper adjectives.

■ A **proper adjective** is formed from a proper noun.
■ A proper adjective always begins with a capital letter.

England	- - - ->	English
France	- - - ->	French
Spain	- - - ->	Spanish
America	- - - ->	American

The rugs from **Turkey** have beautiful patterns.
The **Turkish** rugs have beautiful patterns.

Check your descriptive paragraph. Have you capitalized all proper adjectives?

Proofreading Marks
¶ indent
∧ add
ℐ take out
≡ capital letter
/ make a small letter

Publish: Step 5

Janet shared her paragraph with her classmates. She copied her work in her best handwriting and posted it on the class bulletin board. Several of her classmates asked her about her grandfather. They wanted to know about the things her grandfather built.

YOUR TURN

Make a final copy of your descriptive paragraph. Use your best handwriting. Think of a way to share your description. You might find some ideas in the **Sharing Suggestions** box below.

SHARING SUGGESTIONS

| Read your work aloud to your classmates. | Ask an older relative or friend to read your description. | Make a tape recording of your description. |

SPEAKING AND LISTENING: Describing a Subject

You have just written a description of a person that you know. Your description included an overall impression of the person. It also included some sensory details. Now, you can use what you know about writing a description to give a short talk. In your talk, you will tell your **overall impression** of a person, place, or thing.

First, you will want to make a note card to use for your talk. You do not have to write everything on your note card. The note card should include only the main points and some of the details. Look at this note card.

Notes   Impressions of a Zebra

zebra — horse-like animal of African plains

1. Four and a half feet tall at the shoulder

2. black and white stripes

3. roams in herds in Africa

4. eats grass

5. black mane and tail

6. hunted by lions

Notice that the overall impression is listed on the note card. What other points are listed? How do the details support the overall impression? Are enough details included to give listeners a clear picture of a zebra?

When you give a talk, keep your **purpose** and **audience** in mind. These speaking guidelines will help you to focus your talk.

SPEAKING GUIDELINES: Describing a Subject

1. Remember that your **purpose** is to describe.
2. Tell an overall impression. Include sensory details. Use logical order.
3. Make a note card. Practice using your note card.
4. Look at your **audience**.
5. Speak in a clear voice. Pause briefly between sentences, and do not speak too quickly.

SPEAKING APPLICATION: Describing a Subject

Think of a person, place, or thing you particularly like. Prepare a note card to use to give a short talk about your subject. Use the speaking guidelines to help you prepare. Your classmates will be using the following guidelines as they listen to your description.

LISTENING GUIDELINES: Describing a Subject

1. Listen to "see" the image.
2. Listen for an overall impression.
3. Listen for sensory details.

5 WRITER'S RESOURCES: The Encyclopedia

You have written a description of a place and a person that you know. It is also possible to write a description of a place or person you have never seen. The encyclopedia is a good resource for ideas.

An **encyclopedia** is a set of books that contains information about many topics. Each book, or volume, has articles that are arranged in alphabetical order. Encyclopedia articles give information about people, places, things, and events.

Notice that the volumes are labeled with one or more letters. Each volume includes subjects beginning with that letter. For example, an article about *France* would be in volume 7. An article about *bats* would be in volume 2.

Articles on people are listed under each person's last name. An article on Amelia Earhart would be listed under *E*, in volume 6.

Every encyclopedia has an **index** that lists all the subjects included in the encyclopedia. The index in the encyclopedia above is in volume 22.

Practice

Use the encyclopedia on the opposite page. Write each name in the list below. Then, write the number of the volume that would have an article about that person or subject.

1. Albert Einstein
2. Dorothy Mary Crawfoot Hadgkin
3. Guglielmo Marconi
4. Ivan Pavlov
5. Anna Freud
6. Isaac Newton
7. Marie Curie
8. George Washington Carver
9. Galileo Galilei
10. Robert Fulton
11. Australia
12. Mt. Everest
13. electricity
14. kangaroos
15. computers
16. botany
17. volcanoes
18. ecology
19. Panama Canal
20. irrigation

WRITING APPLICATION A List

Use an encyclopedia to look up information about a famous scientist. Pay particular attention to facts about the person's achievements in his or her particular area of knowledge. You might also decide to make notes about the scientist's date and place of birth and any other interesting information you find in the encyclopedia entry. You may choose one of the scientists listed above or select another scientist. Write a list of details and facts about this person. Keep your list in your writing folder. You will use it in **The Curriculum Connection** page 286.

Albert Einstein

THE CURRICULUM CONNECTION

Writing About Science

Scientists write descriptions every day. They must describe natural things such as the weather and the habits of animals. Astronomers study the universe and describe the movement of the stars and planets, as well as the course of the sun and moon. Geologists describe how the earth was made. In fact, scientists even try to describe things that cannot be seen or heard!

Look at the world around you. Rocks, mountains, oceans, streams, plants, insects, and animals can all be studied and described. The more you carefully observe something, the more details you will find to describe. Scientists may spend years studying one particular plant or animal.

ACTIVITIES

Describe Something Think of something you know well in nature. Try to see it as clearly as you can. Then write notes about this thing. Record any details that describe its shape, size, surface, and any other qualities that help to describe it. Use sensory words and make your notes clear and vivid. When you have remembered everything you can, look carefully at the object and see what you have forgotten to record in your notes.

Describe a Famous Scientist Look at the list of things about the scientist whom you looked up in the encyclopedia. Imagine that you *are* this famous scientist. What would you want people to know about you? Write a brief description of your accomplishments in your special field of science. Be sure to organize your details in a logical order.

Respond to Literature The following selection is a scientific description of shooting stars. The author explains what is happening when a "star" races brightly across the sky. After reading the description, write a response. You might discuss the description, or write your own description of something that occurs in nature, such as a volcanic eruption or an eclipse.

Shooting Stars
from *The Reasons for Seasons*

Shooting stars or meteors are dots of dust on fire. Space is filled with particles. There are two theories about their origin. One is that they are particles left over after the birth of a planet. The other is that they are debris from a dead planet.

Whatever they are, these particles occasionally collide with the earth. Most of them are tiny, about the size of a grain of sand. They burn up when they enter the earth's upper atmosphere. Their glow is what we call a shooting star.

UNIT CHECKUP

LESSON

Group Writing: Description (page 268) Read this paragraph. On a separate sheet of paper, write the sentence that states the overall impression.

> Her eyes are black and lively, and her laugh is always loud. With one hug she can send you gasping for breath. She is always hugging somebody. Mrs. Sanchez is a big, jolly woman who makes everyone feel welcome.

LESSON

Thinking: Classifying Sensory Details (page 272) Imagine that you are going to write a description of a doctor. You wish to create the overall impression that she is hard-working, dedicated to her patients, and kind. Which of these details would you include? Write these details on a separate sheet of paper.

1. workday from 8 a.m. to 7 p.m.
2. came to Buddy's house for an emergency
3. had a salad for lunch
4. made Leslie feel unafraid
5. saw a movie last Tuesday

LESSON

Writing a Description (page 274) What does your best friend think when he or she looks at you? Write a description of yourself as you think your best friend might see you.

LESSON

Speaking and Listening: Describing a Subject (page 282) Imagine that you are about to give a short talk to your class in which you describe one of your favorite paintings or photographs. Make a note card to use during your talk.

LESSON

Writer's Resources: The Encyclopedia (page 284) Select a topic of your choice. Use an encyclopedia to find information about this topic. Write a short summary of the information that you find.

THEME PROJECT

ART REVIEW

You have now written several descriptions and learned how writers create clear and vivid pictures. There are ways to describe things other than with words. One common way is with a drawing or a painting.

Look at the painting below.

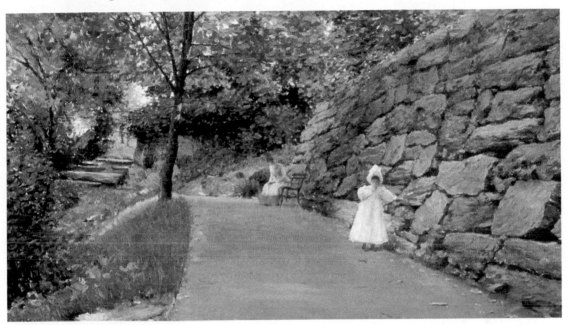

In the Park, William Merritt Chase

Before photography, people drew or painted scenes that they wished other people to see. A painting can tell a viewer about a place. At the same time, a painting or drawing can tell the viewer how the person who made it felt about his or her subject. Talk with your classmates about what you see in the painting.

Write a review of a work of art.

- Choose a picture or photograph that you admire.
- Look at your subject carefully.
- Write a description of what you see in the picture. In your review, tell your readers why they would also like this picture or photograph.

9

Pronouns

In Unit 9 you will learn about pronouns. Pronouns can take the place of nouns. One way to avoid using the same nouns over and over in your writing is by using pronouns.

Discuss Read the poem on the opposite page. What view does the poet have about the destruction of the town?

Creative Expression The theme of this unit is *Views*. When you have a view about something, you have an opinion about it. What views, or opinions, do you have? Work with a partner. Write a few sentences that tell your opinion of something. You could write about a favorite movie, song, book, or food. Write your thoughts in your journal.

JOURNAL

THEME: *VIEWS*

*They're tearing down
  a town, a town,
They'll probably take the rest.
Progress takes its toll, I'm told—
But should it take the best?*

—Jud Strunk,
from "They're Tearing Down a Town"

1 WHAT IS A PRONOUN?

A pronoun is a word that takes the place of one or more nouns and the words that go with the nouns.

You can use a pronoun to avoid repeating a noun or group of words with a noun.

The pitcher was ready. **She** was ready.

	Subject Pronouns	Object Pronouns
Singular	I	me
	you	you
	he/she/it	him/her/it
Plural	we	us
	you	you
	they	them

Guided Practice

Tell which word in each sentence is a pronoun.

Example: We come to the park for relaxation.   *We*

1. Jim brings Dad's paper to him.
2. He always waits for the mail carrier.
3. We discuss the events of the day.
4. The neighbors join us in the park.

 THINK

■ How can I decide if a word is a pronoun?

REMEMBER

■ A **pronoun** is a word that takes the place of a noun.

More Practice

A. Write the pronoun in each sentence.

Example: We plan a picnic together. *We*

   5. They appreciate the trees and flowers.
   6. The Grants have picnics in the park with us.
   7. Paul invited Nan and me to the picnic.
   8. Mother helped prepare food with us.
   9. Nan and I packed a picnic basket.
   10. Nan made a special potato salad for me.
   11. She cooked wonderful food for the Grants.
   12. They loved the food.

B. Write each sentence. Then replace each underlined word or group of words with a pronoun.

Example: <u>Father</u> made a chicken sandwich.
      He made a chicken sandwich.

   13. Sammy thanked <u>Mother and Nan</u> for the chicken.
   14. <u>Mrs. Grant</u> enjoyed the potato salad.
   15. She told <u>Nan</u> some wonderful recipes.
   16. <u>The Grants</u> are all good cooks.
   17. Sammy made popcorn for <u>Nan and Mrs. Grant</u>.
   18. Mr. Grant roasted peanuts for <u>Sammy</u>.
   19. <u>Nan and Sammy</u> supervised the cleanup.
   20. <u>The park</u> is a beautiful place.

Extra Practice, page 318

WRITING APPLICATION An Editorial

Suppose your town council voted to build a park in your neighborhood. Write an editorial in which you state your opinions about the project. Ask a partner to circle the pronouns in your editorial.

COOPERATIVE
LEARNING

2 SUBJECT PRONOUNS

A subject tells *whom* or *what* a sentence is about. A pronoun can take the place of a noun. A **subject pronoun** takes the place of a noun that is the subject of a sentence.

Bill took a bus to the zoo.   **He** took a bus to the zoo.

Subject pronouns are used after forms of the linking verb *be*. Notice the placement of **I** in the sentence below.

The winners of the contest **were** Julie and **I**.

Subject Pronouns	
Singular	**Plural**
I	we
you	you
she/he/it	they

Guided Practice

Tell which word in each sentence is the subject pronoun.

Example: We will visit the aquarium.   *We*

1. I will enjoy the trip.
2. You look forward to the day.
3. It is a new experience for many students.
4. They ask the teacher for information.

THINK

■ How can I tell if a word is a subject pronoun?

REMEMBER

■ A **subject pronoun** can take the place of a noun as the subject of a sentence.

More Practice

A. Write each sentence. Draw a line under the subject pronoun in each sentence.

Example: You will enjoy the dolphins.

  5. He shows the class a filmstrip.
  6. We went to the aquarium on Thursday.
  7. You talked about the dolphins.
  8. They are intelligent animals.
  9. I saw a dolphin last year.
 10. He was named Albert.
 11. Jan and I loved Albert.
 12. We watched Albert for hours.

B. Write each sentence. Use a subject pronoun in place of the underlined word or words.

Example: Sue took photographs of the seals.
She took photographs of the seals.

 13. Simon loved the dolphins and porpoises.
 14. Dolphins and porpoises are similar animals.
 15. Simon and I asked for a tour.
 16. A seal performed funny tricks.
 17. The cutest animals were the baby seals.
 18. Marian loved the sea turtles.
 19. Jack and I saw an octopus.
 20. The octopus scared Betsey.

Extra Practice, page 319

WRITING APPLICATION A Proposal

With a partner write a proposal for a class trip that you would like to take. Tell where you wish to go, and offer suggestions for transportation. Read your proposal to your classmates.

COOPERATIVE
LEARNING

3 OBJECT PRONOUNS

A subject pronoun can be the subject of a sentence. An **object pronoun** is a pronoun that can be used as the object of a verb or after words such as *to, for, with, in,* or *at.*

He plays the **flute**. He plays **it**. He carries **it** with **him**.

Object Pronouns	
Singular	**Plural**
me	us
you	you
her/him/it	them

You and *it* may be subject pronouns or object pronouns.

Guided Practice

Tell which word in each sentence is an object pronoun.

Example: Mother bought a record for us.   *us*

1. The new record sounds great to me.
2. I gave them that record as a gift.
3. John saw it advertised on television.
4. Every song reminds me of the concert.

 THINK

- How can I decide whether to use a subject pronoun or an object pronoun in a sentence?

REMEMBER

■ An **object pronoun** can be used as the object of an action verb or after words such as *to, for, with, in,* or *at.*

More Practice

A. Write each sentence. Draw a line under the pronoun. Then write whether the pronoun is a **subject pronoun** or an **object pronoun**.

Example: Music fascinates <u>us</u>.   *object pronoun*

 5. I watched the commercial with them.
 6. The record is for you.
 7. It was made at the concert.
 8. You will enjoy the music.
 9. The record delights me.
10. Karen told us about the violinists.
11. She likes violins the best.
12. Mother got concert tickets for us.

B. Write each sentence, using the correct pronoun from the pair in parentheses.

Example: Buy extra tickets for (they, them).
              Buy extra tickets for them.

13. The concert will thrill (we, us).
14. Mother will take you and (me, I).
15. Father and (she, her) have many records.
16. She gave (he, him) a new record player.
17. Father bought records for (she, her).
18. The evening will be fun for (we, us).
19. Barbara and (I, me) are excited.
20. I talked to (she, her) about the concert.

Extra Practice, page 320

WRITING APPLICATION An Advertisement

Write an advertisement for an exciting event that will soon take place. Have a partner circle the pronouns.

4 USING *I* AND *ME* CORRECTLY

You already know that the subject pronoun **I** can replace a noun as the subject of a sentence or follow the linking verb *be*.

I won. The winner was **I**.

The object pronoun **me** can replace a noun that follows an action verb or a word such as *with, in, at, to,* or *for*.

Jim explained the rules to **me**.
He tells **me** about the prizes.

Sometimes a compound subject or a compound object contains the pronoun *I* or *me*. To help you figure out whether to use *I* or *me* in a compound, leave out the other word.

Bill and I entered the contest.
I entered the contest.
The rehearsals were hard for **him and me**.
The rehearsals were hard for **me**.

Notice that in the sentences above, the pronouns *I* and *me* follow the other pronoun or noun in the compound. When you use *I* or *me* with nouns or other pronouns, you name yourself last.

Guided Practice

Tell the pronoun that completes each sentence correctly.

Example: The plane trip was exciting for Bill and (I, me).
me

1. The winners of the contest were he and (I, me).
2. The senator welcomed Bill and (I, me).
3. Bill and (I, me) thanked him warmly.
4. The senator took Bill and (I, me) on a tour.
5. Bill and (I, me) learned about government.

?! THINK

■ How can I decide whether to use *I* or *me* in a sentence?

REMEMBER

- Use **I** as the subject of a sentence or after the linking verb *be*.
- Use **me** after action verbs or after a word such as *with, in, at, to,* or *for*.

More Practice

Write each sentence. Complete the sentence correctly with **I** or **me**.

Example: You and _____ loved the tour.
    You and I loved the tour.

6. The tour was thrilling for Bill and _____.
7. He and _____ learned about Washington, D.C.
8. The guide walked along with him and _____.
9. He took other tourists and _____ around the White House.
10. Bill and _____ had discussed the city.
11. The happiest visitors were he and _____.
12. My friends and _____ saw the Smithsonian.
13. That museum was interesting to the other tourists and _____.
14. _____ toured the White House with my class.
15. The monitors were Kate and _____.
16. Badges were given to Bill and _____.
17. John and _____ had a wonderful time.
18. Washington was very impressive to Bill and _____.
19. My friend and _____ shook hands with a guard.
20. At night, Tim and _____ were tired but happy.

Extra Practice, page 321

WRITING APPLICATION An Article

Write an article about a place you have visited with a friend or relative. What did you do there? Whom did you meet? Describe some of the experiences you shared with your companion. Exchange articles with a partner. Check for the correct use of *I* and *me* in each other's writing.

5 POSSESSIVE PRONOUNS

A **possessive pronoun** is a pronoun that shows *who* or *what* owns something. A possessive pronoun can take the place of a possessive noun. Sometimes possessive pronouns come before a noun.

Some possessive pronouns can stand by themselves. They can replace nouns in a sentence.

Possessive Pronouns			
Possessive Pronouns with Nouns		**Possessive Pronouns That Stand Alone**	
my	*My* book is good.	mine	The desk is *mine*.
your	*Your* kitten is tiny.	yours	*Yours* is gray.
his	*His* dog is brown.	his	The dog is *his*.
her	*Her* train is late.	hers	The ticket is *hers*.
its	*Its* purpose is clear.	its	*Its* is clear.
our	*Our* house is quiet.	ours	*Ours* is noisy.
your	Where is *your* friend?	yours	Where is *yours*?
their	*Their* trip was fun.	theirs	*Theirs* was fun.

Your kitten is tiny.

Guided Practice

Tell which word in each sentence is a possessive pronoun.

Example: Several books about space are on my desk.   *my*

1. Our space program is Martin's favorite topic.
2. His ambition is to explore outer space.
3. The model spaceship is mine.
4. Space travel is my destiny.
5. Mars is ours!

 THINK

■ How can I use possessive pronouns correctly?

REMEMBER

- The pronouns *my*, *your*, *his*, *her*, *its*, *our*, and *their* come before nouns.
- The pronouns *mine*, *yours*, *his*, *hers*, *its*, *ours*, and *theirs* can stand alone.

More Practice

A. Write each sentence, using the correct possessive pronoun from the pair in parentheses.

Example: Molly designed (her, hers) space suit.
Molly designed her space suit.

6. Joel and Kim built (their, theirs) spaceship.
7. The idea for the spaceship was (my, mine).
8. We used (my, mine) bicycle for spare parts.
9. They asked (their, theirs) father for nails.
10. I brought (my, mine) telescope.
11. We each had (our, ours) favorite star.
12. Which one is (your, yours)?

B. Write each sentence. Replace the underlined word or words with the correct possessive pronoun.

Example: <u>Donald's</u> drawing shows the rings of Saturn.
His drawing shows the rings of Saturn.

13. <u>Jill's</u> favorite planet is Mars.
14. Pluto is <u>Eddie's</u>.
15. <u>Mars's</u> nickname is "the red planet."
16. The teacher praised <u>Sam and Pete's</u> project.
17. <u>Maria and Yolanda's</u> was wonderful, too.
18. The class admired <u>the one belonging to me</u>.
19. I liked <u>Molly's</u>.
20. The best poster was <u>Ted and Ann's</u>.

Extra Practice, page 322

WRITING APPLICATION A Description

Write a description of your favorite planet. Have a partner circle the possessive pronouns in your writing.

6 USING POSSESSIVE PRONOUNS

As you know, a possessive pronoun shows *who* or *what* owns something. Possessive pronouns never have an apostrophe (').

Remember, some possessive pronouns come before nouns. Possessive pronouns can also replace a noun.

Your bat is broken. **Yours** is broken.

Notice that a possessive pronoun can show ownership of one or more person, place, or thing.

Our game is tomorrow. **Ours** is Saturday.
Theirs are Sunday, Tuesday, and Thursday.

Guided Practice

Tell which possessive pronoun completes each sentence correctly.

Example: We show each other (our, ours) games.   *our*

1. It is time for (our, ours) demonstration.
2. The tennis racket is (her, hers).
3. Sheila and Rene brought (their, theirs) from home.
4. Pete does not use (their, theirs) rackets.
5. He prefers (our, ours).

 THINK

■ How can I use a possessive pronoun to show ownership?

REMEMBER

- Possessive pronouns can come before nouns or stand alone.
- Possessive pronouns can show ownership of one or more person, place, or thing.

More Practice

Write each sentence. Choose the possessive pronoun from the pair in parentheses that completes each sentence correctly.

Example: Mark traded his racket for (my, mine).
Mark traded his racket for mine.

6. You explained the rules of (your, yours) game.
7. Betty explains the rules of (her, hers).
8. Sheila and Mark demonstrate (their, theirs) skills.
9. (Your, Yours) game is difficult.
10. That football is (our, ours).
11. The one in the locker is (your, yours).
12. I described (my, mine) favorite sport.
13. (Our, Ours) jungle gym is fun.
14. Sue and Dave practice (their, theirs) gymnastics.
15. You explain (your, yours) favorite stunts.
16. Lorna shares (her, hers) dance routine with us.
17. Sandy and Paul practice (their, theirs) all day.
18. I demonstrate (my, mine).
19. What will (your, yours) be?
20. (Our, Ours) is fun for everyone.

Extra Practice, page 323

WRITING APPLICATION A Persuasive Paragraph

Write a paragraph that persuades your classmates to learn your favorite game. Write at least three reasons why this is your favorite game. Exchange paragraphs with a classmate. Have your partner underline the possessive pronouns in your paragraph.

GRAMMAR

7 PRONOUN CONTRACTIONS

A **contraction** is a shortened form of two words. Subject pronouns can be combined with some verbs to form contractions.

Some Common Contractions with Pronouns			
Pronoun + Verb	Contraction	Pronoun + Verb	Contraction
I am	I'm	I have	I've
you are	you're	you have	you've
she is	she's	she has	she's
he is	he's	he has	he's
it is	it's	it has	it's
we are	we're	we have	we've
they are	they're	they have	they've
I will	I'll	I had	I'd
you will	you'll	you had	you'd
he will	he'll	he had	he'd
she will	she'll	she had	she'd
it will	it'll	it had	it'd

Guided Practice

Tell the contraction for each pair of words.

Example: I am   *I'm*

1. they have
2. I will
3. she is
4. you will
5. we are

 THINK

■ Where do I use an apostrophe in a contraction?

REMEMBER

- An **apostrophe** is used in place of the letter or letters that have been left out to form a contraction.

More Practice

A. Write the words from which the contraction in each sentence is formed.

Example: They're cooking a big meal for the holiday.

        They're   They are

  6. We're having a holiday dinner with Grandma.
  7. It's a festive occasion.
  8. I'm looking forward to it.
  9. She'll have a big turkey and trimmings.
  10. She's inviting many people.
  11. You'll eat two or three helpings.
  12. I'll eat three or four!

B. Write the contraction for the underlined words in each sentence.

Example: I have bought some flowers for Grandma. *I've*

  13. He is bringing the apples.
  14. She will make a pie.
  15. It will be delicious.
  16. I am excited about the dinner.
  17. She is an expert cook.
  18. She will put the flowers on the table.
  19. I will tie a ribbon around them.
  20. They are my holiday present to her.

Extra Practice, Practice Plus, pages 324–326

WRITING APPLICATION An Invitation

Write an invitation to a friend for a holiday meal. Be sure to include the date, time, and place of the occasion. Your invitation will be informal, so feel free to use contractions. Circle the contractions.

USING *WE* AND *US* WITH NOUNS

You can use **we** and **us** with nouns to make your meaning clear. Remember that the subject pronoun *we* can be used with a noun or after forms of the verb *be*.

> **We** students study journalism.
> The editors of the paper are **we** students.

The object pronoun *us* can be used after action verbs or after words such as *to*, *for*, *with*, or *at*.

> The teacher asked **us** writers for some ideas.
> The principal gave the credit to **us** journalists.

Guided Practice

Tell whether *we* or *us* completes each sentence correctly.

Example: Newspapers are important to (us, we) citizens.

> us

1. (We, Us) students read the newspapers.
2. The papers tell the problems of (we, us) people.
3. (Us, We) fifth graders started a newspaper.
4. The project is fun for (we, us) journalists.
5. It teaches (we, us) students about events at school.

 THINK

■ How can I decide whether to use *we* or *us* with nouns?

REMEMBER

- Use **we** with nouns after linking verbs.
- Use **us** with nouns after action verbs or prepositions.

More Practice

Write each sentence, using the correct word from the pair in parentheses.

Example: The teacher suggested a project for (we, us) writers.   *The teacher suggested a project for us writers.*

6. (We, Us) students plan our articles carefully.
7. It is hard work for (we, us) writers.
8. (We, Us) journalists cover important events.
9. (We, Us) writers interview people.
10. Students speak to (we, us) journalists.
11. (We, Us) writers ask serious questions.
12. Many issues concern (we, us) students.
13. (We, Us) students need more typewriters.
14. Typewriters help (we, us) writers meet deadlines.
15. (We, Us) journalists use notebooks, too.
16. Some of (we, us) writers carry tape recorders.
17. (We, Us) artists make sketches for the paper.
18. Editors are grateful to (we, us) illustrators.
19. (We, Us) artists work closely with writers.
20. (We, Us) readers support the newpapers.

Extra Practice, page 327

WRITING APPLICATION A Statement of Opinion

Write a paragraph or a persuasive article that states your opinion of class parties. Include at least four reasons that support your position. Exchange your work with a partner. Circle **we** and **us** in each other's writing. Read aloud your partner's statement of opinion. Then discuss what makes the writing persuasive.

MECHANICS: More Comma Rules

Sometimes you name the person to whom you are speaking in a sentence. This is called a **noun in direct address**.

Clara, which holiday trip did you prefer?
I know, **Clara**, that you love the ocean.
➡ Use a comma or commas to set off a noun in direct address from the rest of the sentence.

You can begin a sentence with a word such as *well*, *oh*, *no*, or *yes*. These words are called **introductory words**.

Well, Cape Cod is lovely. **Yes**, I agree.
➡ Use a comma after an introductory word.

You may also use an introductory word and a noun in direct address in the same sentence.

Well, Clara, tell me more about the trip.

Guided Practice

Tell where to add a comma or commas in each sentence.

Example: Oh where are your photos?   *comma after Oh*

1. You have a picture Terence of the beach at Truro.
2. Well this is a photograph of our hotel.
3. I stayed there last month Terence.
4. Oh Clara that is a coincidence!

 THINK

■ How do I use commas to set off a noun in direct address or an introductory word?

REMEMBER

- Use a **comma** after an introductory word.
- Use a comma or commas to set off a noun in direct address.

More Practice

Write each sentence. Add a comma or commas where they are needed.

Example: Clara I had a wonderful trip.   *Clara, I had a wonderful trip.*

5. Terence do you prefer lake or ocean beaches?
6. Well I loved our trip to Lake Charles.
7. Where is the lake Terence?
8. It is in Louisiana Clara.
9. Oh isn't the weather hot in Louisiana?
10. Yes Clara but I enjoy hot weather.
11. Terence what did you do there?
12. Well I swam in and boated on the lake.
13. Oh I cannot swim well yet Terence.
14. Have you taken lessons Clara?
15. No but I may sign up for a course soon.
16. Clara why do you prefer the ocean?
17. I like the breezes Terence on the shore.
18. Yes but the lake shore has shady trees.
19. Well is there a good breeze from the lake?
20. No I guess the ocean beach is cooler.

Extra Practice, page 328

WRITING APPLICATION A Dialogue

Write a dialogue that might take place between yourself and a friend about vacations. Your dialogue might contain interesting facts about places you have visited. Include nouns in direct address and introductory words in your dialogue. Have a partner circle the commas in your dialogue. Read aloud each other's dialogues.

VOCABULARY BUILDING: Prefixes

There are different ways to change the meaning of a word. One way to change the meaning of a word is to add other word parts to the base word. A **prefix** is a word part added to the beginning of a base word. A prefix changes the meaning of the word to which it is added.

Some Common Prefixes	
Prefix	**Meaning**
re	again, back
un	not, the opposite of
dis	not, the opposite of
mis	bad or wrong, badly or wrongly
im	not, without, in, into
in	not, without, in, into
il, ir	not, without
non	not, the opposite of, without
pre	before, in preparation for
post	after, later

Guided Practice

Identify the prefix and give the meaning of each word below.

Example: unhappy   *un*   *not happy, sad*

1. refund
2. imperfect
3. misuse
4. nonsense
5. illogical

 THINK

■ How can I figure out the meaning of a word which contains a prefix?

REMEMBER

- A **prefix** is a word part added to the beginning of a base word.
- A prefix changes the meaning of the base word to which it is added.

More Practice

Write each underlined word. Draw a line under the prefix and write the meaning of the word.

Example: The weather became <u>unpleasant</u>.

<u>un</u>pleasant   *not pleasant*

6. On a boat trip, one must take every <u>precaution</u>.
7. We make sure our old boat is <u>refinished</u>.
8. We are <u>unafraid</u> of hard work.
9. Some sailors are <u>inconsiderate</u>.
10. They <u>misjudge</u> the dangers of the sea.
11. We <u>review</u> our maps and charts.
12. A lost crew is most <u>unfortunate</u>.
13. This boat is a <u>postwar</u> model.
14. Eric considers the boat <u>unsinkable</u>.
15. Our captain firmly <u>disagrees</u>.
16. In choppy water we <u>rethink</u> our voyage.
17. On the high seas, our engine is <u>irreplaceable</u>.
18. High speeds become <u>impossible</u>.
19. We cannot <u>refuel</u> at sea, either.
20. The captain <u>returns</u> the boat to the shore.

Extra Practice, page 329

WRITING APPLICATION A Report

Write a report on a trip you have taken or planned to take. Describe in detail what you found interesting and enjoyable about the trip. In your report, include some of the prefixes you have learned. When you have finished, exchange reports with a partner. Underline the prefixes in each other's writing.

VOCABULARY: Prefixes

GRAMMAR —AND WRITING CONNECTION

Using Pronouns Correctly

You know that there are many ways to make your writing clear and precise. You can use pronouns to refer to nouns to avoid unnecessary repetition. You will want to be sure that the pronoun you choose refers clearly to the noun that comes before it.

Look at the sentence below.

I read books about careers, and **it** is interesting.
You may have trouble understanding to which word *it* refers. Now look at another sentence.

I read an interesting book about careers,
and **it** contained important information.
The word *it* in the second part of the sentence refers correctly to the word *book*.

Working Together

COOPERATIVE LEARNING

With your class, discuss how to use pronouns correctly. Supply the correct pronoun in place of each incorrect pronoun in the sentences below.

Example: The children ran toward its parents.
The children ran toward their parents.

1. A bird landed on their perch.
2. The policeman found the little girl and brought us home.
3. Maria saw Andy and told them the news.
4. Andy met his friends and spoke to it about the little girl.
5. Andy's friends knew the little girl and its parents.

Revising Sentences

Kelly wrote these sentences about careers. Help Kelly to make her sentences correct. Be sure that in each revised sentence, the pronoun refers clearly to the noun that comes before it.

6. I chose the book because they was good.
7. The author explains their research.
8. The author knows a great deal about their subject.
9. Some careers require that students complete his work.
10. Students can understand the job market if he tries.
11. The markets are huge; it include many jobs.
12. People should write more books on this subject; he will sell many copies.
13. The book said that students should explore many types of jobs; he will be successful.
14. Students talked about his ideas.
15. My father and Jim told me about his new plans, too.

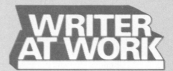

Brainstorm to think of a career or job that interests you. Write a paragraph that persuades other students to learn more about this job or career. When you have finished, check your writing carefully to be sure each pronoun refers correctly to the noun that comes before it.

UNIT CHECKUP

LESSON 1

What Is a Pronoun? (page 292) Write each sentence. Underline each pronoun.

1. Paul asks his friend for help.
2. She is a good history student.
3. The girl studies with him.
4. They prepare for a test.
5. The teacher is pleased with them.

LESSONS 2-3

Subject Pronouns and Object Pronouns (pages 294–297) Write each sentence. Draw a line under each pronoun and write whether it is a subject or an object pronoun.

6. The game was a thrill for me.
7. Dad gave us a ride home.
8. He stopped at a restaurant.
9. We had a delicious meal.
10. The biggest eater was I!

LESSON 4

Using *I* and *me* Correctly (page 298) Write each sentence. Complete the sentence with **I** or **me**.

11. Math is a hard subject for _____.
12. _____ must study harder.
13. The teacher gave _____ extra help.
14. Tom and _____ passed the test.
15. The highest scorers were Dana and _____.

LESSONS 5-6

Possessive Pronouns (pages 300–303) Write each sentence using the correct possessive pronoun.

16. Wayne goes to (our, ours) dentist.
17. (My, Mine) checkup was good.
18. Julie takes care of (her, hers) teeth.
19. We must take care of (our, ours).
20. (Their, Theirs) teeth are strong.

LESSON 7 **Pronoun Contractions** (page 304). Form a contraction from each pair of words. Write the contraction.

21. We are   **23.** He has   **25.** I am
22. It is   **24.** She will

LESSON 8 **Using *we* and *us* with Nouns** (page 306) Write each sentence. Complete the sentence correctly with **we** or **us**. Remember to capitalize the first word of a sentence.

26. _____ tourists like to travel.
27. It is work for _____ salespeople.
28. Bicycles are used by _____ mail carriers.
29. _____ firefighters have trucks.
30. The slowest are _____ walkers.

LESSON 9 **Mechanics: More Comma Rules** (page 308) Write each sentence. Add commas where they are needed.

31. Nancy I read your report on water pollution.
32. Well I agree with your arguments.
33. Yes Jeffrey pollution is a serious problem.
34. We all depend on our water system Nancy.
35. I read your report Jeffrey on pollution.

LESSON 10 **Vocabulary Building: Prefixes** (page 310) Write the meaning of each underlined word with a prefix.

36. Laziness is <u>unacceptable</u> here.
37. <u>Injustice</u> is also frowned upon.
38. He was treated with <u>disrespect</u>.
39. Do not be <u>impatient</u> with us.
40. You will not be <u>misunderstood</u>.

Writing Application: Comma Usage (page 308) The following letter contains 5 errors with commas. Rewrite the paragraph correctly.

41-45. Barbara I have considered your problem carefully. Yes you should make a weekly budget. Your allowance Barbara should cover your needs. Well sometimes you may require some extra money.

ENRICHMENT

TELEPHONE

Play this game with your classmates. One student begins a story with a sentence using a pronoun. The next student continues the story by adding a sentence that tells to whom or what the pronoun refers. Keep playing until the story comes to a satisfying end.

QUAKER QUOTES

The Quakers use different pronouns than *we* do. For *you*, they substitute *thee* and *thou*, and for *your* and *yours*, they use *thy* and *thine*. Rewrite these sentences as a Quaker might say them.

I'd like to thank you.
Your help was appreciated.
I'd like to help you with yours.

I THANK THEE.

ILLEGAL EAGLES

Words with prefixes often lend themselves to puns. For example, *illegal* can also mean a sick bird ("ill eagle"). Have a "prefix pun" contest in your class for the best prefix puns and illustrations. Use your dictionary to look up more words that contain prefixes.

LIFE STORIES

You can do this activity on your own. Write a paragraph about your life, including the interesting details that make your life special. Read over your writing, and circle all of the pronouns. If you like, share "life stories" with a classmate.

Debate Team

Play this game with two teams. Write down some topics for debate, and vote on the one you like best. Start the debate. As you argue for or against an idea, use some words with prefixes to make your point. For instance, if one debater says, "It is fair to hold secret school elections," you might answer, "It is unfair to hold secret school elections." Have the teacher or another student keep track of the number of words with prefixes each debater uses.

EXTRA PRACTICE

Three levels of practice

What Is a Pronoun? (Page 292)

LEVEL A. Write each sentence. Draw a line under the pronoun.

1. Sue and I go to the beach often.
2. She and Tim play a game together.
3. They throw a football back and forth.
4. It sails over Jeff's head.
5. He looks up in surprise.
6. The beach is beautiful to us.
7. We enjoy the water and the cool breeze.
8. You love this sunny weather.
9. Mother tells me about the beaches in Spain.

LEVEL B. Write each sentence. Draw a line under each pronoun. Then, write whether the pronoun is a **subject pronoun** or an **object pronoun.**

10. I pass a bowl of fruit to Grandmother.
11. She sits in a lawn chair.
12. The girls wave to her.
13. She speaks to Grandfather.
14. Grandmother gives him a pair of sunglasses.
15. He reads the newspaper slowly each day.
16. Janet and Kate brought books with them.
17. They read until the sun goes down.

LEVEL C. Write each sentence using a correct pronoun.

18. The children's grandmother supervises _____.
19. _____ lost a towel somewhere on the beach.
20. Dana buys _____ a snack from the vendor.
21. Janet and _____ compare books with one another.
22. _____ are both about horses.
23. _____ enjoyed this day at the beach.
24. _____ should come to the beach next time.
25. You would have fun with _____.

EXTRA PRACTICE

Three levels of practice

Subject Pronouns (page 294)

LEVEL A. Write each sentence. Draw a line under each subject pronoun.

1. I am excited about the contest results.
2. We look forward to the prize.
3. The winners were Sara and I.
4. We went to the circus.
5. I liked the clowns best.
6. She ate too much popcorn.
7. She and I met the ringmaster.
8. We wrote a report for the class.
9. It was about the experience at the circus.

LEVEL B. Write each sentence. Replace the underlined word or words with the correct subject pronoun.

10. Jill bought some souvenirs.
11. The acrobats were graceful.
12. The circus is a thrilling place.
13. Tito and Frank fed peanuts to the elephants.
14. A man applauded wildly.
15. Mrs. Henderson was especially impressed.
16. Sara and I had never seen so many animals.
17. Sara is saving money for another visit to the show.

LEVEL C. Write each sentence. Complete the sentence with a correct subject pronoun.

18. _____ preferred the acrobats to the animals.
19. _____ took a picture of the lions.
20. _____ were amazed by the elephants.
21. _____ was an exciting show.
22. _____ had the best time!
23. When can _____ go again?
24. Jill and _____ bought posters of the event.
25. _____ and _____ loved the clowns.

EXTRA PRACTICE

Three levels of practice

Object Pronouns (page 296)

LEVEL A. Write each sentence. Draw a line under the object pronoun.

1. Airplanes have made life easier for us.
2. On Grandma's birthday the family visits her.
3. Father carries some gifts with him.
4. The flight attendant brought me a magazine.
5. Travel is a thrill for me.
6. This row has a seat for you.
7. Share this magazine with her.
8. Father brought a newspaper with him.
9. Mother gave him a book, too.

LEVEL B. Write each sentence, replacing the underlined word or words with the correct pronoun.

10. The flight seemed pleasant to Father and June.
11. The seat was too small for Uncle Dave.
12. June and Denise slept during the flight.
13. I like to fly with Mother.
14. I played cards with Uncle Dave and Father.
15. I traded seats with Father.
16. Father told Uncle Dave about an article in the newspaper.
17. Mother covered June with a blanket.

LEVEL C. Write each sentence. Draw a line under the pronoun. Then, write whether the pronoun is a **subject pronoun** or an **object pronoun**.

18. Dad explained flight patterns to us.
19. He has experience as a pilot.
20. We have never been afraid of airplanes.
21. The journey is a treat for me.
22. The pilot gave us a tour of the plane.
23. Mother and I enjoyed the movie.
24. The trip was a little long for her.
25. The first passengers off the plane were she and I.

EXTRA PRACTICE

Three levels of practice

Using *I* and *me* Correctly (page 298)

LEVEL A. Write each sentence, using the correct pronoun.

1. Terry and (I, me) joined the school newspaper.
2. It was a great opportunity for Terry and (I, me).
3. The first writers were he and (I, me).
4. The editor sent a photographer with Terry and (I, me).
5. Terry and (I, me) finished our stories.
6. The editor congratulated Terry and (I, me).
7. The artist and (I, me) worked together.
8. She and (I, me) designed the newspaper.
9. The principal gave an award to her and (I, me).

LEVEL B. Write each sentence. Complete each sentence with **I** or **me**.

10. My father bought a typewriter for _____.
11. _____ always type my articles.
12. The research is hard work for _____.
13. The author of the article was _____.
14. The football coach encouraged _____.
15. _____ had written a story about the team.
16. The coach praised _____.
17. The happiest writer was _____.

LEVEL C. Write each sentence, using the correct words from the pair in parentheses.

18. The sports writers were (Charles and I, I and Charles).
19. A new assignment was given to (Sue and me, me and Sue).
20. (I, me) believe in responsible journalism.
21. Honesty is important to (I, me).
22. The editor gave (I, me) an exciting assignment.
23. (Cora and I, I and Cora) were working together again!
24. This is a challenge for (you and I, you and me).
25. (Charles and I, Charles and me) will work with Cora today.

EXTRA PRACTICE

Three levels of practice

Possessive Pronouns (page 300)

LEVEL A. Write each sentence. Draw a line under the possessive pronoun.

1. Our school is really special.
2. The best teachers are mine.
3. Their classes are always interesting.
4. My music class is wonderful.
5. Georgette also likes hers.
6. Her teacher is from Peru.
7. Your new teacher arrives today.
8. Yours will be an exciting week.
9. Our first music class is today.

LEVEL B. Write each sentence, using the correct possessive pronoun from the pair in parentheses.

10. Debra and Joan wrote a story about (their, theirs) class.
11. The article in the paper is (their, theirs).
12. The photograph is (my, mine).
13. I will write (my, mine) own article.
14. It will describe (our, ours) school.
15. I will interview my friends and (your, yours).
16. The editor gave the article (her, hers) approval.
17. (Hers, Her) is a demanding position.

LEVEL C. Write each sentence. Replace the underlined word or words with the correct possessive pronoun.

18. Mary's favorite class is chemistry.
19. The longest paper is Frank's.
20. The one I did was the best experiment.
21. The teacher appreciates Mary and Frank's work.
22. John's favorite science is biology.
23. We students' most interesting hours are spent in school.
24. Gail works all afternoon on Gail's project.
25. Gail's is the most complicated experiment of all.

EXTRA PRACTICE

Three levels of practice

Using Possessive Pronouns (page 302)

LEVEL A. Write each sentence. Draw a line under the possessive pronoun.

1. Our car broke down in the mountains.
2. Ours is an old car.
3. Mr. Charles opened his door.
4. Roberta and Sara opened their windows.
5. Roberta took this photograph with her camera.
6. It shows my surprise at the beautiful view.
7. Sara and I could not believe our eyes.
8. Mine were wide open with delight!
9. Roberta and Sara said the same about theirs.

LEVEL B. Write each sentence. Use a possessive pronoun in place of each underlined group of words.

10. These are the binoculars belonging to me.
11. The picture shows the expression belonging to you.
12. Nadine loves Nadine's new hobby.
13. This photograph was taken with the camera belonging to her.
14. The snapshots belonging to them are the clearest.
15. Fred can see the house belonging to him.
16. Fred's is a big house with a slate roof.
17. The house is two miles north of Nadine's.

LEVEL C. Write each sentence. Complete each sentence with a correct possessive pronoun.

18. _____ sister describes the beautiful waterfall.
19. _____ friends admire the photographs of the trip.
20. Donna expresses _____ surprise.
21. Donna's parents took _____ vacation in those mountains.
22. Brett shows Sara _____ post card.
23. Mr. Charles sent it from _____ trip.
24. _____ was a wonderful vacation.
25. Wanda is saving money for _____.

EXTRA PRACTICE

Three levels of practice

Pronoun Contractions (page 304)

Write the contraction for each pair of words.

1. they are
2. I am
3. we would
4. you have
5. she is
6. he will
7. you had
8. they had
9. we will

Write each sentence. Draw a line under the contraction. Write the words from which the contraction is formed. Remember to capitalize the first word of a sentence.

10. You can tell it's springtime.
11. She's wearing a new dress.
12. We're having a picnic.
13. I'll tell the other students.
14. You've chosen a pretty park.
15. We'll enjoy the day.
16. You've brought your sister.
17. She's an excellent athlete.

Write each sentence. Form a contraction from the underlined words.

18. You had invited a friend to the picnic.
19. He will be there with his baseball glove.
20. It is time for a celebration.
21. You have made a cake!
22. They will really appreciate this.
23. We would like some cake, too.
24. You are ready for the meal.
25. We have planned a perfect day.

PRACTICE + PLUS

Three levels of additional practice for a difficult skill

Pronoun Contractions (page 304)

LEVEL A. Write each sentence. Draw a line under the contraction in the sentence. Write the words from which the contraction is formed.

1. We'll exchange books today.
2. We've both read our books already.
3. I've enjoyed the adventure story.
4. You'd like it, too.
5. We've gotten familiar with the characters.
6. They've become just like real friends.
7. You'll love the hero.
8. She's the bravest girl in the story.
9. I'm certain about that!
10. She'd proved herself courageous many times.
11. I've great admiration for that character.
12. You'd lent some good books to my brother.
13. He's told me about several of them.
14. I'll give two other books to you.
15. They'll surprise and delight you.
16. We'd all read many books this year.
17. Now, we've borrowed more books from the library.
18. It's just a short walk from the school.

LEVEL B. Write each sentence. Form a contraction from the underlined words in the sentence.

19. You had described this character to me.
20. We have met this hero in other novels by the same author.
21. He had written several other adventure stories.
22. They have all been wonderful books.
23. I had discussed the plots with my friends.
24. They will tell you about the other books, too.
25. You will find this story fascinating.
26. I would not spoil the suspense for you.
27. You would never forgive me!

GRAMMAR

28. We are both due for some excitement.
29. I am planning to read your book, too.
30. I have respect for your opinions about books.
31. You had told me your list of favorite authors.
32. We have some of the books at home.
33. They have interesting plots and characters.
34. We would have enough books for the whole summer.

LEVEL C. Write each sentence. Complete the sentence correctly with a contraction that makes sense.

35. _____ collected a wonderful set of mystery novels.
36. _____ enjoy a visit to your private library.
37. _____ received many books from your father.
38. _____ been a mystery fan for a long time.
39. _____ shared your collection with friends.
40. _____ built their own book collections, too.
41. _____ a fascinating hobby for anyone.
42. Now, _____ all bought dozens of novels.
43. _____ also developed an interest in biographies.
44. _____ chosen nonfiction books about fascinating people.
45. _____ studied the lives of some famous artists.
46. _____ often been more interesting than characters in fiction.
47. _____ traded mystery novels and biographies this week.
48. _____ tell me your opinion of the biographies.
49. _____ tell you my thoughts about the mystery books.
50. _____ learn about every type of book.

EXTRA PRACTICE

Three levels of practice

Using *we* and *us* with Nouns (page 306)

A. Write each sentence. Draw a line under the pronoun. Write whether it is a **subject pronoun** or an **object pronoun**.

1. We children love this new pet.
2. The cat is a treat for us animal lovers.
3. We Smiths disagreed at first.
4. We boys wanted a dog.
5. Mother agreed with us girls.
6. The winners were we Smiths.
7. The cat is a good companion for us children.
8. We vacationers bring the cat in the car.
9. The cat sits quietly with us passengers.

B. Write each sentence, using the correct pronoun.

10. (We, Us) girls named the cat Sam.
11. The name seemed silly to (we, us) boys.
12. The boys finally agreed with (we, us) girls.
13. (We, Us) children also got a turtle.
14. The turtle was given to (we, us) Smiths by Jeff.
15. (We, Us) Smiths now have enough pets.
16. Mother gives chores to (we, us) children.
17. (We, Us) pet fans have many responsibilities!

C. Write each sentence. Complete each sentence with **we** or **us**.

18. _____ students study the turtle.
19. The cat is fed by _____ girls.
20. The turtle's bowl is cleaned by _____ boys.
21. _____ children take good care of our pets.
22. Turtles are interesting to _____ scientists.
23. _____ children are quite content.
24. Animals are a fascinating topic for _____ researchers.
25. _____ girls write a composition about the cat.

GRAMMAR

Three levels of practice

Mechanics: More Comma Rules (page 308)

LEVEL A. Write each sentence. Draw one line under each comma that sets off an introductory word. Draw two lines under each comma that sets off a noun in direct address.

1. Mom, where are you going now?
2. Oh, I am going out to the garden.
3. I must do some work in this sunny weather, Glenn.
4. Let me help you, Mom.
5. Yes, there is quite a bit of work for us.
6. Glenn, do you have a pair of old gloves?
7. Well, yes, I have my painting gloves here.
8. Oh, Glenn, the weather forecaster predicts rain!
9. No, he forecast rain for tomorrow, Mom.

LEVEL B. Write each sentence. Add commas where they are needed.

10. Denise what are your plans for today?
11. Well I must shop for a new jacket this morning.
12. Sylvia can you go with me?
13. Oh yes I am free all day.
14. I heard Denise about a sale at our favorite store.
15. Yes Sylvia I saw the advertisement in the newspaper.
16. Do you like long coats Denise?
17. No I need a short jacket for the cold weather.

LEVEL C. Write each sentence. Complete each sentence with an introductory word or a noun in direct address.

18. _____ please come downtown with me now.
19. We should volunteer for Clean Park Day _____.
20. _____ do we sign up this week?
21. _____ _____ we must do it today.
22. Clean Park Day is important for the neighborhood _____.
23. _____ people of all ages participate in the work.
24. _____ I worked in the park last year _____.
25. _____ we all achieved beautiful results.

EXTRA PRACTICE

Three levels of practice

Vocabulary Building: Prefixes (page 310)

LEVEL
 Draw a line under each prefix in the words below.

1. disjointed
2. misplace
3. illegible
4. incredible
5. irrational
6. precaution
7. nonsense
8. unsuitable
9. postscript

LEVEL
 Write each underlined word. Find the correct definition of the word in a dictionary.

10. Researchers deal with common misconceptions each day.
11. Old ideas often fall into disfavor in later years.
12. Postoperative care is important for patients.
13. Ideas about health are reviewed regularly.
14. Old-fashioned theories were often irrational.
15. Scientists exchange information unselfishly.
16. New theories are unveiled at yearly conferences.
17. The age and background of a scientist are unimportant.

LEVEL
C. Write a definition for the underlined word in each sentence. You may use a dictionary, if necessary.

18. One researcher can disbelieve the ideas of another.
19. The contributions of many scientists are irreplaceable.
20. Some speeches are unremarkable.
21. Strange ideas are not illegal!
22. The listeners must not prejudge the speakers.
23. All input should be welcome at the conference.
24. Immature ideas need time for growth.
25. Scientists often reevaluate their work.

UNIT
10

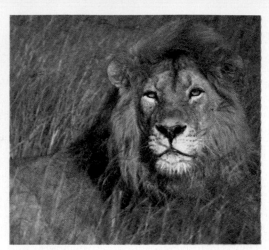

Writing Persuasive Paragraphs

Read the quotation and look at the picture on the opposite page. The quotation was written by Marjorie Weinman Sharmat, the author of a story you will read in this unit. Why might the author have wanted to be a detective or a lion tamer? What is your opinion?

When you write to persuade, you will want to present facts to support your opinion. You will want to persuade your audience to feel the way that you feel.

Focus Persuasive writing encourages the audience to share in the writer's beliefs.

What would be a good topic for persuasive writing? You can use the story and the photographs that follow to find ideas for writing.

*My earliest ambition was to become a writer
or a detective or a lion tamer.*

—Marjorie Weinman Sharmat

Think about an idea that excites or interests you. How might you try to interest someone else in this idea?

Maggie and Thad are both excited about running for class president, but neither is sure how to make a good campaign speech.

As you read the selection, look for the ways Maggie and Thad try to gain the confidence of their classmates. Look for words and phrases that show what the author thinks of the candidates' speeches.

From

Maggie Marmelstein
★ ★ ★ ★ ★ ★ ★ ★ for ★ ★ ★ ★ ★ ★ ★ ★
President

by Marjorie Weinman Sharmat

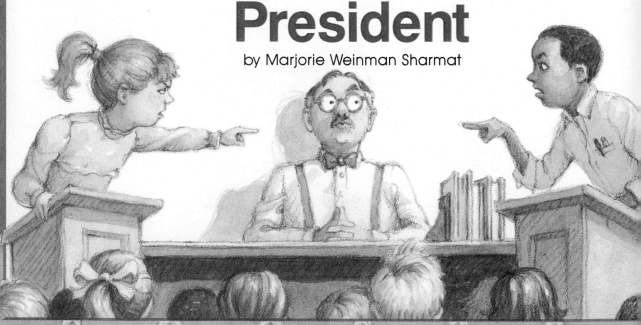

Mr. Krickleman rose and said, "Members of the sixth grade, this afternoon we will hear a debate between the two candidates for the office of class president: Maggie Marmelstein and Thad Smith. They will be introduced by their campaign managers: Noah Moore for Maggie and Henry Emery for Thad."

Suddenly Ralph and Jody stood up. Ralph was holding his guitar, which he had just taken out of its case. He stuck a collapsible cowboy hat, which he had swiftly removed from his pocket and opened, onto his head. He started to play and sing:

Well, I'm walkin' down a lonely road,
And I'm cryin' in a dream,
And I'm needin' help with problems,
And I think of Marmelstein.

'Cause I'm tired of walkin' lonely,
And I'm tired of cryin', too.
So I'm askin' Maggie Marmelstein
To see what she can do.

Notice that Ralph's song is supposed to convince the sixth-graders that Maggie can help them solve their problems.

Henry got up from his chair, almost knocking it over. "I object!" he said. "This is a debate, not a musical show. I know at least six people who can sing and dance for Thad Smith. And do imitations, too, and one can juggle three Frisbees at a time and one can play songs with a spoon and a glass. And I want equal time for them to do their thing for Thad Smith."

Mr. Krickleman spoke. "Henry is right to object. However, since the song did not deal with any issues, it won't affect the debate. But, just to be completely fair, after the debate anyone wishing to perform in behalf of Thad Smith is entitled to three minutes. Now, will the campaign managers please introduce their candidates. Henry, as long as you are on your feet, you may go first."

Henry walked to the center of the stage. "Thad Smith is," he said.

There was a long pause.

"Is Thad Smith," Henry continued. "And who is Thad Smith? He's a great guy. The first time I ever saw this great guy, I said to myself, 'This is a great guy.' Everything about him right away was great. All great. All right away. And when somebody is a great guy, what else can I say about him except one word: president. When I look at Thad, this great guy, I think President Smith. *President* Thad Smith. That sounds right to me. Doesn't that sound right to you?"

A few kids in the audience yelled at the same time, "Right!" "Wrong!" "Right!" "Wrong!"

Henry went on. "I now introduce a great guy, our future president, Thad Smith!"

There was some applause and whistling.

Thad stood up, waved and sat down.

Noah got up and walked to the center of the stage.

This is a good example of persuasive language. The speaker draws the audience to his side.

"My fellow sixth graders," he said, "this election is not a popularity contest. The president of the sixth grade should be chosen on the basis of what *she*—or he—can do for the sixth grade. Is everybody in the sixth grade happy?"

"NO!" some kids shouted.

"Could life be better in the sixth grade? Do we need changes? Can we improve the way things are done?"

"Yes, yes, yes!" cried the audience.

"The sixth grade needs help," said Noah. "And my candidate, Maggie Marmelstein, will help the sixth grade. And here she is—my candidate and yours—Maggie Marmelstein!"

There was some applause and whistling. Maggie couldn't tell whether there was more or less than for Thad.

Maggie stood up, waved and sat down.

Mr. Krickleman said, "We will now flip a coin to see which candidate speaks first." He held up a nickel. "Heads or tails?" he asked.

"Heads," said Maggie and Thad.

Everyone laughed and clapped.

Noah said, "My candidate is willing to speak first or second. It's the words and not their order that's important."

Thad stood up. "I'll let Maggie go first or second."

"No special favors," said Maggie, "I can win on my own."

Mr. Krickleman said, "Will one of you please start the debate."

Maggie stood up. "I should be president because I'll be a better president than Thad Smith, who sometimes isn't very good at all, especially in his **WRITTEN WORK**."

"Please be careful of character assassination, Maggie," said Mr. Krickleman. "Thad, would you care to comment on your written work as it pertains to the presidency?"

"Yes, I would care to comment on that," said Thad. "On that very thing, my written work. In that very way that you mentioned. Yes, I would. Well, my written work is, um, splendiferous."

What do you think of Maggie's choice and ordering of reasons? Is this information persuasive?

335

"What's that?" said someone in the audience. "Wow!"

"Big words. I don't use big words," said Maggie. "Why, I've got a campaign manager, Noah, who knows more big words than every kid in this room put together. But I wouldn't borrow any big words, because a presidential candidate shouldn't be a borrower of words or anything."

Thad spoke. "Well, all I borrow are pencils, and money for the ice-cream machine. I'll be a good president."

"Why?" asked Mr. Krickleman. "Discuss the issues, please."

"So will I," said Maggie.

"Issues, issues," said Mr. Krickleman.

"I'll be better than you," said Maggie.

"No, I'll be better than you," said Thad.

"**ISSUES! ISSUES!**" called Mr. Krickleman..

"I will be a fair and honest president," said Maggie.

"I will be a fair and honest president," said Thad.

"Details, details," called Mr. Krickleman.

Mr. Krickleman wants the candidates to state some facts. Do you think he has been impressed by this debate?

Thinking Like a Reader

1. Why does Mr. Krickleman keep interrupting the debate?
2. If you were in this class, would you be persuaded by the reasons offered by the candidates? Write your responses in your journal.

Thinking Like a Writer

3. What does the author think of the arguments or reasons that Maggie and Thad present to their classmates in order to win votes?
4. Which reasons are convincing? Write a list of these reasons.

Brainstorm *Vocabulary*

In "Maggie Marmelstein for President," the author uses specific words about politics to show the mood of the campaign. Some examples are *candidate, campaign manager, debate, issues,* and *president.*
Think of some topics that excite you. Begin to create your personal vocabulary lists, using words and phrases that tell about things in which you are interested. Use these words and phrases in your writing.

Talk It Over
You, the Candidate

When you want to persuade someone about an idea, you must offer specific reasons. These reasons should support your opinion, or idea. With a partner, imagine that you are running for the office of class president. Tell your partner three reasons why you would make a good president. Use language that would convince an audience to feel as you do. Then, let your partner play the role of candidate.

Quick Write *Write a Speech*

You have been thinking about persuasive language, or how to convince others that your ideas are worthwhile. Suppose that you had been asked to give a one-minute speech about something that is important to you and your classmates. How could you best use this time to create a strong response on the part of your listeners? Write a sentence that tells your opinion of this important issue. Then, write three reasons to support your opinion.

Idea Corner *Your Views*

You have been thinking about ideas that are important to you. How might you persuade someone to accept your views on a topic? What types of facts and opinions can you list in support of your ideas? In your journal make some notes about your views and the reasons that support them. Try to think of words and phrases that could make an audience see a topic from your point of view. Use these notes when you write a persuasive paragraph.

PICTURES

SEEING LIKE A WRITER

Finding Ideas for Writing

Look at the pictures. Think about what you see.
What ideas for persuasive writing do the pictures give you?
Write your ideas in your journal.

1 GROUP WRITING: Persuasive Paragraphs

Good persuasive writing makes a reader think or feel the way the writer thinks or feels. How does a writer persuade a reader?

■ Persuasive Language
■ Logical Order
■ Facts and Opinions

Persuasive Language

Read the following paragraph.

> Families <u>ought to</u> take vacations together. A family trip brings everyone <u>closer together</u>. It can be both <u>fun and educational</u>. Trips to the state parks or to national monuments can be <u>inexpensive and convenient</u>. It is important to <u>relax</u> sometimes by <u>taking a break</u> from school or work.

The writer begins with a topic sentence that states an opinion. Then she chooses specific words to persuade the reader to agree with her. These words show that the writer believes strongly in her ideas. Each of the underlined words and phrases above would probably appeal to a reader, because most people enjoy having fun and taking trips to the countryside.

Guided Practice: Using Persuasive Language

Work with your class to write a topic sentence that tells an opinion about an idea or issue. Then, list reasons that support the topic sentence.

Example: You should not return library books late.

lateness a bad habit   have to pay for overdue books
unfair to others   lose the right to borrow books

Logical Order

In a persuasive paragraph, the topic sentence usually states an opinion. The topic sentence is followed by reasons that support the opinion. It is usually best to state the most important reason *first*.

In the paragraph you read, the writer states that family vacations bring the family closer together. She places this reason right after her topic sentence, because it is the most important point. Look back at the paragraph.

■ What other reasons does she list?
■ How do these reasons support her main idea?

Guided Practice: Listing and Ordering Reasons

Recall the topic sentence you wrote with your class. Check the list of reasons you made to support your topic sentence. With the class, decide on the best order for those reasons.

Facts and Opinions

Look at the paragraph on page 340 again. Notice that the first sentence in the paragraph states an **opinion.** A **statement of opinion** tells what the speaker or writer believes. The writer supports her topic sentence with detail sentences. Some sentences give opinions and others state facts. A **statement of fact** can be proved or checked. A statement of opinion cannot be proved or checked. A writer may use both kinds of statements in a persuasive paragraph.

Guided Practice: Facts and Opinions

With your class, read and discuss the statements listed below. Work together to decide on three reasons to *agree* with each statement. Then, decide on three reasons to *disagree* with each statement. When you have completed your lists, label each reason **fact** or **opinion.**

Loud radio-playing should not be allowed in public.
People who love animals do not like other people.
It is best to exercise in the mornings.

Putting a Persuasive Paragraph Together

With your class you have written a topic sentence that states an opinion about a topic or issue. You have listed supporting reasons and have decided on a good order for your reasons.

Think about your topic sentence. Then look at your list of supporting reasons. Decide which reasons to include in your persuasive paragraph.

Here is how one student chose. Read the topic sentence. Look at the reasons that are checked.

> *Students should read books on their own.*
> ✓ *learn new ideas*
> *won't get bored*
> ✓ *books can be fun and exciting*
> *might get extra credit*
> ✓ *good habit to get into*

Guided Practice: Writing a Persuasive Paragraph

Write three or four detail sentences that support your topic sentence. In your detail sentences, include reasons from your list. Use persuasive language to present your reasons strongly. Write the topic sentence and the detail sentences in paragraph form. End your paragraph with a sentence that sums up your argument or opinion.

Read your persuasive paragraph to your class. Ask the class to suggest ways to make your paragraph more convincing.

Checklist: Persuasive Writing

When you write to persuade, you will want to keep some points in mind. A checklist will help you remember important points to include.

Look at this checklist. Some points need to be added. Make a copy of the checklist and complete it. Keep the copy in your writing folder. You can use it when you write your persuasive paragraph.

CHECKLIST

✔ Purpose and Audience   ■ *Reason 2:* _____

✔ Persuasive Language   ■ *Reason 3:* _____

✔ Order of Reasons   ■ _____

■ *Reason 1:* _____   ■ _____

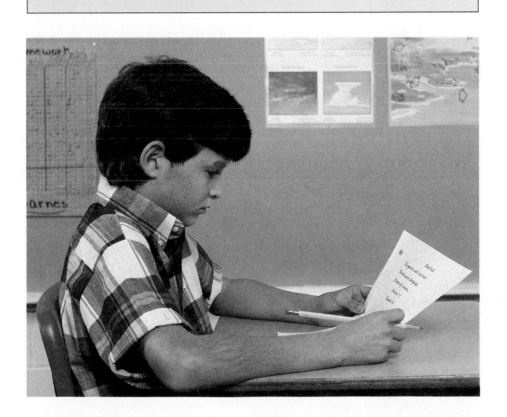

2 THINKING AND WRITING: Telling Facts and Opinions Apart

In persuasive writing, you present one side of an argument. You use facts and opinions to support your ideas. To make a convincing argument, it helps if you know the difference between a fact and an opinion. Remember, a fact can be proved. An opinion cannot be proved.

Look at this page from a writer's journal. The writer plans to write a persuasive paragraph in favor of forming study groups in her class.

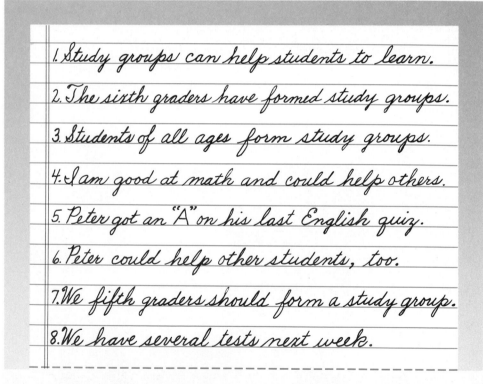

1. Study groups can help students to learn.

2. The sixth graders have formed study groups.

3. Students of all ages form study groups.

4. I am good at math and could help others.

5. Peter got an "A" on his last English quiz.

6. Peter could help other students, too.

7. We fifth graders should form a study group.

8. We have several tests next week.

Thinking Like a Writer

■ Which of these reasons are facts? Which are opinions?

When you write to persuade, you must decide which facts and opinions make the most convincing reasons for your argument.

THINKING APPLICATION Facts and Opinions

COOPERATIVE
LEARNING

Each of the writers named below is planning to write a persuasive paragraph. Help each writer to decide which **facts** and **opinions** to include. Write each reason listed below on a separate piece of paper. Then, write whether it is a fact or an opinion. Remember to consider whether or not the statement could be proved. If there is too much doubt in your mind about a statement, it is probably an opinion. You might wish to discuss your thinking with other students. In your discussion, explain your reasons to each other.

1. Margie wants to persuade her cousin to come to summer camp with her. Which reasons are convincing? Which are facts, and which are opinions?

    Four of our friends are going.   Camp Sunnyvale is in New Hampshire.

    I think you would like tennis.   You would be bored in the city.

2. Saul wants to persuade his father to purchase a computer. Which reasons are convincing? Which are facts, and which are opinions?

    There is a sale on computers this week.   I need one for homework.

    Mom could store her work on it, too.   It would help my grades.

3. Georgia wants to persuade her friend to enter a talent contest with her. Which reasons are convincing? Which are facts, and which are opinions?

    You and I are great dancers.   We were in last year's contest.
    I know we would win.   The entry fee is only $5.00.

4. Chuck wants to persuade his mother to let him take swimming lessons. Which reasons are convincing? Which are facts, and which are opinions?

    I'll still have time for home-work.   The lessons are twice a week.
    Trips to the beach and lake will be safer if I swim well.   The lessons cost fifteen dollars a week.

3 INDEPENDENT WRITING: Persuasive Paragraphs

Prewrite: Step 1

You have learned some important ideas about persuasive writing. Now you are ready to choose a topic of your own. Gina, a student your age, wanted to persuade her classmates to participate in an activity which she believed was important. She chose a topic in this way.

Choosing a Topic

1. First, she made a list of topics.
2. Next, she thought about ways to present each topic.
3. Last, she decided on the best topic.

> Learning to play a flute
> Joining school clubs
> Running a race
> Saving money

Gina liked the third topic on her list best. She narrowed her topic to running in a marathon.

Next, Gina explored her topic by making a list.

Exploring Ideas: Listing Strategy

> I believe it is important to run in the Muscular Dystrophy marathon this weekend.
>
> competition is exciting
> it helps people with this disease
> get to know other runners
> good for your health
> pretty scenery

Gina knew she had some excellent reasons. She knew that her **purpose** for writing was to persuade her **audience** to run in a marathon for a good cause.

Before beginning to write, Gina read over her list and considered each of her reasons carefully. At this point, she made some changes on the list.

> *it helps people with this disease*
>
> *good for your health*
>
> *competition is exciting*
>
> *get to know other runners*
>
> *makes you feel good because you helped*

Thinking Like a Writer

- Which reason did she add?
- Which reason did she leave out?
- Why do you think she made these changes?

Think of a topic about which you have a strong opinion. Use **Pictures** or your journal for ideas. Follow these steps.

- Make a list of topics you believe are important.
- Choose one about which you would enjoy writing.
- Narrow your topic if you think it is too broad.
- Think of some facts and opinions about this topic.
- Think about your purpose and audience.

Make a list. Remember, you can add to or take away from the list at any time.

Write a First Draft: Step 2

Gina knows what her persuasive paragraph should include. She used a planning checklist.

Gina is now ready to write her first draft.

Gina's First Draft

> I believe its important to run in the Muscular Dystrophy marathon this wekend. Running is good for your health. The cause is a worthy one. You will feel good that you did it. You also get to meet other runners. Events like this allow you to compete against your friends, too, but all in good fun. Its going to be a great race.

While Gina was writing her first draft, she did not worry about errors. She wanted to get her ideas down on paper.

Planning Checklist
- ■ Remember purpose and audience.
- ■ Use persuasive language.
- ■ Write reasons in order of importance.
- ■ Include facts and opinions.

YOUR TURN

Write your first draft. As you prepare to write, ask yourself:

- ■ What do I want to persuade my audience to believe?
- ■ How can I persuade my audience to agree with my idea?

TIME-OUT You might want to take some time out before you revise. That way you will be able to revise your writing with a fresh eye.

Revise: Step 3

After she finished her first draft, Gina read it over to herself. Then she shared her writing with a classmate. She asked Teresa to suggest ways she could improve her work.

I'm interested in the marathon, but I'd like to know more about how the race is organized and when it takes place.

Thanks! I will add more facts to my paragraph.

Gina then looked back at her planning checklist. She noticed that she had forgotten one point. She checked it off so that she would remember it when she revised. Gina now has a checklist to use as she revises.

Gina made changes to her paragraph. Notice that she did not correct small errors. She knew she could fix them later.

The revisions Gina made changed her paragraph. Turn the page. Look at Gina's revised draft.

Revising Checklist
- ■ Remember purpose and audience.
- ■ Use persuasive language.
- ■ Write reasons in order of importance.
- ✔ ■ Include facts and opinions.

WRITING PROCESS

I believe its important to run in the

Muscular Dystrophy marathon this weekend.

and
Running is good for your health . The cause is
^
The race begins at two p. m. on Saturday.
a worthy one . You will feel good that you did
^
Each sponsor pays twenty-five cents for every mile
it . You also get to meet other runners. Events
^
a runner completes.
like this allow you to compete against

your friends, too, but all in good fun.

Its going to be a great race.

Thinking Like a Writer

WISE
WORD
CHOICE

- What facts did Gina add?
- How did Gina change the order of her reasons? How does the new order improve the paragraph?
- Which sentences did Gina combine? What do you think of these changes?

YOUR TURN

Read your first draft. Make a checklist. Ask yourself these questions.

- How can I make my paragraph more persuasive?
- How can I improve the order of my supporting reasons?
- How can I make facts and opinions support one another?

Proofread: Step 4

Gina knew her work was not complete until she proofread her paragraph. She used a proofreading checklist while she proofread.

Part of Gina's Proofread Draft

> ⟶ weekend
> Muscular Dystrophy marathon this (wekend).
> and
> Running is good for your health . The cause is
> ⟶ The race begins at two p.m. on Saturday.
> a worthy one . You will feel good that you did
> ⟶ Each sponsor pays twenty-five cents for every mile
> it . You also get to meet other runners . Events
> a runner completes.
> like this allow you to compete against
> your friends, too, but all in good fun.
> It's going to be a great race.

YOUR TURN

Proofreading Practice

Below is a paragraph that you can use to practice your proofreading skills. Find the errors. Write the paragraph correctly on a separate sheet of paper.

> Its always a good idea to eat at Mo's. Mo is the best cook for miles around and its famous from Alabama to Tennessee. Her cornbread and biskits are delicious Whatever you do, don't miss Mo's as you drive through Upton County.

Proofreading Checklist
- ■ Did I indent my paragraph?
- ■ Did I spell all words correctly?
- ■ What punctuation errors do I need to correct?
- ■ What capitalization errors do I need to correct?

Applying Your Proofreading Skills

Now proofread your persuasive paragraph. Read your checklist again. Review **The Grammar Connection** and **The Mechanics Connection**. Use the proofreading marks to mark changes.

THE GRAMMAR CONNECTION

Remember these rules about pronouns.
- A *pronoun* should follow closely the noun that it replaces.
- Make sure each pronoun refers directly to the noun it replaces.

> The **librarian** gave a lecture.
> **She** discussed the card catalog.
> Give the notebook to the **boy**.
> Give the notebook to **him**.

THE MECHANICS CONNECTION

Remember these rules about using apostrophes.
- An *apostrophe* replaces one or more letters in a contraction.
- In a *contraction* of a subject pronoun and a verb, the letters are always dropped from the verb.

> **I would** enjoy a vacation.
> **I'd** enjoy a vacation.
> **He has** shown me a map of Canada.
> **He's** shown me a map of Canada.

Proofreading Marks
¶ indent
∧ add
⌒ take out
≡ capital letter
/ lower-case letter

Publish: Step 5

Gina copied her paragraph in her best handwriting and read it at a school assembly. After the assembly, Gina's classmates told her how much they had enjoyed her ideas. Many of them asked her how they could sign up to run in the next marathon.

YOUR TURN

Make a final copy of your persuasive paragraph. Write as neatly as you can. Think of a way to share your work. Some ideas are given in the **Sharing Suggestions** box below.

> ### SHARING SUGGESTIONS
>
> | Read your work at a school function. | Submit your paragraph to the school newspaper. | Send your paragraph to a pen pal. |
> | --- | --- | --- |

4 SPEAKING AND LISTENING: Listening for Point of View and Bias

When you write to persuade, your purpose is to make your audience behave in a particular way. People who write advertisements for television, radio, and newspapers write to persuade. Advertisements use a combination of persuasive language, facts, and opinions. They are meant to convince people to buy a certain product or to accept a **point of view** or **bias**.

Read these statements from an advertisement for an imaginary candidate named Frank Bardin.

1. Frank Bardin is the best man for the job.
2. Vote for Frank Bardin, the people's choice.
3. Frank Bardin stands for honest government.

The statements above may look like *facts*, but they are really *opinions*. They could not be proved true or false. For instance, statement #2 uses the phrase, *the people's choice*. The writer has used a persuasive device called a **loaded word** or **loaded phrase**. Voters like to feel that they are in agreement with many other people. The writers want their audience to believe that most people are voting for the same candidate, Frank Bardin.

If you listen carefully to advertisements, speeches, or arguments, you can tell the difference between facts and opinions. You can figure out the speaker's point of view or bias, and make your own decisions.

■ How can listening for another person's point of view or bias help me to make my own decisions?
■ How can I make judgments about the truth or accuracy of the advertisements I hear and read?

Careful attention to speeches can help you to understand a politician's bias. Careful attention to advertisements may help you to tell if the product in question could actually be of use to you.

Listen as your teacher or a classmate reads these advertisements.

CRAZY DAVE'S STEREOS
has the best prices in town.

We have special discounts for seniors and students.
IF YOU CAN FIND A BETTER DEAL,
WE WILL REFUND YOUR MONEY!

PLASTIC SOUND

HAS DEALS THAT CANNOT BE BELIEVED!

WE'LL STAND ON OUR HEADS TO GET YOUR BUSINESS.
DON'T BE A SQUARE, AND GO TO THE COMPETITION.

■ Which advertisement makes use of facts rather than opinions and loaded words?

SPEAKING APPLICATION A Statement of Opinion

Think of two products, one of which you like very much. Work with a partner. Describe the two products to your partner. Ask your partner to listen for your point of view. Have him or her try to figure out which product you prefer.

5 WRITER'S RESOURCES: Graphs, Tables, and Maps

In this unit, you have found some resources for persuasive writing. Some possible resources for finding facts are **graphs**, **tables**, and **maps**.

Rock Star Magazine wants to persuade companies to place their advertisements in this magazine. They mail out brochures containing graphs, tables, and maps, to show who reads the magazine. A **graph** compares information.

The Growing Readership of Rock Star Magazine

This bar graph shows advertisers that the audience of *Rock Star Magazine* has been growing steadily larger.

To read the bar graph, look at the captions on the right side and at the bottom. The right side shows the number of readers in each year. The bottom shows the dates being compared.

A **table** can also help you to see and compare information.

This table shows the type of products readers of various age groups buy. The facts might persuade manufacturers of these products to advertise in *Rock Star Magazine*.

	What Rock Star Magazine's Readers Buy		
	product:		
age group:	cars	stereos	vacations
over 50	6%	3%	7%
30-50	21%	7%	20%
20-30	10%	12%	7%

Maps give facts, too. They can show advertisers in different parts of the country where their audience lives.

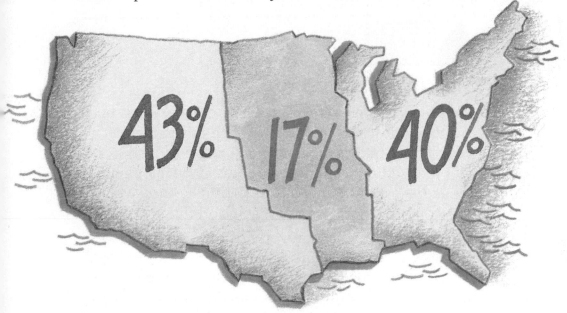

This map could convince a manufacturer in Connecticut to advertise in *Rock Star Magazine*.

Practice

Use the graph, table, and map from this lesson to answer the following questions.

1. By how many readers did the circulation of *Rock Star Magazine* increase from 1970 to 1980?
2. Of the products shown, what do *Rock Star Magazine* readers from the ages of 20 to 30 spend the most money on?
3. Advertising in *Rock Star Magazine* would be most effective for advertisers in what part of the country?

WRITING APPLICATION A List

Find a graph, table, or map in your math book. List five facts that you learned from the resource you found. Save the list in your writing folder. You will use it in **The Curriculum Connection** on page 358.

THE CURRICULUM CONNECTION

Writing About Math

The work of mathematicians applies to many areas of our lives. Mathematics is used in fields such as finance, mapmaking, city-planning, and architecture, as well as in our daily lives. Mathematicians are always developing new theories and uses for mathematics. Each new theory or application must be proved with facts and figures.

Graphs, tables, and maps are all created through the use of mathematics. Numbers and their relationships are used to prove points of view and also to disprove them. Without an understanding of basic mathematical relationships, we would find graphs, tables, and maps useless.

ACTIVITIES

Summarize Facts Use the list of facts you wrote from the graph, table, or map in your math book. Write a paragraph that tells what you learned from the resource.

Use Charts and Graphs Read each of the theories or opinions below. Think of a way to look for numbers that might support it. For example, for theory 1, you might make a graph which shows the distance above sea-level for New York City over each of the last ten years.

Theory 1: New York City is sinking into the ocean.
Theory 2: Girls are smarter than boys.
Theory 3: Eating hamburgers makes you live longer.

Respond to Literature You use mathematics every day. Whether you pay two dollars for a magazine, or use higher mathematics in science, you are using a system that has its roots in ancient history. Read the selection below, then write a response. You might write about some of the ways in which you use mathematics in your daily life. When you have finished, share your writing with your class. Discuss the different ways that mathematics works for each of you.

Counting and Numbers

from *The Penguin Book of the Physical World*

No one knows when man first began to use language or when he first began to count. But primitive men probably matched the things they wanted to count against something else, such as notches in a stick, or pebbles, or knots tied on a cord. As each day passed, for instance, a pebble could be added to a pile. We say now that there is a one-to-one correspondence between the things we count and the things we count them with.

The next step in the development of counting was to use names for numbers. A group of objects could be counted by saying or thinking the names: for instance, we say one, two, three as we count. In the same way it is convenient to use symbols for writing numbers. The ancient Egyptians simply made upright marks from right to left on their papyrus. One was |, two was ||, and so on.

UNIT CHECKUP

LESSON 1

Group Writing: Persuasive Paragraphs (page 340)
Write five persuasive sentences that could support one of the topic sentences below.

Littering is a bad habit.
Public transportation should be free.

LESSON 2

Thinking: Telling Facts and Opinions Apart (page 344)
Write each sentence. Label each one *fact* or *opinion*.

1. Tacos are good for you.
2. Beef is more expensive than jello.
3. Fish and meat contain protein.
4. Eating candy is wrong.
5. Babies like fresh fruit.

LESSON 3

Writing a Persuasive Paragraph (page 346)
Suppose that you are working on the drama committee for your school. Write an article for the school paper that will get people excited about a school play.

LESSON 4

Speaking and Listening: Point of View and Bias (page 354)
Imagine that you will take part in a debate on the question "Should people be allowed to play their radios at the beach?" Write at least three reasons that support your point of view.

LESSON 5

Writer's Resources: Graphs, Tables, and Maps (page 356)
Use library resources to find these facts. Tell whether you found each fact in a graph, table, or map.

1. the difference in size between Texas and Rhode Island
2. the major export of Chile
3. the population of Detroit, Michigan, in 1975
4. the average amount of rainfall in Seattle, Washington, each year

THEME PROJECT A CLASS MAGAZINE

Think about the magazines that you enjoy reading. Magazines give information and present opinions. Journalists who write for magazines are free to look at different sides of issues and report on interesting topics. Though the magazine as a whole may have a point of view, each writer is expressing his or her own ideas and observations about a topic. How do you think that magazine editors choose the topics for the articles in their magazines? What do you think would be some interesting topics or issues for articles?

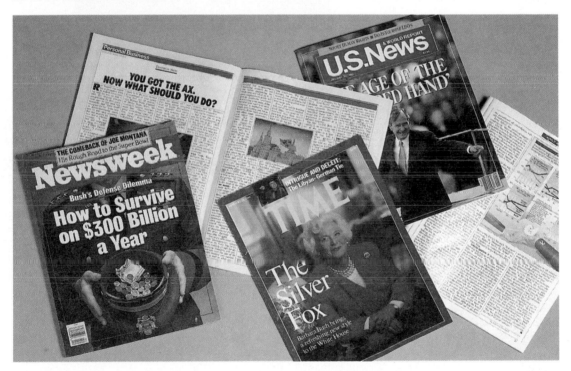

Work with your class to create a magazine.

- As a class, discuss the point of view of the magazine and decide what kinds of topics it should include.
- Choose topics that you think would interest other students in your school.
- When you are finished, share your magazine with the rest of the school.

UNIT

11

Adverbs

In this unit you will learn about adverbs. Adverbs tell more about verbs. Adverbs can help to make your writing more lively and precise.

Discuss Read the poem on the opposite page. What kinds of adventures does the poet describe?

Creative Expression The unit theme is *Adventures*. Where would you go if you could go anywhere in the world? Write a list of all the places you would explore. Write your list in your journal.

JOURNAL

THEME: *ADVENTURES*

When you put me up on the Elephant's back,
I'll go round the world and never come back.
I will travel for miles away from home
To London, Paris, Vienna, and Rome.

—William Jay Smith, from "Elephant"

1 WHAT IS AN ADVERB?

An adverb is a word that tells more about a verb.

You have learned that an adjective describes a noun or pronoun. An **adverb** is a word that describes a verb. Adverbs tell *how*, *when*, or *where* an action happened.

How: The guide **slowly** explains the rules.
When: The tour begins **immediately**.
Where: The entrance lies **here**.

Notice that many adverbs end in *ly*.

Common Adverbs		
How	**When**	**Where**
quickly	yesterday	outside
together	often	there
gracefully	last	below
softly	always	above
hard	next	near
happily	then	ahead
deeply	finally	forward

Guided Practice

Tell the adverb that describes each underlined verb.

Example: Finally, the tour of the caves <u>starts</u>. *Finally*

1. The rowboats <u>creak</u> slightly.
2. The stream <u>winds</u> gracefully around the caves.
3. We always <u>enjoy</u> a boat ride.
4. The guides <u>row</u> smoothly.
5. The boats <u>move</u> forward.

THINK

■ How can I recognize an adverb in a sentence?

gracefully

REMEMBER

- An **adverb** is a word that tells more about a verb.
- An adverb tells *how, when,* or *where.*

More Practice

A. Write each sentence. Write whether the underlined adverb answers the question *how, when,* or *where.*

Example: Marvin sits <u>calmly</u> in the boat. *how*

6. Grace read a guidebook <u>yesterday</u>.
7. She whispers <u>often</u> to Marvin.
8. Marvin looks <u>happily</u> at the cavern.
9. He grasps his camera <u>suddenly</u>.
10. Marvin <u>quickly</u> points at the bats.
11. They hang <u>together</u> from their perches.
12. Marvin gazes <u>above</u> him.

B. Write each sentence. Draw two lines under the adverb that describes the underlined verb.

Example: Water <u>pours</u> <u>loudly</u> from the rocks.

13. The guides <u>tie</u> the boats firmly to a post.
14. Grace <u>looks</u> eagerly at the stream.
15. The stream <u>runs</u> deeply in this cavern.
16. It <u>rushes</u> outside to the sea.
17. The guides <u>walk</u> ahead.
18. The other students <u>follow</u> behind.
19. Marvin <u>steps</u> quickly toward the waterfall.
20. He <u>takes</u> another photograph there.

Extra Practice, page 384

WRITING APPLICATION A Narrative

Imagine that you are an explorer. Write a short narrative or story about your discovery of a secret cave. How did you find it? What did it look like? Underline the adverbs in your narrative.

2 USING ADVERBS TO COMPARE

You know that adjectives can compare two or more people, places, or things. Adverbs can compare two or more actions. Study the chart below.

Comparing with Adverbs		
1. Most short adverbs add *er* or *est* to the adverb.	lowly lowlier lowliest	hard harder hardest
2. Most adverbs of two or more syllables use *more* or *most* with the adverb.	eagerly more eagerly most eagerly	cleverly more cleverly most cleverly

fast   faster   fastest

Guided Practice

Tell the correct form of the adverb to compare two actions and three or more actions.

Example: slowly   *more slowly*   *most slowly*

1. softly
2. cheerfully
3. late

4. quickly
5. soon

 THINK

■ How can I use adverbs when I compare two or more actions?

REMEMBER

- To compare two actions, use *er* or *more*.
- To compare three or more actions, use *est* or *most*.

More Practice

A. Write each sentence. Complete the sentence with the correct form of the adverb in parentheses.

Example: Marco Polo dealt with the Chinese _____ than others. (successfully)
Marco Polo dealt with the Chinese more successfully than others.

6. Marco Polo traveled _____ to China than we travel today. (slowly)
7. The trip took _____ than he imagined. (long)
8. The Kublai Khan greeted him _____ than he had greeted others. (kindly)
9. The Chinese people lived the _____ of any people in the world. (gracefully)
10. Of all the visitors, Marco Polo learned the customs the _____. (fast)
11. Many strangers handled chopsticks _____ than he did. (awkwardly)
12. He wrote the Chinese alphabet _____ than other students did. (skillfully)
13. He spoke _____ than some Chinese children. (easily)
14. The Khan treated him _____ of all the visitors. (graciously)
15. He returned to Europe _____ than he had left. (triumphantly)

Extra Practice, page 385

WRITING APPLICATION A Letter

Imagine that you have traveled to an unfamiliar country. Write a letter comparing the place to your own country. Underline the adverbs.

GRAMMAR

3 ADVERBS BEFORE ADJECTIVES AND OTHER ADVERBS

Adverbs describe or tell more about verbs. Adverbs can also tell more about adjectives or other adverbs.

Adverb Before an Adjective:
The weather seems **terribly** hot.

Adverb Before an Adverb:
The man drove **very** far.

Sometimes it is hard to tell the difference between an adverb and an adjective. Remember, an adjective describes a noun or a pronoun.

The **grateful** man thanked us. **Adjective**
The man thanked us **gratefully**. **Adverb**

Study the chart below.

Adverbs That Describe Adjectives and Other Adverbs					
almost	fairly	quite	slightly	terribly	too
completely	hardly	really	so	very	

Guided Practice

Tell the adverb that describes each underlined adverb or adjective.

Example: We flew in a really <u>big</u> balloon. *really*

1. The day was slightly <u>windy</u>.
2. The preparation was almost <u>over</u>.
3. The crew was so <u>tired</u>.
4. Lulu was quite <u>cheerful</u>.
5. We had worked very <u>hard</u>.

 THINK

■ How can I use adverbs to describe other adverbs or adjectives?

REMEMBER

- **Adverbs** can describe verbs, adjectives, or other adverbs.

More Practice

A. Write each sentence. Draw two lines under the adverb that describes each underlined word.

Example: The crew arrived <u>slightly</u> late.

6. The fire was quite <u>hot</u>.
7. The balloon seemed completely <u>full</u> of air.
8. We were almost <u>ready</u> for the trip.
9. The departure was very <u>sudden</u>.
10. We soared so <u>high</u> into the sky!
11. George looked down fairly <u>often</u>.
12. He was clearly <u>excited</u> about the voyage.

B. Write each sentence. Write whether the underlined adverb describes an adjective or another adverb.

Example: George was <u>fairly</u> comfortable. *adjective*

13. We soared <u>so</u> rapidly in the air.
14. The flight was <u>very</u> smooth.
15. We flew <u>joyfully</u> together.
16. In fact, the ascent seemed <u>too</u> rapid!
17. <u>Quite</u> suddenly, Joe began the descent.
18. The balloon landed <u>fairly</u> fast.
19. It was <u>hardly</u> late in the day.
20. The trip had ended <u>so</u> quickly!

Extra Practice, page 386

WRITING APPLICATION A Journal Entry

COOPERATIVE LEARNING

Imagine that you were on a balloon trip that took off from your neighborhood. What might happen on the trip? Write a journal entry about the trip. When you have finished, have a partner read your journal entry. Ask him or her to circle the adverbs.

4 FORMING ADVERBS FROM ADJECTIVES

Many adverbs are formed by adding *ly* or *ily* to the adjective form of the word.

> Columbus was a **curious** man. **Adjective**
> Columbus looked **curiously** at the island. **Adverb**

When forming adverbs from words ending with a consonant and *y*, change the *y* to *i* and add *ly*.

> The crew was **weary**.
> They stared **wearily** at the ocean.

Good is an adjective.

➡ Use *good* before a noun or after a linking verb.

Well can be either an adjective or an adverb. *Well* is an adjective when it means "healthy."

➡ Use *well* as an adverb to describe a verb.

> The trip began **well**. **Adverb**
> The captain is **well**. **Adjective**

Sometimes it is difficult to tell whether a word is an adjective or an adverb. Remember, adverbs tell more about verbs.

Guided Practice

Tell the word that completes each sentence correctly.

Example: The Arawaks lived _____ on their island. (good, well) *well*

1. Tall ships _____ sailed into the harbor. (slow, slowly)
2. The Arawaks greeted the Spaniards _____. (wary, warily)
3. The Arawaks stood _____ on the shore. (peaceful, peacefully)
4. The Spaniards _____ renamed the land Puerto Rico. (immediate, immediately)
5. The voyage (final, finally) ended.

 THINK

> ■ How can I form an adverb from an adjective?

REMEMBER

- Form some adverbs by adding *ly* to the adjective form of the word.
- Form adverbs from words ending with a consonant and *y* by changing the *y* to *i* and adding *ly*.

G R A M M A R

More Practice

Write each sentence, using the adverb form of the adjective in parentheses.

Example: The Spanish troops acted (forceful).
The Spanish troops acted forcefully.

6. Columbus climbed (weary) from his ship.
7. The sailors cheered (proud) for their captain.
8. They (quick) planned their next move.
9. The Arawaks hunted (brave).
10. Ponce de Leon (easy) conquered the Arawaks.
11. Large plantations were (rapid) introduced.
12. Ships arrived from Spain (regular).
13. The Puerto Ricans (slow) became American citizens.
14. Sugar grows (easy) on the island.
15. Some islanders (strong) want American citizenship.
16. Others (clear) want independence.
17. The governor speaks (forceful) on the television.
18. The islanders listen (careful) to their choices.
19. Some (loud) proclaim their desire for independence.
20. Some (eager) choose United States citizenship.

Extra Practice, Practice Plus pages 387-388

WRITING APPLICATION A Story

Imagine that you discover an island. Write a story about life on your island. What foods and shelter does the island provide? Does anyone else live there? Include some adverbs in your story to make your writing lively and precise. Exchange stories with a classmate. Underline the adverbs in each other's stories.

5 NEGATIVES

You have learned to form a contraction with a verb and the word *not*. These contractions are called **negatives**. The adverbs *no* and *not* are negatives. Study the sentences below.

> Kathy **doesn't** like cold weather.
> She **never** goes to the frozen tundra.

Using more than one negative in a sentence is usually incorrect.

Incorrect: We don't visit nobody.
Correct: We visit nobody.
Correct: We don't visit anybody.

Common Negatives				
nobody	not	nothing	nowhere	no one
aren't	doesn't	haven't	wouldn't	never

Guided Practice

Tell the negative word in each sentence.

Example: The tundra wouldn't be bearable without warm clothing. *wouldn't*

1. Tony can't wait for the departure.
2. We have never been north of Minnesota.
3. Nobody is afraid of the cold.
4. We won't forget our equipment.
5. We go nowhere without it.

 THINK

■ How can I recognize a negative in a sentence?

REMEMBER

- A **negative** is a word that means *no* or *not*.
- Use only one negative in a sentence.

More Practice

A. Write each sentence. Underline the negative word.

Example: Polar bears <u>aren't</u> afraid of cold weather.

6. The subsoil on the tundra never warms.
7. There are no trees on the tundra.
8. We won't see much vegetation on this trip.
9. The forests don't grow here.
10. The moose don't approach strangers.
11. No one has seen a reindeer.
12. Nothing frightens a polar bear.

B. Write each sentence correctly. Use only one negative in each sentence.

Example: You can't never get warm here.
You can't ever get warm here.

13. No musk oxen never leave the tundra.
14. We never see no birds.
15. Haven't you not seen an Arctic hare?
16. This Arctic fox isn't no bigger than a dog.
17. None of the walruses have no tusks.
18. A walrus doesn't eat nothing but shellfish.
19. The wolverine hasn't got no pups.
20. No roses never grow in the tundra.

Extra Practice, page 389

WRITING APPLICATION A Report

Imagine that you have gone on an expedition to a foreign land. You have seen a strange and wonderful animal. Write a report about the animal. Underline the negative words in your report.

6 MECHANICS: Using Quotation Marks

When you write dialogue, or conversation, you record the speaker's exact words in a **direct quotation.** The punctuation marks that set off the direct quotation from the rest of the sentence are called **quotation marks** (" "). The first word of each sentence in a quotation is always capitalized.

➡ Use a comma before the quotation when the speaker's name comes first.

> Julie asked, "What is it?"

➡ Use a comma, a question mark, or an exclamation mark to end the quotation when the speaker's name comes last.

> "It's an incredible invention!" cried Marvin.

➡ Use a period after the speaker's name.

➡ Use commas to separate the name from the quotation when a quotation is interrupted by the speaker's name.

> "I believe," said Julie, "you are correct."

When there are two sentences in the quotation, a period follows the name.

> "Yes," replied Marvin. "It is an airplane."

"It's an incredible invention!"

Guided Practice

Tell which part of each sentence is a direct quotation.

Example: "I am curious," said Julie. *I am curious*

1. Julie asked, "Did this machine ever fly?"
2. "No, it never did," replied Marvin.
3. "I've never seen anything like this!" Julie exclaimed.
4. "It was drawn in the 1400's," Marvin said.

?! THINK

■ How do I punctuate a direct quotation in a sentence?

REMEMBER

- **Direct quotations** are set off from the rest of the sentence by **quotation marks** and end punctuation marks.

More Practice

Write each sentence. Be sure to use punctuation marks and capital letters correctly.

Example: Look at this page said Marvin.
"Look at this page," said Marvin.

5. Julie wondered who was the designer?
6. Leonardo da Vinci designed this, Marvin told Julie.
7. I never knew that! Julie exclaimed.
8. Marvin added, Yes, and he also painted the Mona Lisa.
9. Was he an artist? Julie asked.
10. Yes, he had many talents, said Marvin.
11. Do artists design airplanes? asked Julie.
12. Marvin said, The first pilots were bicycle repairmen.
13. That's the first powered flying machine Marvin said.
14. Julie replied it doesn't look very sturdy.
15. It only flew a few hundred feet Marvin said.
16. Julie asked where was that?
17. It happened at Kitty Hawk Marvin answered.
18. I have been there Julie said.
19. Marvin asked did you see the monument?
20. We drove past it she said.

Extra Practice, page 390.

WRITING APPLICATION A Dialogue

Imagine that you were at Kitty Hawk for the Wright brothers' first flight. Write a dialogue between you and Orville and Wilbur Wright, the inventors of the airplane. What would you ask the Wright brothers? What do you think they might have said? Make sure you punctuate and capitalize your sentences correctly.

7 VOCABULARY BUILDING: Suffixes

A **suffix** is a word part added to the end of a base word. A suffix changes the meaning of the base word to which it is added. It may also change the part of speech of the base word to which it is added.

Suffix	Meaning of Suffix
ful	full of
able, ible	capable or worthy of being
ness	quality, condition or state of being
less	without, that does not
ment	the act, state, quality, or result of
less	without, that does not
ation, ition	the act, state of being, or result of
ward	in the direction of
ly	in a _____ way
er, or	one who _____, something that _____
ist	one who does or makes
an, ian	one who believes in, one who was born or lives in, one who is skilled in _____
y	full of, somewhat, like

Guided Practice

Identify the suffix and give the meaning of the word. Use a dictionary to help you define any base word that you do not yet know.

Example: senator   *or   a member of the senate*

1. determination
2. aimless
3. enjoyment
4. flexible
5. artist

?! THINK

■ How can I figure out the meaning of a word with a suffix?

REMEMBER

■ A **suffix** changes the meaning of the base word to which it is added.

More Practice

A. Write each sentence. Draw a line under the word with the suffix.

Example: The hero looked <u>forward</u> to the adventure.

 6. I read the new book with wonderment.
 7. The hero of the story was very thoughtful.
 8. He was penniless as a child.
 9. The character's mother had a sudden realization.
10. She was the boy's closest relation.
11. Regardless, she sent him on an adventure.
12. His first months alone were joyless.

B. Write each sentence. Change each underlined base word by adding the correct suffix.

Example: The people were <u>fear</u> of the dragon.
The people were fearful of the dragon.

13. The king could not hide his <u>bewilder</u>.
14. The country was in a <u>horror</u> condition.
15. The dragon was a <u>destroy</u>.
16. Each week he caused <u>destruct</u>.
17. A stranger in town suggested his plan <u>calm</u>.
18. The dragon was just a <u>complain</u>.
19. To the dragon's <u>amaze</u>, the boy dampened his fiery breath.
20. The <u>smoke</u> dragon did no more damage!

Extra Practice, page 391

WRITING APPLICATION A Fable

A fable is a very short story with a message about how to behave in a particular situation. Fables teach the difference between wisdom and foolishness. Write your own fable. Have a partner underline the suffixes.

COOPERATIVE
LEARNING

VOCABULARY: Suffixes

GRAMMAR AND WRITING CONNECTION

Combining Sentences

There are words that show the relationship between ideas and events. They can show *why* or *when* an event or experience happens. Words like *when*, *since*, *because*, *until*, *after*, and *before* show a relationship between two or more sentences.

> We were happy. The rain had stopped.
> We were happy **because** the rain had stopped.

> Dad waited. The roads became safe.
> Dad waited **until** the roads became safe.

Notice that in the first sentence, the word **because** gives a reason, or shows *why* something happened. In the second sentence, the word **until** shows *when* something happened.

In both sentences, the joining word makes the writer's meaning clear.

Combining the sentences makes the writing flow more smoothly. It is a good idea to join short, choppy sentences to improve your paragraphs.

Working Together

COOPERATIVE LEARNING

With your class, discuss ways to join sentences using words that tell time or give reasons. Then, find the joining word in each sentence.

Example: I will rest until we are ready for the trip. *until*

1. The sun shone brightly after the rain ended.
2. We can leave when our bags are packed.
3. I am excited because this is my first visit to the mountains.

Revising Sentences

Sam wrote the following sentences to describe a trip to the mountains. Help Sam to revise his sentences by combining each pair below with a joining word that tells time or gives reasons.

4. We drove carefully.
   The roads were narrow and unpaved.
5. The air grew cooler.
   We reached the timberline.
6. We did not see snow at first.
   We reached the higher peaks.
7. We actually kept the windows closed.
   The air grew quite cold.
8. We needed our jackets.
   We climbed out of the car.
9. The snow on the highest mountains does not melt.
   The air remains cold in summer.
10. I saw far beyond the next peak.
    Mother gave me her binoculars.
11. My sister was delighted.
    She looked through the binoculars, too.
12. A large crow flew away suddenly.
    It had seen us.

Brainstorm an experience you would like to describe. Write a story about this experience. When you revise your work, combine related sentences with joining words that show time or give reasons.

UNIT CHECKUP

LESSON 1

What Is an Adverb? (page 364) Write each sentence. Draw two lines under the adverb that describes the underlined verb.

1. The bus <u>rolls</u> smoothly along the road.
2. We cheerfully <u>sing</u> our song.
3. Others quickly <u>join</u> us.
4. The trip <u>ends</u> suddenly.
5. The eager students <u>walk</u> together.

LESSON 2

Using Adverbs to Compare (page 366) Choose the correct form of the adverb in parentheses. Write the new sentences.

6. Betsy finished her lunch (most quickly, more quickly) than I.
7. I finished (latest, later) today than I did yesterday.
8. That was (faster, fastest) than anyone else.
9. Jennie eats (most politely, more politely) of all of us.
10. We finish first (most often, more often) than the other students.

LESSON 3

Adverbs Before Adjectives and Other Adverbs (page 368) Write each sentence. Draw two lines under the adverb that describes each underlined adjective or adverb.

11. Norman was really <u>happy</u>.
12. He very <u>quickly</u> finished his examination.
13. The test was slightly <u>hard</u>.
14. Math nearly <u>always</u> fascinated him.
15. He solved the problem fairly <u>rapidly</u>.

LESSON 4

Forming Adverbs from Adjectives (page 370) Write the correct adverb form of each adjective.

16. peaceful
17. quick
18. careful
19. good
20. slow

LESSON 5

Negatives (page 372) Write each sentence. Draw a line under the negative words.

21. Nobody finished the report.

22. It was not possible.

23. There was nothing in the library.

24. No one could find the books.

25. I never had so much trouble!

LESSON 6

Mechanics: Using Quotation Marks (pages 374) Write each sentence using correct punctuation marks and capitalization.

26. What did we do yesterday asked Diane

27. We studied turtle wings teased Peter

28. Turtles don't have wings yelled Diane

29. The teacher asked what did you say

30. Oh she mumbled it was a joke

LESSON 7

Vocabulary Building: Suffixes (page 376) Write each sentence. Add a correct suffix to the underlined word.

31. Dan is a <u>rely</u> person.

32. He is a <u>fault</u> friend.

33. He gets <u>enjoy</u> from many things.

34. I turn to him for <u>relax</u>.

35. Days with Dan are full of <u>amuse</u>.

Writing Application: Adverb Usage (pages 364-374) The following paragraph contains 8 errors with adverbs and punctuation. Rewrite the paragraph correctly.

36.-43.

    The boy ran quick across the field. He didn't not stop for anything. Wait for me his sister called. He hard heard her voice. He final paused at the edge of the river. His friend quiet stood on the riverbank. I thought you'd be here soonest he said. He swift handed a fishing rod to the boy.

ENRICHMENT

Story Circle

Try this activity with a group of your classmates. One player begins with a sentence containing a subject and a verb, like "The man skates." The next player adds to the sentence an adverb that describes the verb. Build a story as each of you takes turns providing a sentence opener and completing the thought with an adverb. Keep going until the story ends.

ADDING MEANING

You have seen how adding an adverb can change the meaning of a sentence. Add an adverb to each of your responses so that it best answers each question.

How did you buy a camera?
When did you buy a camera?
What did you do today?

NO PROBLEM

Do this with a partner. Sketch a person engaged in an activity. Have your partner sketch the same person unable or not allowed to perform the activity. For example, the first picture might show a jogger running around a lake. The second picture might show the jogger looking at a fenced-in lake. Then, let your partner sketch an activity, and you draw the person unable to perform the activity. Write captions for your sketches. Use negative words where needed.

CREATIVE EXPRESSION

Alliteration

Sea Shell

Sea Shell, Sea Shell,
Sing me a song, O please!
A song of ships, and sailor men,
And parrots, and tropical trees,

Of islands lost in the Spanish Main
Which no man ever may find again,
Of fishes and corals under the waves,
And sea horses stabled in great green caves.

Sea Shell, Sea Shell,
Sing of the things you know so well.
—Amy Lowell

TRY IT OUT!
Alliteration is the repetition of the same first letter or initial sound in a series of words. "Sea Shell" is a poem that uses alliteration. Write a poem of your own in which you use alliteration.

GRAMMAR

Three levels of practice

What Is an Adverb? (page 364)

LEVEL
A. In each sentence, a verb is underlined. Write the adverb.

1. Mrs. Santos graciously <u>invites</u> us to the lighthouse.
2. We cheerfully <u>accept</u> her offer.
3. Mrs. Santos <u>lives</u> there all year long.
4. She patiently <u>watches</u> the ships at sea.
5. We quickly <u>board</u> a ferry boat.
6. The boat <u>glides</u> smoothly through the waves.
7. We <u>peer</u> eagerly through the portholes.
8. We soon <u>see</u> the island.
9. The lighthouse <u>stands</u> proudly on the shore.

LEVEL
B. Write each sentence. Write whether the underlined adverb answers the question **how**, **when**, or **where**.

10. The boat docks <u>rapidly</u>.
11. We climb <u>excitedly</u> from the boat.
12. We do not walk <u>far</u> from the shore.
13. <u>Later</u>, we will swim.
14. <u>First</u>, we have lunch.
15. Our hostess cooks <u>skillfully</u>.
16. We eat our lunch <u>hungrily</u>.
17. We all relax <u>pleasantly</u> in the sun.

LEVEL
C. Write each sentence. Complete each sentence with an adverb that describes the underlined verb.

18. The waves <u>break</u> _____ on the shore.
19. I <u>jump</u> _____ into the water.
20. The water _____ <u>takes</u> my breath away.
21. We all <u>dive</u> _____ into the waves.
22. We _____ <u>see</u> a school of shining fish.
23. They <u>glow</u> _____ in the blue water.
24. The fish <u>disappear</u> _____.
25. The day <u>ends</u> _____ for us all.

EXTRA PRACTICE

Three levels of practice

Using Adverbs to Compare (page 366)

LEVEL A. Write each sentence. Complete the sentence with the correct form of the adverb in parentheses.

1. Long ago, postal service was (slowest, slower) than it is today.
2. Pony Express service was the (faster, fastest) service of all.
3. Riders could travel (most quickly, more quickly) than wagons.
4. The riders rode (more skillfully, most skillfully) than any others.
5. The horses ran (most powerfully, more powerfully) of all.
6. One day, a storm arose (more speedily, most speedily) than a tornado.
7. The winds blew (harder, hardest) of all.
8. Pony Express riders were called (earlier, earliest) than usual.
9. The riders rode (more courageously, most courageously) than anyone had thought possible.

LEVEL B. Write each sentence, using the correct form of the adverb.

10. The first rider arrived (fast) than expected.
11. His horse whinnied (loud) of all the horses in town.
12. Of all the riders, he (clearly) had acted heroically.
13. The wind hit him (hard) than he could believe.
14. He told his story (patiently) than a teacher.
15. He changed horses (often) than the other riders.
16. Each horse ran (poorly) than the one before.
17. The storm raged (harshly) in the country than in the town.

LEVEL C. Write each sentence, using a comparing adverb.

18. The wind screamed _____ than a hurricane.
19. The rain fell _____ in the evening than in the day.
20. He tells this part _____ than the other parts of the story.
21. The rider's path disappeared _____ than ever before.
22. The water rose _____ than the horse's hooves.
23. The wind grew _____ than the screams of the horse.
24. He rode _____ as the path grew muddy.
25. He told his story _____ than any war hero.

EXTRA PRACTICE

Three levels of practice

Adverbs Before Adjectives and Other Adverbs (page 368)

LEVEL A. Write the adverb that describes the underlined word.

1. The launch was completed so <u>rapidly</u>.
2. The crew was barely <u>inside</u> the cabin.
3. The astronauts acted really <u>jumpy</u>.
4. They very <u>soon</u> calmed down.
5. The spaceship was almost <u>there</u>.
6. None of them behaved completely <u>calmly</u>.
7. The earth disappeared fairly <u>quickly</u> from the screen.
8. The crew worked happily <u>together</u>.
9. Our destination was somewhere <u>outside</u>.

LEVEL B. Write each sentence. Write whether the underlined adverb describes an adjective or an adverb.

10. The trip was <u>extremely</u> difficult.
11. The captain shouted <u>terribly</u> often.
12. He was <u>so</u> excited about the adventure.
13. The landing site appeared <u>too</u> quickly.
14. The moon's surface was <u>slightly</u> rough.
15. An engine hummed <u>somewhat</u> more loudly than before.
16. It was repaired <u>soon</u> after.
17. The problems were <u>nearly</u> over.

LEVEL C. Write each sentence. Complete the sentence with an adverb that describes the underlined adjective or adverb.

18. The crew was _____ <u>outside</u> the ship.
19. The sky was _____ <u>bright</u>.
20. The astronauts were _____ <u>happier</u> than they had ever been.
21. The landing was _____ <u>ahead</u> of schedule.
22. The moon _____ <u>often</u> seems ordinary.
23. On the moon they walked _____ <u>quickly</u>.
24. When the mountains appeared, they were _____ <u>there</u>.
25. The crater was _____ <u>below</u> the next hill.

EXTRA PRACTICE

Three levels of practice

Forming Adverbs from Adjectives (page 370)

LEVEL A. Write each sentence, using the correct word from each pair.

1. The forest is a (well, good) place for exploration.
2. You carry that pack (good, well).
3. We hike (good, well) together.
4. The redwoods grow (good, well) in this climate.
5. The heavy rain is (good, well) for them.
6. I feel (good, well) in the warm weather.
7. The trail is marked (good, well).
8. Our campsite is (good, well).
9. We will eat (good, well) tonight.

LEVEL B. Write each sentence. Complete the sentence with the word in parentheses that correctly describes the underlined verb.

10. Peter <u>cooks</u> (quick, quickly) for us.
11. We <u>sit</u> (peaceful, peacefully) together in our camp.
12. The breeze <u>blows</u> (gentle, gently) through the trees.
13. Robin <u>pitches</u> the tent (firm, firmly) into the ground.
14. We (happy, happily) <u>toast</u> marshmallows.
15. A bird <u>sings</u> (sweet, sweetly) from a high branch.
16. Dad (careful, carefully) <u>tends</u> the campfire.
17. Robin and I (slow, slowly) <u>grow</u> tired.

LEVEL C. Write each sentence. Complete the sentence with the adverb form of the adjective in parentheses.

18. In the morning, we (easy) hike three miles.
19. The sun shines (bright) all day.
20. Mom gazes (steady) at the sky.
21. Clouds form (rapid) during the late afternoon.
22. The rain begins (sudden).
23. We pitch our tent (immediate).
24. The rain pours (loud) on the canvas.
25. We sit (comfortable) inside the tent until evening.

PRACTICE + PLUS

Three levels of additional practice for a difficult skill

Forming Adverbs from Adjectives (page 370)

LEVEL A. Write the adjective or adverb in parentheses that correctly completes each sentence.

1. The animal park houses (wild, wildly) animals.
2. Our class travels (excited, excitedly) to the park.
3. The teacher (thorough, thoroughly) explains the rules.
4. We must stay in the (safe, safely) bus.
5. We can see the animals (good, well) from our seats.
6. I (recent, recently) visited another animal park.
7. This park is (different, differently) from the other one.
8. There are more (dangerous, dangerously) animals here.
9. A new tiger has (late, lately) arrived from India.

LEVEL B. Write each sentence, using the adverb form of the adjective.

10. Our bus runs (good) even in the heat.
11. We stop (sudden) in a large field.
12. Giraffes walk (calm) across the field.
13. They hold their heads (stiff).
14. The bus moves (slow) toward another area.
15. We hear the lions growl (loud) at each other.
16. A lion cub rolls (playful) on its back.
17. Its mother stares (fierce) at our bus.

LEVEL C. Write each sentence. Complete the sentence with an adverb that correctly describes the underlined verb.

18. We <u>drive</u> _____ through a jungle area.
19. Monkeys <u>swing</u> _____ from the trees.
20. Parrots <u>screech</u> _____ at the monkeys.
21. One bird <u>flies</u> _____ near my window.
22. Its feathers <u>shine</u> _____ in the sunlight.
23. I _____ <u>enjoy</u> the animal park.
24. The day <u>passes</u> _____.
25. I <u>wave</u> _____ to the animals.

EXTRA PRACTICE

Three levels of practice
Negatives (page 372)

LEVEL
A. Write each sentence. Underline the negative word in each sentence.

1. Nobody knew about the island.
2. It was not on any maps.
3. There was nothing about it in the atlas.
4. No one had ever discovered it.
5. Humans had never landed on it.
6. Nowhere was there a more quiet island.
7. Our ship hadn't stayed on course.
8. None of us realized the danger.
9. There wasn't any warning of the accident.

LEVEL
B. Write each incorrect sentence correctly. Remember to avoid using double negatives.

10. Our ship hadn't never a chance.
11. We never saw no coral reef.
12. Our luggage wasn't never saved.
13. We haven't no food.
14. Our canned food was not nowhere in sight.
15. None of us had no good ideas.
16. At first, we didn't find no shelter.
17. We couldn't not see in the fog.

LEVEL
C. Write each sentence. Complete the sentence with a negative word.

18. What if help does _____ arrive?
19. Later, we did _____ worry as much.
20. I _____ thought we could eat coconuts!
21. This island is _____ bigger than my hometown.
22. _____ is in danger now.
23. The coast patrol has _____ missed us.
24. We have _____ problem any more.
25. The rescue team _____ fails.

EXTRA PRACTICE

Three levels of practice

Mechanics: Using Quotation Marks (page 374)

A. Write each sentence. Underline the direct quotation.

1. "Steve admires horses," said Mort.
2. "That's great!" exclaimed Charlie.
3. Alma explained, "He rides them at a ranch."
4. "Do you like horses?" questioned Charlie.
5. "Yes, but I would never ride one," stated Mort.
6. I whispered, "That explains it."
7. "What does that explain?" demanded Alma.
8. "Steve has a plan," I said.
9. "Did he tell you his plan?" asked Charlie.

LEVEL
B. Write each sentence correctly.

10. I shouldn't talk about it yet I said.
11. Is it a secret asked Alma.
12. Let me explain I began.
13. Please get to the point shouted Charlie.
14. Steve has an idea I continued about a trip.
15. What about the horses asked Mort.
16. His uncle owns a ranch added Alma.
17. Are we invited to the ranch questioned Charlie.

LEVEL
C. Complete each sentence. To each direct quotation, add words that tell who is speaking.

18. "Yes, we can all go" _____.
19. "But horses scare me" _____.
20. "They will not hurt you" _____.
21. _____ "Where is this ranch?"
22. "It is in a beautiful part of the state" _____.
23. "Mort, you should come with us" _____.
24. "I will think about it" _____.
25. "I love Steve's idea" _____.

EXTRA PRACTICE

Three levels of practice

Vocabulary Building: Suffixes (page 376)

LEVEL A. Write each sentence. Draw a line under the word with the suffix in each sentence.

1. Dr. Watson regarded the mystery with amazement.
2. Sherlock Holmes was an insightful detective.
3. Some people considered him scary.
4. All problems got a thorough examination.
5. Dr. Watson was often filled with admiration.
6. His friend got enjoyment from detective work.
7. He held all people responsible for their deeds.
8. Many crimes were thoughtless and cruel.
9. Some crimes were even laughable.

LEVEL B. Write each sentence. Add a suffix to each underlined word.

10. The Governor argued his point firm.
11. He spoke with determine.
12. He was a famous invent.
13. He knew Holmes was knowledge.
14. Holmes had a moment of realize.
15. He had seen the terror crime!
16. His recognize of the criminal was important.
17. His day of relax was over.

LEVEL C. Write each sentence. Complete the sentence by choosing one of the words from the list below.

18. The problem was not _____.
19. Holmes knew the _____.
20. The criminal thought of himself as an _____.
21. The detective cast his mind _____ over the past week.
22. He searched for a _____ solution.
23. Someone had stolen the Governor's _____.
24. He had created a _____ pencil.
25. The thief had caused him great _____.

> irritation
> hopeless
> situation
> reasonable
> invention
> flexible
> artist
> backward

UNIT
12

Writing Stories

Read the quotation and look at the picture on the opposite page. The quotation was written by C.S. Lewis, the author of the story you will read in this unit. How does this author find ideas for his stories?

You can find ideas for stories in many different ways. Ideas can come to you when you are walking in the park or watching a ball game. Sometimes looking at a picture can give you an idea.

Focus A story has a beginning, a middle, and an end. A story tells about characters and events. Very often the purpose of a story is to entertain.

What kind of story would you like to create? On the following pages you will find an adventure story and some photographs that may give you ideas for writing.

THEME: *ADVENTURES*

*All my seven Narnian books . . . began with seeing
pictures in my head. At first they were not a
story, just pictures. The Lion all began with a
picture of Faun carrying an umbrella and parcels
in a snowy wood.*

—C.S. Lewis

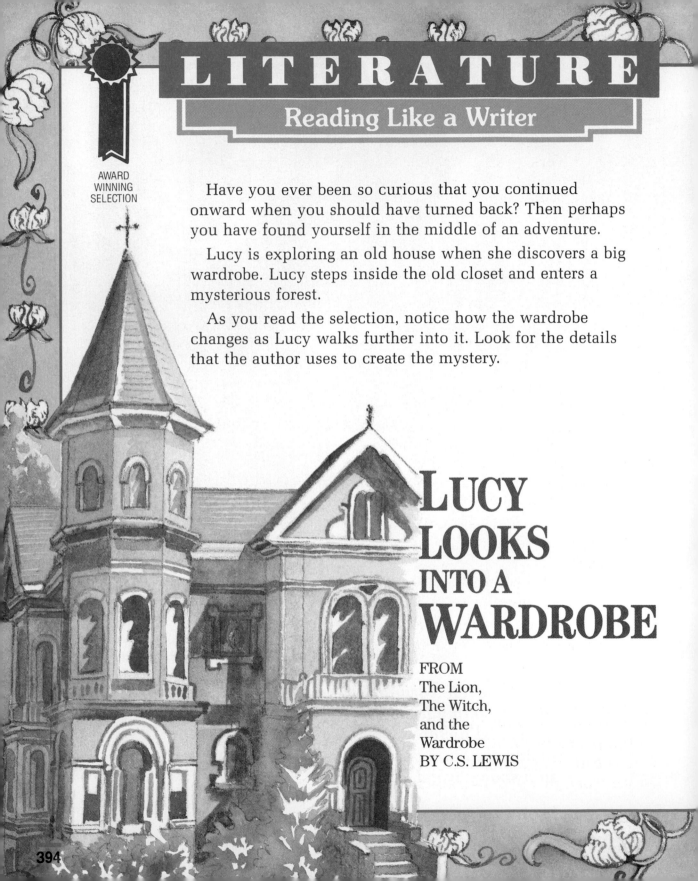

AWARD
WINNING
SELECTION

Have you ever been so curious that you continued onward when you should have turned back? Then perhaps you have found yourself in the middle of an adventure.

Lucy is exploring an old house when she discovers a big wardrobe. Lucy steps inside the old closet and enters a mysterious forest.

As you read the selection, notice how the wardrobe changes as Lucy walks further into it. Look for the details that the author uses to create the mystery.

LUCY LOOKS INTO A WARDROBE

FROM
The Lion,
The Witch,
and the
Wardrobe
BY C.S. LEWIS

"What's that noise?" said Lucy suddenly. It was a far larger house than she had ever been in before and the thought of all those long passages and rows of doors leading into empty rooms was beginning to make her feel a little creepy.

"It's only a bird, silly," said Edmund.

"It's an owl," said Peter. "This is going to be a wonderful place for birds. I shall go to bed now. I say, let's go and explore to-morrow. You might find anything in a place like this. Did you see those mountains as we came along? And the woods? There might be eagles. There might be stags. There'll be hawks."

"Badgers!" said Lucy.

"Snakes!" said Edmund.

"Foxes!" said Susan.

But when next morning came, there was a steady rain falling, so thick that when you looked out of the window you could see neither the mountains nor the woods nor even the stream in the garden.

"Of course it *would* be raining!" said Edmund. They had just finished breakfast with the Professor and were upstairs in the room he had set apart for them—a long, low room with two windows looking out in one direction and two in another.

"Do stop grumbling, Ed," said Susan. "Ten to one it'll clear up in an hour or so. And in the meantime we're pretty well off. There's a wireless and lots of books."

"Not for me," said Peter, "I'm going to explore in the house."

Everyone agreed to this and that was how the adventures began. It was the sort of house that you never seem to come to the end of, and it was full of unexpected places. The first few doors they tried led only into spare bedrooms, as everyone had expected that they would; but soon they came to a very long room full of pictures and there they found a suit

Notice that the selection begins by introducing the main characters In a specific setting.

of armour; and after that was a room all hung with green, with a harp in one corner; and then came three steps down and five steps up, and then a kind of little upstairs hall and a door that led out onto a balcony, and then a whole series of rooms that led into each other and were lined with books—most of them very old books and some bigger than a Bible in a church. And shortly after that they looked into a room that was quite empty except for one big wardrobe; the sort that has a looking-glass in the door. There was nothing else in the room at all except a dead blue-bottle on the window-sill.

"Nothing there!" said Peter, and they all trooped out again—all except Lucy. She stayed behind because she thought it would be worth while trying the door of the wardrobe, even though she felt almost sure that it would be locked. To her surprise it opened quite easily, and two moth-balls dropped out.

The author clearly presents the sequence of events by which Lucy discovers the world beyond the wardrobe.

Looking into the inside, she saw several coats hanging up—mostly long fur coats. There was nothing Lucy liked so much as the smell and feel of fur. She immediately stepped into the wardrobe and got in among the coats and rubbed her face against them, leaving the door open, of course, because she knew that it is very foolish to shut oneself into any wardrobe. Soon she went further in and found that there was a second row of coats hanging up behind the first one. It was almost quite dark in there and she kept her arms stretched out in front of her so as not to bump her face into the back of the wardrobe. She took a step further in—then two or three steps—always expecting to feel woodwork against the tips of her fingers. But she could not feel it.

"This must be a simply enormous wardrobe!" thought Lucy, going still further in and pushing the soft folds of the coats aside to make room for her. Then she noticed that there was something crunching under her feet. "I wonder is

that more moth-balls?" she thought, stooping down to feel it with her hands. But instead of feeling the hard, smooth wood of the floor of the wardrobe, she felt something soft and powdery and extremely cold. "This is very queer," she said, and went on a step or two further.

Next moment she found that what was rubbing against her face and hands was no longer soft fur but something hard and rough and even prickly. "Why, it is just like branches of trees!" exclaimed Lucy. And then she saw that there was a light ahead of her; not a few inches away where the back of the wardrobe ought to have been, but a long way off. Something cold and soft was falling on her. A moment later she found that she was standing in the middle of a wood at night-time with snow under her feet and snow-flakes falling through the air.

L ucy felt a little frightened, but she felt very inquisitive and excited as well. She looked back over her shoulder and there, between the dark tree-trunks, she could still see the open doorway of the wardrobe and even catch a glimpse of the empty room from which she had set out. (She had, of course, left the door open, for she knew that it is a very silly thing to shut oneself into a wardrobe.) It seemed to be still daylight there. "I can always get back if anything goes wrong," thought Lucy. She began to walk forward, *crunch-crunch*, over the snow and through the wood towards the other light.

In about ten minutes she reached it and found that it was a lamp-post. As she stood looking at it, wondering why there was a lamp-post in the middle of a wood and wondering what to do next, she heard a pitter patter of feet coming towards her. And soon after that a very strange person stepped out from among the trees into the light of the lamp-post.

He was only a little taller than Lucy herself and he carried over his head an umbrella, white with snow. From the waist upwards he was like a man, but his legs were shaped like a goat's (the hair on them was glossy black) and instead of feet he had goat's hoofs. He also had a tail, but Lucy did not notice this at first because it was neatly caught up over the arm that held the umbrella so as to keep it from trailing in the snow. He had a red woollen muffler round his neck and his skin was rather reddish too. He had a strange, but pleasant little face with a short pointed beard and curly hair, and out of the hair there stuck two horns, one on each side of his forehead. One of his hands, as I have said, held the umbrella; in the other arm he carried several brown paper parcels. What with the parcels and the snow it looked just as if he had been doing his Christmas shopping. He was a Faun. And when he saw Lucy he gave such a start of surprise that he dropped all his parcels.

"Goodness gracious me!" exclaimed the Faun.

Thinking Like a Reader

1. If you were Lucy, what would you have done when you discovered the world beyond the wardrobe?

2. What kind of adventures have you had or imagined? Were you as curious as Lucy?

Write your responses in your journal.

Thinking Like a Writer

3. How does the author make you interested in Lucy's adventure? How does he prepare you for her unusual experience?

4. Which details does he use to capture your interest?

5. Which details do you like best? Write a list of these details.

Brainstorm *Vocabulary*

"Lucy Looks into a Wardrobe" is written by the English writer C.S. Lewis. Mr. Lewis uses many words and phrases that are familiar to a student in England, but they might seem strange to you. Some examples are *wireless*, *wardrobe*, and *muffler*. Think of an American synonym for each of these words. As you think of words that are synonyms for some of the words in the selection, begin to create a personal vocabulary list. You can use these words in your writing.

Talk It Over
What's in the Woods?

When you tell a story, you include interesting details. Do this activity with a small group. Imagine that you are in a particular place, like a forest or a city. Describe something that you see. The next person in the group should add another detail that describes the place. Everyone should have a chance to add at least two details.

Quick Write
Write a Dialogue

You have been thinking and reading about adventures. Imagine that your class is exploring a cave. Suddenly, you become aware that you are lost! You believe you know the way out, but your friends want to take another route. Write a short dialogue or conversation between you and the other people in which you each argue your reasons for choosing a particular way out of the cave.

Idea Corner
Unexpected Adventure

You have just read an adventure story, and you may already have some ideas for a story of your own. What types of events might make an exciting adventure story? Write your ideas in your journal. **Pictures** can also give you interesting ideas for stories. You might want to include photographs or pictures from newspapers and magazines.

Finding Ideas for Writing

Look at the photographs. Think about what you see.
What ideas for story writing do the pictures give you?
Write your ideas in your journal.

PICTURES: Ideas for Story Writing

COOPERATIVE
LEARNING

GROUP WRITING: A Story

A story connects people, events, and places in a narrative that a reader can understand. How does a writer help the reader to understand a story?

- A Beginning, Middle, and End
- Sequence of Events
- Characters, Dialogue, and Setting

A Beginning, Middle, and End

Read the beginning and middle of the following story. Notice how the events occur in a particular order. How would you end the story?

> Cassandra opened her eyes, but she did not recognize a thing. The sheets were furry, and the bed was made of ostrich feathers. Bozo, her basset hound, was wearing a bowler hat. "Come here, Bozo," she said to the frightened dog.
>
> Cassandra saw a caterpillar-like thing crawling up the sheet. The tiny beast was wearing a suit and eight pairs of tiny shoes. "Welcome welcome, Miss Miss," the beast shouted. "Don't don't be be scared scared. Welcome welcome to to Double Double." Cassandra felt a horrible tug on her shoulder. "Oh, no," she thought, "it's got me."

The **beginning** of the story introduces the main character and the problem she faces. The **middle** of the story develops the plot, or story line, and builds suspense. The **end** of the story shows the final event and solves the problem.

Guided Practice: Using Beginning, Middle, and End
Work with your class to make a story chart. Fill in the events that occur in the middle and at the end of the story.

Example:

> I. Beginning
>
>   Tony wondered if he would ever be found. He had been on the little island for a whole day, and he had not seen another boat. "Oh, well," he thought, "I might as well explore the island."
>
> II. Middle
>   - List things Tony might see/find.
>   - List people/animals Tony might meet.
>
> III. End
>   - List possible final events.
>   - Give ideas for Tony's rescue.

Sequence of Events

Read Cassandra's story again. Notice the order in which the author narrates the events and shows the setting. Ordering the events clearly makes a story easy to follow.

- Which details describe the setting?
- Which events prepare you for the talking caterpillar?

Characters, Dialogue, and Setting

You can tell that Cassandra is the main character because she is introduced first and is involved in all of the events. Who are the other characters?

You know that **dialogue** is set off from the rest of a story by punctuation and quotation marks. Look again at the story. How can you tell who is speaking? What is special about the caterpillar's speech?

The setting of the story is described when Cassandra awakens. How does the author tell you that the dream setting is strange?

Guided Practice: Characters, Dialogue, and Setting

Look at the beginning paragraph and chart you created. List some characters and details to describe the setting. Write some dialogue between the characters.

Putting a Story Together

With your class, you completed a chart that listed some characters, events, and a setting for the story. Think about your story beginning. Then look at your chart. Decide which events and characters to include in your story. Be sure to write the details in a clear order.

One student worked with the beginning and the chart of the adventure story about Tony and the island. Look at the chart below. Notice what the writer has decided to include in the middle and the end of her story. You will probably decide to leave out some of the items on your chart when you write your own story.

> II. Middle   Tony explores the island.
>   List things Tony might see/find.
> - a raft
> - an abandoned house
> - a treasure map
>   List people/animals Tony might meet.
> - a giant tortoise
> - a talking animal
> - another person
>
> III. End   Tony's rescue
>   List possible final events.
> - finds treasure
> - signals for help
>   Give ideas for Tony's rescue.
> - escapes on back of a tortoise
> - is rescued by others

Guided Practice: Writing a Story

Write a story, using the story beginning and the chart that you made with your class. Select details about character and setting to complete the story. Organize the plot and details so that a reader can understand the sequence of events. Write some dialogue between the characters.

Checklist: Story Writing

When you write a story, you will want to keep some points in mind. A checklist will help you to remember important points to include.

Look at this checklist. There is space provided for you to add any points that you feel are important. Make a copy of the checklist and keep it in your writing folder. You can use the checklist when you write a story.

CHECKLIST

✔ Purpose and audience
✔ Beginning, Middle, End
■ _____
■ _____
■ _____
✔ Sequence of Events
■ _____

■ _____
■ _____
✔ Characters, Dialogue, Setting
■ _____
■ _____
■ _____

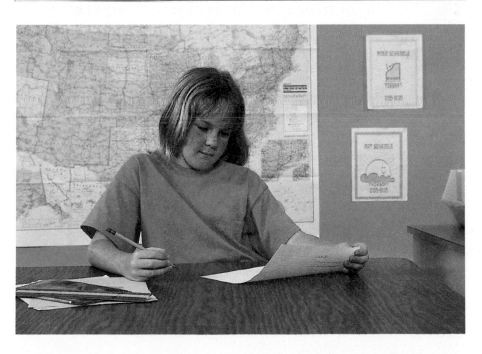

2 THINKING AND WRITING: Understanding Sequence

You know that information in a story is presented in a logical order. The order in which things occur in a story is called the **sequence of events**. The writer presents events in an order that the reader can easily understand.

Look at the following paragraph from the first draft of a story. The writer has presented some of the important events of her story in this paragraph.

> We were in big trouble. Karen looked in the supply room, but she couldn't find it. The doctor called and demanded the vial of bacteria. I knew it had been there yesterday. If we didn't bring the vial, the doctor would surely call the police because the bacteria were very dangerous.

Thinking Like a Writer

- Where should the third sentence in the paragraph be placed so that the events are in a logical order or sequence?

The third sentence in the story is out of sequence. This sentence should be moved to a different place in the paragraph. The reader should learn about the vial of bacteria *before* finding out that it is missing.

THINKING APPLICATION Putting Events in Sequence

Below are three story beginnings, each with a list of events that will be included in the story. Help each writer to put the events in the proper sequence. Write the beginning sentence and each event in logical order on a separate piece of paper. You may wish to discuss your thinking with other students. In your discussions, explain your reasons to each other.

1. After an endless pounding, suddenly the wind halted, and the water became calm.

   ■ Sara continued to bail, and the water level in the boat went down.
   ■ Stan guiltily picked up a cup and started to help.
   ■ Stan breathed a sigh of relief and said, "If you continue to bail, we won't sink, after all."
   ■ Sara said to Stan, "If you don't help, we will sink."
   ■ Sara began bailing water from the bottom of the boat.
   ■ When the rain ended, the boat was flooded.

2. Our cat, Chelsea, disappeared on a freezing December night.

   ■ My father took a flashlight and searched through the garden.
   ■ I couldn't find her in the house, so I told my parents about the problem.
   ■ Chelsea lay peacefully on my mother's sweater, surrounded by four tiny kittens!
   ■ "Oh, I hope she isn't lost," cried my sister.
   ■ Poor Chelsea was nowhere in sight.
   ■ Finally, my brother looked in the downstairs closet.

3. Suddenly, all the lights in the house went out.

   ■ We were grateful for our electricity.
   ■ I couldn't find the stairs.
   ■ Mom lit a candle and led me downstairs.
   ■ My sister finally reached the fuse box.
   ■ The house was completely dark.
   ■ Mom and Dad told us not to worry.

3 INDEPENDENT WRITING: A Story

Prewrite: Step 1

You have learned some important points about story writing. Now, you are ready to write your own story. Ted, a student your age, wanted to write an adventure story. His **purpose** was to entertain his classmates. He chose a topic in this way.

Choosing a Topic

1. First, he made a list of exciting story ideas.
2. Next, he thought about his audience.
3. Last, he chose the adventure he felt was most exciting.

danger on the subway train
lost in a department store
going to wilderness camp
backpacking in the Rockies

Ted liked his first idea best. He narrowed the subject of the story to include one of his own experiences. He was ready to explore his idea.

Exploring Ideas: Story Organizer Strategy

Characters
Tom, a boy from the suburbs
a lady with a dog

Setting
N.Y.C. subway stopped between stations

Beginning
Tom arrives N.Y.C., takes subway to Brooklyn

Middle
subway stuck
dog has puppies

End
puppies wrapped in Tom's shirt
Tom meets aunt

Ted looked at his story organizer. He liked his notes on the setting, but he felt that there were not enough details and characters. He added some details to his chart.

Characters	Setting
Tom, a boy from the suburbs	N.Y.C. subway
a doctor	stopped between
a lady with a dog	stations
	crowded, noisy

Beginning	Middle	End
Tom arrives N.Y.C.	subway stuck	puppies wrapped
takes subway to	dog has puppies	in Tom's shirt
Brooklyn	doctor delivers	people exchange
	puppies	numbers
		Tom meets aunt

Thinking Like a Writer

- Which characters did Ted add?
- Which other details did he include?
- How might these changes make Ted's story more interesting?

YOUR TURN

JOURNAL

Think of an adventure or an exciting event that might make a good story. Use **Pictures** or your journal for ideas. Follow these steps.

- Make a list of ideas.
- Select the idea you like best.
- Think of the characters, setting, and plot.
- Think about your purpose and audience.

Make a story organizer. Remember, you can change any part of the story organizer at any time.

Write a First Draft: Step 2

Ted knows what his adventure story will include. He used a planning checklist.

Beginning of Ted's First Draft

> Tom arrived in New York's Port Authority Bus Terminal. He carefully checked Aunt Kay's directions before he boarded a crowded subway train. "Watch out, kid, A man said to him. Tom moved his suitcase out of the man's way. He noticed a lady with a basket leaning weary against the wall. Her basket started to move.

While Ted was writing, he did not worry about errors. He wanted to get his ideas down on paper.

Planning Checklist
- Remember purpose and audience.
- Include a beginning, middle, and end.
- Make the sequence of events clear.
- Include characters, dialogue, and setting.

YOUR TURN

Write your first draft. As you prepare to write, ask yourself these questions.

- Will my readers be able to follow the sequence of events throughout the story?
- Have I created interesting characters, dialogue, and setting?

TIME-OUT You might want to take some time out before you revise. That way you will be able to revise your writing with a fresh eye.

Revise: Step 3

After he wrote his first draft, Ted read it over to himself. Then he read it to his friend, Mark. Mark had a question about the story.

This story is good, but how do the doctor and the lady leave if the train is stopped between stations?

Oh, no! Some of my events are in the wrong order! I'll fix that.

Ted then looked at his planning checklist. He realized that he had forgotten one point. He checked it off so that he would remember it as he revised. Ted now has a checklist to use when he revises his story.

Ted made some changes to his story. He did not correct small errors. He knew he could correct them later.

The revisions Ted made changed his story. Turn the page. Read Ted's revised story.

Revising Checklist
■ Remember purpose and audience.
■ Include a beginning, middle, and end.
✔ ■ Make the sequence of events clear.
■ Include characters, dialogue, and setting.

WRITING PROCESS

"Do you have anything clean in that suitcase,"
the doctor asked. "Take off the buttons" she ordered.
Tom rummaged in his suitcase. and He brought out a
clean shirt. In a few minutes the doctor was
holding three little puppies in Tom's buttonless
shirt. "Good work, Kid," the doctor said as she
left the train with the lady and the dogs.

Thinking Like a Writer

WISE
WORD
CHOICE

- Which sentences did Ted move? How does moving the
  sentences make the sequence more logical?
- Which sentences did Ted combine? How does combining
  them improve the paragraph?

YOUR TURN

Read your first draft. Make a checklist. Ask yourself these
questions.

- Which paragraphs are in the beginning, the middle, and
  the end of my story?
- How easily could my reader follow the sequence of events?
- What could I add to the story to make the characters,
  dialogue, and setting more interesting?

If you wish, ask a friend to read your story and make
suggestions. Then, revise your story.

Proofread: Step 4

Ted knew that his story was not complete until he proofread it. He used a proofreading checklist while he proofread.

Part of Ted's Proofread Draft

> Tom arrived in New York's Port Authority Bus Terminal. He carefully checked Aunt Kay's directions before he boarded a crowded subway train. "Watch out, kid," A man said to him. Tom moved his suitcase out of the man's way. He noticed a lady with a basket leaning ~~weary~~ *wearily* against the wall. Her basket started to move.

YOUR TURN

Proofreading Practice

Use the paragraph below to practice your proofreading skills. Find the errors. Write the paragraph correctly on a separate piece of paper.

> Inspecter Babette looked into her perse. Her notebook was gone. "Oh no, Sargeant." She gasped. "Someone has stolen my notebook". The too police officers ran quick to there car. Inspecter Babette tried to reach the other police, but she could not contact they.

Proofreading Checklist
- Did I indent my paragraph?
- Did I spell all words correctly?
- What punctuation errors do I need to correct?
- What capitalization errors do I need to correct?

Applying Your Proofreading Skills

Use your checklist to proofread your story. Review **The Grammar Connection** and **The Mechanics Connection**, too. Use the proofreading marks to mark changes.

THE GRAMMAR CONNECTION

Remember this rule about adverbs and adjectives.

- Many adverbs are formed by adding *ly* to the adjective form of the word.

quick – quick**ly**

Check your story. Have you used adverbs and adjectives correctly?

THE MECHANICS CONNECTION

Remember these rules about punctuating dialogue.

- Direct quotations are set apart from the rest of the sentence by quotation marks and punctuation marks.

  "I hear you," said Tom, "but I do not understand."

- Be sure to place the end marks *inside* the quotation marks, as in the example above.

Check your story. Have you punctuated your dialogue correctly?

Proofreading Marks

¶ Indent
∧ Add
ℰ Take out
≡ Make a capital letter
/ Make a small letter

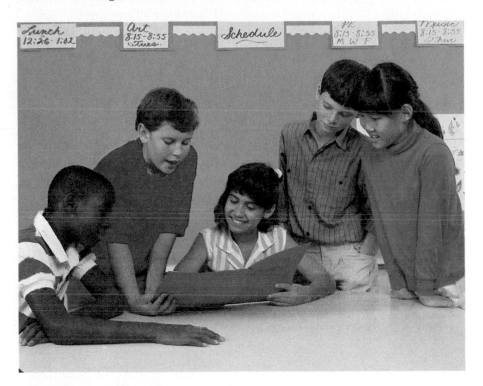

Publish: Step 5

Ted published his story by sending it to the school magazine. The editor agreed to print Ted's story in the next edition of the magazine. Ted's classmates read the story. Some of them told Ted about their experiences on subways. Ted encouraged them to turn their adventures into stories.

YOUR TURN

Make a final copy of your story. Write as neatly as you can. Think of a way to share your work. Some ideas are listed in the **Sharing Suggestions** box below.

SHARING SUGGESTIONS

Send your story to a magazine.	Read your story to the class.	Make a book of stories with your classmates.

WRITING EXTENSION

4 SPEAKING AND LISTENING: Telling a Story

You have just written a story and thought of some ways in which you could share your writing with others. You can use what you have learned about writing a story to tell a story aloud. Your audience will be your classmates. Before you tell a story, you will want to prepare some notes. You can create a story organizer to help you arrange your notes.

A story that you tell, like a story that you write, has a beginning, a middle, and an end. You also tell the events of the story in a logical sequence. You describe the setting for the story and create interesting characters and dialogue.

> **Beginning**
> - The setting
> - Main characters and problem
> - Other characters
>
> **Middle**
> - Events of the story
> - dialogue
>
> **End**
> - Final event
> - Conclusion

The notes on your chart will remind you of specific things that you want to include. Practice telling your story to a friend or relative. The more familiar you are with your story, the better able you will be to tell it. Remember, your enthusiasm will make any audience interested in your story.

The chart above shows a beginning, a middle, and an end. What types of information will be included in each part?

When you tell a story, it will help you to keep your **purpose** and **audience** in mind. These speaking guidelines will help you to focus your story.

SPEAKING GUIDELINES: Telling a Story

1. Remember your **purpose** and **audience**.
2. Plan a clear beginning, a middle, and an end.
3. Make notes that order your events in a logical sequence.
4. Include interesting characters, some dialogue, and a setting.
5. Look at your audience as you speak.

- How can I remember all of the characters, events, and dialogue in my story?
- How do I put the events of my story in a logical order?

SPEAKING APPLICATION A SHORT STORY

Select one of your favorite short stories. Prepare a story chart. Use the speaking guidelines to help you prepare. Your classmates will be using the following guidelines as they listen to your story.

LISTENING GUIDELINES: A Story

1. Listen for the story's beginning, middle, and end.
2. Listen for a logical sequence of events.
3. Listen for interesting characters, dialogue, and setting.

5 WRITER'S RESOURCES: Skimming and Scanning

Sometimes, you might need specific information for a story to make your characters and details seem real. You may know the names of books which contain this material, but you may not want to spend hours reading a book just to find one piece of information. You can *skim* and *scan* when you are looking for specific facts and ideas.

Skimming is reading quickly to gain an overall impression of the subject matter. When you *skim* a book or an article, you are not studying it in depth. You may *skim* the first chapter of a book to see if you want to read the whole book.

Scanning is reading quickly to find one piece of information. If you need to know the exact year when a book was published, you would *scan* the **copyright page** at the front of a book. You would *scan* the **table of contents** at the front of a book to see which topics are included in the middle of the book. You might also *scan* the **index** at the back of a book for the same reason.

Practice

A. Skim the paragraph below. Write the main idea of the paragraph.

This was not to be the best day of Teresa's life. When she put on her warm coat, she left all of her money in her jacket. By the time she remembered, she was in Mrs. Delaney's car on her way to the movies. Then Mrs. Delaney picked up Francis, who already thought that Teresa was irresponsible. How was she going to convince Francis that she was responsible when she had forgotten her money?

B. Scan the **table of contents** and the **index** of this book. Answer the questions below. Then, write whether you found this information by looking in the **table of contents** or in the **index**.

1. On what page would you find information about the **abbreviations of addresses**?
2. Which unit in the book deals with **verbs**?
3. What page in the book explains **entry words in a dictionary**?
4. On which page does the **Curriculum Connection** called "Writing About Science" begin?
5. On which pages does the term *loaded phrase* appear?
6. What is the name of the lesson that begins on page 408 of this book?
7. How many pages long is the **Unit Checkup** in this unit?
8. What page of this book contains **letter models**?
9. On which page would I find examples of **haiku**?
10. Which unit contains the literature selection, "Project Turtle"?

WRITING APPLICATION A Plot Summary

Look at a book that you have recently read. Skim the book to remind yourself of the plot. Write a sentence or two that describes the book. Scan the book to find five important events in the story. Describe each event in one sentence.

THE CURRICULUM CONNECTION

Writing About Literature

Many people write about literature. A **book report**, or brief summary, is a good way to share your reaction.

Nadine, a student in the fifth grade, decided to write a book report about *Eddie, Incorporated* by Phyllis Reynolds Naylor.

EDDIE, INCORPORATED
by Phyllis Reynolds Naylor

INTRODUCTION ⟶ Have you ever wished you could be a boss of a company and make a lot of money? Eddie Anselmino, the main character in the novel, *Eddie, Incorporated*, wants to be a successful Detroit businessman even though he is only in the sixth grade. His big dreams cause big trouble!

BODY ⟶ Eddie and his friends form a company, with Eddie as the boss. They try one line of work after another, but each type of work presents its own special problems. They try recycling aluminum cans, running a newspaper, and many other jobs. Each of the jobs ends up in disaster. Finally, Eddie learns an important fact about being a boss.

CONCLUSION ⟶ If you like funny stories and characters who are a lot like the people you know, you will really enjoy *Eddie, Incorporated*. I recommend this book to anyone who has ever wished he or she had grown-up responsibilities.

Writing a Book Report A book report gives readers a summary of a book. A good book report contains the following information.

1. **The title and author**
2. **The introduction** Your introduction should include
   - whether the book is fiction or nonfiction
   - an opening sentence that will grab the reader's attention
3. **The body of the report** The body should include
   - information about the setting and the main characters
   - a summary of the plot that doesn't give away the whole story
4. **The conclusion** Your conclusion should include
   - a clue about the ending of the book
   - your recommendation to other people to read or not to read the book

ACTIVITIES

Give a Book Report Prepare an oral book report that you will present to your class. Follow the book report model in this lesson.

Write a Book Report Now, use the information you included in your oral book report to write a book report.

UNIT CHECKUP

Group Writing: A Story (page 404) Read the information below. On a separate sheet of paper, write whether each piece of information belongs in the beginning, the middle, or the end of a story.

- the final event
- the setting
- a description of the main character
- the problem the character faces

LESSON

Thinking: Understanding Sequence (page 408) Read these sentences from a paragraph. Write them in the correct sequence.

1. Surprisingly, she was more amused than frightened.
2. She saw that she no longer looked like herself at all.
3. Tara looked into the mirror.
4. She was wearing the face of a total stranger.

LESSON

Writing a Story (page 410) Imagine that your best friend has become invisible. Write a short adventure story about his or her first day as an invisible person.

LESSON 4

Speaking and Listening: Telling a Story (page 418) Remember your first day in a new school or neighborhood. Imagine that you are going to tell a story about that experience. Make a story chart to help you tell your story aloud.

LESSON

Writer's Resources: Skimming and Scanning (page 420) Write each item of information. Write whether you would **skim** or **scan** each item.

1. to review the events in a book that you have read
2. to check the index of a book for the name *Connelly*
3. to find the name of the country in which a book is set

THEME PROJECT Book of Stories

You have been reading and writing about adventures. You have learned that an adventure can happen in a special place, such as an island, or in an ordinary place, such as a street corner. An adventure can happen to a special person or to anyone at all.

A photograph or picture can be the inspiration for an adventure story. Look at the photograph below.

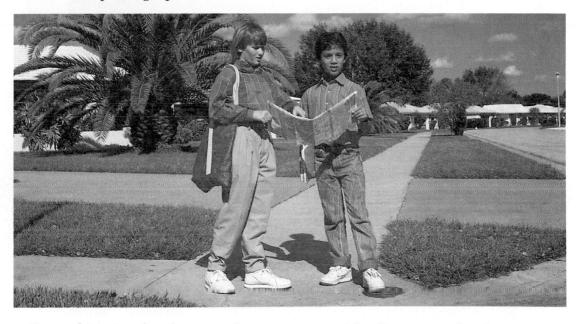

From this simple photograph, a writer could tell a story that begins on a street corner and ends in a hot-air balloon.

Work with a small group of classmates to create a book of stories.

- Bring in pictures from magazines. Select the picture that might inspire the best story.
- Brainstorm for characters, problem, setting, and events. Write a story about what you see in the pictures.
- When all the stories are completed, work with your classmates to make a story collection. Include your photographs as illustrations for the book of stories.

UNIT
13

Prepositions, Conjunctions, and Interjections

In this unit you will learn about prepositions, conjunctions, and interjections. These important words can help you to join related ideas and add variety to your sentences.

Discuss Read the poem on the opposite page. Why do you think the poet encourages the reader to open the door?

Creative Expression The unit theme is *Investigations.* You can investigate, or try to find information about, all sorts of things. What is something that you would like to know more about? Write a few sentences that tell what you would like to investigate. Write your sentences in your journal.

Go and open the door.
  Maybe outside there's
  a tree, or a wood,
  a garden,
  or a magic city.

—Miroslav Holub,
from "The Door"

1 WHAT IS A PREPOSITION?

A preposition is a word that relates a noun or pronoun to another word in a sentence.

In your sentences, you often use words such as *to, for, at,* and *with*. These words are **prepositions**.

Prepositions show relationships between other words. When you write, you carefully choose the preposition that best fits your meaning.

The mystery stories are **in** the library.
Sir Arthur Conan Doyle wrote **during** the 1800s.

The **object of the preposition** is the noun or pronoun that follows a preposition.

I gave my favorite book to **Jeremy**.
I gave my favorite book to **him**.

Common Prepositions					
about	among	down	inside	out	under
above	around	during	into	outside	until
across	at	except	near	over	up
after	behind	for	of	past	with
against	beside	from	off	through	within
along	by	in	on	to	without

Guided Practice

Tell the preposition in each sentence.

Example: Detection was easy for Holmes.   *for*

1. Doyle wrote about Sherlock Holmes.
2. Doyle studied medicine for a time.
3. After medical school, he became a writer.
4. He wrote his mysteries from experience.
5. Medical knowledge is important to a detective.

 THINK

■ How can I recognize a preposition and its object?

REMEMBER

- A **preposition** relates a noun or pronoun to another word in a sentence.
- The **object of a preposition** is the noun or pronoun that follows the preposition.

More Practice

Write each sentence. Draw a line under the preposition. Draw two lines under the object of the preposition.

Example: The sleuth was <u>on</u> a difficult <u>assignment</u>.

6. Sherlock Holmes was created by Doyle.
7. Holmes was the most popular character in England.
8. His popularity traveled across the Atlantic.
9. Dr. Watson was a companion to Holmes.
10. He helped with many cases.
11. Holmes was very wary among criminals.
12. Many mysteries were solved by the brilliant detective.
13. Sherlock Holmes stories are popular in my school.
14. Students find them in the library.
15. The mysteries are stacked by the reference books.
16. Most mysteries are solved after sundown.
17. The solution does not come until the end.
18. Finally, the criminal is under arrest.
19. The reader can guess between different outcomes.
20. The clues are always within the story.

Extra Practice, page 448

WRITING APPLICATION A Case Report

Imagine that you are on the scene when Sherlock Holmes solves a case. Create a scene that includes witnesses, criminals, and an intriguing problem for Holmes to solve. Write a report about the case, including information on how the case was solved and who was involved. When you have finished, underline the prepositions in your case report.

2 PREPOSITIONAL PHRASES

You know how to identify a preposition and its object. A **prepositional phrase** is a group of words that begins with a preposition and ends with a noun or pronoun. This noun or pronoun is called the object of the preposition.

The Curies were a family **of French scientists**.

For several generations, the Curies researched scientific questions.

Marie Curie, **with her family**, studied radium.

Notice that a prepositional phrase can be at the beginning, middle, or end of a sentence.

Guided Practice

Tell the prepositional phrases in each sentence.

Example: Important research took place in Europe.

in Europe

1. During the last century, little was known about radiation.
2. Many scientists did not believe in radiation.
3. Science changed with the discovery of radium.
4. By 1900, everyone believed in radioactivity.
5. The world changed for scientists and everyone else.

 THINK

■ How can I decide if a group of words is a prepositional phrase?

REMEMBER

- A **prepositional phrase** begins with a preposition and ends with a noun or pronoun.
- The noun or pronoun that follows the preposition is the **object of the preposition.**

More Practice

Write each sentence. Draw a line under each prepositional phrase. Draw two lines under each object of the preposition.

Example: The Curies worked <u>on their research.</u>

6. Marie Curie looked for radioactive elements.
7. Her discoveries were of radium and polonium.
8. Uranium was found within pitchblende.
9. Marie Curie was married to Pierre Curie.
10. Their daughter was influenced by them.
11. Following in their footsteps, she won a Nobel Prize.
12. With her husband, Irene Curie studied chemistry.
13. Scientists around the world read Marie's reports.
14. Across the ocean, scientists worked with radium.
15. They experimented within their laboratories.
16. Marie and Pierre talked about their experiments.
17. They worked for scientific progress.
18. Unfortunately, Marie had become sick from radium.
19. Working with uranium was not without risk.
20. Marie Curie received a Nobel Prize for the discoveries of radium and polonium.

Extra Practice, page 449

WRITING APPLICATION A Biography

Research the life of a famous scientist. Use your information to write a brief biography of the scientist. Include information about the scientist's important discoveries in his or her particular field of research. Have a partner underline the prepositional phrases in your report.

The Granger Collection

Marie Curie

3 OBJECT PRONOUNS IN PREPOSITIONAL PHRASES

As you know, the object of a preposition is the noun or pronoun that follows the preposition.

Cats are very special pets for **us**.

I found a cat and played with **her**.

When the object of a preposition is a pronoun, as in the sentences above, use an **object pronoun**.

> **Object Pronouns** me him it us
> you her them

To be sure you have used pronouns correctly in a compound object, leave out the other object in the compound and check the pronoun alone.

Many breeds appeal to **Dan and me**.

Many breeds appeal to **me**.

Guided Practice

Tell which words in the sentence are the prepositional phrase. Then, tell which pronoun is the object of the preposition.

Example: Pets provide company for us.

for us   prepositional phrase
us   object of the preposition

1. Cats share certain traits with us.
2. Teresa read her report to her family and me.
3. She wrote about cats and us human beings.
4. The teacher gave a good grade to her.
5. Teresa illustrated her report for him.

?! THINK

- How can I decide on the object pronoun to use in a prepositional phrase?

REMEMBER

■ Use object pronouns *me*, *you*, *him*, *her*, *it*, *us*, and *them* as objects in prepositional phrases.

More Practice

A. Write each sentence. Draw one line under the prepositional phrase. Draw two lines under the object pronoun.

Example: The report explained animals <u>to <u>us</u></u>.

6. The cat's nose gives important information to him.
7. Cats' eyes do not give as much data to them.
8. Total darkness poses problems for them.
9. My cat cannot always see the food dish below her.
10. She sometimes needs help from me.
11. I leave a light on for her.
12. The cats often jump on Teresa and me.
13. They are good company for my sister and me.

B. Complete each sentence with the correct pronoun.

Example: Teresa shared some ideas with (I, me).
Teresa shared some ideas with me.

14. Teresa's cats sat down beside (I, me).
15. The cats sniffed at (we, us).
16. My parents had brought the dog with (they, them).
17. My father kept the dog near (he, him).
18. He had carried a leash for (she, her).
19. Teresa spoke to (we, us) about animal research.
20. Teresa stroked the gray cat next to (she, her).

Extra Practice, Practice Plus, pages 450-451

WRITING APPLICATION A Summary

Research several facts about an animal and write a short summary. Work with a small group of classmates, and circle object pronouns in prepositional phrases in each summary.

COOPERATIVE
LEARNING

4

WHAT IS A CONJUNCTION?

A conjunction is a word that joins words or groups of words.

You know that the words *and*, *but*, and *or* can join related subjects or predicates. These words are called **conjunctions**. Conjunctions can also join two sentences to form a compound sentence.

➡ Use *and* to join word groups, subjects, or predicates together.
   Louis Leakey **and** his wife Mary worked in Africa.

➡ Use *but* to show contrast.
   Anthropologists study human beginnings, **but** archaeologists study the past.

➡ Use *or* to show choice.
   Were they anthropologists **or** archaeologists?

Conjunctions can also connect other words in a sentence.

   The Leakeys worked eagerly **but** carefully.
   Field researchers work alone **or** in teams.
   They uncover fossils **and** human possessions.

Guided Practice

Tell the conjunction in each sentence.

Example: The Leakeys were famous at home and abroad.
            and

1. Louis Leakey was born in Kenya, but Mary Leakey was born in England.
2. Tools or weapons can help us learn about a society.
3. Fossils in Asia and Africa tell about life long ago.
4. Archaeologists work slowly and patiently on digs.
5. A dig might unearth some pottery or a building.

Louis Leakey

THINK

■ How do I decide which conjunction to use in a sentence?

REMEMBER

■ Use *and* to join, *but* to show contrast, and *or* to show choice.

More Practice

Complete each sentence with the correct conjunction.

Example: I will study either history (and, <u>or</u>) anthropology.

6. The people (and, or) homes of long ago interest me.
7. Fossils look dull, (but, or) they are valuable.
8. This fossil might be a fish (or, but) a mollusk.
9. You find arrowheads in caves (and, but) forests.
10. Mohawk (and, or) Onondaga tribes lived together here.
11. Did Native Americans (or, and) Europeans make these masks?
12. They look old, (but, and) they might be recent.
13. Did the first people come from Africa (and, or) did they come from Asia?
14. I know about history since 1800, (and, but) I know little about earlier times.
15. I have books on American (and, or) world history.
16. Our school library has many books, (or, but) the town library has a bigger collection.
17. Books by the Leakeys (or, but) Ruth Benedict are good.
18. I have nearly finished my report, (and, but) I will need one more day of work.
19. I write my final copy neatly (and, or) quickly.
20. We have learned many new ideas (and, or) facts.

Extra Practice, page 452

Mary Leakey

WRITING APPLICATION A Brief History

Write a short history of the area in which you live. Research some facts of your neighborhood, town, or state. You might include information about the area's famous people, buildings, or geography. Circle the conjunctions.

5 WHAT IS AN INTERJECTION?

An interjection is a word or group of words that expresses strong feeling.

You have learned how to use commas with introductory words. Sometimes these introductory words show strong feeling or call special attention to a statement. These words are called **interjections**.

➡ Use a comma to set off a mild interjection from the rest of the sentence.

My, this is a lovely day.

➡ Use an exclamation mark to set off a strong interjection from the rest of the sentence.

Hurray! We're having a tour of the restaurant.

When an exclamation mark sets off the interjection, the next word of the sentence begins with a capital letter.

Guided Practice

Tell which word is an interjection in each sentence.

Example: Wow! I love this restaurant! *Wow*

1. Oh! We have waited for this tour for weeks.
2. Well, restaurants are busy places.
3. Oops! Be quiet in the dining area.
4. Hey! Follow the teacher quickly.
5. Goodness, the kitchen is huge!

 THINK

■ How do I use an interjection in a sentence?

REMEMBER

■ Use a comma or an exclamation mark to set off an interjection.

More Practice

A. Write each sentence. Draw a line under the interjection in the sentence.

Example: <u>Gee</u>, I wish it were time for lunch!

6. Wow! Something smells delicious in here!
7. Look, the cook is making a stew.
8. Oh! He wears a tall white hat.
9. Gee, I am getting hungry!
10. My, he uses many different spices.
11. Yes! That stew will taste wonderful!
12. Hurray! He will let us taste some dishes.

B. Write and punctuate each sentence correctly.

Example: Oh there is a huge rack of spices
Oh, there is a huge rack of spices!

13. Goodness the cook likes spicy food.
14. Wow his recipes all use garlic and pepper.
15. Aha here is his supply cabinet.
16. Ssh we will disturb his work.
17. Oh he says we can look in the refrigerator.
18. Ah do you see all those kettles and pans?
19. Gee he can cook huge amounts of food at once.
20. Whew it's terribly hot near the stove!

Extra Practice, page 453

WRITING APPLICATION A Dialogue

Write a dialogue between you and other people during a class trip. Where did your class go? Whom or what did you see? Use interjections to make the dialogue lively. Act out the dialogue with your classmates while other students point out the interjections.

COOPERATIVE
LEARNING

G
R
A
M
M
A
R

6 MECHANICS: Capitalizing Titles

There are special rules for capitalizing words in titles. The first and last words in a title are always capitalized. Important words in the title should be capitalized. Most prepositions, conjunctions, and articles are not capitalized.

When you write some titles, you underline them to show that they are written in *italics*.

<u>Time</u> magazine contains many photographs.

A new edition of <u>Treasure Island</u> is in the library.

Other titles are set off by quotation marks.

I read an article called "Summer Fun in the City."
"The Road Not Taken" is my favorite poem.

Underlined Titles	*Titles in Quotation Marks*
books	poems
newspapers	short stories
magazines	songs
movies	articles
	book chapters

Guided Practice

Tell how you would write each title.

Example: the silver chair (book)
<u>The Silver Chair</u>

1. children's times (magazine)
2. black beauty (movie)
3. a wrinkle in time (book)
4. the chicago tribune (newspaper)
5. paul revere's ride (poem)

 THINK

■ How do I write a title correctly?

REMEMBER

- Capitalize the first, last, and all important words in a title.
- Set off titles by underlining them or by putting them in quotation marks.

More Practice

A. Write each title correctly, using the proper punctuation and capitalization.

Example: a special day (story) *"A Special Day"*

6. sleeping beauty (story)
7. lucy looks into a wardrobe (book chapter)
8. the san francisco chronicle (newspaper)
9. casey at the bat (poem)
10. german legends (book)
11. superman (movie)
12. little literature (magazine)

B. Write and punctuate each sentence correctly.

Example: I read the poem titled Two People.
I read the poem titled "Two People."

13. We read Sleeping Beauty aloud.
14. The movie called Robinson Crusoe scared us.
15. I have a book called German Legends.
16. Treasure Mountain is a book of folk tales.
17. We know the words to the song, Dreams.
18. The Earth Is Sore is a Native American poem.
19. We read an article called Poems for Students.
20. The book, The Crane Wife, was recommended by a writer for The Chicago Tribune.

Extra Practice, page 454

 WRITING APPLICATION A List

Make a list of your favorite stories, books, movies, and poems. When your list is complete, have a partner check to see that you have punctuated and capitalized titles correctly.

GRAMMAR

7 VOCABULARY BUILDING: How Language Changes

You may have noticed that people in different regions or parts of the country refer to the same objects by different names. If you buy a sandwich on a long, narrow loaf of bread in Maryland, you might ask for a *hoagie*. If you buy the same kind of sandwich in California, you might ask for a *grinder*. The same sandwich is also called a *poorboy*, *wedgie*, *sub*, and *hero*.

Language can also change over a period of time. The bus you take to school would have been called an *autobus* seventy-five years ago. Words, like clothing styles, change.

Guided Practice

Tell the familiar word from each pair. Your answer will depend on where you live.

1. seesaw/teeter-totter
2. bucket/pail
3. bathrobe/dressing gown
4. sofa/couch
5. bag/suitcase

 THINK

■ In what ways can language change or vary?

REMEMBER

■ Objects can have different names in different regions.

More Practice

A. Look at each object. Write the word that describes the object in your region.

6. a. notebook   b. binder   c. tablet

7. a. snap beans   b. string beans   c. green beans

8. a. skillet   b. frying pan   c. spider pan

9. a. jeans   b. dungarees   c. denims

10. a. pier   b. landing   c. wharf

B. Write each sentence. Complete each sentence with the word that is used in your region.

11. A cold, fizzy drink is a (pop, soda, cola).

12. You comb your hair while looking in a (looking glass, mirror).

13. On cold winter nights, use a (quilt, comforter).

14. The lowest floor of a house is usually the (basement, cellar).

15. The long space that connects the rooms in a house is called a (corridor, hall).

16. On cold days, wear a (ski jacket, parka).

17. For a sore throat, try a (cough drop, lozenge).

18. Keep warm in a woolen (sweater, pullover).

19. (Dinner, supper) is served between 5 and 7 o'clock at night.

20. Carry the groceries home from the store in a paper (bag, sack).

Extra Practice, page 455

WRITING APPLICATION A Report

Report on some words a stranger would encounter in your area. Share your work with a classmate.

GRAMMAR
—AND—
WRITING
CONNECTION

Expanding Sentences

You know that a prepositional phrase adds information to a sentence. You can add more than one prepositional phrase to a sentence to make the meaning of a sentence clear and precise.

Look at the sentences below.

I went **to the animal shelter.**
I went **with my classmates to the animal shelter**.
On Tuesday I went **with my classmates to the animal shelter**.

Each prepositional phrase above adds a particular detail. The meaning of each sentence is different because of the prepositional phrases it includes.

Working Together

COOPERATIVE
LEARNING

With your class, discuss how to add more than one prepositional phrase to a sentence to make your meaning clear. Then, add two prepositional phrases to each sentence.

Example: One dog looked sad.
The face of one dog looked sad for a moment.

1. A volunteer gave us a tour.
2. We saw many homeless pets.
3. I felt sorry.
4. There were many cages.
5. The animals waited.

Revising Sentences

Pete has written these sentences for a paragraph about his visit to an animal shelter. Help Pete to make his sentences more detailed by adding two prepositional phrases to each short sentence.

6. There were dogs and cats.
7. The cages were clean.
8. The animals looked lonely.
9. The volunteers love animals.
10. We walked around.
11. I wanted a pet.
12. I will come back.
13. Mom promised me a pet.
14. I would like a puppy.
15. I saw a picture.
16. Pets need love.
17. Many animals are abandoned.
18. They need our help.
19. Would you like a pet?
20. Visit an animal shelter.

Brainstorm to think of a place you have visited that impressed you. Write a paragraph in which you report on what you recall about the place. When you have finished, check your paragraph to see if you have made your writing more detailed by including prepositional phrases.

UNIT CHECKUP

LESSON

What Is a Preposition? (page 428) Write each sentence. Underline the preposition.

1. The discovery was in the scientist's grasp.
2. He had worked through the day.
3. His assistant worked beside him.
4. They finished their project during the night.
5. They danced happily around the laboratory.

LESSON

Prepositional Phrases (page 430) Write each sentence. Draw one line under the prepositional phrase. Draw two lines under the object of the preposition.

6. The assembly was held inside the old gym.
7. Important news was announced by me.
8. Students learned about the new cafeteria.
9. The school would have another lunchroom for us.
10. The new room would be near the old cafeteria.

LESSON

Object Pronouns in Prepositional Phrases (page 432) Write each sentence, using the correct pronoun.

11. The student had his dog beside (he, him).
12. The teacher smiled sadly at (they, them).
13. The boy asked a question of (she, her).
14. "The dog can't stay," she said to (he, him).
15. "He will wait for (I, me)," said the boy.

LESSON

What Is a Conjunction? (page 434) Write each sentence. Draw one line under the conjunction. Draw two lines under the words or groups of words that the conjunction joins.

16. The fifth and sixth graders are having a picnic.
17. Larry or I will find the best spot.
18. I like the park, but Larry prefers the beach.
19. The beach might be windy or cold in May.
20. Let's call the Commissioner of Parks and Grounds.

LESSON 5

What Is an Interjection? (page 436) Rewrite and punctuate each sentence correctly.

21. Eureka I have found it
22. Hurrah this is a wonderful discovery
23. Why that is nothing new
24. Hey what do you mean
25. Well others have made the same discovery

LESSON 6

Mechanics: Capitalizing Titles (page 438) Write each title correctly.

26. mary's big day (story)
27. math today and tomorrow (book)
28. the high school gazette (newspaper)
29. i love jelly (poem)
30. school times (magazine)

LESSON 7

Vocabulary Building: How Language Changes (page 440) Write the familiar word that describes the object.

31. a. faucet	b. spigot	c. tap
32. a. dragonfly	b. spindle	c. darning needle
33. a. pancakes	b. griddlecakes	c. hot cakes
34. a. parcel	b. package	c. bundle
35. a. soda	b. pop	c. soft drink

36.-40.

Writing Application: Prepositions, Conjunctions, and Interjections Usage (pages 428-436) The following paragraph contains 5 errors of usage with prepositions, conjunctions, and interjections. Rewrite the paragraph correctly.

I arrived of the store with my mother and Jenny. Jenny or I both bought new summer clothing. "Hey You girls look wonderful in those dresses," said our Mom. We paid to the purchases and found a restaurant in the mall. Then we waited for our mother after a few moments as she shopped for a jacket.

WHERE AM I?

Play this game with a small group. Sit in a circle. One player asks the question, "Where am I?" The second player answers with a sentence that includes a prepositional phrase, such as "in a tree." The next player adds a second prepositional phrase, creating "in a tree behind the house." Each person in the group adds a prepositional phrase to the sentence until all the players run out of ideas.

NAME GAME

Some words that you use come from a person's name. The word *sandwich*, for example, comes from the Earl of Sandwich. The Earl did not like to stop for lunch. He ordered his servant to bring him some thick slices of beef between two pieces of toasted bread. From this event, the word sandwich was born. Here are some more words that come from a person's name:

pants   boycott   leotard   spoonerism

Look up the words in a dictionary or encyclopedia to find their meanings and origins. Use each word in a sentence.

CAT MOVES

Draw a comic strip that includes a cat. Under each drawing, write a prepositional phrase that describes what the cat is doing. You might, for example, draw a house with a cat sitting *on the roof*.

CREATIVE EXPRESSION
Personification

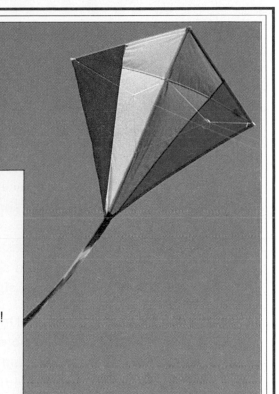

The Wind

I saw you toss the kites on high
And blow the birds about the sky;
And all around I heard you pass,
Like ladies' skirts across the grass—
    O wind, a-blowing all day long,
    O wind, that sings so loud a song!

I saw the different things you did,
But always you yourself you hid.
I felt you push, I heard you call,
I could not see yourself at all—
    O wind, a-blowing all day long,
    O wind, that sings so loud a song!

O you that are so strong and cold,
O blower, are you young or old?
Are you a beast of field and tree,
Or just a stronger child than me?
    O wind, a-blowing all day long,
    O wind, that sings so loud a song!
          —Robert Louis Stevenson

TRY IT OUT!
"The Wind" is a poem in which a child speaks to the wind as though it were a person. **Personification** gives human traits to something other than a person. Write a poem in which you use personification.

GRAMMAR

Three levels of practice

What Is a Preposition? (page 428)

LEVEL A. Write each sentence. Draw a line under the preposition.

1. A Dutch inventor held two lenses in his hands.
2. He looked through both of them.
3. The inventor was peering at something.
4. The lenses were placed inside a tube.
5. The invention was similar to a microscope.
6. A microscope helps us look at tiny things.
7. The lenses are necessary for magnification.
8. The inventor leaned against his chair.
9. He breathed a great sigh of relief.

LEVEL B. Write each sentence. Draw one line under the preposition. Draw two lines under the object of the preposition.

10. We were talking about balloons.
11. Hot air from a flame lifted the first balloons.
12. The inventors learned by accident.
13. A shirt was drying over a fire.
14. Smoke rose above the fire.
15. The shirt sailed into the air.
16. The inventors put their idea into action.
17. They created a passenger balloon through experimentation.

LEVEL C. Add a preposition to each group of words to form a sentence that makes sense. Write the new sentence.

18. Bicycles traveled roads.
19. They bounced the hard and bumpy ground.
20. Boys and girls would fall the bicycles.
21. A man named Dunlop put air rubber tires.
22. People thought they were riding air.
23. Later, a similar type of tire was used automobiles.
24. Tires come different widths.
25. Balloon tires are used children's bicycles.

EXTRA PRACTICE

Three levels of practice

Prepositional Phrases (page 430)

LEVEL A. Write each sentence. Underline each prepositional phrase.

1. Benjamin Banneker lived during the eighteenth century.
2. He was a black man in a slave society.
3. He was a mathematician and a surveyor for the city.
4. He was also an astronomer of great talent.
5. American scientists had all been white until then.
6. Banneker's contributions to almanacs were very important.
7. They were about the location of the planets.
8. Banneker sent Thomas Jefferson a copy of his first almanac.
9. He also sent a letter about the anti-slavery movement.

LEVEL B. Write each sentence. Draw a line under the prepositional phrase. Draw two lines under the object of the preposition.

10. John James Audubon drew pictures of wild birds.
11. Few people know that Audubon was born in Haiti.
12. The artist studied the animals around him.
13. These drawings tell us much about many North American birds.
14. He worked with a Scottish naturalist.
15. They traveled through many states together.
16. Audubon had a deep love of nature.
17. The Audubon Society was founded in his honor.

LEVEL C. Add a preposition to each group of words to make a prepositional phrase that correctly completes the sentence. Write the new sentence.

18. Casimir Funk came _____ the United States.
19. He wrote a paper _____ vitamins and diseases.
20. His papers were also _____ hormones.
21. People gained knowledge _____ his research.
22. Funk explored many fields _____ science.
23. No one had investigated vitamins _____ Funk.
24. The role of vitamins _____ the human body is important.
25. Funk's research caused changes _____ medical science.

EXTRA PRACTICE

Three levels of practice

Object Pronouns in Prepositional Phrases (page 432)

LEVEL A. Write each sentence. Draw a line under the object pronoun in each sentence.

1. Miss Marple brought a clue to us.
2. She carried a magnifying glass with her.
3. A handkerchief had initials sewn on it.
4. One of them was torn.
5. Miss Marple placed the handkerchief before us.
6. She had information about it.
7. She explained her idea to me.
8. I had several questions for her.
9. She spoke intelligently to us.

LEVEL B. Write each sentence, using the correct pronoun.

10. Miss Marple looked at the people beside (she, her).
11. She gazed thoughtfully at (they, them).
12. The detective arrived and she spoke to (he, him).
13. I was the most confused one of (we, us).
14. The detective paid a compliment to (I, me).
15. Miss Marple spoke highly of (he, him).
16. The thief would be caught by (we, us).
17. The handkerchief had been torn by (he, him).

LEVEL C. Write each sentence. Complete the sentence with an object pronoun that makes sense.

18. Jenny thought the mystery was about _____.
19. Leonard believed the culprit was near _____.
20. Miss Marple said the fuss was over _____.
21. Her anger was directed at _____.
22. The clues were beside _____.
23. I had taken my notebook with _____.
24. Miss Marple read my article to _____.
25. The newspapers would have no information without _____.

PRACTICE + PLUS

Three levels of additional practice for a difficult skill

Object Pronouns in Prepositional Phrases (page 432)

LEVEL
A. Write each sentence. Draw a line under the object pronoun in each sentence.

1. Holidays are observed by us.
2. For me, the best part is the feast.
3. With you, I will plan a wonderful meal.
4. Don't start the preparations without me!
5. We'll visit the market near you.
6. The grocer will save a turkey for us.
7. I will bring a list with me.
8. Sit down beside me.
9. Explain that recipe to us.

LEVEL
B. Write each sentence, using the correct pronoun from the pair in parentheses.

10. Joan has shared some recipes with (I, me).
11. We've gotten many good tips from (she, her).
12. I hold the list before (I, me).
13. Mom will bring money with (she, her).
14. Dad will follow after (we, us).
15. We can load the car for (he, him).
16. Mom sits beside (we, us).
17. She keeps her purse near (she, her).

LEVEL
C. Write each sentence, using an object pronoun.

18. This recipe was written by _____.
19. The meal will taste delicious to _____.
20. I will take some vegetables for _____.
21. Please share this turkey with _____.
22. Will you sit beside _____?
23. Mom places a platter near _____.
24. She tells Aunt Dora about _____.
25. You were the biggest help to _____.

EXTRA PRACTICE

Three levels of practice

What Is a Conjunction? (page 434)

LEVEL A. Write each sentence. Draw a line under the conjunction.

1. Find the meaning and pronunciation of the word.
2. You may use the dictionary, but try other reference books, too.
3. Dictionaries and thesauruses help define words.
4. A thesaurus gives synonyms and antonyms for words.
5. Should I use the dictionary or the thesaurus?
6. The dictionary has a pronunciation key, but the thesaurus does not.
7. Look at the first or second definition of a word in your dictionary.
8. The same word might be a noun and a verb.
9. Read every definition, but do not get confused.

LEVEL B. Write each sentence. Draw a line under the conjunction. Draw two lines under the words or phrases that the conjunction joins.

10. Try the school or public library.
11. You must find articles and graphs.
12. Librarians and scientists have something in common.
13. They research and explore sources of information.
14. Our library is good, but Smithtown's is better.
15. Go to Smithtown next Friday or Saturday.
16. Take the bus or the train.
17. You can take some books home, but others cannot leave the library.

LEVEL C. Write each sentence. Complete the sentence with the correct conjunction from the pair in parentheses.

18. Are you reading a book, (and, or) writing a paper?
19. I scanned that book, (and, but) it had no information.
20. The librarian (and, or) I searched the shelves together.
21. Will you check those books out (and, or) read them here?
22. I cannot read (and, or) take notes at the same time.
23. My last paper was good, (or, but) this one must be better.
24. This book is interesting, (and, but) the words are difficult.
25. I read part of your report, (and, but) I haven't finished yet.

EXTRA PRACTICE

Three levels of practice

What Is an Interjection? (page 436)

LEVEL A. Write each sentence. Draw a line under the interjection.

1. Wow! This barn is dark!
2. Well, should we go inside?
3. Gee, let's wait for Alonzo.
4. Ah! Is he so brave?
5. Hush! I hear footsteps!
6. No, that is only the wind.
7. Hey! Where are you?
8. Oops, I dropped the flashlight!
9. Help! I can't find it!

LEVEL B. Write each sentence correctly, using commas and exclamation marks where they are needed. Be sure to use capital letters correctly.

10. Yikes who turned out the lights
11. Oh no I can't see a thing
12. Well what should we do now
13. Oh here is my flashlight
14. Goodness this barn is scary
15. Yes can we leave soon
16. Hey don't be so nervous
17. Heavens is that a monster

LEVEL C. Write each sentence. Complete the sentence with an interjection. Be sure to punctuate and capitalize correctly.

18. _____ have you ever seen anything like this?
19. _____ where is the door?
20. _____ who suggested this idea, anyway?
21. _____ even Alonzo is scared!
22. _____ shall we tell anyone about this?
23. _____ they would never believe us.
24. _____ there is the exit!
25. _____ we're safe at last!

G R A M M A R

Three levels of practice

Mechanics: Capitalizing Titles (page 438)

LEVEL
A. Write each title correctly. Underline or use quotation marks.

1. to build a fire (story)
2. tales of the arctic (book)
3. the anchorage news (newspaper)
4. white desert (poem)
5. blues in the alaska night (song)
6. nanook of the north (movie)
7. how it all began (book chapter)
8. the tundra quarterly (magazine)
9. ice-fishing made simple (article)

LEVEL
B. Write each sentence correctly.

10. The magazine, Science, has an article about igloos.
11. Everyone sang alaska, my alaska very loudly.
12. The teacher had us read the chapter called morning.
13. We thought terror from the north was a silly movie.
14. How to tame sled dogs was the best article.
15. Animals of the tundra is a wonderful book.
16. The bear is one of my favorite stories.
17. The post is a newspaper with accurate sports information.

LEVEL
C. Add a title to each group of words to make a complete sentence. Write the new sentence.

18. The company made a film called _____.
19. It is based on the book, _____.
20. My paper, _____, is about logging.
21. I submitted it to _____ as an article.
22. It was printed with the title, _____.
23. Randy's poem is called _____.
24. The magazine, _____, published her work.
25. The poem will be reprinted in a book of students' writing called _____.

EXTRA PRACTICE

Three levels of practice

Vocabulary Building: How Language Changes (page 440)

LEVEL A. Write the familiar word that describes the object.

1. a. carnival	b. festival	c. fair
2. a. movie	b. film	c. flick
3. a. peanuts	b. goobers	c. goober peas
4. a. shed	b. shack	c. lean-to
5. a. sneaker	b. running shoe	c. tennis shoe
6. a. hero	b. grinder	c. sub
7. a. thongs	b. flipflops	c. beach sandals
8. a. seltzer	b. soda	c. fizz
9. a. porridge	b. oatmeal	c. hot cereal

LEVEL B. Complete each sentence with the familiar word from the box.

10. The gardener turned on the _____.
11. I ate _____ at the picnic.
12. A bright _____ flew over the meadow.
13. I ordered a vanilla _____ at the ice cream shop.
14. Sherri devoured a strawberry _____.
15. I wore my _____ during the cold weather.
16. Do you like _____ baked or roasted?
17. Can you play the _____?

10. a. faucet b. spigot
c. tap
11. a. corn on the cob
b. roasting ears
12. a. darning needle
b. dragonfly
c. spindle
13. a. milk shake
b. frappe
14. a. ice cream soda
b. float
15. a. parka b. ski jacket
16. a. potatoes b. spuds
17. a. harmonica
b. mouth organ

LEVEL C. Use each of the regional words below to complete the following sentences.

18. Instead of a suit, the man wore _____.
19. He carried his things away in a _____.
20. He thought the detective would never _____ him.
21. The detective finished his breakfast of _____.
22. He sat on the _____ for an hour.
23. He suddenly threw some clothes in a _____.
24. He drove toward the local _____.
25. He found the man eating _____ under a tree.

nab   tote   dungarees
johnnycakes   veranda
satchel   filberts
swimming hole

MAINTENANCE

UNIT 1: Sentences

Sentences (pages 2, 4) Label each sentence correctly as **declarative**, **interrogative**, **imperative**, or **exclamatory**. If a group of words is not a sentence, label it **fragment**.

1. That was a wonderful show!
2. Were the tigers terribly fierce?
3. Tell me about them.
4. Tigers in their cages.
5. Yesterday the circus.

Subjects and Predicates (pages 6-13) Write each sentence. Draw one line under the simple subject and two lines under the simple predicate. Draw a line between the complete subject and the complete predicate.

6. Strange plants grow in jungles.
7. Myra will travel to the Amazon.
8. She knows a great deal about plants.
9. The tour guide will give her more information.

Compound Sentences/ Correcting Sentence Fragments (pages 14, 16) Combine each group of words into a complete sentence. Label each compound sentence **compound**.

10. Living things eat. Because they are hungry.
11. We feel hungry. When our bodies need energy.
12. Sometimes I get hungry. But I don't eat.
13. After a few hours. I feel extremely tired.

Using Context Clues (page 20) Choose the correct meaning for each underlined word. Then, write the word or words you used as context clues.

14. The air is so <u>humid</u> it almost drips.
    a. wet   b. dry
15. In some cities people <u>inhale</u> dirty air.
    a. breathe   b. drink
16. Air pollution can <u>damage</u> our health and cause illness in people and animals.
    a. harm   b. help
17. New laws can <u>curb</u> the spread of pollution and control further damage to the environment.
    a. further   b. limit

UNIT 3: Nouns

Singular and Plural Possessive Nouns (pages 84-89) Write the possessive form of each noun.

18. mice
19. lady
20. fox
21. class
22. fish

Compound Words (page 92) Make compound words with the words in the columns.

23. ear   road
24. key   walk
25. rail   fighter
26. side   hole
27. fire   muffs

UNIT 5: Verbs

Action Verbs and Direct Objects (pages 144, 146) Write each sentence. Draw one line under the action verb. Draw two lines under the direct object.

28. A man waved his hand at a cabdriver.
29. The driver stopped the taxicab.
30. The passenger held a map.
31. The passenger soon reached his destination.

Main Verbs and Helping Verbs (page 148) Write each sentence. Draw one line under the main verb. Draw two lines under the helping verb.

32. The horses have eaten the hay.
33. Now they are running wildly.
34. One horse has jumped over the stream.
35. A pony was chasing a mare.

Linking Verbs (page 150) Write the linking verb in each sentence.

36. The weather seemed fine this morning.
37. Now, the sky looks overcast and cloudy.
38. I am not disappointed, though.
39. This cool weather feels comfortable to me.

Contractions (page 152) Write the contraction for the underlined words in each sentence.

40. Michael does not know Cynthia well.
41. She was not in his class last year.
42. I will eat lunch with them today.
43. They have saved me a place at our favorite table in the school cafeteria.

MAINTENANCE

Verb Tenses (pages 154, 156) Write each sentence. Complete the sentence with the correct tense of the verb in parentheses.

44. I (walk, will walk) to the fair tomorrow with my sister and brother.
45. Yesterday, I (promise, promised) my little sister a treat.
46. Now she (looked, looks) tall enough for the donkey rides around the fairgrounds.
47. We always (enjoy, will enjoy) the fair and the exciting rides.

Subject-Verb Agreement (page 158) Write each sentence. Complete the sentence with the correct form of the verb in parentheses.

48. Exercise (is, are) good for everyone.
49. An active person (feel, feels) healthy.
50. I (jump, jumps) rope every day.
51. We each (choose, chooses) our favorite exercise routine for the sports demonstration.

Using Irregular Verbs (pages 162, 164) Write the correct past tense of each verb. Then, write the correct past tense with the helping verb.

52. come
53. give
54. take
55. run
56. sing
57. teach
58. know
59. see

Using the Comma (page 166) Write each sentence, using commas where they are needed.

60. The dark dense mysterious forest is alive tonight.
61. Owls rodents and insects are awake.
62. The moon stars and lake all shine brightly.
63. The bats fly an owl hoots and a cat prowls.

Homophones (page 168) Write each sentence, using the correct word in parentheses.

64. Tonight Robert will eat (meat, meet) and potatoes.
65. He will watch a (miner, minor) league baseball game.
66. Then he will fish in the (creak, creek).
67. Now he makes (doe, dough) for biscuits.

UNIT 7: Adjectives

What Is an Adjective? (page 226) Write each sentence. Draw a line under each adjective.

68. The loud thunder crashed.
69. Bright lightning flashed in the sky.
70. After the terrible storm, the sky cleared.
71. A beautiful rainbow appeared.

Comparing with Adjectives

(pages 226–233) Write each sentence. Complete the sentence with the correct word.

72. The Golden Gate Bridge is the (longer, longest) bridge I have ever seen.
73. The traffic is (heavier, heaviest) today than yesterday.
74. There are (more, most) cars than ever on the roads today.
75. The (better, best) hours of all for a drive are in the early afternoon.
76. Accidents are a (worse, worst) problem than traffic jams.

Using Articles and Demonstrative Adjectives

(page 234) Write each sentence using the correct word in parentheses.

77. (A, An) rodeo came to town.
78. (A, The) event attracted many people.
79. Marie said, "(This, That) horse over there is beautiful."
80. Michael replied, "(This, That) horse near us is my favorite."

Capitalizing Proper Adjectives

(page 236) Write the proper adjective that is formed from each proper noun below.

81. India
82. Canada
83. Italy
84. Germany
85. America

UNIT 9: Pronouns

What Is a Pronoun? (page 292) Write each sentence. Draw a line under the pronoun. Then, write whether it is a **subject** or an **object** pronoun.

86. John watches the children and makes lunch for them.
87. They play football, catch, and tag in the garden until noon.
88. We play soccer with Sue for an hour.
89. John explains the important rules to us.

MAINTENANCE

I and me, we and us (pages 298, 306) Write each sentence using the correct word in parentheses.

90. Sharon threw the ball to (I, me).
91. (We, Us) play baseball every Saturday.
92. Sports are fun for Sharon and (I, me).
93. (I, Me) have organized a game for our class.

Possessive Pronouns (pages 300, 302) Write the possessive pronoun in each sentence.

94. Julie sent a card to her grandparents.
95. Julie had visited their beach house.
96. Its rooms were cool and airy.
97. Theirs is a lovely home.
98. Julie's brother will spend his vacation there, too.

UNIT 11: Adverbs

What Is an Adverb? (page 364) Write the adverb in each sentence.

99. The sun shone brightly.
100. I quickly dove into the pool.
101. Jan and I swim well.
102. I will dive again.

Using Adverbs to Compare (page 366) Write each sentence. Use the correct form of the adverb.

103. I ran (faster, fastest) than you.
104. The storm arose (more quickly, most quickly) than we had expected.
105. Jamie pitched the tent (more speedily, most speedily) of all the campers.
106. Our new tent remained (drier, driest) than our old one.

Adjective or Adverb? (page 370) Write each sentence. Write **adjective** or **adverb** above the underlined word.

107. The local bus stops nearby.
108. It travels slowly up Elm Road.
109. Mr. Lee is a careful driver.
110. He speaks politely to us.

Negatives (page 372) Write each sentence. Draw a line under the negative word.

111. Divers never work alone.
112. Nobody takes foolish risks.
113. I do not swim by myself.
114. Take no foolish risks.

Using Quotation Marks (page 374) Write each sentence, using correct punctuation and capitalization.

115. Lou said let's go to the store.
116. Which store do you like asked Lil.
117. The discount store has nice socks replied Lou.
118. I need new socks too said Lil.

Suffixes (page 376) Write each sentence. Add a correct suffix to each underlined word.

119. The old house looked <u>cheer</u>.
120. Quick <u>act</u> was needed!
121. The poor <u>art</u> required our help.
122. We were <u>response</u> for the repairs.
123. The elderly man thanked us for our <u>charity</u> work.

UNIT 13: Prepositions, Conjunctions, and Interjections

Prepositions and Prepositional Phrases (pages 428, 430) Write the prepositional phrase in each sentence. Draw a line under the preposition.

124. There are beautiful objects on the shelves.
125. Lovely glass bottles shine under the light.
126. A china dog sits near a glass owl.
127. Watercolor paintings hang above the cabinet.

Object Pronouns in Prepositional Phrases (page 432) Write each sentence, using the correct pronoun.

128. Three hawks flew over (I, me).
129. My dog barked at (they, them).
130. Dad talked to (we, us).

131. A small hawk landed near (he, him).

Conjunctions (page 434) Write each conjunction.

132. Take a train or a bus home.
133. Cora and I will meet you.
134. Sandy cannot come, but Danny will be there.

Interjections (page 436) Write the interjection in each sentence.

135. Oh! What is that noise?
136. Well, it is just the wind.
137. Hey, close that door.

Capitalizing Titles (page 438) Write each title correctly.

138. Sleeping beauty (movie)
139. the time machine (book)
140. hiawatha (poem)

UNIT
14

Writing Research Reports

Look at the picture and read the quotation on the opposite page. The quotation was written by George Ancona, who wrote the article that you will read in this unit. Why do you think curiosity is important to a writer?

When you write a research report, you need to conduct an investigation. You will want to find and organize information for your audience.

Focus A research report provides information about a specific subject. The purpose of a research report is to inform.

What topic would you like to investigate and then write a report about? The article and the photographs in this unit may give you some ideas.

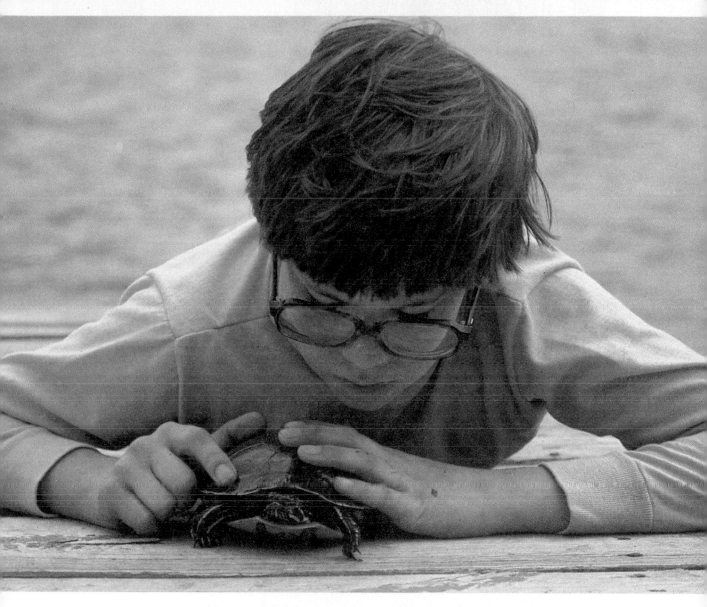

Curiosity is the biggest element in my work. . . . I love to find myself in strange places, meeting people, getting to know them and learning about them.

—George Ancona

Think about the world outdoors. What types of living things do you find there?

Julio and Neca work for TAMAR, a project that studies sea turtles. TAMAR members hope that their work will help to save these endangered animals from extinction.

As you read the selection, notice how the author uses interesting facts in his report on TAMAR and the turtles.

PROJECT TURTLE

FROM TURTLE WATCH *by George Ancona*

Twice every night during the sea turtle's nesting season, a jeep bounces along the beach of Praia do Forte (prī'ä dō fôr'tä), and a searchlight sweeps the sands between the jeep and the ocean.

Now Neca and Julio are covering the fourteen kilometers of beach. Later Guy and Alexandre will take the second watch.

The oceanographers are looking for the tracks of a sea turtle. The tracks will lead them to a nest, where they may be in time to find a female turtle laying her eggs.

Suddenly, above the roar of the wind and the motor, Julio shouts, "Tartaruga! (tär tä rü'gä)" Neca slams on the brakes and switches off the motor. Dousing the lights, they both jump out into the darkness and scramble silently down the slope to the dark shape on the beach.

While still at a distance, Julio and Neca hear the turtle's flippers scrape the sand. Moving slowly behind the turtle, they turn on a flashlight briefly to see the creature. It is a *Caretta caretta* (kä re'tä), or loggerhead turtle. Her shell is encrusted with barnacles. She is building her nest.

The turtle has just finished digging her bed, or body pit, a slight depression in the sand in which she now rests her bulk. She is building her nest above the high-water mark, since saltwater would kill the eggs.

Neca and Julio watch as the turtle begins to dig out the egg cavity. Using her rear flippers, she scoops out a hole in the moist sand. In dry sand, the cavity would collapse.

The turtle raises the front of her body as she works, enabling her to dig a deeper hole. She lifts each flipper full of sand vertically so that she will not disturb the wall of the hole. By now the cavity is about sixteen inches deep. Finally, the turtle widens the bottom of the hole.

Julio scrapes away some sand beneath the loggerhead to reveal the egg chamber. The cavity completed, the turtle releases a thick liquid from the cloaca (klō ä'kä), an opening located slightly in front of her tail. This mucous will protect the eggs as they fall and fill the nest.

Now the turtle's body begins to contract, and the first egg drops into the cavity. As the contractions continue, eggs begin to fall at a faster rate. In about twenty minutes, the turtle has laid from one hundred to one hundred and fifty eggs. The eggs are about the size of a Ping-Pong ball, not hard but leathery and flexible.

While the turtle is laying her eggs, she seems to be in a trance. She is not disturbed by the camera or by the flashlight that Julio uses from time to time.

Julio moves in to attach a metal tag to the turtle's right front flipper and to measure her shell. The tag carries a number and a request that anyone finding the turtle advise TAMAR of the tag number, the location of the sighting, and the dimension of the shell. From now on, whenever this turtle is seen nesting, scientists will be informed and will learn more about the habits of sea turtles.

Notice the author's use of detail in showing how the turtle buries her eggs.

Using her rear flippers, the loggerhead now begins to bury the eggs. She gathers sand from the side of the bed and sweeps it into the egg cavity until the hole has been filled. Then she moves forward and uses her front flippers to fill in the entire bed. Almost an hour has passed since Neca and Julio first sighted the turtle. The turtle seems awake now and aware of her surroundings. Breathing heavily, tired from her efforts, she turns around and begins her return to the ocean. The tracks she leaves parallel those she made when she emerged from the sea. When she reaches the water, she hesitates, lifts her head, then plunges into the waves and disappears.

Neca and Julio know that the turtle will be back. They have learned from the tags on other turtles that she will return to this beach to lay eggs as many as three times each nesting season, which lasts from September through March.

Neca and Julio have followed the turtle to the ocean. Now they go back to the nest for the eggs. If they were to leave them, the eggs might be dug up by other people, or by wild dogs or other animals. With a thin stick, Neca and Julio prod the nest to locate the egg cavity. Once they feel a soft spot, they start to dig with their hands. Soon the eggs are uncovered.

Making sure the eggs remain at the angle at which they found them, Neca and Julio count the eggs and put them inside a Styrofoam cooler. Julio packs them in moist sand to protect them during the trip back home. Then Neca measures the depth of the egg cavity.

Back at the jeep, Julio makes note of the number assigned to the turtle, its species, the size of its shell, the depth of its nest, and the number of eggs found inside.

Then the scientists return to their base and carefully transfer the eggs to a new nest. They bury the eggs at the same depth at which they found them. There the eggs will be protected from the heat while they incubate for about fifty days.

Thinking Like a Reader

1. Would you enjoy working on a project like the one described in the selection? Why or why not?
2. On what projects have you worked? How might you report on one of these projects?

Write your responses in your journal.

Thinking Like a Writer

3. What information does the author give you about TAMAR and the work of Julio and Neca with the turtles?
4. Which facts and details does he use to report on his topic?
5. Which facts do you find most interesting?

Write a list of these facts.

Brainstorm *Vocabulary*

In "Project Turtle," the author tells about a process. Each step of the process must take place at a particular time. He uses time-order words and phrases to show the passing of time. Some examples are *now*, *by now*, *finally*, *while*, and *in about twenty minutes*. In your journal, write any time-order words that come to mind. Begin to create a personal vocabulary list. You can use some of these words when you write a report.

Talk It Over *A Process*

In the selection you read, the author reports on the process by which Julio and Neca work with the turtles. He includes specific details that show the reader exactly how each step is performed. Think of a process with which you are familiar. Outline the steps of this process to a partner. Make the steps of your outline clear for your partner. Then, listen as your partner tells you about a process. Check to be sure you can understand the steps your partner outlines for you.

Quick Write *Write a Proposal*

Before a project gets started, money must be found to support the work. Often, scientists write proposals describing the work they wish to do. People who give money to scientists read many proposals. They choose the ones they think are best.

Write a proposal that tells your idea for a nature study. Explain why it is a good idea to give money for this work. You may want to tell why you are the best person to do the study, or why this study is so important to science.

Idea Corner

Reporting on Nature

You have already started to think about a process in nature. What would you include in a report on this process? In your journal make some notes about facts and details you observe when studying a process found in nature. You can include sketches or photos of the steps of the process. Use these notes when you write a report.

Finding Ideas for Writing

Look at the photographs. Think about what you see.
What ideas for report writing do the photographs give you?
Write your ideas in your journal.

COOPERATIVE
LEARNING

1 GROUP WRITING: A Research Report

The **purpose** of a research report is to give a reader information about a specific topic. How does a writer prepare to write a report?

- Finding Information/Note Taking
- Outlining
- Introduction/Body/Conclusion

Finding Information/Note Taking

Roy went to the library to find information about smog. He read an encyclopedia article and a magazine article. He took these notes on his reading.

> kind of air pollution   smoke + fog = smog
> Two kinds of coal and fuel oil, car emissions
> problems: hurts eyes and lungs,
> damages metal
> worst cases: Mexico City and Denver
> possible solutions: lawsuits, emission control
> Environmental Protection Agency

The notes Roy took contain important facts that will help him when he organizes his report. In a report, facts and details give the reader an understanding of the topic.

Guided Practice: Taking Notes

With your class, choose a topic from the list that follows, or think of one on which you all agree. Go to the library with your class and find an article or encyclopedia entry on this topic. Read the article and take careful notes on specific facts.

  pesticides acid rain endangered species

Outlining

In an outline, the writer lists points in the order in which they will be discussed. Each numbered point will become a paragraph. In the outline, important points of the topic are indicated by a roman numeral.

Smog

I. Introduction
  A. Definition
  B. Kinds of smog
  C. Problems and solutions

II. Problems
  A. Health hazards
  B. Destruction of materials

III. Solutions
  A. EPA and control of smog
  B. Emission controls

IV. Conclusion
  A. Summary
  B. Other Solutions

- How many paragraphs will be in this report?
- Which are the important points in the outline?

Guided Practice: Making an Outline

Using your notes, make an outline for a four-paragraph report. Follow the model above.

Introduction/Body/Conclusion

The main idea of a report is stated in the **introduction**. The **body** of the report contains specific information that supports and develops this main idea. The **conclusion** summarizes the points and adds an opinion about the topic. Look back at Roy's outline.

- Which information belongs in the introduction, the body, and the conclusion?

Putting a Research Report Together

With your classmates you researched to find some information on a topic. You took notes on your reading and organized the notes into an outline.

Think about the main idea of your report. Then, look at the outline you made. Which points would help your reader to understand the main idea of your report? Include those points. Leave out any information that would not help to make your report clear. Read this outline.

Earthquakes

I. Introduction
    A. Causes of earthquakes
    B. Predictions
    C. Problems and solutions

II. Problems
    A. Loss of lives
    B. Destruction of land and property

III. Solutions
    A. Long-term predictions
    B. Short-term predictions

IV. Conclusion
    A. Summary
    B. Other preventive measures

Guided Practice: Writing a Research Report

Use your notes and outline to write a report. Include information that will help you to present your main idea clearly into paragraph form. Organize your report into a logical introduction, body, and conclusion.

Share your report with a classmate. Ask your partner whether you have presented your main idea with enough facts and details to make the topic understandable.

Checklist: Report Writing

When you write a research report, a checklist will remind you of the things you will want to include in your report.

Look at this checklist. It will help you to start writing your report into fully-developed paragraphs. Some points need to be added. Make a copy of the checklist and complete it. Keep a copy of it in your writing folder.

CHECKLIST

✓ Purpose and audience

✓ Finding information/notetaking

✓ Outlining

✓ Introduction/Body/
  Conclusion

✓ Label subheads

■ _____

■ _____

■ _____

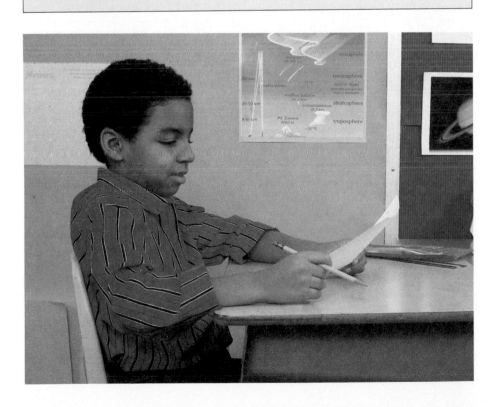

---

2 THINKING AND WRITING: Summarizing

You have learned that a research report presents information on a subject. Each paragraph in a report contains facts and details. The last paragraph, or conclusion, summarizes the information and makes a final point.

When you take notes for your research report, you summarize the information you read. You *paraphrase*, or state in your own words, the important points. A **summary** briefly tells the main idea of a piece of writing.

Reread this passage from the selection "Project Turtle." Then, read one student's summary.

> Making sure the eggs remain at the angle at which they found them, Neca and Julio count the eggs and put them inside a Styrofoam cooler. Julio packs them in moist sand to protect them during the trip back home. Then Neca measures the depth of the egg cavity.
>
> Back at the jeep, Julio makes note of the number assigned to the turtle, its species, the size of its shell, the depth of its nest, and the number of eggs found inside.

Student's Summary

Julio and Neca pack the turtle eggs carefully inside a Styrofoam container. The scientists make careful records concerning the turtle, its nest, and the number of her eggs. Then they take the eggs back to their workplace and put the eggs in a new nest just like the first one.

Thinking Like a Writer

- Which main ideas did the writer want her readers to understand? Which details did she leave out?

When you summarize your report in your conclusion, do not repeat everything you just wrote. Choose the most important point. This is your chance to offer the reader your final thoughts on the topic of the report.

THINKING APPLICATION Summarizing Information

COOPERATIVE
LEARNING

Suppose that you have your own radio news program. Decide which information your audience would need to know from the news article below. On a separate piece of paper, write a three-sentence summary of the article for your broadcast.

October 12, 1990. The investigation continues into the cause of a three-alarm fire at Long Row Mall last Tuesday. Fire fighters had ruled out arson until a witness stepped forward. Jack Flora of 10 Winter Road was parked in the lot to the east of the mall late last night when four youths ran by. Moments later, flames were reported by the janitor in Tidy Homes Hardware, Karen Reeves. By the time fire fighters reached the mall, Tidy Homes and its two nearest neighbors, Tot Togs and HairPower, were engulfed in flames. Captain Turnbull of the Teeburg Police says that he is working "hand in hand" with Chief Phyre. They are asking all citizens with any knowledge of the crime to call 444-3300.

3 INDEPENDENT WRITING: A Research Report

Prewrite: Step 1

You have seen how research reports present information on a specific topic. Now, you can write a report of your own. Mae, a student your age, wanted to write about a topic which would interest the members of her science club. She chose a topic in this way.

Choosing a Topic

1. First, Mae thought about topics she had read about in her science textbook.
2. Next, she started a list of interesting topics for further research.
3. Last, Mae chose the topic she thought she could research easily in the school library.

the life cycle of forests

the causes of earthquakes

how plants make food

Mae thought she could best research how plants make food. She discovered that plants use nitrogen to make protein. Once she had narrowed her topic to the nitrogen cycle, she was ready to explore her idea.

Exploring Ideas: Outlining Strategy

Mae used an outline to organize her notes. Notice that Mae's outline clearly shows how her information will be divided into an introduction, a body, and a conclusion.

Mae can now use the numbered parts of her outline to help her organize her report into clear paragraphs.

Before she actually wrote her report, Mae decided it was important to review her outline carefully. She added information to her outline and changed the order of points.

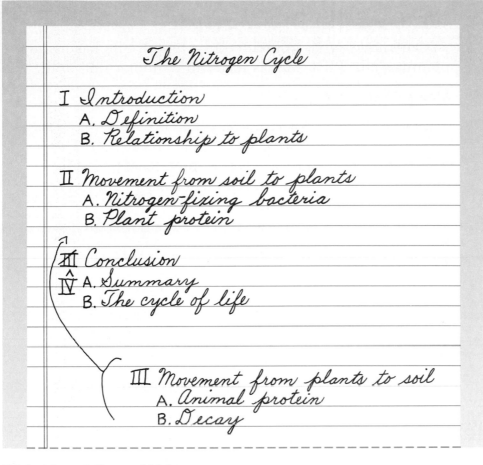

The Nitrogen Cycle

I. Introduction
   A. Definition
   B. Relationship to plants

II. Movement from soil to plants
   A. Nitrogen-fixing bacteria
   B. Plant protein

III. Conclusion
IV. A. Summary
   B. The cycle of life

III. Movement from plants to soil
   A. Animal protein
   B. Decay

Thinking Like a Writer

- What did Mae add to her outline?
- Why did she add these points?

YOUR TURN

JOURNAL

Choose a topic which you would like to investigate. Use **Pictures** or your journal for ideas. Follow these steps.

- Choose a topic that interests you.
- Find information about the topic in the library.
- Narrow the topic if it is too broad.
- Think about your purpose and audience.

Using your notes, make an outline. Remember, you can change any part of your outline later.

Write a First Draft: Step 2

Mae knows what to include in a report. She has made a planning checklist. Mae is ready to write her first draft.

Mae's First Draft

In an artical in Science magazine, Dr Edward Li calls nitrogen ''the stuff of life.'' This gas is found in the air, in the ground, and in all living things. Its movement is called the nitrogen cycle. Nitrogen is important for we.

Nitrogen moves from soil to plants. Bacteria found in certain plants make the gas into something plants can use. Plants convert this to protein.

Nitrogen moves back to the soil. Animals eat plants and convert plant protein to animal protein. As animals and plants die and decay, nitrogen moves back to the soil.

The movement of nitrogen is a basic part of life.

As Mae wrote, she did not worry about errors. She wanted to put her ideas down on paper.

YOUR TURN

Write your first draft. As you prepare to write, ask yourself these questions.

- What will my audience need to know?
- How can I interest my audience in these facts?

TIME-OUT You might want to take some time out before you revise. That way you will be able to revise your writing with a fresh eye.

Planning Checklist
- Remember purpose and audience.
- Find information and take notes.
- Outline points clearly.
- Include an introduction, body, and conclusion.

THE WRITING PROCESS: Writing a First Draft

Revise: Step 3

After she finished her first draft, Mae read it over to herself. Then she shared her report with a classmate, Sandy. She asked Sandy to suggest ways she could improve her report.

Your facts are clear, but your report just seems to end all of a sudden.

You're right. I will write a better conclusion.

Mae then looked back at her planning checklist. She realized that she had forgotten one point. She checked it off so that she would remember it when she revised. Mae now has a checklist to use as she revises her report.

Mae made changes to her report. She did not correct small errors. She knew she could fix them later.

The revisions Mae made changed her report. Turn the page. Look at Mae's revised draft.

Revising Checklist
- ■ Remember purpose and audience.
- ■ Find information and take notes.
- ■ Outline points clearly.
- ✔ ■ Include an introduction, body, and conclusion.

Part of Mae's Revised Draft

nitrogen "the stuff of life." This gas is found in the air, in the ground, and in all living things. Its movement is called the nitrogen cycle. Nitrogen is important for we.

Nitrogen moves from soil to plants. Bacteria found in certain plants *,like peas and beans,* make the gas into something plants can use *.* *and* ~~Plants~~ convert ~~this~~ to protein.

Nitrogen moves back to the soil. Animals eat plants and convert plant protein to animal protein. As animals and plants die and decay, nitrogen moves back to the soil. *If it weren't for nitrogen, we would not exist.* The movement of nitrogen is a basic part of life. *It has a cycle that involves people, plants, animals, and the earth.*

Thinking Like a Writer

WISE
WORD
CHOICE

- Which sentences did Mae combine? How does combining them improve her writing?
- What sentences did Mae add? How do these added sentences make her conclusion clearer?

YOUR TURN

Read your first draft. Ask yourself these questions.

- Does my report contain enough information to be clear?
- Do my paragraphs follow the order of points in my outline?
- Does my report have an introduction, a body, and a conclusion?

If you wish, ask a friend to read your report and make suggestions. Then, revise your report.

Proofread: Step 4

Mae knew that her work was not complete until she proofread her report. She used a proofreading checklist while she proofread.

Part of Mae's Proofread Draft

The Nitrogen Cycle

In an ~~artical~~ *article* in <u>Science</u> magazine, Dr⊙ Edward Li calls nitrogen "the stuff of life." This gas is found in the air, in the ground, and in all living things. Its movement is called the nitrogen cycle. Nitrogen is important for ~~we.~~ *us.*

Nitrogen moves from soil to plants. Bacteria found in certain plants ∧*like peas and beans,* make the gas into something plants can use *∙* *and* ~~Plants~~ convert ~~this~~ to protein.

YOUR TURN

Proofreading Practice

Below is a paragraph that you can use to practice your proofreading skills. Find the errors. Write the paragraph correctly on a separate sheet of paper.

How Kiley Canyon Was Made

A thousand years ago, kiley river was just a streem. Snow melted each spring and fed the trickel. People watched as it grew in size until it became a river to wide for they to cross. Later, the sandstone streembedd was worn away over the coarse of many years. The river widened and deepened, carving out a canyun.

Proofreading Checklist
- Did I indent my paragraphs?
- Did I spell all words correctly?
- What punctuation errors do I need to correct?
- What capitalization errors do I need to correct?

Applying Your Proofreading Skills

Now proofread your research report. Read your checklist once again. Review **The Grammar Connection** and **The Mechanics Connection**, too. Use the proofreading marks to mark changes.

THE GRAMMAR CONNECTION

Remember this rule about prepositional phrases.

- Use object pronouns as objects in prepositional phrases.

    The joke is **on me**.   I laughed **at her and him**.

Check your report. Have you used object pronouns correctly?

THE MECHANICS CONNECTION

Remember these rules about titles.

- Capitalize the first letter of each important word in a title.
- Underline titles of books, newspapers, and magazines to show that they should be italicized.
- Put quotation marks around the titles of short stories, songs, articles, book chapters, and most poems.

    I read the poem, "The Wind," in <u>The Collected Verse of Robert Louis Stevenson</u>.

    The article, "Our Beaches," in <u>The Local Banner</u> was excellent.

Check your report. Have you written all titles correctly?

Proofreading Marks

¶ Indent
∧ Add
ℐ Take out
≡ Make a capital letter
／ Make a small letter

Publish: Step 5

Mae shared her report by reading it aloud to her class. She showed a diagram of the nitrogen cycle and pointed to the diagram as she read. Her classmates said the diagram helped them to understand the cycle.

YOUR TURN

Make a neat final copy of your research report. Think of a way to share your work. Some ideas are given in the **Sharing Suggestions** box below.

SHARING SUGGESTIONS

Illustrate your report and make a cover for it. Keep it in the classroom library.	Make a science magazine with your class. Include your reports and diagrams or pictures.	Read your report aloud to a friend or relative.

4 SPEAKING AND LISTENING: Giving an Oral Report

You have just written a research report. Your report presented your ideas about a topic, which you supported with facts and details. Now you can use what you know about writing reports to give an oral report.

First, you will want to make an outline for your oral report. The outline should include your topic and the main points you plan to discuss. Look at the outline below.

Lemmings

I Introduction
  A. Small rodents
  B. Strange migration

II Facts about lemmings
  A. Live in Arctic
  B. Live in groups

III Migration of lemmings
  A. Caused by overpopulation
  B. Some drown when they reach the sea

IV Conclusion
  A. Summary
  B. What we can learn about overpopulation

Notice that the information contained in the outline shows the main points that the student's talk will include. How does the outline show how the points are ordered?

When you give an oral report, it will help you to keep your **purpose** and **audience** in mind. These speaking guidelines will help you to focus your oral report.

SPEAKING GUIDELINES: An Oral Report

1. Remember your **purpose** and **audience**.
2. Make an outline. Practice using the outline.
3. Make sure your outline has an introduction, a body, and a conclusion.
4. Look at your listeners and speak in a strong, clear voice.
5. Prepare to answer questions when you finish.

- What is the main idea of my oral report?
- Does my information support this main idea?

SPEAKING APPLICATION An Oral Report

Think of a topic that would make an interesting oral report. Prepare an outline to use as you organize the information in your report. Use the speaking guidelines to help you prepare. Your classmates will be using the following guidelines as they listen to your report.

LISTENING GUIDELINES: An Oral Report

1. Listen for the main idea of the report.
2. Listen for a clear introduction, body, and conclusion.
3. Listen for interesting facts and details.

5 WRITER'S RESOURCES: The Atlas and the Almanac

In this unit you have researched information in order to prepare written and oral reports. You have learned that it is important to find accurate facts and details. Two useful resources for the writer are the atlas and the almanac.

An **atlas** is a book of maps. Some atlases have tables of the population, climate, and size of the countries of the world.

Imagine that you are a researcher. You are about to travel to Venezuela to study an unusual bird. You will write a report on your findings. First, you want to learn something about the area you will visit. You would use an atlas to find a map of Venezuela.

This map shows the countries that border Venezuela. You can see where the main river flows and what the capital city is.

Imagine that you will be exploring along the Orinoco River. You might wonder how the river compares in length to other rivers you have explored. You would look up rivers in an **almanac**. Here is part of a table you might find in an almanac.

World Rivers — Length in Miles			
River	Length	River	Length
Niger	2,590	Ohio	975
Nile	4,145	Orinoco	1,600
Oder	567		

From this table you can see that the Orinoco is much longer than the Ohio River, but less than half the length of the Nile.

Almanacs contain many kinds of information. New almanacs are published every year. They contain facts about population, current events and history, people, sports, and many other things.

Practice

A researcher must find the answers to many questions. Write **atlas** or **almanac** to tell where you can find the answer to each of the following questions.

1. Is Angel Falls the highest waterfall anywhere?
2. What islands lie off the coast of Venezuela?
3. Does Venezuela export oil?
4. How much United States aid is sent to Venezuela each year?
5. Do Brazil and Venezuela share a border?
6. Do I cross Cuba when I fly to Venezuela from the United States?
7. What is the average income of a Venezuelan?
8. When did Europeans discover the Orinoco?
9. In what direction does the Orinoco flow?
10. Does the Equator run through Venezuela?

WRITING APPLICATION Questions

Imagine that you are about to travel to some country or place that interests you. Write ten questions about the place you choose. Then use an atlas and an almanac to answer the questions. Keep this information in your writing folder. You might wish to create a record of interesting facts for your own use.

THE CURRICULUM CONNECTION

Writing About Computers

Today, computers aid us in everything we do, from getting a weather forecast to finding a book in the library. Many professional writers use computers. There are also people who write about computers and explain their uses.

ACTIVITIES

Computer Diary Watch for computers as you go through your day. Record everything you do that involves a computer. Remember that some watches and calculators have computers in them. Share your diary with others.

Summarize a Flow Chart People who write software often begin by making a flow chart. Many computers work on a simple "yes-no" system. Read this flow chart. Write a three-sentence summary telling what the flow chart shows.

Respond to Literature Computers have some artistic and entertaining uses. The following selection reports on ways that computers can reproduce pictures. After you read the selection, work with a partner to brainstorm for some uses of computer art. Make a list of your ideas.

from Pixels and Patterns

In some shopping malls, you can find people who will take your picture with a TV camera and reproduce the image with a printer on paper or a tee shirt. If you or your school has access to equipment like this, here is an opportunity to explore the principles of TV imaging, digitizing, and the ability of people to recognize a picture when its detail has been reduced. How is the image from the TV camera converted into picture elements, or pixels? How are light values assigned? How are these values converted into a printed image?

Computer art has practical applications as well, beyond those suggested so far. The designing of quilts, needlepoint, and weaving frequently requires that the artist draw out the pattern and then modify and often redraw it, sometimes many times. Computer programs can produce these patterns on the screen and then perhaps reproduce them on paper later. Such programs would allow the artist to make a small change at the keyboard and see the results instantly.

UNIT CHECKUP

LESSON 1

Group Writing: Finding Information and Note Taking (page 472) Turn to page 491 and reread the selection from *Pixels and Patterns*. Take notes on the paragraph as though you were going to write a report about computers.

LESSON 2

Thinking: Summarizing (page 476) Write a two-sentence summary of this news report.

Port Moresby Three American and two French explorers have settled in a village in the interior of New Guinea in hopes of learning more about the people there. The tribe is so remote that the explorers are believed to be the first visitors they have ever had. Reports from the explorers indicate that the villagers rely on stone and wooden tools and have no written language. A film crew tried to reach the village but was unable to pass through the jungle.

LESSON 3

Writing a Research Report (page 478) Imagine that you are a travel agent. You have been asked to write part of a brochure about island vacation spots. Choose any island you think might be interesting. Find information, take notes, and make an outline. Write a four-paragraph report about the island for your brochure.

LESSON 4

Speaking and Listening: An Oral Report (page 486) Imagine that you will give an oral report on a topic of your choice. Write a topic sentence and three facts that support this sentence.

LESSON 5

Writer's Resources: The Atlas and the Almanac (page 488) Write **atlas** or **almanac** to tell where you could find the answers to these questions.

1. What countries border the Persian Gulf?
2. Who is the American ambassador to China?
3. Through which states do the Rocky Mountains run?

THEME PROJECT

Data Chart

You have been reading about investigations of many kinds. In art, science, literature, and in everyday life, there are fascinating topics for investigation.

Whether you are a detective or a scientist, you follow a series of steps in an investigation. First, you pose a question to which you do not have an answer. You may make some guesses about what the answer is. Finally, you must collect facts, or data, to prove or disprove your guesses. You might do this by observing, simply by looking around and noticing clues. Or, you might set up an experiment and look at the results.

Think of some topics which interest you. Work with a small group of your classmates.

- Begin by brainstorming for some ideas.
- Collect data, or information, on a topic and summarize what the information means.
- After you have collected your data, write it in the form of a chart.
- With your classmates, summarize the results of the data.

Writer's Reference

C O N T E N T S

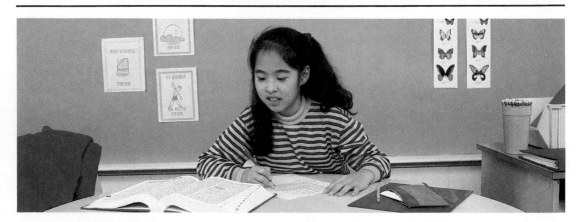

WRITER'S REFERENCE

H A N D B O O K

GRAMMAR

Sentences

A **sentence** is a group of words that expresses a complete thought. A sentence contains a subject and a predicate.

> An Asian cook/prepared the meal.
>   **subject   predicate**

The **subject** tells whom or what the sentence is about. The subject may be one word or more than one word.

> **Sam** skates well. **Sam and Donna** skate well.

The **predicate** tells what the subject does or is. The predicate contains the **verb**, which may be one word or more than one word.

> Cathy **walked** with Jean. The girls **were walking** for hours.

There are four kinds of sentences. Notice the end punctuation of each sentence type.

> I collect stamps. (statement—ends with a period)
> How do you get them? (question—ends with a question mark)
> Ask me questions. (command—ends with a period)
> I love my hobby! (exclamation—ends with an exclamation mark)

A **run-on sentence** joins together two or more sentences incorrectly. Often, they should be written separately.

> I went to the grocery store and on the way there I saw my friend on the other side of the street I called to her and she waved to me.

Divide a run-on sentence into several sentences.

> I went to the grocery store. On the way there, I saw my friend on the other side of the street. I called to her, and she waved to me.

A **sentence fragment** is incomplete.

Add a subject or a predicate to complete a sentence fragment.

The river water rushed past me.

The river water.   (fragment—no predicate)
Rushed past me.   (fragment—no subject)

Nouns

A **noun** is a word that names a person, place, thing, or idea.

student   farm   book   democracy

A **singular noun** names one person, place, thing, or idea.

girl   store   jar   skill

A **plural** noun names more than one person, place, thing, or idea. Add **s** to most singular nouns to make them plural.

girls   stores   jars   skills

If a singular noun ends in **s**, **z**, **x**, **sh**, or **ch**, add **es** to form the plural.

glass—glasses   waltz—waltzes   fox—foxes   brush—brushes
lunch—lunches

If a singular noun ends in a vowel and **y**, add **s**.

toy—toys   boy—boys

If a singular noun ends in a consonant and **y**, change the **y** to **i**, and add **es**.

country—countries   lily—lilies

If a singular noun ends in **f** or **fe**, change the **f** to **v**, and add **es** to some nouns. Add **s** to other nouns.

wife—wives   cliff—cliffs

If a singular noun ends in a vowel and **o**, add **s**.

stereo—stereos   video—videos

If a singular noun ends in a consonant and **o**, add **s** or **es**.

silo—silos   hero—heroes

Some nouns are **irregular nouns**. You must memorize the plurals of irregular nouns.

deer—deer   ox—oxen   foot—feet

A **plural possessive noun** shows what more than one person or thing owns. If a plural noun ends in **s**, an **apostrophe** is added to form the plural possessive.

   horses' hooves   the girls' team

If a plural noun does not end in **s**, **'s** is added to form the plural possessive.

   children**'s** stories   men**'s** hats

A **possessive noun** is a noun that shows ownership.

A **singular possessive noun** shows what one person or thing owns. Usually, **'s** is added to singular nouns to form a singular possessive.

   Sandy**'s** painting   the cat**'s** paw

Verbs

A **verb** expresses action or tells what something is or is like.

   count   counted   is   was

The **time** expressed by a verb is called its **tense**.

Present tense expresses action that is happening now.

   I **close** the door. (present)

Past tense expresses action that has already happened.

   I **closed** the door. (past)

Future tense expresses action that has not yet happened.

   I **will close** the door. (future)

Most verbs add **d** or **ed** to form their past tense.

   dance—danced   work—worked

An **irregular** verb does not add **d** or **ed** to form its past tense.

Present	Past	Past with has, have, had
go	went	gone
fly	flew	flown
break	broke	broken
ride	rode	ridden
throw	threw	thrown

Adjectives

An **adjective** is a word that describes a noun. An adjective tells **what kind** or **how many**.

red dress   **small** cup   **long** hair   **six** elephants

Articles

A, **an**, and **the** are special adjectives called **articles**.

Use **a** before a singular noun beginning with a consonant. Use **an** before a singular noun beginning with a vowel. Use **the** before plural nouns and before singular nouns that name a particular person, place, or thing.

a rock on **a** beach   **an** answer to your question   **the** pages of **the** book

Pronouns

A **pronoun** is a word that takes the place of one or more nouns and the words that go with the nouns.

Subject pronouns are used in the subject part of sentences. Subject pronouns are also used after forms of the linking verb *be*.

Subject pronouns: I, you, he, she, it, we, they

Object pronouns are used after verbs and after words such as *into*, *of*, *with*, and *to*.

Object Pronouns: me, you, him, her, it, us, them

Possessive pronouns show who or what owns something.

Possessive Pronouns: my, mine, your, yours, his, her, hers, its, our, ours, their, theirs

Adverbs

An **adverb** is a word that tells more about a verb. An adverb tells **how**, **where**, or **when**.

She runs **quickly**.	(how)
He ran **downhill**.	(where)
They will leave **later**.	(when)

To make an adjective into an adverb, add **ly**.

polite—polite**ly**   rude—rude**ly**

Prepositions

A **preposition** is a word that relates a noun or pronoun to another word in a sentence.

> Pat saw a parrot **at** the zoo.
> It sat **on** a branch.

A **prepositional phrase** is a group of words that begins with a preposition and ends with a noun or pronoun.

> Pat saw a parrot **at the zoo.**
> The parrot perched **near her**.

The noun or pronoun that follows a preposition is called the **object of the preposition**.

> The parrot flew around the **cage.**
> The bird looked happy to **me.**

When the object of a preposition is a pronoun, use an object pronoun: *me, you, him, her, it, us,* or *them.*

> Pat told Janet about **Robert.**
> Pat told Janet about **him.**

MECHANICS

Punctuation

End Punctuation

Use **end punctuation** to end a sentence.

> A **period** (.) ends a **statement** or a **command.**
> A **question mark** (?) ends a **question.**
> An **exclamation mark** (!) ends an **exclamation.**

> I have a cold.   (statement)
> Take your medicine. (command)
> Will I get well?   (question)
> I finally feel better!   (exclamation)

Periods

Use a **period** to show the end of an abbreviation and with initials.

Apr.   Sat.   Dr.   St.   Co.   Sally K. Ride

Lyndon B. Johnson

Colons

Use a **colon** to separate hours and minutes in time.

3:25   7:15   4:30

Use a **colon** after the greeting of a business letter.

Dear Sir: Dear Mr. Lee:

Commas

Use a **comma** between the names of cities and states.

Bangor, Maine   Houston, Texas

Use a **comma** between the day and the year in dates.

December 7, 1941   July 20, 1969

Use a **comma** to separate words in a series.

Joan's dress is blue, green, and yellow.

Use two commas to set off an **appositive**, a group of words that tells more about the subject.

Joe, a good student, enjoys science class.

Use a **comma** after introductory words or phrases in a sentence.

Yes, I enjoyed the meal you cooked.

Use a **comma** with nouns in direct address.

Jane, are you hungry?

Use **commas** to set off a direct quotation in a sentence.

"Do you know," she asked, "what time it is?"

Use a **comma** before *and*, *but*, or *or* in a compound sentence.

I love winter, but Pat enjoys fall.
The weather is cold, and it is windy.
Mike will buy a copy of his favorite book, or he will borrow it.

Apostrophes

Use **apostrophes (')** in contractions to show where letters are missing.

won't   they'll

Use **apostrophes** with nouns to show possession. Add **'s** to singular nouns or plural nouns that do not end in **s**.

Mary**'s** cat   Joe**'s** house   women**'s** suits

Add an ' alone to plural nouns ending in **s**.

jars' tops   coats' collars

Hyphens

Use a **hyphen** to connect two words to form compound words, or to join syllables of a word that have been separated.

half-hour   drive-in

Quotation Marks

Put **quotation marks** before and after a direct quotation. Do **not** use quotation marks unless you use the speaker's exact words.

"I do not want any potatoes," said Paul.
Paul said that he did not want any potatoes.

Put **quotation marks** before and after the title of a short story, a song, a poem, or a chapter title.

"Cinderella"   "America the Beautiful"

Underlining

Underline the titles of books, newspapers, magazines, and movies.

<u>Black Beauty</u>   <u>The New York Times</u>

Capitalization

Capitalize the names of specific persons, pets, places, or things.

Abraham Lincoln   Spot   Maine   Jefferson Memorial

Capitalize initials.

John F. Kennedy   Franklin D. Roosevelt

Capitalize titles of respect when they are part of a specific name.

President Eisenhower   Doctor Jonas Salk

Always capitalize the first-person pronoun **I**.

Capitalize the first, last, and all important words in the title of a book, newspaper, song, poem, play, short story, or movie.

<u>Julie of the Wolves</u>
''The Elves and the Shoemaker''
''Jingle Bells''

Capitalize family names if they refer to specific people.

I told Father about my project.
The mother penguin protected her chick.

Capitalize the days of the week and the months of the year.

Sunday   Wednesday   May   November

Capitalize the names of holidays and religious days.

Valentine's Day   Memorial Day   Easter

Capitalize the names of specific cities, states, countries, continents, rivers, oceans, and other geographic locations.

Tacoma   Oregon   Spain   Europe
Hudson River   Atlantic Ocean   Niagara Falls

Capitalize the names of streets and avenues.

Main Street   Third Avenue

Capitalize the titles of specific clubs, organizations, and companies.

Explorers' Club
Federal Bureau of Investigation
General Foods Corporation

Capitalize proper adjectives.

German   Mexican   Vietnamese   Egyptian

Capitalize the first word in a sentence. Capitalize the first word in a quotation.

She asked, ''Where does Mickey think he is going?''

Capitalize all the words in the greeting of a letter.

Dear Sir:

Capitalize only the first word in a letter's closing.

Yours truly,

Capitalize the first word of each main topic and subtopic in an outline.
Put a period after each Roman numeral and capital letter in an outline.

I. Types of mammals
    A. Land mammals
    B. Sea mammals

Abbreviations

Capitalize and put a period after abbreviations used in titles of respect.

Sen.   Mrs.   Prof.

Capitalize and put a period after abbreviations of addresses.

Rd.   Ave.   Pl.

Capitalize and put a period after abbreviations for days and months.

Thurs.   Sun.   Sept.   Dec.

Use the **United States Postal Service** abbreviations for state names.
Notice that each abbreviation consists of two capital letters. No period
follows these abbreviations.

AL (Alabama)	LA (Louisiana)	OH (Ohio)
AK (Alaska)	ME (Maine)	OK (Oklahoma)
AZ (Arizona)	MD (Maryland)	OR (Oregon)
AR (Arkansas)	MA (Massachusetts)	PA (Pennsylvania)
CA (California)	MI (Michigan)	RI (Rhode Island)
CO (Colorado)	MN (Minnesota)	SC (South Carolina)
CT (Connecticut)	MS (Mississippi)	SD (South Dakota)
DE (Delaware)	MO (Missouri)	TN (Tennessee)
FL (Florida)	MT (Montana)	TX (Texas)
GA (Georgia)	NE (Nebraska)	UT (Utah)
HI (Hawaii)	NV (Nevada)	VT (Vermont)
ID (Idaho)	NH (New Hampshire)	VA (Virginia)
IL (Illinois)	NJ (New Jersey)	WA (Washington)
IN (Indiana)	NM (New Mexico)	WV (West Virginia)
IA (Iowa)	NY (New York)	WI (Wisconsin)
KS (Kansas)	NC (North Carolina)	WY (Wyoming)
KY (Kentucky)	ND (North Dakota)	

USAGE

Verbs

Avoid changing from one tense to another in a sentence.

> The doorbell **rang**, and Lori **runs** to answer it.
> (incorrect: past to present)
> The doorbell **rang**, and Lori **ran** to answer it.
> (correct: both past)

Subjects and verbs must **agree** in **number**. If a subject is singular, the verb must be singular as well. If a subject is plural, the verb must be plural as well.

> The **dog scratches** its ear. (singular subject and verb)
> The **dogs scratch** their ears. (plural subject and verb)

Adjectives

If an adjective compares two nouns, the adjective usually ends in **er**.

> Saturday was a **colder** day than Friday.
> You need a **heavier** sweater than that blue one.

If an adjective compares more than two nouns, the adjective usually ends in **est**.

> The **loudest** thunderclap of all frightened Sparky. He is the **youngest** of our three cats.

Some adjectives use **more** and **most** to show comparison. Use **more** to compare two nouns.

> Sparky is **more** frightened than Ginger.

Use **most** to compare more than two nouns.

> The **most** adventurous of the cats is Pepper.

Do not combine **er** with the word **more**.
Do not combine **est** with the word **most.**

> Li is **quieter** than his sister. (correct)
> Li is **more quieter** than his sister. (incorrect)
> In fact, Li is the **quietest** person in his whole family. (correct)
> In fact, Li is the **most quietest** person in his whole family. (incorrect)

Pronouns

Use a **subject pronoun** as the subject of a sentence.

> **We** entered the bicycle race.
> **He** was the winner.

Use an **object pronoun** after a verb and after words such as *to*, *with*, *for*, and *at*.

> Mr. Stewart drove **us** home.
> Please take a walk with **me**.

The pronouns **I** and **me** are **personal pronouns.** When you use **I** or **me** with another pronoun or a noun, always put the personal pronoun last.

> She and **I** hurried to school.
> The teacher returned the papers to José and **me**.

The pronouns **we** and **us** have their own rules, too. Use **we** with a noun that is a subject or that follows a linking verb.

> **We** singers practice daily.
> The best cellists are **we**.

Use **us** with a noun that follows an action verb or that follows a preposition such as **to**, **for**, **with**, or **at**.

> The conductor praised **us** musicians.
> The praise was meant for **us**.

Every pronoun refers to a noun. A pronoun must agree with the noun to which it refers.

> Lisa bought the **toy** and handed **it** to the baby.
> The **puppies** wagged **their** tails.

Double Negatives

Negatives are words that mean **no**.

Some examples of negatives are **no**, **never**, **none**, **not**, and **nothing**. Use only one negative in a sentence.

> I **never** saw **any**. (correct: single negative)
> I **never** saw **none**. (incorrect: double negative)

Troublesome Words

Some words or word pairs are easy to confuse.

Good and **bad** are adjectives. They describe nouns.

This is a **good** movie.   That is a **bad** joke.

Well and **badly** are adverbs. They tell more about verbs.

They sing **well**.   She dances **badly**.

Use **well** when talking about health.

Chris felt **well** yesterday.

When you use **good** and **bad** to compare, you must change their forms. Use **better** or **worse** to compare two items. Use **best** or **worst** to compare three or more items.

Breakfast today was **better** than breakfast yesterday.
Maybe breakfast tomorrow will be the **best** of the week.

Its is a possessive pronoun. Do not use an apostrophe with a possessive pronoun. **It's** is a contraction meaning "it is."

The squirrel buried **its** acorn.
Jay thinks **it's** the prettiest tree in the park.

Your is a possessive pronoun meaning "belonging to you."

Is that **your** jacket?

You're is a contraction meaning "you are."

You're going to leave at noon.

Their is a possessive pronoun meaning "belonging to them."

My grandparents have a telephone in **their** kitchen.

There is an adverb that tells "where."

I left my keys on the table over **there**.

They're is a contraction meaning "they are."

They're coming to see us soon.

Two is a number. **Too** means "also" or "very." **To** is a direction word meaning "toward."

William has **two** pets named Fred, **too**!   Her rabbit hops **too** quickly.
They went **to** the park on different days.

THESAURUS FOR WRITING

What Is a Thesaurus?

A **thesaurus** is a reference book that can be very useful in your writing. It provides synonyms for many common words. **Synonyms** are words that mean almost the same thing.

The thesaurus can help you choose more interesting words and more exact words to use in your writing. For example, read this sentence.

Diane **looked** at her sister.

Looked is not a very interesting word, and it says very little about Diane. If you check the word *look* in the thesaurus, you will find these words: *glance, peer, stare*. Using one of these words would make your sentence more interesting and more precise.

Using the Thesaurus

The words in a thesaurus are listed in alphabetical order. If the word is listed in the thesaurus, you will find an entry. For example, if you looked up the word *right*, you would find this **main entry**.

The word *right* is called an **entry word**. The information that follows is called the **entry**.

Cross-references. In some cases you will find cross-references. For example, if you look up the word *small*, you will find this cross-reference: "*See* little." This means that you should look up the word *little*; the word *small* will be listed under *little*.

A

agree *v.* to say "yes"; to have the same opinion; to be in harmony. Jan and Ted couldn't *agree* on what movie to see.

concur to have the same opinion. The members of the jury *concurred* that the witness was lying.

consent to give permission or approval. Will your mother *consent* to your going on the field trip?

allow *See* let.

angry *adj.* feeling or showing anger. When Lenny gets *angry*, he refuses to speak to anyone.

enraged filled with rage; angry beyond control. *Enraged* by her friend's note, Maria ripped it into a thousand tiny pieces.

furious extremely angry. Your brother will be *furious* when he finds out you ruined his bike.

answer *v.* to give a spoken or written response. I wonder whether Celia is ever going to *answer* my letter.

reply to say in response. If he insults you, don't *reply*; just walk away.

respond to give an answer. James did not *respond* to my question.

antonyms: ask, inquire

ask *v.* to put a question to. Let's *ask* that man for directions.

inquire to seek information by asking questions. Tom called the store to *inquire* about the sale.

question to try to get information (from someone). Bill's mother *questioned* him about where he had been.

antonyms: *See* answer.

awful *adj.* causing fear, dread, or awe. The tree made an *awful* noise when it fell.

dreadful causing great fear. Lydia is still in shock from her *dreadful* experience.

terrible causing terror or awe. Jason received some *terrible* news.

B

beautiful *adj.* full of beauty; having qualities that are pleasing. What a *beautiful* dog!

attractive appealing or pleasing but not in an exceptional way. They have an *attractive* house.

gorgeous extremely beautiful or richly colored. What a *gorgeous* rose garden!

lovely beautiful in a comforting way. Ben has a *lovely* voice.

antonyms: ugly, hideous, unattractive

big *adj.* of great size. Do you have any *big* boxes?

enormous much greater than the usual size. There is an *enormous* spider in the bathtub.

huge extremely big. That *huge* man is a football player.
large of great size; big. Paula seldom has such a *large* lunch.
antonyms: See little.

brave *adj*. willing to face danger; without fear. A person has to be *brave* to work with wild lions.
bold showing courage; fearless. Although Kevin acted *bold*, he was really very nervous.
courageous having courage. The pioneers who settled this country were *courageous* people.
daring willing to take risks. The audience gasped at the circus performer's *daring* feat.
antonyms: afraid, fearful.

break *v*. to come apart; to separate into pieces. These glass animals *break* easily.
crack to break without fully separating. Put the egg in the water slowly, or the shell will *crack*.
fracture to break or split a bone. Juan *fractured* his ankle and had to leave the game.
shatter to break suddenly into many pieces. If you drop that vase, it will *shatter*.

bright *adj*. filled with light; shining. Is that light *bright* enough to read by?

brilliant shining or sparkling with light. The king's crown was decorated with *brilliant* gems.
shiny shining; bright. Her blue coat has *shiny* silver buttons.
antonyms: dark, dull

C

clean *adj*. without dirt or stain. Be sure your hands are *clean* before you handle these pictures.
immaculate perfectly clean. For his first day at school, George put on an *immaculate* white shirt and a tie.
pure free from contamination. Is your well water *pure*?
spotless extremely clean. By the time the guests arrived, the house was *spotless*.
antonyms: dirty, filthy, messy

cold *adj*. having a low temperature; lacking warmth or heat. There is *cold* water in the refrigerator.
chilly uncomfortably cool. I put on a sweater because I was *chilly*.
icy very cold. The room felt *icy* because the furnace had been shut off.
antonyms: See hot.

collect *v*. to gather or bring (things) together. Sara and Louis both *collected* stamps.
assemble to gather or bring together, especially people. The marching band *assembled* in front of the town hall.

collect (continued)

compile to collect and put together (information), as in a list or report. They *compiled* a list of the mayor's supporters.

gather to bring together in one place or group. All the campers *gathered* around the campfire.

cook *v.* to prepare food for eating, using heat. Dad will *cook* dinner.

bake to cook in an oven. Alice put the bread in the oven to *bake*.

broil to cook by exposing to a flame or another source of intense heat. We're going to *broil* the hamburgers over charcoal.

roast to cook with very little moisture, in an oven or over an open fire. The directions said to *roast* the turkey for five hours.

cry *v.* to shed tears. The last scene of the movie was so sad that it made me *cry*.

sob to cry with short gasps. The lost child *sobbed* until his parents found him.

weep to show grief, joy, or other strong emotions by crying. The letter from her mother made Sofia *weep* with homesickness.

antonyms: See laugh.

D

do *v.* to carry out. Some days I can't *do* anything right.

execute to complete, often when told to do so; to put into effect. The job of the President is to *execute* the laws of Congress.

perform to carry out to completion. The acrobats will now *perform* a triple back flip.

dry *adj.* not wet; free of moisture. Is the paint *dry* yet?

arid dry as a result of having little rainfall. Nothing grows here because the land is so *arid*.

parched dried out by heat. The lotion felt good on my *parched* skin.

antonyms: See wet.

E

easy *adj.* requiring little mental or physical effort; not difficult. The math problems were so *easy* that Sheila did them in no time.

facile not hard to do or achieve; done easily and quickly. There is no *facile* solution to the problem of acid rain.

simple not complicated. The kit came with *simple* directions that were easy to follow.

antonyms: hard, difficult

F

far *adj.* a long way off; not near. The house is too *far* to see from here.

distant extremely far. Many sailors went to sea so they could visit *distant* lands.

remote faraway, in an out-of-the-way place. It took us three days to

climb to the *remote* mountain village.
antonyms: near, close

fast *adj.* moving or done with speed. A *fast* typist can type more than 100 words per minute.
quick done in a very short time. She gave a *quick* response.
rapid with great speed, often in a continuing way. Jeff kept walking at a *rapid* pace.
swift moving with great speed, often said of animals or people. A *swift* runner was sent to warn the nearby villages.
antonym: slow

funny *adj.* causing laughter. I heard a *funny* story on the radio.
amusing causing smiles of enjoyment or laughter. Harriet found the monkeys very *amusing*.
comical causing laughter through actions. The baby made all kinds of *comical* faces.
hilarious very funny and usually noisy. *Hilarious* laughter came from the party next door.

G

get *v.* to go for and return with. Did you *get* the package at the post office?
acquire to come into possession of through effort. How did she *acquire* so much money?

obtain to get as one's own, often with some difficulty. First, you'll have to *obtain* a parade permit.

give *v.* to turn over possession or control of; to make a present of. I want to *give* you this book.
confer to give as an honor. The college will *confer* an honorary degree upon the guest speaker.
contribute to give or supply in common with others. We are asking you to *contribute* $3.00.
grant to give in response to a request. *Grant* me this favor, and I promise never to ask again.

present to give in a formal way, usually something of value. Miss Kingsley *presented* a check for $5,000 to the Disaster Fund.
antonyms: *See* take.

good *adj.* above average in quality. He wanted a *good* meal.
excellent extremely good. This is an *excellent* book.
fair somewhat good; slightly better than average. He was a *fair* musician but a very good composer.
fine of high quality; very good. *Fine* jewelry is usually expensive.
antonyms: bad, poor
See also great.

great *adj.* of unusual quality or ability. Picasso was a *great* artist.
remarkable having unusual qualities. The actors did a *remarkable* job.

great (continued)

superb of greater quality than most. That was a *superb* dinner. *See also* good.

H

happy *adj.* having, showing, or bringing pleasure. Their visit made Mrs. Johnson very *happy*.

glad feeling or expressing joy or pleasure. We are so *glad* you were able to join us.

joyful very happy; filled with joy. A wedding is a *joyful* occasion.

merry happy and cheerful. Suzanne is such a *merry* person that she cheered me up right away.

pleased satisfied or content. Was he *pleased* with his presents?

antonyms: *See* sad.

hard *adj.* not easy to do or deal with. These problems are *hard*.

difficult hard to do; requiring effort. The hikers planned a *difficult* climb.

tough difficult to do, often in a physical sense. We had a *tough* time finding all our lost sheep.

antonym: easy

help *v.* to provide with support; to be of service to. Mom will *help* me with my homework.

aid to give help to (someone in trouble). The Red Cross *aided* the flood victims.

assist to help, often in a cooperative way. The whole class will *assist* with the project.

high *adj.* located or extending a great distance above the ground. The eagle nested on a *high* cliff.

lofty very high; of grand or inspiring height. Above the valley rose a range of *lofty* mountain peaks.

tall having a height greater than average but with a relatively narrow width. Over the years, the pine trees grew to be very *tall*.

towering of great or imposing height. The city's *towering* buildings made Luis feel small.

antonyms: low, short

hot *adj.* having a high temperature; having much heat. This pan is *hot*.

fiery as hot as fire; burning. Inside the volcano's crater was a *fiery* pool of lava.

scalding hot enough to burn, often said of liquids. I got a bad burn from some *scalding* water.

scorching intensely hot, enough to cause burning or drying. Few plants can survive the *scorching* desert sun.

torrid extremely hot, often said of weather. The pool was crowded during last week's *torrid* weather.

antonyms: *See* cold.

hurt *v.* to cause pain or damage. I fell out of bed and *hurt* myself.

harm to do damage to. An early frost will *harm* the crops.

injure to cause physical damage. Warm up before you exercise, or you might *injure* yourself.

I

interesting *adj.* arousing or holding interest or attention. Mr. Wu gave an *interesting* talk.

captivating capturing and holding the attention by beauty or excellence. The tourists found the village a *captivating* place.

fascinating causing and holding the interest through a special quality or charm. I just read a *fascinating* book about the history of the space program.

inspiring having a rousing effect; arousing interest. Her *inspiring* example gave courage to others.

antonyms: dull, boring

L

large *See* big.

laugh *v.* to make the sounds and facial movements that show amusement. They sang songs to make the baby *laugh*.

chuckle to laugh softly, especially to oneself. The thought of Jo's surprise made Kim *chuckle*.

giggle to laugh in a silly, high-pitched, or nervous way. The two friends *giggled* over their joke.

guffaw to laugh loudly. When Rick *guffawed*, everyone looked to see what was so funny.

antonyms: *See* cry.

let *v.* to give permission to. Will Kyle *let* me borrow his bike?

allow to grant permission to or for, usually in relation to rules. Talking is not *allowed* in the library.

permit to allow to do something. The club members decided to *permit* him to join.

antonyms: deny, refuse, forbid

like *v.* to take pleasure in (something); to feel affection for (someone). They *like* cats.

admire to have affection and respect for (someone). All the team members *admire* their coach.

enjoy to take pleasure in (something). They *enjoy* playing chess together.

love to like (something) a lot; to feel great affection for (someone). The children *love* that old mutt.

antonyms: dislike, hate

little *adj.* small in size; not big. Inside the cage were two big monkeys and one *little* one.

small not large. Violets are *small* flowers.

tiny extremely small. A watch has many *tiny* parts.

wee very small. The dollhouse kitchen had some *wee* dishes.

antonyms: *See* big.

look *v.* to see with one's eyes. *Look at what I found!*
   glance to look quickly. The spy *glanced* over his shoulder to make sure he wasn't being followed.
   peer to look closely. We *peered* through the window of the shop.
   stare to look at for a long time with eyes wide open. Mac *stared* at me as though I were crazy. *See also* see.

loud *adj.* having a strong sound. The band was playing *loud* music.
   deafening loud enough to make one deaf. The exciting goal brought *deafening* cheers from the fans.
   noisy full of sounds, often unpleasant. Their apartment is located above a *noisy* street.

antonyms: *See* quiet.

M

mad *See* angry.

many *adj.* consisting of a large number. Jenna has *many* friends.
   numerous a great many. I have *numerous* chores to get done today.
   plenty (of) enough, or more than enough, suggesting a large number. There is *plenty* of food for lunch.
   several more than a few but less than many. Harold checked out *several* books about mountain climbing from the library.
   antonym: few

mean *adj.* lacking in kindness or understanding. Maya felt bad about being *mean* to her sister.
   nasty resulting from hate. The villain wore a *nasty* sneer.
   selfish concerned only about oneself. Pattie is so *selfish* that she never shares anything.
   spiteful filled with ill feelings toward others. It's best to leave Dan alone when he's feeling *spiteful*.
   antonyms: *See* nice.

N

neat *adj.* clean and orderly. Her homework is always very *neat*.
   tidy neat and clean, often said of a place. We raked the yard to make it look *tidy*.
   well-groomed carefully dressed and groomed. You should be *well-groomed* when you apply for a job.
   antonyms: messy, untidy, sloppy

new *adj.* having just come into being, use, or possession. They are building a *new* house.
   fresh new or seeming new and unaffected by time or use. We put a *fresh* coat of paint on the old kitchen table.
   modern having to do with the present time; up-to-date. Technology is important in *modern* American life.
   recent referring to a time just before the present. Critics have praised her most *recent* book.

antonym: old

nice *adj.* agreeable or pleasing. Her parents are extremely *nice*.
　gentle mild and kindly in manner. Grandpa's *gentle* words made Lisa feel much better.
　kind gentle and friendly; good-hearted. It is *kind* of you to offer to help.
　pleasant agreeable; giving pleasure to. Georgia and Scott are always such *pleasant* company.
　sweet having or marked by agreeable or pleasing qualities. He wrote a *sweet* thank-you note.
　antonyms: *See* mean.

O

often *adv.* many times; again and again. James is *often* late.
　frequently happening again and again. The two families get together *frequently*.
　regularly happening at fixed times. It is a good idea to exercise *regularly*.
　antonyms: seldom, rarely

old *adj.* having lived or existed for a long time. The *old* car broke down.
　aged having grown old. Our *aged* dog sleeps most of the time.
　ancient of great age; very old; of times long past. We visited the ruins of an *ancient* city.
　antonym: young; *see also* new.

P

plain *adj.* not distinguished from others in any way. The meal was *plain* but hearty.
　common average or standard; not distinguished. Measles are a *common* childhood illness.
　ordinary plain; average; everyday. Super Food is just an *ordinary* grocery store.
　antonym: special
　See also unusual.

proud *adj.* having a sense of one's own worth, usually in a positive way. He was *proud* of his family's background.
　conceited having too high an opinion of oneself, in a negative way. Being popular has made Gary *conceited*.
　haughty having or showing much pride in oneself. The actress is too *haughty* to sign autographs.
　vain overly concerned with or proud of oneself. José is *vain* about his looks.
　antonym: humble

Q

quiet *adj.* with little or no noise. The woods were *quiet* tonight.
　calm free of excitement or strong feeling; quiet. Sue remained *calm* as she waited to be rescued.
　peaceful calm; undisturbed. He spent a *peaceful* morning fishing.

quiet (continued)
   silent completely quiet; without noise. The room was *silent* after the principal's announcement.
   still without sound; silent. The house was *still* and dark.
   antonyms: loud, noisy

R

ready *adj.* fit for use or action. Is your costume *ready*?
   prepared ready or fit for a particular purpose. We were not *prepared* for our cousins' visit.
   set ready or prepared to do something. Everything was *set* for the picnic.

really *adv.* in fact. Was your dad *really* in the Olympics?
   actually in fact; really. Grandpa says he's 100 years old, but he's *actually* only 70.
   indeed really; truly. The person you met was *indeed* my sister.
   truly in fact; really. Their garden was *truly* spectacular.

right *adj.* free from error; true. Her answers are always *right*.
   accurate without errors or mistakes. The witness gave an *accurate* description of the thief.
   correct agreeing with fact or truth. Is this the *correct* way to put it together?
   exact very accurate; completely correct. Get *exact* change for the bus.

antonyms: wrong, mistaken

rude *adj.* not polite; ill-mannered. *Rude* people never say thank you.
   discourteous without good manners. It is *discourteous* to keep people waiting.
   impolite not showing good manners. Randy's *impolite* remarks made Mr. Parsons angry.
   antonyms: polite, courteous

run *v.* to go quickly on foot. Milo can *run* very fast.
   dash to go very fast; to run with sudden speed. Lou *dashed* to the telephone to report the accident.
   race to run very fast; to run in competition with. Sharon *raced* Mitch to the corner.
   scurry to move hurriedly. Mr. Flynn *scurried* about town, trying to get all his errands done.
   sprint to run at top speed for a short distance. Janet *sprinted* after the departing bus.

S

sad *adj.* feeling or showing unhappiness or sorrow. I know you're *sad* that they moved away.
   downcast low in spirits; sad. Ollie was *downcast* about the rain.

   miserable extremely unhappy. Peg was *miserable* until she made some friends in her new school.
   antonyms: *See* happy.

same *adj.* being just like something else in kind, quantity, or degree. They both gave the *same* answer.
alike similar, showing a resemblance. All three of the kittens look *alike*.
equal the same in size, amount, quality, or value. Each child got an *equal* share of the cake.
identical the same in every detail. The chair is *identical* to the one in the museum.
antonym: different

say *v.* to make known or express in words. Candidates always *say* they will be fair and honest.
declare to make known publicly or formally. The umpire *declared* that the game was canceled.
pronounce to say formally or officially that something is so. The jury *pronounced* him guilty.
speak to express an idea, a fact, or a feeling. Dr. Garcia will *speak* to the class about health habits.
state to express or explain fully in words. Mr. Jones *stated* his plan.
talk to express ideas or information by means of speech; to speak. We often *talk* about sports.
See also tell.

scared *adj.* afraid; alarmed. "I'm not *scared* of ghosts," he said.
afraid feeling fear, often in a continuing way or for a long time. Nick is *afraid* to fly in a plane.

fearful filled with fear. The child is *fearful* of strangers.
frightened scared suddenly or for a short time. They were *frightened* until the storm ended.
terrified extremely scared; filled with terror. I've always been *terrified* of dogs.

see *v.* to receive information, impressions, etc., through use of the eyes. She could *see* the river from her window.
observe to notice. Did you *observe* anyone leaving by the back door tonight?
perceive to become aware of through the sight or other senses. I *perceive* that you are unhappy.
view to see or look at, usually for some purpose. Hundreds of people visited the gallery to *view* the artist's work.
See also look.

shy *adj.* uncomfortable in the presence of others. Van was too *shy* to ask Angie to dance.
bashful easily embarrassed; very shy. Don't be *bashful*—come in!
timid showing a lack of courage; easily frightened. Deer are *timid* animals.
antonym: bold

sick *adj.* having poor health. Tom was *sick*, but now he is well.
ill not healthy; sick. He was so *ill* that he could not eat.

THESAURUS

sick (continued)
  unwell not feeling well. You should lie down if you are *unwell*.
  antonyms: well, healthy

small *See* little.

smart *adj*. intelligent; bright; having learned much. There are many *smart* students in her class.
  clever mentally sharp; quick-witted. He gave a *clever* answer.
  intelligent able to learn, understand, and reason. Dolphins seem to be *intelligent* animals.
  shrewd clever or sharp in practical matters. The woman's *shrewd* decisions have made her a success.
  wise able to know or judge what is right, good, or true, often describing a person with good sense rather than one who knows a lot of facts. In this folk tale, a boy is guided by a *wise* woman.
  antonym: stupid

smile *v*. to show a smile, in a happy or friendly way. Our neighbor *smiled* and waved.
  beam to smile joyfully. Dan *beamed* when he received the award.
  grin to smile broadly with great happiness or amusement. Walter *grinned* when he saw the picture.
  smirk to smile in a silly or self-satisfied way. Nina *smirked* foolishly.
  antonyms: frown, scowl

strange *adj*. differing from the usual or the ordinary. We heard a *strange* noise in the basement.
  odd not ordinary. Jo has an *odd* pet.
  weird strange or odd, in a frightening or mysterious way. Kids say the *weird* house is haunted.
  See also unusual.

strong *adj*. having great strength or physical power. It took four *strong* men to move the piano.
  muscular having well-developed muscles; strong. That shirt makes you look *muscular*.
  powerful having great strength, influence, or authority. Their new car has a *powerful* engine.
  antonym: weak

sure *adj*. firmly believing in something. I'm *sure* I'll have a good time once I get there.
  certain free from doubt; very sure. Roy was *certain* he had left the key on the counter.
  confident firmly trusting; sure of oneself or of another. Wendy is *confident* of winning the prize.
  definite positive or certain. They have not made any *definite* plans.
  antonyms: doubtful, unsure

surprised *adj*. feeling sudden wonder. He was *surprised* at how cold it was outside.
  amazed overwhelmed with wonder or surprise. Daria was *amazed*

to learn her father had once been in the circus.

astonished greatly surprised; shocked. Everyone was *astonished* to see Mrs. Buford at the meeting.

astounded greatly surprised; stunned. The judges were *astounded* by the gymnast's performance.

T

take *v.* to get into one's hands or possession; to obtain. May I *take* this book?

grab to take roughly or rudely. Brian *grabbed* the phone and said, "What do you want?"

seize to take suddenly and by force. The rebel army *seized* the tower.

snatch to take suddenly and quickly, often in secret. He *snatched* the letter when she wasn't looking.

antonyms: See give.

talk See say.

tell *v.* to put or express in written or spoken words. May I *tell* you an interesting story?

announce to state or make known publicly. The principal will *announce* a new school program at the assembly.

narrate to tell about events, especially a story. Mr. Bell will *narrate* "Peter and the Wolf."

relate to tell or report events or details. Each boy *related* his side of the argument.
See *also* say.

thin *adj.* not fat. His father has always been rather *thin*.

lean with little or no fat but often strong. She has the *lean*, healthy look of a runner.

slim thin, in a good or healthy way. Exercise is important if you want to stay *slim*.

antonyms: fat, plump, chubby

think *v.* to have in mind as an opinion or attitude. What do you *think* of our new math teacher?

believe to accept as true or real. The police did not *believe* the man's story.

consider to regard; to believe. We *consider* her one of the family.

U

unusual *adj.* not usual, common, or ordinary. Jon writes *unusual* stories.

extraordinary very unusual; beyond the ordinary. Monica is an artist of *extraordinary* talent.

rare seldom happening, seen, or found. Some *rare* plants are protected by law.

uncommon rare or unusual. Such a heavy rain is *uncommon* for July.
See *also* strange.

antonyms: common, usual; *see also* plain.

upset *adj.* feeling uneasy; distressed. Ben is *upset* about the math test.
    anxious uneasy about or fearful of what may happen. The family is *anxious* about Grandma's health.
    concerned troubled or worried. We are *concerned* about the flood.
    worried uneasy or troubled about something. Gene was *worried* that he would not finish in time.
    antonym: calm

V

very *adv.* to a great extent. The basketball player was *very* tall.
    considerably to a large or an important degree. It will be *considerably* colder tomorrow.
    extremely greatly or intensely. May Ling is an *extremely* talented musician.
    somewhat a little, to some extent. We are *somewhat* tired today.

W

walk *v.* to move or travel on foot. She takes the bus, but we *walk*.
    march to walk with regular steps. The band will *march* in the parade.
    stride to walk with long steps, usually with a purpose. Just *stride* right in and tell him.

want *v.* to have a desire or wish for. Craig *wanted* to see you.
    crave to want badly, often in an uncontrollable way. I crave pie.
    desire to have a strong wish for. The group *desired* a leader.
    wish to have a longing or strong need for. I *wish* I were taller.
    yearn to feel a strong and deep desire. The boy *yearned* for rest.

wet *adj.* covered or soaked with water or another liquid. Be careful—the floor is *wet*.
    damp slightly wet. The clothes in the dryer were still *damp*.
    moist slightly wet; damp. The grass was *moist* from the dew.
    sopping extremely wet; dripping. Linda took off her *sopping* shoes.
    antonyms: See dry.

whole *adj.* made up of the entire amount, quantity, or number. How could you eat a *whole* melon?
    complete having all its parts. Make sure the kit is *complete*.
    entire whole; having all its parts. The *entire* week was rainy.
    total whole, full, or entire, often referring to numbers. The *total* bill was $14.27.
    stroll to walk in a relaxed or leisurely manner. Why don't we *stroll* around the block?

LETTER MODELS

You can use these models to help you when you write.

Friendly Letter

3400 Broadway
Dobbs Ferry, NY 10522
July 3, 19—

HEADING

Dear Jennifer,

GREETING

BODY

How is summer camp? My sister and I are going to Maine this year for August. I like summer in our town, though, too. There's so much to do, now that I'm babysitting for my baby brother. Write back and tell me all about camp.

Your friend,
Leslie

CLOSING

SIGNATURE

Thank-You Note

88 Monterey Street
Pittsburgh, PA 15212
January 1, 19—

HEADING

Dear Aunt Jean,

GREETING

BODY

I love the sweater you sent me! Everyone says this shade of blue goes with my eyes. It also goes with my favorite skirt. It's just the kind of sweater I love, and I can't wait to wear it next month when you come for a visit. Thank you so much. See you in February.

Love,
Katie

CLOSING

SIGNATURE

Write the receiver's name, address, and zip code on the front of the envelope. Write your name and address in the upper lefthand corner.

SPELLING STRATEGIES

In your writing, it is very important to spell every word correctly. Otherwise, the meaning of what you write may not be clear. Follow the steps below to help improve your spelling.

1. Learn some basic spelling rules.
2. Learn to spell some commonly misspelled words.
3. Learn to spell words by syllables.
4. Check your work carefully when you have finished writing.
5. Use a dictionary to check your spelling.

Spelling Rules

Here are some rules to help you spell certain kinds of words correctly.

Words with *ie* and *ei*

Spell the word with *ie* when the sound is $\bar{e}$, except after *c*.

Sound is $\bar{e}$: brief, relieve, yield, piece
Except after *c*: deceive, ceiling, conceive

Spell the word with *ei* when the sound is not $\bar{e}$, especially if the sound is $\bar{a}$.

Sound is $\bar{a}$: neigh, weight, eighty, sleigh

There are some exceptions to this rule.

Exceptions: either, seize, weird, friend

Adding *s* and *es*

In most cases, **s** can be added to a noun without changing the spelling.

Examples: frog + s = frogs   band + s = bands

If the word ends in *ch*, *s*, *sh*, *x*, or *z*, add *es*.

Examples: bush/bushes   loss/losses
witch/witches   mix/mixes

Changing *f* to *v*

For most words ending in *f* or *fe*, change the *f* to *v* when adding *s* or *es*.

loaf/loaves   elf/elves   wife/wives

There are some exceptions to this rule.

Exceptions: roof/roofs   chief/chiefs

Words ending in _o_	For most words that end in _o_ following a vowel, add _s_ to form the plural.

Words ending in _o_

For most words that end in _o_ following a vowel, add _s_ to form the plural.

Examples: rodeo + s = rodeos   patio + s = patios

For most words that end in _o_ following a consonant, add **es**.

Examples: hero + es = heroes   tomato + es = tomatoes

halo + es = haloes   echo + es = echoes

Irregular nouns

Some words become plural in irregular ways.

Examples: ox/oxen   child/children

mouse/mice   tooth/teeth

goose/geese

Some words stay the same when singular or plural.

Examples: fish/fish   sheep/sheep

Adding _es_, _ed_, _ing_, _er_ and _est_

If the word ends in a consonant and _y_, change the _y_ to _i_ before any ending that does not begin with _i_.

Examples: lady   ladies   bury   buried

However, for most words that end in a vowel and _y_, keep the _y_ when adding an ending.

Examples: employ   employed   stay   staying

In most cases, if a one-syllable word ends in one vowel and one consonant, double the consonant when adding an ending that begins with a vowel.

Examples: grab   grabbed   glad   gladder

hop   hopping   slim   slimmest

For most two-syllable words ending in one vowel and one consonant, double the consonant only if the accent is on the second syllable.

Examples: refer   referred   begin   beginning

If the word ends in a silent _e_, drop the _e_ when adding an ending that begins with a vowel.

Examples: cute   cuter   love   loving

bare   barest   raise   raised

SPELLING STRATEGIES

Adding prefixes and suffixes

When a prefix is added to a word, the spelling of the word stays the same.

| **Examples:** | pre + heat = preheat |
| | mis + understand = misunderstand |

When a suffix is added to a word, the spelling of the word may change. If the word ends in silent *e*, drop the *e* when adding a suffix that begins with a vowel.

| **Examples:** | wobble + y = wobbly |
| | machine + ist = machinist |

However, for most words ending in silent *e*, keep the *e* when adding a suffix that begins with a consonant.

| **Examples:** | care + ful = careful |
| | measure + less = measureless |

When adding the suffix **ness** or **ly**, the spelling of the word usually does not change.

| **Examples:** | like + ness = likeness |
| | near + ly = nearly |

However, if the word ends in *y* and has more than one syllable, change the *y* to *i*.

| **Examples:** | ready + ness = readiness |
| | merry + ly = merrily |

Homophones

Homophones are often misspelled. Knowing the meanings of homophones will help you choose and spell them correctly. Use your dictionary to check the definition of any homophone about which you are unsure.

| **Examples:** | cent | sent | hair | hare |
| | real | reel | scene | seen |

Contractions and Possessives

Use an apostrophe in a contraction.

| **Examples:** | he + is = he's | was + not = wasn't |

Do not use an apostrophe with a possessive pronoun.

| **Examples:** | hers | ours | yours |
| | its | theirs | his |

OVERVIEW OF THE WRITING PROCESS

In this book you have learned that writing is a process. When you write, you follow certain steps. Sometimes you move back and forth between steps, but basically you proceed from the beginning to the end of the process.

Prewrite

- Decide on a purpose and an audience for your writing.
- Choose a topic that would be suitable for your purpose and audience.
- Explore ideas about your topic. You could brainstorm, make a cluster, or make a list.
- Narrow your topic if it is too broad to cover effectively.

Write a First Draft

- Use your prewriting ideas to write your draft.
- Do not worry too much about making errors. Your goal is to get your ideas on paper.

Revise

- Read your draft. Share it with a partner to get some suggestions.
- Ask yourself these questions about your draft.
  What else will my audience want to know? What details can I add?
  How can I make my purpose clearer?
  How can I make my writing easier to understand?
  How can I improve the organization of my writing?

Proofread

- Read your revised draft.
- Ask yourself these questions about your revised draft.
  Have I followed correct paragraph form?
  Have I used complete sentences?
  Have I used capitalization and punctuation correctly?
  Have I spelled all words correctly?

Publish

- Make a clean copy of your revised and proofread draft.
- Share your writing with the audience for whom you wrote it.

STUDY STRATEGIES

Studying is an important part of learning. These Study Tips will help you to study effectively.

General Study Guides

1. Plan your time carefully.
2. Keep a list of assignments.
3. Decide how much time to spend on each task.
4. Find a quiet, comfortable place to work.
5. Keep study materials handy.

Helpful Study Methods

There are many different ways to study. Two methods, 'SQ3R' and PROTO, are described below.

SQ3R The name stands for the five steps you should follow when you read a unit or a chapter.

1. **Survey** the selection to find out what it is about.
2. Think of **Questions** to help you understand the selection.
3. **Read** the material, look for answers to the questions you made up, and look for important points in what you read.
4. **Record** the important points and answers to the questions by writing them down.
5. **Review** the selection and the notes you have written.

PROTO The name stands for the five steps you should follow when you study all kinds of material.

1. **Preview**. First, preview the material to identify the general idea. Look at the title of the selection. Look at the major headings.
2. **Read**. Second, read the material. Read each part carefully, review the headings, and find the most important points.
3. **Organize**. After you have read the material once, figure out how the most important points should be organized. Important information may be organized by sequential order, classification, cause-effect, or comparison-contrast.

4. Take Notes. Use the method of organization to take notes. Write down the important points in what you have read. You may want to write down each major idea or title, and then write notes under each idea. Or you may want to use an outline, a picture, or a time line.

5. Overview. Finally, read through your notes and the list of important ideas again to form an overview or a summary of what you have read.

The PROTO Method can help you to study just about any kind of material. Here are some additional skills that will help you to use the PROTO Method.

Special Study Tips

Follow Directions Carefully

1. Identify the steps you should follow.

2. Ask questions about steps you do not understand.

3. Follow directions step by step.

Set a Purpose for Studying

1. Before you begin studying, identify the purpose of your work.

2. Your goal might be to find out why something happened or to compare two similar events or people.

3. Use the directions to help you identify your purpose.

4. Stick to your purpose as you work.

Outline Your Material

1. Make an outline of what you are studying.

2. Organize your outline according to the important points.

Map Your Material

1. Use a diagram or picture to outline what you are studying.

2. You might use a map, a time line, or a flow chart to indicate what information is important and how it is organized.

Memorize Your Material

1. Speak and write. First, say it out loud. Then, write it down.

2. Classify ideas. Think of a way to classify information you want to remember. For example, you might list important events in time order, in alphabetical order, or in groups.

3. **Invent memory joggers**. A "memory jogger" might be a word or a funny sentence that helps you to remember things. For example, the six states of New England are: Maine, New Hampshire, Vermont, Massachusetts, Rhode Island, and Connecticut. You could remember these states by making up a name or a silly sentence, such as: "Many New Volunteers Make Residents Comfortable." The first letter of each word in the sentence is the first letter in the name of a state.

4. **Repeat** things as many times as you can to help you remember them.

Taking Tests

Taking tests is an important part of your schoolwork. You can use many of the study skills you have learned to make test-taking easier.

1. **Preview the test**. Look through the test quickly to see what it covers and how long it is.

2. **Plan your time**. Your teacher will tell you how much time you have to finish the test. Decide how much time to spend on each part of the test. Some parts may take longer than others. Reading stories, for example, will usually take longer than answering vocabulary questions. Keep track of the time as you work.

3. **Follow directions**. Listen to any directions your teacher gives you. Then read the test directions carefully before you begin the test. As you work through the test, read any directions you see at the beginning of each new section.

4. **Read questions carefully**. Read each test question carefully. Figure out exactly what the question means. Use key words to figure out what kind of answer is required. (Key words might include "why," "when," "who," "because," "after," and "what.") Then, decide on your answer.

5. **Do easy questions first**. Work through the test and finish every question for which you know the answer. Leave the difficult questions for last. Then, go back and work on each difficult question.

6. **Mark your answers carefully**. If you are taking a multiple-choice test, fill in only one bubble for each question and fill it in completely. If you are writing your answers, write each one clearly and neatly.

7. **Check your work**. When you have answered all the questions, use the time you have left to go back and check your work.

SENTENCE STRUCTURE: Diagraming Guide

A sentence diagram shows how the words in the sentence go together. The diagram begins by putting the most important words in the sentence on a line called a **base line**. You will learn how to diagram the most important words first. You will learn how to diagram other words in later lessons.

Simple Subject and Simple Predicate (pages 8-11)

The simple subject is the main word or words in the complete subject. The simple predicate is the main word or words in the complete predicate. An up-and-down line separates the simple subject and the simple predicate on the base line. Find the simple subject and the simple predicate in this sentence.

The class studied the planets.

Look at the diagram below. You can see how the simple subject and simple predicate are diagramed.

class	studied

Sometimes the simple subject is not given. This subject is *you* understood. This kind of subject is found in imperative sentences.

Learn the nine planets.

(you)	learn

Practice Make a sentence diagram of the simple subject and predicate in each sentence.

1. Planets circle the Sun.
2. The Earth completes an orbit in one year.
3. Mercury lies closest to the Sun.
4. Pluto has the longest orbit.
5. Many moons surround some planets.

Compound Subjects (pages 12-13)

A compound subject is two or more subjects with the same predicate. The simple subjects are joined by *and* or *or*. Each of the subjects appears on a separate line in the sentence diagram. The word *and* or *or* is written on a dotted up-and-down line connecting the compound subjects.

Read this sentence. Find the two words that make up the compound subject.

Authors and poets tell about folk heroes.

Look at the diagram. See how the compound subject is diagramed.

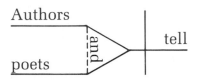

Some compound subjects contain more than two words. Find the compound subject in this sentence.

Pecos Bill, Paul Bunyan, and John Henry have their own tales.

Look at the diagram of this sentence. See how *and* is placed in the compound subject.

Practice Diagram the compound subject and the simple predicate in each sentence.

1. Engineers, steelworkers, and sailors also have folk heroes.
2. Joe Magarac and Stormalong became popular heroes.
3. Paul Bunyan and Babe, the Blue Ox, appeal to many.
4. Sourdough Sam and several other giants worked for Paul Bunyan.
5. Books, movies, and songs tell of these legends.

Compound Predicates (pages 12-13)

A compound predicate is two or more simple predicates with the same subject. The predicates are joined by *and* or *or*. Each part of a compound predicate appears on a separate line in a diagram. The word *and* or *or* is written on a dotted up-and-down line that connects the parts of the compound predicate.

Read this sentence. Which words form the compound predicate?

The students read and talked about the Pilgrims.

Study this diagram of the compound predicate.

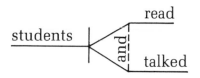

A sentence may contain both a compound subject and a compound predicate.

The leaders and the people planned and made a decision.

Study the sentence diagram. Notice where each *and* appears.

Practice Diagram the subjects and the predicates in each sentence.

1. The Pilgrims left England and sailed to America.
2. The crew and the passengers had a difficult trip.
3. The waves and the wind rocked and shook the ship.
4. My friends and I read and study about the Pilgrims.
5. I planned and built a model of the *Mayflower*.

Direct Objects (pages 146–147)

A direct object is a noun or pronoun in the predicate that receives the action of the verb. A direct object is diagramed on the base line after the subject and the predicate. The direct object is separated from the verb by an up-and-down line.

Read this sentence and identify the direct object.

My club made posters.

Look at the sentence diagram below. Notice that the line separating the verb and the direct object does not go below the base line.

A verb can have more than one direct object. Find the compound direct object in this sentence.

We used paint and photographs.

See how a compound direct object is diagramed.

Practice Diagram only the subjects, the predicates, and the direct objects in each sentence.

1. Our club designed health education posters.

2. We encourage good nutrition and exercise.

3. Our pamphlets list many rules.

4. People study our posters and pamphlets.

5. Our members give intelligent speeches.

Linking Verbs (pages 150-151)

A linking verb joins the subject of a sentence to a noun or an adjective in the predicate. In a sentence diagram, a slanting line separates the linking verb from the noun or adjective in the predicate.

My favorite sport is baseball.

See how this sentence is diagramed. Find the word that names or describes the subject in the sentence diagram.

More than one word may name or describe a subject.

Baseball games are exciting and entertaining.

See how the compound parts are diagramed.

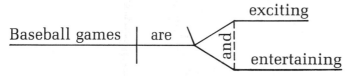

Practice Diagram each linking verb and the two parts of the sentence that it joins.

1. Baseball seems very American.
2. Many people are loyal fans.
3. The games appear complicated and interesting.
4. My favorite players are pitchers.
5. The pitcher is a most important player.

Adjectives (pages 226-235)

Adjectives, including the articles *a*, *an*, and *the*, are diagramed on a slanting line below the noun they describe.

Find the adjectives in this sentence.

The class wrote the first few poems.

Notice how the adjectives are diagramed. Remember that the words *a*, *an*, and *the* are special adjectives called **articles**.

Sometimes adjectives appear in a series. Find the series of adjectives in this sentence.

A poem uses many colorful and exciting words.

See how the word *and* is written with the adjectives in a series.

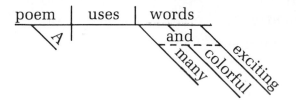

Practice Diagram every word in these sentences.

1. One poem described a large, round, and yellow ball.

2. The yellow ball was the bright summer sun.

3. A short poem seems easy.

4. A longer poem takes patient, hard work.

5. The teacher read the best new poems.

Adverbs (pages 364-371)

Adverbs, like adjectives, are placed on slanting lines below the words they describe.

Find the adverb and the word it describes in this sentence.

A talented child sang beautifully.

Look at the diagram of the sentence.

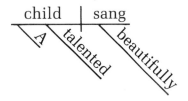

Notice that an adverb does not always appear next to the word it describes. Where is the adverb in the sentence below?

Later, the girl played the violin.

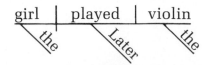

Read this sentence. Notice that an adverb describes another adverb.

The thoughtful student talks very quietly.

Study the sentence diagram.

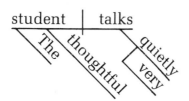

Practice Diagram every word in these sentences.
1. Every student does very fine work.
2. A few kind students help the teacher often.
3. Some people complete homework very quickly.
4. The good student works carefully and seriously.
5. An excellent student studies often and wisely.

Prepositional Phrases (pages 428-431)

In a sentence diagram, a prepositional phrase is written on a slanting line below the word it describes. The object of the preposition is written on a connecting line. The words that describe the object of the preposition are written on slanting lines below it.

Read this sentence. Find the prepositional phrase. What word does it describe?

The girl in the red velvet dress is class president.

See how the sentence is diagramed. Find the prepositional phrase in the diagram.

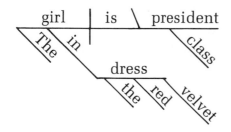

Practice Diagram every word in these sentences.
1. The boy with red hair campaigned very carefully.
2. He and the winner gave speeches from their seats.
3. The people in this room thought very carefully.
4. We voted in a special booth.
5. The winner of the election is a very happy girl.

Compound Sentences (pages 14-15)

A compound sentence contains two or more simple sentences joined by *and, or,* or *but.* Diagram each sentence in a compound sentence separately. Write the connecting word *or, and,* or *but* on a line between the two sentences. Draw a dotted line connecting this word to each sentence.

Read this sentence. Find the two sentences that make up the compound sentence.

Football is a great game, but I prefer soccer.

See how the compound sentence is diagramed.

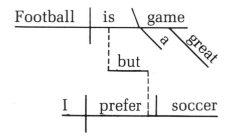

Practice Diagram every word in these compound sentences.
1. Football is very slow, and I like fast games.
2. The game is exciting, or I go home.
3. Soccer is fun, but it takes great skill.
4. I practice often, and I play in school games.
5. The boy in the red shorts plays a hard game, but he is a very polite player.

G L O S S A R Y

OF WRITING, GRAMMAR, AND LITERARY TERMS

WRITING TERMS

audience
the reader or readers for whom a composition is written

detail sentences
sentences that tell more about the main idea of a paragraph

first draft
the first version of a composition, in which the writer gets his or her basic ideas down on paper

main-idea sentence
the sentence that states the overall point of a paragraph

overall impression
the general idea or feeling expressed in a description

personal narrative
a piece of writing in which the writer tells about something that has happened in his or her life

prewriting
the stage in the writing process in which the writer chooses a topic, explores ideas, gathers information, and organizes his or her material before writing a first draft

prewriting strategies
particular ways of gathering, exploring, planning, and organizing ideas before writing the first draft of a composition

- **charting**   a way to gather ideas under different headings—especially useful in comparing and contrasting

Carl Lewis's Victory	My Victory
100-yard dash, Olympics	100-yard dash, school
represented United States	represented my school
won gold medal	won first place
set record 9.9 s	set record 14.9 s

- **clustering**   a way to explore ideas by gathering details related to the writing topic

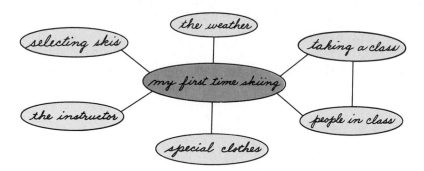

- **flow chart**   a way to organize the steps when writing instructions

- **listing**　　a way to gather supporting reasons and details—especially useful in persuasive writing

> I believe it is important to run in the Muscular Dystrophy marathon this weekend.
>
> competition is exciting
> it helps people with this disease
> get to know other runners
> good for your health
> pretty scenery

- **outline**　　a way to organize topic-related ideas in the order in which they will be discussed—especially useful in drafting a research report

> The Nitrogen Cycle
>
> I Introduction
>   A. Definition
>   B. Relationship to plants
>
> II Movement from soil to plants
>   A. Nitrogen-fixing bacteria
>   B. Plant protein
>
> III Conclusion
> IV A. Summary
>   B. The cycle of life
>
> III Movement from plants to soil
>   A. Animal protein
>   B. Decay

- **story organizer**   a way to gather ideas and details under headings important for story writing

> *Characters*
> *Tom, a boy from the suburbs*
> *a doctor*
> *a lady with a dog*
>
> *Setting*
> *N.Y.C. subway*
> *stopped between*
> *stations*
> *Crowded, noisy*
>
> *Beginning*
> *Tom arrives N.Y.C.*
> *takes subway to*
> *Brooklyn*
>
> *Middle*
> *subway stuck*
> *dog has puppies*
> *doctor delivers*
> *puppies*
>
> *End*
> *puppies wrapped*
> *in Tom's shirt*
> *people exchange*
> *numbers*
> *Tom meets aunt*

proofread   to correct errors in punctuation, capitalization, spelling, and grammar in a writing draft

publish   to share a composition with an audience

purpose   the writer's reason for writing a composition—for example, to explain, to entertain, or to persuade

revise   to improve the first draft of a composition by adding or taking out information, combining and reordering sentences, or changing word choice according to the purpose and audience

sensory details   in a description, the details that appeal to the reader's five senses—sight, hearing, touch, taste, and smell

supporting details   facts, examples, or sensory details that give more information about the main idea of a paragraph

time order   the arrangement of events in a composition according to when they occur in time

topic sentence   another name for the **main-idea sentence**

transition words	words or phrases that link sentences in a paragraph, such as *finally* and *in the meantime*
writing conference	a meeting in which a writer asks and answers questions about his or her writing with the purpose of improving it
writing process	the steps for writing a composition, including prewriting, writing a first draft, revising, proofreading, and publishing

GRAMMAR TERMS

action verb	a word that expresses action The horses *leap* over the fence.
adjective	a word that describes a noun or a pronoun Vermont has *cold* winters.
adverb	a word that tells more about a verb The letter arrived *yesterday*.
article	the word *a, an,* or *the* Tell me *a* story.
common noun	a noun that names any person, place, thing, or idea What *country* will you visit?
complete predicate	all the words that tell what the subject of a sentence does or is The strange noises *remained a mystery*.
complete subject	all the words that tell whom or what a sentence is about *Strange noises* came from that room.
compound sentence	a sentence that contains two sentences joined by a comma and the word *and, or,* or *but* *The lights dimmed, and the audience became quiet.*

conjunction	a word that joins other words or groups of words in a sentence
	We will see a movie *or* a play tonight.
direct object	a noun or pronoun that receives the action of a verb
	The carpenter built a *desk*.
future tense	the form of a verb that shows something that has not yet happened
	Steve *will speak* to our club tomorrow.
helping verb	a verb that helps the main verb to show an action
	Ellen *has* finished her homework.
interjection	a word or group of words that expresses strong feeling
	Wow! What a huge house that is!
irregular verb	a verb that does not form the past tense by adding *d* or *ed*
	The children *found* a baby robin.
linking verb	a verb that links the subject of a sentence to a noun or an adjective in the predicate
	The sun *is* brilliant today.
noun	a word that names a person, place, thing, or idea
	When is the *concert*?
object of a preposition	the noun or pronoun that follows the preposition in a prepositional phrase
	A bird flew through the *rainbow*.
object pronoun	a pronoun that is used as the object of an action verb or after words such as *to, for, with, in,* and *at*
	Will you be traveling with *me*?
past tense	the form of a verb that expresses action that has already happened
	Paul *returned* the book to me last week.
possessive noun	a noun that shows ownership
	Is this the *teacher*'s pen?

possessive pronoun	a pronoun that shows who or what owns something Welcome to *our* house.
preposition	a word that relates a noun or pronoun to another word in a sentence Place the vase *on* the table.
prepositional phrase	a group of words that begins with a preposition and ends with a noun or pronoun The kitten is *in the tree.*
present tense	the form of a verb that tells that something is happening now Eleanor *wants* a new bicycle.
pronoun	a word that takes the place of one or more nouns and the words that go with the nouns *She* would like a ten-speed bicycle.
proper adjective	an adjective formed a proper noun We love *Italian* food.
proper noun	a noun that names a particular person, place, thing, or idea *Carlos* is from *Spain.*
run-on sentence	two or more sentences that have been joined together incorrectly *The explorers drew maps they made careful studies.*
sentence	a group of words that expresses a complete thought *The scientist performed an experiment.*
sentence fragment	a group of words that does not express a complete thought *Came into the kitchen and sat down.*
simple predicate	the main word or words in the complete predicate of a sentence Ana *sang* in the chorus last year.

simple subject	the main word or words in the complete subject of a sentence
	The enormous *tree* towered above us.
subject pronoun	a pronoun that is used as the subject of a sentence
	They arrived during a snowstorm.

LITERARY TERMS

alliteration	the repetition of the same first letter or initial sound in a series of words—for example, ''Linda loves to lick labels.''
characters	the people in a story or play
concrete poem	a poem whose shape suggests the subject of the poem
dialogue	the conversations that people have in a story or a play
fiction	written works such as novels and short stories that tell about imaginary characters and events
haiku	a poem that has three lines and usually seventeen syllables, and that frequently describes something in nature
images	pictures suggested by a description or a comparison, such as ''The stars formed a glittering road in the sky.''
nonfiction	written works that deal with real situations, people, or events, such as biographies
personification	a description in which human qualities are given to something that is not human—for example, ''The wind whispered at the door.''
plot	the sequence of events in a story
setting	the time and place in which the events of a story happen

INDEX

The
HOUSE *of* VELVET
and GLASS

ALSO BY KATHERINE HOWE

The Physick Book of Deliverance Dane

The

HOUSE *of* VELVET
and GLASS

Katherine Howe

voice

HYPERION · NEW YORK

Copyright © 2012 Katherine Howe

Library of Congress Cataloging-in-Publication Data

Howe, Katherine.
   The house of velvet and glass / Katherine Howe. — 1st ed.
     p. cm.
      ISBN 978-1-4013-4091-9
   1. Fathers and daughters—Fiction.   2. Mediums—Fiction.   3. Boston (Mass.)—Fiction. I. Title.
   PS3608.O947H68 2012
   813'.6—dc23

2011034052

Designed by Cassandra J. Pappas

FIRST EDITION

10 9 8 7 6 5 4 3 2 1

THIS LABEL APPLIES TO TEXT STOCK

For my favorite

The
HOUSE *of* VELVET
and GLASS

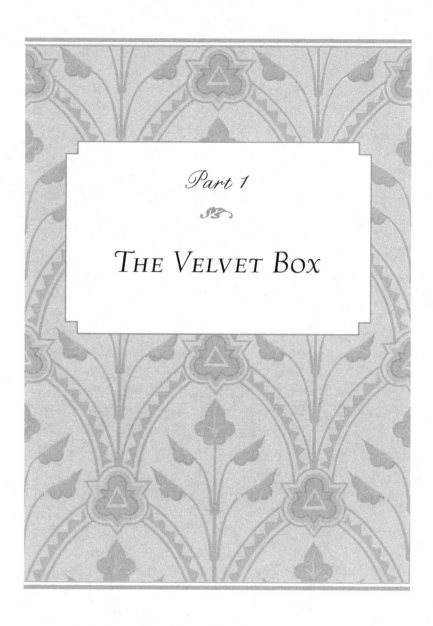

Part 1

THE VELVET BOX

Prologue

জ্ব

North Atlantic Ocean
Outward Bound
April 14, 1912

SOMEWHERE BELOW THE hubbub of the dinner hour, under the omnipresent vibrating of the ship's engines, a clock could be heard beginning
to chime. Helen Allston tightened her grip on her daughter's elbow, brushing aside the lace from Eulah's sleeve to better settle her fingers in its crook.
She cast a sidelong glance at Eulah, whose buoyant anticipation seemed
not to register her mother's weight on her arm. Eulah's face, flushed and
pink, eyelids darkened with such a cunning hand that even Helen, who
knew better, found the change difficult to detect, wore a bright, open expression that few other women's daughters could manage with success.
Helen sighed with satisfaction. She never tired of seeing the world through
Eulah's eyes, young and willing as they were.

But not too willing, of course.

"What a fetching way you've done your hair," she murmured, steering
Eulah with a firm hand toward the grand staircase. Her daughter's blond
curls, too unruly for Helen's liking most of the time, had been twisted off
her forehead and fastened back in a roll, then smothered with a cloud of

fragile black netting fastened at the crown with a butterfly, its enamel wings set *en tremblant*, and so shimmering slightly with Eulah's every movement.

"My brooch?" Helen said aloud, recognizing the ornament, and Eulah turned to her, eyes wide with mock innocence.

"You don't mind, do you, Mother?" she asked, dimpling. "Nellie said that all the New York girls were wearing brooches this way, and I thought . . ."

Helen held her gaze for a moment, sufficient to indicate whose brooch this was really, but not long enough to instill any real remorse. She knew that she was inclined to give Eulah too much, rather than too little, leeway. Eulah had a way of making one see the absolute logic of her preferences, no matter how unorthodox. And she had to admit that the new maid they'd brought with them had a good eye for what was fashionable in hairdressing.

"Well," she demurred, and Eulah laughed, placing her hand on her mother's, knowing the battle was won before it started.

"Just remember, my dear, that for all that New York fashion, you're a Boston girl," Helen whispered, to Eulah's puff of exasperation. This motherly remonstration dispensed with, the two Allston women paused at the top of the staircase, readying themselves.

Helen's gaze traveled over her daughter for a final appraisal, wanting to ensure that everything was in its place before they swept down the stairs and into the first-class dining room. Under the netting Eulah's liquid blue eyes glimmered with anticipation, behind which lurked something else that Helen struggled to identify. She peered closer. Determination, perhaps.

She was accustomed to seeing her youngest child determined. All her children were willful, of course, but Eulah had taken the Allston stubbornness and aimed it outward, at a world that she felt needed fixing, with the same alacrity that Helen's two older children aimed inward, at themselves. Perhaps after all Eulah finally understood the opportunities available to her on this journey, even more than Helen had guessed.

This determination appeared in the obvious care that her daughter had taken with her evening dress. Helen took pleasure in the creativity Eulah showed in instructing the dressmakers back on Tremont Street, and she suspected that her hours with the dressmakers in Paris would only make Eulah's directions more demanding. Well, she supposed they would be, anyway, given all that time poring over *Journal des Dames et des Modes*.

Helen thought it best that Eulah not attempt to look too French, at least not until well after they returned from the tour, so she was glad to see her waist just a little high but still bound with a satin sash, a deep vermilion that she recognized from one of Eulah's coming-out dresses last winter. The reused satin gathered a rich, narrow column of marigold silk with a matching lace overlay around the bodice, which suited her figure marvelously. Granted, the bodice was just a shade low for Helen's taste. But she had to admit that the lower cut set off Eulah's grandmother's cameo beautifully. All in all, Helen concluded that the months in Italy and France had done wonders for her daughter. Eulah had left Boston a fresh, lively girl, and now she had all the freshness of before, but with the sophisticated gloss that can only be imparted by prolonged exposure to certain works of art, performances of opera, and the perfumed air of fashionable restaurants.

Helen cast a melancholy eye down at her own costume, an evening dress a few seasons out-of-date, but still serviceable. Navy taffeta, low on the shoulders, with black beadwork and sashed with pale blue. She wished she had thought to take it over to Mme. Planchette's atelier for a sprucing up, shortening above the floor, at least. Her slippers groped around in puddles of silk, hunting for purchase on the polished deck. Helen frowned, regretting her age, and her hand sneaked up to finger the seed pearl choker nestled in the delicate skin of her throat.

Of course Eulah's loveliness was a credit to her mother. And Helen prided herself on being remarkably well preserved. Her face had only the slightest trace of lines at the edge of her mouth, her eyes were as clear as they ever were, and she only kept the spectacles on a golden lorgnette at her waist for the reading of menus. The rinse that she used was very clever indeed—not even Eulah suspected that Helen's rich dark hair, now heaped in an elegant pouf at her crown, was less than natural in coloring. At least the navy of her dress complemented Helen's skin, pearlescent in the low electric light. She would have preferred gas, at least from an aesthetic standpoint, but she supposed the ship must have all the latest modern conveniences. Lan would disapprove, surely. At the thought of her husband, Helen's face darkened but brightened again almost immediately.

"Why, if it isn't the Misses Allston!" boomed a young man's voice, and Helen felt a familiar hand at her elbow. She turned and met the merry face of Deke Emerson, slick haired and apple cheeked in his tight evening clothes, already flushed from his exertions in the library in the hours preceding dinner.

"Why, Deckie!" Eulah squealed, clapping her hands. "I wondered if we'd see you. Mother says that there're quite a lot of our set on the manifest, but we haven't seen anyone yet. Isn't it just marvelous!"

"It is. Doubly so," Emerson managed, with a little trouble, "now that I've found two such sharming dinner companions."

Helen smiled her most tolerant smile. "My dear Mr. Emerson, what a pleasure. We would be so grateful if you would escort us into the dining room. We've engaged to dine with Mrs. Widener this evening." She emphasized their dining partner's name, and gave him a weighted look.

"Ah!" said Emerson, comprehending, with an acquiescent waggle of his eyebrows. "I approached you with no other object in mind." He offered each woman an arm, and with a gathering of skirts and nerves, they descended the grand staircase to the dining room.

As Eulah nattered to Deckie about the wonders of motor dashes through the Bois de Boulogne and the fashions worn by Parisian women, Helen caught her breath at the glittering scene unfolding before her. The staircase itself was a marvel, more suited to a Parisian hotel than an ocean liner. It was carved out of an elegant wood—Lan would know what it was, and he would probably scoff at going to such expense on the fittings of a ship. Like most seagoing men, Lan could be pigheaded about traveling for pleasure. Well, it couldn't be helped—Eulah *must* go on the tour. When he saw the change wrought in his youngest daughter, the exquisite finish that Europe had applied to her, Helen knew that Lan would agree she had been right.

The staircase was festooned with carved wooden curlicues, lit by a cherub on the central railing holding aloft an electric torch. Overhead soared an illuminated crystal dome delineated by wrought iron, which reminded Helen of the coils and leaves of the shopping arcades in the rue du Faubourg. The landing of the grand staircase featured a clock with

Roman numerals and sharp hands, its face dwarfed by ornate woodwork. She gazed at the clock as they passed down the stairs; presumably the dinner chimes hailed from it. Helen frowned, confused.

"Mr. Emerson," she said, interrupting Eulah's enthused discourse on an opera singer whom she had spotted in a café the evening before they departed for England.

"Yes, Mrs. Allston?" her escort replied, solicitous in his pronunciation.

"Is there anything the matter with that clock that you can see?" she asked, nodding her head in its direction.

"Why, I should think not." He laughed, matching his pace to theirs. "Ship's brand-new, you know. What's the word these sailor types use? Shipshape?"

Eulah giggled, digging her elbow into Emerson, and Helen's frown deepened. The clock bothered her. It looked oddly familiar, but she couldn't have seen its like before. And try as she might, she couldn't quite make herself understand what time it was reading. Even this confusion felt familiar; in another moment she would be able to remember what this reminded her of. It was the most curious sensation.

Just then an elderly couple whom Helen recognized from their Tuesday evening lecture society passed by on the way upstairs to the first-class lounge, and she snapped to attention. They bowed, and she nodded, introducing her daughter and Mr. Emerson. The group joined in a few moments' collective exclamation over the relative fineness of the ship, the dreariness of shipboard life, the delight in continually running into one's Boston acquaintances while abroad, the miserableness of the Popish peasantry in rural Italy, and the great relief to be returning to Boston, where one could have a proper meal at last.

"Gracious, Mother, listen!" exclaimed Eulah once they had freed themselves from the elderly couple. The band had begun to play, and at the bottom of the staircase they swept through the reception hall and arrived at a splendid dining room, tables all laid with crisp white linen. Tiny candles cast the sterling tableware in warm, twinkling light, and the room was filling with murmuring clusters of people, some few couples dancing at the end of the gallery, the men in perfectly turned-out evening dress.

But the women! Helen smiled as she surveyed the flock of women il-luminating each cluster of black-coated men, like tropical birds in a sea of penguins. There was Mrs. Brown, as if Helen needed any help finding her, so insistent was her bellowing western voice, her impressive girth swathed in layers of mink unfitting to April and unmistakably expensive. And there was beautiful young Mrs. Astor, the same age as Eulah, in quiet con-ference with Mrs. Appleton, neither of whom Helen had met, but Eulah often remarked over their doings when reading the columns in *Town Topics*. Mercy, how elegant Mrs. Appleton looked. Her gown was of a shell pink so delicate that it almost seemed not to exist.

The sound of humming broke in on these reflections, and Helen shot a reproving look at Eulah, the humming's source.

"Oh, but I love this song, Mother." Eulah smiled. "Dum dah dee dum dum duuuuum."

"Goose," teased Emerson as he propelled them to their table. "You can't know this song. It's brand-new. Why, I only just heard it in Paree, and at a café where your mother wouldn't ever let *you* go."

"I do so know it!" Eulah mock-pouted. "I can even remember some of the words."

"Is that a fact." Emerson smiled.

"Dum dee dah dah, hmmm hmmmm silver liiiining . . ." Eulah warbled, her gloved hand drawing musical circles in the air at her shoulder.

"Eulah!" Helen scolded. But her exhortations were cut short by their arrival at the appointed table.

"Well, ladies," Emerson said, holding on to the back of a chair for extra support as he executed a gentlemanly bow. "Here is where I bid you adieu."

"You're too kind, Mr. Emerson," Helen said, dismissing him, not un-kindly.

Eulah gifted Emerson with her most celestial smile, and after he had helped them, as best he could, to their seats, he withdrew.

Helen leaned in to admonish her daughter about her conversation, when she was interrupted by the appearance of Mrs. Widener and, just behind her, a mustachioed eminence who could only be her husband, George. Helen sighed, resigned. She hoped Eulah would have better sense than to go on about her absurd political ideas in front of Mrs. Widener. For all Europe's salutary influence, Helen worried that her daughter was still dangerously forward thinking. Helen had even caught her lecturing Lady Rutherford in the dressing room at the opera on the necessity of female suffrage.

Of course, Helen had a few unorthodox interests of her own. Not political of course. Spiritual ones, mainly. Mrs. Dee always said Helen owed it to herself—to the world—to expound about the wonderful things they were accomplishing at her Wednesday evenings. Perhaps Eulah was right and Helen oughtn't lecture her about proselytizing. But babbling on about nonsense in one's sewing circle was one thing, and doing it at dinner on the first real night of a transatlantic passage was something else.

"Eleanor!" Helen smiled up at her dinner companion, nudging Eulah under the table with a slipper to summon her attention. "My dear, how are you? What a long time it's been. And Mr. Widener traveling with you. How nice."

"Helen," Mrs. Widener acknowledged, offering her hand, which Helen took. Mrs. Widener adjusted the ermine at her shoulders, casting a slow, calculating gaze around the dining room. Finally she sighed and sank into the seat next to Helen Allston, rearranging her skirts and settling against the gilded seat with patient assistance from her husband, who then seated himself and proceeded to drum his meaty fingertips on the tabletop. A few moments passed with the table in silence as the band continued, diners in small clusters began to pick their way to their own tables, and Helen fumbled in her mind for something more to say.

"Well," Mrs. Widener said at length. "Here we are." Her husband grunted in assent.

Helen smiled, leaning nearer, and began, "My dear Eleanor, but you remember my daughter Eulah, don't you? We're on our way home from the tour," as Eulah trampled over her mother's introduction with "How d'you do, Mrs. Widener! And Mr. Widener," extending her gloved hand across the little nosegay of lilies at the center of the table.

"Of course," Mrs. Widener allowed, clutching and releasing Eulah's hand. Her husband followed suit.

Just then a breathless young man appeared from within the crush of people and stooped down to Mrs. Widener's ear with a "There you are, Mother. I've just spent five minutes trapped at a table with Eddie Calderhead, listening to some business scheme of his. Picked up the wrong table card.

Nearly had to promise him twenty thousand dollars just so's he'd let me leave."

"You didn't, did you?" Mr. Widener grumbled, but his son paid him no mind.

The young man collapsed into the free chair at his mother's side with a grin. "Nearly, I said," he tossed off with a laugh. Mrs. Widener smiled a mother's indulgent smile, and turned to Helen.

"And you remember my son, don't you? Here, Harry, meet some lovely people I know from Boston. Mrs. Helen and Miss Eulah Allston."

"How d'you do," Harry said, rising with a nod at each, and then seating himself. Helen took in this unexpected development closely. So the Wideners had brought along their son. He was older than Eulah, to be sure, but not so very much. Twenties, thereabouts. A Harvard man, impeccably dressed. Hair a bit messy, but it gave him a sweet, bookish air. Fine jaw. Lovely, straight Roman nose. Roman, or Grecian? Oh, she could never remember. Helen wondered if he was entering into his father's business. Trolley cars, wasn't it? Lan would know. Of course, his mother being an Elkins, what his father did hardly mattered.

"I was just telling your mother," Helen ventured, "that Eulah and I are returning from Paris. Her first time, you know."

Harry's eyes settled on Eulah with interest. "Why, that's capital! Everyone should go to Paris at least once. Some excellent book dealers there as well. How'd you find it?"

Eulah allowed herself a small, mysterious smile, as though she were newly privy to untold mysteries at which Harry could only guess.

"Why, I suppose it was . . ." She paused, pretending to search for the perfect word, and so drawing his attention. He edged closer to hear what she might say, and Helen felt her heart flutter.

"Magical," Eulah finished. "Just so. It was all magical. The art. The opera. The balls."

"The ateliers," Mr. Widener muttered to no one in particular.

"What is it that you do, Harry?" Helen dove in, rescuing the table from Eulah's tendency to rhapsodize.

"I am a bibliophile," he said with gravity, ignoring Mr. Widener's audible snort.

"Are you!" Eulah exclaimed as Helen blinked in confusion.

"Indeed. We were just in Paris as well, as a matter of fact. I was there seeing if I could hunt down this particular volume, and Mother and Father decided they would come along for a change of scene."

"Paris!" Eulah cried. "How funny we didn't see you any sooner. I wish you'd tell me about the book you were looking for. I just love books, you know. Did you find it?"

"It's called *Le Sang de Morphée,*" Harry said, rising. "And I will tell you everything there is to know about it, if you'll only dance with me."

Mrs. Widener suppressed a startled cough as Eulah turned her delighted eyes to Helen. "May I?" she asked, already halfway to her feet, Harry reaching, too late, to pull back her chair.

"Why, of course, my dear!" Helen beamed. "You needn't bother about us. Catch them while they're still playing that song you like."

Giggling, Eulah placed her hand into Harry's and allowed him to help her away from the table, the music seeming to swell in concert with Eulah's growing pleasure. Harry supported her back with a firm hand and, executing a few masterly steps, waltzed them away into the throng of dancers at the end of the gallery.

Helen sighed, pleased, thinking of the cotillion when she first saw Lan. She had felt so grown up, in the stiff silk evening dress her mother ordered, her hair put up for the first time. Helen noticed him right away, even before her mother pointed him out, whispering his marriageable qualifications in her ear with irritating urgency. Helen hadn't heard a thing her mother said. Perhaps his being so much older was a part of it: his face was nut brown, and his eyes looked haunted and knowing. All those years at sea, and it seemed that part of him was forever at sea, unreachable. She shivered at the memory.

Harry Widener might not be as mysterious to Eulah as Lan had been to her, but then Eulah didn't have Helen's taste for mystery. Mrs. Dee had recognized the spark of the unusual in Helen right away, but it was a private spark, one that she kept hidden beneath a well-rehearsed public face.

Eulah, however, was an outward-looking girl. Headstrong, too quick with her desires and opinions. Helen worried that she was hungry for life, almost demanding of it. She would do well with a young man like Harry: well educated, moneyed, bookish, reliable. A trifle boring. He would settle Eulah down. Helen pressed her lips together in resolve. Never mind the four thousand dollars for the ticket, then. Lan could complain about the expense as he might, but it was worth it if she could see at least one of her children settled.

"*Le Sang de Morphée* indeed," Mrs. Widener remarked to herself, surveying the glittering scene before her with a gaze of supreme boredom.

"Blood from a stone, more like," Mr. Widener replied, resettling a pair of gold spectacles on the bridge of his nose and applying his attention to a sheet of heavy card stock in his hand. Helen was shaken out of her reverie long enough to notice that menu cards had appeared. Oysters! Well, she supposed that was apt. And perhaps that boded well for Eulah's chances. Helen placed equal stock in the power of old wives' tales as she did in the newer branches of thought. Consommé Olga, whatever that was. Poached salmon and mousseline sauce with cucumbers.

"What is the name of this tune, Helen?" Mrs. Widener interrupted her thoughts with a poke of her gloved finger on Helen's forearm.

"Why, I'm sure I don't know." Helen smiled, catching a glimpse of Eulah in the crowd of dancers, her head thrown back in exquisite laughter at something Harry was saying. Through the rising babble of dinner conversation, the clinking of cutlery and glassware, the swelling horn section of the band, Helen wondered if she could be hearing the clock tolling again. Was it tolling in actuality, or just in the back of her mind? She pushed the question aside, taking up the menu again to see what gustatory delights lay in store for her and her daughter.

Roast duckling in applesauce. Parmentier and boiled new potatoes. Cold asparagus vinaigrette. Pâté de foie gras, and—oh, Eulah would be so pleased—chocolate and vanilla eclairs! Helen turned in her seat, searching for her daughter's gay face in the crowd of revelers, dropping the menu in her haste on the floor, where it settled against the gilded leg of her chair.

At the top of the menu, engraved in elegant, nautical letters, was written the name of the splendid ocean liner that was carrying them home: TITANIC.

ONE

Beacon Hill

Boston, Massachusetts

April 15, 1915

*G*oodness, but the air was cloying. Sibyl Allston felt a cough rise in her chest and pressed her handkerchief to her lips to silence it. Thankfully she had soaked the kerchief in a little 4711 this time; the astringent, citrusy scent of the cologne sharpened her mind and pushed away the room's miasma. She shifted, feeling her heart turn over in her chest, lurching in trepidation tinted with a strange kind of excitement.

Across the table, Sibyl observed an anonymous man, on the elderly side of middle age, also overcome by the heavy atmosphere. His eyes watered, and skin hung in sallow folds over his detachable collar. She didn't know his name, though she supposed it would have been easy to deduce from the papers if she bothered to look. Sibyl saw him, every once in a rare while, driving down Beacon Street in an old-fashioned brougham, one of the last ones in town, his eyes sheathed in worry. Strange that they should always see each other here, always be seated directly opposite one another, and yet never breathe a word.

Mrs. Dee insisted on that. Absolute secrecy, and absolute silence.

Mrs. Dee had a way of dealing only in absolutes that Sibyl had once found reassuring.

The parlor where they gathered every year had been redone in the modern style some decades ago, in homage to Mrs. Dee's "celebrated" status. The furniture was all carved rococo woods, weighted down with curlicues and waxen fruit and snarling animal faces, the seats upholstered in scarlet silk with golden tassels. The walls bore silk upholstery in a rival shade of magenta patterned with rosebuds, their dignity screened from sunlight by double-hung velvet portieres in deep navy, kissed by sun bleaching at their fringed edges, ends puddling on the floor. The fireplace mantel was black marble, crowded with daguerreotypes and small geodes clustered on a doily, with twin crystal whale-oil lamps at either end.

The mantel also held a small brass dish, shaped like a leaf, with a smoldering cake of incense, its smoke snaking upward to the ceiling. Two ochre Turkish rugs warred for prominence over the floor, rivaled only by the vitrine against the far wall, cluttered with porcelain, bronze sculptures of frolicking nymphs, and glass-eyed stuffed birds frozen in flight. At the center of the riot of objects, each coated in a dignified veil of dust, glowed a glasslike orb nested in velvet. Sibyl eyed this item idly, attracted to its cleanness, she supposed, for it alone seemed to bear the trace of polish and care.

Sibyl herself sat perched on a hassock that positioned her too low relative to the table in the center of the room, her knees drawn up and angled sideways, one hand clasping the opposite wrist. A slender woman, ebony eyed and dark browed, with a long nose and milky skin, Sibyl dressed practically, in shirtwaist and slim dove gray skirt, her hair gathered in a bun at the crown of her head. Her one concession to adornment was a small pin at her throat, of gold and black enamel encircling an ivory wafer patterned with two laurel leaves. The laurel leaves were so cunningly worked that it was almost impossible to tell that they were formed from pale human hair: Helen's mother's. Helen herself had worn the laurel leaves for years; it was a wonder the pin hadn't made the voyage with her. Sibyl reached up to finger it, reassuring herself.

The pin was an outdated ornament, but Sibyl herself was outdated in some respects. Not that she really minded anymore. At twenty-seven she had finally accepted that her life would remain confined to the oversight of her father's household. She clasped her hands in her lap, digging a thumbnail into the flesh of her palm to distract her from the sore spots forming under the bones of her corset. Maybe Eulah had been right about rational dress after all. She shifted her weight, stomach sinking at the thought of her sister. The waiting was the worst part. Soon they would begin.

"If you would all kindly take your seats," Mrs. Dee intoned from the parlor door, where she had appeared with no warning.

The celebrated medium enjoyed making an entrance though sometimes found it difficult, given her small stature. Sibyl appreciated that Mrs. Dee was always the last one in the room, counting on the element of anticipation and surprise to make up for what she lacked in intrinsic majesty. Plump and mono-bosomed, waddling in last year's hobble skirt, Mrs. Dee waved her hands in a herding motion to gather her supplicants around the mahogany dining table. A silent butler drew back the most ornate of the various chairs, a pointed Gothic monstrosity that had been raised on casters to make Mrs. Dee seem taller. She settled herself in her throne as the dozen Bostonians in her parlor picked their way to seats that belonged to them by force of habit.

Sibyl knew a few of them; some she had known from before, in the little world of Boston society with its tight web of marriages and cousinships. Mr. Brown she knew from Belmont: she'd been to dancing school with his niece. Mrs. Futrelle, in from Scituate, her grief making her sharp features more drawn and ethereal with each passing year. Mrs. Hilliard had been in the same Thursday evening lecture club as Helen. The two Miss Newells, survivors both of the gruesome ordeal, the elder of whom, Madeleine, had been in Sibyl's sewing circle. They were put in a lifeboat by their father on that dreadful night, never to see him again.

Not in this life, anyway.

Sibyl shivered, an inward chill raising goose bumps on her arms.

The others, like the sallow man seated across the table, remained a mystery. She knew that she might see them here and there, glimpsed in a church pew, or in a distant row at the Colonial Society; might even see one of their pictures in the *Evening Transcript*. No acknowledgment would be made on either side. What happened in Mrs. Dee's parlor every April fifteenth was for them, and them alone.

"The lights, please," Mrs. Dee commanded the butler, who obligingly turned down the gas in the overhead chandelier as he withdrew. When he slid the pocket doors to the parlor closed, the room sank into an eerie twilight. Sibyl could just make out the faint outlines of the people gathered about the table, and the shadows of the stuffed birds frozen in the vitrine. The rest of the room was murky and black, the smell of the incense almost overpowering. Her heartbeat quickened.

"Let us join hands," Mrs. Dee's voice suggested, swimming out of the darkness. Sibyl placed her two hands outward, palms up, on the cool tabletop, and felt unseen hands grasp them, warm and reassuring. She always found holding the hands strangely troubling, as though she were both tethered to the earth, yet isolated in the void. It felt almost obscene, this pressing of flesh, intimate, yet anonymous. As these uncomfortable thoughts passed through her mind, one of the hands offered an unsolicited squeeze.

"Now," Mrs. Dee's voice continued, distant and placeless. "I would like each of you to inhale deeply." She paused. "And then exhale. And as you feel the air travel out of your body, I want you to relax."

Sibyl did as the voice suggested, drawing the turgid air into her lungs as deeply as she could, and then letting it back out through her nose. As she did so, she felt her scalp begin to tingle, the skin loosening, just as it did when she unpinned her hair after a long day. She breathed in again, more softly, and as she exhaled the close atmosphere of the room receded, and the tingling deepened. Her head nodded forward.

"Very good," soothed the voice, sounding farther away. "Now I would like all of you to clear your minds completely. Wipe them as blank as a chalkboard at the end of a day of tedious lessons."

Sibyl closed her eyes, picturing her mind as the voice suggested. She wiped once, twice, three times. Then the board was empty, and Sibyl exhaled with relief.

"Now," the voice suggested, far at the outer rims of Sibyl's consciousness, "I would like you to focus your attention on the face of the person you would most like to reach."

Sibyl concentrated, trying to recall Helen's face. Her mother, looking younger than her years, though a little jowly. But Sibyl had trouble getting the details right. Her mother's hair, for instance: how had she been wearing it? Sibyl could remember the high pinned curls that Helen wore when Sibyl was small, but she must have changed it half a dozen times since then. Had she started to gray, or was she still dark? What color had Helen's eyes been? Hazel? Sibyl knew they hadn't been brown, like her own. Had they been blue, like Eulah's? Sibyl frowned, mouth pulled down in guilt. As Sibyl had grown, she found herself less willing to look Helen in the face. Her mother lingered in her memory as a voice of disapproval from the corner of the room, no longer attached to a living, expressive face.

For some reason Eulah left a more vibrant image in Sibyl's mind. She'd been so like Helen, in her unconventional opinions and her affection for fine things, making the two women overlap in Sibyl's memory. But Eulah, young, vibrant, suffered none of Helen's worried disappointment. Sibyl had no trouble recalling her sister's liquid blue eyes, the dimples in her cheeks when she said something daring, even the way that Eulah's wild curls could be tamed into an elegant sweep up the back of her head. She could still hear the timbre of Eulah's voice, lower and more earnest than her looks implied. When Sibyl tried to picture Helen, Eulah invariably got in the way. But that was how it was when they were alive, too: Eulah had always gotten in the way. Sibyl had only been out four seasons when their mother gave her up as a lost cause and started plotting Eulah's entree into society instead. Eulah, who wouldn't squander her opportunities, as Sibyl had.

"Try to see every contour of the person's face," the voice interrupted. "The eyes. The nose. The texture of the skin. The hair. Hold your loved one's face before you as if you were sitting right across from him, in this very room."

Sibyl heard murmurs of grief and recognition escape from various ends of the table, and she squinted her closed eyes, trying to do as she was told. So she couldn't picture Helen this time; no matter. She would try to reach Eulah instead. She loved her sister, as everyone had. She had as much cause to reach her as anyone. Yes, there was Eulah's form, the general outline of her face. Her eyes. Her nose—wait. No. Her nose had been smaller. There were her dimples, and her chin. Sibyl pressed her lips together in concentration.

"Ah!" the voice breathed. "I sense that we are being joined from the beyond! Everyone, remain focused and calm. You have nothing to fear. These are your loved ones, come to share their wisdom with us."

Sibyl tensed, worried that she hadn't captured the right qualities of Eulah's face. The image kept unraveling before her, pulling apart and re-forming, hazy and indistinct.

"I sense a male presence in the room!" Mrs. Dee announced, and Sibyl felt secretly relieved. Now she had more time to gather her recollections together. She was afraid that she might hurt Helen or Eulah, as if they could somehow see into the hollows of her mind and perceive the imper-fection of her memory. She was afraid that they would find her love inad-equate and, worse, trembled to think that they might be right.

"Sir, are you there? Can you hear us?"

Three sharp raps vibrated through the wood of the table, causing the backs of Sibyl's hands to slap against the tabletop. A woman's voiced gasped, and Sibyl's pulse beat in her throat.

"John!" the unseen woman cried through the darkness. "John, it must be you!"

"O unworldly spirit," Mrs. Dee's voice beckoned. "Can you identify yourself? Have you come to share your visions of the great beyond with us?"

"John?" the woman broke in, too eager to wait. "Tell me it is you! Oh, how I've missed you, my darling!"

Three more weighty raps shook the table, and the group heaved a col-lective "Ooooooh" of wonder.

"Oh, I knew it must be you!" the woman burst, her voice catching in her throat. "There's so much that I've wanted to tell you."

A long pause lingered over the table, and Sibyl could sense the tension building in the two hands that clutched hers in the dark. She tightened her own grip. No matter how many times she attended the gathering, the first manifestation always shocked her.

"Speeeeeeeeak," groaned another, different voice, something like Mrs.

Dee's, but gravelly and deep, as though the medium's body had been transformed into something larger. The sound was placeless, seeming to come from overhead.

"Well," the woman began, choking back sobs. "I . . . I wanted you to know that . . . that I've missed you terribly." She waited, choosing her next words. The room hung in silence, waiting.

"And Josiah—you'd be so proud of him! His schoolwork goes well. He's growing up to be such a healthy, strapping boy. So helpful to me, and to his sisters. He excels at his lessons, and . . ." The woman paused, as though suddenly aware that a roomful of strangers was listening in on her conference with her departed husband. She swallowed audibly.

"And at chess, just like you wanted. But I make sure he doesn't while away too much time at it. It's not good for boys to be kept too much indoors, you know." This last comment seemed designed more for the eavesdroppers around the table than for the visiting spirit.

"Goooooooood," groaned the mysterious voice, and the listeners all sighed, moved by this benediction from beyond.

"But, John . . . ," the woman broke in, aware that her alloted time was drawing to an end. "I . . . I must . . ." She gasped, sniffling back her tears, and then pausing to collect herself. She drew a deep breath, and continued. "There's something very important that I must ask you."

Sibyl noticed a thrum of interest travel among the seekers at the table. A secret, about to be revealed. She was glad that Mrs. Dee was so adamant about anonymity.

"Asssssssskkk," the disembodied voice groaned, and the assembly held its breath in anticipation.

"Well, since you've been lost to us, we've had some . . . " She paused, her voice strangled with shame. "Difficulty," she finished.

Sibyl's heart contracted. Most of the passengers who drowned with the ocean liner had been men, of course, as they insisted that women and children be the first into the lifeboats. It was even said that the orchestra had played hymns as the ship deck tilted, to give courage to the men remaining. Boston learned of their self-sacrifice with pride, and pointed to it as a sign of the innate manliness and worth of the sons that it had lost. Less often spoken of was the effect on families left behind, so many of whom now lacked the person most able to provide income and support. For some, poverty stalked on the heels of emotional devastation.

"You needn't worry, John. We can manage. And Carlton has been particularly keen on looking after us. He stepped in right away to ensure that no debts went unpaid, never bothering me with any of it. He's so like you, you know, and I was grateful to have his help, that I could concentrate on the children. Josiah took it so hard, you see, and I was terribly afraid it might turn into some sort of nervous condition. And in all that time, Carlton made himself indispensable, and I came to rely on him. I don't know why I never noticed before, but he's grown rather devoted to me, you see. And the children are quite taken with him." Her words tumbled out, one over the other, as if their speed would squash any objection.

"Not that anyone could ever replace you in our hearts," she hastened to add. "Only we've got to think of the future, all of us. And Carlton is really nothing like the brother you knew. If you could only see him with Josiah, I know you'd understand. . . ." The woman's voice trailed off, uncertain, wavering.

A pause lingered over the table, as if the disembodied voice were considering what it had heard. At length it sighed.

"I . . . sssssseeeeeeeee."

"Oh!" the woman gasped, with palpable relief. "Oh, my darling, thank you! I knew you'd never object, if you only could see." She dissolved into weeping, and Sibyl heard the sound of a nose being blown, delicately, into a handkerchief.

"Thank you," the anonymous woman murmured through her tears. And then, more quietly, "Thank you."

One of the hands holding Sibyl's squeezed, as though moved by the family scene playing out before them. Sibyl hesitated, then squeezed back.

"And now," intoned Mrs. Dee, her voice transformed back into its recognizable, if ethereal, self. "I sense the presence changing. Who is there? Who can it be? We must all concentrate very keenly. Everyone, keep your eyes closed. Hold the image of your lost loved one in your mind."

Sibyl did so, allowing her mind to soften. The sniffles of the woman who would marry her husband's brother faded, and she felt herself floating, comfortable and serene, aware only of Mrs. Dee's voice. She redoubled her efforts, painting in details of Helen's and Eulah's faces. She thought of them, in the days before leaving for the tour. The laughter and preparations. Her own envy. Sibyl scowled. It was her duty to remember them.

"The presence is making himself felt to me," Mrs. Dee murmured. "But he asks that all eyes stay closed. He is shy. Spirit, we will honor your request. We only yearn to help you reach us. No matter what happens, we pledge to honor you!"

A low rumbling filled the room, indistinct. Sibyl's heartbeat quickened.

"What are you trying to say to us, spirit?" Mrs. Dee asked. "Are you sad? Could you be angry?"

Sibyl gasped and straightened in her seat. She thought the table had shifted under her hands.

"O spirit!" Mrs. Dee said, her voice rising. "We feel your anger! Your life was over too soon! We hear your anguish!"

Sibyl's heart thudded in her chest, astonished, her mouth falling open, and she fought to keep her eyes sealed shut. For the table was pressing against the backs of her hands. A sudden lurch, and without warning one side of the table lifted itself, then fell back to the floor with a *thunk*. Sibyl cried out, and gasps echoed around the room. Now the other side of the table rose, carrying the séance-holders' hands with it, then threw itself back to the floor. First one side, then the other, until the table was rocking back and forth with gusto, as though on board a ship tossed at sea. The table shook into a crescendo of fury, the clutched hands of the supplicants hopping and slapping against its surface. Then, abruptly, it stopped.

Sibyl felt her palms grown clammy with sweat. Around the table, small sighs could be heard as held breath was let go. The hands gripping Sibyl's loosened. For a moment, silence reigned.

"We may never know whose anger we have just seen," said Mrs. Dee, her voice steady and reassuring. "For he has gone without a further word. But we can rest assured that merely in allowing him to share his distress with us, we've brought comfort to a suffering soul."

Murmurs of satisfaction encircled the table, and Sibyl shivered with the exquisite pleasure that comes from confronting fear. The table-tipping was the most substantial manifestation she had witnessed in all her years attending Mrs. Dee's gatherings. She wondered whose spirit had visited them. But it was a man. It couldn't have been Helen. Or Eulah. They would never have been so angry. In public, anyway.

"We have such time and energy gathered here, that I feel one more spirit yearning to commune with us. Everyone, please turn your gaze to the center of the table."

Sibyl obeyed, excited, zeroing her gaze on the blackness before her. The harder her eyes focused, the deeper the darkness grew. The hands clutching hers on the tabletop tightened their grip, and she felt one of her knuckles shift under the pressure.

After a time, the quality of the darkness seemed to change. She frowned. She thought she could see the faintest gathering of light, coalescing in the space just above the table. The light wasn't strong enough to reach the faces of the supplicants, but it was there. After a time the faint light began to resolve into an indistinct shape.

Everyone around the table was seeing it, too, Sibyl could tell, because she could hear the others breathing. She swallowed, trying to identify the shape. Could it be a face?

Once, years ago, Helen had returned home from one of Mrs. Dee's evenings breathless with wonder, exclaiming that they'd witnessed a full-form manifestation right there in the living room, of a tiny girl, swathed in sheets, who hovered just out of reach, and vanished. Her father scoffed from behind his newspaper, but Sibyl, a girl of seventeen at the time, first turning her mind to questions of death, was moved by the account. And Eulah! Eulah, a little girl herself then, demanded Helen tell them about the tiny girl again and again. How tall was she? Were the sheets very dirty? Did they blow in an invisible wind? Imagine—a full-figure visitation from the beyond, seen with her mother's very own eyes! Sibyl's breathing tightened, her eyes hunting forward in the dark.

With wonder Sibyl perceived that it was a woman's hand. Fully formed, hovering, attached to nothing. A gasp of awe emanated from the group around the table as the ghostly white hand hung before them, illuminated by an eerie internal light. Her heart leaped with hope, faint and dizzying.

"A spirit, reaching out to us for comfort!" Mrs. Dee cried. "We welcome you, O visitor from realms untold!"

Murmurs of assent joined the welcome, and Sibyl looked upon the manifestation with begging eyes. Could it be? She wasn't sure. The hand, she felt she must know it, it had held her as a baby, had cradled her face as a child. How could she be any sort of daughter and not know her mother's hand?

"O spirit, how we yearn to grasp your hand! But we know if we break our circle, you should vanish! How your nearness tortures us!" Mrs. Dee carried on. "For whom have you come? How can we reach you?"

The white hand brushed its fingers against an unseen surface, waving, as though over undulating water. The supplicants gasped, each conjuring his own private horror of being submerged in icy water. Slowly the hand folded itself into a pointing finger, which then rotated in space, aiming at each individual around the table in turn.

Try as she might, Sibyl couldn't tell if the hand belonged to Helen. Too old for Eulah, whose fingers were delicate and tapered, cared for with files and ointments. The hand turned as though on a rotating plate or gramophone, lingering for a moment on each member of the group before moving on. But it must be Helen. Helen had been a Spiritualist since Sibyl's girlhood. Helen, of all people, would pilot herself through the mists and ectoplasms of the beyond to return here, to Mrs. Dee's drawing room, where she herself had passed so many evenings communing with the spirit world. Helen must know that Sibyl would look for her at Mrs. Dee's. What a vast space the beyond must be, for Helen to take so long getting back. Sibyl ached for her mother to see all that Sibyl had had to do since she left, craved for her mother to soothe her. Sibyl's solitude bore down on her like a weight that she could never set down. The hand must be Helen's. It must.

The hand continued its slow rotation. From man to woman. From woman to woman. From woman to man. At last, it came to rest.

It was pointing straight at Sibyl.

Her heart plummeted down through her chest, and she choked, her nose and cheeks flushing with tears. The hands holding hers on the tabletop tightened, rooting her to her seat as her body was overcome with trembling. The hovering hand pointed, motionless.

It was her. At last. Sibyl's mouth opened, closed, opened again as she struggled to choose the right words among everything that she wished she could say, knowing that she had only a few moments before her chance would be snatched away.

Helpless before her awe and relief, she cried out the only word that she could sift from the jumble in her heart and mind: "Mama!"

At that moment, the room plunged into blackness. Sibyl blinked, and the hand was gone. A babble of voices rose around the table. Then the buzzing rose to shouts, and Sibyl screamed. She jumped up from her seat, shaking and sobbing, rubbing her hands vigorously on the material of her dress, trying to bring feeling back to them, to reassure herself that she was safe, appalled at her own horror and fear.

For the table had flooded with ice cold water.

TWO

*A*lighting from the taxicab in the alley behind Beacon Street, Sibyl paused to face the river, flexing her toes inside her tight buttoned boots. Her feet ached, and she wished she could walk without shoes, as she used to.

As a girl, before the Charles River was dammed to make the basin, she used to tie up her dresses around her knees to hunt for eels in the tidal mudflats behind their home. One afternoon she'd collected three glistening fat ones and brought her prize to the kitchen door full of triumph. Barefoot, mud-caked, braids askew, with a basket full of river-rank eels, Sibyl ran smack into the appalled form of her mother, was pronounced "a sight," and banished to the tub, her basket confiscated.

"Don't bother with the hot water, if you like the river so much!" her mother's admonishment followed her up the back stairs. Young ladies did not hunt for eels, she was reminded as the mud was scrubbed off her neck, leaving it reddened and raw. But later that night, her father confided that he saw her catch them out the window, and those were some fine eels indeed.

Sibyl sighed as the sun sank deeper in the sky, and then she turned to the waiting kitchen door.

"SO YOU'RE BACK, then," barked a voice with a subtle burr as Sibyl closed the door, her eyes adjusting to the gloom of the rear hall. "Wipe your feet, or you'll track in the wet."

The white hallway paint was stained with yellowish dinge, layers of smoke from coal fires, tobacco, and leaking fireplaces, and though the gas fixtures were all lit at dusk, the walls absorbed the light rather than re- flecting it. Sibyl shrugged off her overcoat and handed it to the dour ma- tron who awaited it, mustering her best impression of a lady arriving at a house she commanded. Her performance fooled neither of them.

Clara Doherty, the housekeeper, was unchanging, a solid person in an old-fashioned peaked linen cap and long black dress. She might have been Sibyl's age, had not the Allston family employed her since Sibyl was a child. Mrs. Doherty lingered on the periphery of family photographs for over two decades, holding a baby, or standing in the background of a holi- day dinner, and through it all, as the people around her grew and changed, she stayed, arms straight at her sides, face unmoved. She was Irish, but she didn't look it, or at least that's what was always said of her. Her eyes were small, blue, and hard, her cheeks sunken. She wore her dark hair in a coil at the base of her neck, and though it must have been long enough to loop into place, Sibyl had trouble picturing what Clara Doherty might look like with her hair undone.

Sibyl had a fantasy of what warm and friendly Irish maids might be like, drawn from novels and the households of her girlhood friends. They were called "Peg" or "Mary," and they dispensed cakes and merriment in equal measure. They loved saints and little children, and they had amus- ing folk sayings that scarcely made sense. Sibyl sometimes yearned for one of these imaginary Irish maids. She cast a wary eye at Mrs. Doherty as she handed over her hat. The woman accepted it with a sniff of motherly dis- approval, dusting it off with a few thumps of her hand.

"Left your messages in the parlor," Mrs. Doherty said. "Belgian relief committee, and it's your turn to host the sewing circle, Mrs. Drew says. Do you want her to arrange for the flowers, et cetera, and she's very keen that you call her back."

Sibyl's shoulders sagged. Of course Mrs. Drew wanted to arrange the flowers. She wanted to arrange everything. And why couldn't she host the meeting herself? Sibyl wondered, as was her habit when confronted with Mrs. Drew and the sewing circle.

"Thank you," Sibyl said. The housekeeper shot her a reproving look that Sibyl was given to understand meant that other ladies of her standing usually employed a girl to see after the social schedule, rather than distracting the housekeeper with message-taking all day. It was an old argument. Sibyl knew that one day she would lose.

"Mister Allston is at home, I take it?" Sibyl asked, attempting to sound authoritative.

"So he is," the housekeeper said over her shoulder. There was a pause, of instructions needing to be given. "You'll be wanting to see young Mister Allston first, I wager."

"I beg your pardon?" Sibyl said.

"Young Mister Allston's t'home, these two hours ago."

"Harlan? He's home?" Sibyl glanced upward, as if the layers of wood and plaster separating her from her brother could melt into transparency and demonstrate the truth of this unexpected piece of news. Her mouth twisted in a nervous twinge. "But what can have happened? He's not due 'til June."

Mrs. Doherty's face was impassive. She stood before Sibyl, holding the coat and hat over her arm. Behind her eyes flickered a measure of sympathy, held at a far remove.

"Not to worry. We've got the sheets well changed. But the girl's been wanting to know what time she's to have supper for 'em." Mrs. Doherty always referred to the cook as "the girl," for reasons Sibyl never could fathom.

"It's not the sheets that have me concerned," Sibyl said without thinking. She was always saying more than she should. The housekeeper was silent, and in her silence was agreement. Sibyl watched, but the woman's narrow face gave away nothing—no illuminating details that might shed light on her brother's appearance at their door, unannounced, untelephoned, uninvited, in the middle of the week.

"You'll be stopping by the kitchen, then," Mrs. Doherty said, in the neutral tone that was simultaneously an observation and a suggestion. Sibyl noted the comment, reassuming the surface of a woman unfazed.

"I'm sure Betty has it all well in hand," she said with a determined step down the hallway, as if to suggest that she had known all along that Harlan was coming home, had planned for it, had taken it up with the kitchen staff, and that if she had neglected to inform the housekeeping staff, it was her privilege as lady of the house.

"Yes, ma'am." The chill comment followed behind her in the darkness. Mrs. Doherty knew better.

Sibyl hurried to the kitchen, choosing the most easily solved of her fresh problems. She pushed open a heavy door and met the delicious aroma of roasting chicken. Through the savory haze of kitchen air, cloudy with flour and aglow from the gas fixture over the work table, Sibyl observed Betty Gallagher, striped cotton back turned, castigating one of the occasional girls as she crimped the edges of a soggy-looking pie.

Betty, to Sibyl's occasional discomfort, was Sibyl's exact age. She was plumper than Sibyl, healthy-looking, russet skinned with a smattering of freckles, as though her cheeks were spattered with cake batter. Her hair was dark red-brown, and frizzy, tied off her brow in a pouf. Sibyl thought her an ally in the house, and Betty provided one of the few sources of humor to be had within doors. If that humor was tinged with an unbecoming undercurrent of anger, Sibyl tried to overlook it.

"Betty!" she called from the doorway, and the hubbub of the kitchen ceased, with another of the occasional girls, a pale waif in a stained pinafore, actually freezing with her arms raised over a mixing bowl, as though caught in a game of tag.

". . . by God, your ear'll get boxed so hard you'll be spitting blood!" Betty finished upbraiding the cowering girl at the coal stove. As soon as the rebuke left her mouth Betty noticed the abbreviated silence in the kitchen, and turned.

"Forgive my interrupting," Sibyl ventured from the doorway.

"Out," Betty commanded the unfortunate girl, indicating the garden door with a jerk of her head, and the girl ran off with a squeak. Betty wiped her floured hands on her apron and approached Sibyl, casting her eyes sidelong at the other underling.

"Don't stand there gawking," she snapped to the statue at the kitchen table, who unfroze and, with her head down, set batter mixing, eyes averted.

"Too much work, on the dough," Betty remarked, her exasperation tinged with defensiveness. Sibyl gathered that Betty wished to be very clear where blame for the pie should go. "But don't worry, we'll get it fixed. You'll want supper at seven thirty, then?"

"Mrs. Doherty tells me that Mister Harlan's arrived," Sibyl said, watching Betty for clues. News traveled quickly along the back stairs, and most of it found its way to the kitchen sooner rather than later.

"So he did," Betty said, wiping her forehead with the back of a wrist and leaving a smudge of flour behind. She planted her hands on her hips and shook her head, and Sibyl thought she saw a soft look cross fleetingly over Betty's face. "Couldn't miss 'im."

"I don't suppose he indicated to you or Mrs. Doherty how long he plans to say," Sibyl stated.

"I don't s'pose he *did*," Betty bristled. "But his trunk seemed to imply 'twas awhile he planned on. If he's staying, I'll be needing more for the grocer. I've got all the meals planned, but he throws the numbers off, don't he."

"What've you got on for tonight?" Sibyl asked.

"Roast chickens, sausage pie, cold cucumber salad, Madeira, and orange fluff for the pudding," Betty listed. "Had to right stretch to make the pie."

"That should do," Sibyl reflected, avoiding looking at the greasy sausage pie in its deflated raw crust on the edge of the stove. "Mrs. Doherty didn't mention anything at his arrival?"

"Nnnooo," Betty said, drawing the word out. "But it weren't quiet."

"I gather not," Sibyl said.

The two women looked at each other while the girl at the kitchen table stirred her batter with even more vigor.

"All right," Sibyl decided. "Seven thirty, then. Have Mrs. Doherty ring the dressing bell, if you would. Not much more than half an hour, I don't think."

"Ma'am," Betty said, with only a hint of irony, nodding her head. Then she turned to the open garden door and yelled, "You, idler! Back in here 'fore I drag you in myself!"

Sibyl withdrew, letting the kitchen door swing closed behind her, and hurried down the hallway, readying herself to face her father.

Interlude

East China Sea
Yangzi River Delta
June 8, 1868

SHALLOW WAVES SLOPPED against the starboard side of the cutter, tossing up tongues of salt spray. Lannie thrust his hands into his armpits, squinting. Strange to be in such a low boat, within the water's grasp. He could almost reach out and brush a hand over the ocean surface, stroke it like an animal. It looked like an animal, breathing, the surface glassy, or pebbled with wind. In his months at sea Lannie had grown accustomed to looking at the sky for coming weather, or the horizon for other sails, or for wind lines over the swells. He had stopped looking at the water's surface. Now there it was, rolling up and under him, only an arm's length away.

The other men in the cutter murmured, restless, fingers running through the money in their pockets. They'd endured a long journey, longer than planned, and the mood on board the Yankee clipper *Morpheo* had passed from excitement, to tedium, to festering discontent. The passage south was bitter; full on two weeks of foul winds thwarting them, as if forgotten ocean gods, enraged by their presence, stirred up a vile brew of wind and ice to blow the little clipper all the way back to Salem, forbidding them the other side of the world.

Around him the chattering of the others swelled, tension growing in their shifting bodies. Lannie shook himself, alert to the change. He couldn't tell what imperceptible signal meant that the land was approaching. He strained his eyes through the gathering dusk, senses creeping forward. Only blackening mist, and the pull and slop of oars moving them across the surface of the water.

Then, he felt something—a change. The air pulled away from the cool breath of the ocean animal beneath him. Against his face Lannie felt a wave of pressure as the cutter entered the fetid air pouring off the land. He reached up to loosen the buttons on his coat.

In the distance, a line of glittering lights, haloed in mist. The warm mass of air carried shreds of sound: a shout, clattering cart wheels, the faint wail of music. As they neared the shoreline, oars dropping into the water and rising, Lannie's nostrils quivered with the subtle land flavors: familiar wharf smells first, of salt water, rotting fish, seaweed. Then, stranger things: cooking food, something burning, rich animal smells, the cloying scent of flowers. He squinted, peering ahead.

The dots of light resolved into rows of paper lanterns, suspended in the windows of buildings made of bamboo and daubed mud. These modest dwellings hung over the water on stilts; behind them rose hulking forms that slowly revealed themselves to be new stone office buildings; and Lannie understood that he was looking not at some crowded village, but at a bustling modern city. Before his shock could register, it was there..

Shanghai.

The cutter bumped its way alongside the dock, making a hollow sound as it nudged against the wharf, and a flurry of activity broke out as men sprang ashore to secure the lines. The other sailors in the cutter jostled together, assembling on the dock amid whoops and hollers. The sailors' voices mingled with the cries of the street vendors and wharf noise, and Lannie quailed at stepping out of the boat, into a world of which he knew nothing.

"Let's not forget Greenie," a gruff voice admonished, and hands dug into his flesh, hoisting him up, his feet scrambling for purchase on the gunwale, onto the safety of dry land.

Greenie, for greenhorn, was a name he tried to bear with good humor. A sandy boy, with a fine long nose and eyes the color of water, Lannie at seventeen felt confident in his chosen profession. Cocky, almost. He didn't mind the close quarters. He loved the gentle creak of the ship, loved its motion, and the music of snoring sailors abandoned to sleep. At sea he delivered himself into Providence's hands more freely than he ever had back in the brick house on Chestnut Street. At home, Providence always seemed to stalk behind him in the hallways, following him to bed, waiting to pass judgment on his innermost thoughts. On the water, Providence was master; Lannie was answerable only for his actions, and not for the state of his soul.

Even the discomforts of life at sea didn't trouble him. He never cared much about food, always eating absently, whether roast squab at his father's dining table or boiled salt pork out of the galley. He enjoyed the rigor of the watches, the technical precision of the rigging, the clarity of knowing what duty required, and what it did not. While the other men went distracted in their craving for female flesh, Lannie held himself aloof with stern self-assurances of his innate gentlemanliness and piety.

Perhaps that was his mother's voice, stressing piety. Gentlemanliness, at any rate.

He stood on the long wharf off of the Bund, testing his legs, his hands thrust in his pockets. Around him throngs of people pressed, ragged children clawing for money, ageless women with rotted teeth. Multicolored lanterns cast flickering light, and Lannie absorbed the clamor, basking in the mingled fear and excitement that he had craved when signing on as part of the clipper's crew. The mysterious land of his father's stories was not some wild fairyland in a storybook, but was *here*.

"Day breaks on Marblehead," Lannie muttered, grinning to himself.

A shouted discussion was under way as several of his shipmates, already three sheets to the wind, debated which of the needs of men several weeks at sea should be met first, and in what quarter. The old walled city, or the International Settlement? The French concession? But who wants those bony white Shanghailanders, when the land of a thousand flowers is just along the creek?

After a time the group started to move, a decision not having been made exactly, but motion seeming the order of the night. Lannie had gone barely a block before he stumbled as the ground seemed to undulate under his feet.

"Drunk already, Greenlet! Haven't we taught you to hold your liquor better'n that?" bellowed the sailor next to him, a grizzled fellow named Tom, who was missing three teeth from a wide hole on the side of his jaw. Early in the voyage he'd claimed to Lannie that they'd been lost when he caught a musket ball in his teeth, but the bosun's mate informed him later that they'd been pulled by the barber for common rot.

"No!" Lannie protested, looking with confusion at his feet. He lurched, catching himself, without meaning to, on Tom's shoulder.

"You'll be needing those land legs again." Tom smiled with roguish certainty. "We've only little time ashore, then it's back for home and six weeks of salt pork stew for us, by God. And those fancy long three girls won't have yis, if they think you can't handle yourself."

Lannie tried to smile, glancing sideways at his shipmate. Tom's horrible mouth was smiling, but his eyes were harsh in the fragile evening light.

"Right," said Lannie, shrugging his shoulders in a way that he hoped seemed careless, but which, he thought too late, could be construed as haughty. Tom watched him, eyes narrowing. Lannie squirmed under the scrutiny, aware that the verdict on him was out.

He smiled again, more fully this time, looking for a way to reassure Tom of his gameness.

"What's a long three girl?" he asked finally, already fairly certain that he knew the answer.

Tom tossed his head back, guffawing, and clapped Lannie on the shoulder. Lannie felt the tense moment pass as Tom said, wiping his nose on the back of his wrist, "Something tells me you'll be figuring that out soon enough."

THREE

The Back Bay
Boston, Massachusetts
April 15, 1915

The front hall of number 138 ½ Beacon Street, the Back Bay, was a more modern version of the hall that Sibyl had just left at Mrs. Dee's, though darkened by deeper shadows. The town house, a four-story brown creature with a fat bay window bellying out under an elm tree, possessed a facade obscured by twining fingers of ivy, which cast the hall in gloom. In the summertime the ivy leaves spread dark green over every surface of the house; in the autumn they flushed bloodred, and in the winter the leaves shriveled and blew away, leaving dried husks of vines snaking over the house's face like ossified veins. Springtime, the ivy burst to waxy life, tinting the shade inside the house with pale green.

The house was built by Sibyl's father, after his own design, in 1888, and presented as a wedding present to Helen upon their return from a honeymoon tour of Europe. Sibyl's mother had thrown herself into decorating their new house in the height of modern style, and Lan Allston, not usually an indulgent man, acquiesced to almost every desire of his new, and much younger, bride. As such, the interior of the house reflected in its purest form the incoherence of Helen's taste.

The hall stand coiled up the entryway wall, a monument to American aestheticism, but still serving its essential Victorian function by bristling with umbrellas and forgotten hats. A silver tray was cluttered with visiting cards, most of them dropped off by drivers as their owners idled outside at the curb. Lan never received anymore. Sibyl glanced at her reflection in the hall stand mirror, her face cast in green pallor from the ivy over the windows.

To the rear of the grand staircase, which wound its vinelike way up to the canopy of the upper floors, glowed Helen's finest achievement: the La Farge window. She had always made a point of touring visitors past this organizing feature at the far end of the hall to admire its woodland scene of a babbling brook overhung with trailing wisteria, made of nubby layers of stained glass.

"The La Farge," Helen had called it, always leaving off "window," though Sibyl as a girl found the scene unsettling. There was something off-putting about a scene like that, moving water captured so cunningly in shattered and reassembled glass. Like a live bug caught in amber.

The pocket door to the front parlor was closed, and Sibyl's hand hovered above its lacquered surface, twin peacocks furling inlaid tails below her fingertips. There was no telling what sort of mood she might find waiting in the drawing room. Lan Allston wore many discrete faces, and Sibyl suspected that she had only ever seen a handful of them. The one usually reserved for her, a pleasant but closed face, masking general if detached approval, she knew to be different from the one allotted to her brother. Several of Lan's faces, she knew, had vanished years ago under the surface of the Atlantic ocean.

In silence she slid the pocket door aside and slipped into the front parlor, her eyes adjusting to the darkness. The room was done in varying shades of blue, with dark woods and lacquer. Helen's fetish for the art nouveau dominated, with tree boughs and curling birds echoed in the patterns on the Chinese rug and in the *objets* clustered, almost tastefully, on occasional tables. The bay window held benches upholstered in heavy yellow silk, which Sibyl, when small and hungry for sensation, loved to stroke. Velvet curtains blotted out the streetlights. Most of the houses along Beacon had long since run electrical wires to wall sconces and chandeliers; it was a simple process, not even that expensive, but Lan kept the house lit with orange gas flame. He was loath to spend the money, she knew, but she also detected her mother's preferences haunting Lan's choice.

"Electric light does nothing for the complexion," Helen insisted in her mind, as usual delivering instructions. "Women look so well in softer light."

Sibyl turned to the parlor fireplace, its mantel carved and froglike in shape. Above the fireplace was Helen, or rather a life-size effigy of Helen, caught in swirls of paint by Cecilia Beaux shortly after her marriage. The paint-Helen stood frozen, eyes illuminated by globules of white, her hair up in curls at the back of her head, white collarbones exposed, circlet of pearls at her throat. Helen clearly wished to appear "artistic" when she posed. Sibyl could imagine a naïve Helen in the artist's studio, anxious to seem worldly, yet uninformed how to do so. The effect was of a young woman unsure of herself, an awkward slipper peeking out from under her gown, one arm folded at her waist, eyes wide, lips about to speak.

As a child, Sibyl liked to sprawl on the carpet before the fireplace, gazing up at the painting like a miniature supplicant. She was supposed to keep away from the front parlor—no children in the good rooms was the rule—so her hours communing with her mother's likeness were stolen from time during which she was assumed to be sleeping, or working on lessons. Neither Harlan nor Eulah were drawn to the parlor the way Sibyl was; or at least, she had never caught them there on her expeditions to the front of the house. Eulah had no need for a substitute; she could command the attentions of the actual Helen. Harlan, in contrast, spent his energies avoiding close observation. It was difficult, being the son.

Sibyl gazed up at the portrait, her mother looking as surprised and tentative as always. Lately, Sibyl had felt the curious sensation of passing her mother in time. She was now older by some five years than the paint-Helen was. A strange dual awareness situated Sibyl, in the painting's presence, as at once lady of the house, and yet also a small girl, trespassing in a room that was forbidden to her. She always felt the mingled thrill and guilt of getting away with something when she entered the front parlor. Even if she was doing so to receive.

Light from the tulip sconces on either end of the mantel gleamed on the painting's varnish, illuminating it with lifelike warmth. Sibyl could almost feel sorry for Helen as a girl. Her ambition, her curiosity, her fear: everything that Sibyl had known Helen to be could be read in her youthful face. Everything but what was to come, of course. Sibyl's eyes wandered to the soft white hand pressing into the paint-Helen's waist, thumb folded into her belly. The same hand, thirty-odd years older, that had reached out for her from unfathomable nothingness. Sibyl's breath caught in her throat, and she reached her own hand forward, stopping short of caressing the image of the hand that she had longed to touch.

Ashamed, Sibyl pulled herself out of her reverie, realizing that she was dawdling. Castigating herself in silence, she stepped with authority to the pocket doors of the rear drawing room, allowing her footfalls to be audible on the floor. Sibyl hesitated, pressing her palm to the lacquered door, patterned with twin images of whales entwined with tentacled sea monsters. She inhaled, filling her lungs as much as her corseting would allow, and slid open the doors.

THE ONLY FORMS that she could discern in the twilight of the inner parlor were the rounded arms of her father's armchair, a Greek-revival holdout against Helen's aesthetic onslaught, and the hulking shape of Lan Allston himself. He stood with his back to her, busy at the fireplace mantel. A rhythmic grating noise emanated from his corner of the room, and Sibyl saw that he was winding the clock.

She opened her mouth to speak, but he got there first.

"You're back, I take it."

A pause, while the sound of winding continued.

"I've asked Betty for dinner as usual at seven thirty," she said, wary, as she often was when there was a problem to address with her father. "We'll be dressing."

He let out a short bark of a laugh, pulled his timepiece out of a vest pocket for comparison purposes, nodded with satisfaction, and then returned it to the pocket with a practiced motion as he turned to face his eldest child.

Lan Allston, at nearly seventy, was the sort of man whom his contemporaries liked to call "well preserved." By this they meant not that he had managed to hold on to the illusion of youth (he hadn't), nor that he had the too-carefully-groomed aspect of the professional class of man, the bankers and the lawyers. Instead they meant that Lan Allston looked exactly as they felt he should look. Rather than graying, his hair had darkened to the color of pencil lead, and he wore it cropped close and brushed back from his brow, with sideburns longer than fashion allowed for anyone who had not made his fortune at sea. His forehead was high and etched with lines burned by a lifetime of ocean weather. His eyes were an unsettling pale blue. He did not wear spectacles.

As long as Sibyl could remember, Lan had looked nearly the same. He wore elegantly cut brown tweed suits, and she couldn't recall ever seeing him in shirtsleeves. Most importantly, at least to him, he carried a brass marine chronometer tucked into his pocket, won—she had been led to believe—in a card game with another sailor in the Canary Islands. The chronometer was larger than the average pocket watch, and her father made such a fetish of it that his tailor was obliged to render his vest pockets that much larger, and reinforced with silk batting, to accommodate it. His shirt collars were rounded, folded over a plain dark tie held in place with a modest tie pin at his throat.

"It's all very well to dress if you think it necessary," Allston said to his daughter, in a tone that suggested that dressing would do nothing to smooth over the Harlan problem. "Though you'll have to have Mrs. Doherty ring the bell good and loud if you expect me to know it's seven." He cast a baleful eye at the mantel clock.

"You should take it in to be looked at," Sibyl suggested. Lan Allston, she knew, was a man who liked to know, rather than to guess.

Her father grunted in reply. The two enduring Allstons stood, regarding each other in silence. Sibyl had found since she was small that she and her father never needed to say much to know what the other was thinking. Their language was one of implication and assumption, exchanged looks and implied opinions.

"Your afternoon was satisfying, I trust?" he asked. His tone was gruff, but Sibyl could tell by the set of his eyebrows that he was interested in her answer.

Sibyl hesitated. She should tell him. She must tell him, of course. She still felt buoyed by the sight of her mother's hand, and she wanted to share her excitement with someone.

But as she leveled her eyes at her father, she could see that his face was closed.

"I always found that one impossible to read, even when it was working," Sibyl remarked, indicating the clock.

Her father moved away from the mantel, digging a finger into his other vest pocket. The finger withdrew a whole peanut, in shell, and he rolled it between finger and thumb as he crossed to the other side of the room.

"Have you seen him yet?" Allston inquired, each word separated from the last. The chill in her father's voice stopped Sibyl. She could barely see his form moving about in the shadows.

"I felt I should see about dinner first," Sibyl replied, lamely.

"Hm," her father said. Then, more softly, "There, now. Hello. You'd like this, wouldn't you?"

This incongruous last comment was aimed not at herself, Sibyl knew, and so she edged nearer, creeping toward the most unorthodox piece of drawing room furniture. This was a kind of hat rack, or she supposed it had once been a hat rack, fashioned from polished mahogany to simulate a blooming hazelnut tree, with knotty branches twisting this way and that. Her father stood next to it, addressing himself, peanut in hand, to a creature sitting in silent majesty atop the thickest of the carved branches.

"There, Baiji," her father whispered. "Take the peanut, won't you?"

Sibyl frowned. "And you?" she asked. "You've seen him, then?

Her father leaned nearer the creature, murmuring enticements, until it gingerly accepted the proffered tidbit. Then Allston spoke, without looking around.

"Seen, but only in the most cursory sense. Saw his trunk, at any rate. Paid his cab, too. The boy himself?"

He trailed off, as though uncertain which was more offensive: arriving home without telephoning, arriving home without money for the cab, arriving home without having a proper audience with his father, or just arriving home, period. As Allston weighed Harlan's various offenses according to the mental calculus by which fathers are accustomed to judging sons, he reached a delicate fingertip to rub beneath the chin of the animal in the former hat rack.

Baiji, the creature himself, was a macaw. He cast one black, intelligent eye at Sibyl as his beak worked on the peanut meat, withdrawn with uncanny dexterity from the open shell clutched in one claw. The animal was iridescent blue, a compact-bodied thing with a beak curved in a knowing smile and a long, intoxicating tail.

Sibyl recalled one evening, when she was a girl, overhearing her mother joke that she should dearly like to have a few of Baiji's tail feathers to dress her newest hat. Her father had exploded with a rage rarely seen in the Allston family, at least not in the public rooms, where the staff were likely to overhear.

"Lannie, my darling, a joke only!" Sibyl heard Helen protest, her voice muffled through the crack in the pocket door where Sibyl sat, ear pressed, listening. It was some hours before the fracas subsided, with the macaw's tail left intact, as Sibyl knew it would be. Eulah had laughed when Sibyl recounted this argument, saying that of course his tail feathers would just grow back, but Sibyl knew their father would never permit the macaw to be touched.

The macaw was, like the chronometer, like the speaking tube on the library shelf, and like the cracked blue and white porcelain basket on the mantel, a relic of Allston's years at sea. Though a South American bird—Sibyl had no idea which part of South America—he had come into her father's possession in China, another castoff from some long-forgotten sailor. He blinked slowly at her, feathers ruffling under the affectionate finger at his chin. She recoiled, from the strange humanlike expression on Baiji's parrot face, and from his knowing gaze.

"Then you don't know what can have happened," Sibyl stated.

In the years since the sinking Sibyl had assumed the running of the household, complete with the assumption that, should something disagreeable in Allston family affairs arise, it would be delegated to Sibyl to solve. Usually disagreeableness was limited to the firing of a thieving

kitchen girl (one silver spoon, since replaced), or to the settling of accounts with a doctor who failed to treat her father's dyspepsia to his satisfaction. In that vein, Sibyl had expected Harlan's return for the summer to
require her management. His abrupt reappearance, however, hinted that
simple management might not be sufficient.

"I've a pretty good idea. But he'd best hope I'm mistaken," her father
said, his voice neutral, in contrast to the dark clouds gathering in his pale
eyes. Baiji opened his mouth wide, stretching his eerily human tongue out
without a sound, and closed it again.

Sibyl, too, opened her mouth as if to speak, but closed it again without
saying anything. Instead her eyes traveled up to the wooden crown work
pattern on the ceiling, gazing toward the situation that was her brother.

FOUR

*U*pstairs, in a room whose finer architectural points were obscured by an explosion of books and clothing, a young man stood staring at himself in the mirror over his highboy. The highboy was a tall object, a Boston drawer set of strength and gravitas, whose only biomorphic properties were its curving legs and slipper feet, and so it had been banished by the young man's mother into the rooms beyond her reach above stairs. The mirror atop this tall chest of drawers angled downward, for the tying of ties and other details of men's dress. A silver brush and comb rested next to the mirror, together with a half dozen crumpled handkerchiefs and several small glass bottles. The mirror's angle caused the young man to view himself from above, creating the unwelcome sensation of witnessing himself seen as a boy, observed from a superior vantage point.

Harlan Plummer Allston III peered up with disdain at his reflection, propping himself on one leaning arm. The reflection was a near perfect replica of Harlan himself: similar in age, twenty-one, also with his tie loosened and his shirt collar open. His reflection parted his straight brown hair on the left, rather than on the right, and had a black mole in the wrong eyebrow. But the brows themselves were straight and dark, like Harlan's, the smile as rakish. Lips a little fuller than Harlan would have liked, almost like a woman's. Beard could stand to fill in a bit more, too, though the mustache was coming along nicely. Harlan's reflection half-smiled at him, an attempt at reassurance, and tipped a long swallow of amber liquid down his throat. Warmth suffused his tongue, and when he wiped his mouth on the back of his sleeve, Harlan's reflection did the same. He held the tumbler to the corner of his eye, pressing it there, savoring the cool glass on his skin.

A soft scratch at his door caused the young man to start and put the tumbler down.

"Jus' second," he said, swaying, then steadying himself with one hand on the highboy and the other gripping the post at the foot of his bed. Another refugee from Helen's rampant aesthetics, the bed was even older than the highboy. Its mattress was a lumpy horsehair sack still suspended on a lattice of ropes wound through holes in the bedstead.

"Good night, sleep tight," his nurse had sung, putting him to sleep in this bed. When he was a boy it felt huge, an open expanse of starched linens extending around him into an infinity of night. Now, at over six feet, his lanky frame could barely fit within its confines. He had to sleep at an angle, pillows bunched under his head, one foot thrust into space, away from the security of the covers. The mattress sagged, with no nurse there to tighten the ropes. He didn't fit there, anymore, either.

The scratch came at the door again, more insistent.

"Coming," he said, more clearly, releasing his grip on the furniture. He shook his head, trying to snap himself into readiness. After a moment spent balancing he lurched toward the door, only to get tangled in the trunk. Harlan stumbled, and the trunk collapsed, snapping at his thumb. He cursed under his breath.

"Harley," the voice on the other side of the door said. "It's me. Come now, let's open the door."

The young man shook himself free of the scattered clothes, brushed a lock of hair off his forehead, and yanked open the door with irritation.

Harlan hadn't seen his sister—well, his remaining sister—in . . . how long was it since he was home, anyway? Christmas, he supposed. At Easter break he and some of the fellows had run down on a jaunt to New York. To take in the new plays, they'd said. Well, that'd been the plan. And they'd seen a play—after a fashion. He laughed, thinking back to that raucous evening, before drowning the laughter in his mouth with another draft from his tumbler.

"Come in, Sibs," he said, gesturing with a sweep of his arm to the disorder within.

He observed Sibyl cast a roving eye over his belongings, which he had thrown about with almost studied disregard. She hesitated in the doorway.

"Mrs. Doherty assures me the linens have been seen to," Sibyl began.

Harlan groaned in anguished boredom, lolling his head back on his shoulders. "Oh, God!" he cried. "The linens! Whatever are we going to do about the linens?"

He turned away, laughing, from her reproachful gaze, but his smile vanished as soon as his back was to her. Harlan leaned a heavy elbow on the highboy, fumbling with a crystal decanter among the handkerchiefs, and sloshed a finger's width more amber liquid into his glass. Then he flopped into a leather armchair by the fireplace, one leg tossed over the armrest, slippered foot dangling. He glanced up at his sister and saw dismay flicker across her face. A hot explosion of shame and resentment burst in his chest.

"Well?" he snapped. "Let's have it, then. I've waited long enough."

Sibyl swallowed and picked her way into the bedroom. Harlan turned to the fire, prodding it with a poker so he didn't have to look at her. The fire had faltered sometime in the past indistinct hour, and he stabbed at the log on the grate, letting loose a series of pops and exploding cinders until the flames picked up. When he was satisfied he tossed the poker aside and turned to find his sister standing, her hands full of shirts collected off the facing armchair, a look of befuddlement on her face. He snorted. Sibyl turned a sharp eye to him, and then dropped the shirts in a heap on the floor. She settled in the armchair, back straight, and folded her hands in her lap. Then she turned her discomfiting dark eyes on him and waited.

Harlan gazed over the edge of his glass at Sibyl, searching her face. Sibs, his older sister. He was oddly pleased to see that she looked older than he remembered. Girlishness had never been a part of Sibyl, so to have the girlishness carved away from her face, leaving it paler, the cheekbones higher, the nose sharper, made her look more like herself. Beautiful, almost, though he had trouble thinking of his sister as beautiful. Sibyl as a girl had looked ill planned. Now, Eulah had banked on girlishness. Foppy, always talking about hats, dances, boys, hats again. Momentary pleasures, passing fancies. Harlan had never cared for a thing that came out of Eulah's mouth. Yet she'd been petted and coddled to beat the band. What would she have done when time carved her girlishness away? Nothing, that's what. But she'd have been married by then. So perhaps it didn't matter.

Of course, none of it mattered. He frowned into his glass.

"Harley," Sibyl began, leaning forward, reaching out with one hand toward his knee. She withdrew it without touching him. Harlan glanced up at her.

Why wasn't Sibyl married? It looked like it would be all set for a while there. But she seemed all right, didn't she? Tall. Well made. And funny. As a boy he'd cherished the dinner table moments when one of their parents would say something hopelessly Allstony, and Sibyl would catch his gaze to share a fleeting eye roll, as if they alone could appreciate the ludicrous elements of their family life. Sibyl made him feel like he was in on a secret joke. When they were small she often sneaked out of the nursery to go exploring in the forbidden corners of the house, and sometimes he would track behind her in secret, wishing she'd invite him along. He didn't quite understand how that adventurous girl had turned into the stolid spinster sitting in front of him now.

Eulah had been fun, but she'd never been funny. Oh, she'd been able to fool enough fellows into thinking that she was. Plenty of Harlan's friends let slip that they had their eyes on Eulah Allston, even before she came out. Never anything beyond what they knew he'd allow, of course. A man doesn't go around making remarks about another man's sister. Not in decent society.

He smiled ruefully.

"Sibsie," he replied. He chewed the inside of his cheek, waiting for her to say something. The fire spat out another spark, which hit the screen and fell harmless into the ashes below the grate.

"It's just for the weekend, then? You'll be going back to sit for your exams?" she suggested. Her eyes were gentle.

He barked a single laugh, almost identical to the one barked by his father downstairs.

"Not likely," he said, swirling his glass. Harlan couldn't bear her steady gaze—why did she have to look at him like that? Why couldn't she hide how disappointed she was? He cast his eyes sideways to the fire, and the loose lock of hair fell over his forehead.

"Well, you needn't decide all at once. It's a month yet before semester's end, isn't it?" she pressed.

Instead of answering her he got to his feet, ambling to the bay window that looked through the elm branches down to Beacon Street. He'd have preferred the room facing the river, Sibyl's room. She was the oldest, so she always got the best of everything. But he supposed that would have to wait until the old man kicked the bucket. Harlan drew aside the brocade drapery, the glow from the streetlight illuminating the young lines of his face.

"How did the Captain seem?" he asked, trying to sound indifferent.

Sibyl said nothing, and Harlan glanced from the window to her, expectant.

"Oh, Harley," she said at last. "What can have happened?"

Something inside Harlan broke apart, and the full flood of his self-loathing washed through him like a tide of spoiled milk. He turned on her, mouth a tight line, nostrils flared. Sibyl withdrew deeper into the armchair, and he just glimpsed fear in her face before she was able to hide it. As soon as he saw that she was afraid of him, his cheeks flushed with mingled anger and shame: at Sibyl, for not seeing that he wanted to be reassured, and at himself, for his accursed weakness. He stalked across the room to the door, flinging it open with such force that it bounced off the wall, leaving a dent in the paper.

"I have nothing to say to you," he said, too loudly. "I have nothing to say to anyone."

Sibyl rose, and Harlan knew that she was covering over her discomfort with formality. It was typical of Sibyl to respond that way to anything unpleasant, she had adopted it from their father, and Harlan wanted to grasp her by the shoulders and shake her, to force her to see how he was feeling without him having to explain, as she used to when they were children.

He so desperately wanted her to *see* him. In that instant he almost hated his sister. Helen and Eulah had left; and now here was Sibyl, leaving him, too.

She moved past Harlan, head high, lips pressed into a grim line like his own. When she reached the door she lingered, her fingertips on the doorknob. "You're tight," Sibyl said, voice measured and cold, and the judgment in her voice caused the muscle at his jaw to twitch. "No more of that, now. You'd best rest up. I've ordered supper for seven thirty."

She cast her eye down his disheveled self and back up to meet his gaze. "Dressed."

The door closed behind her with a click, and Harlan's fist tightened around the glass until it cracked.

AT PRECISELY FIFTEEN minutes before the dinner hour, but well after the dressing bell, Harlan peeked his head out from his bedroom door, looked left down the carpeted hallway to the main stair, looked right to the rear stair and the door to Sibyl's rooms, and satisfied himself that she was still dressing. No sound stirred the halls of 138½ Beacon Street, save the distant ticking of an unseen clock. He eased one stockinged foot out the bedroom door, followed by the other. His hair was smoothed back, held in place with a combed sheen. His dinner jacket was brushed, with a fresh sprig of mint tucked, in daring defiance of fashion, into his buttonhole. His black silk tie was elegantly knotted, and his cheeks glowed pink with a fresh shave. One hand held a pair of evening pumps buffed to a high sheen, an overcoat draped over his arm, while the other eased closed the bedroom door.

One foot after the other, catlike, exaggerating with high steps of his knees for his own comic amusement, Harlan crept past Sibyl's closed bedroom door. As he passed, the ball of his foot pressed on the joint between two floorboards, which let out a protesting creak. Harlan froze.

Inside, delicate humming stopped. Both parties on either side of the door held their breath, ears straining. No sound but that distant, placeless clock. In a moment the humming began again, the humming of hair arrangement, and Harlan exhaled in slow degrees before resuming his progress. He eased open the door to the rear service stair, slid through it, and closed it with a click.

Down the narrow service stair, silent, as when he was a boy, stalking through the house playing pirate, or Union spy on a raid behind Rebel lines. He'd loved to dress up, winding one of his mother's scarves around his head for piracy, or in a wide sash at his waist to play at being a Zouave, with a cigar-box fez and an invisible cutlass. He'd creep on all fours through the shadows, spying on the kitchen girls, eavesdropping to collect intelligence for the general back at the base, or the pirate captain waiting on shipboard, thrilling at his secret rebellion. He'd write up his notes in a complex code of his own design, borrowed from ship log shorthand and algebraic notation. Harlan loved feeling concealed, on a noble mission, hidden from whatever his father might have wished for him to be doing.

Harlan sat on the bottom step of the service stair and bent to slip into his shoes.

"Oh!" a voice gasped.

His head snapped up, and he beheld the startled face of Betty Gallagher, her hands struggling not to drop a platter of roast chicken.

He leaped to his feet, stepping forward to slide both hands under the platter to help rescue the chickens. His pulse rose, enjoying that Betty Gallagher would now be in collusion with his plan.

"Mister Harlan!" Betty said when she had recovered herself. She took in his dinner jacket, the overcoat on his arm, and glanced at the door into the dining room. "But . . . supper's not been ordered 'til seven thirty."

Harlan, standing close as both their sets of hands supported the platter, gazed down into Betty's face, with its wide eyes and wild hair. Her freckles were delectable. Most fellows didn't care for freckles as a rule, thinking they were tough-looking. But Betty's were appealing. Like cake batter you could wipe off with your thumb, buttery and sweet. He smiled out of one side of his mouth, wondering if she'd pull away, and coiled a tentative arm around Betty's waist.

"Not for me, it isn't," he whispered. "I'm dining at the club." He tightened his grip a little and felt the inviting give of her flesh under the apron and shirtwaist. She wasn't pulling away. He wondered with a shiver of pleasure if he could press further.

She half-smiled in return, gripping the platter with both hands. "Why, Mister Harlan," she chided. "Whatever will your father say."

"Hmm," he said, pretending to look concerned. "Why, I hadn't thought of that. What shall we say to him?" He ducked his head nearer Betty's freckled cheeks, crinkling his eyes in commiseration.

"What indeed?" she whispered. Their eyes met, his sparkling with mischief, hers watchful.

Thrilling at the window of opportunity she seemed to have cracked open for him, Harlan leaned in and pressed his lips to Betty's mouth. He felt resistance, and then beneath his insistent pressure felt that resistance give. She tasted as he knew she would, like flour and salt and cinnamon, and his fingers pressed into the small of her back, sensing the texture of her skin. He pressed himself closer, slipping his tongue between her lips and probing the roof of her mouth. Her mouth was delicious, warm, yielding, but oddly inert under his kiss, accepting without participating. After a moment she broke herself away, wiping her mouth with the back of her free hand and then batting him on the cheek.

"Brute," she scolded, but with a knowing smile.

Harlan laughed. She was a fine, game girl. He'd suspected she would be.

Just then the kitchen door opened to reveal the back-lit silhouette of Mrs. Doherty, her face impassive. "Is the girl bothering you, Mister Harlan?" she asked without preamble.

"Why, not at all, Doherty, not at all," he said, eyes twinkling. "But I am bothered." He reached up to confirm that his tie was in order.

"In that case we've the table to see to," she said, frowning, in a manner both commanding to Betty and dismissive to Harlan.

He winked in Betty's direction, but she wasn't looking. Instead she hurried, head down, to the door into the dining room, opening it with her back, platter of chickens in both hands, eyes averted. Mrs. Doherty turned an icy glare on him and seemed on the point of saying something. Harlan flashed her his most winning smile, brushed his hand over the mint sprig in his buttonhole, and slipped out the back door.

———

"TWO SPADES," SAID Rawlings around the pipe between his lips, coils of smoke leaking out the corners of his young mouth.

"Pass," grumbled Bickering. Harlan wished Bickering would have a better card face. This was bound to be a wasted rubber if he couldn't keep his cards to himself.

"Four spades," tossed out Townsend. He was a smooth fellow, with shrewd eyes. The sort of man who'd have hobbies about which he could be an insufferable bore. Chess? Philately? It didn't matter. It could solve a number of problems, having a bridge partner like Townsend.

"Pass," said Harlan, as evenly as he could.

"Well, dummy's you," Townsend said to Rawlings, who laid his hand out faceup with resignation and rekindled his pipe.

"Well, Allston," he said, slipping the pipe back between his lips. Rawlings cultivated the pipe at college because clenching it in his teeth forced him to flatten out his vowels. Trying to obscure a southern boyhood, was Rawlings.

"Well?" Harlan remarked, eyes on his cards. He shifted a few in pairs, considering his strategy.

"Sir." A murmur by Harlan's ear stirred the fine hairs at the base of his neck. A uniformed porter bent in a confidential attitude by the card table, hands behind his back.

"I'm rather occupied," Harlan said, without looking at the houseman.

"So sorry, sir, but you have a telephone call. Where should you like to—"

"I'm in the middle of a game." Harlan's voice tightened. "I should not like to take it at all."

The porter cleared his throat, saying, "Very good sir. What time shall I tell Captain Allston would be more convenient?"

Harlan looked up at the houseman with a sordid glare, saying nothing.

"An hour then, sir?" the porter suggested, unflappable. Captain Harlan Plummer Allston Junior, Lan to his intimates, Lannie to his wife, had been a member of St. Swithin's longer than his son. His influence there, as in all other venues of Harlan's life, was considerable.

Harlan returned his eyes to his cards, slapping a useless seven of hearts on the table.

"Blast," said Bickering. "If that don't cap all."

"Ninety-five," Rawlings remarked with amusement.

"Well, I reckon we're beat," Bickering said, stretching his arms over-head.

Harlan scowled, heart sinking. Ninety-five! And on top of everything else, too. He should've known better, picking Bickering for a bridge partner.

"Now then, Allston," Rawlings continued, lips moving around his pipe. "Rather early to be slinking out of old Westmorly Hall for the summer, isn't it?"

"What d'you mean?" Harlan asked levelly.

Rawlings laughed as Bickering and Townsend exchanged a glance.

"All right, have it your way," Rawlings said. "But I wish you'd give us the scoop. Otherwise we'll just amuse ourselves with speculating."

Harlan paused, considering how they might respond if he actually told them the truth, and then laughed. Impossible. They'd never believe he meant it. He could afford a variation, at most. He rummaged in his jacket pocket and withdrew a silver cigarette case.

"Well, Rolly, I'll tell you," he began, lighting his cigarette as the three young men pricked up their ears. "It's a pretty good story."

"I knew it," Bickering said to Townsend, who raised his eyebrows.

"It has to do with a certain young lady," Harlan said. "About whom I can't say any more, for fear of her reputation. You understand."

"Oh, come now!" Rawlings protested. "Can't a man speak plainly within the confines of his club, and in the company of gentlemen?"

Townsend and Bickering gave their audible assent.

Harlan made a show of hesitating, and then deciding to persevere. "Very well. I'm sure you're aware, this isn't the first time a member of the fairer sex entered our humble Cantabrigian domicile. So I invited this lady of my acquaintance in for a drink and some companionable conversation."

"That's the boy," said Bickering, elbowing Rawlings in the ribs. Rawlings grinned, teeth still clamped around the mouthpiece of the pipe.

"So there we were, a nice fire going, a couple of excellently made cock-tails," Harlan continued.

"And some *companionable* conversation, no doubt," Bickering interrupted.

"When she comes over faint," Harlan said in feigned surprise.

"The poor thing," Rawlings said through his grin.

"Well, what could I do?" Harlan asked, hands spread in helplessness. "I helped her to loosen her dress. Ladies' underthings can be so restrictive, you know."

"I'm all for dress reform, myself. So much more modern. So much more . . . accessible," Bickering mused.

"Well, wouldn't you know, the tutor chose that most inconvenient moment to drop in." Harlan sighed. Anguished groans broke out around the table. It wasn't a lie, exactly.

"Not Baker, was it?" Rawlings asked.

"I had a few run-ins with Baker myself, before I parted ways with the Crimson Goliath," Bickering remarked to no one in particular.

"So there you have it, fellows. Hoist by my own petard." Harlan took a last drag on his cigarette before rubbing it out in the brass tray on the table. Townsend idly shuffled one of the decks of cards, his hands in constant motion as Rawlings pursed his lips around the base of his pipe.

"Now, Allston," Bickering said, adopting a faux-schoolmarm tone, "there's a rather important detail lacking in your account."

"Oh?" Harlan asked, in false innocence.

"The name of this infamous lady. Mademoiselle Petard," Bickering said.

Harlan stood, hooking his thumbs in his waistband and gazing down on the other men at the card table with a sultry look. "You certain you'd like to know?"

"Her name!" clamored Rawlings, with Townsend and Bickering together.

"Why, Rolly, don't you know? I'd think your sister would've mentioned," Harlan said, before tossing a peanut into his mouth and withdrawing from the table with an ironic salute, as the air seemed to rush out of the room.

AS HARLAN PAUSED in the door of the St. Swithin Club, pulling the collar of his overcoat up under his ears against the chill of late evening, he spotted the form of a man approaching at a laconic pace, streetlights casting his wavering shadow across the brick street. Cursing his luck, a twist of guilt in his belly, Harlan started at a quick clip down the steps, head down, jostling by the man as he started up the stairs to the club. Too late—the man caught his elbow.

"Why, is that Harley Allston?" he said.

"Benton," Harlan said, injecting his voice with the necessary heartiness. "Good to see you. 'Fraid I must be going."

"Hold up a minute," Benton Derby said, keeping a firm grasp on his elbow.

"Wish I could, but I really can't." Harlan smiled, shrugging. "People waiting."

The young man released Harlan's arm, brushing his coat jacket smooth. "All right," he said. "You know, I've got office hours all during reading period. You're welcome, any time."

"Right," Harlan said, still with an uncomfortable smile on his face. "See you, then."

Harlan hurried down the street, hands thrust into his coat pockets, eyes on his shoes. He wished Benton hadn't seen him. Benton must have heard the story by now. Harlan frowned, watching his feet stride down the cobblestones, sidestepping puddles. When he reached the Common he paused, glancing over his shoulder, and saw the silhouette of Benton Derby still standing under the awning of the St. Swithin Club, arms folded, watching him go.

Turning away without a wave, Harlan jogged down the stairs from Beacon Street, enveloped by the anonymous darkness of the Common at night. Hidden in the darkness he felt the shame start to fall away. He crossed southeast, fog thickening around him. The damp created an eerie halo around each streetlight, and moisture beaded on his overcoat by the time he jogged across Charles Street into the Public Garden.

Damn that Benton. Harlan scowled as he passed under the weeping willows by the pond, then through cobbled streets that grew narrower, darker, more clotted with animal waste. The deeper he moved into the center of the city, the more the grip of shame loosened. He paused at an intersection of withered eighteenth-century houses, peeling clapboards and leaning chimneys, places that the historical society ladies treasured without wanting to inhabit. A tiny boy sat in a ball on a stoop, in a pair of greasy boots that were too big for him. The shutters on his house were closed and insulated with wadded newspaper.

"Excuse me," Harlan said. "Would you say I'm nearly at Harrison Avenue?"

The urchin nodded, and then held out a grubby hand.

"Thought so." Harlan smiled, pressing a nickel into the boy's palm. Almost there.

He rounded a corner at a trot, and with a leaping in his chest spotted a brightly lettered placard framed by cherry branches, translated in smaller type as *BOARDING HOUSE*. Beneath the sign stood a nondescript door. Harlan opened this door and stepped into a hallway whose major decorative element was wallpaper covered in bloodred cabbage roses, curling at the corners. A single electric bulb burned in a frosted glass sconce. He mounted the narrow stair, taking the steps two at a time, his footfalls muffled by worn carpeting.

On the third floor Harlan moved down the hallway, a grin spreading across his face. He reached the door at the end, which he knew opened into the front gable garret facing onto Harrison Avenue. A dried sprig of mint hung, upside down, their private signal, pinned to the naked wood of the door, below the hand-painted numeral 8.

Harlan lifted his hand to knock, his pulse quickening.

Just then the door clicked open, and a smiling green eye observed him from behind a brass chain. The door closed as the chain was unfastened, and then opened again.

"I'm so sorry," Harlan started to say. "I couldn't—"

He was interrupted by a delighted laugh, and the sound of shushing. The person behind the door took hold of the lapel of his glistening overcoat, pulled him inside, and closed the door.

FIVE

*S*ibyl's hands plucked at the edge of her overcoat, anxious. The rattling taxicab rocked her to and fro, and every so often her hand wandered up to reassure itself that the edge of her hat wasn't bumping the cab window. The previous day's brilliant light had given way, in the desultory way of New England at springtime, to a thick mist, creeping up the streets in the night and refusing to burn away. On days like this Boston reasserted its stubborn kinship with the water, as if to remind the city that though its swamps might be drained, its air freed of fever, its tide flats filled, it would always be a tiny spit of land in a world of water, river to the one side and sea to the other. The air tasted of salt and wet earth. River bottom.

The cab rounded a corner and approached the Harvard bridge, rising like the back of a sea animal through the fog. Sibyl heard the crack and the groan of metal wheels, the electric 76 streetcar trundling past on its way into Boston, loaded down with writhing limbs, each rider pressing under the overhang to shelter from the drizzle. Sibyl recoiled at the thought of so many bodies pressed together, of the unwanted intimacy of public life. Her busy hands folded themselves around her opposite elbows with a shudder.

A few pedestrians plodded across the bridge, huddling under black umbrellas. Beyond them the slate surface of the Charles rippled beneath the white-gray cloak of fog. The cab moved at a stately pace, motivated, she supposed, by either concern for her perceived gentility or desire for a costlier fare. Sibyl's eyes slid to the back of the driver's head. He wore a wool checked cap pulled low, revealing a beefy roll of neck at the top of his collar. She wondered how many times he must cross this bridge in a day. What did he think about on all those bridge crossings? Did he even notice them anymore?

Out of the fog the outline of Cambridge emerged, the new concrete dome of the technology institute rolling into view first. Sibyl's hands knitted together in her lap. The call had come late, well after her father retired for the night. She herself was only half-awake, already undressed and settled in bed with a book when Mrs. Doherty scratched at her door. The housekeeper appeared, lamp in hand, dressing gown knotted tight, hair in a long braid over her shoulder, grouchy with sleep.

"Telephone. A Mister Derby. I told him 'twas well too late to be rousing the household, but he was most insistent," Mrs. Doherty informed her, in a tone that suggested Sibyl might think twice about accepting such an impertinent overture.

"Benton Derby? Are you quite sure?" Sibyl asked, perplexed, propping herself up on one elbow.

"I've left the handset for you, ma'am," Mrs. Doherty said, and then withdrew, light from her lamp trailing behind her as she made her way to the service stair.

Sibyl rose, pulling a filmy lace dressing gown over her shoulders and taking up her own lamp. Her bare toes gripping the velvet carpet runner reminded her of the nighttime excursions to the drawing room when she was a girl. In the entry hall, tucked behind the stairwell, she found the telephone in its dedicated niche, a technological toadstool, earpiece waiting on the table. In the background loomed the La Farge. Sibyl hesitated, discovering herself to be nervous, even excited, before pressing the receiver to her ear and moving her lips close to the mouthpiece.

"Ben?" she whispered. A loud cough burst through the receiver, and Sibyl held it away from her ear with a grimace.

"Hi, Sibyl? That you? Sibyl? Hello?" boomed a male voice on the other end of the line, then speaking above the mouthpiece said, *How can you be sure if this damn thing is working? What? Well, it would seem to—no, I see. Wait here, would you?*

"Ben? Hello? Can you hear me?" she said, more loudly, feeling conspicuous speaking at full volume in the sleeping house. Her left hand clutched together the edges of her dressing gown at her chest, a gesture toward modesty that she knew to be ridiculous but was powerless to stop.

"Sibyl! There you are." Then, to the unheard other person, *No, it's quite all right, I have it now. Thank you.*

"Ben, what a pleasure," Sibyl began. "Though, I must admit—"

Before she could continue Benton interrupted, "I'm so sorry to be calling so late, and so unexpectedly. You know I'd never wish to trouble you, but—"

"No, no," Sibyl interrupted.

"Sorry? What?" Benton said.

Sibyl smiled, and paused. Her caller paused as well. She took a breath. "Never mind the hour. I was up. Do go ahead."

"Look, it's late, and you can't go around having strange men calling in the dead of night. It's just I wonder if you might have the time to come by my office some afternoon."

"Oh!" Sibyl paused, confused. A strange request, given how much time had passed. What could he want? Sibyl wasn't even sure what business Benton was in. He'd worked with her father for a time, but that was years ago. And she hadn't spoken with him, alone, since just before he was set to sail for Italy. With his new wife. A tiny slip of a thing, with delicate skin and a persistent cough, Lydia's health was too fragile for the New England winter. They'd been sitting together in the bay window when he told her, the cheerful new snow on the windowsill insulting Sibyl with its innocence and freshness. They'd promised to be in touch again upon the Derbys' return from abroad.

They weren't.

Her eyes darkened at the memory, and all the dashed hopes leading up to it, but she pushed her thoughts aside with resolve. That part of her life was over. No point thinking on it now. She recalled that Harley once mentioned that he spotted Benton from time to time, at the club, or around campus. He even remarked with resentful sarcasm that Benton had accepted a position at Westmorly Hall, though in typical fashion Harley failed to supply any illuminating details. Perhaps Harley's indifference was pretense, and he was shielding her from the fact of Benton's return. But perhaps not—her brother took it awfully hard, too, when Benton married Lydia Pusey instead.

"Why," Sibyl said slowly. "I can find a free afternoon, I should think. Any excuse to get out of a committee meeting. But whatever could you need from me?"

"Well, I'm phoning from St. Swithin's." He hesitated.

At once Sibyl understood. She felt her stomach tighten, and she wished she had eaten less at supper. He'd crossed paths with Harlan. That's where her brother had gone when he ran out on supper. Her brother must have embarrassed himself in some way. It would be up to Sibyl to smooth over the ruffled feathers. Benton was only calling as a courtesy.

"Tomorrow," she suggested. "If you'll just remind me where . . . ?"

He laughed, and said aside of the mouthpiece, *In a minute, in a minute!* To Sibyl, he said, "Of course, I'm sorry. I've been teaching in Cambridge, actually."

"Have you!" Sibyl exclaimed with not a little dismay. All that time, and no word from him. Harlan must be in some trouble indeed.

"I have," he said, and she could hear the modest grin in his voice.

"Imagine that. Benton Derby, the professor."

"It is, I wager, even stranger for me to contemplate than for you. Let's say two-thirty. I should be done with actual flesh-and-blood students by then, and on to the paper-marking portion of the afternoon. I'll welcome the interruption. Be desperate for it, in fact."

Despite wishing to seem cool and elusive in her first real conversation with Benton, Sibyl couldn't help but laugh. "And which department? Where shall I find you?"

"Department of Social Ethics. Look for the office with the insufficient light."

THE CAB ROLLED to a halt on a comfortable brick lane, and Sibyl rooted in her pocketbook for change to pay the fare. She stepped down from the cab, which rocked on its springs with her weight, feeling annoyed by the tangle of skirts around her ankles. She'd have to hem this skirt up, no one was wearing floor-length skirts anymore. Sibyl felt foolish and spinsterly, her embarrassment heightened by a gang of underclassmen passing on the sidewalk, completely indifferent to her. The cab shook to life and pulled away.

Sibyl lifted her chin, setting her jaw in a way that made her look fleetingly like Helen. She straightened her hat and crossed under a wrought iron gate onto the campus.

The Yard was dotted with knots of boys in various stages of study and leisure, though rather more leisure than study. Here a gang of them wrestled over a football. There a few stretched in the grass, ties loosened. Chipper music from a Victrola played through an open window, which also contained a pair of socked feet. An older boy coasted by on a safety bicycle, serious under his hat. Sibyl was surprised to see how different the Yard looked, with the new library nearly done.

Sibyl had heard about the library in whispered gossip for three years but hadn't realized it was so close to completion. Faint hammering was audible inside, but the outside looked perfect, a brick and concrete temple to knowledge. Mrs. George Widener had spent a small fortune on this building, a gift to the university, of course, but a monument to her drowned son more than anything. Rumor was that an exact replica of poor Harry's study was to be erected at the heart of the library, designated to hold his most precious books.

Everyone said Mrs. Widener had never fully recovered from losing her husband and son. The Widener men put her and her maid into a lifeboat, after an interminable wait, Sibyl read in the papers, and then stepped back onto the deck of the doomed ship, knowing they had no hope of rescue. Sibyl doubted that she would ever have such courage. What if Lan and Harley had been on shipboard, too; might her mother and sister have been put safely into a lifeboat then? Some men survived. Perhaps they all would've come back to Boston together, on a chartered rail car, giving interviews in all the papers about the horrors of their ordeal, full of the righteous indignation born of safety and security.

What were Helen and Eulah doing, when they first saw that the water was coming? When did they know that the water was for them? For a moment Sibyl's eyes closed, her ears echoing with imaginary screams, frigid water swirling around her mother's and sister's feet. But Sibyl shoved the thought away.

What better way to mourn a bibliophile than through the building of a new library, she reflected, steering her mind to safer waters. Though she supposed that certain future generations of Harvard's men would find reason enough, during exams, to curse the Widener name. Perhaps once the building was open, everyone would stop gossiping about how quickly Mrs. Widener had remarried. Perhaps, but Sibyl wasn't optimistic.

Helen had been so excited to learn the Wideners were on board that she immediately cabled to share the news. It was, in fact, the last word Sibyl had from her mother.

While she was alive, that is.

SET TO DINE WIDENERS THIS EVE NOT CAPTS TABLE BUT
WILL HAVE TO DO STOP EULAH BRIGHTEST BUD YOUNGER
SET STOP TAKE CARE PAPA TAKES MEDICINE LOVE MOTHER

Helen never could keep herself under the limit.

Sibyl turned away from the new library and hurried across the Yard, following a half-known path to the Department of Social Ethics, hurrying to make her appointment with a man she hadn't seen since before he chose another woman for his wife.

ON THE SECOND-FLOOR landing of the Social Ethics building as she climbed the stairs, a sudden pain in Sibyl's stomach stopped her. A black fog crept into the corners of her vision. She leaned on the banister, taking long breaths. Her father was right—she hadn't eaten enough at breakfast. In truth, she'd had only some sweetened coffee and a few bites of Betty's oatmeal.

Perhaps less than a few bites.

She breathed, feeling the compression of her corset around her rib cage and belly. It would pass in a minute. It always did.

Before long the fog began to dissipate, and the pain receded, replaced by the familiar sensation of perfect emptiness. Of control. She could face him now. Sibyl exhaled in perverse triumph.

Benton's office was at the end of a dark hallway, the door propped open. Voices traveled down the hall, and she glimpsed a suited figure leaning in the doorway of Ben's office, shoulders moving in lively discussion.

"Oh, you can't be serious!" She heard Ben's voice, friendly, but challenging.

The man in his office laughed. Sibyl, curious, crept closer to listen.

"I'll tell you the problem, Benton," said the man. "Hobbyists and charlatans. I read in the *Globe* about a chiseler who was holding séances for impressionable women. Seducing them, and then taking their money. Article said when he was arrested, his pockets were filled with love letters, blank prescriptions, and clairvoyant calling cards. True Spiritualist inquiry should happen in an academic context for just that reason. Don't we owe it to science to have an open mind?"

Sibyl swallowed, excited by their vigorous intellectual discourse, but also intimidated. All the women of her acquaintance couched their opinions in such polite language that it could be difficult to know the depth of their convictions. Eulah had been different, of course. She would say anything to anyone. But Eulah had been beautiful enough that she could afford to be shocking.

"Whoop, you've got a visitor." The man had spotted her, and beckoned her over with an easy gesture. She started, a blush creeping over her cheeks.

"It's a waste of time and energy," Benton's voice countered from inside the office. "I'm much more concerned with the practicalities of a life well lived, in the here and now."

While Benton spoke the man in the door smiled at Sibyl. She edged nearer, reminding herself that she had been invited. The man, younger than she first guessed from the way he was talking, rolled to the side out of the door to make room for her, smiling behind a pair of gold spectacles. His hair was parted in the middle, worn in thin shellacked waves close to his skull, and his suit was of a weathered tweed.

"Practicalities, Professor Derby," the man rejoined, indicating her.

Sibyl stepped into the doorway and found a room barely larger than her closet, stuffed to the gills with papers, a desk, a chair, books, a filthy brass ashtray, and a few trinkets scattered across the upper bookshelves. One window was wedged open with a telephone book, letting in the wet afternoon fog. A desk lamp cast the office in a greenish tint. Behind the desk, leaning back in a swivel chair with his muscular arms folded, leaned Benton Derby, associate professor of psychology. When he spotted her, he got quickly to his feet, scattering a few papers to the floor in his haste. He blushed and bent to retrieve them, cursing under his breath.

Benton would be about thirty-five now, perhaps a little less. Older, at any rate, than the fellow in the doorway, who was around Sibyl's age. Ben still had the build of a man who'd wrestled at school: overmuscled for his suit, which bunched in places, sewed by a tailor accustomed to slight society men. His hair had gone carbon gray in the past three years. The graying hair on a young frame gave Benton a funny air of exoticism, and it was cut short, a sign of an impatient man who doesn't wish to waste time on his appearance. Benton had round wire-rimmed glasses pushed up the bridge of his nose, making his steel eyes seem smaller than she remembered. Sibyl wondered if he truly needed the spectacles, or if he were trying to seem professorial. Of course, all those years of study were bound to ruin one's eyes. That was one reason Helen had been dead set against Sibyl going to college.

Sibyl smiled, waiting to be introduced.

"Here, let's ask her," Benton said, waving a hand in her direction, as though she had been present for the entire duration of their argument. "A neutral party."

Sibyl was taken aback by Benton's informality until she saw that he was shuffling the papers in his hands with more vigor than was called for. His eyes settled on her, lit up, and darted to the bookshelf. It occurred to her that Benton might have been nervous about seeing her again, too.

"Ask me about what?" Sibyl said.

"You'll have to forgive him." The man leaning in the doorway smiled, extending a hand. "It's a truism about psychologists that they should all probably be put away. I'm Professor Edwin Friend."

She accepted his hand, laughing. Benton pretended to glower. "And it's a truism about philosophers," he said, "that they don't make a lick of sense when they talk. Professor Friend, meet Miss Sibyl Allston. Go ahead. Ask her."

"I'd hate to bore Miss Allston before you get the chance to do it yourself," Friend said, smiling.

Benton wrinkled his nose at the other professor and tossed the papers onto his desk.

"The question," Professor Friend said, folding his arms, "concerns the American Society for Psychical Research. Dissension in the ranks. One faction thinks we should concentrate on psychic phenomena, like telepathy and precognition. It's possible that the human mind has qualities that aren't fully understood, which could be explained within the laws of physics."

Sibyl nodded, aware as she did so that Benton was staring at her. Her eyes flickered off of Friend's face and caught Benton's gaze, which darted back to his desk surface. He cleared this throat.

"The alternative view," Professor Friend continued, "wants to emphasize Spiritualist phenomena. Communicating with the dead, ectoplasm, spirit writing, and so on. Which is a kind of human potential, but of a very different sort. So which direction can most reveal something meaningful, something *true*, about human existence? Expanded talents in this world, or transcendence with the next?"

Sibyl smiled, intrigued. "My goodness. What weighty concerns you professors have on a spring afternoon."

"See, Edwin?" Benton exclaimed. "Miss Allston's far too practical a woman to be concerned with nonsense. I can't imagine what *your* excuse is."

"On the contrary," Sibyl said, giving Benton a long look. "I have a rather strong opinion on this matter."

"There," Professor Friend said, talking over Benton's incredulous "You do?"

Benton collapsed into the chair behind his desk and made a show of sinking his head in his hands. Sibyl laughed. "Now, Professor Derby, you have no idea what mischief we practical ladies get up to away from prying eyes. I think you'd be surprised." She turned to Professor Friend. "Of course I would never presume to comment on what's worthy of scientific inquiry. But as it happens, I have, myself, witnessed some remarkable events."

Benton suppressed a gasp as Professor Friend's ears perked up. "Have you, then?" he said. "Of which type, may I ask?"

Sibyl had never discussed her involvement with Mrs. Dee. Mrs. Dee insisted on discretion, and revealing her activities to two members of the Harvard faculty would hardly qualify.

"Of . . ." She hesitated.

Professor Friend leaned forward. Benton rested his chin on his fist, watching her with apparent amusement.

"Of the . . . spirit type. As a matter of fact." She could obfuscate who was involved. And she found herself wanting to impress them. Helen had warned Sibyl that men didn't appreciate women who were too smart, but she had always found herself wanting to seem serious for Benton.

"Is that so?" Professor Friend said, keen with interest. "Can you tell me any details?"

"I'm afraid that I'm required to keep most of it in strictest confidence," Sibyl said, enjoying the suggestion that she might have secret knowledge that this eminent scholar could not fathom. "But suffice it to say that, for my own part . . . Well, we experienced some loss. In our family. Within the past few years."

He nodded in sympathy, accepting her euphemisms, encouraging her to continue. "There's a regular meeting, not far from my home. Of people who've suffered the same loss."

Benton may have mouthed the word *Titanic* to Professor Friend, but Sibyl only caught his mouth moving out of the corner of her eye, and so she couldn't be sure. She shot a lowered eyebrow in his direction, but he affected not to see it.

"How extraordinary," Professor Friend said, bringing a finger to his chin. "And you have, yourself, seen . . . ?"

Sibyl smiled a private smile. "It would be breaking a confidence to say in any great detail. But I must assure you . . ." She paused, creating the impression that more should be read into her words than was being made explicit. "I'm of the opinion that communication with spirits is not only possible, but offers real comfort to those of us left behind."

"Fascinating, Miss Allston," the philosopher said, scratching under his chin and gazing up at the ceiling in thought. "Thank you. A vote, then, in favor of researching life after death. Most intriguing."

He thrust his hands into his pockets, rocked on his heels, and then shook off his ruminations and grinned at Sibyl and Benton.

"Well!" Professor Friend said. "You have matters of grave import to discuss, no doubt. I should let you get to it. You're at Radcliffe then, Miss Allston? You must drop by one of my lectures sometime. You'd be quite interested by phenomenology, I think."

"Oh!" Sibyl exclaimed, laughing. "Oh, no, no. I'm not a student."

"Ah, no?" Professor Friend said, raising his eyebrows. He lingered, perhaps waiting for one of them to explain why, if she were not a student, Sibyl might be visiting Benton in his office hours. When no explanation was forthcoming, he remarked, "I see. Well! Onward and upward," rapped on the doorjamb in a genial farewell, and ambled away.

Benton's eyes tracked the other professor's movements. He lifted a hand in a polite wave and listened for the footfalls as they receded down the hallway. When their sound finally disappeared, he burst. "Can you *believe* that?"

"Believe what?" Sibyl asked, perplexed.

"We finished our doctorates at about the same time, you know. A prodigy. One of the finest minds I've ever seen, and now he fritters his time away on nonsense. Do we look at telepathy, or do we commune with the dead instead? For Pete's sake. What about real life? Does he know how many children scrounge in the Boston city dump for food and ice and fuel every day? It's in the hundreds. What do they care about mental telepathy? What good will table-turning with their dead grandfathers do them? Ed's a fine man, but he wants to spend his time on this hocus-pocus. What good's the soul, without knowing the mind?"

Benton's cheeks were flushed, and his breath came quickly with the force of his assertions. Sibyl stared at him, taken aback. Then he seemed to recover himself, wiping a hand over his face before he pushed back from the desk and rose to his feet.

"Listen to me," he said, shaking his head with a laugh. "Ranting like a madman. Let's blame the undergraduates, shall we? Hello, Miss Allston. It's such a pleasure to see you again." He paused, his unsettling gray eyes taking in Sibyl's face. She smiled out of the side of her mouth.

She drew her glove off, one finger at a time, and offered him her hand. He pressed it between his. His grip was warm, familiar. Her hand tingled at the contact, and she returned it quickly to her lap.

"Benton, really," she protested. "Haven't we known each other long enough?"

"Sibyl, then," he said, pleased. He gestured to the disorderly pile of student papers that he had rescued from the floor. "You should see what some of them think will pass for a term paper. Even gentlemen must know how to put words together, I tell them," he remarked as he took his seat again.

"I'm sure you do your level best." They looked at each other, and Sibyl felt a heavy thud in her chest. She breathed deeply, trying to push her nerves aside. She wanted to bring her hand to her cheek, to toy with the hair at her temple. But she didn't. "He seems very smart, your Professor Friend," she ventured. "I'm afraid I don't see why he bothers you so much. If science can reveal new truths about the human condition, how can that be bad?"

Benton sighed heavily. "Oh, he is, he is." He paused in turn, mouth contorted as he chewed the inside of his cheek. "I didn't know you were going to séances," he said finally. It wasn't an apology, exactly. But it almost was.

"I never used to. Well, that's not true. Mother would take me, from time to time. When I was younger. They were always interesting, you know, in an amusing sort of way. But, then, since it happened. Well. I've found it's been rather . . ." She trailed off, unsure how to explain.

A pained look crossed Benton's face. "I have no wish to upset you," he said, a little formally. "But you know, if the loss of Eulah and your mother pains you, there are ways of addressing that."

"Oh. Yes, well." Her words were vacant, deliberately so, for she wished to move the conversation away from such abrupt intimacies. There had been a time, perhaps, when she could have imagined telling Benton these things. One time.

"But how long have you been teaching? The last we heard from you,

you were in Italy," Sibyl said, giving little thought to her choice of words in her haste to change the conversation's direction. Immediately she wished she had said nothing.

"Yes," Benton said, voice vague.

Perhaps they could maneuver around it, Sibyl thought, watching Benton's face. A shadow passed through his gray eyes, but it didn't linger.

He pressed his lips together and then smiled gamely. "About two years. Since I've been back. They've been very good to me. Gave me a cupboard of my very own." He swept a hand out, indicating his minuscule office.

Two years. But then, after Lydia died, no one had expected him to come back at all. Sibyl's eyes flicked down to observe his hands and saw that he still wore a gold band on his left ring finger. She brought her eyes back to his face, hoping that he hadn't noticed.

"How nice, to have important work to keep you busy," Sibyl remarked.

As she spoke, she heard how inane the words sounded. She had been trained from girlhood to smooth over uncomfortable silence with platitudes. She slipped into this rhythm without thinking about it, like a clock that moved its hands without knowing why. She leveled her eyes at Benton, his features at once familiar, as known to her as her own brother's, and yet changed, nearly unrecognizable. Time had pressed itself onto Benton's massive shoulders and into the skin of his face, time and care. She wished that she could reach forward and cup his cheek in her hand. She imagined the texture of his skin, him closing his eyes at her touch. Sometimes she wished she lived in a world that would let her do the things she imagined.

Impatient with her own restraint, Sibyl spoke. "Do tell me the reason for your call, Ben, pleasant though it is to see your cupboard. Something happened with Harley?"

He widened his eyes and leaned back, surprised at her pointed inquiry. His expression betrayed a man who had assumed he must conduct a further twenty minutes of discourse on the changing seasons, or on upcoming charity amusements to benefit displaced Belgian orphans, or starving Russian widows, or conscripted Italian peasants that they both might attend. Sibyl found that she enjoyed seeing him surprised.

"Well," he said, one hand reaching for a nub of cigarette in the ashtray, "I'm afraid you're right."

"He's come home from school. I suppose you know that," she ventured.

"I didn't, not officially. But I bumped into him coming out of the club rather late last night. Not usual to see undergraduates away from campus this time of year." Benton watched her.

Sibyl sighed. "Of course. We rather thought he'd gone there. He skipped out on supper. And we hadn't even known to expect him yesterday."

Benton smiled. "I imagine that didn't sit well with Captain Allston."

A groan of exasperation slipped between Sibyl's lips before she was able to stop herself. "You have no idea. Papa was in a terrible state all evening. His nerves, you know. A worser attack of rheumatism than I've ever seen. We had to use nearly double his usual amount of tonic."

"Hmmm," Benton said, brows furrowed. He didn't comment further.

"We telephoned," Sibyl continued. "But Harley wouldn't take it. And he's yet to be home today. It's not like him, to stay out all night. Why, when you called I feared there'd been an accident."

"Nnnooo." He drew the word out, rubbing his brow with one hand. "Nothing like that. But he did his best to avoid speaking with me; he would've cut me dead if I hadn't waylaid him. Even so he was most anxious to get away. And then when I arrived I found . . ." Benton paused, uncomfortable.

Sibyl leaned forward in her chair.

"Well, I'm afraid he owes some clubmen rather a lot of money," he finished.

Sibyl sat back in her chair, confused. "But that's impossible," she said. He watched her.

"No, there must be some mistake," Sibyl insisted, getting to her feet, agitated. Benton rose when she pushed back her chair and stood with his arms crossed as she paced in the narrow room.

"Why do you say that?" he asked.

"Why, because Harley's got an allowance," Sibyl said, blanching at the mention of money. "Ample for his needs. The income from his trust. Surely if he lost at cards he'd merely pay his debts."

"Surely," Benton agreed, his eyes tracking her movements across the room.

Sibyl stopped pacing and faced the professor. His gaze was neutral:

decidedly so. She frowned, disliking her inability to read what he might be thinking.

"Well, of course he would!" she insisted, too loudly.

His expression stayed the same.

"I—" she started to say. "He—" She realized that she was sputtering. Sibyl felt her control slipping and knew that she must leave to avoid making a scene. She realized with surprise that she was angry—but at whom? At Benton? At her brother? She gathered her pocketbook and hat and stalked to the door.

"Sibyl—" Benton started, reaching out with one hand to stop her.

"Thank you, Benton," she said, her voice newly chill with formality. "You are so kind to have brought this to my attention."

"Wait," he said, frustrated. He moved from behind his desk to meet her halfway out the door.

"It won't be necessary to see me out," Sibyl said. Her head buzzed with rage at her brother for putting her in this situation. For making her solve his problems, and for making her seem vulnerable in front of Benton. This layer of formality protected her from how she was feeling. But she knew she sounded haughty, and it annoyed her.

"No, listen." Benton stopped her, taking hold of her elbow. She started at the familiar gesture, his warm fingers pressing into the firm flesh of her upper arm under layers of linen and wool. "That's not even why I called. I mean, it is, but there's something else, too. I have the distinct impression that Harley has been asked to leave school permanently." Benton spoke quickly, with urgency.

"Leave?" Sibyl echoed, eyes wide.

"I can't account for it any other way."

"But why?" Her dark eyes searched his, but they betrayed no secret knowledge to her.

"I don't know yet. That's why I telephoned. He didn't say anything to you?" Benton still held her elbow, more gently now that she wasn't pulling away.

"He never says anything to me anymore," she said, her voice almost a whisper.

As Sibyl gazed up into Benton's concerned eyes, she sank into a curious sense of déjà vu.

Harley, slow down! she cried in her memory as a ten-year-old boy skidded through the drawing room, just missing a vase with his elbow. He was snagged, squirming, by a laughing man in his twenties, the son of her father's business partner, his clear gray eyes shining with mischief.

Gotcha. The young man grinned, wrestling the boy to the carpet and pinning him over sputtered protests.

What're you thinking? Can't you see what kind of damage you could cause? You should be more careful, her sixteen-year-old self demanded of the wiggling boy as Benton held him firm, elbow on the boy's back, laughing. *Ben, let him up before Papa sees.*

Sibyl sighed, remembering. Things had seemed so much more straightforward, when they were younger. She wasn't sure what had changed.

Benton's eyes softened as he watched her. She looked up into his face.

"What I wouldn't give," she said, "to be able to know his mind."

Interlude

❧

International Settlement
Shanghai
June 8, 1868

SHABBY, *LANNIE THOUGHT*. He stood behind the shoulders of his shipmates, in a long, narrow room, lit by lanterns and smoking oil lamps. The furniture looked European, of medium quality, since cast off: heavy armchairs upholstered with threadbare silk, horsehair stuffing spilling out through their bellies. The walls were hung with landscape scrolls, illuminated by calligraphy that he was helpless to read. Lannie both recoiled from and felt attracted by the strangeness.

Along one side of the room stretched a bar, crowded with Western stools, on which a few men perched, backs hunched. Upstairs, a woman's voice sang high and wailing, eerie, and to Lannie's ear, tuneless. The room smelled musky, and Lannie fidgeted, too hot in his overcoat but unwilling to remove it. He dug his hands deeper in his pockets, balling his fists to give himself confidence that he didn't otherwise feel.

A woman approached the knot of sailors, in her fifties, dressed in a hooped Western skirt and long corkscrew curls, brushed over her ears in a way that reminded Lannie of his mother. The woman's hair was glossy black, shot through with ribbons of steel, and her face was locked closed. She wasn't Chinese, exactly, though her eyes were narrow and glittered black in the lamplight. Lannie stared, unaware of his open mouth until one of the other men chucked him under the chin with a knuckle and a gruff laugh.

The woman rested a bony hand on the shoulder of their agreed ring-leader, a merry fellow of about twenty-five named Richard Derby. He was a Salem Derby, but Lannie didn't know where he hung on that august tree. None too high up, if he was shipping out himself. But Dick was a modest man, compact and well spoken, and Lannie trusted him.

Now Dick stood, eyes twinkling, his head bent in conference with the woman, letting her hand linger. Lannie could tell that negotiations were under way. At first there seemed to be disagreement, nothing too substan-tial, as she was smiling, mouth open to show her wolfish teeth, and Dick was laughing, flirting, or pretending to. Finally a bargain was struck. The woman patted his shoulder in a motherly way, and then barked a few words to an underling. The underling hollered up the stairs, clapping her hands. A rumbling of footsteps, and then Lannie felt his mouth fall open again.

Down the rickety staircase, hand balanced lightly on the banister, moving slowly, eyes lowered, strode a young woman—a girl, not much older than Lannie, though the paint on her face and the looped-up ropes of her hair made her look much older. She wore a loose silk robe, partway open in the front, and with each descending step he glimpsed a black-stockinged leg, ending in a silken high-heeled slipper. His eyes followed her, drinking in her porcelain skin, the rich dark mass of her hair, her downcast eyes. He felt a sickening lurch in his stomach, the nausea that resulted from a warring sense of propriety, offended by the spectacle of his base desire. Lannie swallowed.

Behind the girl followed an older woman, in a differently patterned robe lined with red ostrich feathers. This woman gazed straight out over the banister, unblinking, sizing up the band of Americans who clustered together under the frank challenge of her gaze. Some of the men mut-tered, making jokes to cover their embarrassment. The woman was tiny, less than five feet tall even in her high-heeled shoes, and so thin that she looked like she would weigh nothing at all. Lannie was amazed that such a minute creature could render his fellow sailors into squirming boys with only her gaze, shaming them with her raw power.

On the heels of the second woman strode a third, more coquettish, age impossible to determine, obscured as her features were by garish paint and lacquered curls. Her robe was splashily patterned, her giggling laughter high pitched and false. She moved with an artificial waggle that Lannie found distasteful, but he could tell that the woman's baser charms worked a perverse magic on several other members of the crew. Some hooted, clapping louder with each dipping step she took down the stairs.

In the coquette's wake strode a statuesque woman, her heaped-up hair a strange pale auburn, possibly the result of chemical intervention, though her features, like those of the woman in charge, seemed placeless, as though she were from everywhere and nowhere. She held her head in a haughty attitude, her nose high, neck sinewy, a rope of pearls—was that possible?—draping over her collarbones and disappearing into the folds of her black silk gown. Lannie's eyes widened, entranced.

The young girl, the first down the stairs, never lifting her eyes, drifted to a spot along the wall opposite the bar and stood, hands folded, stockinged knee extended. Each woman after her stopped, lining up, some gazing levelly at the band of sailors, others staring into the middle distance, others with their eyes locked on the floor.

For a surreal instant Lannie was reminded of the vivid *tableaux vivants* mounted by the young women of his acquaintance: Diana the huntress, attended by woodland nymphs, depicted in motionless splendor by proper young ladies swathed in drapery, green vines coiled through their hair. Of course the tableaux were "artistic," conceived as paintings brought to life. But this row of women, so close to him that Lannie could smell their competing perfumes, was not some abstract paean to female beauty. These women could be talked to. Could be touched. The idea simultaneously thrilled and repelled him.

The Western-dressed madam paced in front of her merchandise, straightening robes, adjusting posture with sharp slaps against a shoulder, a cheek. In response to these brusque ministrations the row of women organized into their most attractive display, and waited.

The madam started at the end of the line, resting a proprietary claw on the last prostitute, a plump woman with a lavish bosom hidden behind the clutched-closed top of her pink robe. The madam smacked her hand away, and the robe parted, revealing a soft swell of flesh from which Lannie averted his eyes. The madam spoke a long torrent of Chinese—Lannie was at a loss to know what dialect—and Richard Derby, laughing, said, "Well, fellows, you need me to translate that, or have you pretty well got it?"

The group bellowed their appreciation, and one of the sailors whooped, bounded forward, and grabbed the curvy woman around her waist, hoisting her into the air and jostling her like a child. She squealed in surprise, one curl of hair tossed loose, and her squeal morphed into simulated laughter. The sailor slung her over his shoulder and carried her to the stairs, ignoring the madam, who followed beside them like a clucking chicken.

—"Right, then!" Tom leered, jabbing his elbow into Lannie's flank.

Lannie recoiled at the rough gesture but fixed a game smile to his face. The older sailor rubbed his hands together, as if approaching a vast banquet. The madam was still following their crewmate up the stairs under his heavy burden of squirming woman, and so Tom, half-toothed mouth grinning, elbowed forward and caught the wrist of the first girl, the young one with the downcast eyes. She gasped in protest, twisting her arm to free herself, but the sailor took this for play and held on tighter.

"Aw, she's feistier than she looks, eh?" He laughed. The girl's struggle intensified as Tom started to drag her, first with subtle insistence, then with impatience, toward the stairs. The girl's eyes widened, and she called out, trying to summon the madam. Lannie frowned. Out of the corner of his eye he spotted one of the anonymous men at the bar swivel in his seat, placing his glass down.

"Just because you're in the *yichang* doesn't mean you can act like an animal," the man said.

Yi was a word that had been banned in Shanghai, at least in reference to white people. It meant "barbarian." *Yichang* meant "barbarian quarter," and Lannie understood that the man had just issued the most mortal insult to Tom at his disposal.

"What?" said Tom, pausing. The girl struggled, but he held fast to her with no more effort than if he were dangling a line for trout.

A space cleared as the group of sailors withdrew, sensing the shift in the room. Lannie glanced at the speaker and was surprised to find that he was Chinese, for his voice had a slight British inflection. He was young, in his early twenties, dressed in the plain tunic and pantaloons of a scholar, with a long queue down his back. His body, though shorter than the Western men, was muscular, and his cheeks were pitted from pox, giving him the appearance of being able to back up his words with more than his intellect.

"You have made a mistake," the man by the bar said, his hands relaxed by his sides.

"What in God's name is he talking about?" Tom laughed, addressing himself to his shipmates. Silence passed from one to the next, born of tension and watchfulness.

"You are treating her as a *yao'er*," the scholar continued, unfazed by the sudden quiet. With quiet came stillness. The other men at the bar had new bands of tension running up their backs. "Like someone unworthy of respect."

"Why, I believe the Chinky bastard might be talking to *me*," Tom said, mirth draining out of his voice, his eyes narrowing.

At that moment the madam reappeared. She leaned over the banister and called out to the young girl, her curls trembling. The girl started to respond, voice high. The scholar cut in, barking something to the madam, and she hurried downstairs, coming to a stop near the bar.

"I will explain, so that you may apologize," the scholar continued, still betraying no sign of anxiety, his voice steady and calm. Friendly, almost. "She is a *shuyu*, from Suzhou, where the women are uncommonly beautiful. An artist. She tells stories. She plays marvelous music. Her voice is like water pouring over stones. And she has excellent conversation."

Tom's face contorted in confusion, and he tightened his grip on the girl's wrist. "You talk pretty good English for a Chinaman," he snarled. "But that doesn't mean I've gotta listen."

The scholar smiled, a thin, frosty smile, and continued as though Tom had not spoken. "It is a simple mistake to make. She must be courted. Her attentions must be won, at great length and with effort, and then only if you are to her liking, or very fortunate. You have taken her for a saltwater sister, because you are a sailor, and you have money in your pocket. This is understandable, but it is most offensive. Of course, uncivilized people cannot always be expected to understand. But now that you have been told of your mistake, I must insist that you release her. And apologize for your error."

Tom looked around in growing disbelief. Then a slow smile dawned across his face, and he released the young girl's arm. She scurried back to the line of women, resuming her place, eyes downcast. The sailor, meantime, started rolling up his shirtsleeves.

"I see," he said, drawing the words out, taking his time with the sleeve rolling. "A mistake's been made. An apology should follow. That right?"

"That's correct," the scholar affirmed. He pressed the knuckles of one hand into the palm of the other. Through the silent room Lannie distinctly heard the young man's knuckles crack.

"Well, all right," Tom said. The room froze, all attention focused on the humming space between the burly, half-toothed American sailor and the compact Chinese youth.

"Tom, don't!" Lannie started to cry out, too late, for the older man had lunged, swinging a fist that grazed off the younger man's shoulder.

The scholar pounced, landing three blows in quick succession, bursting the sailor's nose. Tom let out a furious roar, blood streaming into his mouth, and without thinking Lannie dove between them.

"Stop, Tom, stop!" Lannie bellowed, his voice deepening, hands warding the sailor off, but his words fell on deaf ears as Tom's fists barreled forward, landing first on the scholar's trunk with the dull *thwack* of a hammer hitting a side of beef. Then there was an abrupt explosion of white light and dancing stars and a cracking sound, like a snapping tree branch, and the floor was suddenly rushing up to meet Lannie, smacking him in the face.

A gasp rose from the group of sailors, a flurry of boots rushing across the floor, the floor that was now pressing against his face, the boots tracking through a spreading pool of something sticky and red. Shouting, cursing, and across his narrowing field of vision Lannie saw the thrashing form of Tom being subdued by Richard Derby and three others.

"God dammit, Greenie!" Tom hollered, veins in his neck standing out.

Lannie blinked, dazed, felt strong hands take hold of his shoulders, and the floor pulled away as someone rolled him up to a seated position. For a second every figure in the room split into two, vibrating and blurring before snapping back into their regular shapes, and he brought a hand up to his head. His skull seemed intact. His fingers hunted through the sandy mop of hair, searching for blood. Nothing.

"Aw," a voice by his ear laughed, and under his lowered lashes Lannie observed the smiling face of the Chinese scholar, squatting down to inspect him. "That's going to smart."

He gestured to Lannie's face, and Lannie brought his fingertips up to his jaw. The light pressure of his fingers caused his eyes to squeeze closed in pain.

Lannie's tongue probed his cheek, tasting copper and salt. He discovered an object in his mouth, like a boot button, rolled it onto the tip of his tongue, and spat it out. The object hit the floor with a clack, bouncing once, twice, then skittering to a rest against the toe of Tom's boot.

It was a tooth.

"Christ almighty, Tom!" he slurred through the blood pooling in his mouth.

"Serves you right, you little rich bastard," Tom spat, still enmeshed in the restraining hands of the crew. He lurched, and was subdued. Richard Derby peeled away from the knot of men, coming to kneel at Lannie's other side.

"Lannie," he said, voice low. "Look, I know what you were trying to do. And I admire it. You've got sand. But perhaps . . . look, why don't you light out for a bit? Meet up with us later? Tomorrow, maybe." Dick rested a hand on Lannie's shoulder, giving it a reassuring squeeze. "Let it blow over."

Lannie looked into Dick's face, then glanced over the Salem man's shoulder to Tom, surrounded by the other sailors. Their murmurs obscured what was being said.

"C'mon," Dick said, hoisting him to his feet. "It'll be all right. You'll see. Happens all the time, first night in port. Men get twitchety. Doesn't mean anything."

Lannie's eyes slid to Dick's face, testing to see if his friend was speaking the truth. He couldn't be sure. If Dick was telling him to leave, though, he'd best make himself scarce.

"You heard the man," the scholar said, clapping a hand on Lannie's other shoulder. "Let's leave this sink of iniquity."

He took Lannie's elbow, tossed a fistful of yuan onto the bar, and steered him to the door. The madam bustled up, thrusting a cold compress into Lannie's hand.

He started to slur a "thank you," but the scholar spoke over him, shooing the woman away.

The door swung open, and they plunged into the humid night.

SIX

Harvard Square

Cambridge, Massachusetts

April 16, 1915

*T*he cab wove through the student throng of Harvard Square, dodging two dinging trolleys, a hod-carrier pulled by a flea-bitten horse, and half a dozen boys on bicycles, their coat-tails flapping. Sibyl gripped the hard leather seat with both hands, terrified that some new threat would appear out of the mist just in time to be pulled under the wheels of the car. The cabbie, a sallow man with bristly gray whiskers and a low hat, seemed unperturbed. He spun the steering wheel this way and that, depressing brakes, leaning on the horn. Sibyl despaired of ever learning to drive herself.

"To know another's mind," Benton had said before she left his office. "Some question whether that's even possible."

Sibyl looked up at him, cross and impatient. "What good is it, then?" she said, pulling free of his grip. She pressed her lips together in mingled annoyance and shame at her own worthlessness to those in actual need. Her mind roved a catalogue of balls attended, new dresses worn, reworked, and discarded, all for the betterment of those less fortunate, or so the invitations always stated.

Oddly, Benton hadn't seemed offended. "Professor James—he was my mentor, before he died—said that facts only become true insofar as they are useful to an understanding of our place in the world. But I agree with Doctor Freud—the human mind is like a machine, assembled by circumstances in childhood, which can be tweaked with attention and care. We can change ourselves, Sibyl. I believe it."

She had gazed up into Benton's face, his pale eyes softening against the blow of what he was implying about Harlan. Sibyl had reached down to take Benton's hand and squeezed it, smiling a grateful, yet sad, smile up at him, and then turned to go.

Now she stared out the cab window at the gray world outside, her mind shuffling through different options to solve the problem of Harlan. Well, if they'd had him leave school for some reason, she supposed they could just accept him back, couldn't they? And if he owed money to some of his friends, well, her father would have a solution in mind. Harley'd known all those fellows since boyhood. He'd be able to set it right. If it was just a question of money, she supposed her brother could borrow the necessary sum from her father, against his share in the estate. Or could take up some sort of job in Lan Allston's shipping company.

He could find an answer.

He could.

If he came home.

The spoiled sot.

The thought burst behind Sibyl's eyes, anger flooding her chest and mind and mouth. She thrust her ungloved fist up to her mouth, pressing her teeth into the groove between her knuckles, keeping a scream of rage locked inside. What excuse could Harley possibly have, for gambling so recklessly? For worrying her? For drawing trouble to himself like this? Where was he?

Without warning the cab bounced over a hole of missing bricks in the road, rattling Sibyl in the backseat. The jolt caused her skin to tear on her teeth, and a coppery taste of blood touched her tongue. She scrambled to keep upright, hands hunting for purchase on the slick leather.

"Sorry, miss," said the driver in the front seat, the cab's progress smoothing.

Sibyl sagged against the backrest in the cab. She knew the strain was just from worry, rather than any physical exertion, but her energy drained away anyway, as though someone had opened a tap in one of her toes. The blood ebbed from her face, and the oily black haze rolled into the far corners of her vision again. Her mouth went dry, and Sibyl pressed a hand to her cheek to maintain consciousness.

"Excuse me," she managed to say, voice thick with effort.

"Yes, miss?" drawled the driver, cocking an ear over his shoulder to catch her instructions.

"I'm afraid I've given you the wrong address," Sibyl said, pronouncing each word with care. The man nodded as she gave him a new house number, and then she reached up, unpinned her hat, and allowed her head to loll back against the seat, her eyes closed against the darkness.

THE CAB ROLLED up to the house on Beacon Hill, and the cabbie leaped out, leaving the engine running, to open the car door. Sibyl looked up at him, wan and grateful, and he helped her out of the car with surprising gentleness. She stood, unsteady, fingertips touching the roof of the car for balance.

"All right, then?" he asked, his face furrowing with concern. Sibyl was taken aback by this stranger's noticing of her, his interest and concern. What was she, to him, beyond another anonymous face attached to a pocketbook?

"How kind of you," Sibyl said, a phrase that fell often from her mouth, usually without much meaning behind it. Today, however, was different. "I'm perfectly well. Thank you."

The man accepted his fare without another word, but tipped his hat as he withdrew.

Sibyl mounted the stairs of the town house where she had been—was it really only a day earlier? Impossible, but true. The door already stood open, the same butler standing motionless in the entry, as though carved out of wood and cunningly painted to imitate life.

Sibyl's father found the keeping of a butler to be pretentious. *Stinks of New Yorkism*, he had remarked to her once. Sibyl wasn't so sure; in a way, she thought it lent the house a certain continental panache. Helen certainly thought so. More than once Sibyl's mother lobbied Lan that they should have a man to open the door.

"It's so much nicer," Helen insisted, in her usual opening salvo in the drawing room after supper. The last time Sibyl remembered them discussing it was the November before Helen's fatal voyage with Eulah. The house in those days was seized by a months-long festival of preparation for Eulah's debut, a heady blur of dress fittings, decoration, redecoration, calls paid and repaid. At night Sibyl more than once came across her little sister brushing her teeth in their shared lavatory, her feet moving automatically through the dance steps that were likely to be called at her cotillion, head nodding to imaginary music. Sibyl hadn't practiced half so much, as Helen rarely failed to point out.

"Nicer than what?" Lan grumbled.

"Oh, you know," Helen simpered, looking at her husband from under her lashes as her busy hands worked at their needlepoint. "It says something. About one's standing."

"I can stand just fine on my own, thank you very much." At that point, Lan rose from his armchair by the fire and strode without another word to the inner drawing room. As he went, leaving behind his chuckling wife, her head shaking with resignation, he dug in his pocket for some crumbs to tempt Baiji, perched like a blue gnome on his hat rack. Sibyl had never known a man who could end conversations like her father.

Full of hope and trepidation, she looked up into the graven face of Mrs. Dee's butler, whose name she still did not know, and wondered if he would admit her. These were not usual visiting hours, and she was not expected. Her card was already in her hand, ready to substitute for an audience with the medium if necessary. The butler's eyes traveled down his nose and rested on Sibyl's upturned, taut face. Without a word he stepped into the shadows of the entry hall, holding the door ajar.

Relieved of her coat and hat, Sibyl was shown into Mrs. Dee's receiving room, where she held her Spiritualist meetings. It looked much the same, with its stuffed birds frozen in flight, their dead eyes watching. Sibyl moved, restless, knowing she should sit and wait with some composure, but helpless to keep still. The air was cloying, from years of incense seeping into the upholstery. Sibyl traced an idle finger along the sideboard, testing the texture of a pheasant wing, traveling through the dust on the walnut cabinet, creeping around delicate heaps of loose crystals. It stopped at the edge of a small box, open, lined with black velvet. The box cradled an opalescent orb of polished quartz, gleaming in the low light. Its smoothness invited Sibyl to pick it up.

"I'm not surprised you would be drawn to that," a woman's voice said from the parlor door, and Sibyl turned with a start.

There, her arms extended with hands resting on the doorjamb in an unusually sumptuous posture, stood Mrs. Dee, as small and stout as ever, clothed in a tapestry robe lined in ermine. A winter dressing gown, unseasonable and unfashionable, fastened all the way up to her round little chin. The medium brought her hands to toy with the fur at her throat as she moved into the room and seated herself in her Gothic throne.

Sibyl gawked before recovering herself. "I am so sorry to burst in on you like this," she began, flustered by the woman's taking her deliberately by surprise.

"It's no trouble, for I knew you were coming," Mrs. Dee interjected, raising her eyebrows with implied meaning. "I foresaw it."

Pausing by the sideboard, Sibyl frowned against a glimmer of doubt. But Mrs. Dee looked so authoritative as she sat on her elevated armchair, hands folded in her lap.

"But I . . ." Sibyl started to protest, stopped by Mrs. Dee's holding up of one bejeweled hand.

"Shhh. Come. Sit. Bring the orb, if you like." She smiled and gestured with a sweep of her hand for Sibyl to take the armchair opposite her, by a low teak tea table.

Sibyl hesitated, then took up the small box and seated herself in the armchair indicated by the medium. She placed the box on the tea table, crossed her feet tight at her ankles, and straightened her posture. Sibyl wished for clarity with such keenness that it felt like an ache in her limbs.

Speaking with Benton tied Sibyl up in knots, filling her with confusion and dread. She stared into the medium's face, willing her to lift the horrible uncertainty away.

Mrs. Dee leaned forward and scooped the trinket out of the box, keeping it wrapped in its scrap of black velvet. She cradled the ball in her hands, a perfectly round egg in a nest of darkness. Mrs. Dee started to roll the ball to and fro, slowly at first, though the orb's surface was so polished that it appeared motionless, its movement perceptible by the working of the medium's hands, but not by any change along its surface.

"Now then," Mrs. Dee began, her voice low. "You have nothing to worry about."

Sibyl felt the skin of her face loosen. Mrs. Dee always knew what to say. Helen certainly thought so. Her mother consulted the medium on everything of import to their family. What day was best for Eulah's first tea? Would everything go well with Lan's latest investment? Helen always returned home from these conferences feeling more confident in whatever decision she had already made. Mrs. Dee's signal strength, it seemed, was to reassure Helen that she was usually right. Sibyl felt herself settle into the embrace of the armchair, craving for her own sense of clarity to return.

"There," Mrs. Dee suggested. "You're much more comfortable now."

Still the orb rolled in her palms, winking and beautiful. Sibyl yearned to touch it. She wished that Mrs. Dee would pass it to her. Sibyl's eyes followed the ball, rolling, rolling, silent in the velvet.

"Perhaps you'd like to tell me what's troubling you?" Mrs. Dee inquired.

Sibyl sighed with relief. She could never speak about her fears to anyone. Always, people observed her—her friends. Mrs. Doherty. Her father. Her brother. She had to perform for all of them, and none of them knew the dark corner of her heart, where her secret self dwelled afraid and alone. More alone now. Sibyl had taken the adventurous girl she had been and stuffed her into a box, hidden her away in a dark and cold place while her adult self bent to duty and expectation. She didn't know where to begin. So many . . . There were . . . so . . .

Sibyl's eyelids dropped halfway over her eyes, and she struggled to keep them from closing completely.

Blackness—they had closed after all.

"My dear," said Mrs. Dee's voice, insistent, breaking into Sibyl's thoughts and wrenching her eyes open. "I sense that you are gravely worried."

"Oh, Mrs. Dee, how right you are." Sibyl sighed, her eyes traveling to the medium's face.

"I know," she soothed. Still the ball rolled, though Sibyl wasn't watching it. Instead she searched Mrs. Dee's impassive eyes, craving to be seen, to be shown how to unlock herself from the careworn woman that she had become.

"I don't know what to do," Sibyl said, voice catching in her throat.

"It's a lot to bear," Mrs. Dee agreed.

"I had no idea things were getting as bad with him as they seem to be," she continued. "Because he never tells me anything. He used to, you know. When we were small. But he's pulled away. First the problem at school, and there's the question of debts. But then, Benton seems to think he understands what the trouble is."

"And does he?" pressed Mrs. Dee, in a manner that seemed to suggest that she, herself, already knew, but was waiting for Sibyl to see it for herself.

"Perhaps. Perhaps he does. But I can't believe it. Well, perhaps I can believe it, if I'm being truthful." Sibyl brought a hand up to her forehead and massaged her eyebrow. Mrs. Dee waited.

"He's been moving that way for some time. Even Papa sees it. But I'd have thought . . . that is, what Benton thinks, it can't quite explain everything. Can it?"

Mrs. Dee fixed her with a small, knowing smile.

"Maybe," the medium said after a time, "we can find out." She nodded with authority to the butler, who had appeared in the parlor door at some point within the past several minutes, unobserved, and was lingering for instructions. He moved silently about the room, extinguishing lights, until just one old-fashioned oil lamp burned on the end table by Mrs. Dee's well-upholstered elbow. Sibyl watched these preparations with a mixture of unease and excitement.

"Do you know what this is?" Mrs. Dee asked, holding the crystal, the pale color of skimmed milk, nestled in its velvet.

Sibyl wasn't sure. It seemed as if it could only be what it was—a small-ish, polished crystal ball, about the size of a chicken egg, if chicken eggs could ever be made perfectly round. And blue.

"I'm afraid I couldn't say," she said, feeling foolish, then adding, "It's very pretty." She still wished that Mrs. Dee would pass it to her. Her fingers craved its touch.

"This, my dear, is a very particular tool of mine. We use it to see pictures of things beyond the normal powers of vision. It's especially adept at revealing the true nature of things within the past, and of unlocking the secrets of the human soul. It is, Miss Allston, a scrying glass."

Sibyl had never encountered such a strange word before. It sounded to her like *crying*—a crying glass. At this unwelcome suggestion Sibyl felt a prickling sensation within her nose, the heated hard crumpling of her cheeks. No, she must push that feeling away. She couldn't start weeping in Mrs. Dee's parlor. Granted, in the years she had been attending the séances Sibyl had overheard much behavior that was not accepted in drawing rooms. But somehow that was different; they were all shielded by the darkness of the room, and by the assured silence of their collective weaknesses. She couldn't bear to think she might break down in Mrs. Dee's closely observing presence, alone.

"Why, Mrs. Dee," Sibyl said, fighting through the prickling with a forced smile. "Whatever can you mean?"

"*Scry* is a rather outmoded word," Mrs. Dee said, in the tone of a schoolteacher delivering a lesson. "We oftentimes find we must resort to older words, even to describe new phenomena, for our modern age sadly lacks the language necessary to speak of the world beyond normal perception. It's a pity that the world of science fails to interest itself more fully in the work that we're doing."

Mrs. Dee shook her head, mourning over what a pity it was. Sibyl was confused; Professor Friend's group had been active in Boston for some time, investigating human potential along scientific principles. Sibyl had assumed that Mrs. Dee knew this, and wished to keep herself a secret from them. But at least Mrs. Dee wouldn't disapprove of her earlier indiscretion.

"It means," Mrs. Dee continued, "to consult a reflective surface in hopes of revealing images beyond our ken. The reflective surface can be most anything. Some use mirrors, painted black. Some use little dishes of oil dropped in water. I've even heard that in earlier days, they'd break an egg into a glass of water, and use the egg white for divining. How clever of them, don't you agree? But by far the most effective, all the books suggest, is a polished ball of pure crystal. Like this one."

Sibyl returned her eyes to the beautiful toy in Mrs. Dee's hands. Its surface shone almost mirrorlike, now that most of the lights had been extinguished. The orb caught the oil lamp's glimmer, gathering the small light within itself, and returning the light to its surface in a smattering of spangles, like tiny stars in a miniature firmament.

"How does it work?" Sibyl asked, entranced.

Mrs. Dee laughed. "It's the spirit guides who reveal the hidden truths to us. They've crossed over and so can see far beyond what we can. I'd think, given your particular problem"—she eyed Sibyl, knowing—"that your dear mother and sister would wish to give us their aid and comfort. Don't you think?"

Sibyl held her breath, sitting perfectly still, warring with the burning tears collecting in the rims of her eyes. So that was why she had led herself back here. Sibyl wanted Helen to solve Harlan's problem. Helen had always been soft with Harlan, admiring and permissive. If Sibyl was honest, she could admit that as a girl she had sometimes envied her cherished younger brother.

Of course, it was rather a hard lot, to be cherished. The beloved can so easily disappoint when they inevitably prove to be human. And Harlan was certainly that. He was prone to solitary imaginary games as she was, never as good in school as he knew he should be. Harlan had been given to understand that he was constantly at risk of being a grave disappointment. But even with Harlan's flaws, Sibyl knew her mother would worry over the recent changes that had come over her son.

"Oh, I hope so," Sibyl wished, eyes fixed on the glittering trinket rolling in Mrs. Dee's palms.

"As do I," Mrs. Dee assured her.

"What do we have to do?" Sibyl asked.

"Just rest your eyes on the ball," Mrs. Dee urged. "And concentrate as hard as you possibly can. It's the magnetic forces in the mind, affecting the latent magnetism of the crystal, that opens a fissure between our world and the next, like a cable wire to the beyond. We need all of our concentration."

The explanation of the crystal's mechanism slid past Sibyl. Instead she nodded, furrowing her brow with effort as she stared into the medium's hands. Several minutes passed in silence as both women fixed their gaze, barely blinking, on the sparkling ball.

Somewhere in the distance, muffled by walls and upholstery, a clock began to chime the dinner hour, and Sibyl realized with a sinking in her stomach that she was being missed at home. Lan would be dining by himself, assuming Harlan hadn't returned, and her father hated dining alone. Sibyl frowned with mingled guilt and dismay. She could already hear his objections when she returned to the town house. Couldn't she have called? Surely she hadn't been out, alone, with Benton Derby, at this late hour?

She scowled, plotting out the coming argument in her mind. An explanation of her true whereabouts would do little to placate him after his lonesome supper in the dining room, attended by the withering gaze of Mrs. Doherty, her very silence serving to underscore her disapproval of his recalcitrant children. Sibyl's grim anticipation of this homecoming kindled warring desires to hurry home immediately, and to flee and never return.

Sibyl noticed that she had forgotten to keep concentrated on the crystal ball. Her mind had wandered. She glanced at Mrs. Dee to see if the medium had perceived her inattention, but the lady appeared absorbed in her work. Sibyl let out her breath by a small degree, relieved, and turned her guilty attention to the orb.

Its surface had changed. The tiny points of light seemed duller, less playful. Almost as if obscured by smoke. Sibyl blinked, bringing moisture to her eyes. No, her eyes were clear, but the orb seemed smokier. There was no fire going in the parlor that could be leaking smoke from the flue, since she had burst in on Mrs. Dee unexpected. But wait, Mrs. Dee said she knew Sibyl was coming. Odd. And it had been gray and chilly all day, her father even thinking they'd have frost by nightfall. But in any case, no fire. The lamp's wick was well trimmed; it wasn't smoking, either. She peered closer.

Sibyl imagined she could see clouds moving over the surface of the glass. Smoke, or clouds? Sibyl couldn't tell. As she stared the smoke coiled back on itself in whorls, moving, slow, silent.

"There!" Mrs. Dee cried, and Sibyl jumped from the unexpected intrusion of the medium's voice. "There, I see her! Her face, just as it was. Ah, Helen, my lost and most mourned friend!"

Sibyl looked back at the glass, confused. The smoke had vanished. The orb had reverted to a pretty, sparkling, inert object.

"How blessed I am to rest my weary eyes on your countenance!" Mrs. Dee cried, delivering her lines with flair. Sibyl sometimes wondered if Mrs. Dee formed her persona in part from watching the representations of mediums in films. Still, the drama suited the small woman. The language lent her a gravitas that was lacking in her physical form.

Sibyl's gaze oscillated between the medium's face and the ball, watchful and alert. Mrs. Dee gave every appearance of beholding a clear vision in the glass, but try as she might, Sibyl saw nothing. Less than nothing. She saw a round lump of rock.

"Mrs. D—" she started to say, but was stilled by the medium's holding up of one pudgy finger. Sibyl sat back, chastened. When she was still, Mrs. Dee continued.

"Helen, my dear, you surely must know why we summon you. Why we reluctantly rouse you from the paradise where we know, in our hearts, that you now reside."

Mrs. Dee paused, her eyes closed, the corners of her mouth turned up in a willful smile. When her eyes opened again they darted to Sibyl, who caught their look for an instant before they returned to the glass orb.

"I am here with Sibyl, your loving daughter. She has such worries, my dear. I know you ache to soothe her. Would that it were possible for you to reach out from beyond the grave and smooth the cares from her fevered brow!" Mrs. Dee's voice rose in pathos, her chin lifting to carry her exhortations to the ceiling of the dim parlor.

Sibyl folded her hands in her lap, brows lowering over her eyes. Her nostrils flared.

"But what? What's that you say?" Mrs. Dee cried, bringing the orb up to her nose and peering inside, as a child might into a Christmas present.

There was a long, excruciating silence. One of Sibyl's thumbnails dug into the flesh of her palm.

"Ah!" Mrs. Dee sighed.

Sibyl sat forward.

"Oh, how wonderful," the medium exclaimed. "Helen, I shall tell her. I shall tell her immediately." Then the medium closed her eyes and lowered the orb to her tapestried lap.

Her low simmering skepticism cast aside, Sibyl gripped the armrests of her chair. Feeling at once foolish but full of hope, she forced herself to stay in her seat. Her breath came fast and high in her chest, and her heart thudded so that she thought it must be visible, trembling under the delicate linen of her blouse.

After a time, Sibyl wasn't sure how long, she observed Mrs. Dee's eyelids fluttering, like moths' wings, over her rounded cheeks. The woman roused herself from an unspecified altered state, sighed with satisfaction, and turned to Sibyl.

"My dear, I have wondrous news to report," Mrs. Dee began. "I have communed with your mother's spirit, yet again. How blessed we are! Could you see her? Could you?"

Sibyl's shoulders vibrated near her ears, humming with anxiety and frustration.

"No, Mrs. Dee," she said, her voice small. "I couldn't see her. Please. Please, just tell me what she said. Tell me how I can help Harlan."

Mrs. Dee reached a soft hand forward and patted Sibyl on her knee. "You poor darling," she murmured. "But you have nothing to fear. Your mother asks me to tell you that she sees your troubles. She is sorry that the household depends so much on you. She wishes you to know that she loves you, and so does your dear sister."

Sibyl's mouth twitched, out of relief partly, but mostly out of guilt, for all that afternoon she had scarcely thought of Eulah. Eulah, who was worth the cost of the ticket to go on the tour. Eulah, who was sure to marry well. Eulah, who'd been pretty like Helen, not staid and Allstony, like Sibyl. At times Sibyl worried that, in a black and tarry corner of her heart, she was relieved that Eulah had been the one chosen to go on the ocean liner, and not her. As soon as the uninvited thought began to form,

Sibyl rejected it as impossible. She loved her sister. Everyone loved her sister. She was young, she was vibrant, she was glamorous and unconventional, she . . .

Without Sibyl's noticing that it was about to happen, a teardrop coalesced in the inner corner of her eye, brimmed over, and traced down her cheek, around the groove at the side of her nostril, to the ridge atop her lip. The salty taste brought Sibyl back, and she cast dejected eyes into her lap. Without looking up, she whispered, "What of my brother, Mrs. Dee? What did Mother have to say about him?"

The hand on her knee lingered there and squeezed in a way that was probably meant to be reassuring. "She sees your fear for him," Mrs. Dee murmured. "She sees, and she pities. But she wishes you to know that all will be well with your brother."

Sibyl glanced up, her brimming eyes searching Mrs. Dee's face.

"He will," the medium affirmed, answering Sibyl's unspoken plea. "You must be patient. You must wait. But all will be well."

"Really?" Sibyl whispered.

The medium smiled a tiny, self-satisfied smile.

The two women sat, regarding each other across the tea table, the oil lamp flickering. Sibyl had no idea of the time. Her father would be anxious. But what if what the medium was saying was true? Perhaps she didn't need to do anything at all. Harlan could even have come home while she was away.

Sibyl stood, fumbling a wrinkled handkerchief out of her sleeve and dabbing under her eyes. Mrs. Dee stood also, signaling to the butler, who moved about on silent feet, illuminating lights. He drew apart the velvet curtains at the window, but night had come to Beacon Hill, extinguishing the last of the weak afternoon sunlight. Sibyl caught sight of herself broken into pieces and reflected by the lozenge-shaped panes of glass.

When Sibyl turned, tucking the moist scrap of linen back up her sleeve, she found Mrs. Dee gazing on her with a look of sincere-seeming concern. The medium stroked her arm, saying nothing. Sibyl smiled, but it was a stoic smile. The medium took her elbow and walked her to the front hall.

There, the butler proffered Sibyl's overcoat and hat, which she accepted. In principle, she ought to feel relieved. Sibyl glanced back to Mrs. Dee, whose face wore an expression of worry. The medium lifted her chin to the butler, gesturing with a flick of her eyes back into the parlor.

"What a difficult few days you've had," Mrs. Dee murmured to Sibyl as he disappeared.

Sibyl hesitated, and then nodded.

"Have you spoken with your father about this?" she asked. Sibyl wasn't sure if by "this" Mrs. Dee meant the séances, or her worries for Harlan. Perhaps both. She shook her head.

Mrs. Dee nodded sagely. The butler reappeared and passed something to the matron without a word. "I'd like you to have this," she said, taking Sibyl by the hands and pressing the object into them. It was the velvet-lined wooden box containing the scrying glass. Sibyl's brows rose in surprise.

"There's no need to thank me," Mrs. Dee assured her with a final squeeze of Sibyl's hands. "I'd like to think it could ease your cares, if you keep the tool whereby your mother came to us. Whenever your worries grow most acute, I'd like you to hold the orb to your breast and remind yourself that you are loved, and that all will be well."

Sibyl stood mute with surprise as the small woman, smiling sweetly, withdrew. Then she was gone, swallowed by the shadows in the town house. Mrs. Dee enjoyed her exits as much as her entrances.

For the first time that day, Sibyl felt the iron grip of worry begin to loosen. Instead, she felt clear about what she must do. Confident. Sibyl paused by the hall stand to affix her hat, wondering if the butler could be persuaded to summon a taxicab to carry her home. Sibyl turned from the hall stand mirror, on the point of asking the butler if he would be so kind as to . . .

He was hovering just at her elbow. She jumped, having not known he was there. His eyes traveled down from her face, to the hall stand, to the small marble shelf on the hall stand, all the way down to the hall stand's genteel silver visiting card bowl, standing empty.

He cleared his throat and fixed her with a long and meaningful stare.

Cheeks burning with shame, Sibyl understood. She rummaged in her pocketbook to withdraw Mrs. Dee's standard fee.

SEVEN

ibyl found him in the inner drawing room, as she expected she might. Her father's form was obscured by an open newspaper, turned to the international affairs page. A cheerful fire crackled in the hearth, bathing the normally grave room in a dancing orange glow. The room's air was tinted with the homelike aroma of pipe tobacco and old port, opened and left to breathe. The hour was later even than she realized, and Sibyl half thought she would return home to find her father already retired for the evening. Instead Mrs. Doherty showed her, or rather marched her, to the pocket doors and left her there, making it clear that Sibyl had no option but to go in. Obediently Sibyl edged into the room, hugging the wall with its silk upholstery covered in arcing cherry blossoms and painted junks, unsure which of Lan's many faces she might find when the newspaper dropped.

"It's a damned dirty business," her father growled from behind the newsprint. Sibyl made her way over to the somnolent macaw perched on his hat rack, one claw tucked into his chest feathers, beak almost smiling under watchful avian eyes. She extended a finger and scratched under the animal's chin. He let her do so, cheek feathers bristling.

"I know it," Sibyl said, resigned. "Though I'm hoping it'll shake out soon enough."

"Shake out!" he father barked, lowering the paper just enough for her to catch his cool eye, flashing under a graying fringe of eyebrow. "With nothing holding down the western front but a sorry lot of colonials? And *Belgians?*"

"Oh," Sibyl said, recovering herself. She turned away from the eye gazing at her over the paper and pretended to busy herself with the parrot. "No, of course not," she said, her back to him, abashed that she had misunderstood. "I suppose you're right."

Her father lowered the newspaper farther to reveal the other icy eye. "You're referring to something different, I take it," he stated. Usually conversations between Lan and Sibyl began in the middle, both being aware what the other was thinking.

Sibyl sighed and moved to the armchair opposite him. He was seated in his Greek revival seat, its sturdy wooden swoops seemingly designed with Lan's specific body in mind. His legs were stretched out toward the fire. When she glanced at her father's face, Sibyl found that he was wearing the cordial expression of a man who is not easily surprised. She didn't see that face very often anymore.

"How was supper?" she asked, lamely.

"Bah," he said, bringing the paper to eye level again with a rustle. "Stopped in to Locke-Ober. I fancied some proper lobster bisque." He arched his eyebrow at his daughter, who chuckled in recognition.

"I'm not sure Betty'll ever forgive you," she remarked, leaning back into the armchair and letting her head rest against its wing. Some years ago, near the beginning of her tenure at 138½ Beacon Street, Betty Gallagher, wishing to impress her new employers with her skill and economy, made a lobster bisque from shellfish given to her, Sibyl discovered later during a confidential, weepy moment in the kitchen garden, by a young man she met at a dance hall. A present, he'd said, though she hadn't known where he had gotten it, as the man himself had not been a lobsterman. Betty claimed he told her it had fallen off the back of a truck.

Sibyl always enjoyed hearing what little Betty would share of her evening exploits, which consisted of making the rounds of moving picture shows, vaudeville revues, and the occasional night out dancing with other young women who, Sibyl gathered, Betty knew from her parish. Betty's origins were mysterious, to the Allstons at least. Sibyl knew that their young cook lived a complex and multipeopled life outside of the kitchen garden, though its specific contours were kept well obscured—certainly from Lan, and they had been from Helen as well. At any event, the lobster turned out to have been relieved by the dance hall boy from the castoffs of a local restaurant, and Betty was too besotted by his handsome, well-made face to care. Betty had an unfortunate tendency to let beautiful male faces distract her from her better judgment. Her error, in this case, had sent the entire household to bed for three days with what Lan persisted in calling "the bloody flux," to her mother's horror.

Helen responded to the crisis with decisiveness, placing an unequivocal ban on all future lobster dishes, which she insisted was preferable anyway, as lobster was common, and none of the good people ate it anymore. Helen used to carry in her mind the judgments of an invisible panel of social approval, to which she was in the habit of submitting everyday household decisions. Lobster failed. The family caved to her decree, to Lan's dismay, for lobster simply prepared with drawn butter and rice was one of his favorite dishes. Though Helen herself was vanished from the household, her dictum remained, and Lan could satisfy his longing for lobster only through subterfuge.

"What about you?" her father asked, folding his newspaper and laying it to the side. "Did you manage to scratch something together for your own supper? Here I was worried about leaving you alone, and instead I find you've been out on some mysterious business of your own design. We're risking upsetting the staff, you know." He gazed on her with indulgent kindness, and Sibyl smiled.

"Not at all mysterious," Sibyl said, sidestepping the question of her own supper, whatever it might have been. Or whether it had been at all. "I was repaying some calls, and lost myself so thoroughly in conversation that the hour quite escaped me."

"Hmmmm," Lan Allston said, leaning a weathered cheek on one fist.

The firelight played over his sparkling eyes, long nose like her own, grayed overlong sideburns, narrow mouth, and for a moment Sibyl could see the outline of the face her father must have had as a young man. The angle of the shadows in the inner drawing room made Lan look as if the youth he had been was still locked somewhere inside the form of the worthy gentleman who was her father. A smile played about his mouth, as though he were about to call her out on something, as he used to do when she was a child. No, the candles weren't being stolen by thieves in the night—they were being burned by a young girl up late reading novels. No, Helen's scarf wasn't lost—it was stained with ink from a young girl's blotting a letter. Sibyl sometimes forgot how well her father could see past her subterfuges. She twisted her hands together in her lap, failing to elaborate on her whereabouts. He watched her, and she knew that he was weighing whether or not to press her further.

"You know," her father remarked, never taking his eyes from his daughter, "I was always sorry we didn't see too much of Benton Derby after his marriage."

Sibyl's mouth twitched into an involuntary smile of its own and settled down again. "Well, they traveled abroad so soon after," she remarked, not meeting his gaze. "For her health."

"Mmmmmm. So they did."

She waited.

"You saw quite a bit of him, for a while there, if I remember correctly," he ventured.

"I suppose so," Sibyl said, giving away nothing. Her father watched her.

"I was always glad to've been in business with his father. They're sober people," he tried again.

"They are," Sibyl agreed.

Silence settled between the two sober Allstons. The fire popped.

"He seemed most concerned about your brother, when he telephoned today," Lan continued, watching for her reaction.

"Yes," she said, her voice coming out almost as a squeak, but not quite. "As a matter of fact, he's one of the friends on whom I called today. For that very reason."

"So he mentioned," Lan said, smiling out of one side of his mouth. She was caught. "I'd like to have called on him myself, as a matter of fact. No idea he'd even returned from Italy."

"I may have heard something from Harley," Sibyl said, wrapping her hands around her opposite elbows to hide her embarrassment at being seen through. "That Benton was back."

"And how is he? A professor now, he said."

She paused, considering. "He looks older."

Her father nodded, his cheek resting on his fist. "Widower, can have that effect, you know," he murmured, gazing into the hearth under lidded eyes.

In the corner, on the hat rack, Baiji stretched his wings out like a well-fed hawk and then settled them along his back.

For a time the two sat in quiet, each thinking his and her own private thoughts. Sibyl wondered what Benton had said to her father. Perhaps he had found out from the school why Harlan was asked to leave before the semester was over. She sensed the moment she set foot in the house that her brother hadn't returned from wherever it was that he had fled after St. Swithin's. The town house was too quiet, too dull, too lacking in the thrumming energy that emanated from Harlan.

She glanced at her father and saw a scintilla of pain contort Lan's features for a passing moment, before melting back into his skin. He didn't move, but the residue of pain was palpable in his expression. She frowned.

"Did you have your medicine today?" she asked, leaning forward to rest her elbows on her knees. He sometimes forgot. More rarely, he might refuse. Lan could be stubborn. *Pigheaded* was Helen's word when she was cross with him. His rheumatism was more acute when the seasons changed. His doctor kept them supplied with a tonic for the pain and nerves, but every few years he would try to go without it.

"Hm?" he grunted. "Oh, yes. Earlier."

She folded her arms over her chest, doubtful. But his eyes were lowering under the warmth of the hearth fire, drowsing. It was hardly worth the argument. Sibyl settled back into the armchair, turning her face to the fire.

"It's good, you go to those things," her father's voice whispered. "Good for you, I think. I worry. Sometimes."

Surprised, Sibyl smiled, but said nothing.

The mantel clock ground out a sigh before it began to chime midnight, its tones sweet and jewel-like in the silent house. One. Two. Three . . .

Sibyl counted each chime as it passed, reflecting that in doing so she could feel the slippage of time as it drifted away from her like a paper boat on a slow river. The clock chimed, and she felt herself floating as well, borne along on the heavy wave of time as she sat in the comfortable inner drawing room of her father's town house.

On the eighth *pling* of the mantel clock, Sibyl and Lan both started bolt upright in their chairs. Voices burst into the front hallway—an argument. Baiji let out a protesting squawk at the commotion. Shouting. A door slammed.

In an instant Sibyl was on her feet and pulling aside the pocket doors with a rattle of lacquered wood against metal. The toe of her boot snagged the velvet carpet while she dashed through the front parlor, and she stumbled, catching herself with a barked elbow on the credenza. At the collision a crystal candlestick on top of the credenza wavered, wavered, wavered, and tumbled over in an exploding starburst of shattered glass.

The voices grew louder, one of them Mrs. Doherty, agitated, protective, imperious, but Sibyl didn't recognize the other one, the angry one, and she fumbled at the latch to the door separating the front parlor from the hall, her fingers clumsy with haste. She couldn't see; the latch was engulfed in shadow, and her fingers tripped over the mechanism in the dark, refusing to obey. The lights in the front parlor were all extinguished, and Sibyl squinted in the darkness, bent over, her face lit in relief by the single bar of light from under the hall door.

"I will see them! You can't stop me seeing them!" the unfamiliar voice insisted, shrill and panicky.

Sibyl swore under her breath as she jostled the door, trying to force the latch open. Finally the catch gave. She hauled the door open with a grunt and stood, arms splayed, her heart pressing into her ribs, a ribbon of hair loosened from her bun, her breath coming in short anxious bursts.

Sibyl's eye fell first on Mrs. Doherty, the housekeeper's face a taut confusion of panic, irises ringed in white, still in her black taffeta uniform, peaked hat thrown askew, hands thrust out. The front door was flung open, its yawning mouth breathing a blistering breeze from outside. Standing in the doorway, framed by the dim glow of the streetlights burning through the mist, arms raised to fend off the housemaid, was a woman Sibyl had never seen before in her life.

She was young, younger than Sibyl, but the youthful curves of her face had been roughened somehow. Her form was compact, small, slim, square shoulders, her face heart shaped, with a turned-up nose, a mouth reddened to the shape of a tiny bow, and hypnotic bottle green eyes. The skin under her eyes was purpled, and her eyelashes were damp. Her skin looked sallow, pale not only from lack of sun and air but also from ill use, for its texture was fragile where it should have been flush. Her hair formed a frizzy halo of pale blond, bobbed to her jawline, leaving exposed a creamy expanse of neck. She was dressed in a long, loose tunic of vermilion silk over a black silk underskirt, hemmed to midcalf, with elegant heeled black boots. The tunic hung from her shoulders in a luscious column, gathered at the waist with a black satin sash. But it wasn't the woman's dress that seized Sibyl's attention.

It was the deep, browning splash of blood soaking into the silk.

In shock, Sibyl's lips parted, but no sound came out. She registered that Mrs. Doherty's mouth was moving, she was saying, "I tried not to let 'er in, I said she mustn't—"

At the same time the strange woman herself was wailing, and before Sibyl could understand what was happening she had twisted free of Mrs. Doherty's grasp, bounded across the room, and flung herself into Sibyl's arms, clutching with her fingernails at Sibyl's blouse and waist, her breath hot on Sibyl's cheek. The woman—or girl, she was nearly still a girl—had a strange smell about her, something like the incense in Mrs. Dee's parlor, but spicier, and Sibyl recoiled from her grasp.

"You must come, you must," the crazed stranger insisted, twisting her fingers in the linen of Sibyl's shirtwaist. Her grip was strong, wiry little arms under her yards of silk, and Sibyl felt their desperate pressure before Mrs. Doherty was there, wrenching her hands between the girl's arms and Sibyl's ribs, pulling, the three of them roiling while the girl screamed, "Listen to me! You must listen!"

"Enough!"

The word was bellowed from behind Sibyl, and the struggle ceased as abruptly as it had begun. The girl's grip loosened, and Mrs. Doherty jerked her away from Sibyl by the shoulders, more roughly than would have seemed possible for the aging housekeeper. The girl stood, panting, gasping for breath, the bloodstain on her tunic deepening to a hideous burnt brown-black.

Lan Allston, drawn up to his full height, stepped out on deliberate feet from the shadows of the front drawing room. He cast a slow eye over his daughter, assessing for damage, and upon finding none turned to the struggling girl, Mrs. Doherty still holding her in an iron grip. The housekeeper's face showed fear and motherly panic, and the girl was spitting and fighting like a cornered cat.

"You must listen!" the girl burst. "They're going to kill him!"

Sibyl gasped, horrified. Benton said her brother owed money to some clubmen, more than he could pay. His debts must have been mounting for longer than she had imagined. Rather than tell their father, he must have borrowed from some street criminal. With his recent losses, he couldn't repay the loan. So he hadn't run away to hide from the family after all. He'd been waylaid and beaten within an inch of his life. The color drained from Sibyl's cheeks as she realized the true depth of her brother's depravity.

Lan Allston just folded his arms.

For a moment nothing happened. Sibyl turned to face her father, looking for her own shock to be reflected in his weathered face.

But he only frowned, and said, "Frankly, I'm surprised she had the nerve to come here."

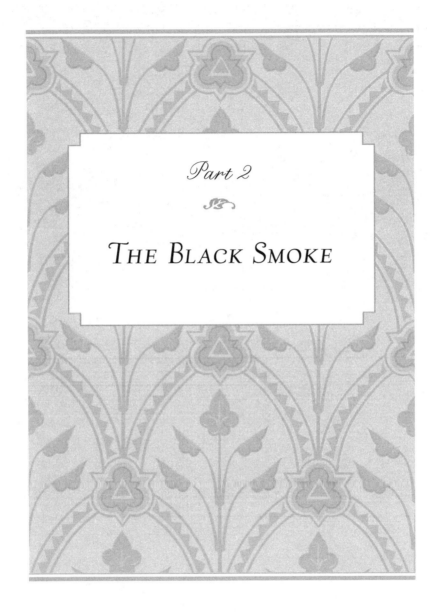

Part 2

THE BLACK SMOKE

Interlude

North Atlantic Ocean
Outward Bound
April 14, 1912

EULAH ALLSTON GLANCED back over her shoulder as Harry Widener steered her deeper into the throng of dancers at the end of the gallery. Her mother was stretching up in her chair, hands clasped in her lap, eyebrows raised, watching them go. Eulah rolled her eyes. She wished Helen wouldn't look so eager all the time. With her neck stretched up like that Eulah thought she looked like a chicken, her wattle quivering, all eager and watchful. Not that Eulah had much experience with chickens. But her mother sometimes had the ridiculousness and vanity of a chicken, her dyed hair teased like glistening feathers on top of her head. Annoyed, she let Harry's pressure at her waist carry her behind a sheltering screen of other dancers. She tossed her head back and looked up at him with lidded eyes, smiling.

"You were telling me about that book," she prompted, wishing to impress him with her seriousness. *"Le Sang de Morphée."*

In her quick observations of Harry Widener, Eulah had already concluded that he would be most drawn to a woman who could keep up with his interests. Some men enjoyed being given private windows into the world of women—hearing about dress fittings, maybe, or gossiping about people known in common. They liked to see into women, while staying separate from them. But Harry, she could tell, was different. Frippery would not suffice. Harry might indulge a woman, but he would never find an indulged woman interesting.

"Oh, that," he said. "It's a kind of storybook. Very rare. Remarkable engravings. A travelogue, something like Coleridge, or the story of the lotus-eaters in the *Odyssey*. Terribly sordid. A proper girl like you would never like it."

She grinned, enjoying that he would tell her about his prized discovery. Eulah had never been able to talk books with any real authority. Not the way Sibyl could, anyway. In fact, Sibyl could talk books entirely too much for most men. Her older sister had never learned what came to Eulah by instinct, which was that the surest way to convince a man that you were a fascinating creature was to ask him all about himself.

At the thought of Sibyl, Eulah felt a twinge of guilt. Sibyl had so wanted to come with them on the tour. And in a way, Eulah had wanted her to come, too. She felt more confident when Sibyl was there. She managed to be both more reasonable than their mother, and more adventuresome, too. Sibyl would have gone to the cafés with her, no matter how late the hour, and would have loved the carriage rides through the Bois as much as she did. But the money, it really was outrageous. She had overheard her parents discussing the matter—not arguing, as one didn't argue in the Allston house—late at night, after their children were assumed to be asleep. Eulah, nervous and excited to learn her father's decision, had crept to her mother's bedroom door and pressed her ear to the keyhole, listening.

"Have you any idea what four thousand dollars can buy?" her father thundered. "Why, I'd just as soon marry her to a lawyer and build the two of them a house, for that price. And a pretty fine one, for that matter."

"Now, Lannie," her mother countered, in her most reasonable tone. "Don't be so hasty. Just consider who she'd be likely to meet, though. Just once in a lifetime will so many quality people be all gathered together like that. It'll be in all the papers. Wouldn't it be worth the expense, to see her settled?"

"Hmmph," Lan Allston grunted.

"You can afford it, if you set your mind to it."

"Afford!" he protested. "And even if I could, why wouldn't we spend the money on Sibyl? She's the eldest. Don't you think she might like to see Paris?"

"My dear, I know how you feel about it. But you must acknowledge," his wife insisted, dropping her voice to show she was serious. "Eulah's got the best chance."

When Eulah heard that, she knew with a sinking in her stomach that Sibyl's fate was sealed. Her sister's moment was past. Sibyl'd had such a good opportunity, too. For a time, in 1911, even *Town Topics* had whispered in its circumspect way that an engagement was imminent. Opinions differed on the likeliest candidate, but the gossip magazine cast the most popular lot: "Which hyphenated shipping company is likely to have to change its name before the year is out? Maybe they'll get a break on the new letterhead if they order the invitations there, too."

All that year Eulah had watched Sibyl's comings and goings with mounting excitement, waiting poised behind potted palmettos at dances and peering over staircase banisters, not wanting to miss it when it happened. There were a few others, Leonard Coombs most notably, but after a time he receded, and they were always together, Benton and Sibyl, always whispering and laughing. And then Eulah noticed that Lydia Pusey girl loitering on the periphery, with her fragile skin and that tubercular pallor that some men find appealing. She played the part of the romantic invalid with great aplomb, but Eulah wasn't fooled. She saw the mechanism turning in the girl's eye.

Damn that Lydia.

"Don't you think she's around an awful lot?" Eulah ventured to Sibyl in their lavatory one night, each girl wiping cream under her eyes. "I never used to see her at all, and then suddenly she's everywhere."

"I think it's nice people are including her," Sibyl said brightly. "She never used to be well enough to go to parties, you know."

"Hmmm," Eulah said, looking at Sibyl out of the corner of her eye. Her sister. Always too trusting. And not forthright enough. Did Benton even know how much she doted on him? Eulah would never play it so coy.

And then, nothing. Invitations for Sibyl dwindled. Eulah saw the disappointment in their mother's face, which quickly morphed into fresh, anxious attention paid to Eulah. Suddenly Helen was after her about her hats, was discovered rummaging through her wardrobe and flinging away outmoded things. And something seemed to change in Sibyl, too. Some of the verve seemed to go out of her. But not even in the late confidential hours with the two of them alone, Eulah brushing out the waves in Sibyl's hair, had Sibyl let slip what fatal mistake she had made that had condemned herself to spinsterhood.

Eulah felt a little strange, or disloyal, being the focal point of all of Helen's aspirations. She supposed her siblings' paths were already well plotted out, though. Harlan, just starting college, would finish with undistinguished grades but with some good social contacts, and would step into a position of responsibility in their father's shipping company. He'd marry, eventually, maybe one of those small-town horsey girls from out west who'd taken to showing up at fashionable eastern watering places, looking to merge their new money with a respectable old name. Sibyl would stay at home, caring for their parents as they aged, gradually assuming the running of the household. Probably even staying on in that role when Harley's equine-faced wife proved too absorbed in her committee work and charity amusements to be bothered with things like keeping the house going, or raising the children.

And Eulah herself? She sighed. Well, she supposed her mother had her plans. Eulah'd never really been one for plans herself. She could push aside the schemes her mother was weaving around her, the moves she was no doubt masterminding back at the dining table next to Harry's mother. Eulah was here now. The music was exquisite. Through her feet she felt the ship's mighty engines rumbling under the deck of the ocean liner, felt the warmth of Harry's hand on her body. She leaned her weight deeper onto his shoulder, watching the bright dress of the women swaying near them, brushing against them, and the flickering of the candlelight. Around her, laughter and music merged into a splendid cacophony of pleasure.

"You're a marvelous dancer," Harry said, breaking into her reverie, and she felt his voice vibrate deep in his chest as he pressed her nearer to him.

"I'd better be." She grinned. "All those cotillions. If I weren't, you can bet Mother'd want her money back."

Harry laughed, moving his hand from her waist to the small of her back. He was a pretty good dancer himself, actually. Better than she expected. Bookworms usually weren't much in the dance department. She cast an appraising look up at his face from under the netting of her hat, which he affected not to notice. Better-looking than your usual bookworm, too. She hesitated, and then rested her cheek back against his shoulder, letting him lead.

Inside his chest, she could feel him humming in tune with the music.

"Are you melancholy?" he asked.

"Me? Why, no. Quite the opposite, in fact. Why do you ask?" she murmured.

"The tune," he said. "I wonder if you could be my melancholy baby." He sang softly along with the music as they swayed, and she felt his voice deep in his throat as he held her.

A wave of pleasure began at the top of her head, washing down her body in cascades. Her arms broke out in goose bumps, and she shivered. "Perhaps." She sighed, smiling into his dinner jacket. "Perhaps I could be."

Eulah let her eyes drift closed and tried to pretend that her mother wasn't surveilling them from across the room.

EIGHT

Massachusetts General Hospital
Boston, Massachusetts
April 17, 1915

The first sensation was pain. Vague and difficult to locate or explain, but pain it was, and Harley met it with a strange detachment. It suffused his body like a heat, or—because heat wasn't quite right—encompassed him as though the pain were a pool of salt water, wrapping around his body, supporting it, moving along him in waves. Harley could not ascertain where his physical self ended and the pain began. Harley heard someone whimper, a frightened animal sound, and to his horror realized that the whimper emanated from his own mouth.

He tried to shift and found that his body ended after all, met by the pressure of a cot with a thin, sagging mattress. Each point of contact brought him closer to consciousness as the pain fractured apart, concentrated first down the side of his ribs, inserted into his flesh like a railroad spike, next stretching in a web across his face. Harlan attempted to open his eyes. A tiny crack of light penetrated the darkness, and Harlan winced, realizing that his eyes were open as much as they were able. The flesh of his face was swollen, his eyelashes glued together with a dried crust of blood.

Harley groaned, letting the sound pour out of him in a shuddering wave. The stabbing in his side twisted deeper, and Harley's groan deepened out of shame.

"Shhhhhh," a soft female voice soothed, and Harley felt a cooling sensation on his swollen eyes as someone placed a moist cloth over his face. Discovering that he wasn't alone with his weakness and failure, Harley felt the shame tighten its grip. Another groan fought to come out, but he clenched his jaw against it. The cool cloth passed over his eyelids and then wiped gently along his cheeks and jaw. It brushed his lip, sending a jolt of fresh pain through the muscles of his face.

Under the bruising of his skin Harley flushed with disgust. Beaten. He'd been beaten, soundly. He lay in his hospital cot, imprisoned in his weakness, and in the certain knowledge that he was a disgrace, as he'd always secretly feared he would be.

Harley pushed through the fog in his mind, thinking. A few images swam by, none of them particularly clear. Nighttime. And Betty, sturdy Betty with her freckles and her wild hair. He'd kissed her. Finally. He'd wanted to do that for years. Harlan tried to smile, but his face refused to obey. The memory of Betty's buttery taste on his tongue pushed away the pain. But only for a moment.

Then, with sickening certainty, he remembered. Had he even landed a punch before he went down? A wave of nausea washed through him, and a white explosion of pain burst across his eyes. As the expression on his face changed, the person holding the cloth, whoever she was, caught her breath.

"Don't," the woman said. "Just relax."

Again the soothing pressure of the cloth over his eyes. It was delicious, the gentle care being lavished on him. Quiescent, he allowed himself to be tended to, saying nothing.

Maybe the woman didn't know how it had happened. Maybe she would assume that he had behaved with bravery and was overpowered through unfairness, or lack of sportsmanship, or . . .

He grimaced again, his shame intensifying. He inhaled, and the pressure of pain from a cracked rib tore through him with new urgency.

"Harley," the visitor's voice whispered close to his ear. "Are you waking up?"

The visitor's elbow depressed the edge of the mattress, and the faint jostle of the bedding sent arrows shooting through his trunk, causing him to gasp, a fresh tear rolling out of the corner of his eye.

The woman emitted a worried murmur. "Shall I call the nurse?" she asked.

"Not yet," barked a gruff voice, and then Harley knew with a sinking certainty who was in the room with him.

"Papa, he's clearly in pain. He needs morphine," said the soothing voice, which Harley now recognized as belonging to his sister. His mortification deepened. To have his weakness revealed before Sibyl, perfect and judging Sibyl, was bad enough. But now he would have to face Lan Allston, too.

"I have no doubt of that," his father's voice agreed, sounding hard around the edges. "But not before we've ascertained how he got himself into this mess. And what he plans to do about it."

"But, Papa," Sibyl started. "He's hardly in a state to—"

Their father cut her off with a grunt.

"I'd like a word alone with the boy, if you don't mind," the Captain's voice said, its chill cutting into Harley's bones. "It'll just take a moment."

Harley heard his sister protest and felt her weight rise, pulling away from his cot. Sibyl spoke with a hushed urgency to their father, but Harley couldn't hear what was being said. He wished Sibyl wouldn't go. He wished she would stay and protect him.

"Of course, my dear, I understand," their father soothed, setting aside whatever her objections might have been. "Why don't you take a moment to go out and talk with that"—he paused, and cleared his throat—"young woman."

Harley's mind reeled at this reference, confused, before finally realizing, with a sour sinking in his stomach, how his family came to know where he was, and in what state he might be found.

Dovie.

Dovie had gone to the Beacon Street house. He should never have told her where it was. He certainly shouldn't have driven her past it one laughing, carefree night after they stumbled together, drunk and happy, out of Mabel White's evening salon. It was reckless of him, stupid. But he'd wanted to impress her. He never thought for a moment that she would dare to . . . but she did. And now they'd know.

They'd know everything.

Harley's breath quickened with mounting panic, wishing his eyes would open fully so that he could see what was happening, so that he could prepare to face his father.

"But, she's . . . ," Sibyl said, leaving her thought unspoken, but no less certain for what she did not articulate.

"Yes, I know. But all the more reason we might wish to know her a little better, wouldn't you agree?"

Harley was surprised to hear his father suggest that cosseted Sibyl, who circulated only among the nice and the good, whose world was bounded by so many ladies' committees and drawing room teas, who could barely bring herself to operate the telephone, should be seen speaking, in public, with the likes of Dovie. It would be comical, if it weren't so tragic.

He heard his sister swallow, thickly, and then without another word her footsteps moved across what he now understood to be his hospital room, making a hollow, echoing sound of brisk boot heels on cold tile. His lower lip trembled, willing her to return, for her not to leave him alone.

A leaden silence descended on the room. Harley heard rustling fabric, which indicated his father's pulling out the chronometer from his vest pocket to consult it, or perhaps just to finger it, as was his habit when agitated or angry. Harlan lay motionless, wondering if he could feign sleep and so push away the inevitable, but also knowing that the pain was holding him awake, prostrate but conscious, presenting him to his father like a gutted fish on a platter.

Lan understood this kind of pain, Harley suspected. He would have experienced it himself in some distant port years ago, and so for that reason could not be expected to sympathize the way that Sibyl might. He would expect his son to bear it. Any failure to do so would bring nothing but contempt, Harley reminded himself as his father settled himself in a chair at his bedside.

Lan Allston cleared his throat. Harley stiffened.

"It's no business of mine," his father began, the words measured and deliberate, "if you want to gad about with whores."

In a flash of righteous anger Harley's mouth worked, and he tried to object, but before any words could come out Lan continued.

"I should think, however," his father continued, "you'd have better sense than to become the *patron* of one." He spat out the word with such dismissal that Harley physically recoiled. "Particularly given the opinions on such patronage likely to be held by her *pimp*."

The word sounded wrong, even obscene, spoken in Lan's elegant Boston accent. Harlan felt in his father's hostile pause the appraisal of his roving gaze, taking in the bandaged ribs, the battered face, the split mouth. So his father assumed that Harley had been beaten by Dovie's procurer. Harlan would have smiled, a cruel smile it's true, but a smile all the same, if he had been able. He said nothing.

Lan continued, "But it's the privilege of the young to be stupid, and so stupid you must be."

A sour ball of resentment knotted itself in Harlan's stomach. He knew his father disapproved of him. He knew he was a disappointment. He was bound to be one, no matter how successful he might seem to the rest of the world. But he would show his father that he had honor of his own. Lan Allston couldn't take that from him, too. Harley summoned his strength, building the words in his mouth before speaking. The effort of moving his tongue caused tears to squeeze out of the corners of his eyes.

"Yes?" his father prodded. "You have something to say for yourself? Well, I'm at your disposal, my boy. By all means. Speak."

Harley's nostrils flared with anger. How could his father know so little! He held himself aloof, hidden away in his precious Beacon Street house. Blind to the world, the way the world really was. Not like Harley, who craved experience, who refused to lock himself away as Sibyl allowed herself to be locked up, a prisoner in that infernal life. That tomb of his dead mother's taste. It was time Lan Allston got a dose of the real world. Harley steeled himself, and spoke.

"I . . . love . . . her," he said. He spoke each word with perfect clarity. His heart swelled when he said it, speaking the truth aloud for the first time to someone other than tender Dovie, or his own reflection.

His father leaned in close to his face, close enough that Harley could smell the port and tobacco on his breath.

"*The hell you do,*" his father hissed.

Harley lay in his cot, resolute, and tried to force his eyes open. The white splinter of light pierced the darkness, and then widened into a thin band, vanished as he blinked, then opened to the blurred blob of a face that could only belong to his father. Harley riveted his eyes to his father's, hoping that he looked like a deadly serious man, and not a frightened little boy.

"She'sshh . . . not . . . a whore," Harley slurred through his blistered lips as a door opened to admit a nurse in a starched apron, white gaiters pulled up over her sleeves, carrying a glass syringe on a tray. She noticed the man in conversation with her patient and hesitated in the door.

Harley's father leaned in, blotting out the form of the nurse behind him. Lan placed a hand on Harley's arm with the steel grip of a man whose life had depended on a firm grasp of ropes while at sea. Harley clenched his teeth against the bite of his father's thumb digging into the flesh of his arm.

"That is *precisely* what she is," Lan stated, voice too low for the nurse to hear. "Whether you believe her to be or not. I'd think that your current state would convince you."

"Here now," the nurse interrupted, appearing at Harley's bedside. Lan released his grip, moving his hand to the vest pocket that held the chronometer. "He's awake, then, is he?"

Lan rose to his feet, his gaze on his son as he folded his hands behind his back. "He is."

A long pause ensued, with Lan's cool eyes resting on Harley's face. Harley held the look as long as he could, his innards tightening in anger and shame, his lip trembling. Finally, with a miserable exhalation of breath, his eyes slid away.

"I think you'll find," Allston said, "that the boy is in quite a lot of pain."

"Oh, we'll fix him up right enough. Needs his rest," the nurse assured the gentleman as she busied herself with the syringe. She held it up to the light, withdrawing amber liquid from a small glass ampule, tinking the syringe with her fingernail to clear away the air bubbles. She bent over him, and Harley smelled the ripe scent of her body as she drew near with the needle. He closed his eyes in delicious anticipation.

"I've no doubt about that," he heard his father say. Harley tensed his arm, waiting for the needle's sting in his inner elbow. "But I'm afraid we can't allow him to have any morphine."

The nurse glanced up, confused, needle poised in the air. At the tip, a tiny bubble of liquid trembled, catching the light. "But, you yourself said . . ."

Harley's eyelids flew open, and he turned to his father with naked panic. A punishment. He had been given morphine before, knew its power to fill his limbs with delicious warmth, to spread from the crown of his head along his skin, into his mouth even, down his neck, to wash away every last iota of suffering. His body remembered the delectable feeling, and the indifference of it, the drug's profound power to free him from care, and every cell of his body cried out, weeping for release.

"This is not open for discussion." Allston gave the nurse a sharp look. "We'll have to rely on Providence to relieve him while he heals."

Not bothering to conceal her troubled expression, the nurse placed the syringe back on its tray and drew herself up to her full five feet. She glanced down at her patient, and Harley worked his mouth, the pain clawing at his body. He felt himself floating, the sensation of the bed receding.

"Well then," the nurse's voice said, distant, as though spoken through a speaking tube like the one in his father's parlor. "Sir, I'm afraid I'll have to ask you to leave. The boy's injuries place him at great risk of infection, and we must limit his contact with visitors. For his own protection, you understand."

"Indeed. But no morphine, or I'll have your job," said his father, but his voice was muffled, spoken from the bottom of the ocean itself. Lan Allston started to say something else, something that might have been "This conversation is not over," but Harley couldn't be sure, because he was floating very far away, alone in a river of pain.

SIBYL MOVED DOWN the hospital hallway, her hands cupping her opposite elbows, throat closed against the stench of sickness. Her pace quickened as she planned out in her mind what she would say to the young woman who awaited her.

Sibyl strode past a succession of open doors, each ward a hangar of identical white cots, each cot holding a suffering body. Sibyl quailed in the face of so much need, at the smells of the bodies and the cries for help. The wards were nothing but a holding pen for hunks of human flesh, soul prisons, before they were finally freed from whatever miserable indignity was tormenting them.

An abattoir.

Sibyl hesitated by a bank of wooden telephone booths, thinking. Making up her mind, she pulled a door aside and stepped in.

She supposed it was Benton's comments about the everyday horrors of human life, his sympathy, that made her want to telephone him. Sibyl sat on the Women's Hygiene and Improvement Committee, and had toured tenements with baskets of fresh linens to distribute. She had flattered herself that she knew what it was, to be poor in Boston. But she had never seen suffering like this.

"Boston, I have Cambridge, Massachusetts, for you," said the distant, nasal operator at the other end of the line. "Go ahead, Boston."

"Hullo?" rasped a sleepy male voice. Sibyl suppressed a shiver of pleasure as she imagined Benton, in his bed, asleep, roused by the jangling of the telephone. She pictured what he might look like while he was sleeping: rumpled striped cotton pajamas, with a thrown-on dressing gown. Then she pushed the thought aside, appalled at herself.

"Ben, I'm so sorry to wake you," she began, voice thick with mortification, worried that he might be able to somehow overhear her thoughts underneath the neutral words.

"Miss Allston?" he exclaimed, voice growing instantly more alert. "Sibyl," he corrected himself. He sounded sleepy, confused, but growing more awake. "What time is it?"

"So late that I can't possibly tell you," she said, voice low. "I'm so sorry. But you see, I'm calling about Harley."

"Harlan?" Ben said, his voice stiffening. "Has something happened?"

"Something has," she said, her fist pressing against the telephone booth glass. "I'm afraid that Harley was badly beaten this evening. I can only assume"—she paused, horrified at what she was about to say—"I can only assume it has something to do with the debts. That you mentioned to me. I have to believe he took out a loan from some unsavory people to pay them. But the truth is, I don't know."

She heard Benton take a sharp inward breath. Then he said, "And?"

Sibyl closed her eyes, hating having to tell Benton these things. "He was in a roominghouse, on Harrison Avenue. They expect that he'll live, but he's unconscious. A broken rib. And his face, Ben . . . I could barely recognize him."

"I see. He's expected to recover, you say?"

"Yes," she confirmed. Then, swallowing, preparing herself, she whispered, "There's something else."

Sibyl paused, pressing her cheek to the glass and peering down the hall to the room at the end, where she was meant to be waiting for her father to emerge from his conference with Harlan, if her brother had been conscious enough. She inhaled, and let the air out in a long hiss.

"What something?" Ben pressed. She found the sound of his breath in her ear oddly reassuring.

She swallowed again, trying to decide how to say it. Finally, for lack of anything more delicate, and too tired to be circumspect, she simply said, "There's a girl with him."

If she had expected him to sound shocked, or even surprised, Sibyl was mistaken. He only said, "I'll be right there."

NINE

*P*ulling aside the glass partition of the telephone booth, Sibyl peered down the hospital corridor. A few scattered patients in wicker wheeled chairs, abandoned alongside the whitewashed walls, blankets tucked around their knees; a cluster of nurses bustling through doorways, heads bent together. No sign of her father. Perhaps she shouldn't have left them alone. But there was no way around it. The Captain would have his say whether she was there or not.

Sibyl started down the hall, eyes on her feet, arms folded over her chest. Her head ached, as though metal bands had been wound around her skull and tightened with screws. A hand found its way to her temple and massaged it as she walked. She couldn't remember the last time she was up so late. It would probably have been for a party, when she was still being invited to the big winter balls and receptions. So, perhaps . . . three years?

Three years.

Not that she wasn't invited places still—she was. But there had been a subtle shift. Those first few seasons had been nights of dances, cards full of scribbled names attached at the wrist with a minute gold pencil, rounds of waltzes, breakfast served in the morning room while the music played, trays of scrambled eggs and bacon, stewed tomatoes and fried codfish balls. Leaning in the shadow of a giant porcelain urn, the corner of her dance card grazing her lower lip while she laughed into the face of a steady progression of college boys. Nighttime was for pleasure, for enjoying feeling young. Pleasure first, later tinged with increasing pressure, the dark shadow lining the sparkling edge of a night spent dancing, which was the knowledge that she had better secure one of those boys for herself. Soon. And Benton . . . Well.

Benton.

Her steps slowed. She should be in the room with Harley, shielding him from their father's rage. The rage would be there, she knew, but her presence would temper its expression; it always did. Sibyl was the baffle between Lan and Harley. She stepped in when Helen was no longer there to do it.

Her brother was just a boy, really. He pretended, puffed himself up like all boys do. Gradually, they forgot they were performing. Sibyl had seen it dozens of times. One day, the playacting of manhood ceased being a joke and became the actual man. Maybe her error was her tendency to see through the puffery to the frightened boy underneath. Too late, she realized that the men of her world might not appreciate being seen through.

But Harley wasn't there quite yet. Sibyl wondered if this woman knew what a boy her brother really was. She imagined Harley moving with his self-satisfied smirk through sordid places, God knew what kind of people, which seemed through their sordidness to be more authentic to him than the carefully wrought drawing rooms of the Back Bay. Worlds where he could pretend to be another person, where he found this woman who would let him pretend. Sibyl's breath came faster, her pace agitated.

Of course, his little jaunt had gotten all too real this evening. She wondered what sort of hideous men could have been responsible for rendering her strong and healthy sporting dog of a brother into a battered heap. She pictured thugs, drunken, snub-nosed simians like she saw in the illustrated newspapers, carrying clubs, grubby hats pulled low, bearing down on him with their base heft and greater numbers. Or some shylock gangster, piggy eyes, greasy hair, caring only for the debts, ballooned by outrageous interest and unfair terms. It was unconscionable, such people preying on a fine boy like him.

A boy! She corrected herself with scorn. He was twenty-one years old.

He could be married at that age. He could have children of his own. A bitter wave of contempt washed over Sibyl. Harley's helplessness was learned, was handed to him by birthright. It was a privilege, his naïveté, his guileless wandering through worlds where he had no business. And she participated in this petting of him. He was like an infant, dead set upon throwing itself into the fireplace because the flames were so bright and pretty.

Perhaps the time had come for it to stop. Perhaps Harley should be allowed to fail.

But first, she must address this . . . *woman*.

Sibyl rounded the final corner, her mouth flattened into a dour, spinsterish line. She marched to the room at the end of the hall, pressing her hand to the swinging door and flinging it open.

The woman—girl—spun from where she had been pretending to gaze out the waiting room window. The room was a grim whitewashed void, furnished with uncomfortable-looking bentwood armchairs and a few cheap tables heavy with ashtrays. Low electric light from two bulbs overhead cast the woman-child's face in a sickly pallor and transformed the multipaned casement windows into so many dingy mirrors, reflecting in fragments the scene within. The girl was alone, but the windows reflected a dozen different angles of the back of her head and tops of her shoulders, as if she were guarded by an army of versions of herself, each one slightly different from the last.

The girl stood with one arm wrapped protectively around her waist, left hand flickering close to her face like a moth, tossing ash in unconscious movements from the end of a cigarette. Her green eyes were open wide, translucent lids blinking, and the violet circles under her eyes had deepened in color. When she spotted Sibyl standing in the doorway the girl took an involuntary step back, the blood-stiffened tunic making a rasping sound as she moved.

The two young women regarded each other across the empty waiting room. The only motion was the faint coil of smoke drifting up from the girl's cigarette. The moment dragged on as Sibyl took in the details of the girl's fragile face and roved through her mind for the right way to open the conversation. How could she possibly understand the first thing about this woman's lonesome nights in that awful room above Harrison

Avenue? What could she say to bring them into any understanding? Sibyl's shuttered mind cracked open for an instant, affording her a fleeting, imagined view of this young woman's life, with its own parade of men offering security and support, but of a very different type.

Perhaps not that different. The men passing through this girl's room, this girl's pasty thin arms even, must have interests as peripatetic, as subject to fits of whim, as dependent on money and all it could offer, or take away, as the string of boys sharing late-night scrambled eggs with her. She imagined the girl's false laughter, the sparkle that she would conjure in her eyes to make whatever man she was with feel special, and understood, and seen in the way he would most like to be, and so trick him into drawing nearer, into giving the girl what she wanted. In a sickening flash of recognition Sibyl understood that the differences between them were, possibly, academic. In fact, she saw with sudden certainty, they must have smiled up into the faces of some of the very same boys. But all Sibyl did was smile, of course.

Sibyl's nostrils twitched from the burning tobacco. She opened her mouth, wondering what she was about to say, when without warning the girl cried out, dropping the cigarette to the floor, and plunging her fingertips into her mouth. Her lips were dark ruby red, and as she soothed her burnt fingers between her lips she gave the appearance of a terrified child.

Sibyl ground the cigarette ember under the toe of her boot, and then took the girl's unoccupied hand and eased her down into one of the armchairs. She turned frightened eyes on Sibyl, fingers still in her mouth. The eyes looked frightened—at first, anyway. As Sibyl peered closer, she saw the twin green pools under the darkened brows were representing frightened eyes, without conveying a depth of feeling that would have been true.

"He's—" Sibyl started to say, but the girl cut her off.

"He'll be all right, won't he?" she cried. Her fingers out of her mouth now, both of the girl's hands fumbled for her tunic, twisting it into a ball in her lap.

"We'll have to see," Sibyl said. "He's receiving the best care, and they're keeping him comfortable. But there's a great risk of infection. One of his ribs is fractured."

The girl choked out a sob, bringing her knuckles up under her chin, eyebrows rising in a peak over her nose. It struck Sibyl as a theatrical gesture, done by an ingénue in a flicker show to demonstrate misery, rather than a real expression. She nevertheless reached a tentative hand to the girl's knee, attempting to be soothing.

"Broken!" the girl exclaimed. She fumbled in the folds of her dress, pulling out a handkerchief and dabbing her eyes. Sibyl had never seen a woman, up close anyway, who wore so much face paint. Eulah, she knew, had lined her eyes, reddened her lips on occasion, had even tried whitening her skin with some lead-based concoction from an advertisement in one of her fashion magazines. She had done all this with Helen's tacit approval. This girl, however, had blackened her eyes so thoroughly she almost looked beaten herself. Her tears washed some of the kohl from her eyes, spreading it in pitiful streaks down her cheeks. Sibyl reached a hand to the girl's cheek, trying to wipe away some of the blacking with a thumb.

As she did so, she murmured, "I'm sure all will be well. But perhaps . . ."

The girl cast her eyes down, tucking her lower lip under a tooth, then glancing up to meet Sibyl's patient gaze.

"What?" the girl said. Sibyl started at the girl's tone but smoothed over her discomfort with a detached smile.

"Your name," she asked gently. The girl was skittish. "I'd like to know what it is."

She gave Sibyl a dark look, as though trying to weigh her intentions. It crossed Sibyl's mind that the girl might lie. Why wouldn't she? She had little reason to tell the truth.

"It's Dovie," she said, as though challenging Sibyl to disagree with her.

"Dovie," Sibyl repeated, smiling. Preposterous. It must be her stage name, or whatever it was these women call it. But it wouldn't do to seem quick to judge. Already Sibyl was surprised to have gotten that much out of her. In fact, it was a wonder that she was still in the waiting room at all. "And what is your last name, Dovie?"

"Whistler," said the girl, before adding, "I didn't make it up."

"Of course you didn't," Sibyl agreed. It might not be a lie, exactly. If she didn't make the name up, perhaps someone else did.

The two women sat, their hands tangled together on Dovie's knee as Sibyl took curious measure of Harlan's lover. Her clothes were fashionable, the skirts hemmed well up. Most startling was her hair. Instead of the dig-nified bun that crowned Sibyl's head, Dovie's frizzy waves were chopped short. The hairs at the base of her neck were as soft and downy as a little boy's, trimmed to a narrow point. Sibyl watched the curve of the girl's neck when she bent her head forward to press her handkerchief against the fresh trickle of tears leaking from the rims of her eyes, amazed that the short hair could somehow make her appear more feminine, rather than less.

"Aw, I can't believe it." Dovie sighed.

"There now," Sibyl said, hearing Helen's voice in her choice of words. "I'm sure it'll be all right."

"Yeah, but I think it's gonna blister," Dovie said, holding up the singed fingers of her left hand for Sibyl to see. Shocked into silence, Sibyl said nothing. She released Dovie's other hand.

The girl rummaged in a concealed pocket in her underskirt and with-drew a gold cigarette case and matching lighter. She busied herself with lighting a fresh cigarette, careful of the two wounded digits, using her ring and pinkie fingers to hold the cigarette. Sibyl stared at this process while it happened, at a loss.

She was so absorbed in watching Dovie's hands move through their steady preparations, illuminating her hard features with a flame from the lighter, that Sibyl didn't notice the waiting room door opening and quick, heavy footfalls approaching her until a hand fell on her shoulder.

"Oh!" Sibyl gasped, turning in her seat. She was met with the sleep-rumpled face of Benton Derby. His tie was askew, as though pulled on and knotted in the dark, and his suit jacket was a subtly different pattern of tweed from his pants, donned without a second look to see if they matched. His cheeks were shadowed with stubble, and his hair stood up in bristles, giving him the comic aspect of an awakened hedgehog. Without meaning to Sibyl smiled, both in pleasure at his presence and at seeing the junior professor in an unguarded moment, a window through his reserve into what she imagined his private self might look like.

"Had the damnedest time getting a cab," he grumbled, hand still rest-ing on her shoulder. "I would've been here sooner, otherwise."

"But it's so good of you to come," she countered, smiling up at him with relief. He moved to take the seat next to her, hand traveling with a light touch down her sleeve to rest on her forearm. The gesture surprised her with its intimacy. Sibyl was aware of Dovie watching their exchange from behind her cigarette. She crossed her legs at the knee, bobbing a foot, saying nothing.

"And may I present Miss Whistler, Harley's . . . that is, she was . . ." Sibyl trailed off, gesturing to Dovie with a helpless hand.

"Of course. How do you do." Benton nodded in the girl's direction, too casually, without bothering to stand. Dovie accepted the acknowledgment with a nod, an impression of a polite smile flitting across her face and then vanishing. The cigarette found her mouth, and her eyes narrowed as she drew the smoke into her lungs.

"I came directly here," he continued, as if the introduction had not taken place. "So I haven't had a chance to make inquiries yet. Is there any news?"

Sibyl shook her head. "Papa's in with him now, but I'm not sure he's awake enough to talk. We still don't know what really happened."

"Well, he'll have to be soon enough." A shadow crossed Benton's face as he glanced at his pocket watch before tucking it back into his vest pocket. Sibyl noticed that the vest was of another competing pattern of tweed, and wrinkled enough to suggest that it had been retrieved off the back of a chair. Her mouth twisted into a smile before she quashed it with an expression of seriousness sufficient to the situation.

"What do you mean?" she asked. "He needs to rest. He could've been killed."

"Just so," Benton agreed. "All the more reason he'll have to give a full account of what happened to the police."

"Police!" Dovie burst. Sibyl and Benton swiveled their eyes in her direction, watching her, but rather than adding anything to her outburst she pulled her gaze away, busying herself with the folds of her dress.

"But of course," Sibyl said after a pause. "I didn't think."

"I phoned them before leaving my rooms," Benton continued. "They'll be here within the hour. In fact, I thought they might even beat me here."

Without warning Dovie stood, wandering back to the casement windows. The darkness outside meant that all she could see in the glass would be the multipaned reflections of her own ravaged face. Benton's and Sibyl's eyes followed her as she moved, and then turned wordlessly to each other.

His eyebrows knit together in inquiry. Sibyl shook her head and then gave the barest hint of a shrug.

Later, Benton mouthed. Sibyl nodded.

They sat that way for a while longer, Sibyl couldn't quite be sure how long, though her fingers twitched for the enameled watch at her waist. Voices came and went in the hallway. Dovie loitered by the window, back vibrating with tension, not making any further attempt to engage them in conversation. Sibyl's gaze traveled from the point of baby-fine hair at the nape of Dovie's neck, along the tiled waiting room floor, up the tweed pant legs extended from the chair next to her, to Benton's hands folded in his lap, one of his thumbs toying with the skin of the back of the opposite hand. There were short hairs on his knuckles, and Sibyl's eyes settled there, absorbed in the texture of his skin.

Time trickled to a stop while they waited.

Without turning around, Dovie sighed and said, "He was so gentle with Harley, you know? Your father. I wasn't sure if coming to get him was the right thing to do. But he was so kind, when he came with me back to the boardinghouse. I was out of my mind, I was so afraid. So much blood. But he held Harley in his arms, smoothing his hair, telling him it would be all right while we waited for the ambulance. *Don't be afraid*, he said. *You'll be all right this time*. I knew it was the right thing. Coming to you all."

Sibyl, surprised, was about to press Dovie further when the door to the waiting room opened and admitted the stooping form of Lan Allston.

Interlude

Outside the International Settlement

Shanghai

June 8, 1868

LANNIE'S FEET FLOPPED at the end of his legs, the compress against his jaw warm and sticky with blood, trying to follow the dark shoulders of the young scholar, his queue swinging as he strode through the crowd. Lannie blinked, not clear where in the city he was, hurrying to catch up with the young man at an intersection thick with wheelbarrow pushers, carriages, and a cow.

"Hey," Lannie said, attempting conversation. The scholar did not turn. Instead he bounded across the street, ducking around other pedestrians. Lannie scrambled behind him, desperate to keep up.

What should he do now? He didn't speak the language, though it seemed that the *lingua franca* of Shanghai was broken English, scrambled grammar interspersed with words in Chinese. The neighborhood around them morphed into a sedate Second Empire quarter, with brick avenues and elegant shop fronts, and Lannie heard snatches of rapid-fire French.

As he trotted behind the scholar Lannie attempted to reason with himself. He could get along speaking good, clear English, if he had to. He felt in his coat pocket for the wad of bills secreted there. He'd grown up in a port town. He could make his way back, he felt certain. Find a place to berth for the night. Sort everything out.

The scholar, as if overhearing Lannie's thoughts, glanced over his shoulder at the boy. "It hurt much?" he asked.

"As a matter of fact," Lannie slurred through the congealing blood in his mouth, "it does. Like you wouldn't believe."

The young man laughed. "You'd be surprised what I'd believe," he said, plucking at Lannie's sleeve to get him moving.

"Where are we going?" Lannie asked.

"You'll see," the young man said. "Got to know where to go, or you'll end up in some stinking sampan on the Huangpu, paying a trollop for a little *tangchai* that'd disgust even a sedan-chair carrier."

Lannie recoiled until he saw that the scholar was smiling.

"Wait," Lannie protested. "Tell me your name, at least."

"I'd sooner cut out my tongue than hear my family name in a filthy barbarian mouth," the scholar bellowed. But Lannie could tell he was being teased.

"Oh, come on," Lannie protested. "I lost a tooth, for Christ's sake." The blasphemy felt good on his tongue. He grinned, knowing his teeth to be stained red.

The scholar shook his head. "Too hard for you. Unless you've got Shanghainese I don't know about." The young man paused. "Let's say it's Johnny. That'll do."

He stuck out a hand, in mimicry of hearty Americanism, and Lannie took it. The man's grip was strong and dry.

"Lan," he said, and their hands pumped once.

"*Lan*," Johnny repeated, sarcastic. "I do speak English, you know. No need to make up some fake Chinese name on my account."

"It's a nickname," Lannie replied, confused. "For Harlan. My father's also called Harlan, so they gave me a nickname for simplicity's sake."

He felt foolish explaining, more so when he saw that Johnny, or whatever his name was, had immediately lost interest in the intricacies of New England naming traditions.

After a time, Lannie began to understand where they were headed.

His knowledge of the city was schematic, assembled from anecdotes spun on shipboard as they neared port, and so skewed with hyperbole and misunderstanding. From those piecemeal accounts he knew that the old center of the city was shuttered with dense fortifications that once wound through the entire countryside. Now, at the end of a narrow alleyway festooned with lanterns and drying laundry, they met an imposing stone wall.

"Nanshi," the scholar said. "The walled city. Come on."

The trailing end of a drying sheet brushed over the top of Lannie's head as he passed beneath it. The wall before them stretched up into the sky, as oblivious to the passage of time as a sheer cliff face, or as the ocean itself.

"Three hundred years old," Johnny said proudly in response to Lannie's wordless gape.

Lannie felt himself to have come from an old place. Salem was a long-memoried town, its streets stalked by ghosts. As a boy his mother told him of witches who liked to fillet disobedient children, and even though he knew she was spinning fairy stories he nevertheless grew up with the weight of past generations on his shoulders. He carried the burden of tradition with a mixture of pride and disquiet, or even resentment. Every choice bore the implied judgment of these ancestors he never knew, whose memory must not be sullied, whose expectations for him must not be let down. At times Lannie bristled that his future must be given over to maintaining the supposed honor of the past. At other times, that sense of honor provided him with welcome clarity.

Nothing in Salem approached this wall for age and majesty, which protected old Shanghai from the incursions of the new. There were a few old-fashioned houses, of course, inhabited by poorer people, crowded together in their darkness and dampness, the stench of two hundred years' worth of mice and sweat and woodsmoke and whitewash. But when New England was still a wilderness, this wall was already over a hundred years old. Lannie felt small and insignificant before it, a passing rill on an otherwise unbroken stream of time.

"A model settlement!" Johnny exclaimed, a sarcastic echo of the British term for Shanghai. Behind the wall Lannie spied the silhouettes of peaked pagodas, curled at the corners like dried leaves.

"Now," Johnny said. "We attend to your jaw."

Lannie thought that he would just as soon present his shattered tooth to the ship's surgeon than some strange doctor with foul-smelling herbs and terrifying needles. He smiled, trying to convince Johnny to forget it.

"It's nothing. Really."

"Ha, ha," the scholar said, speaking the words rather than laughing them. "Come on."

The two young men wended their way to the center of the walled city district. They passed a squatting row of artists executing placid, if nearly identical, landscapes. Lannie brightened, wondering if he should pick one up as a gift for his mother—a lark, maybe, or a mountain range. Then he remembered that a scroll rather like these, dried and yellowed, hung in the pantry of the house on Chestnut Street, a souvenir brought back by his father when he and Lannie's mother were young.

"Johnny," Lannie said.

"Mmmmm?" he answered without looking around.

"How is it you speak such good English?" Lannie asked.

The scholar glared over his shoulder, and Lannie backed away, attempting to cover his mistake. "I mean, that I would think . . . that is . . ."

"My profession." The young man cut him off.

"But what's your profession?"

Johnny stopped, rolled his eyes heavenward, and pinched the bridge of his nose between a forefinger and thumb. "I'm a translator," he said. "If you think my English is good, you should hear my Latin."

"Latin?" Lannie exclaimed. "Who do you translate for?"

"Anyone who'll pay," Johnny said. "But these days, the American Heritage Bible Mission."

"You're a Christian, then!" Lannie was surprised, and curious.

"Stupid," the scholar muttered. But he didn't answer.

Before long they arrived at a street that Johnny called Xuexiang Lane, a modest quarter of shop fronts and shuttered houses. The street crawled with painted women, leaning in doorways, beckoning, their eyes flat under the red lantern glow. Fingertips trailed over Lannie's shoulders as he passed, and his hands thrust deeper into his pockets. He still hadn't taken his coat off, despite the sheen of sweat at his hairline and on the downy fuzz of his upper lip. Inside his coat, he felt safer.

"How do you like the ten thousand flowers?" Johnny asked. "There aren't really ten thousand of them, you know. Or at least, I don't think there are."

"Is that what you call this?" Lannie asked, his eyes sliding by an older, haggard woman sitting on a doorstep, her arms folded, meeting them with a glare as they passed.

"Pssshhh, this isn't what we're here for," the scholar said, waving his hand in dismissal. "The *changsan* in Madam's house would never stoop to address these *yao'er*."

"*Changsan?*" Lannie asked.

"Long three," Johnny translated. Then, with a wicked smile, he added, "It's from the mah-jongg tile." He laughed, and Lannie, not understanding why this was funny, smiled and nodded his head.

"*Changsan* deserve respect. These"—he flicked his fingertips at a woman of indeterminate years leaning in a doorway, one sallow shoulder peeking out from within folds of silk—"these, you just pay. Not for us. And anyway, there's your jaw to think of."

Lannie brought a hand up to his cheek at the mention of it, abashed that his injury wasn't escaping notice. His lip felt pulpy, and the sharp pain had receded, leaving a throbbing ache. Some whiskey would help. Did they drink whiskey in the old quarter of Shanghai?

He was on the point of posing this question when Johnny stopped before a low wooden door, hung overhead with a prettily lettered banner. The scholar caught Lannie by the shoulder.

"Here," Johnny said. "A *huayanjian*. Good for your jaw, good for your mind." He wagged a cautionary finger under the boy's nose. "There'll be girls here, too. But I don't recommend it. That's not why we came."

Lannie swallowed, uncertain. The door looked like the mouth of a cavern leading into subterranean worlds. He felt as if he were standing aside, observing himself. He'd had the same disembodied sensation when being photographed at the new studio on Tremont, buttoned into his school suit, conscious that he must not move a muscle, driven to distraction by roaming itches that appeared first in an eyebrow, then under his chin. He'd posed before the Roman ruin backdrop, powerless to act, and gradually he pulled away from his body, observing himself. Here was this young man, this Lan Allston, who was him, and yet not him, half a globe away from everything that he knew.

"What does *huayanjian* mean, Johnny?" he heard himself ask.

The scholar arched one eyebrow at Lannie and smiled.

"It means 'chamber of smoke and flowers,'" came the answer. As he spoke the door opened, into a blackness that Lannie's eyes could not penetrate. And he watched himself step inside.

TEN

The Back Bay
Boston, Massachusetts
April 17, 1915

The light behind Sibyl's eyelids turned rosy pink, and though she could no longer deny that she was awake, she pulled the needlepoint coverlet up under her chin, resisting the intrusion of day. Stubborn, she nestled deeper into the feather mattress, as if she could will herself to stay asleep. Her muscles tightened from the effort, her eyes screwing shut.

She was not awake yet. She was asleep.

She waited, poised in the hope that she might fool herself.

A minute ticked by.

Two.

Sibyl brought the heels of her hands to her forehead with a groan, pressing into the ache that still gripped her skull from the previous night. It was no use. She was awake. The world outside awaited her, or more immediately, the world downstairs. Sibyl rolled onto her side, a beam of sunlight falling across her cheek, warming her skin as she bunched the coverlet to her chest. She closed her eyes against the daybreak, resenting it.

Sibyl felt as though she had been asleep for only fifteen minutes. Her arms were leaden with fatigue, her fists balled under her chin. Even the soles of her feet were tired. Steeling herself, she drew her body up amid her nest of linens. She gazed, eyes puffy, through the leaded glass of the bay window, out over the winking surface of the Charles River.

Her feet pressed to the floor as she struggled into her dressing gown, tangling one arm in a filmy sleeve, a few strands of hair hanging into her face. She could scarcely remember what time they'd gotten home. Before first light, but only just. As she stumped through the rear entrance of the house behind her father, she had heard the first tittering of the sparrows who nested in the ivy on the face of the town house. A few of their tiny bodies fluttered under ivy leaves and burst forth to swoop through the darkness, protesting the opening of the back door.

"The sound of morning," her father murmured to himself before closing the door behind them.

Sibyl shuffled into the lavatory that she used to share with Eulah, bent over the claw-footed bathtub that Helen had chosen, and twisted the hot water tap. How had Helen been so certain that she would have daughters, who would need a claw-footed bathtub? It was as though their mother had willed Sibyl and Eulah into being, because the existence of such a fine lavatory required it.

Steam began to rise off the porcelain, filling the room with a fragrant cloud, and Sibyl leaned against the marble vanity, peering at herself. In the thin morning light Sibyl's skin looked older, more papery, her eyes ringed in shadow from the previous night.

She squeezed her eyes closed, thinking about the policemen with their questions and scribbling pencils. Harley hadn't been able to say anything of use, of course.

"Should be a quick recovery," the dapper young doctor assured her and her father as Dovie loitered within hearing range. "I should say the rib's merely cracked, rather than fully broken, and I think you'll find that his youth and vigor will set him to rights sooner than you might expect. We'll keep him for a few days, just for observation. We're in a better position to keep him comfortable."

As the doctor spoke, the nurse shot her father a nasty look. Sibyl didn't understand why. Lan seemed unperturbed by the nurse's disapproval, agreeing to leave his son in their care. But not before the police were satisfied.

Sibyl sighed, opening her eyes and staring at the disheartening spectacle of her face.

With Harley slipping in and out of consciousness, unable, or unwilling, to articulate what had transpired, the two policemen determined there was little reason for them to be present at the hospital. Benton grew insistent, pushing himself into the policemen's faces with all the righteous fury at his disposal.

"Can't you see he's been beaten?" the young professor insisted, too loudly. A few heads turned in the hallway, looking. "He's lucky they didn't do worse! He could've been killed. I fail to see how you're going to find the men responsible if you don't speak with him. I insist you try again."

Sibyl observed the policemen's response to Benton's wrestler's bluster. The two uniformed men (one of them, she noted, with a cauliflower ear, and probably not from wrestling, either) passed first through bemusement, then to placation, before finally growing angry and dismissive.

"Well, if the young man ain't gonna tell us what happened, there isn't much to be done about it, then," one of them said, tucking his pencil into his breast pocket with finality. "Sure, we understand, Professor Derby. You're upset and all, but I'm afraid it can't be helped. If the victim don't want to complain, then there's no complaint, is there? Unless the young lady wishes to make a statement?"

Dovie, her back to the group, face reflected in the multipaned window, held as still as if she had not been addressed at all. Sibyl's eyes darkened behind the drifting steam in the lavatory at the memory. Well, what did she expect the girl to do? Just blurt out everything? Including why Harlan was in her rooms in the first place? Surely not. And did Sibyl want to hear it, if she did?

The policemen, Benton, Sibyl, and Lan all waited, watching the tension rippling down the girl's back, which, with the rhythmic flick of her cigarette, was the only sign that she was a living thing, rather than some wax replica of herself. When she did not so much as shift her weight on her feet, much less speak, the group re-formed, closing her out. The policemen were disinclined to inquire about her relationship, whatever it might be, to Harlan. Perhaps they didn't wish to embarrass the family. Or perhaps they just didn't want to be bothered. Benton's fists balled at his sides as each person in the group wondered what should happen next.

Finally, Lan Allston cleared his throat.

"It's right good of you lads to be so concerned for my son's welfare," he said, sounding less the noble patriarch and more the genial sailor who has risen through the ranks. "Perhaps when the boy's more himself would be a better time."

Her father rested a rough palm on the shoulder of each policeman in turn, squeezing with seriousness, and shook each man's hand, leveling his ice blue gaze square in the other men's eyes. The policemen, shrugging, both ready for a long day to draw to a blessed close, minds on cold roast beef at kitchen tables and sleeping children at home, withdrew without argument, and with evident relief, laying the authority to resolve the situation at the feet of the aging sailor.

Draping her dressing gown over the back of a chair, Sibyl eased first one bare foot, then the other, into the scalding water in the bathtub. She lowered herself with care, her senses awakening from the mingled sensations of steaming water and chilled porcelain against her skin. Sibyl rested her head against the tub back, eyes drifting closed, feeling her aching limbs loosen.

In a few short days, they said, Harley could come home. He'd have to be tended to, of course—wounds cleaned, bandages washed and changed, food more tender than usual while his lip and jaw healed. There was the question of school. And the debts. Harley, a bundle of situations, as always. Sibyl slipped deeper into the tub, knees emerging from the soapsuds, water meeting her lips.

Her father had circumstances well in hand at the hospital. But it was fitting, and typical, for him to step forward in a moment of acute crisis. Once the crisis had passed, or rather shifted into the new shape of normal, the minor details of its resolution would be left to her. Sibyl folded her arms over her breasts, sliding down still farther, pulling away from the weight of her responsibilities. Her head slipped beneath the surface of the water and she was alone, suspended, listening to the movement of her blood in her body and the rhythmic pulse of her heart.

A bubble slipped out from one of her nostrils. Sibyl felt the tantalizing pull of nothingness, of warmth and vacancy, and she lingered in it. Another bubble slipped from her nose.

Without warning, a steely hand clamped over her upper arm and hauled upward. Sibyl gasped in surprise, breathing water into her nose and down her throat, tinged with the sour floral taste of lavender soap. Coughing and sputtering, Sibyl scrambled upright with a splash, wet hair plastered to her face as she heaved for breath, water running off her lips, her fingertips, her chin.

"Miss!" a voice exclaimed.

Sibyl looked up into the shocked and worried face of Mrs. Doherty, one sleeve rolled to the elbow, holding a bath towel. She was accustomed to entering without knocking, as had been her habit since Sibyl was old enough to bathe herself. Behind the housekeeper's deliberately unflappable stare, Sibyl saw worry mingled with contained panic. Sibyl drew ragged breaths, her hands clutching the sides of the bathtub, face flushed and clearly alive. Seeing that Sibyl was safe, the housekeeper's expression resolved from alarm to disapproval.

"Oh!" Sibyl panted, wiping the hair out of her eyes with one hand while trying to cover the modest parts of herself with both arms. Sibyl's cheeks reddened in embarrassment and aggravation. Mrs. Doherty stared closely at her, more concerned with Sibyl's mental state than her physical one. Sibyl glared back, wishing the woman would go away.

Finally, Mrs. Doherty said, "I can't have Betty hold the breakfast," as though that were a credible explanation for hoisting Sibyl out of the water with such urgency. She waited, keeping a wary eye on the young mistress of the Beacon Street house, pretending to be readying to offer Sibyl the towel.

"Breakfast?" Sibyl asked, aware that she had overslept. The staff had a schedule to keep, which she herself had set for them, and which it was her duty as mistress of the house to maintain.

With a sniff of annoyance, which she could afford now that the safety of the situation was clear, Mrs. Doherty laid aside the towel and turned her attention to the vanity table. Her back to Sibyl, she rearranged the bottles by order of size with a brisk hand while she spoke.

"The eggs'll be getting cold, and you know how he hates cold eggs." Neither of them felt the need to specify whose eggs would be growing cold.

The housekeeper hazarded a worried glance over her shoulder at Sibyl, who affected not to notice. Then with a grunt of resignation the woman bustled out, the door clicking closed behind her.

Sibyl sighed again, dropping her head back into the cooling water, feeling its surface close over the tip of her nose as she knew with sickening certainty that she could hide from this day no longer.

THE DOOR TO the dining room squeaked open, and Sibyl edged into a room so encased in walnut paneling that even the cool springtime sun through the bay window failed to relieve the impression of night. Efforts had been made at brightening the space in deference to the season: a cheerful arrangement of paperwhites and daffodils sat in the center of the dining table, perfuming the air. The table held a white linen runner, needlepointed by Helen as a new bride, with white roses and young fawns in repose among tiny ivy leaves. Someone had taken the time to polish the silver and the candlesticks, which caught the morning light with a chill glimmer. Even so, the room managed to absorb these gestures of sunshine, swallowing them up.

At one end of the table a straight-backed chair stood out at a careless angle, overlooked. In the vicinity of the chair rested a crushed napkin, half obscuring a few coffee stains and a sprinkling of crumbs. A fork, clotted with eggs, sat tines down on a greasy plate. Sibyl ignored this tableau, which happened to be arranged at her customary seat, and settled instead at the opposite end. At the table's head, behind a newspaper, Sibyl found her father, steam still rising from his freshened coffee.

"Good morning, Papa," Sibyl said, announcing her presence, her voice rusty from sleep. As she spoke Mrs. Doherty appeared, sliding a silent plate of eggs and buttered toast into place before her. Coffee poured, as if of its own volition, into a waiting cup at Sibyl's fingertips. Sibyl felt the housekeeper's gaze on her, as though confirming her safety once and for all. She did not speak.

The newspaper rattled.

"It's unconscionable, I tell you," Lan Allston said from behind the morning edition.

Sibyl sighed, unwilling to revisit the previous evening's events in any detail before she had had so much as a sip of coffee. She brought the cup to her lips, her eyes on the tablecloth, saying only a noncommittal "Hmmm," sufficient to indicate that she was listening.

"Chlorine gas," her father continued, head shaking in disapproval. "You can't even imagine the depths the Hun will stoop to. And I always thought they were an honorable people."

Sibyl let out an inaudible sigh of relief that her father was wrapped up again in accounts of the war, rather than in the situation within the Beacon Street house. She had no idea what he could be referring to. Whatever it was, it sounded wretched.

Sibyl wrestled with the habit, inculcated by Helen, of closing her ears, and so her mind, to unpleasant things. Few aspects of Helen's and Sibyl's overlapping characters would send Eulah on a tear faster.

"How can you be so horribly ignorant, Mother?" Sibyl's memory heard Eulah demand, sitting one morning at that very breakfast table. Her imperious younger sister always insisted that there was little worse than willful ignorance of harsh human truths. "I can't tolerate it, I really can't."

Eulah's dominant theme just before her death had been votes for women, a passion unshared by the other members of the Allston household.

"Really, my darling," Helen clucked. "You act as though women don't hold any sway over men already. Whatever would I need the franchise for? Then I'd have to start reading newspapers and following party platforms and all sorts of bother. Who has the time?"

"Mother!" Eulah cried. "You can't go about having Papa speak for you all the time. Don't you want to have your own views put forward? Haven't you anything to say on your own account?"

"Why, my views are Papa's," Helen soothed. "And Papa's views are mine on everything that's important. In any event, I wouldn't want to have to deal with the consequences of lawmaking, would you? Imagine, if one made the wrong decision. Why, it makes me tired just thinking about it."

"Sibsie," Eulah squealed in rage, turning to her sister for moral support. "I can't believe her! And you just sitting there like a lump, not even saying *anything*!"

At that her younger sister had tossed down her napkin and stormed out of the dining room, tipping over a chair in her haste with an abrupt *thunk*. Eulah always had a flair for the dramatic.

"Must be her special time," a sullen Harlan muttered, to which her mother hissed, "Harlan! None of that." She may have even swiped at her son's elbow with the back of her butter knife, but Sibyl didn't remember. Helen had been a great one for propriety enforced by butter knife.

Sibyl detected the same streak of self-righteous impatience in Harley, though his point of view was shot through with a naïveté that Eulah, despite her cosseted upbringing, had never had. He certainly preferred to speak rather than listen. Whereas Eulah voiced her politics at club meetings and marches under banners, Harlan limited his activism to grumbled disagreements within the safe confines of the Beacon Street house. Harlan was clear in his sense of how the world *ought* to be, his opinions formed from the view out of the drawing room window. He had so far proven unable to act toward those ostensible ideals, of course. But he was flush with ideals all the same.

Sibyl half smiled, certain that Harley would object to such an unforgiving characterization. And what of Sibyl? She had usually been content to hold back, observing the larger personalities of her mother and siblings as they clashed together. But she chafed at it.

Sibyl straightened in her chair and inquired, "Really? Chlorine gas, you say?"

Her father lowered the newspaper and leveled his blue gaze on her face. She sipped her coffee with a pleasant smile, then took up her fork and stirred the eggs around the plate in a practiced gesture of simulated eating.

"Hm," her father said, perhaps trying to evaluate the true depth of his daughter's interest in current affairs. "Well, I suppose we can discuss it this evening. It's hardly appropriate breakfast conversation." His eyes traveled from her face to the fork moving around the edges of her plate.

"Indeed?" Sibyl asked.

"Suffice it to say," he continued, "the Kaiser is a ruthless man. Ruthless. And without honor."

Sibyl's eyebrows rose, knowing that to disparage a man's honor was Lan Allston's most cutting insult.

"If you leave the paper for me, I'll read it this afternoon," she said, bringing a tiny morsel of egg to her mouth. "Be sure you tell Mrs. Doherty, though, or she'll throw it out."

"It'll be in the *Evening Transcript* as well, I'm sure," her father said, still observing the slow progress of her fork. She brought another, equally minute tineful of egg to her mouth and slid it between her teeth. She made a show of chewing, swallowing, affecting enjoyment.

"Betty does the best eggs, doesn't she?" Sibyl remarked, to push away her father's close attention.

"Mmm," he agreed, watching her.

He reached over and let out a sharp ring of the silver bell that rested by his seat. Mrs. Doherty appeared, not bothering to conceal her aggravation at the summons. She was chewing, Sibyl noticed, which suggested that her own breakfast had been interrupted.

"Sir?" the housekeeper inquired, concealing the bite in her cheek.

"Bring Miss Allston some bacon, if you will. We have bacon, don't we?" he said, telling rather than asking. It was clear the existence of bacon was not subject to debate. "Good and fried. In butter."

"Very good, Mister Allston," the housekeeper said, bobbing a fleeting curtsy before disappearing into the pantry.

"Papa, that's really not—" Sibyl was silenced by a reproving look from her father.

"You need your strength," he said, more gently than Sibyl expected. "It was a long night, after all. And it's shaping up to be a long day today, I should think."

To her surprise, her father reached a rough hand across the table and grasped her wrist with a reassuring squeeze. She blinked, taken aback by the unaccustomed expression of affection. A smile passed between them, and the meal continued in silence. When Mrs. Doherty reappeared after a few minutes bearing some fragrant fried bacon arranged artfully on a small plate, Sibyl accepted it with a nod, and ate.

Neither of them remarked on the vacant chair at the opposite end of the table.

As breakfast drew to a close, and her father commenced rummaging in his coat pockets for the first pipe bowl of the day, Sibyl decided that the time had come to speak. She cleared her throat, and her father cocked a wiry eyebrow at her, seeming to know what she was about to say.

"Well then. Is she . . . ?" Sibyl began.

Her father nodded, gesturing with his chin to the drawing room across the hall. "I believe you'll find Mrs. Doherty helped her into some of your clothes. Quite an improvement, it must be said."

Sibyl started to frown, not knowing that any of her blouses and skirts were missing, and discomfited that they would be taken without her approval. But she stopped herself, feeling churlish. Of course the girl needed clothes to wear.

The previous evening, in a wordless agreement on placing duty over propriety, Sibyl and Lan had pressed Dovie to return with them to the town house for the night. Both the practical Allstons were fearful of letting her travel home alone at such an unwholesome hour, and uncertain of the safety of her rooms, given what had happened. She was a stranger to them, but not to Harlan, discomfiting though that was. And once she was in their home, the girl couldn't very well be expected to stay in her bloodied tunic, could she? Sibyl covered over her irritation with a determined smile.

"All right," she said, loitering with her fingertips resting on the dining table.

"I'm swinging by the office," her father said, one eye on the chronometer in his hand. "I've a few things to take care of, I'm afraid."

"Shall I have Betty hold dinner, then?" Sibyl asked. She knew that the implicit message of Lan Allston's comment was that the entertainment, or confinement, or investigation of Dovie Whistler was Sibyl's designated assignment for the day.

"No need," he assured her, rising to his feet in turn. "I should think he'll be ready for another visit this afternoon. And while I'm there I'll see about bringing him home. Ought to be back in plenty of time for whatever Betty's got in store for us. Lamb chops, I'm hoping." He gazed on his daughter with a smile.

She smiled back. "Lamb chops would be a nice change, wouldn't they?" she said.

"They certainly would," her father agreed.

"A little mint jam."

"I do enjoy mint jam." Lan sighed.

He looked on her, his eyes softening, and Sibyl knew without him saying anything that her father wished to reassure her about Harlan. It was a look that she hadn't seen in some time, and she paused, returning it with a tiny, if unconvinced, smile.

Without another word they drifted apart, Lan busying himself with his pipe, Sibyl moving to the pocket door, squeaking it open on its sticky wheels. Her nerves tingled with anxiety, her stomach clamping down on the rich food, as if a leaden ball had been sewn into her belly.

She usually preferred to feel empty, on the inside. Empty was more manageable. Cleaner. When Sibyl was worried about something—it seemed like she was often worried about something these days—a sure way to keep that worry under control was to maintain the emptiness of her body. Empty was control. Empty was free. She wasn't sure if her father had cottoned to this long-simmering habit of hers, but she suspected that he might.

Sibyl brought a hand to her waist, massaging her belly to reassure both it and herself as she crossed the front hallway toward the drawing room. The hall stand caught her eye as she passed, its mirror reflecting a wan face, nose sharper than she remembered, eyes rimmed with fatigue. She turned away from the unwelcome specter of herself and opened the enameled peacock door.

ELEVEN

Sibyl found the front parlor brimming with pale spring sunlight. Motes of dust glittered in the sunbeams, held in the air by the stirring breath of the long dormant room. Someone had thrown back the velvet drapes, tying them open, and had fluffed and rearranged some of the throw pillows on the divan, heaping them up in inviting disorder. Sibyl surveyed the room, blinking, surprised.

"I'm sorry," a youthful voice spoke from the yellow silk bench under the bay window. "It was just so gloomy in here, I could hardly see."

Sibyl followed the voice, losing it first in the glow of sunshine through leaded glass. A slim figure was stretched out on the window seat, leaning on one elbow, toying with something that gathered the light to itself and then sent it out again in sharp, brittle splinters.

For a baffling instant, Sibyl felt transported. Three years ago, maybe, or four, coming into the drawing room after breakfast, with the curtains pulled back just like they were now, squinting her eyes against the spring sunlight pouring through the bay window.

"Oh!" the voice in her memory laughed from its perch on the window seat. "She vexes me so, I can hardly stand it. It's just too much, to think of going on the tour with her. For months, can you imagine? First on the steamer going over, and you know she'll want to share a stateroom. With her snoring! Then train after train after train. It just wears me out. I so wish you'd come with us."

Sibyl furrowed her brows, remembering the mingled envy and resignation that weighed on her that year. She almost hated her mother for giving up on her so quickly. She struggled not to fold that bitter feeling into her affection for Eulah. "I wish I could," she said. "But you know the cost is just ridiculous. And anyway, I think Mother's persuaded it'll do you much more good than it will me. I can't say I blame her."

"Nonsense," Eulah chided from her spot on the bench in the bay window. "Why, if nothing else, you should be there to keep me from throwing her overboard in a fit of pique."

Sibyl remembered laughing at Eulah's feigned misery, settling in the windowed enclave across from her youngest sibling.

"Now, now," she said, already growing into her coming role. It was the duty of Boston spinsters to encourage and reassure marriageable young women, and Sibyl slipped into that performance with worrisome ease. "You mustn't talk that way. You know Mother dotes on you. You'll have fun. Just think of all you'll see. The pictures. A real opera. The cafés, full of artists and writers and singers. I'd love to visit a Parisian café, you know. You'll order your clothes, and if I'm very lucky you'll lend me a few of them when you get back, provided I haven't gotten too fat pining for your return, of course. You'll meet all sorts of interesting people."

"*Titled* people," Eulah said with a mischievous smirk. "Why, I don't think she's liable to rest until I'm married off to no less than a duke."

"She'd settle for an earl, I'm sure."

"An earl! Long as he's got a proper country house for Mother to oversee on my behalf. I always thought she fancied herself too good for Gloucester." The two Allston girls laughed, leaning their heads together in the conspiracy of sisters united in shared opinion of their parent's folly.

"Anyway, you'll go. You'll enjoy yourself, you'll see. Even if Mother's along, hounding you the whole way."

"What will you do?" Eulah asked, some of the merriment falling away from her eyes. Sibyl knew that Eulah felt guilty for supplanting Sibyl in their mother's attentions. "It's just too sad to bear, leaving you here alone, with old Doherty watching you like a hawk, and the Captain as conversational as ever."

"I suppose I'll also have Harley passing through every three days complaining that the laundries in Cambridge can't starch his shirts properly," Sibyl mused, laying a gentle hand on her sister's knee. Sibyl understood her guilt. Even appreciated it. But it wouldn't make any difference. "But really, you mustn't worry about me. They've put me on the committee for the historical society lecture series. There's a poetry group starting up at the Athenaeum. And if it gets too hot in town, we'll take the train up to the shore house for a while. It's humble, by your European standards, I realize, but it'll have to do. I've got plenty to keep me occupied."

Eulah smiled on her, a smile born of relief. She had wanted Sibyl's permission, Sibyl realized. She wanted to be excited about the coming trip, to not have to conceal her excitement from her sister. Unapologetic unfairness was a part of the Allston family, as it was in all the other families of their acquaintance, and both of them knew it. "Maybe my earl will have a brother?" Eulah suggested.

"A dissolute one, I hope." Sibyl smiled.

"Hideously ugly, with bad teeth!" Eulah laughed, clapping her hands.

"Provided he has a large fortune, and travels very frequently on business," Sibyl insisted.

"And a country house close to mine. Then Mother can run both the estates for us while we lie around reading novels in the English sunshine."

"Ah, that's a lovely plan. A lovely plan indeed." Sibyl sighed, smiling on the lively girl across from her. She wouldn't put it past Eulah to snag an earl. Though for his sake, she hoped he favored female suffrage.

"Sure, that's a great plan. Though, you know, I'd always thought that Benton Derby was . . ." Eulah trailed off with an uncertain smile.

"What!" Sibyl gasped, shocked to the quick.

"You think I didn't know? Oh, I know plenty," her sister teased.

When Sibyl didn't respond, instead sitting back in the cushions, her hands clutching the dress fabric at her knees, Eulah added, "Maybe more than you, even." Her smile melted away and in a quiet voice Eulah added, "Whatever could have happened, Sibs? I just can't see why he'd wind up with Lydia and not you."

They both leaned on the silken window seats, a warm puddle of spring sunlight between them, arms wrapped around their middles in an identical posture. Sibyl sighed, and then looked at Eulah from under lowered brows. "Maybe it was me? Maybe I told him that until he was titled aristocracy with his own yacht, I'd never even consider it."

The two Allston girls stared at each other for a long minute, and then burst at the same time into gales of laughter, at everything the future might hold for them.

"MISS ALLSTON?" THE voice interrupted, shaking Sibyl out of her daydream. She was still standing in the drawing room, but her déjà vu released its hold, and she shook her head, bringing herself into the present. It was strange to walk into the drawing room and find another young woman stretched in repose in the puddle of sunshine that belonged, rightfully, to her sister.

"Yes, I'm so sorry," she said, aware that she had probably stood gawking at Miss Whistler for an uncomfortable span of time. "I'm afraid I'm not quite myself today. We returned so late, and . . ." She trailed off, unsure how to fill her patter with this stranger.

With a tentative step, Sibyl approached where Dovie was sitting. Well, lounging; one slippered foot was tucked under the girl's haunch while her compact body loafed in the cushions. Sibyl felt a twinge of envy; she never had the nerve to drape herself over the window seat with that much abandon anymore.

"You don't mind that I opened the curtains, do you? It's just so nice out, you know, and I wanted to watch everyone going along Beacon Street. There's this little old man out there who's been working his way up the block for, oh, it must be an hour or more. Never saw someone so slow in all my life. It's a wonder he hasn't been trampled." The girl's voice was sharp and bright, merry, accustomed to filling rooms.

"It's quite all right," Sibyl said. "In fact, I don't know why we don't draw the curtains back more often. It's much cheerier in here now."

Dovie Whistler leaned up on one arm and looked at Sibyl with a welcoming smile. Her figure, now that Sibyl could make the girl out through the halo of light around her, was, she had to agree with her father, much improved by the simple shirtwaist and dun-colored skirt that Mrs. Doherty had pilfered from Sibyl's closet. Scrubbed free of paint and kohl, her face glowed younger and rosier than Sibyl expected, eyes wide and rich emerald, and her hair was brushed close to her head in tidy waves, curling just under her chin.

In the light of day, Dovie looked barely out of her teens; twenty, at the most. Sibyl felt a swell of sisterly responsibility, the same sense of entitlement mingled with obligation that marked all her interactions with Eulah. She moved to the window seat, wondering if complimenting Dovie on her improved appearance would be considered forward, or too intimate.

"Sure is a nice house you've got," the girl said brightly. "Harley always made it sound like some kind of tomb or something, but I think it's much nicer than a lot of the houses I've seen."

The girl's voice was softer too this morning. Her accent was difficult to place, flat and matter-of-fact, untinted by the lingering Anglophilia of Sibyl's Boston circle. Sibyl smiled, bemused at the girl's backhanded compliment.

"Why, thank you. My father designed it," she said. "The house. For my mother, when they were going to be married."

"Oh!" Dovie's eyes widened, with new, though possibly feigned, appreciation for the aesthetic achievements of their home.

"And my mother chose the furnishings. Well, nearly all the furnishings. She was very particular."

A knowing smile dawned across the girl's face. "Particular. An Allston. Imagine that."

Sibyl laughed. Deep in the inner parlor, Baiji the macaw let out a plaintive squawk, sufficient to inform the inhabitants of the drawing room that he was finding their conversation tedious.

"Did your mother choose this, too?" Dovie asked. "I've been playing with it. When I'm nervous, I pick things up. It's a bad habit, I know. But I find I just can't help myself." She held up the polished blue crystal orb, balancing it on her fingertips.

Sibyl's eyebrows rose in surprise and momentary annoyance. The ball had been hidden away in its enameled box and secreted in the sideboard. For Dovie to find it, she would have had to open drawers, peer under lids, rummage. Attempting to be magnanimous, Sibyl reminded herself that Dovie had been awake for some time, unoccupied and alone. Lonely, probably, and anxious in a new place, with people she didn't know. Sibyl extended her hand, palm open, and Dovie slipped the ball from her fingertips. It was cool and round and perfect, polished, smoky blue, like a chunk of arctic ice.

"Ah," Sibyl said, cupping the ball in her palms. "No, not hers. That's mine."

Dovie swallowed, growing worried. So she knew how impolite she had been to find it. Perhaps she had been seeing what she could get away with. "Oh! I didn't realize."

"It's no bother. It's meant to be held, actually." Sibyl forced a fresh smile and offered the trinket back to Dovie, who accepted it, folding it in her tiny hands with unconcealed pleasure.

"Really?" she asked, bringing the item to her face for a closer look. "What is it?"

Sibyl leaned back in the yellow silk of the window seat, crossing her arms and smiling. She waved a foot. "I'm not sure you'd believe me if I told you."

"Oooooh!" Dovie exclaimed, rearranging her feet and leaning forward, elbows on her knees, in an attitude of confidentiality. "Try me."

Sibyl laughed, resting her head against the leaded window. Outside a fresh breeze stirred the new ivy leaves, causing sunlight and green shadow to dance across the blue velvet rug, bringing unaccustomed gaiety to the drawing room. A corner of sunbeam brushed against the portrait of Helen over the fireplace and danced away. Under the leaves the sparrows tittered.

"Well," she began. "It's a bit difficult to explain."

Dovie grinned, rolling the crystal ball in her hands with glee. "I love it! You *must* tell me," she pressed.

Sibyl cast a watchful eye on the eager young woman perched across from her, as slight and airy as a bird herself. Would she understand? It was difficult to tell. Sibyl had heard that Spiritualist interests abounded in the artistic circles in Boston, much as they did among society. Perhaps more so. And this girl, in her travels, must have seen some marvelous things. Marvelous, or horrible, in turn. Looking into Dovie's smooth face, green eyes shining with curiosity, Sibyl felt that her interest was genuine. However, Sibyl also guessed that beneath the sheen of interest was a heavy curtain behind which no one was ever allowed to see.

"Oh, I will. Only there's so much I want to know about *you* first," Sibyl said.

A shadow flitted across Dovie's face, and she straightened in her seat. "Me?" she echoed.

"Why, certainly," Sibyl said, attempting to sound reassuring. "Your accent, for example. I don't think I've heard one quite like it before. Where do you come from?"

Dovie stiffened, her eyes shifting, as though she wanted to move away but couldn't without drawing inappropriate attention.

"Why, California," she said. "San Francisco."

Sibyl saw that Dovie was trying to keep her real emotions hidden. A pretty credible job she was doing, too—if Sibyl had a less sharp eye, Dovie would have come across as careless, or disinterested in discussing her origins. But the carelessness was a ruse.

"Ah," Sibyl said, wistful. "I've often dreamed of California, you know. But I've never been. Is it true that the air there smells like lemons? I read that somewhere."

A train, billowing smoke with a mournful whistle, wended its imaginary way across Sibyl's mind, chugging through tunnels blasted in mountains, past plains dotted with buffalo, and noble red Indians on horseback. Did they still have buffalo out west, and noble red Indians on horseback? She didn't know. Had they ever? To think Dovie had seen all that. It seemed incredible, that such a small, young person could have traveled such a great distance.

Dovie only smiled, still tightly. She let the lemon comment pass unremarked.

"And how long have you been in Boston?" Sibyl continued, undaunted.

"Oh, you know. A little while now. I can hardly remember, to tell you the truth. Seems like I've always been here." Dovie kept her smile vague.

Her eyes were on the scrying glass, rather than on Sibyl's face. She rolled it between her palms, then brought it to her lap.

"Ah," Sibyl said. "So I suppose you consider Boston your real home, then?"

"Yes, yes indeed," Dovie agreed, relieved to leave the question of California behind.

"And yet you live in a boardinghouse, don't you?" Sibyl pressed, keeping her voice gentle.

"Sure." The girl's eyes darkened to a deeper emerald. "It's quite affordable, you know. Respectable, too. I haven't got any family anymore, and Mrs. Lee, she's the one who runs the house, she keeps an eye on me. We're a very congenial bunch, in the boardinghouse."

"I see," Sibyl said. She wondered what this creature did for money. She had her assumptions, naturally. But it was impossible for her to ask. Wasn't it?

Sibyl paused, and the girl smiled at her, perhaps thinking the question of lodging had been addressed.

"I suppose you support yourself, then?" Sibyl ventured.

The girl pressed her lips together but kept her expression bright and open. "Well, sure! I have my own money. I've been on my own for ages."

"Ah," Sibyl said, nodding. "So."

"And now that I've told you all about myself, you must tell me what this funny ball's supposed to do," Dovie said, teasing, but also firmly enough that Sibyl perceived that further details of Dovie's upbringing would not be forthcoming. At least, not today.

"Well," Sibyl began slowly. "There are many ways to answer that, I suppose. It's a little hard to know where to begin." She paused. "Perhaps Harley told you that we had another sister as well? Who died?"

Dovie's face closed, arranging itself into the proper representation of pity and understanding. "Yes, he mentioned." She hesitated, unsure what words would be best to choose, and so choosing—as so often was the case with people faced with another person's tragedy—to say nothing.

"She was a remarkable person, Eulah," Sibyl said, eyes softening. "So opinionated! Very involved in the franchise. So pretty and gay. She loved music, and dancing. I never knew a girl so happy to be alive, so open to what the world had to offer. Mother was very attached to her—of course, we all were."

She took a breath, and then let it out slowly, releasing the miserable tightness that she always felt in her chest when she thought about Eulah and Helen. If she strained her ears, she could imagine she heard the sound of Eulah's laughter, tinkling upstairs.

Dovie watched her with a tentative smile.

"Well, Mother decided that Eulah, after she came out in society, should be taken on the grand tour. Meet all the fashionable people in Europe, go to the picture galleries and cafés."

Sibyl's dark brows lowered at the memory. She could never escape how bitterly the news of this decision sat with her when it was first delivered, in Helen's trademark singsong voice, over a late-night supper four years earlier.

"*Her?*" Sibyl spat, throwing her napkin down in annoyance. "Her, by herself? I suppose Harley and I don't have a yen to see Europe, then?"

"Mother, Sibsie at least should come with us," Eulah suggested, though at the time Sibyl had thought Eulah was saying so out of filial loyalty rather than any real desire for Sibyl's company. Her sister's love of being the center of attention could sometimes offset her basic goodness.

"Really, darling," Helen said, with a firmness that the Allston children didn't often hear from her. "I'm sure your brother can find a time to go later on. When he's done with school."

"My brother!" Sibyl exclaimed, her anger coloring her cheeks a rich scarlet. Eulah's eyes vacillated between the two of them, nervous, unwilling to say something that might jeopardize her own opportunity to go. "And what about me?"

Helen smiled on her eldest daughter with a patient, immovable smile. "Well, there's the matter of cost, I'm afraid. The tickets I have my eye on are terribly expensive. And someone has to stay here and keep an eye on Papa," her mother said, as though explaining a terribly obvious point. "You don't think I can count on Harlan to do that, do you? What do you think will become of Papa if he's left here all by himself?"

"But," Sibyl protested, sputtering, feeling like a young child being cheated at a game. She grappled for the right argument to make, perhaps that her father had lived on his own at sea for half his life and so could surely make do in Boston, or that Sibyl herself was still young, still beautiful enough to be worth marrying.

"You're so reliable, Sibyl," her mother said, closing the discussion. "I simply can't see any other way. And you wouldn't wish to deny your sister such a grand opportunity, would you?"

What followed was a dreadful row of which Sibyl was still ashamed. She hardly ever raised her voice; usually it was Harley or Eulah who was the maker of scenes in the Allston universe. Perhaps even worse than her initial anger was the fact that Sibyl would never be able to forgive herself for thinking, in the first black instant when they heard that *Titanic* was lost, that she was relieved not to have been with them.

Dovie placed a gentle hand on Sibyl's knee, inviting her to continue. The gesture shook Sibyl out of her sadness and guilt, bringing her back to the sunlit bay window.

"Yes," Sibyl said. "Well. They were on their way home. They'd been away for months, you know, and I knew from the postcards and telegrams that they'd had a wonderful time. Especially Eulah. They were embarking at Southampton, and we were all set to meet them in New York when they arrived. And the boat they were taking was so grand and fine, there was an awful lot of excitement. Its maiden voyage. We were going to meet them to celebrate when they landed at New York."

She paused, searching Dovie's face for understanding, possibly even for forgiveness. Sibyl yearned to be released from the crushing, noxious weight of her mingled guilt and relief. Of course Dovie couldn't know that. Even if she could know what Sibyl wanted, forgiveness wasn't in her power to bestow. Sibyl knew this, but she searched for it anyway in the young woman's face. Dovie nodded, slowly.

"Well," Sibyl finished, with a stoic smile. "I suppose you know what happened. They never arrived."

Dovie's hands reached forward to clasp themselves together on Sibyl's knee.

"As you can imagine," Sibyl said, voice catching, "it was a terrible shock. For all of us. It was in all the papers. We couldn't get away from it. Harlan took it very hard. He'll never admit it, but he did."

Dovie smiled a private smile, her eyes softening at the mention of Harlan's name, and Sibyl wondered what he had told Dovie about those first few days after the sinking. As she'd passed his rooms Sibyl had heard the muffled sound of him weeping like a little boy, and whenever he emerged for meals his eyes were puffy and red. Their father was impatient about it. She once overheard the Captain upbraiding Harley in the inner parlor, hissing that he must pull himself together for Sibyl's sake. Even then, Sibyl suspected that the real reason Harlan must contain himself was for their father's benefit, rather than her own.

Looking at the young woman across from her, Sibyl wondered what other parts of Harlan's secret self he had been able to share with this young woman that he had had to keep hidden from his family. Still Dovie said nothing, only watching, with those magnetic green eyes.

"Well. You're probably wondering what that has to do with—" She gestured to the crystal orb in Dovie's lap, loath for some reason to give it its proper name. "When she was alive, Mother had been—that is— she had rather enjoyed the fashion for . . ." Sibyl hesitated. "Oh, it sounds so silly when you say it aloud. Table-tipping. You know. Those sorts of things."

"Did she really!" Dovie exclaimed. Sibyl watched her, trying to weigh how open the girl might be to what she was about to say.

"Yes," she affirmed. "I was never all that interested when I was younger, to be honest. Not at first. I mean, she used to take me with her. When I was a girl. I was always afraid that the spirits would hurt me. I was terribly scared during the séances most of the time. Of course nothing bad ever happened. It was always just music, and strange images, and sometimes"— she paused, embarrassed—"manifestations. Mother placed great stock in it. She'd consult a medium on anything. I eventually stopped attending, when I got older. Eulah and Harlan never went at all."

"Why, I'm amazed you'd stop going, once you saw it wasn't as scary as all that," Dovie remarked. "I should think it'd be amazing, to communicate with spirits. Imagine! I always thought that was just a lot of stage magic, you know. Like climbing into a box and pretending to be sawed in half."

"Yes." Sibyl faltered. "Well. I suppose I can see why you'd think that.

But. At any rate. Losing them, the way that we did." She took a breath, and then smiled gamely. "It's just that it was so sudden, you know. We weren't prepared for it at all. So when, on a day shortly after the sinking— That is, a woman, a most remarkable woman, who ran the evenings Mother always used to attend, she gathered a group of us together. For the purposes of—"

"A séance," Dovie finished for her, smiling. "You started going to séances, that's it, isn't it?"

Sibyl glanced at her, seeing delight in Dovie's face, as though her proximity to Sibyl might edge her nearer to the beyond herself.

Sibyl continued her abbreviated thought as though Dovie had not spoken. "Of contacting those lately lost. I was in the group that first week, yes. And I've seen her each year since. It was that woman who gave me the crystal ball."

"So this is for conjuring, is that it?" Dovie asked, holding the ball up before her eyes with a newfound gleam of interest. "Well, it doesn't look like much, does it? But I suppose you should know."

"I don't know about conjuring," Sibyl demurred. "It's for seeing. Of a sort."

"How does it work?" Dovie demanded with enthusiasm, laughing like a girl about to play a practical joke. "You've got to show me. Shall I draw the curtains?"

Sibyl brought a hand up to her face, cupping her chin, tired. The bacon weighed heavily in her belly, and she was unaccustomed to dealing with someone of such high energy as Dovie. How was the girl able to put on so many different faces while still managing to appear sincere?

"In truth," she said, "I'm not really sure. The medium showed me how, once. But it only worked for her, and not me. So I put it away."

"Away!" Dovie cried in dismay. "But that's a shame, to have such a remarkable thing, and not use it." She toyed with the crystal, playing it about her fingertips. Sibyl watched her play with it, feeling a curious sour jealousy that Mrs. Dee had been able to make it work, while she had not.

The two sat in silence, Dovie still rolling the orb in her hands, absorbed. She was very like Eulah in many ways. The same quick, credulous energy. The same enthusiasm. Dovie seemed, like Eulah, the sort of person who would answer yes to things as a matter of course, rather than no. Small and bright, compact, faster moving than Sibyl, who was more languid. Sitting in the bay window, sunshine falling between them, talking with Dovie, it felt familiar. Homelike.

Sibyl sat up with a thrill of sudden resolve. "Let's get your coat," she said.

"My coat?" Dovie asked. "What for? I'm actually not sure where it is. That gloomy-looking housekeeper took it away last night."

"We'll have her find it, then. We're going out. For tea. Come along." Sibyl got to her feet, holding a hand out, without thinking, for Dovie to take. Smiling, surprised, Dovie slipped the ball into her skirt pocket, accepted Sibyl's hand, and got to her feet.

Interlude

✦

North Atlantic Ocean
Outward Bound
April 14, 1912

LAUGHING, HER ARMS wrapped around herself for warmth, Eulah stumbled over the doorjamb from the gallery out to the deck, narrowly avoiding tripping over a neglected steamer chair in her haste to reach the railing.

"Wait up!" Harry called after her, closing the door behind him.

She leaned her elbows on the railing, pressing her face to the frigid night air and inhaling deeply. The night was moist and heavy with fog, and a damp chill spread through Eulah's bones as soon as she left the warm safety of the dining gallery. The breeze from the ocean stirred her skirts around her ankles, moving the heavy silk against her body and flapping it out to the side. She brought a hand up to secure her hat against the breeze. Her breath escaped her mouth and nose in a cloud of warmth, and she grinned, imagining that it was her soul that she could see, moving in and out of her body, instead of her breath. She was on the point of sharing this observation when she felt Harry's arm slide around her shoulders, and his voice whispered low in her ear. "It's freezing out here. Now what was it you wanted to show me?"

The warmth of his body in the cold night caused her to shiver. Eulah brought a hand up alongside his cheek, and her eyes danced up at him. "Me?" she asked. She dropped her voice to a whisper and said, "This."

She tipped her head back, offering her lips to him, and he pressed his mouth to hers. He tasted like warmth and whiskey, the perfect male flavor, and Eulah found herself smiling around the kiss, helpless against the laughter that came bubbling up from her chest. She laughed into his mouth, and he laughed, too, pulling back to place a kiss first on her cheek, and then on the tip of her nose.

"You're very forward this evening, Mr. Widener," Eulah chided, nestling into the crook of his arm. He was right, it really was freezing outside. Her arms were all gooseflesh, and soon her teeth would start chattering.

He laughed, looking out over the water. "I am?" he asked, rubbing a hand over her upper arm to warm her up. "Well, I suppose I am, then."

They paused, both gazing out through the depths of fog, a low haze hiding the surface of the water and deadening its sounds. They heard the tinkling and laughing of voices inside the dining room, the scrape of chairs as dancers reclaimed their seats. Somewhere on a lower deck, they could discern the faint sound of voices and fiddle playing. The entire ship throbbed with life. Within its teeming soul, they felt the engines vibrating beneath their feet, and the churn and roll of water as it was muscled aside by the cutting bow of the steamer.

"We'd better not stay too long," Harry remarked. "Your mother will miss us."

"I can think of few things my mother would like better," Eulah said, "than to think she might have reason to miss us."

"She making plans for you, I take it?" he teased.

Eulah sighed, glancing at him under the netting of her hat. It tickled against her nose, and she brushed it away with a finger. "Always," she said. "Mother always has plans."

"Just for you?" he asked. "Or for everyone?"

"Well," Eulah said, thinking of her siblings. "Just everyone south of Gloucester. But it seems like her hopes really rest on me."

"How's that?"

"Oh, you know. My brother's all decided. He'll finish out school, and then Papa'll take him in hand. Put him to work. He'll marry somebody eventually. He'll get the house. That'll be that, I guess. And my sister—"

Eulah hesitated, wondering if it was disloyal of her to speak so freely. But she didn't care. She knew she shouldn't speak her mind as much as she did, but was usually powerless to stop herself.

"I think she's missed the boat, in a way. It's a shame. She's awfully clever. Much cleverer than I am." She paused, thinking about Sibyl. "I was always a little jealous of her, to be honest. People listen, when she says things. But she's been out for a while now, and nothing's ever come of it. She'll keep on with her committees, I imagine, and she'll take care of Papa. So yes, I suppose you could say Mother's settled the better part of her ambition on me. She'll just about die if I'm not engaged within the year. I don't know how she's standing the heartbreak, me not coming home a duchess already."

"I know how you feel," Harry said, frowning.

Eulah searched up into the young man's face. "You do?" she asked softly.

"Sure. You think old George in there thinks book collecting's a worthy pursuit?" Harry laughed with dismissive candor. "No, sir. Not when I could go into transportation, or finance. Or anything else, when you come down to it, that's not spending his hard-earned money on books nobody wants to read. He'll make me give it up eventually."

Eulah placed her hand over his on her arm. "But you're good at it, aren't you?" she asked.

"Why, I guess it doesn't matter if I'm any good at it or not." He glowered. "My father thinks it's frivolous, and that's all there is to it. But that's to be expected, I think."

He turned his gaze down to Eulah's face.

"Is it?"

"It's the way of all things, from what I can tell," he said. "A man works hard. Makes something of himself in business. He marries the right woman, who'll help him achieve his goals. He has children. He wants those children to achieve the way that he achieved. But instead they develop arcane interests that take up their time and attention, and have no use in business. I try to tell him, you know, it could be worse. I could fence. I could race yachts, which is basically like standing in the bath and tearing up hundred-dollar bills for fun. Instead, I research and collect rare books. I'm persuaded there's a value to my passion. But he'll probably never see it that way."

"You should meet my brother." Eulah smiled ruefully. "He's in the same boat as you. Only he doesn't have your drive, I don't think."

"What does he do?" Harry murmured, moving his nose behind her ear. A chill gust blew over them from across the ocean surface. Eulah shivered.

"He plays cards," Eulah said, gazing into the middle distance.

"And?" Harry asked, lips distractingly close to Eulah's neck. She felt his breath against her skin.

"And, he plays more cards."

"That's all?"

"Well, in theory he's going to school." She chuckled. Her skin tingled whenever he brushed against it. Her eyes traveled up to the night sky, an impossibly black and moonless night, the stars like tiny points of shattered crystal scattered over a dark velvet cloak. She thought she had never seen a night as dark as this one. It was a formless void, this darkness. She felt that the steamship, massive as it was, was just a tiny point of life alone in the middle of a giant universe. The feeling made her stomach roll over, uneasy.

"Maybe," Harry murmured, "he just hasn't found his right calling yet."

"Maybe," she said. Her eyes drifted closed. For a time she was aware of nothing but the frigid air on her skin, bringing the blood to her cheeks, and the warmth of Harry's hands on her waist. At length he spoke.

"And what are your plans, I wonder, Miss Allston?"

"Me?" She laughed, leaning into his chest. "At this point my only plan is to dance a little more. With you."

He grinned. "Then that's what we shall do. And not a minute too soon, because it's far too cold to stay out here!"

Laughing, arms around each other's waists, Eulah and Harry made their way back to the door to the gallery. Just as Harry was fumbling with the door latch, an icy blast burst along the deck, snatched up Eulah's hat, with Helen's butterfly brooch still attached, and blew it skittering along the deck before hurling it over the railing into the blackness of the ocean night.

"Oh!" she squealed in dismay, her hand darting to the top of her head. Coils of pale brown hair blew in spirals around her face, over her eyes, into her mouth.

Harry laughed. "I like you better without it," he assured her. "Come along. I think the band's starting up again."

He led her back with a protective arm through the door into the dining room, but Eulah looked back over her shoulder to the spot along the railing where her hat had disappeared.

TWELVE

Commonwealth Avenue
Boston, Massachusetts
April 17, 1915

"What'd you say this place was called?" Dovie hissed as Sibyl led her down a stately hallway, carpeted in cabbage roses. "The Oceanus Club."

"What kind of crazy name is that?" the girl asked in an anxious whisper. "It doesn't look very nautical to me. I'd expect there to be—I don't know—figureheads and boat models and mermaids and things. Shippy things."

Sibyl laughed, helping Dovie off with her coat, which, in the light of day, looked shabbier than Sibyl remembered. "I suppose it is a silly name when you come to it. It's named for the baby born during the *Mayflower* passage. Oceanus Hopkins. Course, he didn't survive the first winter, so I suppose there's a certain fatalism in it. But that's the name they picked."

"What is it?" Dovie asked, shifting her eyes to take in the quietly sumptuous surroundings.

"It's, oh, I don't know. A club. Luncheon. Cards. There's a lovely garden," Sibyl said. She peered into the front sitting room, at the clusters of women sitting, ankles folded, hats bent over cups of tea. She recognized a few faces, women she knew from committees. She felt a twinge of anxiety about bringing Dovie there. But it passed, replaced with self-satisfied rebellion.

"I'm glad my name isn't Oceanus," the young woman grumbled.

"Oh, I quite agree. Dovie's *much* more preferable," Sibyl said. Dovie glanced over to see if she was being teased, and Sibyl smiled to show that she was, albeit gently.

"Psh," Dovie said, and poked Sibyl on the upper arm.

"Sibyl is even better, of course," she added. "Nothing like being named for obscure elements of Greek mythology, don't you agree? Why, when I was a girl I wished for nothing more than a nice normal name. Like Bertha."

Dovie laughed through her nose, with delicacy, and the two women moved down the hallway toward the sound of silverware clinking against china, and murmuring women's voices.

"Why, is that Sibyl Allston?" a practical woman's voice declared, and Sibyl turned to find Mrs. Rowland, a member of Mrs. Dee's secret *Titanic* séance circle, sandwiched at a small table between a young woman with the identical round features as Mrs. Rowland's own, only twenty years younger, and a beaky spinster in old-fashioned dress reform bloomers.

"Why, Mrs. Rowland. Speak of the devil," Sibyl said, pausing by the table.

"You can speak of him as much as you like, but it won't make him any realer," the Unitarian matron said. "May I present my daughter, Mrs. Leopold. And this is our friend Ellen Baxter, up from Rhode Island." Heads nodded. The spinster adjusted her spectacles and gave Sibyl a long look.

"And this is Dovie Whistler, from California," Sibyl said.

"How d'you do," said Mrs. Leopold, eyeing Dovie's bobbed hair with mixed curiosity and envy.

"California!" Mrs. Rowland exclaimed. "Why, I can't see why you'd ever leave a place like that. I hear the weather's near perfect. So unlike New England, isn't that right, Ellen?"

The spinster flared her nostrils. "Oh, I don't know," she said. "Too nice weather can make a body morally weak."

"Well!" Sibyl exclaimed, hastening their escape. "Such a pleasure running into you."

"You're looking well, Miss Allston," Mrs. Rowland said with significance. "Worlds better."

Sibyl smiled and took Dovie by the arm. "Thank you," she said. "I am well."

More heads nodded as they said their good-byes, and Sibyl led the girl away.

"Were they friends of yours?" Dovie asked.

"In this world," Sibyl said, "everyone is friends with everyone else. In a way."

They reached the woman who ruled over the reservations book, and Sibyl said, "Let's have a table outside, if you please."

They were led past tables of women, young and old, mothers and daughters, college girls, all whites and organdies and crisp blouses and well-fitted long sweaters, pearl earrings, and elegant straw hats. Deep glasses of iced tea, perfect roseate pats of butter, and tiny sandwiches served on ironed tablecloths. Nervousness poured off Dovie in waves, and Sibyl rested a reassuring hand on the girl's forearm, guiding her through French doors into the stone garden at the rear of the clubhouse.

They sat at an iron table, framed by starbursts of lush fern, sedate in the spectacle of a perfect spring afternoon.

"So," Dovie said, grasping for something to say. "Gosh. This is just lovely. Do you come here very often, then?"

"Sometimes," Sibyl said. "My sister rather liked it. When I did come, it was usually with her. Most of her regular meetings were held here. Mine as well. Temperance society. The suffrage. Tenement reform. They've got quite a lively lecture series."

"That sounds perfectly dreary," Dovie said without thinking.

Sibyl laughed, shocked. "You're right," she said. "I suppose it does."

Dovie froze, aware that she had made a mistake. But when she saw that Sibyl was smiling out of the side of her mouth, Dovie relaxed and smiled back.

Their tea and sandwiches appeared, and Sibyl gazed over the rim of her teacup at Dovie as the girl bent to help herself to a scone.

"You know," Sibyl began, as though the thought had just occurred to her, "I don't think you ever told me how you and Harlan first became acquainted."

"Didn't I?" Dovie said, feigning surprise. "I could've sworn I did."

Sibyl shook her head with a knowing smile.

"We were introduced at Mrs. Allerton's artistic salon," Dovie said, setting her teacup down and folding her arms.

"Oh?" Sibyl said. "I don't think I know Mrs. Allerton."

"But you must," Dovie protested. "Harlan said he'd been going there for years. He knew everyone there."

"Did he?" Sibyl said. She thought with warmth of her crafty brother, gadding about in secret, away from the Captain's prying eyes. No wonder they saw him so rarely. She felt a twinge of envy that Harlan had been free enough to build his own secret world, while she still moved through the one she had been born into. "Well, isn't that interesting. Tell me, what goes on at one of her evenings?"

"They're every Tuesday," the girl said, growing animated. "Louisa— that's her Christian name, she insists everyone go by their Christian name, she's very unconventional that way—anyway, she always said that there was never anything diverting going on in the Club on Tuesday evenings, and that it was high time someone hosted an evening that would bring together artists and society types."

"Hm," Sibyl mused. She wondered, privately, what sort of milieu this Louisa Allerton took for "society," given that at least one of the most prestigious and exclusive historical lecture series had been meeting Tuesday evenings since time immemorial, possibly even before the Pilgrims dropped anchor at that apocryphal rock. "What an innovative idea. And how do the evenings usually go?"

"Well," Dovie said, "the members of the salon will bring in some artist or other to give a performance, followed by some lively discussion on aesthetic principles. They'll have a painter come in to talk and do some drawings in charcoal, or they'll have a writer come and give a reading. They try to rotate who's invited, so that each week they have someone different. Sometimes there'll be music, and dancing. In fact, most nights it ends with dancing, even if there isn't a musician invited. Louisa's got this wicked punch recipe, you know, it's just deadly." She let out a simpering laugh, before remembering that there might be temperance ladies within earshot.

"It sounds like quite a festive bunch of people," Sibyl remarked, keeping her voice mild, punctuating that mildness with a genteel sip of her tea. In a corner of her mind Sibyl reflected that such an evening would be the stuff of Eulah's dreams. "And how did you come to be invited, again?"

"Oh!" Dovie exclaimed, through a mouthful of tea cake. She caught some crumbs under her chin with a napkin while saying, "I was giving a dramatic recitation. Of 'Kubla Khan.'"

She smiled, dimpling, as Sibyl's eyes widened.

"Harley said he'd never heard anyone who could recite poetry with as much passion as I could. That was the word he used, *passion*." She shivered with pleasure at the recollection, little starbursts twinkling in her eyes, and Sibyl sighed inwardly. Eulah used to talk that way. Eulah always preferred an overstatement of feeling to an understatement.

"So you're a performer, then?" Sibyl asked, nudging closer to the question of how exactly Dovie Whistler supported herself.

The girl's face closed behind the veil that Sibyl was learning tended to fall when Dovie wished to avoid discussing something.

"Yes," she said, without elaborating. "Anyway, they'd just asked me for the one evening, but Harlan took such a shine to me that he kept inviting me back as his guest. I've met some very lovely people there." It felt strange, to Sibyl's ears, to hear her brother called by his first name by someone from outside their family. He must have been moving in some progressive circles indeed.

"And how long ago was this?" Sibyl wondered aloud.

"Oh, several months, I should think."

Sibyl coughed, having aspirated some of her tea. She brought a fist to her chest, hacking, and Dovie looked up from her teacup with concern.

"Why, are you unwell, Miss Allston?"

"No, no," she sputtered, setting her cup down. "Fine. I'm perfectly fine. Thank you."

The girl nodded, concerned. Then Sibyl saw the girl's eyes shift, with wariness, over Sibyl's left shoulder. Dovie's eyes narrowed in a frown.

"Well, if it isn't the elder Miss Allston," a voice tittered, and Sibyl felt her heart sink with dismay. She turned her face up to meet the speaker.

Behind her, arms folded, stood a woman about Sibyl's age, with an equine face topped by an expensively maintained chestnut cloud of hair, beaming a chill nonwelcome down at them.

"Why, Miss Seaver," Sibyl said. "It's been such a long time."

"So it has!" the woman-pony agreed. "Ages. But it's not Miss Seaver anymore. I'm Mrs. Leonard Coombs now."

"How silly of me," Sibyl said with a tight smile. She knew Mildred Seaver was married. And she knew Mildred was married to Leonard Coombs. Leonard Coombs, a mild-mannered Yalie who, during Sibyl's first season out, had been vying with Benton Derby for Sibyl's attention. Instead of dancing, at which Sibyl failed to excel, they ended up sitting on staircases, knees pressed excitingly together, talking in hushed voices about books. Mildred Seaver, in Sibyl Allston's sewing circle and dance class, gawky but persuasive, had, through a series of maneuvers that Sibyl still lacked the social virtuosity to untangle, insinuated herself with the bookish young man, locking him down in a matrimonial triumph trumpeted across all the regional newspapers the following winter. *Ten thousand* orange blossoms, the papers breathlessly chronicled.

"And how is Mister Coombs?" Sibyl inquired.

"Just topping, thanks!" the former Miss Seaver beamed, exposing the full panoply of her teeth. "He's just been named partner in Daddy's firm. And he positively dotes on Lenny Junior."

"Ah," Sibyl said. Lenny Junior. Proof, as if she needed any more, that the Allstons had fallen well off the Coombses' visiting list. They hadn't even been sent a card. "Why, I hadn't heard. Congratulations."

Mrs. Coombs simpered, shifting her hips. "Oh!" she moaned, a hand to her chest to show how stoic she was. "Well, thanks. It was just awful, you know. Really, too awful to be believed. You are *so* lucky, to be spared all that. I'd just as soon never go through any of it, to be honest. It really is better, I wager, not having to be married at all. Now, who's this?"

She turned an appraising eye on Sibyl's luncheon partner, who responded by sinking lower in her garden chair.

"Mrs. Coombs, I'd like you to meet Miss Dovie Whistler," Sibyl said. When she faced Dovie, waving her hand at her in introduction, she found the girl's face purpling with slow-simmering rage.

"Whistler!" Mrs. Coombs whinnied, bringing a thoughtful finger up to her chin. "Whistler. Hmmmm. New York?"

"Never been," Dovie said, arms folded.

"No? Well, that's odd. The only Whistlers *I* know are in New York. We see them every summer at Newport, when we go down for the regatta."

"No relation," Dovie said, emerald eyes darkening.

"Well, that's a shame. They're lovely people. He's from a banking family, and they race the most gorgeous little ketch, why it makes me just blue with envy. Blue!"

"People don't turn blue with envy," Dovie said, using a voice that sounded like a regular conversational tone but that managed to fill the room. "Must be that good Newport blood you're thinking of. Sounds like *you* would know."

"What?" Mrs. Coombs sputtered.

Sibyl laughed before she could help herself. "I'm afraid she's right, Mildred," Sibyl said, heart thudding with enjoyment at adding to the woman's shock. "Green's the color of envy, not blue. Why, you should know that."

"Well!" the woman clopped backward on one of her low-heeled hoofs, reeling from surprise. "My goodness. *Miss* Allston. I don't know where you could have found such a creature." She glared down at Dovie, radiating waves of social contempt.

"I guess we're just too regular to know from blue, aren't we, Sibyl?" Dovie remarked, settling back in her seat, legs crossed at the knee, looking up at the woman with an expression of open challenge. "But then, I've heard that the thin air up there on Mount Olympus can do terrible things to the mind. And don't even get me started on what it can do to a girl's *face*."

Sibyl gasped in both shock and, if she admitted it, pleasure. She'd never had the nerve to say what she really thought about Mildred Seaver to anyone but Eulah, and here Dovie had almost sensed it without her having to say a thing. She almost hesitated to look at the young woman sitting across from her at the garden table, for fear that she would give away her delight.

Mrs. Coombs opened her mouth, as though she had been hit in the chest and couldn't catch her breath. Sibyl glanced at Dovie, who met her look with a mischievous smile. Twin sensations of mortification and mirthful joy rose within her, and Sibyl felt her cheeks flush. She was terribly afraid that she would start laughing.

"My goodness," Mrs. Coombs managed, struggling to regain her upper hand by addressing Sibyl alone. "What *unconventional* company you're keeping. But I suppose those Allstons always did have rather distinctive taste in friends. It's one of your great strengths, you know. I've always said so. You are so openhearted, you'll just keep company with anyone. How very progressive you are!"

Mrs. Leonard Coombs then turned on her substantial heel and marched through the French doors, through which the sound of whispering could be clearly heard. Sibyl managed to last until the moment when she thought Mildred might be out of earshot before laughter burst out of her mouth, and she folded her arms around her waist, whooping, shoulders shaking.

Dovie watched the woman go, waves of hostility vibrating off her small form. Then a slow smile broke across the girl's face. It widened, and she, too, started to laugh.

"Oh! Oh!" Sibyl cried, wiping the corner of her eye with her napkin. "Oh, if you had any idea how long I've wanted to say something like that to her. She's been insufferable since we were girls."

Dovie grinned, and shrugged her shoulders.

Finally, as her laughter died down to snicker, Sibyl grew aware of the silence within the lunchroom. She leaned forward, gesturing for Dovie to incline her ear.

"I think, my dear, we'd better be going," she whispered.

"I haven't even finished my cake yet!" Dovie protested in mock-innocence. "But if you think we must, then we must."

"Oh, by all means, finish your cake," Sibyl said, through a nervous giggle. The silence in the clubhouse puddled deeper.

Dovie took the last chunk of tea cake and crammed it into her mouth, puffing her cheeks out like a squirrel. "Done," she said, word muffled through the mouthful of cake, a few crumbs escaping between her lips, and she brought her hand up to keep the rest of it in.

Sibyl, eyes twinkling with merriment, got to her feet. "All right," she said. "Let's be off, then!"

She threaded her arm around the girl's waist, and they tripped out in lockstep together, heads high. They marched through the dining room, past several dozen silent, watching, judging pairs of women's eyes. She spotted Mrs. Rowland, a wicked smile twisting the corner of the matron's mouth. Sibyl and Dovie picked up their pace to an almost-jog, leaving behind a trail of cake crumbs, never to set foot in the Oceanus Club again.

THAT EVENING, THE two young women perched across from each other in the inner drawing room, a fire going in the fireplace, Sibyl bent over some needlepoint in Lan's old Greek revival armchair while Dovie flipped through a fashion magazine, her feet tucked under her. They had no other company besides the observing macaw, at whom Dovie cast the occasional worried glance as he sat, immobile as a sculpture, on his hat rack. Lan Allston had yet to return from his business downtown, and the two young women had shared a plain dinner in the dining room, talking with excitement about fashions and magazine stories and society gossip, and revisiting the scene of Dovie's shocking triumph.

"I swear," Sibyl said, smiling over her needlework. "The expression on Milly Coombs's face was priceless. I could bottle it and sell it."

"She really stole your fella, huh?" Dovie said, flipping another page and tapping her chin in thoughtful consideration of the coat sketches spread across her lap.

"I guess she did," Sibyl confirmed, pulling the thread tight and knotting it with a quick motion. "I was pretty disappointed at the time, but I don't really care anymore. He was pleasant enough. Collected stamps. Just think, if I'd married him I'd have spent the rest of my life pretending to be interested in philately. Ugh. But even so, he was rather sweet to me for a time. That's all."

Dovie sniffed. "A girl'd get slapped for less," she muttered.

"Beg pardon?"

"Oh, nothing," Dovie said, flipping another page. After a long pause, she asked, "And there wasn't ever anyone else?"

Sibyl hesitated, looking aside into the fire. Her heart thudded once, twice, heavily, as it always did when she thought back to that snowy afternoon with Benton on the window seat. He had said, *Lydia tells me she thinks we should be married.* And then he had stared at her. Waiting. After an interminable silence, in which her heart collapsed into her stomach and her head grew light with misery, Sibyl had said what she thought he wanted her to say, which was *Oh, indeed?*

When she said that, his face crumpled. It was the wrong answer. She still hated to think of it. She knotted the thread of her needlepoint with unnecessary vigor, frowning.

"No one to speak of," she said at length. "No."

Dovie gave her a long look. But instead of pressing the question further, she flipped another page. After a time she reached the end of her magazine and cast it to the floor with a bored sigh. Sibyl leaned forward, squinting in the firelight, concentrating on her work. Dovie sighed again, loudly enough to indicate that she was trying to get Sibyl's attention.

Sibyl glanced up and found the young woman squirming in her armchair, rummaging in the pocket of her skirt. Dovie brought forth the polished crystal ball, which she had been toying with during their conversation in the morning. In the soothing firelight the ball glowed with an inviting warmth, and Dovie folded her legs Indian style in the armchair, resting her elbows on her knees and holding the ball nearer the firelight.

"It's so pretty," she remarked, rolling it along her fingertips. Behind her, the macaw let out a sumptuous yawn.

Sibyl smiled, setting her needlework in her lap. "It is," she agreed. "I'd forgotten you still had it."

Dovie gazed on it intently for a few minutes, her eyes almost crossing with the effort. Sibyl laughed aloud, sensing what she was trying to do, and Dovie blushed. Then a slow smile awoke in her features, the same smile of collusion that had lit up the girl's face that afternoon.

"It's for seeing, you say?" she asked, her eyes twinkling with secret mischief.

"Yeeees," Sibyl said, drawing the word out, dubious.

"Ah," Dovie said. She drew her lip under a tooth, staring at the ball, rolling it in her palms, and then leveled her green gaze on Sibyl.

"I know what we'll do," Dovie said, abruptly reaching forward and taking Sibyl by the hand. "The best way to see anything. Only you'll have to come with me tomorrow."

"Come with you?" Sibyl echoed, her hand still in Dovie's.

The girl's grip felt warm, reassuring, and despite her initial misgivings Sibyl found herself wanting to keep Dovie's attention. She felt privileged to have been invited into a secret confederacy with the younger woman. It reminded her of the unique pleasure she used to feel when Eulah would grab her shoulder as she passed in the hallway after a late dance. Sibyl would sit in Eulah's vanity chair, her chin resting on a fist, nodding and laughing while her sister recounted what had been said to whom, and why, and what it might mean, and didn't Sibyl think that's what it meant, really? She had envied her sister's beauty and social success, it was true, but their nights of discussion made Sibyl feel invited into Eulah's charmed sphere. Now she felt drawn to Dovie in the same way. It was uncanny how much Dovie reminded her of Eulah.

"Come where?"

"You'll see. You've taken me to your club, now you have to let me take you to mine. I insist."

Sibyl blinked with uncertainty. "Yours? But I don't—"

"Trust me." Dovie smiled, cheeks dimpling, her hand tugging gently at Sibyl's. "We'll bring the crystal ball with us. It'll be fun, I promise. What else have we got to do tomorrow, anyway?"

"Well," she demurred. "As long as we're home by suppertime, I don't suppose . . ."

"It'll be great," Dovie insisted. "You'll see."

Laughing, almost cackling, with pleasure, Dovie released Sibyl's hand and leaned back in her armchair, her eyes glowing in the firelight.

THIRTEEN

Chinatown
Boston, Massachusetts
April 18, 1915

ibyl lost track of which street they were on after a series of
turns that carried them around the Common, across Boylston
Street, and past the electric marquees of the theater district.
The street where she and Dovie stood was busy at midday, the spring sunshine quickening everyone's step, casting everything with the golden gloss
of possibility. Sibyl stood half a head taller than all the hurrying people in
that quarter. All of the signage was written in unfamiliar, oddly beautiful
characters: Chinese. She turned to ask Dovie what they were doing here,
but her companion's attention was absorbed in her silk evening bag, still
speckled with Harley's blood. The girl rummaged, muttering under her
breath.

"Dammit, I know it's in here."

Sibyl's eyes roved over the faces jostling in the street. She felt conspicuous, too tall, alien, shaded into anonymity under her broad straw hat. Dovie
was smaller, and though fairer than Sibyl, she fit in the streetscape with
ease, having none of Sibyl's self-consciousness.

"Dammit!" Dovie said again, and Sibyl shifted on her feet, willing herself invisible. Sibyl thought of shushing her but didn't. Dovie wasn't Eulah. Sibyl had no business correcting her. She had no business here at all.

"Oh, here it is." Dovie sighed with relief. She unfolded a square sheet of paper, browned around the edges from handling, on which was scrawled a hasty series of Chinese characters. She stepped up to the nondescript doorway and rapped on it with her knuckles.

A porthole slid open, and one eye, as dark as Sibyl's own, peered out with suspicion. Dovie held up the paper with a broad, sparkling smile. The eye took in whatever message the paper had to offer for a long minute. Then the porthole slid closed.

Several minutes ticked by, Dovie rocking back on her heels like a girl eager to begin a footrace. Murmured discussion could be heard going on inside. Sibyl's stomach rolled over with a growl.

"Miss Whistler, what—" Sibyl was interrupted by the cracking open of the door. No explicit invitation issued from within. In fact Sibyl wasn't entirely certain that the door had opened on purpose.

"It's Dovie, you silly goose. C'mon." Dovie smiled, threading her arm through the crook of Sibyl's elbow. Sibyl allowed herself to be pulled forward.

A watery man waited inside, greeting them with a wary glance and the subtlest incline of his head.

"Creesy, it's so good to see you again!" Dovie trilled, waggling her fingers at the man in a coquettish way that Sibyl found both endearing and calculated. The man didn't register her greeting, instead gesturing with an outstretched arm that they could advance down the hall. Dovie responded with a delighted laugh and tightened her grip on Sibyl's elbow.

"Don't worry, he's always like that. I don't think he's really a mute, though." Dovie said this last part loudly enough so that the watery man would overhear.

Sibyl blushed at Dovie's rudeness, but let herself be led deeper into the building. Narrow, dark, thickly carpeted, with wall sconces casting a weak glow, the hall swallowed the two women up, its dimness cloying after the bright springtime afternoon outside. Dovie lit their way with the pure force of her enthusiasm. They reached a steep staircase, echoing with the distant sound of a gramophone. Creaking footsteps, but no conversation, circulated in the room overhead. Sibyl hung back.

"I don't. That is, I'm not—" Sibyl started to protest.

"Oh, come now," Dovie teased. "There's nothing to be afraid of."

Dovie bestowed a celestial smile on her, and Sibyl felt bathed in the girl's confidence. Dovie started up the stairs, and Sibyl followed, one cautious step at a time. At the top of the stairs draped a crimson velvet curtain, lined with golden tassels. Dovie folded herself through the curtain, disappearing into the unseen room. Sibyl paused, screwing up her courage, and then passed through.

She found herself in a sumptuously appointed drawing room, with double-height ceilings and carved wood moldings. Red tapestry drapes shuttered away the sunshine, creating a cozy dimness of indeterminate time. The only light came from two massive brass chandeliers, their arms outstretched like arching insect legs, with lights glowing on the ends of their feet, and a few brass candelabra placed at odd intervals. Two fireplaces dominated opposite sides of the room, both with walnut mantels, and fires crackling behind their screens.

The furniture was like something out of the Arabian nights, or a cartoonish fantasy of it. Several patterns of exotic carpet, both Turkish and Chinese, battled for dominance on the floor in a riot of reds and ochres, geometric patterns and biomorphic leaves. Along the edges of the room, in confidential groups of two and three, long chaises lurked in the shadows, holding reclining figures of men and women whose faces were difficult to make out.

A few overstuffed silken pillows were heaped in inviting nests before the fireplaces. Low enameled tables bore small trays, each with a lamp. The gramophone, its blooming tube like a giant morning glory rendered in brass, crooned a song that Sibyl recognized, a popular one from a few years ago. She almost remembered the words.

Something something melancholy baaaaby . . .

Next to the gramophone towered a Gothic revival grandfather clock, crowned in wicked-looking turrets. The clock's hands promised that it was still the middle of a springtime afternoon, but the darkness of the room made Sibyl unsure that the clock could be trusted.

Dovie, grinning, slid out of her coat and searched with eager eyes in the dim recesses of the room, Sibyl didn't know for what. Sibyl edged nearer to her, closing her own coat around herself. No one spoke. A few plumes of smoke drifted to the ceiling. Under the music and the steady ticking of the clock flowed a current of deep silence that Sibyl found unnerving.

A small man of indeterminate middle age approached them with a smile and a low bow. The man was probably Chinese, Sibyl guessed, but his outfit was a bizarre mishmash of crimson Zouave pantaloons, full through the leg and gathered at the ankle, silk blouse embroidered with cherry blossoms, and odd long slippers with coiled toes. She almost broke out laughing, seeing his elaborate and fantastical costume, but managed to keep quiet.

"Miss Whistler!" the costumed man cried with evident pleasure, taking Dovie's hands in his. "Such a pleasure to see you again."

"And you, Mister Chang," Dovie said, bestowing on him the full force of her dimpled smile. "But it's so crowded today. I do hope we won't have to wait?"

"You? Wait?" the man brought a shocked hand to his chest and seemed appalled at the very thought. "No, no. No wait."

He clapped his hands, and a young boy, uncostumed and surly, appeared at his side. Dovie heaped her coat into the boy's arms without a word, and Sibyl followed suit.

"Splendid. I really think we should have something close to the fire, don't you? Won't the light be so much better?" Dovie said, bringing her hands to her waist, imitating a posing film actress, and tossing her hair off her forehead.

Her comment seemed aimed at both Sibyl and the proprietor, a demand rather than a suggestion. Sibyl shrugged, a neutral smile on her face.

"Come this way," the man said, nodding his head. "Fireplace, yes. I have just the thing."

He walked along on quick, shuffling feet, careful of the turned-up toes of his slippers, and showed them to a pair of chaises by the far fireplace.

The lounges were both carved Victorian monstrosities, heavy with cherubs, upholstered in rival shades of purple, silk on one, velvet on the other. Their raised ends, for resting arms or heads, were nestled together. A low table stood between them, empty save for a taper candle, burned to a nub and smoking. The fire popped, casting the corner between the chaises in an inviting orange glow.

Dovie flopped onto the silk chaise with a sigh of relief and reached down to begin unfastening her buttoned boots. As she did so she said to Sibyl, "I think some tea would be good, wouldn't it? And aren't you hungry?"

Sibyl, smile still careful and arranged, said, "If you are."

Dovie turned to the proprietor, who waited, bent and attentive, his mouth in an expectant smile, and said, "Green tea, please, Mister Chang. And some of those funny little cakes that you do. I'm famished."

"Very good, Miss Whistler," he said, still half bowing. "And, may I be so bold as to recommend the Burmese this afternoon? It's very fine. Very fine indeed."

Dovie's eyebrows rose as she freed one foot from a boot and flexed her stockinged toes. "You know I always defer to you," she said. "Let's have one for each of us. And give us Quincey, if you please. My friend's never been before."

"Of course," the man said and shuffled off on his slippers.

Dovie let out a happy laugh, leaning on one elbow while she freed her other foot from its boot. Sibyl sat erect on the velvet chaise, hands folded in her lap. Dovie curled up on the chaise and lounged back, resting her cheek against the end of the sofa. She leveled hypnotic eyes on Sibyl and smiled, free hand toying with a fine chain around her neck.

"There's nothing to be nervous about," she said, watching Sibyl.

"I'm not nervous!" Sibyl chirped, knotting her hands in her lap. Dovie laughed.

The surly boy reappeared, kneeling to unload a fat ceramic teapot, two cups with no handles, and a plate of sticky sweets—the cakes. The boy lifted the teapot lid, took a disdainful sniff, and clattered it closed before pouring. Sibyl took a tentative sip. It was different from the tea that she was accustomed to drinking—paler, astringent.

Dovie took up one of the cakes in her fingers. She chewed and laughed at the same time, shaking her hair, and Sibyl smiled, feeling her sense of unease begin to loosen.

"You brought the crystal ball, right?" Dovie asked.

Sibyl rummaged in her pocket and withdrew the blue crystal. Dovie wiped cakey fingertips on her skirt—Sibyl's skirt—and reached for the trinket. Once in possession of the prize the girl flopped back on the silk chaise, folding up her knees and chuckling with mischief. She rolled the ball between her palms while Sibyl watched, sipping her tea.

"Look how it sparkles," Dovie exclaimed. It was true—the surface of the orb drew the firelight into itself until it was wrapped in pale, swirling colors, as if it had been dipped in oil.

"You think it just requires different light?" Sibyl teased. "I tried it in the medium's own drawing room, you know. I'd think you'd be hard-pressed to find better light than that, for divining."

Dovie said, "Hmmmmm" and sent Sibyl a knowing look under her eyelashes.

Across the room, someone wound the gramophone, and the same mournful song started to play.

A man shuffled up, balancing a tray on unsteady arms. He was leathery and old, or at least, he seemed old, but on closer examination Sibyl decided that he could be anywhere between thirty and sixty. His skull showed below the sallow flesh of his face, his cheeks caved in, clinging to the contours of his teeth. His clothes, simply cut and linen, drooped as though meant for someone else—perhaps for the man that he had once been. This ghost knelt by their table, moving the teapot aside with a practiced gesture. His eyes did not rise. They might as well have not been there at all.

"Quincey's the best," Dovie whispered, watching his labors with appreciation.

The man eased the lacquered tray onto the table, making certain of its stability before running his slow hands over the various implements resting there. A cut crystal lamp, with no chimney, already lit. Two long needles, like knitting needles, but thinner, with their narrower ends propped on a stand. A slender pair of gilt scissors, bent in the shape of twin swan necks. One delicate silver spoon. A polished wooden box, inlaid with mother-of-pearl and gilt wire in the shape of a flower. And, lastly, two lengths of bamboo, with chased silver caps on one end, and shallow blue-and-white ceramic bowls about two-thirds of the way down, attached with ornate silver scrollwork.

Sibyl watched the man shuffle these mysterious items on the tray, sitting on his heels, absorbed in his work. The man's mouth was pursed, and as his hands moved over the inlaid box his jaw worked the way a starving person would when touching a plate of ripe fruit. Sibyl felt vague disquiet, and she glanced over her shoulder. The Gothic clock ticked, the gramophone played. Nothing was amiss.

When she turned back she found Dovie already leaning forward, bow-shaped lips pressed to the silver end of the bamboo. She tipped the ceramic bowl, angling it nearer the lamp. The man, kneeling, held one of the needles between fingertips and thumb, pointed end angled to a tiny hole in the bowl, twirling. He and Dovie concentrated their full attention on this enterprise, and with sudden certainty Sibyl, flushing at her own ignorance, grasped where she was.

"Dovie," she began but was interrupted by the girl's eyes fluttering closed, her soft cheeks drawing in as she pulled at what Sibyl now understood to be a pipe.

The girl paused, reclining on her side, stockinged feet crossed at the ankles, and then leaned her head back with a sighing smile, the pipe slipping in her hands. Under heavy lids Dovie's eyes traveled to Sibyl. They glittered in the firelight as a slow smile spread over Dovie's features, softening them, making her seem even younger than she was.

"It's okay," the girl murmured, drawing the syllables out. "Really. Quincey'll show you."

Dovie took a deep breath, keeping hold of the pipe with one hand while the other stretched, languid, over her head, coming to rest along the back of the chaise with exquisite indifference.

"But, I . . . ," Sibyl groped for what she was supposed to say.

She listened inside her mind for her mother's chastening voice, the voice that always told her how to behave. Usually it chattered along with a steady commentary, as though Helen herself were looking over the shoulder of Sibyl's life. Sibyl found it silent on this question. Should she be shocked? Angry? Should she have known this was where Dovie was taking her?

"I don't understand," Sibyl said.

"The visions," Dovie breathed, settling more deeply into the silk chaise, thumb playing over the shaft of the pipe.

Her hand swam downward, smoothing itself into the folds of her borrowed skirt and withdrawing the crystal ball. She brought it to her face, rolling it onto her forehead, down her nose, to her lips, over her chin, along her neck, to her throat with a torpid smile.

"I wanted you to see," Dovie said. "It gives the most beautiful dreams."

FOURTEEN

*Q*uincey busied himself over the table, balanced on his heels. He dipped the long needle into a glob of brownish stuff nestled in tissue paper inside the box, rolling it until a perfect bead of opium clung to the needle's end. He balanced the needle on its stand so that he could present the remaining bamboo pipe to Sibyl. She took it, gingerly. How bad was it, really? The Captain had tried it in China, years ago. Made it sound boring, actually. *Not worth going to war over,* he'd said, with characteristic dismissal. She glanced at Dovie, watching as the flower of pure bliss blossomed on the girl's face.

"I don't know what to do," Sibyl said, as much to herself as to Dovie.

"Quincey'll show you," the girl whispered. Her hand danced, slowly, tracing the contours of unseen shapes. Sibyl watched its movement, entranced.

Quincey waited, fingertips balancing the needle, eyes downcast. The moment had come.

Visions, Dovie said. She had tried so many times. When she was at Mrs. Dee's the spirit world always seemed to be hovering just out of her reach, barely visible, almost near enough to touch. The pull of a window into that world was tantalizing, seductive.

A long dormant part of Sibyl finally stirred, as though the curious girl she had been was finally able to crack open the lid of the box in which

Sibyl had locked her. Her hands holding the pipe at an awkward angle, Sibyl leaned forward, elbows on her knees. Quincey grunted, indicating through a series of gestures that she was to recline on the chaise.

"Oh," Sibyl said, abashed.

She prized off her shoes and settled back, stiff and awkward, propped on her elbow. Her corset bit into the flesh of her hip, and she shifted against the discomfort. Quincey nodded, not looking at her, then beckoned for her to lean forward. Sibyl did so, rolling the top of the pipe bowl nearer the lamp. She held the silver mouth of the pipe nearer to her own, without touching.

Quincey hissed in irritation and smacked his index and middle fingers in a V shape against his mouth. Sibyl pressed the silver hole to her lips, feeling the metal grow warm under the pressure of her mouth, and leaned the ceramic bowl nearer the flame. Concentrating, Quincey brought the tip of the needle to the bowl. Sibyl inhaled through her open mouth.

The brown bead at the end of the needle vaporized in an instant of whitish light, and Sibyl's mouth flooded with a curious numbing that tingled on her tongue, lips, cheeks, throat. She squinted, pushing the pipe away. Quincey laughed, his mouth a horrible grin of gums speckled with teeth. Sibyl coughed, and a wisp of smoke escaped through her teeth. Startled, she fell against the worn velvet of the chaise, feeling it prickle against the skin of her cheek.

Sibyl lay motionless, the pipe held loose in her hands, feeling her heart beating, aware of the movement of her blood. Nervous, she supposed she was nervous, and so she told herself to concentrate on the croon of the gramophone, and breathe.

Come to me, my melancholy baaaabyyyy. . . .

In. Out.

In. Out.

There.

She was fine.

There was nothing to worry about.

Except . . .

The velvet. The purple velvet on the chaise, it was distracting. Sibyl nestled into it, feeling its prickle on her chin, her nose, her eyelashes. It was softer, more perfect than any other velvet. It brushed against the corner of her mouth, and she opened her eyes, trying to focus on the texture. That close up her vision was blurry, and after a minute of intense staring at each individual tuft of velvet in its fullest detail, she surrendered, letting her eyes drift closed.

She brought a hand up, and it moved as though dragging through a dish of molasses, before coming to rest on the velvet next to her face. Her grip around the pipe loosened, and she felt it lifted lightly away, by Quincey she supposed, but she was too absorbed in the velvet to care.

Somewhere, far away, she heard laughter. She wondered where it could be coming from. Who was laughing? Was *she* laughing? Sibyl thought about her mouth and found it closed and smiling. No. It wasn't her.

With some effort Sibyl opened her eyes, drawing her eyelids back like the curtains in her father's drawing room. She was gazing into the fire. Why had she never noticed all the different colors in a fire before? The yellows and reds and oranges and blues and whites and . . . there it was, the laughing again.

Her gaze swiveled from the dancing fire behind the grate down to the carpet, to the low table where Quincey was at work, scooping ash out of the pipe bowl with the little coffee spoon. He didn't seem to be laughing. In fact, he seemed unaware of anyone. He was absorbed in his task, a hand brushing the lid of the inlaid box with the intimacy of a lover. Her eyes slid past him, moving up the violet silk chaise opposite her, where Dovie lay stretched on her back.

The young woman's stockinged toes were massaging themselves together, and Sibyl heard the joints crack. There it was—the laughing again. It was coming from Dovie. Sibyl's eyes ventured up the girl's form, blurry as Sibyl's vision slipped in and out of focus, Dovie's saucer eyes and short blond hair swimming together. The green saucers were fixed on her, the red bow mouth was laughing. Dovie rolled onto her side, her pipe laid on the table, and in her hands she toyed with the blue crystal ball.

"It's so pretty," she said, and the words reached Sibyl as though spoken from under water.

"Yes." The word formed in her mouth, heavy and moist, like speaking through a mouthful of raspberries. "So pretty."

They lay silent for a time, gazing at each other, motionless except for Dovie's soft fingering of the scrying glass. In the distance, a world away, the grandfather clock began to chime. A part of Sibyl's mind attuned from habit to count the number, but the chiming reverberated, each *bong* overlapping with several others, the sound vibrations moving in the wrong direction, so that Sibyl was at a loss to determine the time.

The light remained a steady glow of candle and lamplight, separated from the day. The gramophone had wound down, and she heard someone moving in the room, winding it, shuffling through records. The scene in the firelight swam before her eyes, and so she closed them, swallowing down a sour bubble of nausea. Closing her eyes was no better; the chaise moved beneath her as though floating atop a gentle swell.

"Sibyl," said a voice close to her ear. "Are you nodding off?"

"Hmmm?" she mustered enough will to answer.

The chaise bobbed on a passing wave, and Sibyl dug her fingers into the velvet to keep from falling off.

"Can you open your eyes?" the voice, Dovie's, asked, her breath stirring the fine down along Sibyl's ear.

Another wave rolled in, lifting the chaise and settling it down, and the nausea turned in her stomach. She was afraid she would slide off. A crush of panic burst in her chest, and she gasped. A hand settled on her cheek, and the sweet voice said, "Don't frown so. Nothing's wrong. Open your eyes."

Sibyl obeyed.

"There," the girl said, smiling. "You'll feel better if you don't nod off the first time. Have a little something to eat."

"Eat?" Sibyl echoed.

"Trust me," Dovie urged, withdrawing with trailing fingers from Sibyl's chaise and melting back onto her own.

Sibyl eyed the cake with suspicion. She sank her teeth into a corner of it, sugar melting over her tongue, her molars sticking together as she forced the morsel down. There. She had eaten some of it.

"All of it," Dovie insisted. "I promise, you'll feel scads better."

Her lip curling, Sibyl forced herself to finish it, one nibble at a time, rabbitish.

Sibyl settled back on the chaise, waiting for the wavelike motion to resume. She was surprised to discover that Dovie was right—the chaise now felt sturdy and safe, and the nausea had passed. She closed her eyes, finding her unease replaced with a pervasive sense of warmth, tingling from her scalp all along her neck, her shoulders, down her legs and into her toes. Sibyl stretched her arms overhead, bending like a cat, reveling in the feeling, letting it wash through her.

"You've . . ." Sibyl paused. "Do you do this a lot?"

"Hmmmm?" Dovie asked. "Oh, well. You know."

She hesitated.

"Sometimes."

"Sometimes," Sibyl whispered, lidded eyes on the ceiling, with its dark carved molding. She traced her gaze along the curlicues and shapes, letting her attention wander.

"It's useful," the girl said. "For my art."

The word hung there between them for a time as Sibyl turned it over in her mind. A euphemism? Though she had been brought to that salon to recite "Kubla Khan," hadn't she? Sibyl was prepared to let it slide past, let it be carried away as if it hadn't been spoken, when Dovie continued.

"I'm an actress."

Sibyl laughed out loud, pressing her hands to her middle, bringing her knees up, rolling on her back like she used to do when she was a girl. Tears rolled down the corners of her eyes, and her laughter intensified, dissolving into a fit of hiccups. Even the laughter felt delicious, roiling through her body, crinkling her eyes. Her cheeks began to hurt.

After a time she became aware of a deep silence emanating from the opposite chaise.

"Oh!" Sibyl exclaimed, collecting herself. "Excuse me. I can't . . . I can't think what came over me."

"I *am*," Dovie said, her voice unusually tight.

Sibyl rolled to her side, cheek pressed to the velvet again, and cast a twinkling gaze on the younger woman. "But of *course* you are, dearest," she said, grinning.

Dovie, green eyes cool, gazed on Sibyl for a long moment. Then she, too, burst out laughing. They both held their arms around their middles and guffawed. Their giggles finally subsided with two long sighs, and the two women quieted, half staring into the fire and half looking at each other. At some point in the past hour Quincey had withdrawn, leaving them alone. Hiccuping with residual laughter, Dovie leaned forward for a sip of tea.

"Oh, I know what you all think," she said, answering an unspoken comment from Sibyl. "But I am. Really. I got started out in California. Musicales. Then I got a chance to join a traveling company. We went all through the Midwest. It went okay, but I was never made the lead. Just ingenues and understudies. My coming here really did start out that way."

"What way?" Sibyl asked.

"Well," Dovie said. "When you prepare for a role, it can be helpful to . . ." She paused, looking for the right words. She turned an idea over in her mind, and then continued. "To forget yourself. To delve into your mind and see what else is there."

"What else is there," Sibyl repeated, almost turning the repetition into a question, but not quite.

"Oh, Sibyl," the girl exclaimed. "What tremendous visions you can have, once you get accustomed to it. Like Coleridge. Or that English fellow, who wrote the book, whatever his name was. I found it fueled my imagination like nothing else. They never made me . . . That is, I'd always been a credible mimic, but something was lacking when I tried to—"

She paused, frustrated, unable to articulate what she meant.

"With this, you don't need to have any imagination of your own, I guess is what I mean. You just lie back, and images will come to you, things you never dreamed might be in your head. Once, I even saw a silver dragon form in the air right above me, fire coming out of its nose, and it bent around like a snake until its tail was in its mouth, then rolled itself in a circle whirling faster and faster, before it disappeared in a puff of smoke. After that I spent a whole day not really knowing who I was."

Sibyl reflected on this idea.

"But that wouldn't be real," Sibyl mused. "Just dream stuff, is all you'd be liable to see. They must all be ideas that you picked up from somewhere else, stored away, and forgot about."

"Course, it doesn't hurt that it feels marvelous." This last word Dovie let out with a groan and leaned back on her chaise with a delicious sigh. They sat for a time listening, under the ticktock of the clock and the winding-down gramophone, to the deep silence emanating from the other motionless forms in the room.

Sibyl knitted her fingers across her midsection and settled on her back, contemplating the ceiling. An actress. So that's how Dovie Whistler paid her way at that awful boardinghouse. Well, she couldn't be a very good one. Successful or not, if that's how Dovie thought about herself, it would explain how changeable she seemed. Sibyl wondered if this worldly, yet oddly innocent, girl was the true Dovie Whistler. Was this the same person Harlan saw when he squired her around town, to artistic salons and who knew where else? This tiny blond westerner, who could stand amid the bustle of Chinatown in Boston on a spring afternoon and blend in completely. And in the hospital the night of Harlan's misfortune, performing the role of the concerned sweetheart, all exclamations and facial expressions technically correct, without necessarily being natural. Which was the real Dovie Whistler? Perhaps there wasn't one.

Sibyl supposed that everyone assumed different roles, depending on the circumstances. The version of herself that presided over the breakfast table with Lan Allston was Sibyl-as-dutiful-daughter, and different from Sibyl as Helen's stand-in running the Beacon Street house, warily circling Mrs. Doherty or prodding Betty for gossip in the kitchen. Sibyl-as-sister looked different in Harlan's wary and suspicious presence than she did consulting with Benton over Harlan's future at college.

Sometimes, when she was alone, unobserved, Sibyl tried to disentangle her inherited notions about what she ought to be from what she truly wanted. Sometimes she found disentanglement impossible and wondered if she had any true self at all.

Sibyl squinted her eyes closed, tired of her busy mind.

"Dovie," she brought herself to say. "Let me see the scrying glass for a minute."

"How come?" Dovie asked, loath to give it up.

"Just want to play with it, I guess," Sibyl said. "I'm bored of myself. Trapped inside my head."

Dovie laughed, passing the box into Sibyl's hands. "That can happen. Never know what you're going to find in there, do you?"

Without answering Sibyl placed the box on her belly and opened the lid. The crystal orb glinted in the firelight, safe in its velvet nest. She ran her fingertips over it, tracing minute circles around its edge, over the top, enjoying its smoothness. Her mind turned away from herself, enjoying the mingling sensations of the cool stone against her skin, the warm lap of the firelight, the sagging cushion of the chaise.

In its lining of black velvet, the scrying glass pulled the light deep into itself, faintly glowing under her fingers. She could see the rock's milky veins, shifting as she rolled the ball with one thumb. Sibyl sighed, feeling her weight release into the chaise. Her eyes slipped out of focus.

Time passed, but Sibyl didn't know how much. She was floating in a half-sleep in which she was conscious, but unconcerned. The surface of the ball darkened, as though the light were drawing away from the crystal's surface, collecting into a pinpoint at its center. As Sibyl focused on the pinpoint of hard white light, a transformation began to take place.

Under her fingertips, the surface of the scrying glass appeared to be roiling. The ball itself was motionless, but its surface looked contorted, moving, slippery. Sibyl felt her blood moving in her veins, and her lips parted while she watched, entranced.

The ball had blackened, the inside of its membrane obscured by billows of smoke, puffing out from its fiery core. The billows thickened, coiling back on themselves, tiny storm clouds clashing together inside the sphere, as though the scrying glass were hollow, though it was not. Her fingertips twitched where they rested on the ball, and the smoke moved faster.

After a time, the smoke slowed, thinning into nearly recognizable shapes, like storm clouds parting in a distant sky. She beheld a nighttime as dark as what she had once seen arcing over a mown field out in the countryside, away from the electric lights of the city. The spherical firmament inside the glass was speckled with pinprick stars, an entire night sky perfectly rendered in miniature.

Sibyl let her breath out in slow degrees. She had been holding it without knowing. She sat up on her elbows, drawing into a seated position, her back curved so that she could have a clearer view into the velvet-lined box. Moving with care, deliberately enough that the springs in the chaise didn't make a sound, Sibyl brought the box with its microscopic universe into her lap.

The stars inside the scrying glass winked, and she brushed a thumb over its surface, scarcely able to believe what she was seeing. Then, the stars began to move. They shifted, rotating down, like sped-up film, until deep within the glass the tiny night sky met a dark, distant horizon.

Sibyl peered closer, whispering to herself, "It's just a dream, a Xanadu, I'm seeing."

Dovie might have said something in response, but Sibyl didn't hear her.

The horizon was smooth, reflecting a mirror image of the stars. Sibyl's brows knitted together in concentration. Then she understood: water. She was seeing the surface of some body of water, late at night. Sibyl's lower lip drew under her tooth in thought.

Across the surface of the water, a subtle change. A ripple, foaming white. Sibyl's hands, thumbs resting on the crystal ball, fingers wrapped around the base of the wooden box, brought the scrying glass up out of her lap until it was level with the end of her nose. She breathed carefully, not wanting to cloud it with moisture from her breath.

The foaming along the surface of the water continued, impossibly small, difficult to see but unmistakable. The perspective inside the glass shifted, and when Sibyl understood what she was seeing her shock was so deep and disturbing that she let out a cry.

On the periphery of her vision, she sensed Dovie sit up, concerned, and from far away heard the girl's voice say, "Sibyl? Are you all right?"

Sibyl made no answer. For there, with perfect clarity, slicing with pride through the silent ocean night, Sibyl beheld the prow of an ocean liner.

FIFTEEN

The Back Bay
Boston, Massachusetts
April 29, 1915

*H*arley lay on his side, feet dangling over the edge of his rope bed, head propped on his hand. His hair stood up in a rumpled mess, the bedclothes bunched at his feet. Someone had crept in while he slept and cranked open the window, letting the breath of spring freshen the room. Outside, a warm rain drummed on Beacon Street, punctuated by a roll of thunder in the distance, out over the water.

Harlan yawned, wondering if that afternoon's baseball game would be postponed again. Boston had been drowning under days of soporific rain, blurring the streets and fields in a gray haze. He scratched his stubble and turned the page of his newspaper. His eyes skated past the war headlines, bored. Something about the Turks, and the British on Hill 60. Just as well the United States was staying out of it.

Harley rolled onto his back, careful of the bandages around his midsection, and sighed. The newspaper slid to the floor as he played his hand over his belly, wishing someone had thought to send up his breakfast. He supposed he ought to get up. At first, they'd been pretty stern about trying to get him up, mornings. Well, his father had, anyway. Sibyl'd been a softer touch.

"He needs his rest," she insisted to their father in the hallway, two days after his return home. There'd been some argument, talk about whether he was being coddled, but Sibyl had actually won that one. And he did need his rest, didn't he? Cracked rib and all. They could at least send up a tray or something. Some bacon. He'd really do with some bacon.

Harley propped himself on his elbows, surveying the room under its wreckage. A soothing breeze crept through the ivy, bringing in the loamy scent of the Common. It smelled like purity and decay at once, reminding him of playing soldier in the woods, or wading in the river basin after Sibyl when she went on her solitary eel-hunts. It felt good, being home.

Maybe if the rain let up he'd run over to the Fenway and see about the Sox and Senators game. It couldn't stay rained-out forever. Who'd want to go with him? Feet on his desk and a lazy toothpick jutting from the corner of his mouth, Bickering would be ensconced in his office, idle, but would probably insist on staying there "for show." Townsend would be at the club, hustling for a hand of bridge. Perhaps he could be scared up. Baseball was a good game for betting men.

And Rawlings . . . well. Harlan laughed, shrugging off the passing idea for what it was.

He stood up, stretching his arms overhead, feeling the bandage pull on the skin over his ribs, and then shaking himself like a puppy emerging from the river. He made his way over to the highboy, planted his hands on either side of it, and turned a crooked gaze up at his reflection in the dressing mirror.

An angry boy glared back at him. He was surprised. Could just be an effect of the bruising, he supposed, but his split lip was almost healed, just a faint crust where the laceration had been, and the dull purplish splotch across his cheek had faded to a pale blue. Just enough to make him look interesting. Well, that's what Dovie said. At the thought of her, Harley's reflection broke into a smile.

He peered up at himself, raising his chin with arrogance, furrowing his brows. It's true, the pummeling had taken away some of the gloss of prettiness that had galled him when he was younger. He grinned out of one side of his mouth, trying to seem rakish and mysterious, and enjoyed the effect. He looked like someone with a past, someone who knew things.

He looked more like a man.

BY THE TIME Harlan made his way, at an unhurried shamble, smoothing his slicked hair back with both hands and buttoning the cuffs of his shirt, down the main staircase, the mantel clock within the drawing room was chiming one o'clock. He heard voices, laughing, a young woman in the dining room calling out "I'll be there in just a minute!" and then the sliding door squeaked open to reveal the laughing form of Dovie Whistler. His heart leaped with a mixture of nerves and pleasure.

She looked well. Her face was flushed with health, and she had put on a little weight. Maybe she was eating all the food Sibyl didn't touch, he reflected, finishing with one of his cuff buttons. Her clothes were neat and simple, well fitting, crisp from where they had been folded on the shelf at Filene's, and considerably different from the flowing tunics and sleeveless shifts that she favored when he first met her. Maybe he missed the tunics, which hung from her shoulders in a way that often intruded on his thoughts when he was alone. But even in the proper shirtwaist, she was arresting.

He thought he detected his sister's influence in the tidying of Dovie Whistler, though he also knew her to be a malleable person in general. She might have sized up the situation in the Allston house and made whatever adjustments were necessary to blend into the scenery. Like a chameleon. He smiled on her with proprietary pride and moved to meet her.

Dovie stopped midstep when she saw him, her face breaking into a sparkling smile. He loved it when she smiled like that. Her smile remade her entire face, transforming her from a painted china doll to a twinkling girl, throwing light into her eyes. She glanced over her shoulder into the dining room, craning her neck with swift, birdlike motions back and forth, and seeing no one, skittered up to him on her toes, silently flinging herself into his arms. He took her porcelain face in his hands, cupping it in his palms, feeling the smooth skin of her cheeks under his thumbs, tilting her face up to meet his kiss.

She let out a happy protesting squeak, yielding for a delicious moment before squirming out of his grip, laughing.

"Harley! You bounder," she scolded, keeping her voice soft so as not to be overheard. "Someone could see."

"I don't care." He grinned, moving nearer. He brought his lips close to the pearlescent curve of her ear and whispered, "I thought I might see you last night." Knowing that she was housed just down the hall from him had been an exquisite torture.

She laid a hand alongside his cheek.

"You're still recuperating," she said, in a voice so low and quiet she might not have been speaking at all. "And anyway, I—I was— It seemed too risky."

He folded his arms around her waist, pressing her to him, burying his nose in her soft halo of blond hair. He indulged in a long sniff, enjoying the warm girl-smell of her, punctuated with a hint of lavender soap, likely borrowed from his sister. She allowed him to hold her, his arms tightening, before she gently slid her fingers under his forearms, prizing his grip from around her middle.

They heard footsteps padding across the floor of the drawing room on the other side of the staircase, and the enameled sliding door rolled open just as Dovie had freed herself from his grasp.

"Oh!" Sibyl exclaimed, coming with apparent surprise upon their conference in the entryway. "Excuse me."

"I was just telling Harley a joke I read in the paper," Dovie said quickly.

"Were you now?" Sibyl said, folding her arms. A knowing smile settled on her face, which caused Harlan's temples to flush.

"I just love jokes. May I hear it, too?" his sister asked, leaning in the doorway.

Grinning, ducking her head, Dovie peeked up at Harlan through lowered eyelids and placed her hands on her hips in that film ingenue way that she had, the fingers pointing down along her flanks. She tossed her bob back out of her eyes, exposing her creamy expanse of neck.

"So did you hear about the daring bank robbery last week?" she asked, in the rote teasing tone of a vaudeville actress about to deliver a real groaner.

"Oh, no," Harlan replied, crossing his arms over his chest, in the attitude of a man in the audience playing along. "Do tell."

"Oh, yes," Dovie said. "It was very daring indeed. The villain walked right into the bank, pulled out a pistol, and then he held up the cashier in broad electric light, before running out and escaping under cover of day!"

A pause while Harlan brought his hand up to his forehead with a groan of dismay, while Sibyl spoke the single syllable "Ha!"

"Doves," Harlan said, shaking his head with a smile. "That was terrible."

"Wasn't it grand? You simply cannot top me for skills as a comedienne," she replied, batting him on the shoulder. But as she did so, her eyes traveled past him, coming to rest on Sibyl. Out of the corner of his eye Harlan noticed his sister incline her head, beckoning Dovie into the drawing room. Dovie giggled, bringing her gaze back to Harlan's face.

"I've just left your father in the dining room," she said. "We had a splendid lunch, didn't we, Sibyl?"

"If you can call cold meat and cabbage splendid," Sibyl muttered, turning her back.

Harlan realized that his sister hadn't said anything to him that day—no good morning, no how are you feeling, no oh your lip is looking well isn't it. He frowned, put out and overlooked. Dovie pulled away, but he held on to her hand as she started toward the drawing room, only letting her go when she moved past the limit of his arm's length. She waved at him over her shoulder, mouthed the single word *Soon*, and the enameled door slid closed, cloistering them away. He heard murmured voices but couldn't discern what was being said.

Harlan scowled, the corners of his mouth pulling down. Well, he'd just show himself into the dining room, then. He wasn't about to give up the chance of some bacon just because his father happened to still be in there.

As Harlan turned toward the dining room, he caught a flash of movement at the periphery of his vision. Deep within the recess behind the stair, by the kitchen corridor, he glimpsed a striped cotton skirt disappearing around a corner, followed by the bitter slam of a door.

"Betty," he started to say. But the skirt was already gone. Clearly she had been eavesdropping while he whispered to Dovie. He couldn't understand it. So he'd kissed her. So what? It didn't mean anything. He thought Betty was a fine girl, who knew he was just horsing around. But when he went skulking after her again, to steal another one, she'd slammed the kitchen door in his face. And now Dovie occasionally complained that her food was underdone.

With a sigh of self-pity at the complicated dealings of women, Harlan steeled himself and stepped into the dining room.

HE FOUND HIS father pushing back his chair, brushing off his suit with a carelessness that usually signaled his return to the business of life outside of the Beacon Street house. Mrs. Doherty was bent at the opposite side of the table, gathering soiled dishes. In a lazy puff on the back of one of the dining chairs perched the iridescent blue macaw, his head tucked over his shoulder in sleep, a claw pulled into his chest. Mrs. Doherty edged around the chair that held the parrot, giving him a wary glare, and hoisting the dishes unnecessarily high for clearance over his head. A few peanut shells lay scattered before the chair where Baiji dozed.

"I can't believe you bring that animal in here, Papa," Harley said, easing with splendid indifference into the nearest chair and propping a knee on the edge of the dining table. He folded his hands behind his head and lolled his gaze up to the ceiling. While he sat, Mrs. Doherty silently placed luncheon-size silverware and a napkin on either side of him, unsparing in her disapproval despite her failure to voice it.

Without answering, Lan Allston reached a finger over to scratch the creature under a wing. The macaw's feathers stretched outward in a slow pouf of disturbance, and his mouth yawned. Then the bird returned to his nap while Lan pulled the chronometer from his vest pocket, rubbed a meditative thumb over its face, and turned his eye at last to his son.

"Finally awake, I see. Well, I suppose that's a relief. You'll have to hurry," Harlan's father said.

"Hmmmm?" Harlan asked as he tried, and failed, to summon Mrs. Doherty's attention. She exited the dining room by pushing through the door to the kitchen with her back, hands laden with dishes, her eyes avoiding both of the Allston men.

"Say," Harlan remarked, "do you think old Doherty'll be able to fix me up with some bacon?" He rubbed a hand over his slim belly, wishing that bacon could be made to appear by force of will.

His father scowled down at him, returning the chronometer to its allotted pocket. "As I was saying. The car's coming for you in ten minutes," Lan announced. "Whether you've eaten or not by then is immaterial. But you'll need to look more pulled together than that, I should think."

"Car?" Harlan echoed, only half listening.

Mrs. Doherty reappeared through the kitchen door and approached Harley's seat. She carried a plate with some slices of meat—roast beef, maybe, cold and unappetizing-looking, with a grayish sheen—and a disappointing spoonful of cabbage. The plate was laid before Harlan with a minimum of ceremony, and she started to withdraw when Harlan stayed her with a hand on her sleeve.

"Come on, Doherty. Can't Betty get me some bacon or something? I'm starved," he said, turning plaintive eyes on her and sticking out a satirical, puppyish lower lip.

The housekeeper flinched, clearly annoyed, but she said, "I'll see, Mister Harlan." She disappeared back into the kitchen.

"The car," Lan Allston reiterated. "It's coming to take you to your appointment this afternoon."

"What appointment? I haven't got any appointment. I'm going to the Sox game," Harlan said, pushing the cold meat around his plate with a fork. This would not do, this cabbagey stuff. Maybe some coddled eggs, to go with the bacon. That'd be the ticket.

"You have an appointment with Benton Derby at the college at two o'clock, and the car has been ordered to ensure that you make it in plenty of time," he father informed him.

"Since when?" Harlan replied, laying the fork aside and folding his arms. He tossed his flop of hair off his forehead, lifting his chin to make certain his father knew that he was an adult now, and so not one to be pushed around.

"Since I made it for you this morning, while you were still, incredibly, asleep," Lan said, his hands tightening on the back of his dining chair.

Mrs. Doherty reappeared through the kitchen door and made her desultory way back to Harlan.

"This morning!" Harlan exclaimed, attention still on his father. "Well, it'll have to wait. Got plans already, I'm afraid. Like I said."

"Plans, have you?" his father said, his eyes chilling by perceptible degrees, and the lines deepening around his mouth. The skin between his father's knuckles turned white with the force of his grip. "Unless those plans that you claim to have hatched involve returning your belongings to Westmorly Court and sitting your final exams this very afternoon, then they *do not exist*. Attendance at a baseball game, I can assure you, my dear boy, does not qualify as *plans* in this household."

"Move back to Westmorly!" Harlan protested, voice carrying just a hint of a whine. "But I'm still recuperating, dontcha know. It's way too early for me to move. Anyway, I'm done with school. I guess I'm just not meant to be a college man." He smiled, his face resolving into the same pleased expression he wore when taking a trick with an unexpected trump, and folded his hands behind his head again.

"Done!" his father said, with a laugh of disbelief.

"How 'bout those eggs, then, Doherty?" Harlan said to the housekeeper, who was loitering at his elbow, melting into discomfited invisibility while the altercation between father and son played out its course.

"I'm afraid," Mrs. Doherty said, her voice strained with formality, "that eggs will be quite impossible this afternoon, sir."

"What?" Harlan protested. "Since when?"

"Unfortunately," Mrs. Doherty reiterated, a hint of desperation threading through her voice, "there simply won't be any eggs available today, Mister Harlan."

"Well, we'll just see about that," Harlan said, starting to his feet in a lather of disappointment. He was waylaid by the housekeeper's insistent hand on his shoulder.

"Sir," she said, voice and grip equally tight, insisting on his attention. "The cook has said in no uncertain terms that it will not be possible for you to have eggs this afternoon." Her dark eyes bored into his, and Harlan read the intensity of warning to be found there.

"Oh," he stammered.

She held his shoulder a moment longer, staring into his face with motherly coldness. The young man swallowed. So that was how it was. Betty was jealous. As if he didn't have enough to deal with.

He was startled out of his dismay by the sound of his father pushing the dining chair back into place with a sharp report. The jolt caused the macaw to jump, cawing in protest before resettling himself on the back of his dining chair, one glittering eye observing the discussion.

"Never mind," Lan Allston said. "There's no time anyway. You've got to be on your way. You're going to Cambridge. And you're going to meet with Benton Derby, who has offered to take time out of his schedule to speak with you. And you're going to listen carefully to everything that he has to say."

As the patriarch spoke he strode around the dining table, more quickly than Harlan expected, and dug a hand into his wayward son's armpit, hoisting him to his feet. Harley was always taken aback by his father's vigor. The Captain was in the habit of moving deliberately, carrying his long legs like a marionette's, as though he still expected the floor to shift under his feet like the deck of a rolling ship. In some respects Harlan never imagined that his father had been anything other than weathered and elderly, authoritative and decisive. Harlan often forgot that his father was a physical man.

"I believe I hear the car," Lan said into his ear, in a tone of forced friendliness. "You'd better get your coat and hat. Don't want to keep Professor Derby waiting."

Harley frowned, considering twisting free of his father's grip. But he reconsidered. He wasn't a child. What harm was there in seeing Benton? What could the professor do, anyway? He'd go, he'd hear Ben out, his father would be placated, and maybe there'd even still be time to scoot over to the Fenway afterward. Hell, maybe he'd talk Ben into going with him. At this thought Harlan's mouth twisted in a mischievous smile, and he tossed his hair back.

"All right," he said. "But if I'd known I had some big appointment today, I'd have gotten more dolled up before I came down."

Without releasing his grip on Harlan's armpit, Lan Allston steered his son from the dining room, through the front hallway, and over to the hall stand by the front door.

"Careful, Papa," Harlan protested as Lan plucked rain gear from within the indistinguishable jumble. "My rib's still awful tender."

Inside the front drawing room, behind the closed door, Harlan overheard a musical giggle, which he knew belonged to Dovie. He wondered what secrets could be passing between Dovie and his sister. Harlan almost envied their confederacy, the late-night giggles and whispering. Much like he'd felt when Sibyl and Eulah cloistered themselves away in their lavatory after coming home from dances. More than once he'd pressed his ear to their keyhole, aching to be let in on their secrets, to hear what they were saying about the people they'd met. Harlan felt terribly alone, those nights.

His father said nothing but buttoned Harlan into his overcoat as though he were still a little boy, even going so far as to wind a knitted muffler around the young man's neck. At first Harlan found this treatment irritating, but deep within himself, the sensation of his father's hands on the buttons of his coat, somehow more sure, more *buttoned* than when he did it himself, filled Harlan with reassurance.

"There," Lan Allston said, brushing off Harlan's shoulders with finality. "Now then. We'll have the car drop me at the office, and then it'll take you into Cambridge. Should be plenty of time. Come along."

Harlan looked into his father's weathered face and felt his obstinacy soften.

"All right," he said.

The two Allston men moved, one after the other, with identical gaits, out the front door of the Beacon Street house and into the drizzling springtime afternoon.

In the dining room, in the quiet void of their abrupt departure, Mrs. Doherty picked up the plate of uneaten roast beef and cabbage, frowned, and carried it back into the kitchen.

Interlude

❧

Shanghai
Old City
June 8, 1868

LANNIE'S EYES REBELLED against the dark. He heard shuffling, and his nose sensed old wood, damp earth, and warm bodies clustered together on a humid night. He deduced that he was standing in a long cavern, with a floor of packed mud covered in straw and windows blotted out with old paper advertisements. The atmosphere was heavy. Though he sensed that he was surrounded by people, he heard no talking.

"It doesn't look like much," Johnny whispered in his ear. "But you'll see."

They stood near the door, waiting. A bead of moisture traced from Lannie's hairline to the bridge of his nose, and he shrugged out of his peacoat.

A faint glow swam toward them, resolving into a minute young woman, simply dressed, her jet hair worn in two long braids over her shoulders. She nodded to Johnny, looked over Lannie, and indicated with her head that they should follow.

The room was lined with plain bunks, two and three high. Every bunk contained a supine figure, some curled into the wall, feet folded, backs bony. Lannie passed faces with blackened, hollow eyes, hands coiled under chins like mummified children. Most of them were dressed in tatters, their bare feet weathered in a way that suggested a perpetual lack of shoes.

"You're worrying," Johnny murmured. "Don't. The only ones who get like that're the ones that never leave. We're gentlemen with self-control. Aren't we?"

Lannie laughed, a bark born of discomfort rather than amusement.

They were shown to two empty bunks, one over the other, covered in mats that had not been changed in some time. Johnny vaulted into the higher bunk, stretching out with a sigh. Lannie held back. He'd had bedbugs plenty of times, of course, those itchy devils, but he didn't relish having them *and* fleas, all at once. Not when hot baths were hard to come by on the *Morpheo*.

"Priss," Johnny scoffed, folding his hands behind his head.

Lannie drew himself up and blustered, *"I* don't care where I sleep. I can sleep anywhere. This'll be luxury, compared to a hammock."

"Sleep?" the young man echoed. "Who said anything about sleep?"

Gingerly Lannie spread his peacoat over the bunk's filth, and lay down. His spine popped, cracking with relief at being allowed to lie flat for the first time in weeks.

His eyes drooped, and before he knew what was happening he was falling backward into a sleep as black as a midnight pond.

"You closing your eyes, Yankee with the fake Chinese name?" the translator's voice said, and Lannie's eyes flew open, startled. He had no idea where he was.

"What?"

"Don't fall asleep, now."

"I wasn't! That is, I . . ." Lannie trailed off, licking his lips, confused.

"Course you weren't," the translator agreed.

Time passed. Lannie couldn't tell how much. He was accustomed to the rigid order of watches on the ship, of the *dong*ing of the ship's bell, and was disturbed not to sense the time. How could there be no clocks here? Of course, there wasn't much of anything here. He would give most anything for a clock.

"Johnny," he ventured.

"Mmmmm?" came the voice from above.

"Do you know what time it is?"

"Time is just point of view." The scholar yawned. "A single day is nothing to a rock, and a lifetime to a mayfly. What's the difference?"

Lannie chuckled. "Well, I guess you're right. But I don't suppose you've got any idea what time a clock would read right now, if I were to look at one?"

The young man sighed at Lannie's apparent thickheadedness.

"No idea. But if you're really that concerned about it, just ask." He called out a short, declarative syllable, and a small boy scampered over. Johnny issued a command, and the boy dashed off. In a moment he reappeared, presented an object to Lannie on outstretched hands, bent his head, and waited.

"What are you waiting for?" Johnny asked, gazing down from overhead.

"What?" Lannie said. "I don't understand."

"He's brought what you asked for. You'd better pay him."

Lannie propped himself on an elbow and peered at the object in the boy's hands. To his surprise, he found a small marine chronometer, of polished brass, its crystal crusted with salt.

"What's this doing here?"

"I imagine someone used it to buy goods in trade. Looks too old to be much use, anyway. I'm surprised they took it."

Lannie knew better. A sailor would have to be of some rank to warrant a chronometer. He would have to be desperate to part with it. Lannie smiled, brushing his fingertips over its burnished surface, wondering what ports it must have passed through to go from London, where it was made, to this dank corner of Shanghai. Valparaiso? Tortuga? New York? Salem, even?

"Pay him," Johnny said.

"I don't know how much." Lannie hesitated. He could never afford to buy such a fine timepiece in a chandlery. They were so prized for longitudinal navigation that old chronometers wound up on fireplace mantels, not in pawnshops. But Lannie suspected that dens of iniquity were unaccustomed to dealing in fine marine instruments and wouldn't know its worth.

"Bah." The scholar dismissed Lannie's concern. "Just give him something for his trouble."

Eyelids fluttering with excitement at his good fortune, Lannie rummaged for his wad of bills, peeled one off, and presented it to the boy with an affectation of reluctance. The boy pocketed the money and moved off, with a touch of smugness at the good bargain.

Lannie settled on his back with his new prize cradled in his hands. He held it up to his ear, listening to its reassuring ticking. Sure enough, it was late enough at night to qualify as morning. But no matter. He had a chronometer!

The young woman with braids reappeared, carrying a tray. She set it on the floor with a thud and placed a small lamp at Lannie's elbow, reaching up to place another by Johnny. Next to the lamp she dropped a length of bamboo with an earthenware bowl attached, a metal knitting needle, and a grubby spoon. Johnny exchanged a few words with the girl, who argued, looking put out. Johnny argued, and the girl muttered in annoyance, but acquiesced.

"I'm getting her to help you," Johnny explained.

"Help me?" Lannie said, tucking the chronometer under his arm. "Help me with what?"

The girl leaned nearer, and a braid fell from her shoulder, swinging down and brushing against his arm. Lannie swallowed, muscles tensing.

"Johnny," he said.

"Hmmmmm?" He heard rustling as the scholar shifted himself on the mats.

"Do you think I could get something to drink? I'm parched."

"I don't see why not." He fired off a request to the girl. She snapped back in a tirade, pointing down in front of her at what she was doing. Johnny insisted, and the girl threw down her implements with irritation. When she reappeared, it was with a smeared glass of something watery.

"I was hoping for whiskey," Lannie confessed.

"Tea is better. You'll see." He paused. "Sometimes you find people who can read the leaves, you know. Ever try that?"

"Reading the leaves?" Lannie said, peering into the glass. An unappetizing scum of leaf fragments swirled at the bottom, caught in muddy eddies of tea. "I wouldn't know how."

"Give it a try after," Johnny suggested. "Give you something to do."

The girl with the braids held a long match to the lamp and then shook it out. She pushed the bamboo stalk into Lannie's hands. He took it, uncomprehending. "What?" he said.

Irritated, she mimed bringing the end of the bamboo to her lips. The gesture struck Lannie as strangely obscene.

"Are you arguing with the nice lotus flower?" the scholar chided, invisible in the gloom. "Didn't your barbarian mother teach you manners?"

Lannie snorted at the characterization of the redoubtable codfish aristocrat Sarah Allston as "a barbarian."

Keeping his eyes on the girl, he brought the end of the bamboo to his mouth. As he did so, she pressed the knitting needle to the opening in the clay bowl, while steering the bowl nearer the lamp flame. The wick needed trimming, and the lamp gave off an oily coil of smoke that made Lannie's eyes smart.

The girl issued an order, and Lannie inhaled. The end of the knitting needle exploded in a blue ball of flame, and Lannie's mouth flooded with bitter numbness. Surprised, Lannie slipped, thudding to the bunk. The room tipped on its side, obscured by ragged ends of straw and his peacoat's collar.

"Ow," he heard someone say.

The girl was watching him closely and, noticing his expression, emitted a tiny smile before disengaging the pipe from his slack fingers. She laid it beside him, within reach, and moved the forgotten glass of tea nearer. She rolled the lamp wick down, and its smoking subsided. Then she crept away.

He sighed. His lips felt funny. The numbness inside his mouth spread to his face. He brought a hand, with some effort, up to his cheek, and was surprised to find it gritty with dried blood. His jaw felt fine. He worked the muscles in his face, brushing the remaining molars over each other, and felt no pain. In its place Lannie found a splendid wholeness, as though deep in his body rolled a calm, smooth ocean, lit by the sinking pink of an evening sun. Lannie gazed into nothing, glassy eyed, letting the sunset creep along his limbs.

"Tea." The syllable drifted from the bunk overhead and hovered before Lannie, devoid of context.

Tea. His mouth felt gummy, coated in a film of disuse. He groped around, hunting for the forgotten drink.

The liquid was tepid, but it washed the moss out of his mouth. He shifted to his side and propped his head in his palm. The rolling ocean and glowing sun still illuminated the inside of his head. He surveyed the room, no longer perturbed by its dessicated occupants, or the silence.

"How's your jaw?" The words moved slowly, reaching Lannie one at a time.

"Good," Lannie said.

"*Good,*" the scholar echoed with a sleepy laugh. "Maybe have a little more tea."

Lannie brought the glass to his face, swirling its contents with a meditative gesture. His eyes slid down to the surface of the tea, the liquid membrane broken by flecks of chopped leaves.

Lannie's eyes moved, following the leaves. The bits of leaf came together and pulled apart, swirling within the light on the surface of the water, drawing the light behind them in tiny eddies.

A soft sigh of astonishment escaped Lannie's mouth.

The leaves. They had formed a pattern.

SIXTEEN

Harvard Square
Cambridge, Massachusetts
April 29, 1915

Harlan realized, as he was halfway across the Yard and closing in on the new library, that perhaps he ought to have given it more thought before setting foot on campus again. Already he had passed two or three boys he knew, and though they greeted him with the jollity and hallooing that were de rigeur among the slick-haired boys of Harlan's class, he could tell by the nervous flicker of their eyelids that they had heard . . . well, something. How much credence they had given the rumors depended in large part on which of Harlan's disgraces were under consideration. The conversations were strained, all undertaken with the pretense of sharing news as though Harlan were just back from an extended trip, rather than removed from their world with abrupt finality.

Harlan pulled his coat collar up around his ears, feeling conspicuous for his lack of haste. The clock in the tower of Appleton Chapel struck the half hour, and Harlan's pace slowed, despite the certain knowledge that he would now be late to his appointed meeting. Harlan frowned at his feet.

Well, the library was looking pretty fine, wasn't it? Harlan invented a reason to stop walking, indifferent to the creeping damp in his clothes. He turned to the neoclassical row of columns that would soon guard Harvard's vast collection of books, a mere month away from opening with suitable pomp and ceremony. Imagine, a man who would be not that much older than himself, if he weren't dead, with a grand new library all erected in his honor. He hadn't known Harry Widener, himself. Poor fellow. Course there were plenty of ways that Harlan would prefer to be remembered, than with a library. He was never really one for books.

But even so . . .

Harlan stood, stock-still, letting the bustle of campus fall away, thinking. He had avoided considering too closely the fact that his classmate had perished on the same night—probably within moments—as his mother and sister. He hated having to think about them every time he set foot on campus. The library facade was like a giant sign that read HARLAN, YOU DIDN'T HELP THEM. Impossible to attend a club meeting, a party, a graduation . . . at every turn, the library would be standing there, a silent testimony to meaningless horror and death. And him, just going along, living. It offended him, being alive like this.

How come some man hadn't been there to see them safely into a lifeboat? That was the question that Harlan couldn't escape. The papers had been filled with eyewitness accounts of the heroism of men ushering women and children into the boats, of standing aside, facing their fates without qualm. But not his mother and sister. No one had bothered to help them. Did no one have honor anymore?

His mother had been a helpless duck, cunning with people, but when it came to practicalities, Helen Allston had been a prisoner of nicety. Despite her unorthodox Spiritualist beliefs, Helen belonged to an earlier age. She could never make herself understood on the telephone, railed against every advance of modernity as less refined than some imagined, long-past standard of propriety, which Harlan was pretty sure dwelt only in his mother's imagination.

Eulah'd been just the opposite, of course. His sister had struck him as a mouthy and large-hatted memorandum sent directly from the future, with her votes and her shorter skirts and her dancing. She surely would have had the wherewithal to. . . . Well, in any case, she would've felt no compunction whatever about asking someone to . . .

Harlan folded his arms over his chest and traced a circle in the mud with his toe.

As he turned his desultory way toward Benton Derby's office, he scowled over his shoulder at the library's indifferent facade, hating it.

Someone should have helped them.

Someone.

WHEN HARLAN CAME upon Benton Derby's office upstairs from the Department of Social Ethics, he found the door already open and occupied by a lanky professorial fellow, who looked to be about Sibyl's age.

Harlan came to a stop, his hands jammed into the pockets of his coat, hair falling forward into his eyes, and wet. He cleared his throat.

"Oh!" the other professor exclaimed. "A visitor, Professor Derby. I've monopolized you yet again."

Harlan peered around the door and observed Benton getting to his feet behind his desk, drawing off his spectacles, and bringing the earpiece to the corner of his mouth. Benton's face looked pinched, the face of a man with something on his mind. Harlan knew perfectly well that the pinched expression was reserved for him.

"Ah," Benton said. "Professor Edwin Friend, I'd like you to meet Harlan Allston."

"How d'you do," Harlan mumbled, sticking his hand out in front of him.

"Harlan Allston," Professor Friend repeated. "Harlan Allston . . . What year are you, then, Mister Allston?"

Harlan's eyes shifted left and right, settling uncertainly on Benton Derby's face before answering. "I was a senior, sir. Class of 'fifteen."

"*Was*," Professor Friend said, also glancing to Benton. All at once he seemed to recollect something, and he said, "Oh, yes, now I remember. Well, in any event, a pleasure to see you, my boy. Best of luck to you, and all that."

"Thanks," Harlan said, for lack of anything better.

"When are you off on your travels, then, Edwin?" Benton asked, still standing behind his desk.

"I sail from New York on a Saturday, May first. First stop, Liverpool. Can't wait."

"Your wife not going with you?" Benton asked.

Professor Friend chuckled. "Not this time," he said. He paused, as though on the point of imparting some secret to Benton, but then he glanced to the waiting boy. Professor Friend only smiled.

"All right," Benton said, sliding his spectacles back into place. "I'll be seeing you before then, I'm sure. Thanks for stopping by."

Harlan felt a dismal sinking in his entrails, knowing that soon the other professor would leave, and then he would be treated to the full spectacle of Benton's disappointment. He couldn't fathom why Benton would care. Fellows left school before graduation all the time. Look at Bickering, he'd left their sophomore year merely out of boredom. The college would have been happy enough to cash Bickering's father's checks and issue him his due allotment of gentlemen's Cs until he slouched his way into a diploma, with rosy memories sufficient to inspire a fat contribution some twenty years down the line. What difference did it make?

"No doubt. Well, onward and upward!" Professor Friend said, rapping his knuckles on the doorjamb in departure. He shambled out of the office, leaving Harlan and Benton to stare at each other across the cluttered expanse of Benton's desk.

Harlan swallowed, more nervous than he realized. He reminded himself that he didn't care what this young professor thought of him. He thrust his hands into his trouser pockets with the force of the reminding.

"Take a seat, Harley," Benton said.

A flash of annoyance contorted Harlan's face. He didn't appreciate the young professor addressing him as though he were his father. All right, they weren't peers, but even so. Harlan was only in his office as a courtesy. He wasn't a student anymore. Benton should speak to him like a man.

"Thanks, Ben," he said, making his reply deliberately casual, and using a nickname that he knew Benton would fail to appreciate hearing in a professional context.

He settled into the pitted armchair situated at an angle to Benton's desk, a sturdy and uncomfortable hunk of wood whose back was fashioned into a shield that read VERITAS. Harlan pulled a pant leg back and brought his ankle up to his knee, slouching, insouciant. He rummaged in his pocket for his cigarette case, pried one out, and slid it into the corner of his mouth. He was on the point of striking a match when he was stayed by Benton's clearing his throat.

"I'd rather you not smoke, if you don't mind," the professor said. Harlan glanced up to Benton's eyes, drained of the ironic merriment that Harlan was accustomed to finding there.

He paused, looking into Benton's face for a long, challenging moment. Then he smiled.

"All right," he said, removing the cigarette from his lower lip and placing it with care back into the case. "Whatever you say. It's your office."

A full brass ashtray sat at Benton's elbow. So it was to be *that* kind of conversation. Well, he supposed he was ready. Harlan folded his arms over his chest and tossed his head back, brushing the flop of hair out of his eyes. Then he waited, keeping what he hoped was an easy, confident smile on his face.

Benton leaned forward, knitting his fingers together and resting his considerable weight on his desk. Benton had been a wrestler at college, and even as he grew from the college boy Harlan had known when he was a child to the man who sat before him, Benton would always have that dense wrestler's build. His body was compact and muscled, slightly the wrong shape to look fashionable in suits. His shoulders were too broad. There was something unrefined about Benton's body, though that was offset by the sharpness of his mind. A psychologist, that's what Sibyl said he was. So Benton Derby liked to study crazy people. Well, bully for him. Harlan had better things to do with his time.

"How've you been, Harley?" Benton asked, more gently than Harlan was expecting. He shifted in his chair, made uncomfortable by the care in Benton's words.

"Why, all right I guess," Harlan said dubiously. "Rib's getting better. Been resting up."

"So I'm told," Benton said. He paused. "Had a rough few weeks."

Harlan snorted. "'S nothing too much, I don't think," he said. He wished that Benton would let him have a cigarette. It was pretty cheap of him, not to allow it when he smoked himself.

"When we ran into each other, outside the Swithin," Benton said, "you were in an awful hurry to get away, seemed like."

"Nah." Harlan waved off the suggestion. "I'd just . . . I was late to meet someone, that's all."

"Uh-huh," Benton said. The two men stared at each other, neither of them speaking.

"When the trouble started here," the young professor said, "I wish you'd thought to tell me. Perhaps I could've helped."

"Man's got to stand on his own two feet, I guess," Harlan said, flushing.

"Well, sure," Benton allowed, "but even so. We've known each other a long time. Why, I remember when you were born, even."

"Thought you were away at school when I was born." Harlan frowned, chafing under the unwelcome intimacy.

"I was, but I remember Father's letter telling me about it. The Captain was pleased as punch, he said. Come on, Harley. Why didn't you come to me? You knew I was here."

Harlan just stared at him, impassive expression covering the simmering anger in his belly. "You'd been away a long time," he said, at length.

Benton stared into his face, and it occurred to Harlan that the professor looked sort of sad. "I suppose that's true," he said, voice quiet.

Harlan waited to see if Benton really understood why he wouldn't have come to him. He couldn't be as dense as all that. For at least a year everyone seemed sure that Benton and Sibyl would marry. Especially after Sibyl was rid of that weaselly Coombs fellow. Harlan remembered Eulah monitoring their every interaction, reporting back to Helen the slightest conversation, the merest brush of hands. Everyone was waiting. Eager. Perhaps Harlan most of all.

Harlan had always yearned for a brother. Someone to be in confederacy with him the way that Eulah and Sibyl were with each other, someone to share the weight of their father's expectations. Sibyl was almost as good as a brother sometimes, especially when he was small. She'd go adventuring with him. She taught him to fish. And the burly son of their father's shipping partner had been around as long as Harley could remember. Harley used to look forward to Lan's business dinners with the Derbys at the Beacon Street house. Benton would sit over cigars and cognac with the Captain and Mr. Derby after dinner, one eye on the door where he knew Harlan was hiding. He'd peek around the door, and slowly Benton would cross his eyes at the boy with a grin before going back to the adult conversation.

And then Benton dropped the ball. Jilted his sister for Lydia Pusey! Maybe *Lydia's* brother would call him up, if he had trouble at school. Did Lydia even have a brother? Who cared? Harlan scowled, hating the young professor for not sensing the wellspring of hurt that still festered in him.

"Now then," Benton said. "I've made a few inquiries into your situation. And I think I see a way through it."

"Ben," Harlan interrupted. "Look. It's real nice of you to be so concerned. But I'm fine. I wasn't much of a student, anyway. In fact, I was hoping we could just skip the talk. You want to ditch your afternoon classes and catch the Sox game with me instead?"

A shadow passed through Benton's eyes. "The Sox game," he said.

Harlan grinned at him and laced his fingers together behind his head. "Rain's finally letting up. We'd have a fine time."

Benton shifted his weight on his elbows, looking down at his hands, and then glancing back up to Harlan. "I think you know that's not going to be possible. Frankly, Harley, it concerns me to see you taking this so lightly."

The smile melted off of Harlan's face. "Well, how d'you suggest I take it? I'm out. They've made that perfectly clear. And I'm just as happy they did."

"You're happy, are you," Benton said.

"Sure. I hated it, anyway." Harlan heard the petulance in his voice and was irritated by it, sliding his gaze away from Benton's face and onto the corner of the desk.

"Didn't seem like you hated it. From what I can see, you were doing fine. Made some good clubs. Grades all right. A good group of fellows around you. Looks to me like you'd found your way, all things considered. Should've been no reason you wouldn't graduate this spring."

Harlan frowned, still staring at the corner of the desk. "So what if I did? Doesn't matter."

Benton took a deep breath, as through preparing for something unpleasant. "I had some difficulty getting a straight answer from the administration, since I wasn't inquiring in any official capacity. But it seems as though the real issue was the girl."

Harlan turned his clear blue eyes back on Benton's face, his mouth flattening in a defensive line.

"Well?" Benton prodded.

"Well, what?" Harlan said, defiant. The reference to Dovie filled Harlan with an unaccustomed protectiveness, alert to the faintest hint of denigration of her character.

The young professor sighed, shaking his head. His face betrayed a world weariness, even pity, that made Harlan fantasize about smashing his fist into Benton's face, perhaps connecting right where those damned spectacles sat on his patrician nose, breaking them both at the same time. The fantasy pleased Harlan, and he smiled, a cold, cruel smile, settling his arms more tightly across his chest.

"Look," Benton began. "Everyone fools around. Am I right? Young fellows such as yourself, no attachments. It's to be expected."

"If you say so," Harlan said, giving away nothing.

Benton cleared his throat and leaned forward, dropping his voice. "But to have her in your *rooms*, Harley . . ."

"Plenty of fellows've brought girls back to Westmorly," Harlan said, dismissive. "You hear about it all the time."

"Not all the time," Benton said, voice cool. "And certainly not"—he cleared his throat—"in the condition. In which you two were found."

Harlan scowled, dropping his pretend-casual foot from his knee back down to the floor with an impatient *thunk*. His gaze transformed from defiant to openly hostile. Benton felt the force of Harlan's look, and sat back in his desk chair, unknotting his fingers and spreading his hands flat on the desk.

"I only bring it up," Benton continued, "because the . . . flagrancy . . . with which you flouted the rules of the dormitory would tend to suggest . . ."

The two men locked their eyes across the narrow office. Outside, a sheet of rain washed up against the office window, and Harlan felt, rather than heard, the low rumble of thunder prowling the sky over Cambridge. No game today after all. He waited. Benton clearly wished for him to finish the thought left hanging in the air between them. But Harlan wasn't about to give him that satisfaction.

"It would tend to suggest," Benton started again, his voice low, so that it might not be overheard by anyone passing in the hallway outside the office. "Deliberation. On your part."

"Deliberation? What are you talking about?" Harlan challenged him.

"That you meant to be caught," the professor clarified. He watched Harlan's face carefully.

"That's preposterous!" Harlan burst. He sank lower in the chair, feeling its carved VERITAS dig into his spine. His gaze tore away from Benton and landed back on the corner of the desk. Harlan was growing intimately acquainted with the whorls of wood grain in that square inch of academic furniture.

"Is it?" Benton pressed, a new gentleness in his tone. His hands knitted themselves together again on the top of his desk, and he lowered his head to look at Harlan over the rims of his spectacles.

"Of course it is," Harlan growled. "What would I want to get kicked out of school for? You think I *liked* coming home to the Captain like that? You think I *like* being hounded by my sister every minute of the goddamn day? And that housekeeper watching me like a hawk?"

"Well," the young professor said, drawing the thought out, "sometimes we do things without really knowing why we do them. You've certainly gotten a lot more attention from them now that you're home. They're concerned about you."

"Attention!" Harlan exclaimed, sitting forward with his hands gripping the armrests of the office chair. "As if that's what I were after. *More* attention from them. And what about Miss Whistler? You think I'd have brought this on her willingly? I know what everyone thinks, and she doesn't deserve any of it. What kind of man do you think I am?"

Benton sat back, keeping his expression mild. "That's an interesting question, Harley. A very interesting question indeed. What kind of man do *you* think you are?"

Harlan scrambled to his feet, blinded with confusion and anger. There was no reason in the world that he had to sit here and listen to this. Who did Benton think he was talking to? Why, just because he'd known him as a boy was no reason . . . And anyway, he'd disappeared from their lives when he married and left for Italy. Abandoned them. In truth, he didn't know Harlan at all. Then just because Harlan got into a spot of trouble at school, he thought he could just insert himself in his affairs. He wouldn't stand for it. These thoughts warred together in Harlan's mind as he stood, breath coming fast in his chest, fists knotted at his side, piercing gaze ze-roed in on Benton's mild face.

"You're upset," Benton remarked.

"You're damn right I'm upset," Harlan hissed through clenched teeth. "You have no business making light of what's happened after vanishing like you did. You don't know me at all."

Benton brought a finger to his lips, watching Harlan, and seemed to con-sider his response. Harlan waited, wondering why he hadn't left yet, annoyed at himself for not having left, but arrested where he stood, waiting. For some reason, it mattered very much to him what Benton would say.

At length the professor took a long breath, still with the finger pressed to his lips.

"You're right," he said. He slid his spectacles off and worked a hand over his forehead, then tossed the spectacles onto the desk.

Harlan was taken by surprise.

"I beg your pardon?" he said. The rage in Harlan's belly bubbled lower, as if the heat had been turned down. Not off entirely. But down. His hand found the back of the chair and clamped down on it, but he didn't leave.

"I said, you're right. Have a seat."

Harlan, startled, plopped himself back into the seat across from the professor, feeling simultaneously mollified and chastened.

"Now then," Benton said, leaning forward on his elbows, leveling his gray eyes on Harlan's watching face. "The fact of the matter is, your rea-sons for your actions, whatever they might be, are beside the point. Our main enterprise here is looking at ways to get you back into school. You want to get back in, don't you? Sit for your exams? Walk with the rest of the 'fifteen fellows?'"

Harlan wondered why the young professor was trying so hard. Benton didn't stand to benefit from helping a sad sack case. If anything, Benton would be running a substantial risk. If Harlan failed, if he violated the tiniest college rule, Benton's reputation would suffer for having vouched for him. And even if Harlan were successful, if they found a loophole whereby he could be readmitted, if he sat for his exams and walked the following month, the administration wouldn't care that Benton had helped.

A fissure opened in Harlan's mind, allowing him to see past himself for a moment, and he wondered if Benton felt guilty. If he missed the Allston family as much as they missed him.

"Maybe," Harlan said. His comma of hair slipped over his forehead, and he brushed it out of the way with a toss of his head.

Benton nodded. "All right. We'll give it some thought, then. Now, I have one other question. Don't mean to pry, of course. . . ." He trailed off.

Harlan waited, giving away nothing.

"The girl," Benton said, cheeks reddening. Harlan could tell that the professor found the entire matter distasteful, though perhaps not shocking. In some respect his friend's disappointment was the most unbearable part of the whole sordid situation, worse than his father's censure, or his sister's cloying worry. "Where do things stand? Were promises made?"

Harlan sat forward, suddenly exhausted. He was tired. He was tired of worrying about what he was supposed to do, tired of hiding, tired of trying to be the kind of man that he knew he was supposed to be. His side hurt. His split lip was sore. He brought his hands to his face, sinking his cheeks into his palms with a heavy sigh. The sigh was almost long enough to turn into a sob, but Harlan choked back the fear and shame rising in his chest with a gurgle. He felt, rather than saw, Benton's expression grow both more concerned, but also softer.

"I know what you all must think of her," Harlan began, his voice small behind his hands.

Benton waited. Then he asked, "Are you planning to marry her?"

Harlan held his head in his hands, shrugging his shoulders.

"She's . . . I want to, Ben, I want to, so much. But I don't see how. . . ." Harlan left the thought unfinished.

Harlan heard the professor shift his arms on the desktop, as though one hand were worrying the gold band that he still wore on his left ring finger.

"She ran off from her family. In California. She's been on her own for ages. She goes on the stage. You think I don't know what that means? It's just that . . . I love her. I know I'm not supposed to. But I do," Harlan said. He dropped his hands between his knees, head hanging, avoiding Benton's gaze. He felt the weight of a hand descend on his shoulder. The hand squeezed.

"So I see," the professor said.

Wiping the corner of his eye on the back of a wrist, embarrassed, Harlan struggled to his feet, shuffling them together in his haste to escape his admission. Benton's hand fell from Harlan's shoulder, and Harlan helped it go, shrugging him off.

"I should go," Harlan mumbled to his feet.

Benton nodded, hands in his pockets. The two men stood like that in Benton's office for a little while, each waiting to see what the other would do.

"Going to try to catch the game?" Benton asked, failing to sound jovial.

Harlan shook his head. "Nah. Too wet," he said, eyeing the dismal spring world waiting for him outside in the Yard. "Guess I'll just . . . Oh, I don't know."

Benton shifted his weight and made a noise of assent.

"Well then," he said after a time. "Why don't I have another word with the dean, and then we'll just see where we are?"

"All right," Harlan allowed. Head still hanging, he turned to leave.

As Harlan reached the office door, his cheeks scarlet with shame, he was waylaid by Benton's clearing his throat. Harlan glanced over his shoulder to find the young professor rocking back on his heels, as though he had something else to say.

"Harley," Benton began.

"Huh?" Harlan grunted.

The professor paused, one hand clasping his opposite wrist. "Ah. You'll give my regards to Miss Allston, won't you?"

If Harlan didn't know better, he would have said that Benton looked nervous.

"Sure," Harlan said, lowering an eyebrow before pulling the office door closed behind him.

SEVENTEEN

Bosworth Street
Boston, Massachusetts
April 30, 1915

*T*he door swung open on a merry crowd of fancifully hatted women, clinking glassware, low-hanging cigarette smoke, and the smell of cooking butter. Sibyl loitered in the entry, pulling off her gloves. She flopped them against her palm, craning her neck to look over the heads of the diners. She spotted him, pressed into the corner of a wooden booth, and Sibyl shot her hand up, waving to get Benton's attention. Lifting his chin with an answering smile, Benton started to get to his feet, nearly shouldering aside a long-aproned waiter balancing a platter laden with covered dishes. The waiter unloaded a torrent of French on him that Sibyl gleaned rather than overheard, due to the ambient roar of the restaurant, and she laughed.

By the time she wove her way to his table Benton was standing, hands in his trouser pockets, ducking his head with embarrassment after his tongue-lashing. He took Sibyl's hand in both of his and said, "I thought for sure I'd be thrown out of here before you made it to the table."

"Serve you right if you did! He almost lost his Welsh rarebit, you know. That would've been a disaster," Sibyl chided.

He helped her out of her coat, settling it on the hooks on the high end of the booth, and gestured for her to take the seat across from him. Sibyl didn't usually dine in restaurants, and she enjoyed being in the noise and bustle of the room at midday. The restaurant, a venerable French institution in downtown Boston, echoed with wooden chairs scraping under the weight of diners, voices rising to make themselves heard over the din. The room was narrow, tiled in black and white, with a marble bar along one side and the row of wooden booths along the other. Several waiters swanned among the tables, platters overhead.

Benton gazed at her over his spectacles, and then looked down at the menu, chuckling.

"What is it?" Sibyl asked, noticing his laugh.

"Nothing," he said, shaking his head.

"What? Now you have to tell me," she insisted.

He looked back at her across the table with a small smile. "It's nothing much," he said. "You had the biggest grin on your face just now. I wasn't used to it."

Sibyl's eyebrows rose, and she brought an abashed hand to her cheek. "I did?" A blush crept down her hairline, warming her skin.

He smiled more broadly. "You did."

Sibyl laughed softly, through her nose, and hid behind the menu under pretense of studying it closely.

The indifferent waiter reappeared, jotting down Benton's poorly accented order with a hint of disapproval, including a request for a *pâté en croute* over Sibyl's napkin-twisting objections. Then, after they each swallowed a long drink of water, and spent the requisite amount of time admiring the surroundings, exclaiming over how delicious everything looked at other tables, and expressing relief that the rain had begun to let up, Benton leaned forward, resting his elbows on the table.

He hesitated, and then closed his hand over Sibyl's where it rested next to her water glass. She twitched in surprise but didn't withdraw. His hand felt warm to the touch, softer than she expected, but with a latent strength.

The contact point where her skin met his tingled, and Sibyl swallowed, able to concentrate on his face only with difficulty.

"It's good of you to join me," he said. "I know you don't usually . . . that is, I'm not accustomed to seeing you out and about. During the day."

"Oh!" she exclaimed. "Well. I was glad for your call. It's a treat, really. To have lunch."

"Well," he said. "I'm glad of it."

Again, the awkward silence. "I suppose you know," he continued, "that I spoke with Harley yesterday."

Sibyl nodded, eyes on her salad fork. "That was good of you."

"Well, your father asked." Then he added with haste, "I was happy to oblige, of course."

"Of course!" Sibyl agreed.

"Your family," Benton said, "felt like a second home for me, you know. After my father . . . well."

"Papa always liked you," Sibyl said. "I think he'd have been happy for you to join the firm. If you'd wanted to."

"Oh!" Benton exclaimed. "Yes. I never was much of a businessman, I'm afraid. And then, I was moving to Italy, so . . ."

"For Lydia's health. I remember," Sibyl said. She kept her voice neutral with difficulty.

"Right. Anyway," Benton said, perhaps realizing his mistake, "I was happy to help."

Sibyl shrugged, as if she could roll off the unpleasant memory "Harley He seems to be feeling better, I think. Though we're no closer to him telling us anything."

"I'd be surprised if he did. He's an awfully proud fellow. And rightfully so."

"Rightfully!" Sibyl exclaimed. She was on the point of pressing him when the waiter appeared, sliding a platter of *mignons de porc bordelaise* with *haricots verts* before Benton, who waited, cutlery at the ready, and a small bowl of onion soup before her. She glanced at Benton's plate of delicious steaming meat, into which he was sawing with gusto, and then looked back at the bowl before her, an inviting cap of browned cheese melting over its edge. Between them slid a baked pâté wrapped in pastry, as browned and crisp as leaves of burnt tissue paper. Benton was five bites into his dinner before she managed to pick up the soup spoon, dip it into the broth, and bring it to her lips.

"Yes, rightfully," Benton continued, stabbing a tiny green bean with his fork. "You should try this," he said, without asking, depositing the vegetable on her plate.

Sibyl blinked. She could hardly refuse. He would notice. And anyway, it was just a green bean.

"It's normal for a man your brother's age, or a bit younger, to push against what's expected of him," Benton said, chewing with evident pleasure. "All part and parcel of him figuring out what sort of man he wants to be. He looks at the rules bounding his behavior, and by God, he wants to test them."

"Oh, there's no one like Harlan, for testing," Sibyl said drily.

Benton eyed her with a smile. "Could be worse. There's no need to go into details, but I've spoken with the administration and gotten a clearer picture of what happened. I think, with some promises made to the right dean, we can eke him back in."

"Well, that is good news. Papa will be so pleased." She paused. "And what did happen?"

Benton laid his fork aside and looked at her over his spectacles. "If it's all the same to you, Sibyl, I'd rather not mention the specifics. There was some"—he paused—"ungentlemanly behavior."

Sibyl pressed her lips into a disapproving line, irritated. "Well, of course there was, Ben," she said, laying her spoon aside with a sigh of impatience. "A boy doesn't get asked to leave college for behaving himself *too* well, does he? I wish you didn't feel the need to protect me from my brother's considerable shortcomings. I can assure you I've a pretty good idea what they are already."

"Have you?" Benton asked, one eyebrow raised.

"I have. She's actually very nice, you know," Sibyl said briskly. She took a bite of the bean and chewed, not meeting Benton's gaze.

Benton laughed in surprise. "Oh, is she now!"

"She is," Sibyl affirmed. "Papa was adamant. After what happened to

Harlan, he insisted we help extricate her from what was doubtless a very complicated situation. It was the decent thing to do."

The professor waited, resting his chin on his palm. The surprise on his face occasioned by Sibyl's comment softened into an indulgent smile. "And . . . ?" he said.

"And so she's staying at the house now. Temporarily." Sibyl, still avoiding Benton's gaze, leaned forward, blowing a delicate stream of air over the soup in her spoon.

"Temporarily," Benton repeated.

Sibyl sat back with a sigh and looked him in the face. "Oh, you needn't conceal what you really think. Of course I was against it at first."

"Of course," Benton agreed.

"But Harley's quite attached to her, and given what happened in that awful boardinghouse, well . . ." Sibyl trailed off. She added "It's no place for anyone, that boardinghouse. It's dreadful. After all the work I've done with settlement houses, how am I going to object when the girl needs our help? Besides, Harley is the real problem here, not her."

"I don't suppose the Captain thinks Harley's really going to marry this girl?" Benton asked, voice low. "I can't see him allowing that. Or you, for that matter."

A curious expression crossed Sibyl's face as Benton voiced this idea. "If there's been any discussion of marriage," Sibyl said, stumbling over the last word, "I haven't been party to it."

"I see," Benton said. He returned to the plate in front of him, sawing off another morsel of pork and forking it into his mouth.

"But in any event," Sibyl continued, stirring her cooling soup, "Miss Whistler's a much nicer girl than I would've anticipated. Even if she has had an unconventional upbringing."

"Unconventional," Benton said, spearing another few green beans and depositing them, again without asking, on the edge of Sibyl's plate. "That's one word for it."

"Ben!" Sibyl said, irritated. "I'm surprised at you. She's had a tougher time of things, all right. But Miss Whistler's a lively girl, and she's devoted to my brother. Of course I don't know what Papa's plans are, but she's been perfectly fine to have in the house. In fact, I've grown quite fond of her."

Benton sighed, massaging an eyebrow with his fingertips.

"What is it?" Sibyl pressed, folding her arms over her chest. "I wish you'd just say what's on your mind, and not make me guess at it all the time." *I so often guess wrong*, she thought without saying.

"Frankly," Benton said, looking at her, "I can't believe this. What, are you going to bring her along to Junior League meetings now? Lectures at the Bostonian Society?"

"Why not?" Sibyl challenged him. Perhaps she hoped to shock Benton with her worldliness.

"I don't think you understand. It's not just a matter of Harlan's having a romantic, ill-fated love affair, like something out of one of your women's pulp novels."

"I don't read pulp novels!" Sibyl objected, but he cut her off.

"She was in his rooms, Sibyl. She was found there. In a—" he cleared his throat—"a compromising way. An *immediately* compromising way."

A long pause settled on the table between them while Sibyl digested this piece of information. Her dark brows furrowed over her eyes. Benton waited, watching. She kept her face composed. Then she took up her spoon.

"Nonsense," she said. And followed this pronouncement with a prim sip of broth through her pursed lips.

"I'm afraid it's true," Benton said.

"You're mistaken," Sibyl said. "She's an actress. She has some unconventional ideas, I'll give you that. An artistic temperament. That's all. It's quite refreshing, actually. I don't know why I haven't made more of a point of going to the artistic salons, as Harley has."

Benton peered at Sibyl, and she saw behind his gray eyes the turning wheels of calculation. "What makes you say so?" he asked.

"Why, I've gotten to know her quite well these past few weeks," Sibyl said with authority. "I have," she reaffirmed before he had the chance to argue with her. "We've been going around together. She's lovely. And not at all the way that you imply. I think we've all misjudged her."

Sibyl looked at Benton under her lidded eyes, enjoying the shock on his face.

"Well, how do you like that," he said. "Going 'round with her. Going 'round where, pray tell? I don't suppose you've gone to catch the Griffith picture, then, or take in a show?"

"As a matter of fact, I've had her to lunch at the Oceanus. And that's not all," Sibyl said with a slow smile. She looked left and right over her shoulder, with an air of happy conspiracy, and leaned forward, beckoning for Benton to do the same. She moved her mouth only a hairsbreadth away from the curve of his ear and whispered, "There's something else I've rather wanted to discuss with you."

THE CAB HAD nearly arrived in Harvard Square, and Benton was still so angry that he hunched away from her on the seat, glaring out the window. But Sibyl was sure. She knew what she had observed over the past several weeks. She had never been more certain of anything in her life.

"It's remarkable, I tell you," she reiterated, but he only responded with an aggravated snort.

The cab bounced over a pothole, and the two rocked against each other, his shoulder pressing momentarily against her own. He felt solid, reassuring, but in his solidity Sibyl sensed a new remoteness.

The cab rounded a corner, and Sibyl glanced at the driver to see if their argument was being observed. From the faint twitch in the driver's ears, she saw that it was. She dropped her voice to a barely audible whisper.

"I'd think you of all people would be most interested in what I have to say," she said. He, too, shifted his gaze to the back of the driver's neck, then ducked his head to argue in a harsh whisper of his own.

"Miss Allston," he said, and she noticed that her Christian name had fallen away over the course of their drive to Cambridge. "What you de-scribe is simply impossible. Now I have every certainty that you *believe* that you've experienced something real. But your believing it doesn't make it so. Frankly, it concerns me."

"Concerns you!" she exclaimed.

"If it happens the way you've described it to me, how could I help but be concerned?" His voice rose, agitated, and the driver's head inched back to hear what was being said.

"Don't be ridiculous," Sibyl said. "It's perfectly safe."

"I don't see how you, an otherwise reasonable woman, would claim such things are safe. There's a reason the law was changed, you know."

She started to protest, but by then the cab had stopped on Massachusetts Avenue and Benton was already out of the cab, tossing some coins at the driver and not bothering to see if Sibyl was following him or not. She scrambled after him as he strode through the brick arch leading to campus with the forward-leaning gait of a man on a mission.

"Ben!" she called, feet skittering beneath her, her skirts gathered with one hand and the other placed squarely on top of her hat. He didn't look around. "Ben!" she cried again, breaking into a jog.

He slowed, only enough for her to start to catch up, then continued without looking at her. The Yard elms whispered together, their leaves waxy green from the rain, and Sibyl sidestepped a puddle.

"Perfectly safe," he muttered under his breath, apparently indifferent to her struggles to keep up. "I'll show you perfectly safe. It's lunacy. You're making a terrible mistake, and I'm going to prove it."

He marched to the philosophy building, up the concrete steps, through an echoing marble entrance, down a long hallway, and through a heavy oaken door with the word FRIEND in black letters. Benton flung the door open.

"Edwin!" he cried. "If you don't see the harm of your damn fool experiments when you hear what she's been up to, then by God, you've lost your senses completely."

Professor Edwin Friend glanced up from a stack of undergraduate term papers, over which he was bent with a blue fountain pen, and smiled.

"Why, Miss Allston!" Friend said, breaking into a smile, eyes crinkling with pleasure. He stood, tossing the pen down. "Do come in! And you might as well bring Professor Derby with you. We can put up with him for a little while, can't we?"

Sibyl laughed but brought her gloved fingertips to her lips with a hasty glance at Benton. Their merriment only seemed to make him angrier. His ears were deep scarlet, and his nostrils flared. Sibyl placed her hands on Benton's shoulders, and felt them drop in response to her touch. She moved around him, edging into the office and beckoning him to follow with her eyes.

"Tell him," Benton said, his voice tight with rage as he took a seat across from the philosopher's desk. "Go on. Tell him what you've been doing."

"Professor Derby is terribly uncomfortable with madness as a general rule," Professor Friend remarked. "But in any event, I'd love to hear about whatever you've been up to. I did hope you'd stop by my class, you know."

"We were dining downtown," she said, "and I told Professor Derby about a recent experience of mine. But I'm afraid he doesn't approve."

"Approve!" Benton burst, smacking his hand on the armrest of his chair. "My God, spit it out already!"

Professor Friend looked mildly on his colleague, and then leaned toward Sibyl with confidential interest. "I'm fascinated. Anything that could get Professor Derby so riled up must be worth doing."

"Well," she began, "you recall that I had been involved with a . . ." She cleared her throat, glancing at Benton. His pupils formed pinpoints of rage. "A Spiritualist gathering."

"Yes, of course," Professor Friend said, nodding his encouragement. "As so many of us are."

"Yes," she faltered. "Well. The medium presented me with a present. A sort of crystal ball."

The philosopher's eyes gleamed. "Oh, really? Not one of those glass balls that gypsies use?"

"Oh, no," Sibyl protested. "This one is small, just a toy, really. I didn't think much of it at first."

Benton drummed his fingers on the armrest of his chair. "That's it, just work your way up to it slowly, no rush at all," he said. Sibyl scowled at him.

"How big is it?" Friend asked.

"Small. It can fit in a palm. But I usually keep it in the box. Mrs. Dee told me that—" Sibyl stopped, clapping her hand over her mouth when she realized what she had done. The name didn't seem to mean anything to the professors, however.

"She told me that it was a tool," Sibyl continued. "For seeing."

"Clairvoyance," Friend exclaimed. Benton made a pshawing sound and rolled his eyes. "Now, Professor Derby," the philosopher said, his voice friendly, "surely you know what clairvoyance is?"

"I suppose there's no stopping your telling me," Benton said, rolling his head against the backrest of the chair in exasperation.

"Clairvoyance," Friend said, "is the ability of gifted individuals in a mesmeric state to see beyond the normal realm of perception. Often by using tools like tea leaves, cards, or a glass."

"Just so!" Sibyl exclaimed. "At first I didn't think I could do it. But lately I've been seeing the most remarkable things, Professor Friend."

"Like what?" he asked, eyes gleaming with excitement.

"Well," Sibyl said, relieved at having an appreciative audience, "as you know, I'd been trying to contact my mother and sister for some time. I'd grown terribly frustrated, and I was skeptical of ever being able to accomplish anything like that on my own. After all, I have no special gifts."

"That's not true at all," Benton growled.

She glanced at him, surprised, but made no comment. Then she turned back to Professor Friend. "At first, I just saw water. Or at least, I thought it was water."

The philosophy professor leaned forward on his desk as Benton squeezed the bridge of his nose between finger and thumb.

"Lately," Sibyl whispered. "I've been seeing the ship. I can see it down to every detail. The hull, the dining room, the clock in the stairwell . . ." She trailed off, eyes shining. "I've been amazed. I think . . . I think I'll be able to see them. If I only practice a bit more."

"Remarkable," the philosopher breathed. "Seen *Titanic*, have you? As though you were there yourself? Simply remarkable."

"Remarkable!" Benton grumbled. "Tell him how you attain the mesmeric state necessary for these remarkable visions of yours, Miss Allston." When he said the phrase *mesmeric state*, Benton waved his fingers on either side of his head, as though they were quotation marks.

"Well, Professor Derby, it's usual for clairvoyants to experience visions in a trance state," Professor Friend said. "I can think of a number of your colleagues who've done research into hypnotism and altered consciousness. I understand it has tremendous therapeutic potential."

"Tell him," Benton said to Sibyl, ignoring him.

Sibyl ducked her head, looking sheepish. "I assure you, Benton, there's no harm in it."

"Tell him," Benton hissed, "or I'll tell him myself."

"He's very concerned," she said to Friend. "Though frankly I can't imagine why."

"Because it's against the law, for one thing," Benton burst, "and because of the unpardonable risk to your health for another!"

"Whatever is he talking about?" Professor Friend wondered, looking at Sibyl.

"In truth," she confessed, "the first few times I tried to use the glass nothing happened."

"Why, that's not unusual," the professor said. "Like any mental exercise, clairvoyance requires patience. And practice. And a certain amount of innate capacity. Occasionally, the skill is found in families. Some people try for years before achieving even modest success. Most never succeed at all."

"You see, Benton? It's not so terrible as all that," Sibyl said, wishing to elide the question of how she might have discovered this innate capacity of hers.

Unable to restrain himself, Benton leaned forward into Professor Friend's face. "She's been smoking opium, Edwin. She!" He pointed at Sibyl, who sat, prim and ladylike, shoulders drawn back as though prepared for a ballet recital. "That's how she's been accessing your so-called mesmeric state. And you're encouraging her! I can't believe it. The unmitigated gall!"

He turned to Sibyl. "I suppose you know that everything you think you've seen with this so-called scrying glass has been a fever dream, don't you? That's all opiates do—create vivid dreams. Same kind of thing you'd get with scarlet fever. There's no reason to give it any credence whatsoever."

Scarlet fever. The disease that had taken his wife in Rome. He never mentioned it, never mentioned Lydia at all. The comparison hung there, in the room.

"Now, Professor Derby," Friend started to mollify.

"And you! Doesn't this bother you at all? How would a woman like her even go about obtaining opium, I ask you? What sort of people must she be coming in contact with? You haven't seen what addiction can do to a person. But I have."

He got to his feet and strode over to Friend's bookshelf, leaning on it and resting his forehead on the back of his hand.

"They become hollow shells of people, Sibyl," he said without looking at her. "They lose their very humanity. I can't believe you'd dabble in such things. I won't tolerate it. Certainly not in the name of pseudoscience. You're far too . . . you're . . ." Benton trailed off, helpless in his rage. His shoulders moved under his suit jacket, as if they could roll off his anger.

"You see." She smiled, turning to Professor Friend. "He's terribly upset."

"So I see, so I see," Friend remarked, brushing his fingers over his mustache in thought. "I must say, Miss Allston, he makes a point. I share his worry about the people you might encounter with such an experiment. But"—he turned his cool gaze on Benton—"I differ from Professor Derby in one important respect. I don't think your experiences aren't legitimate. Perhaps the answer lies in a change of venue, rather than method."

"Preposterous," Benton said, still by the bookshelf, hands clenched at his sides.

"Now, see here, Benton," Friend said, weary of Benton's outburst. "There's nothing wrong with opiates per se. So they've instituted a licensing scheme. Better to keep unscrupulous doctors from creating addicts just to bolster business. But Miss Allston isn't putting her health in danger, necessarily."

"It's true, Ben," she said. "Why, Papa takes laudanum almost every day, for his rheumatism. It's in the tonic we give him, which his doctor prescribed. He's taken it for years. It's all perfectly natural."

Benton prowled the narrow office like a caged panther, muttering. Sibyl glanced at the philosopher, who sat back in his desk chair, fingers still grooming his mustache, watching.

Finally, Benton stopped.

"All right," he said. "I can see there's only one way to convince you both that this is folly."

"What do you mean?" Sibyl asked, twisting in her seat to look up at him.

"We'll call on this Dee woman," Benton announced. "Then you'll see."

"Call on her!" Sibyl exclaimed, aghast.

"That's an excellent idea," Friend said, getting to his feet. "But we must go immediately. I leave for New York tomorrow."

"Immediately?" Sibyl repeated, eyes widening with panic.

"Immediately," Benton affirmed, and stepped forward with a hand to pull her to her feet.

EIGHTEEN

*A*n interminable span of time had passed since Benton rang the bell, and Sibyl drew herself behind his bulk, as if she could swallow herself up and disappear. They hadn't even phoned. Sibyl was appalled at herself for leading them to Mrs. Dee. The three of them, Sibyl, Benton, and Edwin, had piled into a taxicab in the trolley-heavy heart of Harvard Square, and Benton turned to her, saying only, "Go ahead. Give him the address."

And she did.

Sibyl knew that the medium would be angry with her, but in a secret corner of her heart Sibyl was excited. She thrilled at the idea of revealing Mrs. Dee's talents to the skeptical psychologist, thrilled at the prospect of Professor Friend's legitimizing their work, and was also anxious to unveil her own recent discoveries to the woman who had guided her.

Sibyl always felt as though she were a disappointment to Mrs. Dee. Not that Mrs. Dee ever said so, but Sibyl feared that she wasn't sufficiently committed to the work of their séance circle, and that her detachment indicated a failing of character. She worried that she was not a true enough person, a good enough daughter and sister, to be worth reaching. As though her soul were deficient.

Sibyl was so tired of disappointing people.

But the past few weeks had transformed Sibyl's feelings about herself. First, that tantalizing moment when her mother's manifested hand reached out for her, almost near enough to touch. Then, the deepening images revealed in the scrying glass. She could feel the contours of her world changing. For a long time Sibyl had felt imprisoned within herself, locked in a room she couldn't get out of. But now, for the first time since she was a girl, she felt alive to possibility. Loosed.

Almost . . . free.

"Well?" Benton said, turning to Sibyl. He wasn't going to let her hide behind him.

Sibyl squared her shoulders and said, "I suppose you could ring again."

"You're certain she's home, Miss Allston?" Professor Friend asked, peering up at the forbidding face of the town house.

"I've never known her not to be," Sibyl said. All three of them turned pale faces to the door, and Benton reached a hand up to grasp the knocker. It was brass, the shape of a spiny pineapple.

As Benton's hand hesitated, the door squeaked open to reveal the watchful stare of the butler. Disapproval glimmered across the man's face.

"Welcome," he intoned, a flicker of recognition in his eyes as he surveyed Sibyl's upturned face. "If you will follow me into the drawing room, please."

Sibyl muttered, "Thank you," in the butler's direction and allowed herself to be shown through the door, the two professors following close on her heels.

Sibyl watched Benton out of the corner of her eye as he surveyed the room with a curled lip of skepticism. Professor Friend wore a bemused smile as he circumnavigated the room, bending for a closer look first at a book, then at one of the sparkling, opened geodes on the fireplace mantel.

Benton brushed a fingertip along the carved back of the medium's Gothic armchair, lost in thought. Then he sauntered from the table to the cabinet at the far corner of the room. He stood, hands folded behind his back, gazing at it for a while. Sibyl thought she caught him steal a glance at her before turning his attention back to the cabinet, but she couldn't be certain.

"Ah!" Mrs. Dee announced from her position in the doorway, the butler looming behind her. "My dear! What a pleasant surprise. And you've brought some gentlemen with you, I see."

The small woman's eyes roved over first Benton, and then Professor Friend, with a gleam of interest overlying a deeper suspicion. She was in her ermine-lined tapestry dressing gown; in fact, she looked so similar to the way she appeared when Sibyl last called on her that the effect was disconcerting.

"Good evening, Mrs. Dee," Sibyl said. Her voice pierced the thick atmosphere of the room, sounding loud to her ears. She paused, unsure how to account for their sudden appearance in Beacon Hill, or how it would be received. "You know I would never wish to interrupt you—" she began.

The medium made a mild snorting noise of disapproval as she moved into the room.

"You know I always so enjoy your visits, Miss Allston. Though I prefer to be given a bit more warning if I will be entertaining guests." She settled her eyes on Professor Friend first, moving toward him with her small hand outstretched.

"I confess the responsibility lies with me, madam," Professor Friend said, his voice injected with a warmth that even Sibyl found reassuring. "You see, we were most anxious to speak with you, and as I'll be traveling abroad on an extended trip tomorrow, it necessitated our sudden appearance on your doorstep."

"If I may," Sibyl interjected, "this is Professor Edwin Friend, of the Harvard philosophy department."

"Ah! But not *only* the Harvard philosophy department, surely," Mrs. Dee said with a knowing smile.

"Indeed not, madam," Friend said, executing a courtly bow. "I have long been involved as well with . . ."

". . . the American Society for Psychical Research," Mrs. Dee finished for him. "Of course. Professor Friend. How good of you to come. To my home." She accepted the young professor's hand while also casting her eyes toward Sibyl, so that she would feel that the imposition wrought on the medium had not gone unnoticed.

"And . . . and this is Benton Derby. Professor of psychology," Sibyl added, gesturing in a helpless way toward Benton, who still loitered by the cabinet in the far corner of the room.

"Derby! Why, that's an old seafaring name, isn't it?" The medium smiled. "You are a voyager, then. I can see it in your very bearing."

Benton cleared his throat with mixed aggravation and discomfort, and managed to say, "You're very good to welcome us on such little notice. Miss Allston spoke so highly of you, my colleague and I were most anxious to start right away."

"Well!" Mrs. Dee exclaimed, moving to her customary chair, eyes downcast in false modesty. "Miss Allston is very kind. I only hope that I can be of help to you. Do join me."

While speaking she had settled at the head of the table, her hands folded in her tapestried lap. Sibyl dragged her hassock over, placing it in her usual spot, while Professor Friend seated himself in a side chair. Benton lingered for another moment, rubbing a thumb with close attention over a hinge in the cabinet, and then, nodding with satisfaction, strode to join them. He sat, leaning his chin in a cupped hand, leveling his pale gaze on the medium with a smile that struck Sibyl as almost smug.

"I must say, Mrs. Dee," Professor Friend began, "it's amazing to me that you've been able to escape the Society's notice."

She smiled, dimpling at the perceived compliment. "Well, I'm afraid I have a very exclusive circle, Professor Friend. The people who come into my home insist on my absolute discretion. And in return I expect the same from them. We've had no wish to draw attention to ourselves."

The medium settled a pointed look on Sibyl, who lowered her gaze to the surface of the table. The hassock was low, and the effect of this position was childlike, making Sibyl feel smaller than she was. She felt chastened by the medium's rebuke.

"Of course," Professor Friend agreed, nodding. "These matters always require tact and understanding. You must be of particularly keen sensitivity."

Mrs. Dee watched the professor with the faintest air of suspicion but softened as he spoke. Even gifted mediums, it seemed, were susceptible to flattery.

"Yes." She sniffed. "Well."

A moment of quiet settled on the table as Professor Friend beamed on the woman in the Gothic throne, and Mrs. Dee enjoyed his attention. Benton cleared his throat, edging Sibyl's foot under the table with a nudge of his toe. She gurgled at the suggesting pressure, and then brought herself to speak.

"I was telling them, before we arrived, how invaluable your friendship and guidance have been to me and my family since the sinking," Sibyl said. "The scrying glass, in particular, has— Well. You must know. I was—at first, that is . . ." In her enthusiasm Sibyl stumbled over her words.

The medium bestowed a proprietary smile on Sibyl and nodded. "You've been practicing." She made this announcement not as a guess, but as a statement of fact.

Sibyl shrugged and smiled her assent.

"And as you have practiced, you have had greater success," the medium said, also as though making a statement of fact that was already known to her.

Sibyl looked up, her dark eyes searching the medium's face for understanding. "Oh, Mrs. Dee," she breathed. "You can't believe what I've seen."

"And these worthy gentlemen," Mrs. Dee said, with a slow sweep of her hand to encompass the two men on either side of her table. "They expressed doubts, did they not?"

Benton let out a humorless laugh, chin propped on his hand, as Professor Friend hastened to say, "Oh, no indeed! We merely wished for more details."

"Oh?" Mrs. Dee said, arching an eyebrow.

"Confirmation," the professor clarified. "You see, the Association prides itself on using scientific principles to research the paranormal. We wished to consult with you on Miss Allston's experience. I think you will find us"—he glanced at Benton—"to be a very credulous audience."

"Ah," the small woman said, bringing her fingertips together in a tented shape before her mouth. "Why stop with consultation?"

Sibyl's eyes widened, and her eyelids started to flutter.

"Why indeed?" Benton said, watching Sibyl. "I was rather hoping we'd have a demonstration."

"Benton," Sibyl said out of the corner of her mouth.

"Well, why not?" he said. "What better place than here? She's the one who gave you the glass, isn't she? And taught you how to use it? In this very room?" He turned to Edwin Friend for support. "You can't object to having another talented medium to evaluate, Edwin. Why, this could be vital for your research. We'd be doing science a great disservice otherwise."

Sibyl's brows lowered, unable to tell if Benton was mocking her. She didn't appreciate his treating the situation so lightly. What did he know of loss? But as soon as the thought occurred to her, Sibyl flushed with shame.

Of course. Benton knew enough about loss. She glanced at his face, and when she did she found there a limpid look of desire and pain so palpable that she had to catch her breath.

"Why, that would be . . ." Professor Friend trailed off, stumbling over the look that was passing between Sibyl and Benton. He cleared his throat, and Sibyl cast her eyes back to the tabletop. "Yes. That would be remarkable. Yes. If Miss Allston were willing, of course."

"Well, I don't—" Sibyl stammered. "That is, I've had some successes, yes. But they were always in rather particular circumstances."

Benton, watching her closely, said without looking around, "I feel certain we can approximate the necessary circumstances."

Sibyl caught his gaze and shook her head, a fraction of an inch. He reached a hand across the table and took Sibyl's in his own.

"Miss Allston's been suffering a slight cough today. Nothing serious, but I'm sure she's concerned that it might be distracting. Mrs. Dee, surely you keep a cough remedy handy?"

The medium's eyebrows rose, and she gestured with a careless hand over her shoulder, bringing the butler to her. "Why, I had no idea she was feeling unwell. You do look rather pale, Miss Allston." She turned to the butler and said, "Bring some of those drops I keep in the medicine cabinet."

"Very good, madam," the butler said, tilting his head in acquiescence.

While they waited for him to return, Professor Friend leaned back in his chair, brushing thoughtful fingers over his mustache, as he was wont to do when considering a vexing question. "Now, Mrs. Dee," he said. "You are familiar with the work of the Seybert Commission, no doubt?"

"Professor Friend, is it? I can't say that I am. I'm sure you understand that my desire for privacy keeps me from willfully entering any sort of controversy."

"But of course. The Seybert Commission"—he leaned forward on his elbows—"was established some years ago at the University of Pennsylvania. It was one of the first university-based inquiries into Spiritualist phenomena. In that vein, I'm anxious to learn how you structure your mediumship. For instance, do you employ slate writing?"

"Oh! Indeed not," Mrs. Dee said, as though shocked by the very idea. "No, I find that those spirits who are kind enough to visit our gathering don't go in for parlor tricks."

Professor Friend nodded his approval.

"No, most of the time we are blessed with manifestations of a visual sort," Mrs. Dee continued. "Images, and voices. I'm sure Miss Allston has told you. Occasionally the table will lift itself clear of the ground. And at times, we will even have a strong physical manifestation, brought about by ectoplasmic condensation."

Sibyl thought she heard Benton muffle a snort under his handkerchief.

"The water," she whispered. She turned to Mrs. Dee. "That night. When we reached my mother. The table flooded with ice cold water." Sibyl crossed her arms with a shiver at the memory, cupping her elbows in her hands.

"So it did," the small woman said, her voice gentle and serene.

Sibyl felt Benton's eyes still on her, soft with concern.

"Fascinating," Professor Friend said. "So what structure shall we follow this evening?"

"Well," the medium said slowly. "I'm most concerned for Sibyl's well-being, of course. I should dearly like to observe her newfound talents for myself. I'm sure you gentlemen would as well."

At that moment the butler reappeared, carrying a teak tray with a stoppered glass bottle, a cut crystal sherry glass, and a silver teaspoon. He brought the tray around the table and set the implements one at a time in front of Sibyl.

She looked at Benton with confusion and whispered, "But I don't see how . . ."

"Trust me," he murmured in response.

Sibyl took up the bottle and saw that the label read PEEKMAN'S PRE-FERRED CHERRY COUGH ELIXIR. The label featured a drawing of a smiling young woman, with lidded eyes, surrounded by swirling locks of hair dotted with pink lotus flowers. It promised IMMEDIATE RELIEF OF COUGH, PAIN, RHEUMATISM, FATIGUE, NERVES, DROPSY, FEVER, AND SHINGLES, together with quotations from doctors attesting to its efficacy. She measured out four teaspoonfuls into the sherry glass.

The liquid was dark reddish brown, and smelled foul. Nothing at all like cherries. She lifted the glass, with another long look at Benton. He nodded in encouragement. She tilted her head back and swallowed the elixir, its harsh chemical taste causing her to gasp and cough.

"My goodness!" Mrs. Dee exclaimed. "But she *is* ailing. What good fortune we had some drops on hand."

"Indeed," Benton said, his attention still on Sibyl. She wiped the corner of her mouth with a handkerchief, clearing her throat of the sticky, bittersweet fluid. He watched her with a hand resting on the back of her chair. She squirmed under his attention, returning the cough syrup to the tray and nodding her thanks as the butler cleared it away.

"Now then," Mrs. Dee said, assuming control as Sibyl always knew her to do. "Do you have the scrying glass with you, my dear?"

Sibyl nodded, rummaging in the pocket of her skirt and pulling out the wooden box. "But I'm not certain that I'll be able— That is, I'm so unaccustomed to having an audience."

"There's nothing to worry about," Professor Friend assured her. "We're just a friendly group, aren't we? No need to feel embarrassed in the least. Isn't that right, Professor Derby?" Sibyl thought she heard in Professor Friend's voice a cautioning note to Benton.

"Quite right," Benton said, close to Sibyl's ear. She swallowed, watching him as he watched her.

Mrs. Dee motioned to the butler, and he moved around the room, extinguishing lights one after the other, until only a crystal oil lamp burned on a table in the far corner of the room.

"There now," Mrs. Dee said, her voice soothing and soft. "Let us begin."

SIBYL SAT, HER fingertips resting on the surface of the crystal ball, se-creted in its nest of black velvet. Her mind felt soft, and the muscles in her neck and arms had unwound perceptibly over the past several minutes. She was aware of Benton sitting next to her, of Professor Friend across the table, an indistinct form in the dim light of Mrs. Dee's drawing room, and of course of Mrs. Dee herself, presiding in solemn majesty at the head of her séance table. The nameless butler, after setting up the lighting in the room until it matched Mrs. Dee's precise instructions, had withdrawn, leav-ing them cloistered in the room, a stick of incense smoking on the fireplace mantel.

With each passing moment Sibyl felt more peculiar. She worked her tongue over the surface of her teeth, finding the feeling of her tongue in-side her mouth alien. Benton was right—she felt similar to the detach-ment she experienced while lying on the velvet couch in Dovie Whistler's secret club. Though the sensation wrapping around her now was more leaden. And she was sitting up, rather than lying down, which made the whole enterprise dizzier. She felt herself sway where she was sitting on the backless hassock, and a hand pressed to her lower back.

"Are you all right?" a voice murmured in her ear, close enough to stir the fine hairs at the base of her neck, yet echoing as though coming from a great distance away.

"Yes," she found herself saying. "I am perfectly fine. Thank you."

"Is she unwell?" another voice asked—Professor Friend, possibly. Who-ever it was seemed concerned.

"She's fine," the first voice replied—Benton, of course. Still the hand rested on the small of her back, steady and reassuring.

"Miss Allston," Mrs. Dee said. "The method that I usually use is—"

"Yes," Sibyl said, cutting the medium off without meaning to. "Yes, I know. But I just watch."

She exhaled softly, leveling her gaze on the polished blue surface of the crystal. It worked so quickly now, Sibyl hardly had to wait at all before the surface darkened, the ball filling with billows of black smoke, swirling back on themselves. Sibyl let her breath come easily, allowing the room around her to fall away.

Under her fingertips the smoke intensified, coalescing around a tiny pinpoint of light at the center of the ball. The pinpoint grew brighter, twinkling with increasing fire as it drew the smoke into itself.

"What's she seeing?" someone asked, but Sibyl was barely aware of it.

"Miss Allston?" someone else pressed her. "Can you tell us? What are you seeing?"

The voice reached Sibyl after what felt like several minutes, and though she perceived the sense of the question, it didn't seem to bear any relationship to her, didn't seem to have any meaning. She made no answer.

"Miss Allston?" the voice asked again, coming from even farther away.

The smoke had all cleared away by now, sucked down into the burning center of the light inside the ball. The pinpoint intensified, its glow spreading, and then it burst into a million tiny fragments, scattering into the perfect constellations of a cold night sky. Sibyl's lips parted, and she sighed with satisfaction. This was how it always went. Next, she would be able to see the water.

Sure enough, her point of view shifted within the ball under her fingertips, rotating from the sky overhead down to the surface of the water, skimming along the rippling surface of the ocean as if in flight. The water looked close enough to touch, as if she could reach through the membrane of the ball and dip her fingers into its star-spangled surface. Faster, speeding up, ducking and weaving like a tern chasing a school of fish, the image zoomed close alongside a giant ocean liner, brushing along the white foam break rolling off the prow of the ship. Sibyl caught her breath, excited. With each experiment she had been able to glimpse just a tiny bit more.

"I'm not at all convinced," someone whispered, and at the same time someone else wished aloud that she would comment, or explain something of what she was doing, to offer a narration perhaps, but the whisper had nothing whatever to do with her, and so she ignored it.

Instead, she watched, fingers still lightly pressed to the scrying glass, as the image lingered over the ship's prow, chasing after it as the prow thrust itself forward through the night. Then, with deliberation, the point of view within the glass pulled away from the waterline, tracing along the side of the ocean liner, traveling up and over a polished railing and moving onto the open bow.

Now, for the first time, Sibyl saw faces, and she let out a gasp of surprise and delight. She didn't know how much longer she had before the smoke would swirl closed again; usually the image only held together for a few minutes at most, and then it would sink below the black cloud and disappear. She narrowed her eyes, peering closer.

The point of view within the orb floated along, drifting past one laughing, smiling face after another. They were dressed for the evening, these unfamiliar people, the women wrapped in gossamer robes lined with fur against the North Atlantic chill, the men in white ties and long tailcoats. A young couple rose into view, the boy with his hair slicked back as he leaned in to whisper a joke to a young woman with a flower affixed over her ear. Sibyl looked closely, thinking that the laughing girl with the sparkling eyes might be Eulah. But no, this girl had black hair, in tight curls. Whoever she was, she looked happy. The unknown girl tilted her head back for a swallow of champagne, and the point of view within the orb swerved away, searching through the crowd.

Through the muffling haze enveloping her body Sibyl felt her heartbeat quicken, heard the *lug lug, lug lug* of the blood moving through her veins. Inside the scrying glass, her vision drifted through a cluster of couples dancing, well-fed men with cheeks the color of roast beef, sturdy matrons draped in old-fashioned jet beads. She recognized no one. Where could her mother and Eulah be? She remembered her mother's telegram, that they weren't at the captain's table, but she couldn't recall any details about where they would be sitting. Then she remembered—with the Wideners. But Sibyl didn't know Harry and his parents. Sibyl frowned, peering into the glass, hunting for what she imagined a bibliophile might look like. Young men in spectacles, moving past people's shoulders, gleaming candlelight on glassware . . .

Then Sibyl gasped, biting down on her lower lip in alarm. The image in the glass jolted, everyone in the dining room stumbling at once, falling into tables, men grasping at women's elbows, people's mouths opening in screams. But she still hadn't . . .

"Dear me," someone whispered, voice muffled as though from miles away. "Is she all right? Miss Allston?"

But no, she wouldn't be distracted, she wouldn't be pulled back, not when she was on the point of finding them. Now the ship lurched again, and the crowd in the dining room shifted in character. No longer was it a staid and plush gathering of individual people, cultured and urbane, enjoying their voyage between Europe and New York. Instead, the dining room transformed into a panicked mass of black and white dotted in shocking colors, moving as one to run away from something.

Sibyl couldn't see what was going on. Her breath came faster, and she leaned in closer, bringing her nose almost to touch the stone's surface, hunting through the surging crowd, desperate for a familiar face. Eulah would have been dancing, surely. Would she have been happy?

The point of view inside the glass moved, but not entirely in response to Sibyl's will. One of her fingers twitched with tension as she observed the ripples of panic shooting through the crowd in the dining room, here a uniformed man attempting to issue instructions, ignored by the onrushing crowd. Chairs turned over, a man threw aside a table, sending glassware exploding in all directions. Sibyl held her breath as inside the glass the dining room began to list.

Then the point of view inside the glass floated up to the face of a person standing motionless in the center of the crowd. A person who Sibyl recognized.

Her mouth fell open, gaping in shock and incomprehension.

In her ear, the insistent whisper came again, worming into her conscious awareness. "What is it, Sibyl?" Benton's whisper asked. "What do you think you see?"

A scream rang out.

Sibyl, blinking, was shaken awake with a shock. She looked around, confused, unclear where she was, or what had been happening. Where had the scream come from?

"Oh!" the cry came again, and Sibyl turned to Mrs. Dee, her outline just visible in the dimness, sitting at the head of the table. The medium's eyes were fixed in a horrified stare at the scrying glass, her mouth open, chin trembling with apparent emotion. "Oh, the horror! My poor Helen! How she suffers! And the water is so cold!"

Sibyl moved her eyes back to the crystal ball, warm from the pressure of her fingertips on its surface. The image had vanished, the crowd, the boat, the water, the starlight, even the coils of black smoke, all of it gone.

The orb lay in its velvet depression, an inert ball of rock. Sibyl glanced at Mrs. Dee under her eyelashes.

"See how it rises!" the medium cried, her head lolling against the high back of her Gothic armchair. Her eyes rolled back in her head, revealing their lower whites, and a deep, altered moan started to pour forth from her mouth.

As the moan deepened, keening and otherworldly, both Benton and Professor Friend, whom Sibyl could barely discern through the gloomy half-light, leaned forward, alternately baffled and enthralled. Sibyl kept her hands resting on the table, the scrying glass in its box held between them. Then, under her palms, the table shifted.

"What the—" Benton said aloud.

It shifted again, scraping against the floor.

"Remarkable," breathed Professor Friend, his hands also resting on the table. Sibyl had trouble making out his face, but his voice sounded both pleased and surprised.

Still the medium moaned, the sound emptying out of the woman's body and filling the room. The table jolted, rattled with a thumping vibration, and then, it slowly, surely, began to rise.

Sibyl felt the table pressing her hands upward, and she let it happen, didn't resist the pressure as it floated, her mind still occluded with the residual haze of her altered state. Next to her, she heard Benton inhale sharply and caught a glimmer of movement out of the corner of her eye, which she thought must be Benton's yanking his hands away from the table's surface. She heard Professor Friend let out an appreciative sigh of wonder.

At last the moan drew to a close, petering away to a hoarse whisper, and then the medium took another deep breath, which she let out in a piercing wail. The table floated, about six inches higher than when they began, vibrating, otherwise motionless, hanging in midair.

Sibyl trembled, her hands twitching with tension. Then she gasped, her stomach contracting in horror. Out of nowhere the tabletop overran with a sheen of ice cold water, which crept under Sibyl's wrists and soaked her dress to the elbows. She gurgled a scream of misery and dismay, and heard Professor Friend cry out, "Good God in heaven!"

Then, without warning, the room flooded with artificial light, and the table fell to the floor with a thud. Rivulets of water dripped from the edge of the table, leaving wet plops on the floor.

Mrs. Dee's wail stopped as surely as if someone had stuffed a cork in her mouth. Sibyl squinted, the light glaring in her eyes, which had grown accustomed to the darkness.

"Professor Derby!" bellowed Edwin Friend. "What in God's name do you think you're doing?"

Sibyl spun in her seat to find Benton standing by the electric light buttons on the wall. His hand rested on the switch, and his face bore a satisfied smile.

"Throwing a little light on things," he said.

NINETEEN

Mrs. Dee's face contorted in rage, blotching crimson from her neck to her cheeks, her wattles trembling, little hands knotted into fists on the tabletop.

"How dare you!" she cried. "Who do you think you are, young man? Have you any idea how dangerous it is, what you've just done?"

"Dangerous for whom, madam?" Benton asked, walking at a leisurely pace back to the table.

"Why, dangerous for all of us! For Miss Allston, who is in a most delicate psychological condition. And nearly fatal for me."

"I should say it *is* nearly fatal for you," Benton agreed. "Look here, Edwin."

Benton took hold of the edge of the table and hoisted it up. It resisted at first, then rose with a mechanical creak, stopping at a sharp angle. Benton let go, and the table stayed tilted. Confused, Sibyl bent to look under the table and saw Benton tap the end of the table leg with the toe of his shoe.

"Ingenious," he said. "It's on mechanical leg extenders. Mounted from beneath the floor. And controlled, I expect . . ." His voice trailed off as he moved to the head of the table, where Mrs. Dee sat, apoplectic with rage.

"Ah, yes. Pardon me," he said to the woman. Her mouth was pinched, but she made no move to stop him. Benton leaned over her and reached under the table. He adjusted some kind of dial, and the table lowered itself again. A very faint whirring could distinctly be heard, of gears gnashing together. Faint enough to be obscured by a loud moan, or a wail.

"But—" Sibyl started to protest.

"That's not all," Benton said. Still leaning over the medium's chair, he fiddled with another control, and a hole opened in the center of the table, another faint chugging, whirring sound could be heard, and then the opening emitted a thin spreading puddle of water from somewhere underneath.

"A pump?" he asked. The medium said nothing.

"I thought so," Benton said. He straightened, sliding his hands into his pockets. "Now, Mrs. Dee. Is there any need for me to open the cabinet in the corner?"

The medium stared at him, her eyes livid with hate.

Professor Friend's attitude, Sibyl noticed, had traveled in the past several minutes from surprise, to dismay, to mild amusement. He leaned back in his chair, arms folded.

"Well, well," the philosopher said. "I, for one, would love to have a look in the cabinet, Professor Derby. I can hardly see how the lady is in a position to object."

Mrs. Dee said nothing, her hands gripping tighter at the armrests of her chair. Through the lingering confusion left over from the séance, Sibyl absorbed the full force of what Benton was suggesting. Her gaze traveled to Mrs. Dee, coming to rest on the familiar face, the face that had offered her solace.

A face that had lied to her.

And taken her money while doing it.

A storm cloud gathered in Sibyl's chest, and the corners of her mouth pulled into a frown.

Benton strode to the cabinet and opened it. Inside were shelves with tidy stacks of folded table linens, napkins, tea towels. It was in every respect a standard and uninteresting linen cupboard.

"I fail to see," Mrs. Dee hissed through clenched teeth, "what interest you could possibly have with my table linens."

"Ah," Benton said, holding up a finger. He turned back to the cabinet, ran his hand alongside the outside of the door hinge, and tripped a concealed catch. He reached inside the cabinet, threaded his finger through a small opening in the wall behind the napkins, and pulled. Sibyl heard a distinct click, and the inner portion of the cabinet swung open. The shelves masked a false back, and behind the inner doors formed by the false shelves were none other than a small Victrola, a long speaking tube, a strangely altered violin, a tambourine, and a bin containing a grayish heap of what appeared to be gauze soaked in some unidentifiable liquid.

"There's your ectoplasm," Benton said, grimacing at the pungent smell. "Ugh. What *is* that?"

Professor Friend laughed, clapping his hands together with appreciation. "I say, you *are* clever, finding the catch for that cabinet. I suppose that's where music emanates from as well?"

"But—I don't—" Sibyl said. No one else in the room paid her any attention.

"More interesting than the cabinet, even," Benton theorized, "is what I suspect we'd find concealed in her chair. Madam? I don't suppose you would be so kind as to stand up?"

"All right!" the woman spat, getting to her feet, her hands planted on the table. "There's no need to look. If you must know, the chair has a compartment under the seat. In that compartment you'll find a few wigs, some stage makeup, and a wax hand. Are you quite satisfied now?"

The door to the drawing room flung open as the butler, hearing the commotion inside, rushed to the aid of his mistress. When he saw the cabinet standing open, its secret contents revealed with all the horror of a gutted cadaver, he stopped short, aghast.

"Madam!" he exclaimed. "But what can have happened?"

"It's likely," Benton continued to Professor Friend as though the two of them were carrying on a conversation in his office, paying no mind to the other individuals within hearing distance, "that the butler is her confederate. She'd need someone who could come in under cover of darkness and operate the mechanism to play the music, or the voice recordings, on cue. And possibly to smuggle her the box of gauze before the manifestation portion of the evening."

"But how could he bring it to her unobserved?" Professor Friend wondered, also speaking only to Benton. "They'd have a whole roomful of people, and some of them would be bound to sit facing the cabinet."

"Why, along the floor, I should think," Benton said. "Look at him. He's spryer than he looks. Could just shimmy along there, on his stomach, easy as you please."

The butler's face flushed bright crimson. He said nothing.

"Aha. You see? That's what I thought," Benton said, smiling.

"I'll thank you," Mrs. Dee said with hauteur, ignoring the butler and addressing herself to the two professors, "to leave my home at once."

Benton moved to stand behind Sibyl, who sat beetle-browed, her mind warring over what had just been revealed. He rested his hands, lightly, on her shoulders.

"I should think," he said, "that you owe this young woman an apology. And possibly, a great deal of money."

Mrs. Dee stood at the head of her table, drawing herself up to her fullest, albeit unimpressive, height. "I do no such thing," she said. The butler moved to stand behind her.

"The hand," Sibyl said, blinking. "My mother's hand. It was . . . ?"

Mrs. Dee looked on her with a new, closed hardness in her eyes.

"And the voices? All those voices, of people's husbands? People's children?" Sibyl searched the medium's face, as if she might find a logical explanation there. A logical explanation, that is, other than the obvious one.

"You charge a fee for your services, don't you?" Benton said.

"I do not," Mrs. Dee replied, her voice brittle as a cracked crystal glass.

"Yes, you do!" Sibyl burst, shaken out of her numb denial, awakening to the anger boiling in her chest. "You most certainly do!"

"My dear," the woman said. "You've had a terrible shock today. I feel dreadful that you've been put in such a delicate position by these thoughtless acquaintances of yours. But on that count, you are mistaken."

"I'm not mistaken." Sibyl rose to her feet, buoyed up by her disillusionment. She turned to Benton. "Every time! Every time I've come here, they all leave money for her. In the card tray on the hall stand. No one's let out of the house without leaving something. Some people leave quite a lot. You should see the bills. Hundreds of dollars. Every time."

"Nonsense," the woman said smoothly. "If the people who visit me feel moved by their experience to make some sort of donation, why, that's their own affair. It has nothing whatsoever to do with me. And at no time have I ever suggested such a thing. To think, me, talking openly of money."

"The time I was here, and you gave me the scrying glass," Sibyl exclaimed, pointing at the butler. "He wouldn't let me leave. I had to pay."

"A misunderstanding," Mrs. Dee said. The butler didn't speak, instead staring with leaden eyes at the assembly from his position behind the medium's chair.

"I—" Sibyl's voice caught in her throat, her anger subsiding into disappointment and shame. "I believed you." She turned her face away, hiding it behind her hand, trembling.

Professor Friend got to his feet, brushing his hands along his coat sleeves in a gesture of finality. "Miss Allston," he said. "You aren't the only one. It's nothing to be ashamed of. If anyone should be feeling shame in this room, it certainly isn't you. It's to combat the reckless and coldhearted manipulations of charlatans"—he paused, to ensure that all hearers knew to whom he was referring—"that the Society conducts the investigatory work that it does. She was preying upon your better nature, upon your love of family, and on your sense of loss. She's no better than a vulture." He turned to look at Mrs. Dee, an expression of rancid disapproval settling on his otherwise friendly features. "Truly, the expression of a baser instinct I've rarely had the displeasure to see. I've a good mind to notify the authorities. Though if the fees were never explicitly stated, I'm afraid we have very little legal recourse."

"Oh, nothing is ever explicit, is it!" Sibyl spat. She slapped closed the box containing the scrying glass and thrust it into her pocket. "That's all anyone ever does, is imply. I can't believe what a fool I was."

"But don't you see?" Mrs. Dee said quietly. "That none of it makes a particle of difference?"

"What?" Sibyl said, anger burning in her pale cheeks. "How can you possibly say that?"

Benton reached a steady hand to take Sibyl's elbow, and he made a soothing noise through his lips, an effort, perhaps unconscious on his part, to calm her rising temper.

"Consider, my dear," Mrs. Dee said, hard and unapologetic, fingertips resting on the tabletop. "That we all have different ways of understanding what is authentic, and what isn't."

"That's a fine person, to talk of authenticity," Benton growled. He exerted gentle pressure on Sibyl's elbow, to begin steering her to the door. She hung back, baffled as to what the little woman could be driving at.

"What do you mean?" Sibyl demanded.

"What were you looking for, when you came here?" she asked, watching Sibyl.

"I was . . ." Sibyl started to say, but trailed off.

What had she been looking for? Reassurance that her mother and sister were well. And perhaps she was looking for absolution. Sibyl's grief and sorrow weighed on her with leaden pressure, deepened and soured by her all-encompassing guilt. Guilt for not being with them when the ship went down. Guilt for resenting their voyaging without her, and guilt for being secretly relieved that she yet lived. Perhaps she came seeking permission. Perhaps she came to the séance seeking permission to live.

Sibyl glanced back at the medium's face and saw that she knew what Sibyl had been looking for, and did not judge her. Mrs. Dee's face softened, a half-smile bending her puckered mouth.

"Were you looking for a *true* experience?" Mrs. Dee asked. "Or were you looking to have your grief soothed? Which is more important, do you think?"

She paused, to let her point sink in, not only for Sibyl but for the professors as well. Benton and Edwin Friend exchanged a pointed look.

Mrs. Dee continued, without agitation or defensiveness. "I offer succor to suffering people, that's all. When you come down to it, what difference does it make, the methods that I use? What matters, in the end, is that the succor you found in this drawing room was real."

The woman stepped from behind the trick séance table and moved toward Sibyl. She stiffened as Mrs. Dee approached, a carapace of anger and bitterness settling over her. Sibyl resented the physical proximity of someone who had abused her trust. Yet she wondered if the medium had a point. If she found what she was looking for, did it really matter if it was found under false pretenses? Sibyl frowned, uncertain, hating feeling tricked. Her gullibility was the most horrifying realization of all.

The tiny woman edged nearer, taking Sibyl's hands in hers. Mrs. Dee's hands felt fragile and small, warm, reassuring even, and Sibyl felt for the last time a twinge of the deep relief that she had grown accustomed to finding in Mrs. Dee's company. In a sense this revelation of Mrs. Dee's duplicity, this drawing back of the complex curtain of dissembling that Sibyl now knew had cloaked her awareness every time she entered the Beacon Hill house, felt like yet another loss. In the glaring light of truth revealing the technology of deceit, this realm of safety, of anonymity and reassurance, was closed to her. She would never be able to fool herself so thoroughly again.

The woman turned her round face up to Sibyl, her gaze boring deep into Sibyl's eyes. "You must understand," she said, almost in a whisper. "I didn't mean to hurt you. I do hear spirits, you know, I always have. I could see the smoke, but I could never see through it. They speak so quietly, sometimes. You mustn't think, just because I've added a few bells and whistles to heighten the effect, that your experiences with me have no meaning."

Sibyl swallowed, her brows drawn in a furrow over her nose, unsure what she was supposed to say in the face of this nonapology. The medium rose on tiptoe, reaching her lips for Sibyl's ear. Obediently, Sibyl dipped her head to capture the last words that Mrs. Dee would ever say to her.

"I know that you can see, too," the woman said, her whisper so faint that it seemed to occur inside Sibyl's head. "Don't let anyone else tell you what's true, when you *know*."

Sibyl drew her head back, looking down at the false medium in shock. Her mouth twisted as she wondered how to respond. Mrs. Dee held her gaze for an instant longer, nodded once, as if to say, *You know that what I say is true*, and then stepped back, releasing her hold on Sibyl's hands.

Sibyl's confused reverie was abruptly broken by the voice of Professor Friend, who announced, "Well, I think we've seen all that there is to see here, haven't we? Come along, Miss Allston. It's getting late. I'm sure you're wanted at home, and I have an early start tomorrow."

"Yes," Benton said, still holding her elbow with a delicate grip. "Sibyl, let's go."

The two men moved to the drawing room door, Sibyl allowing herself to be led away, stumbling on feet made uncertain by the combined effects of cough syrup and her odd trance during the séance. Mrs. Dee watched her go, the butler looming behind her, sepulchral and silent.

"Madam," Professor Friend said, "it's been a most enlightening afternoon. I thank you for your hospitality."

Mrs. Dee did not respond, only flaring her nostrils in annoyance. Benton glared at her, not bothering to conceal his malice as he wrapped a protective arm around Sibyl's shoulders.

Sibyl climbed into her coat and hat, feeling strangely detached, as though the afternoon had happened to someone else. As the two men flagged down a taxicab and bundled her out the medium's front door for the last time, Sibyl looked over her shoulder into the drawing room. The butler was sliding the inner door closed, and Sibyl caught sight of the little woman, whose first name, Sibyl realized, she did not even know, disappearing by slow degrees behind the rolling pocket door. Just before the medium vanished from view, she caught Sibyl's eye, and mouthed *I know you see*.

And then she was gone.

IN THE TAXI bumping alongside the Common in the gathering darkness, Benton and Edwin chatted between themselves, digesting the turn of events. Sibyl gazed out the window, listless and perturbed.

"There you have it," Benton was saying. "They're all just cunning manipulators. It's fascinating, in a perverse way. The psychology of her. I don't deny she had tremendous personal magnetism, but you know, there are personality disorders that'd account for it. I grant you she probably *believed* she could communicate with spirits. But, Ed, that doesn't mean Spiritualism is legitimate. You should know. After all, you've debunked more than anyone, I'd wager."

Sibyl pressed her fingertips to the cab window, her breath fogging the glass. Outside, beds of tulips rolled past, their pale flower heads wet and glistening, receding into the shadows of the park.

The philosophy professor let out a hearty laugh and said, "I do believe Houdini has debunked more. Strange work, that a stage magician would align himself with academic science. But you must admit, Benton, that people's very willingness to believe in her speaks to the profound, nearly universal desire to commune with the spirit realm. Isn't that desire itself evidence that the spirit realm exists? The idea of the soul is an abiding belief, across cultures, across history. The callousness of a few manipulative people can't make the entire enterprise unworthy of study."

Sibyl let out an audible sigh, without meaning to, and both men paused, noticing. Benton let his hand drift to her knee and leaned his mouth close to her ear.

"There now," he said. "There's nothing to worry about."

"Why?" she said, voice fragile and small.

"Why what?" he murmured.

Observing their confidential discussion, Professor Friend pretended to be absorbed in the staid house fronts of Beacon Street passing outside as the taxicab rolled its stately progress down the hill and into the Back Bay.

Sibyl swiveled her eyes to Benton's face, dark and pleading. "Why would you want to do that, Benton? I feel so—"

The lines around his eyes contracted with concern. "Me? But, I just—" he started, then stopped. He took a breath, and then tried again.

"Because. I thought— You're so very—" he started, then stopped again. Still she gazed at him, searching his pale gray eyes for comprehension of why he would want to pull away this bit of solace. He squirmed, dropping his eyes to his lap, threading the fingers of his hand together with hers.

"I want so badly for you to be happy," he confessed, having some difficulty assembling the words. "Truly happy, I mean. I couldn't stand the thought that some charlatan would—"

She waited, wondering what he was going to say next. She let her thumb explore, almost by accident, the skin of his knuckle, with its few tiny dark hairs. Something about those few dark hairs compelled Sibyl, though she was at a loss to explain what that might be.

Finally, he spoke again. "I thought this interest of yours might be standing in the way, that's all." He cleared his throat, forcing himself to say what he was thinking. "Of your moving on. It's natural to mourn their loss. Of course it is. But you're still alive, Sibyl. There's so much of life waiting for you." He brought his eyes up to her face again, and she felt his stare enter into her.

"But, Ben," she whispered, dreading what she was about to say, or rather, dreading that the accepting look on his face would fall away when she said it.

"What is it?" he asked, tightening his grip.

"I . . ." she began, then paused, biting her lip. "I wish I could explain. But you must know. I *did* see something in the glass. In fact, each time I try it, I see more."

He frowned, worried. "The power of suggestion is very strong, Sibyl. You mustn't feel strange about that. Anyone would have thought they saw things, who had sufficient desire to do so."

"No," she said, shaking her head. "You don't understand. What I saw—"

"What was it?" he asked, his tone unexpectedly gentle, willing to listen.

"I saw the night sky over the Atlantic, and I saw the prow of the boat, which I've been seeing for a few weeks now. But this time, it was different. This time, I was finally able to see people."

"People? What people?" he asked.

"They were all in a very fine dining room, the first-class dining room, and there was dancing. And then all at once everything shook, and everyone started to panic. There was running every which way, and then the boat started to list. Oh, Ben." Her voice caught, horrified by the memory. "It was horrible." She brought her hands to her face with a shudder.

Benton spoke slowly, drawing his words out. "Did you see them?"

Sibyl swayed with the motion of the taxicab, her face buried in her hands. Professor Friend cleared his throat, possibly to remind them that he was still within hearing distance. Sibyl dropped her hands halfway, peeking at Benton from above her fingertips.

"Not them," she whispered, eyes reddening.

"Who?" he whispered. "Who did you see?"

Sibyl swallowed, then dropped her voice until it was little more than an exhaled breath.

"Him," she whispered, pointing at Professor Friend as he gazed, lost in his own thoughts, out the taxicab window.

Interlude

Old City

June 8, 1868

ONCE, THE SUMMER before he shipped out on the *Morpheo*, at an after-noon musicale at the home of Eunice Proctor, two blocks down Chestnut Street from the Allston home in Salem, Lannie encountered a zoetrope.

"How's it work?" he inquired of his young hostess. Of Eunice Proctor that particular afternoon all Lannie could remember were two dainty cross-stitched bloomer cuffs extending below a full plaid taffeta skirt, as his gaze hadn't so far been able to stray farther north than the giant bow at her waist. He spent most of the musicale addressing himself to her shoes.

"It's simple," she said. "You take a strip of this paper, here." She held out a long coil printed with successive images of a horse in midrun, each silhouette depicting the horse's legs in a slightly different position. "And then you put it in the barrel, here."

She leaned forward, adjusting the mechanism with purpose. It was in that moment that Lannie had made it as far as the bow.

"And then you look through the slats," she urged. He leaned forward, bringing his nose near to the barrel. Out of the corner of his eye he grew aware that Eunice was also leaning forward. He might have just spotted a glossy corkscrew of hair, tantalizing in its nearness, but he daren't look.

"And then you spin it!" she said. The barrel burst into motion, and Lannie caught his breath. Flashing through the barrel slats, the horse broke into a run before his eyes.

"Why, look at that! It's moving!"

The girl tittered, enjoying showing off her sophisticated parlor entertainments. It spun and spun, the horse galloping in a circle to nowhere, gradually slowing along with the dwindling rotation of the barrel, devolving into flat flickers which, finally, resolved to stillness.

"Want to see another one?" she asked.

"You bet I do!"

Scene after scene was fitted into the barrel, and in each instance the illusion took Lannie's breath away. A lion, leaping over a ball. An elephant walking with an acrobat on its back. A long-tailed blue parrot bursting into flight. He quickly forgot Eunice Proctor's bloomer cuffs in his astonishment at discovering movement in images that had, moments before, been devoid of life.

This long ago afternoon, in a Salem parlor half a world away, lurked now in the back of Lannie's mind as he lay in the Shanghai house of smoke and flowers.

Just as he had stared through the slats of the zoetrope, now his full attention focused on the strange scenes forming within the light on the motes of tea at the bottom of his cup. He stared, entranced, pulled in by the illusion.

"Like a zoetrope in my hand," he whispered.

He saw water, mostly. At first. Not water in the teacup, not tea, but *water*—the ocean. Whitecaps, ripples, and swells. As though he were there in person, staring at the surface of the sea while riding to shore on the cutter. He had never, outside Eunice Proctor's well-appointed drawing room, experienced a moving image reproduced, and he couldn't tear his eyes away. The perspective within the teacup changed, as though he were skimming along the water like a seagull, and he came upon a clipper, the *Morpheo*, he thought, slicing its way through a canal.

"The ship," Lannie whispered.

The image shimmered and transformed into another ship, similar to *Morpheo* but larger. A steam-sail hybrid, and his perspective zoomed over the deck until it hovered by a man of about thirty bent over a navigation table. With a chilled gasp Lannie saw that this man was *himself*, with long muttonchop whiskers, and that he was giving instructions to a younger man standing next to him.

"Steam?" he whispered. He knew of steamships, but had yet to work one. He spoke the word aloud, and the scene melted apart, unveiling a ship that boggled Lannie's mind. Impossibly large, massive, more like a European hotel laid on its side than any oceangoing vessel. The behemoth had no sails, pushing itself forward through a starlit night, muscling aside the ocean as it went, with four striped smokestacks belching coal smoke. A craggy shape floated in the distance.

"But, what? How does it—?" Lannie sputtered. Was it another command? When he was even older? Was it all just a phantasm of his twisted imagination?

"You're muttering," the young man overhead commented. Lannie didn't hear him.

Inside the tea glass, the sea boiled away to reveal a college campus in the full flush of autumn. Blurred faces passed by, young men his age, none of them familiar. And then he saw himself.

His cheeks were fuller, tanned still, his hair less moppish, and his mustache had finally come in. This grown Lannie was not doing anything in particular, just striding along past Massachusetts Hall, shuffling his feet through chestnut leaves, hands in his pockets, lost in his thoughts.

Lannie imagined he could hear *bonging*, the university clock tower perhaps, and then the college campus dissolved, its buildings melting like spun sugar in boiling water. Out of the swirling tea fragments resolved the form of a fine house, rising from an empty riverside vacant lot within scaffolding, brick by brick, in a time-lapse succession.

"My!" he exclaimed.

As he watched, a man, himself he guessed, only older, in a dark waistcoat, his whiskers touched with dignified gray, ushered a very young, very beautiful woman on his arm up the stairs.

"Having pipe dreams, are you? They can be awfully nice, sometimes." The scholar's voice wedged itself into his ear. Lannie pushed it away.

He wanted more. He wanted to see inside the house. He watched himself fumbling with keys at the front door, the beautiful woman tossing her head back and laughing, waving her hands with excitement while she explained something. His older self smiled and nodded, but there was something behind the smile that looked a little sad.

"I don't see what you want a clock for, anyway." The voice intruded again.

What was he wanting to talk so much for? Lannie wished he could be left alone with his teacup. He was entranced. Pipe dreams, maybe, but everything he saw fit the plan he had hatched, with his father's guidance, in the months leading up to the ship's departure for the Far East. He'd finish out his time on *Morpheo*, make some money. He would arrive home older, wiser. Then he'd be ready for college down in Cambridge. After Harvard he'd get his own merchant command. With this new command he'd make his fortune. He'd make his name.

And someday, he'd meet that exquisite girl. Who was that girl?

Absorbed in his plans, Lannie grumbled an incoherent nonresponse to Johnny. He wanted to see more. He wanted to see all that the sea would make of his life.

"A clock can't actually tell you anything about time," the scholar mused, oblivious.

"I luh?" Lannie said, irritated. The image in the teacup grew difficult to discern. He needed to concentrate, or it didn't work. Whatever "it" was. He wished the young man would stop distracting him.

"It's useless to know what time it is *now*," Johnny insisted. His bowl's worth of opium must have worn off, making him chattier. "Knowledge of the past makes a man wise. Knowledge of the future, well"—he laughed— "that could make a man rich. But neither will make him happy."

"You don't think being wise and rich is the same as being happy?" Lannie asked, still with one eye in his teacup. Johnny wasn't making any sense.

"Yankee with the fake Chinese name," the scholar said, peering over the edge of the bunk and looking into Lannie's face. "Only by being present can you be happy. Too much attention to the past and the future takes the *now* away. And once it's gone, you never get it back."

Lannie laughed, shaking his head. "You're crazy, you know that?" he suggested.

The scholar's face withdrew back to the top bunk. "Maybe," he muttered. "Maybe not."

Lannie pulled his chronometer from its hiding place and gazed on it, as if consulting the timepiece would prove his acquaintance wrong. But something was off. He screwed his eyes tighter. Lannie had trouble telling what time the chronometer read. God knew what poisons were in his blood, souring his humors and fogging his brain. Try as he might, he couldn't derive any sense from the chronometer face. With a sigh of irritation he secreted the instrument back in the safety of his armpit. If he nodded off he had no wish to be relieved of it before he even had the chance to use it at sea.

He ruminated, swirling the liquid in his cup, watching the patterns shift with the motion of the tea. "Johnny?" Lannie said without tearing his eyes away.

"Mmmmmm?"

As he'd said his companion's name, the scene in the leaves shifted, focusing. He saw Johnny, in the same clothes that he was wearing now, in the thin light of early dawn. An argument. A crowd had gathered. Someone stepped forward and shoved him in the chest. The group cheered, like the braying audience at a bare-knuckle boxing match. Johnny shoved back, and the crowd clustered nearer, egging them on.

Then the other man had his hands around Johnny's throat. The hands tightened, and Johnny's face started to turn cherry red. His fingers clawed at the other man's hands, and his feet beat against the ground.

"Oh, my God!" Lannie exclaimed.

"You shouldn't swear, Yankee," Johnny muttered from the bunk overhead. "Unchristian barbarian."

"Oh, stop it!" he cried, forgetting himself, speaking to the figures that he saw in the glass.

At the moment that the words escaped his mouth, the scene shifted. Someone broke through the crowd around the two men, who were locked together, grappling, each man pushing the other's face away with a clutching hand, teeth bared in animal strain.

Johnny's tongue protruded in a grotesque perversion of a mask from Greek tragedy, his limbs slackening. Then the third figure was upon them, there was a flash of something bright and a splash of red, a spreading blotch on the larger man's shirt, and the hands around Johnny's neck loosened. Freed, Johnny doubled over, collapsing on the ground, coughing and clawing for air.

Through the zoetrope of Lannie's teacup, the larger figure fell to his knees, his hands wrapped around his middle, surprised. With each slosh of the teacup the man's face changed, as though viewed through a prism. The third man stood over him, and Lannie could see that the third man was breathing heavily, his head down, his hands at his sides. Both of the third man's hands were stained red, and at his side, held loose, was a short knife dripping blood.

"Johnny," Lannie started to say, baffled. The scene was like a version of what had happened in the whorehouse, but the time was clearly different, and the outcome was as well. He didn't understand. Was he just now feeling the fear from the earlier fight, when Tom had beaten a tooth out of his jaw?

"Don't spend too long in the pipe dream," the scholar admonished. "You might never make it back."

But Lannie didn't say anything. Deep within the shifting forms of tea, in the strange dreamworld the drug had woven in his mind's eye, the third man, the one holding the dripping knife at his side, had lifted his other arm to wipe the sweat from his forehead, and turned at a different angle, so that Lannie could clearly see his face.

"Oh, my God," Lannie whispered. "It's me."

TWENTY

The Back Bay
Boston, Massachusetts
April 30, 1915

"Shhh! She'll be back anytime," Dovie whispered, disentangling herself from Harlan's grasp and rolling out of his reach. Harlan grinned, making a show of grasping at the air where she had lately been.

"No, she won't," he insisted. "Come on. Just another minute."

"She will," Dovie said, with a lowered eyebrow at him. She turned her back and faced his highboy mirror, bunching her fingers in her hair to fluff it back into place. "I expected her an hour ago. It's a wonder she hasn't gotten home already."

Harlan propped himself on an elbow and looked at Dovie, enjoying the quick movements of her slim arms as she rubbed a fingertip over her lips to redden them. The rumples in the shell-colored slip hanging from her shoulders accented the shape of her body, with its slim boylike hips and narrow shoulders. She looked like a fledgling with her hair mussed like that, all baby feathers and bony legs. A delicious, almost painful twinge of affection caught his breath up short, and he smiled at her, eyes soft. She glanced up into the highboy mirror reflection, meeting his eyes. And returned the smile.

"Oh, who cares what she thinks, anyway," Harlan said. His hand stretched forward and caught the hem of her slip.

"*I* care," Dovie said, turning to face him. The slip hem twisted around her legs, tying itself like a bow. He tugged on it, enjoying watching the silk move over her skin. "She's been real nice to me, you know."

"Well, sure she has," Harlan said, still with an easy grin on his face. "You're wonderful."

"I mean it," Dovie said as he drew her slowly to him with the slip in his hands. Her shins met the edge of his rope bed, and she climbed on, standing on her knees with her hands angled down along her flanks. "I know they all think it was my fault."

"What, this?" Harlan brushed his free hand over the bandage on his ribs. "Oh, they don't know."

"They do," she countered, looking down at him with what he knew was her real serious face, and not her simulated one. "They think I'm some whore you tried to rescue, and my procurer beat you. They do!" she argued over his beginning protest. "Or else they think you got jumped by gangsters, which I probably introduced you to, since I'm so unrespectable."

"As if I'd borrow money from gangsters. Come on," Harlan said, grinning out of the side of his mouth. "I haven't lost *that* much."

"Harley, you should—" Dovie started to say, but she stopped herself as the sound of footfalls moved past the locked bedroom door. The footfalls stopped, followed by the sound of rustling taffeta, as though someone were listening at the keyhole. Harlan widened his eyes and clapped a hand over his mouth in pretend silence. Dovie smiled down at him, a finger pressed to her lips. A few seconds ticked by, and then the distinct music of an Irishwoman clearing her throat could be heard in the hallway, before the steps moved away.

Laughing, Harlan took up a pillow and swung it at Dovie, hitting her fragile shoulder with a muffled *plumpf*. She squealed, laughing, collapsing into the bedclothes as Harlan rolled onto her on his elbows. "Shhhh!" she whispered, her hands threading through his hair as he rained kisses on her forehead, her cheek, the corner of her ruby mouth, the hollow at the base of her collarbone. "Harley!" she protested, silent laughter shaking her body.

"Shhhh," he countered, brushing his nose along the creamy planes of her neck where it met her shoulder. Her skin was delectable, the fine hairs at the base of her skull tickling when he pressed his lips there. He loved the warm girl-smell of her, spicy, like incense lingering on her skin.

"Really, you've got to tell them the truth. They'll never like me otherwise."

"Later," he whispered into her hair. "Plenty of time for that. Later."

"SIBYL, PLEASE LISTEN," Benton was protesting downstairs as they entered the front hallway of the Beacon Street town house, Sibyl moving quickly, as if she could abandon his doubt behind her on the stoop. Outside in the street, the taxicab containing Professor Friend pulled away with a sputter of engine backfire, the professor waving farewell through the back window as the cab rolled down Beacon Street.

"I don't care," she insisted, shrugging off her coat with impatience and flinging it in the general direction of the hall stand. It missed and fell to the floor in a heap, which Sibyl didn't even bother to pick up. "You can say whatever you want to say, you can analyze it as much as you like. But I know what I saw. I was there. I know that it happened."

In the shadows of the rear hallway, silhouetted by the La Farge, the immobile form of Mrs. Doherty watched their arrival. Sibyl met her eyes only briefly, finding them concerned and preoccupied, as if she had something to say to her, but Sibyl dismissed the housekeeper with a curt shake of her head, and the woman scowled and disappeared into the kitchen.

She marched into the drawing room, one thumbnail brought to her lip for a chew. The afternoon was wearing into evening, and she knew that within the hour the other members of the Allston household would trickle back into the house. Lan would arrive from his office, after a day spent mulling import figures. Dovie was probably upstairs dressing, or lolling on her bed, flipping through one of her gossip magazines. Sibyl had prom-

ised to be home hours earlier, and in the back of her mind she worried that
Dovie would be annoyed with her for being so late.

Harlan either would or would not appear in time for supper. He had
been vanishing with increasing regularity as his health improved, and often Dovie would be absent at the same time. Sibyl presumed that they
crept away to escape all the watching eyes of the house, though neither of
them elaborated on their movements when Sibyl wasn't with them.

The mantel clock in the inner drawing room chimed the thirty minutes before their usual dinner hour. She heard the bustling sounds of Mrs.
Doherty laying the flatware in the dining room, lighting candles, arranging flowers. Sibyl ought to check in with Betty in the kitchen. Betty should
be informed that Benton was staying. And perhaps that Harlan's appearance wasn't assured.

This minutiae of household maintenance crowded in on Sibyl's mind in
a way both tedious and comforting as she crossed the drawing room. Over
the fireplace, the portrait effigy of a youthful Helen, still frozen in doubts
of her own, seemed to track Sibyl's movements with her painted eyes. Sibyl
glared up at the image of her mother, feeling cross and betrayed. She threw
herself onto the window seat in a froth of petulance, slouching with her
arms crossed, not looking at Benton.

"Sibyl," Benton said, following close on her heels. "You mustn't think I
don't respect you. You mustn't think I don't give credence to what you're
saying. Please. You've been deceived by someone you've trusted."

She glared at him with open defiance. "I don't see how else I'm meant
to take it," she said. "You're saying I'm mistaken, that I didn't see what I
know perfectly well that I saw. I'm not mad, Ben. But I know that I can't
explain it in a way that'll persuade you, so there's really no use in our continuing to discuss it."

He lowered himself with care onto the window seat opposite her, elbows on his knees, hands knitted together. "I'm the one who's failing to
explain." He paused, probing with his eyes to meet her gaze. She avoided
him. "Let me see if I can do better. Will you at least listen? Please?"

Sibyl softened. She didn't think she'd ever heard Benton say "please"
quite so many times at one stretch. He was usually too stubborn to be
that solicitous. She flicked a glance at him, just enough to test his intent,

but it was enough. He caught her eye and held it, smiling, leaning closer. From somewhere in the inner drawing room, they both heard a leisured squawk as Baiji the macaw reminded them that he was bearing witness to their conversation.

"All right," she relented. "But you won't be able to persuade me. I can see that I was wrong about Mrs. Dee, all right. She's not the first person I've been wrong about, is she? Don't you think I feel foolish enough already?"

Benton's face took on a pained cast. "You needn't," he said, voice low. "I never meant—"

"I take no pleasure in being made a fool of," Sibyl whispered, her quietness signaling the depths of her fury.

"Of course you don't," he said. A tentative hand edged nearer, coming to rest on Sibyl's knee.

"So," she said, noticing the pressure of his hand there. Her anger simmered lower. "Explain it, then. Tell me how I didn't see what I know that I saw."

Benton took a long breath and said, "I'll try. Let's consider first the actual content of this vision, all right? What was it?"

"You know what it was," Sibyl said, irritated. "I saw the ocean, and the night sky. And then I saw the ocean liner. After practicing, I could move around on the ship and see into the dining room. I was looking for Mother and Eulah, and while I was looking something happened to the ship. Everyone starting running, and it listed to one side. Then, instead of finding them, I saw Professor Friend."

"Right," Benton said. "Now, forget the vision for a moment. Have you ever had the experience of thinking about someone right before you get ready for bed, and then having a dream about them?"

"I suppose so," Sibyl said slowly. "Though I don't generally remember my dreams."

As she said this, she heard a distant *thunk* from somewhere upstairs. She glanced upward. Then Sibyl turned her attention back to Benton, doubting that he could persuade her to abandon what she knew, in her innermost self, to be true.

"That doesn't matter. I'm speaking in hypotheticals. Oftentimes dreams seem nonsensical, don't they? Cause and effect will be jumbled, laws of physics won't apply, scenes will change without reason. Am I right?"

Benton's cool eyes bored into Sibyl's own as he spoke, making her feel revealed, as though he were looking directly into her thoughts. The sensation was somehow both awkward and pleasurable at once. She shifted, her cheeks coloring.

"Well, yes. I guess," she demurred.

"And yet, within that nonsense you usually find recognizable elements, don't you? People or places that you know, perhaps juxtaposed in an unexpected way. We generally don't awaken thinking we've dreamed about things that have no meaning, after all. In dreams the sense might be drained away, but most of the elements will be familiar, possibly even familiar enough that we can guess why we might have had a given dream on a given night. Someone lately seen might appear, or a scene lately visited, but the two ideas won't naturally seem to belong together. At first."

Sibyl furrowed her brows. "Maybe," she allowed.

"Some men working in my field have a term for that phenomenon. It's called condensation. In dreams, a single image can reference multiple different experiences. So a single element of the subconscious can appear as a symbol in juxtaposition with something that seems initially unrelated to it. But if we look more closely at the symbol, if we evaluate its chain of associations, then we begin to understand all its different meanings." He looked intently at her, and she read in Benton's face the eager hope that she was seeing ahead to the conclusion that he wanted her to draw.

"I'm afraid I don't follow," she said, stubborn. "What do the visions that I've been seeing have to do with dreams? I told you I never remember my dreams anyway. And the visions are nothing at all like being asleep."

Benton rubbed his free hand over his forehead, battling frustration. Overhead, another *thunk* vibrated through the rafters of the town house. Sibyl glared at the ceiling, and looked down again.

"So you've said." Benton spoke from behind the hand on his forehead. "But you must see the connection. When do you have these visions most clearly?"

"When I—" Sibyl started to say, but didn't finish.

"Am under the influence of a very heavy, very dangerous narcotic," Benton finished for her.

"Really, Ben. It's not so bad as all that." She frowned, sitting back in the window seat cushions. "And what about Mrs. Dee's? I was perfectly myself. I fail to see what that has to do with anything."

The young psychologist blinked at her, astonished. "The cough syrup," he said.

"What do you mean, cough syrup?" Sibyl said, baffled.

"Oh, come now."

"I have no idea what you're talking about," she said, gaze floating to the ceiling again out of frustration.

"I thought you'd know. Sibyl, there're opiates in that cough syrup. In most cough remedies and tonics, in fact. That's one reason they've finally started regulating them." He stared at her. "Didn't you know? Why, they're all the same, chemically speaking. Opium. Morphine. Cough syrup. Laudanum."

"Laudanum, too?" she said, a thought flashing through her mind, not fully formed. It vanished before she could get hold of it.

"Certainly. Same thing. They all have the same effects, just in varying strengths. That's why they're so dangerous, these patent medicines. It's all too easy for people to become dependent on them without even knowing it."

"But," Sibyl protested, aggravated with Benton but not understanding why. "I fail to see what that has to do with this condensation business that you're talking about."

"Opiates," Benton said, "cause vivid waking dreams. It's the same, psychologically speaking, as what you might see while you're asleep. Only you're awake, and the interference of the drug makes the imagery even more intense."

"So?" Sibyl glared. She thought she might see where Benton was going.

Overhead, an even louder *thunk*, and the sound of something metallic dropped and rolling across a wooden floor.

"What on earth . . . ?" Sibyl muttered to herself. Benton paid no attention.

"Consider. Your mind has been much on your mother and sister lately.

You're reminded of them every day here in the house. And then it's the anniversary of the sinking, always a difficult time. Yes?"

"I suppose," she said.

"So naturally your subconscious might turn to images of the sea, of an ocean liner even, in reference to them around this time of year."

"Even so—"

"Even so. And you'd just been looking at Professor Friend across the table from you. His was the freshest face in your mind before Mrs. Dee shut off the lights. Further, he'd provided you validation and support when I myself did not. You were grateful to him. He encouraged your wish to contact them, and so became tangled up with the idea of them in your mind. It's only natural that you'd superimpose him into your dream."

"But—" she started to object.

"Sibyl," Benton said, his voice gentle, eyes probing, pleading for her comprehension. "It's just a dream. That vision you've been having—it's a projection of your unconscious mind. A manifestation of your grief over losing Helen and Eulah. It's perfectly understandable, and nothing whatever to be embarrassed about. But you must see that there's nothing of clairvoyance or spirit communication or anything else about it."

She watched him speak, weighing what he was saying. Sibyl had to admit that it made sense, what Benton argued; that the image she kept seeing in the scrying glass could just be fragments from deep within her mind, creating what looked like a coherent picture as a way of giving her what she yearned to have.

"But," she said, dropping her voice to a whisper, "it seemed so real." She searched his eyes for understanding, and probing there, found patience and sympathy. But not anything that might be called belief.

"I know," he whispered back. He seemed on the point of saying something further, his eyes hunting deep into her own.

"As real," she said, "as you are now." She placed her hand over his where it rested on her knee, and pressed there. She waited, lips parted.

A stricken look crossed Benton's face, and he murmured, "Sibyl, I . . ."

She edged nearer, wishing to hear what he was about to say. "Yes?"

And then his lips were pressed to her mouth.

Sibyl barely had time to register what was happening before a thumping of chair legs on hard wood and rustling of papers caused them to leap up from their intimate conference in the window seat, abruptly dropping their hands. The outline of movement emerged from within the darkness of the inner parlor, and out of the shadows stepped the form of Lan Allston, one hand propped on his vest pocket, and the other with a newspaper at his side, tapping the side of his leg meditatively. His icy sailor's eyes were dark, his mouth flattened into a disapproving line.

"Oh!" Sibyl exclaimed, taken by surprise. "Papa. I didn't realize you were—"

"Good evening, Professor Derby," Allston said with a curt nod at Benton. Then he turned his attention to his daughter. "I don't suppose you've told the staff that we'll be having another guest for supper this evening, have you?"

"Really, Captain Allston, I wasn't—" Benton started to say.

"I was . . . that is, I was just—" Sibyl stammered, talking over Benton. She glanced sidelong at the young professor, grappling for an explanation. He looked back at her, with the faintest of shrugs and a half-smile.

"I thought not. Well, no matter. I'll do it myself." He pulled the chronometer out of his vest pocket to reassure himself of something and stuffed it back while tucking the newspaper under his arm. "Well. We'd best be excusing ourselves to dress, I suppose. Derby, you'll be fine the way you are. I can't see Mrs. Doherty causing too much of a fuss. No more than usual, at any rate."

"Ah," Benton started to say. Abashed, he hunted around himself, as though searching on the floor for something to say. Instead of finding it, he folded his hands behind his back, rocked on his heels, and said, "Well, that's kind of you, sir. I'd be glad to stay."

"Excellent," Lan said, though his tone indicated that the invitation was not meant to be regarded as optional. He crossed the front parlor and offered Sibyl his arm to lead her upstairs. For lack of anything better to do, she took it.

"Make yourself at home, Ben," she said with a resigned smile. "We'll only be a minute."

Sibyl allowed herself to be led out of the drawing room and toward the stairs, in part relieved to be freed from her puzzling interaction with Benton. She wondered what her father might have overheard. She watched his weathered face under her eyelashes, waiting for a sign. In the vestibule behind the stairs the La Farge window, its forest glade scene lush with leaded and pebbled glass, glowed with the last of the early evening light.

"You know, my dear," he said as they started up the stairs, "he's a clever man, that Benton Derby. I've always thought so."

Sibyl wasn't sure where her father was heading with this vague insight, and had no wish to reveal more of their conversation than was necessary. "So he is," she said, speaking with care. "I'm fortunate to have him for a friend."

"Hmmm!" her father rejoined. Halfway up the stairs, he stopped. Sibyl looked up into his face. The corners of her father's eyes crinkled, and he smiled down at her. "I think you should listen to his judgment," Lan Allston said.

"What do you mean?" she asked, unsure how much her father knew.

A long moment passed, Lan Allston smiling that unnerving and unpersuasive smile, but there was an abiding sadness somewhere behind his cool pale eyes, and for a moment Sibyl found herself feeling something she had never felt for her father before—pity.

"I mean," he said, "that I believe I was wrong, to encourage you to keep seeing that woman. I thought it would help. I did. But Professor Derby's right. It's better you not go anymore. It's all just dreams and childish nonsense. None of it means a fig. And, worse than that, it stands in the way of a clear view of the real world. Better for us to look ahead with hope, than look back with regret."

"But, Papa," she started to object. Her father's face closed to her interjection.

"No," he said, in the tone that Sibyl recognized as signaling the end of a conversation. "I should never have let you get so involved. That was wrong of me. Now, I'd like you to stop. Immediately."

Sibyl was puzzled at this unexpected admission from her usually reserved parent. She searched his eyes, looking for some clue as to the source of that profound sadness that she saw there.

"All right," she said.

"That's my girl," her father said, using a phrase Sibyl hadn't heard since she was in pigtails. She yearned to question him. But it wasn't the Allston way to elaborate. Instead, they stood for another interminable moment, in silent agreement, before starting their ponderous way back up the stairs.

As they neared the top another thumping could be heard, followed by peals of laughter rolling down the second-floor hallway. Harlan tumbled out one of the bedroom doors, his hair mussed, fumbling with the cuff link of one sleeve.

"Good gracious!" he exclaimed, embarrassed and laughing, coming upon Sibyl and Lan Allston making their way up the stairs. "What, is it time to dress already?"

Sibyl and her father exchanged a wary glance before looking back at the youngest Allston family member. He grinned at them, and Sibyl thought she detected a faint smear of lip rouge at the corner of his mouth.

"It certainly is," her father said, voice returned to the stern detachment that was his usual idiom when addressing his son. "We won't wait up for you, you know."

Their father turned to make his stately way down the second-floor hall, and Sibyl caught Harlan's eye. She motioned to wipe at the corner of her mouth with a thumb, and raised her eyebrows at him. His eyes widened, and so did his grin as he followed her direction, wiping away the smear with the back of a wrist. Sibyl thought about registering her disapproval with her wayward younger brother, but instead rolled her eyes and sighed before shooing him back to his room. He retreated down the hall at a trot, still laughing.

As she passed the guest room, she thought she heard giggling from within.

LATER THAT EVENING, after a supper that consisted of Benton and Lan discussing developments in the war in Europe while Harlan and Dovie exchanged limpid glances over the flower arrangement and Sibyl stirred her food around her plate with dismay, followed by sherry and a hand of bridge in the drawing room, at which Harlan lost his temper when he was beaten, Sibyl sat at her dressing table, listening to the silence in the house. Downstairs she heard the remote chiming of the mantel clock, telling her that it was midnight. Sibyl raised her hands and withdrew the pins from her hair one at a time, tossing them aside with a *tink*ing sound into the porcelain tray on her dressing table.

With her hair falling loose around her shoulders, clad in her dressing gown, Sibyl settled in the armchair by the fireplace in her room, stretching her feet toward the last of the glowing embers. The room was lit only by the cold light of a waxing moon, hanging in the sky over the river basin. She rummaged in her pocket, pulling the wooden box out from the silken folds of her gown. Sibyl opened the box and withdrew the bluish crystal, holding it before her in the moonlight. It looked murky in the half-light of the room, as though dipped in milk.

Sibyl turned over everything that Benton had suggested as she balanced the ball on the ends of her fingertips. Just a waking dream, he said. A construct of her subconscious. She sighed. Everything he said made perfect sense. She trusted him. And her father, who had apparently overheard every bit of her conversation that afternoon, agreed. In fact, he had made her promise to stop.

Without her permission, her mind seized on the kiss, on the feel of Benton's mouth against hers, and she felt her head swim. She leaned against the side of the armchair, wondering what he meant by it. Perhaps nothing. Perhaps he was just overcome with a sense of protectiveness toward her, overwhelmed and forgetful of himself. She would pretend as though it hadn't happened. He would be ashamed of himself, of abusing their confederacy that way. Benton Derby was a gentleman. She would rise above it. She would let him feel that she still trusted him. But she would be careful.

Then again, she considered—turning back to the content of their discussion rather than its conclusion—wasn't Professor Friend also trustworthy? And he disagreed with Benton. He was no less persuaded in his beliefs by the revelation of Mrs. Dee's fraud. If anything, he appeared more assured of the authority of his own dispassionate approach. Sibyl frowned, staring at the scrying glass.

The vision seemed so different from the stuff of a dream. So much realer, more vibrant. Like a moving picture. Sibyl never went to movies anymore. But she had gone a few times with a group of girls from school, remembered sitting in the audience, her face turned up to the flickering light, piano pounding merry commentary on the adventures on the screen. The whole roomful of people, young people like herself, all jumping back as one from the oncoming train, caught up in the tension of a Keystone chase, horses, gunfire, evil villains twirling their mustaches, heavy makeup around their eyes. The images in the glass were more like that, like something that she was watching, than like dreams.

Sibyl glanced left and right, assuring herself that she was alone. Hearing the deep silence of the slumbering house, she felt reassured. No one would know if she tried again. Just one last time.

Reaching for the glass decanter on the table at her elbow, Sibyl dropped about ten drops of reddish amber liquid into a glass that already contained the dregs of her sherry from the bridge game. She held the glass up, examining it as the red drops dispersed like blood in the liquor, and then tossed the mixture back with a grimace of distaste. She couldn't imagine that her father took laudanum almost daily. The taste was really dreadful. It must speak to the severity of his pain, if he was willing to brave that bitterness in his mouth.

She set the glass aside, settling back in her armchair and holding the scrying glass between finger and thumb. Her weight relaxed, her head leaned against the cushion, she felt the warmth of the embers tingling on her bare feet. The grip of her worries loosened, and her face softened. A sweet sigh escaped her lips.

After a few silent minutes, with her gaze leveled on the scrying glass, its surface started to change. Black, coiling smoke filled the sphere, billowing and bending back on itself. Sibyl smiled with satisfaction. Each time the image resolved more quickly. She was improving.

The smoke parted, drawing open like curtains on a stage, revealing the rippling ocean surface, only this time the waves glinted under a bright midday sun. Sibyl frowned, confused by the change of time. The point of view within the glass skimmed along the water as it had before, ducking and weaving with intoxicating freedom. She caromed along the hull of a gigantic ocean liner, its hull bright in the afternoon sunshine, then veered up and over the gunwale to the laughing faces on board, the women in their lacy daytime finery, the men in their impeccable suits. She peered at each passing face, and though she recognized some of them from her earlier experiments, none were Helen or Eulah.

As she gazed, Sibyl argued with herself. It was all a dream. Benton was right. Everything she saw could be explained away by the particular state of her mind, altered by the substance that she had taken. But the sensation felt nothing like a dream. She felt as though she were watching something happening, in real life, that she couldn't possibly see.

The glass wandered from person to person, laughing faces most of them, some of them locked in grave conversation. She moved from the deck into the dining room, past waiters moving about with platters held overhead, swerving around dining tables. All the same, all she had seen before, only set, for some reason, in a different time of day. Dinnertime, the midday meal, rather than a late-night party, but everyone else was identical, all the people located in the same positions. Still no sign of Helen or Eulah. Sibyl squinted her eyes, wishing for more. She couldn't understand where they could be, and she was running out of time. Soon enough, she knew, it would happen.

And then, it did happen. The ship lurched, everyone in the dining room stumbled, and there he was again—young and handsome Professor Edwin Friend, in his tweedy suit, his mouth open in a shout, or possibly issuing instructions. People breaking into a run, the surface of the boat starting to list sharply to starboard. This was the moment when the vision ended.

But this time, it didn't end. She watched as Professor Friend hurried forward, helping an older woman who had stumbled, saw him wrap his arm over her shoulders and usher her through the throng. Sibyl's point of view paused, a still point within a panicked crowd of people scrambling for the high side of the dining room. Then the glass floated to the window of the ship's first-class dining room.

Outside, through the window, she saw a sudden bright explosion, followed by a hellish tower of smoke and water and debris shooting up into the afternoon sky. She trembled where she sat in her armchair safe at home, her body wracked by the vibrations shaking the ship within the scrying glass.

While she stared in horror the glass slowly filled with billows of black smoke, condensing into a boiling mass. When the blackness looked nearly solid, it abruptly pulled apart, dissolving, leaving the glass perfectly clear.

The orb slipped from Sibyl's exhausted hand, rolling from her lap to the floor, and she buried her face in her hands with a sob.

TWENTY-ONE

St. Swithin Club

Beacon Hill

Boston, Massachusetts

May 7, 1915

*T*his afternoon was never going to end. Harlan slouched lower in his club chair, folding and unfolding the napkin on the table before him. He bent first one corner, then the other, fluffing the linen until the napkin had transformed into the shape of a swan.

"Impressive," Bickering said from behind his fan of cards. "Looks like you've got some latent talents after all, Allston."

"Too bad they're not anything to do with card playing," Townsend remarked, rearranging his own hand with a meditative eye. Harlan blew a frustrated hiss of air through his nose, nervous hands working the napkin again until it transformed from a folded swan into a compact elephant.

"Where'd you learn how to do that, anyway?" Bickering asked as Townsend took the trick with a miscounted trump. "Damn," Bickering said in response to Townsend's move, out of a sense of obligation to appear dismayed.

Bickering's partner, a watery fellow with pale whiskers and red stains of acne on his cheeks, frowned with more feeling. Harlan wondered if this fellow, whoever he was, was as ill equipped to lose a hundred dollars as he himself. They'd been hesitant to let him play at all. If he should lose, he'd be finished in Boston. At least, his lines of credit would at last be exhausted. Which was all it took, to be finished in society.

"Oh, I don't know," Harlan said, ignoring Pale Whiskers' aggravation. "You just mess around with things long enough and you figure it out." A few more folds and twists and fluffs, and the elephant became a dachshund. Harlan mock-walked the dog over to Bickering, and made sniffing sounds while pressing its napkin-nose to Bickering's wrist. The other man pulled his hand away with a funny look.

"Hmmm," Bickering said, taking a trick from Townsend with a triumphant arch of his eyebrow. Harlan folded his hands behind his head, stretching his legs out below the table. At least they were fifty points up. Two more tricks and Townsend would make the rubber. Harlan knew Townsend'd make a better bridge partner. Few more games like this and his debts would be square. Nearly. In his worried hands the napkin transformed into a cat.

His mood was pierced by a commotion breaking out near the front door, shouts and thumping of feet. Harlan raised his eyebrows, curious, without moving from his slouch. The other three men sat unperturbed, bent with intense attention over their game.

A slick-haired young man whom Harlan half recognized—what was his name, Peter?—burst into the card room, waving a newspaper, breathless, his face flushed.

"Well, they've gone and done it now!" he cried, rushing up to the foursome of bridge players. He flapped the newspaper open on the table, ignoring their protests at the interruption. "The unmitigated gall. I can't believe it, I tell you. I just can't believe it!"

More shouts and excited conversation thrummed through the club, and through the window in the street outside Harlan spotted a man and two young women clustering over a newspaper as well, bending their heads together and talking excitedly.

"What's going on?" Harlan asked, stirred enough to lean forward and look at the headline splashed across the late edition. The other three card players joined him, their shoulders bumping into one another, a hand of hearts (look at all those trumps, a part of Harlan thought wistfully) scattered forgotten, like leaves, over the floor.

The headline blared SAILED WITH SENSE OF DISASTER IMPENDING.

"They've torpedoed *Lusitania*. Torpedoed it! Damn thing went down in thirty minutes!"

"What?" Harlan asked, confused, as the other young men started to talk excitedly.

"Hard to believe these are the same people who brought us Goethe and Schiller," Townsend remarked, unflappable as usual. "Guess it just goes to show you." He didn't go on to elaborate on what, specifically, that goes to show you, as the rest of the table was all talking over each other, rustling through the newspaper pages for more details.

"Torpedoed!" Bickering cried, cracking his knuckles with excitement. "But she's an ocean liner! A civilian cruise ship! What could those damnable Huns be thinking?"

"Says here the embassy issued a warning before the ship departed last week. Reminded everyone that a state of war existed between Germany and her allies and England and her allies, and that the waters around the North Sea were patrolled by U-boats. They as good as promised the ship'd be bombed. As good as promised."

"But it's an ocean liner!" Bickering repeated. "What would they want to torpedo a bunch of vacationers for? How in God's name could they possibly justify it?"

"Says here," Peter went on, "that some of the more prominent people who're set to sail on her received telegrams on the pier warning them not to go, signed with fictitious German names. Says here Alfred Vanderbilt just crumpled the telegram up and threw it aside."

"That's what any man would do," one of the boys commented.

"But why would the Cunard people let her go, if the embassy sent out a warning the previous week? Seems to me you might want to pay attention when the German embassy notifies you they've got U-boats carrying torpedoes with your name on 'em."

"Says here," Peter continued, "that everyone thought the liner was safe. She could make twenty-five knots easy. They thought for sure she could outrun 'em if they tried to make good. But nobody really thought they'd do it."

"How could they?" Bickering said, fingernails digging into the table-top. Harlan reflected that he might never have seen Bickering look so upset before. Bickering was never one for politics; he cared nothing for his profession. He treated all the girls he'd seen with magnanimous indifference. He lost money and won it with precisely the same level of detached bemusement, as if the details of his life were all part of the same grand joke. Now the young man's face was starting to burn red. "I don't see how Wilson can keep us neutral. Not after this . . . this . . ."

"Outrage," Townsend finished. Still calm, unmussed, and calculating, but clearly even Townsend was upset.

Harlan sat, benumbed with shock. A shock that felt almost welcome in its familiarity. In fact, Harlan could barely remember a time without it. An elegant ocean liner, sunk. Torpedoed by a German submarine this time. Men. Women. Children. Thirty minutes, the paper said. All over in less than thirty minutes.

His eyes widened as he pictured the explosion's impact shaking through the ribs of the vessel, the deck sharply listing, moving like some hideous heaving sea animal under all the passengers' feet. Harlan heard the screams in his ears of passengers scrambling for higher ground, of tables turned over and glassware shattering. He imagined with perfect clarity the roiling panic of people clawing to get into lifeboats, trampling over one another, a lifeboat swinging free from its hoist and crashing through the windows of the dining room in an explosion of splintered glass.

"Was anyone saved?" he heard himself ask. At the center of his imagination—the still point of his cold and miserable shock, the image that haunted his sleep—stood his sister and his mother, arms knotted together in each other's clothes, faces stained with weeping, with ice cold water rolling long tongues toward their feet.

"Anyone?" he asked again, in a smaller voice. "Anyone saved at all?"

The young men didn't heed his question, instead bellowing over one another in self-righteous indignation, loudly announcing their thoughts for what ought to be done to the Germans now that the States would have to enter the war.

Another thumping of feet approached, and Rawlings appeared in the doorway of the card room, his pipe in his hand. "You fellows hear the news?" he cried, before spotting Harlan.

A long moment of frigid silence descended on the assembled company as the men clustered around the card table exchanged rapid, knowing glances. Harlan settled his hands on the armrests of his chair, gripping them, swallowing, a rush of guilt and anxiety bubbling up in his chest. Rawlings stepped back, as though reconsidering entering the room. The men all waited, watching, wondering who would be first to speak.

A shadow crossed over Rawlings's face, followed by one of his hands wiping across his eyes. Then he slid the pipe between his teeth, thrust his hands in his pockets, and moved over to where Harlan was sitting. Without intending to, Harlan slouched lower in his chair, keeping a weather eye on the approaching young man.

Rawlings reached Harlan, and the other boys all stood up as a body, stepping back to give the two room. Rawlings cleared his throat, looking at his shoes.

"Look here, Allston," he began.

Bickering coughed, nervous from tension. Peter, not the usual companion of the boys, started to say "But what . . ." and Townsend silenced him with a quick "Tsssst." Pale Whiskers, whoever he was, watched the proceedings as though he were at a baseball game, his arms folded across his chest.

"Rolly," Harlan acknowledged, looking up at him, defiant, but only just.

The other boy paused, hazarding a glance at Harlan's face. "How's that lip of yours? It mending all right?"

"I guess it is," Harlan allowed.

Rawlings nodded, looking relieved. His hand wandered up to fiddle with the pipe at his mouth, which, when he withdrew it for a long look into its bowl, Harlan observed to be more chewed on the mouthpiece than usual.

"Glad to hear it," Rawlings said finally. "Glad to hear it." Another pause while Harlan waited, bringing a fingertip to his scabbed split lip.

"I'll tell you," Rawlings said, flexing his hand. "Just about broke my knuckle, there."

Harlan didn't say anything, waiting.

"Way I see it, Allston," Rawlings continued, voice tight with embarrassment. "We've known each other a long time, and—"

When he saw where Rawlings was going, Harlan let out a sigh of relief. "See here, Rolly," he said. "I should never've said that. About your sister. You know I think she's a fine girl. And nothing at all like—like I implied."

Rawlings looked at him, stricken.

Harlan shifted in his seat, uncomfortable under the judging gaze of the other young men.

"You've got to know I didn't mean anything by it. I was just running my mouth off. Like a jackass. You know that, right? Rolly?"

After weighing what Harlan said, the other young man nodded, and stuck out his hand. Harlan got to his feet and took it, bringing in his other hand as well to clasp them together.

"Okay. I—I know," Rawlings said. "And I'm sorry about all that . . . that business." He gestured with his chin to Harlan's battered face. "But I couldn't very well let it stand, could I? I mean, could I? You didn't give me much choice, you know."

"Frankly," Harlan said with a half-smile, "I never thought you had it in you. I've got you to thank for this new shape my nose's in, huh?"

The group of clubmen watching this exchange let out a collective sigh of relief. The two former combatants smiled at each other, hands still clasped together. Then the smiles broadened into grins, and they flung their arms around each other in a quick, tight embrace. The boys watching their exchange had to restrain themselves from breaking out in applause. Instead they muttered a few phrases of hearty approval, slapping backs and laughing.

"It needed the help," Rawlings joked, elbowing Harlan, who cried, "Oh, did it? You bounder," to a round of guffaws.

The group then bent themselves back to the newspaper spread around the card table, gesticulating with excitement over their plans to travel across the Atlantic and wreak revenge on Germany as soon as they possibly could.

SIBYL SAT IN the front drawing room, attempting to knot the thread on the underside of her needlepoint, and failing. She tried again, bending closer and squinting her eyes for a better view. She was on the point of getting it when her hands trembled, slightly, and the needle fell from her grasp.

"Drat," she muttered under her breath. At her feet, Baiji waddled past, pausing to tongue the end of Sibyl's shoe to see if it might taste as good as a peanut shell. It didn't, and so the bird continued on his meditative way, shimmering tail trailing behind him.

"You'd better not chew the carpet again," Sibyl remarked to the passing macaw. "I'll make you into a hat after all. You see if I won't."

As she said this the pocket door opened and Dovie flounced in, a fashion magazine tucked under her arm. She flopped into the armchair across from Sibyl and stuck her feet out straight in front of her with a long sigh.

"Feeling any better?" Sibyl asked without looking up.

"Mmmm? Oh," Dovie said, waving her hand in dismissal. "Sure. Just ate something funny, I guess." She paused, and Sibyl didn't respond. "You know, I don't think that Betty of yours likes me so much."

Sibyl glanced up from her work and regarded the young woman draped over the chair across from her. Dovie's face was faintly green still, but her color did seem to be coming back.

"Oh? What makes you say that?"

"Nothing in particular," Dovie said, with a strange look on her face. "Just a feeling. She won't look at me when I try to talk to her. And I don't think— Well. You all seem to enjoy her food more than I do, is all."

Sibyl laid her work in her lap and leaned back in her chair, thinking about Betty Gallagher. It was true that she'd seemed more curt than usual when Sibyl went to the kitchen to consult her on dinner plans. Once, Sibyl enjoyed loitering in the kitchen to soak up the details of Betty's various affairs, which were always touched with drama and intrigue. But she'd been less good humored, and more likely to snap at the kitchen girls lately. Sibyl had gotten into the habit of keeping her conversations with the cook to a minimum over the past few weeks, if only to spare the sculleries Betty's wrath.

She was on the point of saying this to Dovie when the two women were interrupted by the slamming open of the front door, followed by the sound of pounding feet. Harlan burst through the door into the parlor, the stubborn forelock of hair flopping into his eyes. He panted, out of breath, and his eyes sparkled with a new kind of determination that Sibyl didn't recall ever having seen in her otherwise laconic younger brother.

"Harley!" Dovie turned and gasped, seeing his excitement. "Why, what's happened?" She rose to her feet, balancing one hand on the back of the chair.

Troubled by the sudden outburst of excitement, Baiji squawked, flapped his wings, and returned with a leisured soar to the hat rack in the inner parlor.

"You haven't heard?" Harlan burst, rushing across the room to take Dovie's hands in his.

"Heard what?" Sibyl asked from behind her needlepoint at the same time that Dovie cried, "No, my darling! What is it?"

"The Germans. There'll be no way we can keep out of the war now."

"War!" Dovie exclaimed, looking confused.

"What's happened, Harlan?" Sibyl frowned, dropping her work into her lap. She didn't like seeing him so. . . . Sibyl struggled to find the right word to describe Harlan's attitude, and her stomach rolled over when she realized that this was *enthusiasm*, what she was seeing in her younger brother. He was excited. Thrilled. He was almost . . .

Happy.

"Look here," he said, eyes shining with excitement as he pulled the newspaper from under his arm. He hurried to the coffee table, and the three of them gathered around as he spread it out for them to read. The paper was black with two-inch headlines, of which she caught the words TERROR and SEAS in the commotion. "I tell you, Wilson's mad if he thinks we can stay neutral now. Soon enough they'll get a real taste of what we've got to offer, you see if they won't."

"But what—" Sibyl started to say, but she was interrupted by the sound of a man speaking from the doorway.

"*Lusitania*," the man announced. Harlan, Sibyl, and Dovie all looked up at once in response to the sound and discovered Benton Derby standing in the drawing room entryway, hands propped on either side of the door jamb, his face ashen. He looked as though he had been kicked in the stomach. "They torpedoed it."

"Torpedoed?" Sibyl breathed. "You mean, it sank?"

"In eighteen minutes," the professor confirmed. "Broad daylight."

"But—" Dovie started to say.

"How many passengers were there?" Sibyl asked, her voice hollow in her ears.

"One thousand two hundred fifty-three," Benton said. "At least, that's the number I heard. I don't know how many crew." A strange look crossed his face, as though he had something important to add. "Sibyl, there's—" he started to say with some urgency, but she cut him off without meaning to.

"Great God in heaven," Sibyl whispered.

"Well, Ben," Harlan interjected, drawing himself up to his full height and thrusting his chin forward with manful determination. "Looks like we'll be going to war after all."

"What do you mean?" Dovie asked, looking up at him from where she was kneeling by the coffee table, her hand on the newspaper.

"Well, sure," Harlan said, with a new determination in his voice. He folded his arms across his chest, and the gesture made him look broader. Older. "Think about it. I don't see how we'll stand for this. Why, there were Americans on that boat. A hundred of them at least. It was en route from New York! We can't take that kind of thing lying down. I'd say it's only a matter of time before we throw our hat in the ring. Should've done it a long time ago, if you ask me. Some of the fellows were down at the club talking, and we decided we're all going to head to this camp they've got in New York, at Plattsburgh. It's for civilians who want to start training. That way when it's made official, we'll be ready."

"Harlan!" Sibyl exclaimed, aghast.

"Now wait one second," Benton said, moving into the room and stopping behind Sibyl's chair. He looked down at her, face haggard and drained. "Let's just keep our shirts on."

"Shirts on!" Harlan burst. "How can you say that, in the light of all this? Broad daylight, you said it yourself! They don't even know if anyone made it off alive. Why, the loss of life could be enormous. Are you going to stand here and tell me we should accept that kind of barbarity? Why, it's an open act of war. It goes against every sense of common decency and humanity."

Benton cleared his throat, lines around his eyes contracting with tension that Sibyl couldn't entirely read. "Nobody's saying otherwise, Harley. But remember all that fuss on campus last year, over the Mexican question. We've got to consider every angle. The torpedoing could be a mistake. I heard the boat had been repainted, making it look less like a passenger ship. Who knows if her name was even visible, or what flag she was flying. The Germans might try to make reparations. There's no telling what will happen. I understand the president hasn't even issued a statement yet."

Harlan straightened where he stood, throwing a look of venomous spite at Benton. "I could care less about Wilson and his goddam statements," the boy exclaimed. "There's right, and there's wrong. The Germans have crossed the line, and I'm not going to stand for it. Some of us were talking about joining up with the Canadians, to get over there even sooner. Show Fritz what we're made of."

"Harley," Sibyl said, slowly rising to her feet and placing a hand on her brother's sleeve. "What about school? I thought you were going to—"

"School!" he spat, throwing her off. Dovie stood up also, her eyes darting between the two Allstons, weighing where her allegiance should lie. She edged nearer to Harlan, looking on Sibyl with pleading eyes, willing Sibyl to calm her brother down. "What could I possibly learn by going back to school? You expect me to go back to Westmorly, write up my term papers like a good little boy? What have term papers to do with anything that's real? Nothing. Don't you see?"

"Harlan," Benton said. "She only meant that—"

"No!" Harlan bellowed, cutting him off. His eyes flashed with a certainty and clarity that Sibyl had never seen in him before. "I wouldn't expect either of you to understand. Sibyl, you never even set foot outside this goddam house. You're like a ghost. And you!" He spun on Benton. "Shuttered away in your office with your books and papers. Don't you see? I've been given a chance. I can *do* something about this. After all this time, I've finally been given a way to make it right!"

At this last word Harlan pounded his fist against the wall, so hard that

Sibyl felt the vibration through the soles of her feet, turned on his heel, and stormed out of the room. Dovie looked around, a helpless expression on her young face, before hurrying after him. Harlan's feet could be heard stomping up the front stairs, and Dovie disappeared through the parlor door behind him, calling out, "Harley, wait. Wait!"

In the sudden calm following Harlan's departure, Sibyl exhaled and sat with an "Oof" back down in her armchair. She leaned forward, her elbows on her knees, resting her head on her hands. She was aware of Benton's moving to take Dovie's chair, sitting, placing his hands on his knees. As always her gaze was drawn to the little hairs on his knuckles. He held himself more stiffly than usual, and his hands gripped his knees as though reminding himself to stay restrained.

"Sibyl," he began. "I have something very difficult to tell you. The *Lusitania* . . ."

She sat back and dropped her hands with a sigh. "What a tragedy," she said, looking at him. "Though I'm a little surprised to see Harlan taking it so hard. Whatever can that be about?"

"Yes," Benton said, uncertain. "About that. There's something else. That Harlan doesn't know." He looked down, working his hands together.

"Why, what is it?" she asked.

"It's—I can hardly think how to tell you," he stammered. Benton stopped speaking, and Sibyl waited. The only sound in the house was the omnipresent ticking of the mantel clock.

Finally Sibyl couldn't stand the wait anymore. "Benton, I wish you'd tell me what's—" she started to say, but she began speaking at the very instant that he said, "Tell me again, what was in that vision you've been having?"

"I beg your pardon?" she asked, confused.

He leveled his steely gaze on her, and she saw that his eyes were watery and pink behind his spectacles. She frowned.

"That vision of yours," he said, voice nearly breaking. "The one you've been having. The one you had when I persuaded you to go to Mrs. Dee's. Could you tell it to me again?"

"Well," she began, uncertain why he'd be asking. "It starts with me skimming along the surface of the ocean." Benton nodded, urging her to continue. "And then it shows me the ocean liner. And then I move up over the side and travel among the people inside. And I go looking for my mother and sister. But it—happens. The boat begins to founder. Before I find them. People running and screaming. And then, sometimes, right at the end, I see Professor Friend in the crowd."

Benton hung his head, looking down at his hands. "Right. Yes. And what time of day did you say it was?" he asked.

"Time of day?" she repeated. "Why—well, that's the odd part. When I first started, it was during the night. Late, but not so late that people weren't still up. But the last few times, it's been during the middle of the day. I couldn't really figure out why that should be, but that's how it's seemed to go. I was beginning to think you might be right."

"Has it," Benton said, still quiet. "And did you never find your sister and your mother? Not even once?"

"No," Sibyl said, her voice dropping to a whisper, her dark brows drawing together over her eyes. She leaned forward until she could just feel his soft breath on her face. "Why, Ben? Why are you asking me these questions?"

"Sibyl," he said, meeting her eyes with his. "What time of day did *Titanic* sink?"

She sat and thought for a moment. "Why," she said, "I'm not sure. But I believe the papers said they struck the iceberg a little before midnight. And then it"—she paused over the word, swallowing—"sank. Within a couple of hours. Before dawn, at any rate. Why?"

He nodded, searching her face. "Just so. And, for the sake of argument, why do you think the time of day would have changed?" he asked. "In your vision. If it was *Titanic* you were seeing, shouldn't the vision have always been set in the middle of the night?"

A vague sense of ill ease spread through Sibyl, and her eyes widened. She sat back in her chair, feeling the same sickening dizziness that sometimes crept in on her when she hadn't eaten enough. The dark, oily blackness started to swirl in on the edge of her consciousness, and she took hold of her armrests, willing herself to stay present. "Ben," she said. "What are you saying?"

Benton leveled his gaze at Sibyl, boring into her as though if he stared into her eyes hard enough he would be able to see whatever strange images she was privy to.

"Sibyl," he said. "I'm asking because of Edwin. You see, Professor Friend was traveling to Europe this week for a conference."

"He was?" Sibyl asked, her voice sounding hollow in her ears.

"Sibyl," Benton said, struggling over the words. "Edwin was on *Lusitania*."

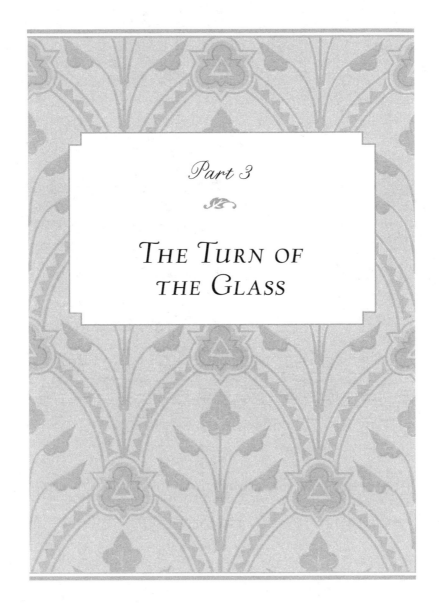

Part 3

The Turn of
the Glass

Interlude

North Atlantic Ocean
Outward Bound
April 14, 1912

HELEN TWISTED HER napkin between her hands and stretched taller, trying to see over the throng of dancers at the end of the gallery. She'd lost sight of them. Her instincts told her to stand up and see if she could get a better view, but she battled the impulse away. She mustn't meddle. Or she mustn't seem to be meddling. Oh, but it was too stressful to be believed. Where had those two sneaked off to? She hoped Eulah wasn't talking the Widener boy's ear off. Course, she also hoped he wasn't boring her daughter stiff with all that book-collecting business. Eulah wasn't such a book person. Gracious, who was?

Tinkling laughter reached Helen's ears, and she turned to find Eleanor Widener laughing behind her dinner napkin. Her eyes were resting on Helen, bemused and kinder than when they first sat down.

"Oh, Helen." She sighed, dropping the napkin back to her lap. "It's hard, being the mother, isn't it?"

Helen sighed with relief when she saw that the laughter was friendly, and reached for the glass of Madeira that had appeared at her place while she watched her daughter dance. "It is," she admitted. "It really is."

"I don't know about you," Eleanor said, leaning closer. "But I never expected it to be so difficult. Did you?"

"Difficult?" Helen said. "Why, I don't know that it's been as difficult as all that."

"Perhaps difficult isn't what I mean exactly," the other woman said, resting her chin on a papery white hand, heavy with jewels. She ruminated on the question for a time, and Helen reflected that Eleanor Widener had the most rosy and exquisite skin she'd ever seen on a woman her age. In the candlelight she looked twenty years younger than she probably was, and her eyes were shining from the wine. "George, what word am I looking for?" the lady asked her husband.

"Hmmmph?" he grunted. "Oh, I'm sure I don't know."

"Men never pay attention, do they?" Eleanor smiled. She dropped her voice. "Of course, sometimes that's for the best." She waggled a ring finger suggestively when she said it.

"On the contrary," Helen said with a sniff. "Lan is rather involved with the children. From a distance, you know. But he always has been."

"Has he?" she said, surprised.

"Oh, yes. They'd tell you otherwise, I'm sure. But they just don't know him as I do. He always had it in his head that we'd have three. Even had their names all picked out. And he pays close attention to everything that they do, knows all their little peccadilloes. How a man seems and how a man is can be so different sometimes, don't you agree?"

"Hear that, George?" Eleanor said with an arch of her eyebrow. But Mr. Widener was busy winding his pocket watch and didn't respond.

"He'd never admit it, but he's quite fond of them. They'd probably be shocked to hear me say so. You know how children are. Scared of their fathers, sometimes. Intimidated. But I can tell. He dotes on them," Helen said with a pleased smile.

"Well, of course he would. Eulah's quite the butterfly, isn't she? Just lovely," Eleanor agreed, and Helen beamed.

"She's a pistol. That's what her father says. Personally, I think she takes after me." Helen pressed a modest hand to her chest and fluttered her eyes as she made this pronouncement. "But you know," she said, dropping her voice to confidential tones, "his real favorite is our eldest."

"Which one is that?" Mrs. Widener asked, taking another sip of her wine.

The band tuned up and launched into a sedate foxtrot, and Helen lifted her chin, looking for a glimpse of Eulah's vermilion silk. "Sibyl," she said, eyes still scanning the crowd. No sign of Eulah. Where could she have gone?

"That's a beautiful name."

"You think so? I thought it was awfully queer, when he chose it for her. But I guess it's grown on me," Helen said, giving up her search and turning back to her tablemate. She pressed her lips together, thinking about her older daughter. Such a serious girl. Even playing, as a child, she did so with a seriousness of purpose. Harley toddling along after her, Sibyl giving him instructions. He was her little lieutenant. And so stubborn! No one could ever tell Sibyl anything. It was a relief that she was so reliable. Imagine, a child with Eulah's freewheeling outlook and Sibyl's independence! Why, her heart quailed to even think of it.

Sibyl grew up pretty enough, Helen supposed. A little dark. A shade too thin. But she had suitors, perfectly fine ones. The Coombs boy. He was innocuous, but adequate. She had liked that Derby fellow well enough, and he might have taken up Richard's stake in the firm. Give Lan a proper heir apparent. For a time it looked like Sibyl would be all right. Lan had been so certain! But something happened. Helen never understood what. She worried that Sibyl had been too coy. Too much the friend, and not enough of a woman. Finally Helen had to accept that Sibyl was a lost cause. They would be just as happy to keep her at home, if that's how it was going to be. Particularly when Lan got older. Sibyl would be invaluable then.

"Well, I think it's rather elegant," Eleanor said, lifting her nose with a sniff. Her fingers turned her wineglass on the tablecloth.

"She's so like her father," Helen mused, gazing at the nosegay of lilies forming the table centerpiece.

"Oh? How's that?"

Helen paused, thinking. She had been seventeen when she first met

Lan Allston. It was at a dinner dance given by her Boston Edgell cousins, and Helen remembered that that night was the first time her mother let her wear her hair up. She'd felt awfully mature, with that heap of curls pinned on her head, and the high bustle in the back of her dress rustling with taffeta formality. She'd taken the train in all the way from Framingham for the occasion with her mother, whose ambition for Helen made her own for Eulah look laughable in comparison. It wasn't often she was invited to dances in Boston. Her mother was determined to make it count. Most of the train ride was spent listening to her mother emit a stream of commentary on who might be there, and who Helen should endeavor to meet, and what Helen must, under no circumstances, say.

But Helen was never very sure of herself, especially not at seventeen. When they finally arrived at the dance she loitered on the periphery of the drawing room, alone, watching as crowds of young people laughed and stepped their way through a quadrille. Twisting her hands together in her purple taffeta, Helen wished she could disappear behind the potted fern. None of the other girls were wearing purple. Maybe it was old-fashioned? She didn't know anyone except her cousin Constance, who was older, anyway, and who always seemed like she was being nice to Helen out of a sense of duty, and not because she wanted to.

"Go on," her mother hissed in Helen's ear. "Circulate, at least!" Helen felt a sharp pinch on the flesh of her upper arm, and she squeaked.

"Mother!" she hissed back. But there was no arguing with Mehitabel Edgell. Helen felt her mother's eyes boring holes in the back of her neck as she propelled her recalcitrant daughter from behind the fern around the edge of the room, and deposited her within a crowd of strange men's shoulders. Helen's heart thudded in her chest, and she broke into a clammy sweat.

"Why, it's you!" a merry voice said in her ear. "I wondered if I'd find you here."

Helen jumped and looked around to see who had spoken. There, standing at her shoulder, was an elegant man who looked to be in his early thirties. He was tall and regal-looking, with his hair longer than was fashionable, and sideburns reaching almost to his jaw. His eyes were an unsettling shade of pale blue and had creases around them that had been burned there by the sun. He was smiling down at her.

"Me?" she said, taking a step back. "Have we met before?"

"I don't believe we have," he said. "I apologize for not arranging a more proper introduction. I'm Harlan Plummer Allston Junior." He half bowed with an air of ironic seriousness. "But, of course, no one calls me that."

She laughed before she could help herself. He was old, but he was sort of funny. "Oh? And what do they call you, then?" she asked.

"Lan," he said. "And you're called Helen, aren't you?"

She gasped, so surprised that she grew light-headed. Her mother had laced her too tight, as usual. "Why," she stammered. "Yes. Yes, I am. Helen Edgell."

"I thought so," he said. She stared at him, her lips parted in wonder. Something about Lan Allston soothed her. Most of the other men in the room struck Helen as arrogant, overcompensating by putting on airs of sophistication. But something about Lan Allston was serene and unreachable. She gazed into his eyes, seeing depths of experience there that she knew she would never understand, which lent him a gravitas that the other men were lacking. And this man, whose respectability struck Helen as hard won rather than given, was focusing his attention on her.

"You haven't danced yet, have you?" he said, offering his hand. "Did you lose your card?"

"N-no. I haven't. It's . . . you know, I'm not sure where I put it," Helen said. She placed her hand in his without a moment's hesitation. The skin of his hand was rough and weathered in a way that made Helen shiver. It was a hand that had been places far beyond Framingham.

"Then we must remedy that," he said with a smile. Helen let herself be led into the center of the dance floor, to be spun around the room with ease in the sturdy arms of the man who, she knew with sudden clarity, would be her husband.

"Helen?" Eleanor Widener prodded her.

"Oh?" What was she talking about? Oh. Sibyl. Of course.

"Your eldest? She's like her father, you said."

"Ah." Helen paused. And so she was. There was something of the Allston stillness in Sibyl. The same uncanny certainty that Helen had sensed in Lan that first night she met him. "I suppose that Sibyl has her father's"— Helen groped for the right word—"resilience. They take everything in stride.

Most things, anyway." She paused again, and Eleanor leaned forward, waiting for Helen to continue.

The tune changed, and several couples made their way back to their tables as a bevy of waiters deposited the first course of supper, starting with the captain's table.

"Where could they be?" Helen asked aloud, searching the crowd for Eulah and Harry. "You don't think something can have happened, do you?"

Eleanor Widener laughed. "Indeed not, Helen," she said, placing a hand on Helen's forearm. "There's nothing to worry about. Not a thing in the world."

TWENTY-TWO

The Back Bay
Boston, Massachusetts
May 7, 1915

"But that's impossible," Sibyl said. Her stomach dropped, the same sensation she had riding the roller coaster at Revere Beach one ill-advised summer afternoon years ago. The tottering and tipping at a high apex, and then the sickening fall and spin, the sound of screams in her ears. She thought she was going to be sick.

"We only just saw him! He couldn't have been."

"He was," Benton said. Sibyl saw that his eyes were red-rimmed and raw. He reached a hand to Sibyl's knee, and the warm pressure of his fingertips told her that this was real, what he was saying. This was really happening. "Edwin Friend was definitely on *Lusitania*."

"But I don't understand," she protested. A bubble of panic rose in her chest, panic tinged with despair.

"He told us he was sailing, remember? That was why we had to hurry and see Mrs. Dee the day we went to his office. That was why it couldn't wait. He was set to sail from New York the next day. May first, it was. I had a cable from him on the dock, as a matter of fact. They were delayed by a couple of hours as they took on some passengers from another ship that had just been requisitioned."

"Requisitioned!"

"For the war. They can do that, you know."

"Oh. The war. Of course." Sibyl let her breath out, a confused coldness spreading within her, as though she had taken a long drink of ice water. She looked down into her lap and then glanced up to Benton's face. "But is he . . . ?"

"There's no knowing," Benton said. "None of the newspapers can agree about how many casualties there've been. I've tried calling Cunard, but there's no getting through. The operator told me not to bother, nobody's getting through at all. She suggested I watch the papers instead. But so far half of them say everyone's been lost, and the other half say everyone's been saved. I can't tell what's true. It's madness."

Sibyl's grip tightened on her own hands in impotent worry, her needlepoint slipping to the floor unheeded. She blinked back the hot tears that were trying to force their way out of her eyes. "But. He could be saved, then couldn't he?"

Benton watched her, and his own eyes reddened. "I'm hoping. I'm—" He paused, not meeting her eyes. "Praying, even. I'm praying."

They sat for a long silent moment, each weighing in private horror the feeling of an ocean liner shifting underfoot, listing, being swallowed by the gaping maw of the sea.

"Then all we can do is wait. We have to wait," Sibyl said. "Oh, my God," she added, remembering the ring on his hand. She looked with new horror at Benton. "He has a wife, doesn't he?"

Benton looked down and nodded, wiping his eye with the back of his wrist. "He does. And she's going to have a child. In four months."

Sibyl's breath caught in a stifled sob. "Oh," she whispered, placing her head in her hands. "Oh, poor Edwin. I didn't know that."

"It was in the cable he sent me. Asked me to look in on her while he was away. I'd thought something was up, you know. He'd been even punchier than usual the past few weeks. But I can't believe he'd go overseas at a time like this. That damned fellowship that he got. Meeting with the British Society for Psychical Research, or some nonsense. The consulate as good as warned the passengers that it would happen. Did you see the announcement? In the paper, no less!"

"They did?"

"They did. Here it is."

TRAVELLERS intending to embark on the Atlantic voyage are reminded that a state of war exists between Germany and her allies and Great Britain and her allies; that the zone of war includes the waters adjacent to the British Isles; that, in accordance with formal notice given by the Imperial German Government, vessels flying the flag of Great Britain, or any of her allies, are liable to destruction in those waters and that travellers sailing in the war zone on the ships of Great Britain or her allies do so at their own risk.

IMPERIAL GERMAN EMBASSY
Washington, D.C. 22nd April 1915

"They said it. It's practically a promise."

"Why in God's name would he go? Why would any of them? I had no idea they'd issued a warning like that. What could have been in his head?" Sibyl exclaimed, a tear escaping her eyelid and streaking down her cheek. Her face was blotchy and hot.

"I wish I knew. But he's always been so damnably confident. He'd have been too excited thinking about his conference. And anyway, plenty of people thought they'd never have the nerve to attack an ocean liner. He'd have said the same."

Benton's face blackened with anger at his friend and colleague. "Stubborn as a mule," he added, voice breaking again. He sank his head in his hands, and Sibyl saw his shoulders shuddering. She didn't comment, instead letting him sit like that, resting her own hand on his knee.

"Ben," she whispered. She moved her hand to his back and stroked his shoulder. "Ben," she whispered again.

UPSTAIRS, SIBYL UNWOUND her hair and ran a brush through it, listless. They'd had a nearly silent supper, Benton pushing vegetables around his plate, responding in monosyllables. He was still downstairs, playing a disinterested hand of cards with Harlan while her brother chattered about what Wilson would do next. Benton seemed unwilling to go home, and no one mentioned the time.

Half undressed, her blouse undone at the throat and hair loose around her shoulders, Sibyl sank into her armchair and gazed into the fire, thinking about Edwin Friend. His warm, sparkling eyes. His expectant wife. She must be frantic with worry. Benton had phoned her from the front hallway, just before dinner, and Sibyl had done her best not to eavesdrop. But the hopeless expression on Benton's face after the call told her that there was still no news.

The fire popped. Sibyl brought a thumbnail to her mouth and gave it a meditative chew.

She caught sight of her reflection in the window glass, her face drawn and pale, faint purplish circles under her eyes.

"*It's because you're such a worrier,*" Eulah's voice suggested in Sibyl's mind. "*Look, you're making yourself older just by fretting. There's no use fretting, you know. I never fretted, did I? If you fret, it'll just make him not notice you.*"

"What?" Sibyl whispered to herself.

A scratch came at the door. Then another. Sibyl glanced up. The scratch turned into a soft knock.

She quickly fastened the buttons on her blouse and moved to open it.

"Oh!" Benton exclaimed, seeing her hair undone. "I'm—I'm terribly sorry. I didn't mean to disturb you."

Sibyl swallowed, her eyes darting around her room to check for any improper signs of female residency. A corset lay abandoned on the floor in a tangle of laces, and her dressing gown was draped over the back of the armchair near the fireplace, a drooping puddle of silk. The bed linens were mussed, the pillows still deformed from the pressure of her sleeping head.

"Not at all," she said, recovering from her surprise, and nudging the errant corset under the bed with a toe. "That is," she corrected herself, "I'm afraid it's a bit of a mess."

He edged around the corner of the room, trying, and failing, not to let his eyes roam around this private feminine cloister. "I would never wish to intrude," he began, "but I was thinking. About Edwin. And I had a question that I wanted to ask you. If you don't mind."

She reached forward and drew the dressing gown away from the back of the armchair, the silk making a soft whispering sound as she did so. Benton swallowed, visibly.

"All right," she said. "Sit down, then."

He did so, perching on the edge of the chair, as though settling comfortably would betray an inappropriate degree of ease with being where he was. She seated herself across from him, running a hand through her loose hair without thinking.

"What is it?" she asked.

He looked around, as though he might find a clue for how to begin secreted somewhere in the carpeting. "I was wondering," he said. "How much you knew. Of Edwin's travel plans."

"What?" Sibyl asked, perplexed.

"Edwin told us he was traveling. What did you know about his trip?"

Sibyl's dark brows knotted together over her eyes. "Why, nothing," she said.

"You didn't know he was going overseas. And that he was taking a steamer."

"No," she said. "I only ever spoke with him when you were there. He didn't tell us his exact plans. Did he? I don't think he did."

"That's what I thought," Ben said, bringing a finger alongside his temple and staring into the fire.

"Why are you asking me this?"

He hesitated, shifting uncomfortably in his seat. "I don't know. Something's bothering me, but I can't put my finger on it."

"Poor Edwin," she said, thinking. The young professor's face hung before her, the image of him from her vision crowding in on her thoughts. Sibyl reached for the newspaper on the end table, scanning the late edition for more details on what precisely had happened to the ship.

"Can this be right?" she asked, peering at the paper. The newsprint was so fresh that it peeled off the page, staining her fingers as she read. "They don't know how many torpedoes it was?"

"They don't. Some reports say it must have been two, as the ship was too grand and powerful to be breached by just one."

Sibyl sat, eyes wide, thinking back to the closing image of the vision that she had been revisiting, daily, in secret, alone in her rooms for the past few weeks. First came the one explosion, the shattering impact of something striking the hull, which she didn't see, but rather felt. Then a second, deeper explosion, the one that she could see through the dining room window, that blew itself outward, shooting water and debris into the sunny afternoon sky.

"The boiler," she remarked to herself, eyes widening. "It must be." She turned to him, growing increasingly certain the more she considered it. "Ben! Oh, my God." As the realization dawned on her, Sibyl sank beneath a crushing wave of guilt.

She'd known. She'd seen it. And she hadn't done anything to stop him going. She hadn't understood in time.

Benton leaned forward, his elbows on his knees, looking at her with concern. "What is it, Sibyl? What's the matter?"

"Lusitania." She moaned, holding her temples between her hands. "Oh, my God, why didn't I tell him? Why didn't I say something?"

"What are you talking about?"

She climbed from her chair and knelt before him, searching up into his face, her lip trembling. "Benton," she whispered. "I was wrong. In that vision. The one I kept having. I was wrong."

"What do you mean?" Benton looked stricken.

"It must be. In all those times I never actually saw the name of the ship anywhere. I didn't see the stern, and didn't find it written anywhere inside. I just assumed . . . I assumed . . ." She trailed off, still on her heels, newspaper dropping to her lap, hands covering her face. Her voice caught in a sob, and she groaned, "Oh, no."

Benton looked at her strangely, uncomprehending. "I don't follow. What were you wrong about? Sibyl, tell me. Please."

She placed both her hands on his knees and said, "What if—" She paused, afraid to give voice to what she was thinking. "Benton, what if it wasn't *Titanic* I was seeing after all?"

He frowned in confusion. "What? Impossible."

"But you said yourself, the image changed as I practiced. At first all I saw was ocean. Then I saw the ship, but it was nighttime. What if I was seeing the ship at night at first because it's what I was expecting to see?"

"But your expectations never changed. You always thought you were seeing your family's last moments. You never wavered."

"You're right," she said, looking desperately up into his face. "But, Ben, I was mistaken. I must have been. The daylight? And then at the very end, Professor Friend? I wasn't seeing *Titanic*. I was seeing *Lusitania*! Oh, poor Edwin." She choked, the guilt and horror of her mistake squeezing the breath out of her like a vise.

"Coincidence. It must be."

"How can it be? I couldn't just make it up. Not and have so many of the details be accurate. Things I couldn't possibly know."

Benton stood, moving away from her to stand with his hands propped on the fireplace mantel, his head low between his arms. He shook his head, pressing his weight into the mantel, as if he could push the very idea away from him. "What you're saying," he said, his back to her. "I can't accept it. It's just not possible."

Sibyl scrambled to her feet, moving near to him and placing her hand on his arm. His muscles tensed under her touch. "Ben," she said. "It can't be a coincidence. It can't be. The daylight? The explosions? Professor Friend being there, without his wife? I couldn't possibly imagine all those things. Maybe one or two of them, but not all." Two tears squeezed out from the corners of her eyes. A baby would grow up without a father because she hadn't understood. "How else do you explain it? I didn't understand. I failed. I thought I was seeing the past. But I wasn't. I was seeing the future."

He spun and looked at her with a wild expression. "Then why would the image have changed?" he demanded. "Explain that. If you were seeing something real, something that was really happening out there, in the world"—he swept his hand out in an all-encompassing gesture—"then it wouldn't change, would it? What you're seeing, it's just dream stuff, Sibyl. It has to be. You put yourself into a kind of . . . a kind of. . . . Oh, I don't know. A trance. Self-hypnosis. It's been known to happen, I've seen it myself. And then your imagination shows you a cluster of symbols that pertain specifically to you, to your own subconscious mind. That's the only explanation that could possibly make sense. It's nothing to do with what happens to people out in the real world."

"I know. You're probably right," she said. "But what if—what if this scrying glass were like playing music? Or—oh, I don't know—sewing? You can't just pick those things up and do them perfectly the first time. They've got to be practiced. You should see the first pillow I tried needle-pointing. I threw it away, it was so awful. And Eulah! Everyone thought she was this marvelous dancer, but she used to practice her steps so much at night that she'd even do it without thinking, while she was brushing her teeth."

He eyed her, wary. Sibyl tightened her grip on his arm. "She said," Sibyl tried again, "Mrs. Dee said the scrying glass was for seeing. But she never told me *what* I might see, did she?"

"She's a fraud, Sibyl," he said, and his voice had a chill in it that she hadn't heard before. "And you know it. The only thing you're liable to see in that glass is what's already in your own mind. You're just sad that Edwin's likely been lost. It's grief. That's what it is. And you feel guilty. But you couldn't have done anything. None of us could have. The only thing that would've saved Edwin is if the Germans didn't torpedo that liner."

She released his arm, dropping her hand to her side and squaring her shoulders with resolve.

"All right," Sibyl said, her voice calm. "So it's all imaginary. It's all in my head. In that case, then, there's no harm in trying again, is there?"

"What do you mean?" He straightened, staring at her.

"If the images I've seen are nothing but a collection of ideas in my sub-conscious," Sibyl said, "subject to changes that are also within my mind, then the vision should stay basically the same if I try it again, despite what's just happened. Right?"

"Do you hear what you're suggesting?" he asked with a wretched expression. "When both your father and I have warned you about the dangers?"

Sibyl's eyes blackened to the color of obsidian, and she folded her arms over her chest. Standing with her arms crossed kept her hands from trem-bling. "I don't care. I'm going to try it again."

"Sibyl," he started to object, but she ignored him.

Turning away, she busied herself at her dressing table. Sibyl still had the bottle of laudanum that she had stolen from her father, and it had a few measures of amber liquid left. She lit a stub of candle, tossing the match into the grate of her fireplace, and paused, running her fingers over the wooden box that held the scrying glass.

She mixed a measure of laudanum in the sherry glass that was now a permanent resident on her end table. She carried it, together with the candle and crystal ball, over to the low table by the fireplace and dropped into the chair. Watching her, face bent in a worried frown, Benton lowered himself back into his armchair and knotted his hands together.

"This is a bad idea," he muttered. But he made no move to stop her. The space between them hummed with sudden tension. The fire popped.

She took a delicate sip from the sherry glass. Oddly, the bitter taste didn't bother her as much as it had before. She wouldn't say she liked it, exactly, but she found herself almost . . . anticipating it. While she swallowed the noxious liquid, Benton fumbled in his coat pockets for his cigarettes and leaned forward to light one on her candle.

He leaned back up, inhaling with a squinted eye against the smoke of his cigarette, watching her closely. She took another sip of her laudanum mixture, and as the liquid passed her lips she observed him lick his own lips, unawares.

"It's all right, Ben," she soothed, setting the glass to one side and leaning her head against the back of her chair as the intoxicating weight spread through her limbs. "I'm perfectly fine."

"We'll see," he said, still watching her.

She frowned, but put his comment out of her mind. The smoke coiled up from his cigarette, the only movement in the otherwise silent room. She waited until the weight, the wonderful sluggishness, felt familiar, telling her that she had reached the right level for what she wanted to do. Then she opened the wooden box and withdrew the glass from its velvet nest.

The scrying glass's surface appeared a dull milky blue, shot through with veins of quartz. Sibyl leaned back in her chair, bringing the ball close to her face. She focused her gaze on its surface, where the glimmers of light thrown off by the candle scattered in warm orange speckles. In the background, Benton's face grew fuzzy and out of focus.

Earlier in the year Sibyl had attended an exhibition of pictures at the Copley Society of Art. Standing in the narrow Newbury Street gallery, she gazed on a painting that at first looked like nothing but blotches of paint, different colors all rioting in a nonsensical mass. She leaned in closer, bringing her nose almost up to the canvas (so new it still smelled of linseed oil), and the colors blurred together. But then, as she moved away, stepping backward one foot at a time, the colors resolved into a recognizable form. If she softened her eyes and stopped trying to see the component parts of the painting, then its internal structure revealed itself—a narrow bridge, arcing over a shimmering pond dotted with lilies. Sibyl gasped with sudden recognition as it happened, and once she saw the image she didn't understand how she hadn't seen it earlier.

In some respects using the scrying glass felt similar to that, like seeing without being aware that she was seeing. Sibyl let her gaze play about, not looking at the surface, instead absorbing the interplay of light and shadow. At first she saw nothing. She let her eyes relax. When Mrs. Dee showed her how to use the glass she made a fetish of hard concentration, but that didn't seem right to Sibyl. Of course, Mrs. Dee was a fake. Or, if not a complete fake, as she claimed, then her fakery long ago eclipsed any real talent the woman may have had.

Sibyl let these thoughts drift through her mind, and set them aside. The spots of candlelight on the orb's surface glowed, merging together in a web of light and then drawing into the center of the ball. The collected pinpoint of light deep inside the scrying glass began to release familiar coils of rich black smoke. Sibyl released an audible sigh of pleasure.

"Sibyl?" Benton asked, his eyes growing concerned. When she didn't respond, he muttered, "I knew this was a bad idea," and took a long drag on his cigarette.

Inside the ball the black smoke thickened, rolling back on itself. Her lips parted in anticipation, looking for the familiar ocean surface. She waited, and she waited, but for some reason, the image didn't change. The smoke stayed, moving, always moving, but it stayed.

Her eyebrows lowered in a scowl over her eyes, and Benton edged nearer to her, near enough that she was aware of his breath on her cheek, and he asked, "What is it?"

Then, deep within the smoky haze, Sibyl saw flickering lights. In clusters. A flash here. Another flash there. Like lightning, but not quite. Not the cold white light of lightning, but a hotter light, reddish, and each burst attended by tiny bits of what looked like dirt or debris. She watched this rumbling series of explosions within the smoke as it went on for several minutes. Then, with no further clarity or explanation, the lights slowly receded within the coils of smoke, growing fainter and farther away. The smoke drew into itself, pulling away from the surface of the orb until it vanished, leaving the scrying glass perfectly clear.

Sibyl sighed, dropping the ball to her lap.

"Well?" Benton prodded, stubbing out the end of his cigarette and leaning in to hear what Sibyl had to say.

"What?" she asked, shaking herself awake. She was startled to find Benton staring at her with those delving gray eyes. Benton, in her bedroom. What was Benton doing in her bedroom? She couldn't remember how he had gotten there. She opened her mouth to speak, and when nothing came out he sprang to his feet and fetched her a glass of water from the decanter on top of the vanity table.

She swallowed, grateful, rinsing away the unpleasant aftertaste of the laudanum.

"Better?" he asked. Benton sat down again across from her. She nodded, setting the glass aside.

"Yes," she said, pasting a reassuring smile onto her face. But the smile was troubled.

"So," he began. "Was it as you suspected? Was the vision the same?"

She looked him in the face, her dark eyes wide. She shook her head.

He leaned back in the armchair, bringing a meditative hand up to his chin. "Really," he said.

"No," she whispered. "I thought it was at first. It started the same, with the black smoke. But then it was completely different. Perhaps I . . . perhaps I wasn't doing it right this time."

"What did you see?" he asked. Sibyl could hear in his tone the faintest sliver of doubt.

"Well," Sibyl said, trying to sift sense from what she had seen. "There was the black smoke, sort of billowing in on itself. That's how it always starts. And then usually it parts and reveals the surface of the ocean. I waited, but the smoke never parted this time. Instead, there were these sorts of flashes of light. Inside the smoke. Almost like explosions, because after a time it looked as though with each flash of light there was some . . . stuff . . . dirt, maybe? I don't know. It would go shooting up in the air. But I couldn't be sure, because the smoke never cleared."

"And then?" he prompted, hanging on her words.

"And then," she said, frowning as she gazed into the middle distance between them, trying to remember. "Then, nothing. The lights receded. The smoke went away. And it was over. That was all."

Benton got to his feet with a strangled growl, as though his thoughts were racing beyond his control. He stalked back and forth in the small space behind the armchair. "Impossible," he muttered. "I don't see how it can be possible."

"Ben!" Sibyl cried, getting to her feet. "What is it?"

He moved over to her and took her hands in his. His grip was warm and dry, reassuring, and Sibyl's skin tingled from the pressure of his hands. "The vision. It changed, just as you surmised it would," he said. "You said that if I were right, and the glass only showed you what was in your own mind, then it wouldn't change. But if it was showing you something real, something true, then it would."

"Yes," she replied, searching his face.

"Sibyl, I— There are those who don't hold that psychology is a science." He faltered, his grip on her hands tightening. "But I've always considered myself a serious person. A scientific person."

"But of course," she said.

In his voice, the sliver of doubt deepened. "If what you're saying is true . . ." he started, then stopped himself, looking down at his shoes. Then he glanced up again. "I think we should test you. In controlled circumstances. Then we'll know for sure."

"Test me?" she echoed. His face was close to hers, close enough that she could see the texture of his cheeks, nubbled with beard. She could smell the tobacco on his breath.

He paused, looking down at her, and his eyes filled with a tenderness that she had never seen in them before. He held her gaze for a long, excruciating moment. Sibyl gazed up at him, feeling her heart thudding in her chest. Benton leaned nearer.

"But there's . . ." he said, hesitating. "There's something that I'm afraid I must do first."

"What?" she asked, eyebrows rising.

He brought his hands to trace along the line of her jaw, cupping her face. His thumbs brushed over the corners of her mouth, testing them. She held her breath, searching into his eyes.

"I'm sorry," he whispered. "But I have to."

With that his mouth found hers, pressing there with tingling warmth and urgency. Her eyes drifted closed, relishing the sensation of his lips on hers, the nearness of his body, breathing him in. The perfect feeling lasted only an instant before he broke away, smiling down on her.

"Come on," Benton said. He took her hands, and gave them a squeeze. "There's no time to waste."

TWENTY-THREE

Harry Elkins Widener Library
Harvard University
Cambridge, Massachusetts
May 7, 1915

Clusters of college boys strode past the marble stairs of the new Harvard college library, their shadows stretched long by the streetlights that dotted the pathways through the Yard, like the shapes cast by a spider perched on a glass lamp.

"Ben," Sibyl started to say. "I don't know."

Benton gave her a mischievous glance. "I'm a professor, remember? They'll be open."

The main library vestibule smelled of fresh polish and paint, and their footsteps echoed through an elegant marble hall. Mrs. Widener would be proud to see her considerable fortune so well spent. Sibyl followed close behind Benton into a room lined with wooden card catalogue cabinets.

"Scrying," he muttered. "Let's see, here."

His sturdy fingers riffled through the cards with astonishing speed. Flip, flip, flip, flip, and then they settled on the card they wanted. "Well,

Miss Allston," he said, in a teasing tone, "it appears that there is a single book in all of fair Harvard's library collections that addresses our subject matter. And it's in French. How about that?"

"French!" she exclaimed.

"You read French, don't you?" He smiled. "I thought all proper Bostonian young ladies could read French and play pianoforte and do needlepoint pillows and dance a cotillion."

Sibyl rolled her eyes. "But of course! That's how you can tell we are *accomplished*," she said, placing artificial emphasis on the last word.

"Well, that's a relief," he said. "Because mine's pretty rusty. When we moved to Italy, I'm afraid the Italian pushed aside whatever meager French Andover had managed to impart to me." He smiled, a sadness behind it. Sibyl rested a reassuring hand on his arm.

At the circulation desk, the laconic young man working his rubber library stamp said, "Working late tonight, then, Professor Derby?"

"Seems so," he said, passing the boy the call slip.

"*Le Sang de Morphée*, huh? That's some kinda strange title."

"The Blood of Morpheus," Sibyl translated. She glanced at Benton, worried. He smiled at her, and she felt his hand come to rest on the small of her back.

"Right you are," the boy affirmed. "But you're not the first person to ask for that book this week. Thought it was a weird title then, too."

"Beg pardon?" Benton said.

"Hang on," the boy said, riffling through a box of note cards. "Aha! Yep. It's charged out to another professor. You want I should recall it? Take a few weeks, probably."

"Perhaps whoever it is will just let me take a quick look," he said, leaning forward on a conspiratorial elbow. "I don't suppose you could tell me who's got it, could you?"

The boy gave Benton a long look. "You know I'm not supposed to do that," he said.

Around them footsteps and rising voices signaled the closing of the building for the night. In the adjoining periodicals room the lights snapped off.

"Oh, sure," Benton said. "But listen. I just need a peek at it. I'm sure whoever it is won't mind if I just drop by. Saves us all the trouble of having to recall it and charge it out all over again. Right?"

The boy weighed this idea, calculating the time and energy necessary to fill out the needed paperwork. "Okay," he demurred. "I suppose it'll be all right. Don't make a habit of it, though." He gave the professor a wily look, and said, "Maybe I'm just persuaded by your research assistant, here."

Sibyl blushed. Benton, however, smiled. "And a better research assistant I've never had," he said. His elbow nudged her ribs.

Without a word the boy passed the card to Benton, and then leaned on his elbows, chin on his hands, sending his most inviting smile in Sibyl's direction.

"Ha!" Benton exclaimed, looking at the card. "Well, I'll be damned. Thank you."

He slid the card back and took Sibyl's elbow. She glanced over her shoulder as they went, and the boy behind the desk waggled his fingers at her in a coquettish wave.

"Where are we going?" she asked as they hurried ahead of snapping-off lights, out the front doors of the library, and into the deepening darkness of the Yard.

Benton looked away and sighed. "I don't know why it should surprise me. His curiosity is insatiable. Always was." He then leveled his gaze at Sibyl, and she saw the red rims of his eyes. "Edwin," he said. "Edwin has it."

Sibyl bit her lower lip, sickened with guilt and sadness. "Professor Friend," she whispered. She stopped in her tracks, bringing her hands to her face. He paused, looking left and right before enfolding her in a quick embrace.

"Come now," he whispered to her. "Can you think of anyone else who'd be more excited by the idea of precognition? Real, provable precognition? Can you?"

She snuffled, eyes on her feet, shaking her head.

"Can you imagine how excited he'd be? If he were here, don't you think he'd insist on testing you right away? He would, wouldn't he?" Benton brought a hand up to Sibyl's hair and smoothed it off her brow. The hand then traced along her jaw and lifted her face to meet his gaze. She saw that his eyes had cleared, in fact were glimmering with resolve.

"He would," Sibyl agreed, wiping her damp eye with the back of her wrist.

"You bet he would," Benton said.

She stared up at him, probing. "Yes," she agreed. "All right."

He took her by the hand, gave it a reassuring squeeze, and they hurried to the philosophy building. With his free hand Benton rummaged in a pocket for a set of keys. He shook his head and muttered, "Dammit, Edwin. I don't see why you had to get on that blasted boat."

The door lock gave with a creak, and Benton held the door open for her to enter ahead of him.

"Ben," she asked, hesitant in the empty building. "How are we going to get it out of his office?"

"I'm not sure yet," he confessed.

All the lights were out. Sibyl shivered against the forlorn atmosphere haunting the philosophy building at night. Benton produced a silver cigarette lighter from his pocket and lit it, holding the flame overhead to guide them. Sibyl edged nearer, threading her arm around Benton's elbow.

"Nothing to worry about," he said, though she could tell he was injecting his voice with confidence for both their benefits. They moved down the hall, the flickering flame tossing their shadows about in a way that made Sibyl dizzy.

"I'm not worried," she lied.

They arrived at a glass door with the name FRIEND inked on it. Benton tried the door.

Locked.

"Drat," Sibyl said. Benton glanced at her, amused.

"*Drat?*" he repeated.

"What?" she said, folding her arms.

"Drat," he said again, smiling out of the side of his mouth.

"Now what do we do?" she asked.

"Hmm." Benton tried the door again, but it was just as locked as before. The two of them stared at the doorknob, each silently willing it to open of its own accord.

Benton glanced at Sibyl with a small, mischievous smile. "How daring are you feeling today?" he whispered.

"Well. I'm already in an abandoned classroom building in the dead of night with a strange—dare I say *very* strange—man. So I guess I'm feeling more daring than usual today."

"Touché," Benton said. He reached over and pulled a hairpin from Sibyl's hair. She gasped with surprise and brought a hand up to stay the slipping lock of hair. He grinned, said, "Thank you, Miss Allston," handed her the cigarette lighter, and knelt before the office door.

"Ben!" she hissed. Benton slid the pin into the mouth of the lock.

"Could you bring the light a bit closer, please?" he asked, concentrating. Gingerly, she knelt on the floor next to him, moving the flame as close as she dared without singeing his eyebrows.

"Wherever did you learn how to do this?" she whispered, peering down her nose as he made delicate, gentle probing movements with the pin inside the lock.

"They don't just teach French at Andover," he said. They heard a soft *click*. Benton reached up and turned the handle of the door. He looked at her with a small smile. "I read about it once in a book of detective stories. When I was a boy."

She laughed and accepted his help getting to her feet.

The room was illuminated only by shafts of pale moonlight falling through the windows behind the central wooden desk. Sibyl could just make out the ghostly shapes of furniture and books. She imagined she could almost see the form of Edwin Friend, bent over the pile of undergraduate term papers still heaped before his empty desk chair. She swallowed. If only she'd understood sooner.

"Ben," she whispered. "You're sure Edwin wouldn't mind?"

"I'm sure. In fact, knowing him, I think he'd enjoy it. You saw his face when I opened that cabinet at the Dee woman's place. But all the same, I think it would be better"—he kept his voice near a whisper—"if we didn't turn on the lights."

"I don't suppose the university would look kindly on a professor's rummaging in his colleague's office late at night," Sibyl agreed, scanning the bookshelves, eyes narrowed.

"Better to skirt the issue entirely," he suggested, seating himself behind the desk. He started sifting through papers. Sibyl moved to the bookshelf, squinting to read the spines of the books. She found numerous works of William James, together with other philosophers that she had never heard of. On a lower shelf, the full-bound edition of the *Proceedings of the American Society for Psychical Research*, and the companion volumes of the organization's British counterpart.

"Benton," she ventured. "How is it you and Professor Friend both studied with William James, yet you've come to such drastically different conclusions? I've never understood the feud between the two of you."

"Feud?" Benton said, opening desk drawers for a quick look. "There's no feud. I'd characterize it as a debate, rather than a feud. Edwin is—" He paused, and Sibyl thought he was considering his choice of verb tense. "A good friend of mine. And I had only the utmost respect for his intellect."

"Yet every time I saw you together, you seemed to be arguing."

Benton closed a drawer, leaned his head in his hands, and sighed. "Well, you're right that we both studied under Professor James. But Professor James held some contradictory beliefs, you see. He was the original Pragmatist. Any idea had to be tested for truth before it should be believed. Yet parapsychology—which, to my mind, is a matter of faith rather than science, and is therefore untestable—informed everything that he thought about the human mind. I guess" he paused "Edwin and I, we each took hold of opposing sides of James's thought. I espoused a pragmatic approach in the use of psychology. But Edwin, he was after something that, even if it *were* true—and I didn't think it was—but even if it were, it wouldn't really help anyone."

"The séances helped me, when I believed in them," Sibyl said slowly, dragging her fingertips along the book spines without looking at him. "I've never felt so soothed as when I believed Mrs. Dee was able to reach my mother. That one night, when I saw her hand . . ." She trailed off. "Well," she finished. "It helped."

"I know," he said. "But the thing of it is—" Benton paused, looking for a way to explain himself. "I suppose I can understand that. I can certainly sympathize with it. Don't you think there was a time in my life when I wanted nothing more than to live my life in the past?"

He waited. Sibyl looked at him and nodded without speaking. Benton held her gaze for a long moment, and looked away.

"But," he continued, his hands busy among the papers on Friend's desk, "a life spent only looking back, at the past, or ahead, after death, is a life that has no meaning. Edwin thought just the opposite. He thought that we should try to understand the beginnings and ends of a human life, the frame of it. But frankly, I'm much more interested in what happens in between."

Sibyl held the cigarette lighter overhead, rising onto her toes to scan the higher shelves of Professor Friend's books. "What was the title again? *Le Sang de Morphée?*" she asked, pulling a plain bound library book from a high shelf.

"That's it," Benton said, looking up. "Did you find it?"

"I believe I did," Sibyl said, her eyes lit with triumph. She held the slim volume out to show him the title on the cover.

"Excellent!" Benton exclaimed. "Now I propose we take it back to my laboratory. Then if anyone happens upon us, at least we won't have to explain ourselves."

"*You* won't, at any rate," Sibyl muttered. "Come to think of it, wasn't Harley expelled for a similar offense? Who'd think that Harvard would give so much more leeway to its junior faculty than it does its senior undergraduates?"

"I don't think it was quite the same set of circumstances." Benton grinned.

Benton restored Professor Friend's desktop to its undisturbed state, and the two of them crept out of the office. He paused in the doorway, taking a last look around the bookshelves and the desk, Sibyl's hand on his shoulder.

"Well," he whispered. "I guess that does it."

Her hand tightened.

"Thank you, Edwin. It's been my privilege, working with you." His voice caught, and he cleared his throat.

Benton and Sibyl glanced at each other, and she nodded to reassure him. He relocked the door, and Sibyl found his hand in the darkness, weaving their fingers together, their warm palms meeting with sureness as they hurried away.

"WELL?" SIBYL ASKED from inside the crook of her elbow. Her head drowsed in her folded arms on the cool soapstone of the laboratory table. The pipes in the psychology department clanked, the noise in the otherwise empty building causing her to twitch back to consciousness. Benton pored over the French book, reading, his mouth sounding out the words.

Sibyl sighed and sat up.

"Are you sure you wouldn't rather I read it?" she asked.

"No, no," he said, waving her off. He continued reading.

She crossed her arms, impatient. "I'll wager you a dollar my French is better. Is it a bet?" She held out her hand, trying to tempt him to shake on it.

"I have no doubt you're right," he said, pointedly refusing to take her hand. "But unfortunately, for the experiment to work, I must be the one to read it. We must keep you in the dark."

She sighed again, exaggerating the sound to indicate her boredom, and dropped her head back to the table.

"What sort of book is it, anyway?" she asked, voice muffled within her arms.

"Well," he said, flipping a page and jotting notes. "It seems to be a sort of report-cum-travelogue. Written, I think, by an anthropologist. The publication date is given as 1888."

"Mmhmm," she said, eyelids drooping. "And what's it got to say about scrying?"

"Some interesting things," he said, keeping coy. "Mostly it catalogues the cultural uses of opium. There's a long chapter on China. Indochina, also. The wars with Britain in the last century. Afghanistan. California, interestingly, especially San Francisco. I wouldn't have thought of that at first, but of course they have quite a lot of Chinese there. And then it goes into the uses. Medicinal. Spiritual. Escape. Pleasure."

She half raised her head to look at him, but the loose ribbon of hair freed by her stolen hairpin drifted into her eyes, and so she rested her head back down.

"You know, it's curious, Benton. I can't tell whether you believe it's true, what I've been seeing."

He laid his pen to the side and rubbed his fingertips over his eyes, under his spectacles. Then he dropped his hands to the laboratory table and looked at her.

"I can't tell, either," he confessed. "My heart is shocked that Edwin has likely died, in such a tragic and spectacular way, and astonished that you might have seen it before it happened. My mind, of course, knows this is impossible. And now your vision has changed. My mind tells me that the change is merely a result of suggestibility, of the changes within your psyche in response to shock and nervous strain. My heart—" He trailed off, gazing beyond Sibyl into an undefined middle distance.

Sibyl placed her hand on his forearm. Her touch brought him back to himself, and he picked up the pen, turning to his notes, leaving his unfinished thought hanging in the air.

"Now then," he said. "One of the reasons paranormal skills are so difficult to test is that they often take place outside of a laboratory setting. They happen in a medium's parlor, say, which as you know can feature all sorts of sophisticated gadgetry. Surrounded, furthermore, by people with a vested interest in the outcome, which can cause a subject to behave, consciously or not, in a way designed to please the spectators. Further, in settings such as that, a naïve subject—"

"Naïve!" she protested.

"It's not a judgment on your character," he assured her. "It means in this case only that you are not actively trying to fool the researcher. You aren't, are you?" He smiled at her in good-natured collusion, and his foot nudged hers under the laboratory table.

"Of course not," she said, straightening in her chair.

"Well, all right," he said. "As I say, the challenge lies in conducting the experiment in a controlled setting, free of suggestion. And in your case, there's also the question of . . ." He trailed off.

"Of?" she pressed.

"Well," he said. "Of dosage."

"Ah." She looked down at her hands.

They trembled. Just a little.

"The book has a chapter which posits that whereas most people under a heavy dose of opiate experience vivid flights of fancy, a select few acquire unusual self-knowledge. Which raises an interesting question."

"Yes," Sibyl said, uncertain.

"That is, what, exactly, are you seeing? How do these events, if that's what they truly are, relate to yourself specifically?" He watched her.

Sibyl twisted her fingers together in her lap and looked with worried eyes into Benton's face.

"I don't know," she said in a small voice.

"All right. Perhaps that's something we'll find out, then. Are you ready to begin?" he asked.

Sibyl squared her shoulders and tucked the loose strand of hair out of her eyes.

"Yes," Sibyl said. "I'm ready."

Interlude

Shanghai
Old City
June 8–9, 1868

"ME," LANNIE BREATHED.

There inside the tea leaves stood himself, dressed in his present clothes, feet planted apart, holding a dripping knife. His left arm wiped across his forehead, smearing grime. Lannie's pale eyes glowed an unsettling blue. At his feet lay two men, one curled up, leg twitching, and the other, Johnny, stretched out on his stomach, motionless.

Lannie stared into the teacup, overwhelmed with horror, insensible to everything but the imperative that he must change what he'd just seen. He squinted his eyes closed, but the image lingered behind his eyelids as if burned there.

"Hmmmm?" inquired an unconcerned voice. Lannie wrenched an eye open. He was met with the scholar's dangling arm over the edge of his bunk.

"I told you not to spend too long in the pipe dream. Not always so pretty, is it."

"But you don't understand," Lannie started to protest. His hands clutched the teacup so hard that his knuckles were white.

"No, don't tell me," the young man said, waving his arm back and forth like a pendulum. "I have no desire to see into the twisted soul of a Yankee barbarian. Less than no desire."

"It seemed so real. . . ." Lannie trailed off. Johnny's arm swam in and out of focus.

"That's the funny thing about lotus eating," the scholar mused. "What's real, and what's not real, turns out to be more fluid than we expect." He paused, as though weighing whether or not to say more. "Once, I spent too long in a pipe dream. I saw my father's house explode in a giant ball of hell-fire. I could hear my mother screaming. I saw my sister run out the door with her hair in flames. I screamed and wept, I was so persuaded it was real. For hours, I was inconsolable. They threw me out of the den because I was upsetting the others. I roamed the streets, blind with grief."

"And did your father's house really explode?" Lannie asked, in a remnant of the voice from when he was a child.

"Of course not. He lives to this day, in the same fine house as always. Spending his days counting his money and wondering why I haven't married. It's just a dream, you know. Called up from your mind. And easily changed. Look again, you'll see what I mean."

"I couldn't," Lannie said, his voice breaking. "It's too horrible. I can't stand it."

"Nonsense," the young man said. "Look again. Maybe hold the glass differently this time. It'll change your point of view."

"What do you mean, change my point of view?"

"Parallax," said the voice from overhead. "Boy, you must be one terrible navigator. Remind me never to go sailing with you."

Frowning, Lannie looked back into his teacup. Parallax. Objects seeming to move or change position based on the perspective from which they were viewed. It was an important part of celestial navigation. He swirled the watery tea in the bottom of his cup, watching the light scatter across its surface. This time, he tipped the glass toward his face, elongating the surface area of the water, causing the leaves to swirl together in a subtly different way.

The pattern formed a dark black cloud, thick and oily. Then the cloud pulled apart like the curtains of a *tableau vivant*, revealing the circle of braying men, frozen like insects in amber.

"Well, how d'you like that," Lannie breathed. He shifted the angle a hairsbreadth, and the scene sprang to animated life. The men shouted, urging on the two fighters. But something was different: this time, the other man didn't lunge for Johnny's throat. Instead, Johnny's fist connected with the stranger's jaw. When the man's head rocked back from the blow, Lannie saw that he was Tom. The older sailor reeled, and the crowd roared its approval.

On the outskirts of the crowd, struggling to shoulder his way through, Lannie saw himself. His muscles tensed as he willed himself to hurry, to stop the fight. But this time the crowd held Lannie fast, and though he was screaming for them to stop, his cries went unheeded.

Johnny, younger and faster, landed two blows for every one of Tom's, but the sailor was larger, a meaty slab of a man. He absorbed Johnny's fists, and the young scholar's face purpled with each strike. Every explosion of blood egged the sailor on to a greater intensity of fury.

"Hurry," Lannie urged himself. "What d'you think you're doing? Hurry! You've got to stop it!"

"See?" Johnny's voice interjected from overhead. "Told you it would change."

Lannie didn't respond. His hands tightened around the teacup, tension causing the surface of the water to tremble.

Then a glinting flash, so fast that he felt rather than saw it, and Tom's hand darted forward like an eel from inside a reef hole attacking a passing fish. A red dot appeared on Johnny's chest, and Tom stood back, his face a twisted grin of triumph. Johnny's mouth opened in surprise, and he slid to his knees, bringing his hands up to the dot, which spread to the size of a saucer, then a dinner plate. Johnny's hands reached forward, grasping at nothing, and he collapsed forward. A puff of dust billowed up when his body hit the ground.

The men watching the fistfight shifted, and Lannie finally freed himself, elbowing forward until he reached Johnny on the ground. Lannie knelt, placing a hand on the scholar's back. The other men pulled away, making room. Lannie bent down, shaking his shoulder, receiving no response.

He shook again.

Out in the real world, Lannie's eyes widened in panic, and he whispered, "Wake up. You've got to," though he wasn't sure if he was addressing Johnny in the tea leaves, or himself.

No response from the boy on the ground. Lannie slowly got to his feet, unfolding to his full height. His face contorted with a righteous fury that the real-world Lannie had never experienced.

He swiveled to face Tom, who was shouting at the other men, his face red, pointing first at himself, and then at the boy on the ground. The crowd parted as Lannie prowled nearer the older sailor. He carried a knife. Instead of acting in defense of Johnny, Lannie saw that he had transformed into an instrument of revenge.

"I can't!" Lannie cried out, overcome with horror.

He hurled the teacup aside with a sob and threw himself onto his stomach, burying his face in his arms.

"Yankee?" the scholar asked. Lannie felt rustling as Johnny peeked over the edge of his bunk, then climbed down and sat alongside him. Lannie trembled, not looking up.

"Lan? Are you all right?" the young man asked. A tentative hand on his shoulder. He shook his head, not wanting Johnny to see his face.

"I'm sorry," the scholar said, hesitant. "I thought it would help with your jaw. I never thought it'd hit you so hard. I didn't. I guess I shouldn't have brought you here."

Still Lannie trembled, gulping down his sobs. A wave of homesickness swept through him, so crushing that it squeezed his breath away. He hated being in this strange country, surrounded by people he didn't understand. He hated the ship, and everyone on it. He longed to be home, tucked under a quilt in the four-poster bed in his room at the top of the stairs in the Chestnut Street house, his sister thumping down the hall and rapping on his door, the sound of his mother singing downstairs as she bent over her sewing.

At the thought of his mother Lannie's sobs broke through his shame and reserve. Under the cover of his arm, his face buried next to the chronometer, Harlan Plummer Allston Junior keened for himself, for his lost childhood, for his loneliness, and for the horrors that he had conjured from within his own mind.

"Lan," Johnny tried again. "It's not real, you know. None of it's real. Didn't it change?"

Lannie opened one eye and let it swivel to peer through a mesh of his hair back at the scholar.

"It did, didn't it?" Johnny said.

Lannie nodded, wiping his bubbling nose with the back of a hand, which served only to smear mucus into the sleeve of his already filthy linen shirt.

"Well, there, see? It's nothing to be worried about. It's all just made-up lotus flower craziness from inside your miserable Yankee head."

"It was—" Lannie's voice caught on a fresh sob. "It was so much worse. Johnny, I saw—I saw—" He couldn't finish, squinting his eyes against the memory.

"Ah," Johnny said, sitting back. He rubbed a hand over his face and sighed, resigned. "I think you're very tired. And I think you're far from home. And I think I've forgotten you're younger than me."

At this gentle challenge Lannie sat up, wiping his face. "I'm not much younger than you."

"Oh, no? How old are you, cabin boy?" Johnny asked with a wry smile, folding his arms.

"Seventeen," Lannie grumbled, cross at being made to feel like a child.

"Seventeen!" the scholar exclaimed. He laughed, throwing his head back. "Oh, dear. It's worse than I thought. But you're so tall! You are like a baby giant. What do they feed you, anyway, in the New England?" He got to his feet, still laughing. "Come on. Time to go."

"Why," grumbled Lannie. "How old are you, then?"

"I," Johnny said, pulling himself up to his full height, which was half a head shorter than Lannie, "am twenty!" The young man pounded a fist against his chest with pride of manhood attained.

"Oh, I see. You think you're more man than I am? 'Cause you're older?" Lannie asked, smiling, folding his own arms over his chest.

Johnny smiled back, relieved at the change in Lannie's mood. "I never implied such a thing. Never."

"That's good. 'Cause I couldn't let a thing like that stand."

"Of course you couldn't. Now come along."

Lannie climbed back into his coat, stuffing the chronometer in his pocket, and the two young men stepped back into the streets of the Old City of Shanghai.

TWENTY-FOUR

Harvard University
Department of Social Ethics
Cambridge, Massachusetts
May 7–8, 1915

"Right," Benton said. "Are you ready?"

Sibyl folded her hands before her on the soapstone laboratory table and slowly nodded her head.

The front of the laboratory classroom featured a chalkboard, marked with chapter assignments on mental hygiene. By the chalkboard hung an orangutan skeleton, its skull in a disturbing, sharp-toothed grin. A few specimen jars stood grouped on the desk at the front, full of parasitic worms preserved in alcohol. The room was lit by an electric fixture overhead, and the building was so quiet that Sibyl could hear the filaments buzzing within the lightbulbs.

Benton arrayed before him the implements of his experiment: a notebook, a fountain pen, a pocket watch with a sweep second hand, the library copy of the anthropological textbook *Le Sang de Morphée,* turned to a page titled *Hypothèse sur les opiacés et la précognition,* a glass ampule of amber fluid, a leather zipper case, and the wooden box containing the scrying glass. Benton checked this array against the list in the textbook, and he nodded.

"Here's how it'll work, everything on the level. To begin with, we're in a sterile laboratory environment, without any spectators." Sibyl's eye wandered to the ape skeleton and the jars of worms, but she didn't bother to disagree with him. It certainly wasn't like Mrs. Dee's parlor, or Dovie Whistler's secret club. She turned back to Benton and nodded her assent.

"Right. The first thing to do, is we give you a shot of morphine."

"We do what?" she exclaimed.

"But of course," he said, unzipping the little leather pouch. It was actually a small medical kit, containing a metal syringe and several different gauges of interchangeable hypodermic needles. At the sight of the needles, some of which were quite large, she felt a slippery faintness creeping over herself. The blood drained from her face, leaving her skin clammy and green.

"Is that . . ." she struggled to say. "Are you sure that's necessary?"

"Why, I should think so. It's the only surefire way to control the dosage we give you. Everything else is too variable. Syrups, opium from poppies, even laudanum varies drastically from batch to batch, and among manufacturers. That is, incidentally"—he paused, cocking a pointed eyebrow at her—"one of the things that makes these substances so dangerous. Morphine, on the other hand, we can measure out down to fractions of a grain. And that's just what we're going to do."

Sibyl started rolling up one of her blouse sleeves, knowing that Benton was right. "It's just that I'm rather . . ." She swallowed, the clamminess spreading under her arms and into her belly. "I'm rather uncomfortable with needles, I'm afraid."

"It'll be over before you know it," he said. He chose one of the smaller gauges and wiped it off with a dampened cloth before screwing it into place on the syringe. "Now then," he said, examining the textbook. He made a brief calculation in his head, and snapped the top off the glass ampule. "While I'm doing this," he said, "why don't you tie a tourniquet around your upper arm?"

At this suggestion the oily cloud bubbled up in the corners of Sibyl's vision, and she had to struggle to keep herself sitting upright on the laboratory stool. "Benton," she said, voice thick. "I'm not so sure about this."

He lowered the syringe and fixed a cool eye on Sibyl. "Oh, come now. You can't be afraid of this. It's nothing." He waved the needle for emphasis.

Without warning Sibyl leaped from the stool and stumbled out of the classroom, one hand over her mouth, groping for the door. Her footsteps echoed as she blundered through the dark, finally shouldering open the door to the lavatory at the end of the hall. She caught a passing sight of herself in the mirror and, seeing the gray pallor of her face, leaned over the sink and was violently ill.

After collecting herself in the men's room of the social ethics building, Sibyl, with more pink to her cheeks, stepped back into the laboratory. The orangutan skeleton grinned its skinless grin at her.

"Feeling better?" Benton asked, his tone light. She found him sitting with his arms folded across his chest, trying not to smile at her.

"It's not funny," she said as she retook her seat on the laboratory stool.

"Mmm," he said, busying himself with the syringe. Without looking up, he added, "It's a little funny."

"It's not!" she countered, but she was fighting back a smile. She rolled her sleeve up and fitted a tight band around her upper arm.

"I don't suppose I have to point out to you the fact that you don't bat an eye trying a strange drug among a bunch of nefarious people down in Chinatown, but the same substance in a safe, scientific context causes you to faint?"

"No," Sibyl said. "You don't have to point that out. I was well aware of that already."

"You're a spitfire, Sibyl Allston. I would never've thought it."

She rolled the pale expanse of her inner elbow upward and rested her arm on the laboratory table. Then Sibyl turned her face away, eyes and nose scrunched together in anticipation of the coming prick.

But it didn't come.

"What are you waiting for?" Sibyl asked, opening one eye to peek at what Benton was doing. She saw that he was staring at his watch.

"I have to note the time," he said absently. "Few more seconds. And—there."

As he spoke the needle slid into her arm, and Sibyl squeaked, turning her face away. When she looked again, Benton was cleaning and putting away the syringe.

"Precisely ten o'clock," he said. "Now, we wait. Shouldn't be too long." Sibyl watched as he set aside the medical kit and began to unpack the wooden box containing the scrying glass. She felt the tiny tremors in her hands subside.

"How long?" she asked. Already her lips felt loose and numb, and a puddle of bliss was spreading through her shoulders.

Benton set the crystal ball before her and took up the fountain pen. "Any time. Whenever you're ready. Now, your job will be to narrate for me. You have to tell me what you're seeing. Even if it's nothing, or you don't understand what it is. All right? I'll note everything down, and keep track of the time. And then we'll see where we are."

Sibyl's gaze sank from Benton's face to the scrying glass, cold and inert under the dim electric lights. She raised her hands, which moved with slow deliberation, as if under water, and brought her fingertips to rest on its surface.

Nothing happened. It sat there, a lump of cloudy, polished quartz.

"I don't know, Ben," Sibyl managed to say. "I'm not sure it's going to work like this."

Benton didn't respond, instead scribbling notes in his notebook. "That's all right," he said, eyes on his notes. "Just tell me whatever happens. Remember. Even no result counts as a result."

Sibyl let her gaze soften, pushing aside the worry that she would fail.

"Narrate for me, Sibyl," he reminded her. "Don't forget. I can't see it, remember."

"Nothing," she murmured. "I don't see anything."

He nodded, and checked the pocket watch.

She sighed. It wasn't going to work. Benton was right, it was all just in her head. She'd been a fool to think any part of it was real. She was tricking herself, just as Mrs. Dee had tricked her.

There was nothing to see.

"Narrate," Benton prodded her gently. "Go on."

She sighed. "I'm trying to see," she whispered. "I'm trying. I truly am."

As she spoke, she squinted her eyes. The glass had darkened. She was sure of it.

Sibyl swallowed, a curious mixture of excitement and trepidation surging through her. "It's . . ." she started to say, and Benton's ears pricked up, pen poised.

"Yes?" he said.

"It's darkening," Sibyl said. "Yes. Definitely darkening."

"Is that what usually happens?"

"Yes," she said, but her voice sounded strange to her. "It starts to darken, and then it looks as though the ball is filled with black smoke."

"Is that what's happening now?" Benton asked, pen moving quickly.

"Yes," Sibyl said. She almost felt as though she were not the one speaking, as though she were floating, watching herself. "It's filled with black smoke, as though it were hollow. But it's not."

Keeping his voice neutral, Benton asked, "And what happens, after the black smoke?"

Sibyl leaned forward, bringing her face closer. Inside, the smoke coiled and bubbled over. Underneath the smoke, she thought she could detect a landscape. "Usually, it parts." She paused. "And before, I'd see water."

"And this time? How is this time different?"

"This time, it's not parting. It's still there. But I can see—" She narrowed her eyes, unsure. "I think I can see land. Like a field. With grooves in it? But that doesn't make any sense."

"Don't worry about whether it makes sense," Benton said. "Just tell me what you see."

Sibyl nodded, detached. "I see the smoke, only now it's not as thick. Drifting. Like a haze."

"Good," Benton encouraged. "What else?"

"Under the haze, there's definitely a landscape. A field, I think, but with those grooves. And some flashing lights. In the haze. They're far away."

"Are all of them far away?"

Sibyl jumped, as one of the flashes burst nearby, sending a smattering of dirt high into the air. Her fingers twitched over the glass. "No," she said. "One of them just came very close. An explosion."

"Interesting," Benton said, writing furiously in his notebook. "Tell me more."

Sibyl gazed closer, uncomprehending. "Ah," she said, furrowing her brows. "They're not grooves after all. They're deep. And things are moving inside them. It's hard to see with the smoke." A flash went off, nearby, and more dirt burst through the air.

"Things?" Benton asked, frowning. "What sort of things?"

Sibyl peered into the scrying glass, willing herself to understand. "Round things?" she asked.

"Can you give me any more details? What variety of round things?"

She grunted with effort, and her fingers pressed harder on the glass, as if she could wring the sense out of the confusing images it was showing her. Inside, her perspective crept nearer, floating through the haze, impervious to the showers of dirt and flashes of reddish light. She drifted over the landscape, its frost-tipped ruts of mud, outlined by long undulations of sharp-looking wire. Then, her perspective nudged up to one of the grooves, and peered in.

"Oh!" Sibyl exclaimed. "It's— Ben, it's people. Men."

"What did you say?" he asked. He laid his pen to the side.

"Inside the grooves. They're like hallways in the earth. Full of men, wearing helmets. Round. Like dinner plates? Round, anyway. They're covered in mud. They're holding rifles."

"Sibyl," Benton said slowly. "When you say grooves, or hallways in the earth. Could you mean trenches?"

"Ah," she said. "Yes, trenches. That's what I meant."

"Good God," Benton breathed, unable to hold back his shock.

"Trenches," Sibyl reiterated. She floated over the ragged edge of the bulwark inside the scrying glass and drifted past the men inside. Under the smudges of grime and the boils on their frightened faces, she saw that most of them were boys, as young or younger than the ones in Harvard Yard. The trench was shin deep with filth and slush.

"Sibyl," Benton said, clearly trying to keep his voice steady. "What has any of what you're seeing to do with you?"

"What do you mean?" Sibyl asked. Her vision was hazy, clouded with smoke and grit. She floated past the form of a boy half submerged in slush at the bottom of the trench, his one visible eye open and glassy, the skin of his cheeks waxy gray.

"With you," Benton reiterated. "What you're seeing. It must pertain to you somehow."

"But I don't understand what I'm seeing," she murmured. "I don't know."

"Think," he urged her, picking up his pen again. "The book is very clear. No matter how remote it seems, something in this vision has direct bearing on your life. If what you're seeing is what we think it is."

We? Sibyl frowned. But she didn't recognize the landscape, she didn't understand the situation, she didn't see herself, she didn't see anyone that she— Wait.

Sibyl gasped.

"Oh, Ben," she breathed. "It's Harley. I see Harlan."

TWENTY-FIVE

"Here," Benton said, handing her a glass of water. Sibyl accepted it, her shoulders drooping. She gulped the water eagerly, wanting it to wash away the residue of what she had just seen.

Benton sat down across from her with a grunt of fatigue. He pulled his notebook over so that they could both see it. "Well," he said, resting his cheek on his fist. "I must say, that was a surprising turn of events."

"How do you mean?" Sibyl asked, setting the water glass aside. She thought she had never been more tired in her life.

"Look here," Benton said, indicating the notebook. "Ten o'clock, morphine administered. Ten oh one, no change. Ten oh two, no change. Then finally, at ten oh eight, the black smoke appears. At ten sixteen, the black smoke reveals a strange grooved landscape, that was how you described it. The vision proceeds like this, in a reasonably regular progression, with each interval revealing a new level of detail. It went that way for nearly an hour, right to the moment you saw your brother. In fact, I think it would have continued if you hadn't been shocked out of your receptive state by the sight of him."

Sibyl watched Benton while he spoke, weighing what he was telling her. She'd had no real awareness of time while she gazed into the glass. "So," she hazarded, "you don't think I'm just dreaming, then?"

"Sibyl," he said, taking her hands in his and looking with intensity into her face. "Have you even read up on the war?"

"Why? What do you mean?"

Benton pressed his lips together in frustration and tried again. "The war in Europe. Do you read about it? Are you aware at all of what's been going on?"

Sibyl paused, annoyed at herself. "Well, I—" She thought. "I know Papa was all incensed that the Kaiser used chlorine gas."

"Whom did he use it on?"

"Um," she demurred. She couldn't look Benton in the face. She knew about the poor Belgian orphans, and that was about it. "I don't know," she admitted. "I've been meaning to read up on it, you know, but Wilson seemed so dead set on keeping us neutral, and I thought . . ."

"As I suspected," he said, sitting back and drumming his fingers on the laboratory table.

"I've been so busy, you know." She started to excuse herself, but he held up a hand.

"No, no," he said. "That's not what I mean. I don't fault you for not knowing. I only mean that your lack of exposure to what's happening in Europe makes the vision that you've just had all the more compelling. You didn't even come to the word *trench* until I supplied it to you. Did you even know that they were fighting in trenches along the western front?"

"No," she confessed. "No, I didn't."

Benton's eyes locked on Sibyl's and softened. He brought up his hand, brushing his knuckles along her jaw and bringing his fingers behind her ear, threading them into her hair. Gently, slowly, he brought her face to his, while her eyes widened, and his lips found hers.

Sibyl lost herself in the feeling, the salty, earthy taste of him, the prickle of his cheek against her skin. Her hands hovered at shoulder height, like confused moths, before she had the presence of mind to lower them to his shoulders and close her eyes. They lingered, sipping each other, and Sibyl felt Benton shift on the stool opposite her, bringing a hand to the small of her back and drawing her to him. Her hands roamed to the nape of his neck, and as the pressure of his mouth deepened, she slid her palms down the front of his shirt to his waist. She sighed, and he broke their embrace with a breathless gasp. His gray eyes bored into her, alight with certainty.

"I believe you," he whispered. "I believe that somehow, some way, even though it goes against all logic and common sense, you are able to see the future in the scrying glass."

"But if what I'm seeing is true," she whispered, "then we've got to hurry home. We have to stop Harley's going."

"You're right," Benton said, getting to his feet. "Come on. It's time we went home."

WHEN THEY ARRIVED back in the Back Bay, Sibyl expected to find all the lights extinguished in the Beacon Street town house, and everyone long since asleep. To her surprise, every window in the house was lit, silhouetted forms moving behind filmy window curtains. The bright windows and forbidding front door gave the house the disturbing aspect of a creature with an open mouth, covered in a fur of ivy, waiting to gobble them whole.

Sibyl and Benton mounted the front steps with trepidation, and before she could knock, the door was opened by Mrs. Doherty.

"There she is. And not a moment too soon. I suppose you know you've missed supper," the housekeeper said by way of welcome as she relieved them of their overcoats. Sibyl opened her mouth in explanation but was interrupted by the sound of feet thumping down the stairs, a blur of flying blond hair and sniffling, and Dovie Whistler flinging herself into Sibyl's arms.

"You're back! Oh, thank heaven you're back. He'll listen to you," the girl gasped, her eyes wide with panic.

Sibyl raised a tentative hand to the girl's back as Dovie coiled her arms around Sibyl's waist and pressed her face into her neck with a dramatic sob. Sibyl's eyes met Benton's over the fuzz of the girl's hair, and he shrugged.

Unmoved by the display of misery snuffling into Sibyl's blouse, Mrs. Doherty said, "I think you'll find, miss, the Captain's been waiting for you in the inner drawing room."

"He has?" Sibyl said, eyes widening in surprise. "Well, that's odd. I'd best go in, then."

"Yes, I guess you'd better," the housekeeper agreed.

Gently Sibyl started to prize Dovie's arms from around her waist, but the girl tightened her grip.

"Oh, Sibyl," she cried. "Please go upstairs first. Please! Go talk to Harley. I can't make him listen. He said he's dead set on it. I've never known him to be so stubborn."

She looked up into Sibyl's face with pleading eyes. Sibyl saw a well-spring of need behind those eyes that startled her. She had seen the girl upset before, and she had seen her insistent, but she had never seen her nakedly fearful. The sudden change in her usually bold and independent friend was disconcerting.

"I'll talk to him, dearest, I promise," she whispered into Dovie's hair. "But I must see what Papa wants first. It's his house, you know. I'm sure whatever's going on with Harlan will keep for another quarter of an hour."

Sibyl managed to free herself from the girl's grip, only for Dovie to attach herself with a fresh sob, barnaclelike, to Benton Derby.

"Well!" he exclaimed, taken by surprise, holding his hands up at shoulder height as though someone had just pressed a knife to his back and demanded all his ready cash. "I suppose I'll just stay here, then," he said. "And make sure Miss Whistler's all right."

"I suppose you shall," Mrs. Doherty said, unmoved by the histrionics being performed in the front hallway. Her expression suggested that they had been under way for some hours. "He's asked to see Miss Allston alone."

"Oh," Sibyl said, exchanging a look with Benton. "Well. That settles it."

"Come, Miss Whistler," Benton said to the trembling girl attached to the front of his shirt. "Miss Allston tells me you used to go upon the stage. We must hear you recite some evening. I wonder if you've ever seen Bernhardt?"

He ushered her, with a steady stream of theater prattle, to the window seat in the front parlor, glancing over his shoulder at Sibyl with a look of curiosity mixed with concern. Sibyl returned the look, then hesitated outside the lacquered pocket doors leading to the inner parlor, and rolled them aside.

"CLOSE IT BEHIND you, if you would," Lan Allston said from behind his newspaper.

He was sitting, as was his habit, in the Greek revival armchair with its horsehair upholstery, a castaway on an island in an ocean of Helen's taste. A pleasant fire burned in the fireplace, and the mantel clock announced that the hour was well past midnight. Baiji the macaw perched, one claw tucked up in a puff of iridescent blue feathers, fast asleep on his hat rack. Everything seemed as it should be, except for the lateness of the hour. Sibyl obeyed, rolling the door closed behind her.

"You're up late, Papa," she remarked, moving to take the armchair across from him.

"Mmmm. Well, I've been awaiting my daughter's arrival from some mysterious late-night errand," the old sailor said, cocking a graying eyebrow at her. She met his gaze with a polite smile.

He waited, and when she didn't volunteer any information that would clarify her whereabouts, he cleared his throat, folded the newspaper with a rustle, and leaned forward with his elbows on his knees.

"My dear," he said, employing a term of endearment rarely heard in the Allston house, which alerted Sibyl to pay closer attention. "I see you're as little disposed to idle chitchat this evening as I am. So I will come to the point. I've waited up to persuade you not to talk Harlan out of going to Plattsburgh."

"I beg your pardon?" Sibyl asked, confused.

"You're going to try to talk him out of it," her father said. "You can't. You mustn't. I know why you feel that you must, but it is imperative that you obey me in this respect. It's very important."

"Papa, I—" She started to protest, baffled as to how her father might know of her plan. It was impossible. She'd only just formulated it. And no one had been in the social ethics building with her and Benton. No one could possibly have told him. Her mind tripped along at a mile a minute, leaping ahead to figure out what she was supposed to say, but falling short, baffled.

"I don't know what you're talking about" is what she finally came up with, but her eyes slid down to her fingers, toying with a loose thread on the armrest of her chair.

"Oh, you don't?" he asked.

"No," she said, her attention absorbed in the threads. This armchair was much more threadbare than she remembered. She would have to see about getting it recovered.

"Sibyl, hold out your hands, please," he commanded.

She glanced up, her heart thudding faster in her chest.

"Hold them out?" she faltered. "Whatever for?"

"Do it, if you will, my dear. Please. Hold up your hands."

She did so, facing up, palms to her face, like a magician about to do sleight of hand, showing that he has nothing hidden up his sleeve.

"No," Allston said. "Out straight in front of you, please. Like this." He demonstrated, extending his arms out straight from his shoulders. His hands had a slight tremor as he held them there, the ravages of his rheumatism.

She followed suit, extending her arms out slowly from her shoulders.

Her hands trembled.

She frowned, commanding them in her mind to be still.

Still, they trembled. She looked at her father with frightened eyes, and found him gazing on her with a wounded expression, the same helpless worry in his eyes that he tried to hide when she would appear at the kitchen door with scraped knees as a child, weeping for him to pick her up.

"As I suspected," her father said, leaning back in his chair and bringing a thoughtful finger alongside his temple. "You haven't stopped. In fact, I wager that you've increased your usage. Even though I specifically asked you to give it up."

Sibyl, ashamed, folded her arms tightly across her chest, and half turned her body away from her father to face the fire.

"I'm just tired, is all," she insisted, hiding her face from him. "It's awfully late."

"It isn't that late. You used to stay out 'til much later than this, you and Eulah. And I'd appreciate it if you wouldn't lie to me."

Chastened, Sibyl hung her head. Her father sighed, the long sigh of a man disappointed and not knowing where to begin. When she hazarded a look in his direction, she found him slouching in his chair, arms draped over the swooping armrests, legs stretched out straight before him. There was something oddly youthful about this posture, like a teenaged boy drooping in a chair out of sight of his mother, and Sibyl felt that she was being given a glimpse of the young man her father had been, years ago, before the weight of dignity settled so heavily on him.

"How did you know?" she whispered, dismayed to hear in her voice the timbre of a little girl caught standing over a broken punch bowl.

He sighed again, staring into the fire, his eyes open wide, and though the rims were pink with fatigue his eyes themselves were still the aquamarine color of a tropical sea.

"How. Did. I. Know," he said, enunciating each word. The aquamarine eyes swiveled from the fire to his daughter's face and settled there. She waited, knotting her hands together so that he would not see them tremble anymore.

"You might well ask," he said. "How I knew about Miss Whistler. Or how I knew that the sea would make my fortune. How I knew it would take away my wife and youngest daughter."

When these words met her ears all of Sibyl's breath squeezed out of her body at once. She sat, frozen in her seat, trying to absorb what he had just said to her. Trying, and failing.

"What do you mean?" Sibyl stammered. "What are you saying to me, Papa?"

"Well, to begin with, I don't have rheumatism, if that's what you're wondering," he said with a wry, but sad, smile. "Never have. The prescription, the laudanum drops, I take only to keep the symptoms of withdrawal at bay. And those symptoms are wretched, I assure you. The addiction itself is my ailment, my dear, as I fear will yours be if we don't act quickly. But the drug, as I gather you've come to know, is only a small part of what I'm talking about. Perhaps not even the most important part."

"So it's true, then," Sibyl said, her voice sounding hollow in her ears.

"I don't pretend to understand the mechanisms of it," her father said. He got to his feet, standing with a stretch and then leaning an elbow on the mantel. The firelight cast itself upward over his face, and the soft quality of the light smoothed away some of his weatheredness, continuing Sibyl's strange impression of her father standing before her as a younger version of himself. "I don't know why it's not this way for other people, or if it's the work of God, or the devil. But yes. It's true. It's been true for me for the past fifty years."

Sibyl let out her breath by slow degrees. "Incredible," she said. "I thought it was true. But Benton was so persuasive. He wouldn't be convinced. Not until—well . . ." She trailed off, watching for her father's response.

"Yes, well. Professor Derby. He's a scientist. And at root, a practical man. Like Richard, his father. Sometimes there's just no reasoning with practical men about impractical matters."

"Fifty years? Really?" she asked with amazement, watching him. He gazed with an absent look into the fire.

"Fifty years," he repeated. "Or a little more."

"But how . . . ?" she started to ask.

"In China," he said. His tone, Sibyl knew, did not invite discussion of the circumstances of Lan Allston's introduction to scrying. A dark shadow crossed his face, the ghostly shadow of horror and regret, and for a sickening instant Sibyl wondered if she would see her father cry.

"I see," she said, looking away. She paused, and asked, "Do you know what I've seen, then?"

Her father moved from the mantel out of the circle of light cast by the fire, into the shadows in the deeper recesses of the inner parlor. Sibyl heard a pleasant clucking sound, the sound of Baiji being scratched gently under his chin.

"Yes." Her father's sepulchral voice floated out of the darkness. "I have."

"Yet you're telling me not to stop him?" Sibyl got to her feet, growing angry. Surely her father couldn't resent his prodigal son so much that he would wish him dead. She couldn't imagine her father being that cold. Not when there were so few of them left. Not when it would mean leaving her alone.

A heavy, resigned sigh, and he spoke again. "I am not telling you. I'm asking you. Begging you, really. Not to try to stop him."

"But why?" she demanded, digging her fingers into the back of the armchair, her voice rising. "How can you condemn him like this? It's impossible, you can't have seen it, otherwise you'd never ask such a thing of me. How can you?"

"Because," her father said, in tones of deep sadness and resignation. "Because I have also seen what happens to Harlan's life if you succeed."

A long, leaden pause plunged the room into abrupt silence. In the silence the fire popped.

"What do you mean?" Sibyl hissed.

The shadows parted to reveal her father moving back toward the light, the seams of his face craggy with fatigue.

"Ah," he said with a grim smile. "You haven't discovered the parallax then, I take it. Well, it's probably for the best."

"Parallax?" Sibyl asked, dark brows furrowing. Her eyes flashed black. "What parallax? What does that mean?"

"It means," he said, drawing the words out in a meditative way, "that objects—or in this case, events in time—can sometimes look different if viewed from a different vantage point."

Sibyl grew light-headed and leaned her weight into the back of the chair. In the dim recesses of the room, Baiji released a quiet sneeze.

"Different," she breathed. "Are you telling me there's some way to see different alternatives? Each time I've tried I've just seen the one event, and then when it came to pass, I saw the beginnings of another one. Every time, it gave me more details. And sometimes the details changed, but I couldn't control it. I couldn't control it at all."

Her father sighed, running his fingertips along the back of his armchair. "I shouldn't have said anything," he said finally. "Let's leave that aside."

"Tell me," Sibyl commanded, her heart rising in her throat. She tightened the hand on the back of her armchair into a fist, her nails digging into her palm. "Tell me how it's done. You must."

"I must!" he exclaimed, looking up at her with mild surprise. "Well, well. What a willful daughter I have, all of a sudden. Your mother always thought it was Eulah who was willful, you know. But I knew better."

"Oh, won't you tell me!" she burst, blind with rage.

Her father met her outburst with a raised eyebrow. "You know," he remarked, circling the edge of the firelight and coming back to the mantel, "that I grew up in Salem, don't you?"

Confused by the apparent shift in topic, Sibyl shook her head, and frowned. "What? Of course. You even took us to visit the house when we were small. What of it?"

"Chestnut Street." Lan sighed, momentarily wistful. "I had some happy days there. A boy running loose in a bustling seaport town, ships arriving every day from the Far East, odd fruits, spices, curious men with gold in their ears. A real seagoing city it was. Well, it was a different time." He shook off his passing thought and settled again in the Greek revival armchair, cupping his chin in his hand.

"Papa," Sibyl interjected, but he raised a hand to quell her.

"My own father, your grandfather," Lan continued. "The first Harlan Allston. Like me, he married a woman many years his junior, after a successful career at sea. That means he was born in the very first years of the last century. Practically an eighteenth-century man. Can you imagine that? The Revolution was still fresh in people's minds when he was a boy. The old houses still stood. People frightened him with stories about witches cooking up naughty little boys in giant cauldrons, and then Mother frightened me with the very same stories. I sometimes wonder what my father would have to say about Boston today, if he could see it. The automobiles. Electric lights. The people. So many people! From all over the world. This is really an Irish city, you know, Sibyl. The times are changing, and they will never change back. Our set may hold ourselves aloof, but we are fooling ourselves."

Sibyl watched, still standing, her face frozen in a grimace of confusion and anger.

"Well, those days are past. I don't pretend to know whether for good or ill. I moved down to Boston with your mother, because she wanted to be among fashionable people. Salem's seagoing days are gone. It's a different city now. Shoe factories and salt water taffy. But I mention it only because the Salem where I grew up, you know, the Salem of a generation ago. It was still, in its way, a rather religious place."

"*Salaam*," Sibyl said, watching him. "It means peace."

"Just so," her father said with a tiny smile. "All the other Essex county towns took their names from English towns. Even Boston. Marblehead took its name from the cliffs it was built on, of course. Always were a stubborn people, those 'Headers. But only Salem took its name from a religious idea. From the hope of peace. And you may not know this about me, my dear, but I am a rather religious man. I believe that God has a particular plan in mind, for each of us. And we have no way of knowing what that plan might be. But whatever it is, it must be for the best. Because Providence— God—has willed it so."

Sibyl's eyebrows rose, surprised to hear this deeply buried vestige of old Puritanism lying hidden in her father's heart.

He stared hard at her, compelling her attention with the force of his gaze. "It is not our place," he said, enunciating each word with care, "to monkey with what God has planned. It is hubris. Of the very worst kind."

She swallowed. "But—" she started to protest.

He held up a hand.

"Why do you think I've never told you about this particular skill I have?" he asked.

"I—" Sibyl stammered. "I don't know. Why didn't you?"

"Because I wanted to protect you from it. I never wanted you or your siblings to know. Ever. Why do you think I denied Harley the morphine in the hospital? I'm no sadist, no matter what the boy might think of me. I would never wish one of my children to suffer unnecessarily."

"But look at what you're asking of me," Sibyl said, her voice catching in her throat. "How can you say you want to protect us? Wouldn't this skill, or whatever it is, wouldn't this be a way of setting ourselves free?"

Her father sighed, massaging his forehead with his fingertips. Deep in the shadows the macaw let out a sleepy caw. "I suspect," he said, "that most people would hold your opinion. But this is still new to you, I gather. It's not new to me. It's weighed on me for almost as long as I can remember."

"But why should it?" Sibyl asked, not understanding, hurrying over to kneel at her father's knee, looking up into his face.

"I suspect that most people, hearing our family has the wherewithal, under specific, and dangerous, circumstances, to see what God has in store for us, would be envious. But that envy would be misguided, Sibyl. You see this as a great gift now. That's only because you haven't lived with it long enough. Do you think I liked knowing that the sea would give me my livelihood, while taking away what I love? Even before I met Helen, I knew how she would die. Do you think I liked knowing, even before you all were born, that I would outlive all my children, save one? That my efforts to change the plan, my struggles to be free, would only make the outcomes worse? It's actually—" He paused, resting his hands gently on his daughter's shoulders.

"What?" she whispered, looking with terrified eyes, obsidian in the firelight, into his weathered face.

"It's a curse." He said the word softly, so softly that Sibyl at first didn't register its gravity.

"A curse?" she repeated, a deadly chill spreading through her limbs.

He nodded. "Yes. It doesn't look that way at first. But it is. In truth I feel myself," he spoke gently, "to be damned. I have sinned. I know this. And I must bear my punishment as best I can. I only ask that God not visit the same punishment on my children. Not on you, my dear. Not on you."

Sibyl dropped her head, wiping at the corner of her eyes with her fingers. She felt her father's hand descend on her head, patting her hair with a soft, reassuring stroke.

"There, there," he murmured. "Don't cry, my dear. Please don't cry."

She didn't respond, bringing her forehead to her hands, still knotted together on his knee. She choked back her sobs, keeping silent, and he stroked her hair. They sat like that for a long while.

At length Sibyl swallowed her tears and said, "But, Papa. What shall I—what shall I say to him?"

"You shall say nothing," Lan Allston said. "You shall let him make his own choices, guided by God's hand. Even God cannot make us other than we are, but he can, in his love, show us the best possible path. That is the kindest, the truest thing you can do for your brother. You must let him feel himself to be free."

She searched his face, horrified by what he was asking her to do. "But how can I face him?" she said, aghast. "How can you ask me to say nothing, to let him go away? What can I say to Dovie? To Benton?"

The old sailor smiled wanly down on his distraught daughter. "You have the strength. And in asking these questions you begin to see how dangerous, how horrible, this skill is. You must give it up, before it's too late. I'm begging you. Give it up. We'll find a way to help you. But you must give it up."

He clasped his hands around hers, pressing them between his rough sailor's palms. Sibyl felt their tremor, which she now understood was a sign not of tired hands beaten by a life at sea, but of his addiction, his enslavement, to the hideous seduction of scrying.

Sibyl looked down, and then she pulled her hands away and struggled to her feet. She drew herself up to her full height and looked down at her aged father, who gazed up at her with sorrowful eyes.

"I'm sorry," she said. "I can't."

TWENTY-SIX

$\mathcal{S}$ ibyl hurried back to the outer drawing room, her arms wrapped around herself, and when Benton and Dovie saw her horrified face they both leaped to their feet.

"Darling," Benton exclaimed, stepping to meet her. He placed his hands on her shoulders and peered down into her face. "Why, what is it?" he asked when he read her distress. "What can have happened?"

Sibyl forced a smile, tossing the loose strand of hair off her forehead with a quick motion of her head, which made her look fleetingly like Harlan. "It's nothing," she said, placing a soft hand alongside Benton's cheek. His skin was rough and sandpapery to the touch, a hallmark of the lateness of the hour. She allowed herself to rub her thumb along the corner of his mouth.

"It's not nothing," he insisted, gray eyes darkening with concern.

"No, really," she said firmly. "It's just the lateness of the hour. I'm so tired I can barely see straight. Surely you must be tired as well."

"I suppose," Benton demurred. Hesitant, Dovie, her face streaked with tears and rivulets of kohl, approached from the bay window and hovered at the outer rim of their conversation.

"I confess, I'm awfully tired, Sibyl," the younger woman said, resting a hand on Sibyl's arm.

"Well," Sibyl said, placing her own hand over Dovie's and then smiling

at them both. "That settles it. Benton, perhaps you should head home. I'll
see Miss Whistler upstairs, and we'll regroup to take on the Kaiser tomorrow. All right?"

Benton looked doubtful but pulled out his pocket watch and let out a
low whistle when he observed the time. He replaced the timepiece in his
waistcoat pocket, and threaded his arm through Sibyl's free elbow. "Reasonable to the last," he said. "All right. I don't have any classes until tomorrow afternoon. Shall I drop by for breakfast, then?"

"I'll tell Betty to expect you," Sibyl said. She and Dovie, arm in arm,
walked Benton to the front door and waited while he climbed into his
overcoat. He met Sibyl's eyes and seemed on the point of leaning in for a
kiss. She didn't move, keeping her arm in Dovie's and smiling at him.

"Well," he said, hesitating.

"Good night, Professor Derby," Dovie said, tightening her grip on
Sibyl.

"Good night, Miss Whistler. No welshing, now. I get a recitation of
Longfellow from you. I'm holding you to it."

"Good night, Benton," Sibyl said. They exchanged a look that promised further discussion tomorrow.

Benton then cocked his hat, said, "Ladies," with a mock salute, and
vanished through the front door.

"Come, dear," Sibyl said, leading Dovie up the winding front staircase.
The girl leaned on Sibyl's arm, as though the strain of Harlan's possible
departure had robbed her of her strength. Her body felt small and fragile
next to Sibyl, birdlike, and as they mounted the staircase Dovie rested her
cheek against Sibyl's shoulder.

"You'll talk to him tomorrow?" she murmured.

"I will," Sibyl said, voice grim.

"You promise?" the girl pressed.

Sibyl reached across and patted Dovie's hand. "I promise," she said.

They reached the top of the stairs, and Sibyl, her arm around Dovie's
narrow shoulders, ushered her to the door of what had been Eulah's room.
The light under Harlan's door was out, and the sound of gentle snoring
could be distinctly heard from within. Sibyl stopped and rested her hands
on Dovie's shoulders.

"Now then," she said. "You get your rest. All right? I'm sure we can reason with Harley tomorrow. It won't do anyone any good to have you up all night worrying, will it?"

"No," Dovie allowed. "I suppose not. Good night, Sibyl." She rose on tiptoes to place a quick kiss on Sibyl's cheek. Sibyl smiled at the sleepy girl, who gave her a wave before stepping through the door to Eulah's room.

Sibyl stood alone in the hallway, and while she stood there the smile dissolved off her face. She listened to the sounds of the house: a creak, a snore, the ticking of the mantel clock downstairs. Then she turned on her heel and hurried down the hall toward her bedroom.

But when she reached the door, she passed it without entering.

Instead, she glanced left and right, and started down the back service stair. The lights had all been extinguished, and Sibyl had to grope her way down the narrow stairs to the lower hall, which led to the kitchen entrance of the house. Once there she fumbled for one of the castoff overcoats that often hung on some pegs by the back door and struggled into one.

A creak of the kitchen door opening, and Sibyl exclaimed, "Oh!"

She was met with the drawn, freckle-spattered face of Betty Gallagher, one arm propping the kitchen door open, the other holding aloft a small oil lamp.

"Miss Allston!" she exclaimed.

"Betty!" Sibyl gasped, bringing a hand to her chest to quiet the thudding of her heart. "Oh, my goodness, how you startled me. But you're still here. Whyever haven't you gone home?"

The cook looked haggard, her red-rimmed eyes blinking rapidly. The fatigue didn't suit her, Sibyl thought meanly. For the first time, Sibyl thought that Betty looked a little rough around the edges.

"I . . ." Betty started to say. "That is, I had a few things I had to do in the kitchen, and—" She grappled, in search of a credible lie, and then decided to dispense with pretense. "See here, he's not really going, is he?"

"Who?" Sibyl asked, buttoning up the overcoat. "Harlan?"

"Of course, Harlan!" Betty said, crossly, and Sibyl frowned, hearing the impatience in the other young woman's voice. Betty had worry lines around her eyes, and sadness around her mouth. If anything, the cook wore the expression of a woman who feels herself too alone.

"Well," Sibyl said, keeping her reply neutral, "I couldn't rightly say." She gazed levelly at Betty, wishing the cook to feel the subtle assertion of her authority. Betty returned the look, glowering under her pale reddish eyebrows.

"I warrant it might be right dangerous, don't you? If he went," the cook pressed.

Irritated at the line of questioning, Sibyl said, "Well, I suppose it might be, yes. In any event, I'm glad to run into you. Professor Derby will be joining us for breakfast. I'd like you to plan accordingly."

A look of pure hatred passed through Betty's features, so hard and abrupt that Sibyl nearly stepped backward to escape it. The look said that she knew her feelings were of no account, that she was wasting her time, and that she resented them for it.

"Very good, Miss Allston," the cook said, a perceptible chill in her voice. The anxiety had vanished from Betty's face, replaced with the subtle, constant anger of the household servant. At that moment Sibyl knew she'd lost her confederate for good. But perhaps she'd never really had her in the first place.

A pause, while Betty seemed on the point of saying something else, when her expression changed again upon noticing that Sibyl had put on an overcoat. "You going out again tonight, then?" she asked, her hostility mollified by curiosity.

"I am," Sibyl said. Betty hesitated, waiting for Sibyl explain. But she did not.

"Well, all right. We'll do a Benedict for breakfast, I think," Betty said, eyeing Sibyl with wariness, shifting into the role she knew was expected of her. "With Canadian bacon. I think we've got enough. And I'll have Rose make the English muffins."

"Very good, Betty. That sounds fine." Sibyl paused again, before dismissing the cook by saying, "That'll be all for tonight."

The cook, openly frowning, bobbed a quick almost-curtsy—something Sibyl had never seen Betty do in all her years of employment on Beacon Street—and stalked back into the kitchen.

Alone in the darkness and silence of the rear hallway, Sibyl squared her shoulders, drew the shabby overcoat more tightly around her, and stepped out into the night.

SHE WAS SURPRISED that she could remember the address. And in truth, the cabbie—when she was finally able to get a taxicab—nearly refused to take her there.

"You wanna go *where*?" he asked, turning around in his seat and roving his eyes over her body, from the crown of her head to the tips of her boots. She fixed him with a defensive stare, folding her arms across her chest. He confirmed his apparent suspicion that she was not the sort of woman who would normally be venturing to that quarter, and so added, "At this hour, miss? You sure?"

Sibyl extended a bill held between her index and middle fingers until it just reached his peripheral vision. "I'm sure," she said. He plucked the bill from her grasp, shrugged his shoulders, and gunned the car.

They arrived at the nondescript door a short while later, making the trip briskly through the empty streets of nighttime Boston. A few horse-drawn refuse carts made their somnolent way down the alleys, and a handful of private cars rolled past full of fur coats and merriment, either coming from or going to parties. As they went Sibyl gazed out the taxi window, glimpsing isolated men lounging against brick walls, a few ragged boys asleep in a pile. On occasion the cab trundled past clusters of brightly dressed women, idling on street corners and staring at the taxicabs. One of the women caught her eye as Sibyl's taxi rolled past, and smiled a smile of commiseration at her, showing incongruously yellowed teeth within a still young and attractive face. Sibyl recoiled at first, but then half-smiled back.

She alighted from the taxi and approached the door that she remembered, though the street now was a completely different universe from its afternoon incarnation. Rotting heads of cabbage and bok choy festered in stinking heaps in the gutter, along with splinters of produce crates and refuse. An elderly woman, bent double with age and malnutrition, picked among the shattered crates, collecting the largest pieces for fuel. The rest of the street stood deserted and dark, a few lamps burning in windows, but that was all.

"You want I should wait?" the cabbie called.

Sibyl glanced back at him, a coil of trepidation tightening in her gut. She'd never been here by herself. She'd always come with Dovie there to smooth her passage. Sibyl considered turning around, climbing back into the taxi, and heading straight home again. But the thought of Harley crowded in on her; the incomplete, suggestive image of her brother hovered before her like a taunt.

"No," she whispered.

"What's that?" the cabbie hollered. "Miss?"

"No," she said, raising her voice, firm. "Thank you. There's no need to wait."

Without saying anything, shaking his head, the cabbie gunned his car again and bounced away down the cobblestone street.

Alone, Sibyl approached the unmarked door. She knocked, softly, with her knuckles.

There was no response.

She scowled and rapped harder, this time with the end of her fist.

The aperture in the door slid open and an eye appeared. It stared at her.

Cursing to herself, Sibyl remembered that Dovie always had to show a slip of paper, like a letter of introduction written in Chinese, in order to gain entry. She didn't have one. Determined, she stepped nearer to the door so that the thin red lantern light could pick up her features. She stared at the eye, waiting.

The eye blinked once. Twice. Then the aperture closed.

Sibyl cursed again, under her breath. She knew she shouldn't have let the cab go so cavalierly. She ruminated, hands in the pockets of her shabby overcoat, wondering what she should do next.

Then, to her surprise, the door cracked open. Trying to act as though she were expecting this, Sibyl drew herself tall and stepped inside.

"Hello, Creesy," she said to the withered man who opened the door for her.

"Good evening, Miss Allston," he replied in a clipped colonial accent, which caused Sibyl to jump. He had never spoken when Dovie addressed him. In fact, Sibyl thought the man might have been a deaf mute. "Go right on up. I've taken the liberty of telling them you're here."

Sibyl shivered, anxious, but managed to keep her voice steady as she said, "Thank you." Then she made her way up the stairs.

When she arrived on the landing, she found the elegant den sparsely populated, but warm and inviting. The usual fires were going, and the giant brass chandelier cast a soft glow over the room's various textures of carpet and brocade. A few forms lounged on the couches or in nests of cushions on the floor, some fast asleep, but most lost in waking dreams of their own. A man bent over the Victrola, shuffling through records. There was no sound beyond the crackles of the fire, the ticking of the grandfather clock, and the occasional indolent snuffle of one of the patrons. Sibyl waited, shrugging off her overcoat and scanning the room. The Victrola started up, a woman's voice warbling about clouds with silver linings and kissing away her lover's tears. Such a maudlin song. Yet it always seemed to be playing when she was here.

Presently the proprietor shuffled forward on his ludicrous Turkish slippers, and Sibyl smothered a smile at seeing him in his self-consciously "Oriental" costume. But then, she supposed that he was selling the fantasy of the Far East, as much as he was selling anything else. He smiled broadly when he saw her and took her hand. He betrayed no apparent surprise at finding her on the doorstep of his establishment, alone, in the middle of the night. She supposed that the rules of decorum were different in the world of opium dens. "Miss Allston," he said with a gentlemanly bow. "Such a pleasure to see you again."

"And you," she said.

"Shall I show you to your usual spot?" he asked. "It's very nice over there, by the fire. Very private. You shan't be disturbed."

"That would be lovely, thank you," she said, somewhat stiffly. He led her to the purple velvet chaise. Her hands twitched. She swallowed, nervous and ashamed. Under the shame, the insistent gnaw of hunger asserted its painful presence in her body.

"Here we are," Mr. Chang said, gesturing to the chaise, which did indeed look inviting, bathed in firelight, with a low lacquered table close at hand.

"Perfect," she said. She felt in her skirt pocket for the item that she needed and was reassured to find it still there, its slight weight soothing among the folds of her clothes. Then she settled herself on the couch and started to unlace her shoes.

"I'll send Quincey over right away," the proprietor said. "We have a lovely selection from Afghanistan this evening. Very delicate and refined on the palate, perfect for a lady. Perhaps you'd care to try it? Or would you prefer your usual Burmese?"

"Ah," Sibyl demurred. "I think, the Burmese, just at the moment. Thank you."

"Very good, Miss Allston," the man said, with another tiny bow. "And," he added, looking sidelong at her from under his slight brows, "I'm pleased to say that we've just acquired a supply of very fine gunpowder tea." He paused.

"Oh?" she said, unsure what response was expected of her.

"Yes," he said, watching her. "Your father's preferred blend, if I'm not mistaken. Shall I bring you some?"

She turned wide black eyes on the smiling, courtly man in silk floral pantaloons, topped with an incongruous kimonolike robe, with his curly-toed slippers and pleasant, patient face. But of course. In fact, she wasn't even surprised.

"Why, that would be delightful," she said, smoothing her skirts with both hands. "How thoughtful you are."

He inclined his head and shuffled away, gesturing to unseen people in the back of the den to bring her what was requested.

Sibyl sat motionless on her velvet seat, staring for long minutes into the heart of the fire. After a time she rummaged within her skirt pocket, withdrew the wooden box containing the scrying glass, and cradled it on her lap. She slid the catch of the box open with her thumb, and brushed the fingertips of one hand over the polished ball, lost in thought. Parallax, her father said. Sibyl rubbed one stockinged foot on top of the other, flexing her toes. If there were different possibilities, then she must see all of them. She must come up with a way to save Harlan from himself. And she would stay there, in the plush den above a shop front in Chinatown, until she'd seen every last one.

SOME HOURS LATER, the embers of the fire glowed a deep molten red, and Sibyl rested on her back, immobile, her eyes glassy and unseeing. Her breath came fast and light, rasping over her parted lips. The skin of her lips was parched, and her tongue crept out to moisten them. On the table at her elbow sat the implements of her habit: the slender needle, the box with the brown lump lovingly wrapped in tissue paper, the long bamboo pipe, the lamp trimmed low and flickering. A cup of what had held tea, nearly empty, sat cold and unheeded, beads of moisture trickling down the side.

Her hands were slack but kept their loose grip on the crystal ball. Through the haze of her fatigue Sibyl mulled what little it had told her in the previous several hours. So far she hadn't mastered the parallax question, the seeing of other alternatives if she could view the glass from a different angle. Over hours of repeated efforts she experienced the same vivid, progressive revelation of detail. But the details all added to one consistent picture, a picture that she could not accept.

Sibyl saw first the smoke-shrouded landscape, scored with trenches and coils of barbed wire, explosions in the distance. She crept along the edge of the trench, then lowered behind the rampart to scroll through the faces of the boys cowering within. She saw the rancid slush around their feet, she saw the dead boy with his hideous, open eye half submerged in the slurry. She approached Harlan's face, under a lopsided circular helmet, his cheeks smudged with mud and spatters of blood, his eyes wide and frightened. Her brother's uniform was different from the other boys around him, as if he didn't belong where he was, but she hadn't been able to discern why. And then, she saw the explosion. Every time, the explosion shook her out of herself, shocked her back to awareness, as if her mind couldn't withstand the horror of what followed.

She had gone through the whole vision four or five times now, and nothing changed. More details, no alternatives. The dramatis personae didn't change. The order of events didn't change. She groaned and blinked.

The backs of her eyelids felt like sandpaper scraping over her eyeballs, and she lolled her head back, gazing up at the ceiling.

A face leaned over her, moving into her field of vision like a ghost. It was Quincey, the man designated to help her with the complicated ritual necessary to prepare the opium. His head was hideous, his hair scraped back and thin on his scalp, the skin clinging to every contour of his skull. His mouth opened in a grin of rotted teeth when he saw that she was awake.

"Miss?" he croaked. "You want more?"

Sibyl coughed, raising herself on her elbow and casting a haggard look at the scrying glass in her lap. Then she turned to face Quincey and said, "Yes. Another bowl. Get it ready, please."

Smiling and nodding with the hunger of a man in agreement, he knelt over the lacquer table, fixing and preparing and kneading and rolling. While she waited, Sibyl settled along the velvet couch, feet drawn up under her spread-out skirts, resting her cheek in her hand. She brought the crystal ball even with her nose and gave it a hard glare. It glowed with a faint light from within, not sparkling as it sometimes did, but emanating a deeper light, as if polished from heavy use. She'd try again. There was still time. She'd make it work. She must.

Quincey passed her the pipe without a word, and she pressed its end to her lips, leaning forward and holding the bowl angled to the flame. He brought the needle-end pearl of opium to the opening in the pipe bowl, and Sibyl breathed deep, watching the pearl burst into a tiny perfect flame, relishing the delicious numbing through her mouth. She leaned back, feeling the pipe lifted out of her hands, and exhaled. But the effect was deadened. Gone was the initial spreading warmth of pleasure that she yearned for. Instead she felt steady, and without pain, but the implication of pain to come lingered.

She cupped the scrying glass in her hands and brought it to her face, staring hard into its milky depths. She didn't have to wait more than a second or two before the smoke started to fill it, black and greasy-looking. A minute or two of its ominous billowing, and then the tendrils parted, revealing the blasted earth with its deep grooves. All as she knew it would be.

Deep in the muscles of her back, Sibyl felt, under the comforting artificial softness of the drug, the twinge of spasm. She hadn't stirred in hours, and her corseting dug red stripes into her flanks. Still holding the ball, Sibyl shifted, rolling from her back onto her side. The light moved over the surface of the orb, sliding along it like a silken scarf, and as it did so the image of the grooved landscape shimmered. The subtle shift in light within the crystal ball looked like the dropping of a shard of colored glass inside a kaleidoscope, a tiny movement that causes the entire image to shift.

Sibyl peered closer, angling the ball nearer the light from the fire so that she could get a better view. She still saw Harlan's face, and it still looked wide-eyed and frightened, the same expression as it had before, but now his face wasn't smudged with mud. It was clean, and his hair was combed. He looked older, but not by much—he had freshly minted lines around his mouth and eyes, and the texture of his skin was coarser, the face of a man in his mid-twenties. The same age that Sibyl was now. Sibyl strained her eyes to see more.

Her perspective drew back, and her brother was sitting at a large desk, surrounded by crumpled papers. The hour was late, his face lit from below by a green desk lamp, which cast his features in ghoulish relief. His eyes were rimmed with red and had deep gray-purple circles around them, and his skin was waxen. His nose was red with burst capillaries, and his features in general looked blurry, smeared by hard living and regret. At his elbow sat a bottle of liquor, nearly empty, and a tumbler stained with fingerprints. As she watched he buried his face in his palms, shoulders trembling.

For a long while Sibyl watched while her brother shuffled through the papers on his desk and grew more visibly stricken. The desk might have been in an office at their father's shipping company, but Sibyl couldn't be sure. Her brother looked wasted, as though his very soul had been eaten away. He leaned down, opening a drawer in his desk and rooting inside. Whatever he found there he drew into his lap. He turned to the bottle, tipping the dregs of its contents into the tumbler and tossing it down his throat with a trembling hand.

"Oh, Harley," Sibyl whispered, unaware that she was speaking.

The apparition of her brother inside the glass, of course, could not hear her. Instead he slowly lifted the object from his lap and laid it with care on the desk.

It was a pistol.

Sibyl's eyes widened in horror, and she whispered, "Oh, my God, Harley, no," but it didn't matter, he couldn't hear her, he was just a vision of one possible future that lay in store if he didn't go away to Europe. Sibyl understood that if he didn't leave as he planned, her brother could continue to sink into a life of dissipation and anger. He would eventually be given some menial job in their father's company, but he would never distinguish himself. He would never become the kind of man that he yearned to be.

Sibyl shook her head, saying, "No, that can't be possible, there must be some other way."

Holding the glass between finger and thumb, she swiveled it by ninety degrees, the firelight sliding over its surface, and the light inside the scrying glass turned over, again like a kaleidoscope. Inside, the image shifted, the setting around Harley rearranging itself. This time her brother was facing down a pistol still, but in the hands of a ragged-looking man on a dark street corner. Shaking her head, she turned the glass another ninety degrees, the image folded over on itself yet again, and there was her brother, still the same, the pistol back in his own hand, moving it slowly up to press against his temple as he sat in the armchair in his bedroom at the Beacon Street house.

"It can't be possible!" Sibyl repeated, her voice rising. At the edges of her consciousness she grew aware of stirring as heads lifted from their own chaises in response to her cry.

She twisted the glass again, swiveling it upward this time, and the light inside the orb tumbled over itself, around Harlan's face, resolving into an image of him still the same age, still with the pistol pressed to his temple, his eyes closed, but now he was in a bar, it looked like, with shattered glass around him on the floor and a rivulet of blood trickling from his hairline along the inside of his nose.

"It can't be possible!" Sibyl cried, voice growing shrill as she twisted the glass, seeing Harlan back in the office, slightly younger, with different furniture, sunlight streaking into the window at a different angle. His finger started squeezing the trigger, slowly, slowly, and Sibyl screamed, "It can't be! It can't be! There must be a way! There must!"

She turned the glass again, but as it moved the image inside exploded in a sudden burst of red.

Sibyl let out a guttural, hysterical wail, wordless, desperate, her head thrown back, hair falling loose around her shoulders, hot tears squeezing out of the corners of her eyes. She felt hands on her shoulders, shaking her, heard voices calling out her name, trying to wake her, but she twisted free, struggling, holding the glass before her eyes for another look, just one more look, she had to see, there must be some alternative, something she hadn't thought of. . . .

But the scrying glass was deep crimson red, and she turned it, and she turned it, and she turned it, and it didn't change.

She saw that it never would.

With a cry ripped from deep within her soul, Sibyl hurled the scrying glass into the brick fireplace. It exploded in a tinkling burst of shards, scattering through the embers and across the floor, glittering splinters winking like teardrops, or stars. Sibyl sobbed, moaning, "It's not possible, it can't be possible," sagging into the arms of the people who were trying to restrain her.

She gulped for air, exhausted, weeping, and through the blurred haze of her tears she watched as the color of the shards melted from red, to perfectly clear, and at last back to milky bluish white.

TWENTY-SEVEN

Westmorly Court

Harvard Square

Cambridge, Massachusetts

May 8, 1915

*T*he sound of sparrows rustling about their morning business struck Sibyl as perverse. She looked through eyes blistered with weeping out at a world that was unchanged, and its indifference offended her. The morning light was thin and gray, watery, the beginning of a soft, cool day. A produce cart rolled along Massachusetts Avenue, its nag sleepy and nickering, its driver urging her on with minimal flicks of the reins. A squirrel paused in the grass by the gracious dormitory building where she found herself, rooting at the base of a tree for its cache of nuts. She leaned her cheek on the dormitory's door, resting. Just for a moment. Then she lifted her hand and beat her palm on the door.

Pound.

Pound.

Pound.

She waited, her lips chapped, hair plastered to her forehead with a sickly sheen of sweat. Through the ear pressed to the door she thought she could hear stirring within. She closed her eyes.

Her arrival in Cambridge was unclear. The last thing that she could remember was wailing, deep and horrid keening, and the sensation of hands on her arms and waist, of being pulled from her seat under a rain of admonishments to be quiet. She was hustled down a flight of stairs—had she fallen? Or tripped at the bottom? She wasn't sure—and then thrust, with force, out onto the street. A coat came flying out the door after her, and she staggered, losing her balance, trying to gather the coat up in her arms. It was impossible to pick up, like trying to carry aspic in her arms, so she reeled away without it. There had been a car—a taxicab? A stranger? No, she would never have accepted a ride from a strange man, at the break of dawn, surely not—and it had taken her here. Why had it taken her here?

She opened her eyes and rolled them up in their sockets, looking at the snarling face of a concrete gargoyle grinning down at her. She lifted her hand, her heavy arm, and beat on the door with her fist.

Pound.

Pound.

Pound.

From deep inside the building she thought she heard a youthful male voice cry out, "Christ Almighty!" Then, from a nearer vantage point, she heard the same voice say, "Andersen, you forget your key again?" while fiddling with locks and dead bolts.

The door opened inward, and Sibyl fell inside, collapsing into the surprised arms of a tall blond boy in striped pajamas and robe. "Wha—holy cow!" the boy exclaimed.

"Harley," Sibyl murmured, her hand pawing at the air. Her head lolled on her shoulders, and she tried looking into the boy's face, but his features were blurry. She was dimly aware of the sound of pounding footfalls, and another boy's voice saying, "Great Scott, Lester, who've you got there?"

"Why, I dunno," the boy holding her up said. His arms felt spindly and young under her weight, and she tried to get her feet organized enough to pry herself off of him, but they weren't obeying.

"What well have you been wishing at, I'd like to know?" the second boy asked with a laugh. "She looks a sight, though, doesn't she."

"Yeah. I think you'd better get the professor," the first boy said.

"I think you're right," the second one said, and his feet thumped away.

"Miss?" her rescuer said, loudly, into her ear. "Miss? I'm going to help you to this bench, all right?"

"Mmm," Sibyl said. "Harley." She felt herself being moved, her feet dragging along behind her.

"Huh?"

"Harley," she said again, her head flopping forward, chin on her chest.

"What, Harley Allston? You know him? Why, he doesn't live here anymore. Got sent home." Then, as an afterthought under his breath, he added, "And I can see why."

The sound of more feet, and the second boy saying, "Right over here, Lester's got her."

"And you don't have any idea who she is? On the level, now, Cooper. You've got to tell me the truth," an older male voice said. A voice that sounded familiar. Sibyl tried to force her eyes to work, but the faces all swam together.

"Honest, we neither of us ever saw her before in our lives," said the second one, Cooper.

Then the older voice said, "Oh, my God."

"Why, Professor Derby! You know her?"

Benton. Sibyl redoubled her efforts to make herself understood, but she was having trouble controlling her limbs, and her tongue lay in her mouth like a foreign object.

"Boys," Benton said, without commenting on whether he knew her or not. "You did the right thing. Here, help me get her upstairs. I'll call for a doctor."

Sibyl felt her arm lifted over a broad pair of shoulders, with another hand or two at her waist, helping her down a long hallway. A door opened, her feet were dragged along a richly patterned carpet, before she was lowered onto a couch. A wonderful brocade couch. She sank onto it with a sigh of immeasurable relief, resting her cheek against its nubbly surface.

The voices around her faded into a background drone of murmurs and discussion. Doors opened and closed. Sibyl rooted her cheek against the brocade, covering her face with one hand. She felt herself loosen and begin to drift. Then she sank into a delicious, perfectly deep sleep.

"WELL, I CAN see why you were concerned, but I think she'll be all right," someone said. Sibyl's eyes flew open, instantly alert.

She saw Benton standing a little ways off, in conference with a spectacled man holding a black leather bag. Benton? Why would he be there? Where was she? Her eyes roved over the room where she lay, shoes off, stretched out on her side on a brocade couch. It was a dark-paneled drawing room, lined with books. Deep leather armchairs, a Wardian case full of ferns under a leaded glass window. An antique globe, yellowed with age, over in the corner. A brass telescope trained out the window. A side table, on wheels, holding an assortment of Scotch, glassware, and a cut crystal seltzer bottle. Over the fireplace, a small, rather bizarre painting, all jagged edges that half suggested the shape of a guitar. It was a well-appointed, masculine room, small and comfortable, unassuming. Benton's room. How on earth could she have gotten to Benton's rooms?

"Just needs some rest and something warm to eat, I should think. But I can take her over to the hospital if you like. Just to be sure."

"No, no," Benton said. "Unless you think it's really necessary." He lowered his voice, angling his body away from her, and said, "I'm a friend of the family. As you can imagine, I think they'd prefer to avoid any notice."

"Of course," the doctor said, glancing at her over Benton's shoulder. "I understand completely. I think the young lady should be fine in a few hours. Although—" He paused, and then lowered his voice to match Benton's. "I don't think I need to point out to you that this is worrisome behavior. The family should be informed. Should they wish, I can refer them to a very fine sanitarium. One that's accustomed to dealing with such situations. With discretion."

"That's good of you," Benton said, ushering the doctor to his door. "I'll be sure to mention it."

"It's quite common, you know, Professor Derby," the doctor said as he readied to leave. "You should tell them that. Nothing to be ashamed of. It's happened to some very fine people."

"I'm sure you're right," Benton said. The two men parted at the door with the customary thanks and assurances, and then the doctor was gone.

Benton moved back into her field of vision, settling with a grunt in one of the leather armchairs, crossing his ankle on his knee. He rested his chin on his fist and looked at her.

She focused her eyes on him and gave him a wan smile. He was in a crewneck sweater over an oxford cloth shirt, unbuttoned at the neck, the sleeves pushed up on his forearms. She didn't think she'd ever not seen him in a suit. The quality of the light suggested midmorning. She raised herself up on an elbow.

"Benton," she began.

He returned her smile, with tired eyes, and held up a hand. "Would you like some coffee? I was just going to make some."

"Why, yes," she said, rubbing her fingertips over her eyelids. "I would. Thank you."

He nodded, getting to his feet and vanishing down a hallway. She heard cheerful morning kitchen sounds, clattering and water running. A whistling kettle. Sibyl waited, enjoying lying there, watching the sunshine lengthen into the room.

When he reappeared, he carried a tray holding a silver pot, two cups and saucers, spoons, and two bowls of oatmeal with butter and brown sugar. Sibyl struggled into a seated position. Wordlessly he fixed up her coffee with sugar and two precise droplets of milk, then passed her the cup. He must have noticed her idiosyncratic coffee-doctoring habits at some point, as he didn't even inquire. She accepted the cup gratefully, and sipped. Its warmth started to bring color back into her cheeks, and she sighed with pleasure.

He started to pass her the bowl of oatmeal, and out of habit she said, "Oh, no, I couldn't possibly."

He scowled. "I know you were awake while the doctor was here. And that means that I know that *you* know that this is not optional. Eat it."

"But I . . ." She trailed off, looking at the oatmeal. The sugar had melted into a delectable puddle of brown syrup. She felt saliva spring into her mouth.

He gave her a sharp look. "Don't think I don't know what this is about. But you can't be in control of everything all the time, Sibyl. Now come on. Eat it. It's only oatmeal."

Abashed, unaccustomed to being seen through, Sibyl reached for the bowl and took a small bite. It was delicious.

They sat for some time, breakfasting, drinking coffee, avoiding discussing the state in which Sibyl had appeared on his doorstep. She had forgotten that he was in residence in the same dormitory where Harlan used to live. Or perhaps, in some cobwebby corner of her mind, she hadn't forgotten. Perhaps she hadn't wanted to arrive home in such a state. A flush of shame crept over Sibyl's cheeks. She set down her coffee cup and looked away.

"Sibyl?" Benton asked.

She shook her head, face hidden behind her hand.

He got up from his seat and moved to join her on the couch. Sibyl emitted a pathetic sniffle, and Benton slid his arms around her. She buried her face in his neck, hot tears dampening his sweater.

"Oh, Ben," she sobbed.

"Shhh," he whispered into her hair. She felt his hand on the back of her head, his fingers in her hair, stroking her, soothing. She coiled her arms around his waist, not caring anymore what he might think of her, abandoning herself to her grief.

When her sobs subsided he gently disengaged from her hold and sat back, looking at her.

"Are you ready to tell me what happened?" he asked. There was no judgment in his voice.

She looked at him, then down at her hands in her lap. She nodded.

Quickly, with nervous glances from under her eyelashes to weigh his reactions while she spoke, Sibyl recounted her conversation with her father. When she told him that Lan had used a variation on the scrying glass himself, in fact had become addicted to it from a young age, he rubbed a distracted hand through his hair but said nothing. She finished by describing what she had seen of Harlan's future, his inevitable early death, in misery and dishonor.

"That's why I sneaked out," she finished, speaking to the seam along the edge of her skirt as she toyed with it. "When Papa told me it was possible to see alternatives, I thought—I knew I had to do something. To help Harlan. But I wasn't doing it right. Every time I turned the glass, I saw the same thing." Her voice caught in her throat.

Benton sat next to her, listening. After a time he said, speaking with care, "You know, there are worse things than dying."

Sibyl stared at him, aghast. "What do you mean?" she asked. "What could possibly be worse than dying?"

He looked sidelong at her, his expression mild. "Well," he said. "We all die. Right?"

She blinked, sitting back.

"Perhaps worse than the dying itself," he mused, "is living a life with no meaning. A life that's wasted."

"Wasted," she whispered.

"Yes," Benton said. "You said that in all the alternatives for Harlan, if you stopped him from signing up to fight, he died after living a short, miserable, and dissipated life."

"Yes," Sibyl said, waiting for him to finish his thought.

"And we must admit," Benton said, treading lightly, "that's not such a surprising outcome. Given the way things have been going for him lately."

"But I can't accept what Papa said. He said that everything is foretold, and all we can do is submit to our fate. Why can't things be different? Why can't Harlan just stay here, and be happy?"

Benton got to his feet and moved to rest his hand on the globe under the window. He gave it a thoughtful spin.

"I don't know," he said at last. "I approach the world scientifically, Sibyl. I don't believe in God, at least, not the way your father does. But I do believe in Newton. If I pick up this coffee cup and drop it, I believe it'll fall. Is that fate? It's just obeying the laws of physics. But then, so are we. There simply aren't infinite possibilities in the universe. Either for this coffee cup, or for ourselves."

"Then you agree with him," Sibyl said, her face crumpling with dismay.

"If we can't control what happens to us, then there's no point. We can't be moral people."

"What do you mean by that?" Benton asked her.

"Papa said that he knew he'd sinned. He sees this—skill—that we have as a curse. He thinks he's damned. It's as though the ability to be a good person has been stolen from him."

She paused, feeling an emotion for her father that was so alien she at first could not identify it. After a moment's reflection she knew it for what it was: pity.

Benton stopped the spinning of the globe with an abrupt hand. Sibyl saw that it had come to rest on the eastern coast of China.

"I think," he said, toying with the globe, "our childhoods create the template for the people we become. But that's not the same as fate. Not exactly." He paused, gazing in meditative silence at the globe under his hand, rolling it this way and that. "It's character," he said finally. "We are the men that we are. Whether that is because of our childhoods, or God's hand, or nature, doesn't much matter. Perhaps your father's wrong. It's not a curse at all. Your father, and you, have actually seen the best possible outcome of Harlan's life. And it's the path that he wants to choose."

She stood, running her hand along the telescope at the window. "I hate it," she whispered. "I hate that we can't be free."

She paused, feeling his surprised eyes on her back. Without looking around she said, "I suppose that shocks you, coming from me. Who's always lived the life that's been laid out for me."

"That doesn't shock me at all. But don't misunderstand me. Those basic laws hold sway over us like the laws of physics hold sway over this cup. But as we attain reason, we become free to act. We're free to assign whatever meaning we wish to our lives. We act, and in doing so, the choices that we make have meaning."

"That's a very perverse kind of freedom," Sibyl said, irritated.

"It's the best kind," he countered. "Freedom of thought. What matters isn't Harlan's death, as such. Harlan's death is assured. As is yours." He paused, glancing at her. "As is mine. What matters is the life he chooses to live. The meaning he gives it. He must have the opportunity to choose to live his life with honor."

Sibyl stared at Benton with a sinking heart.

"You're right," she whispered, her obsidian eyes wide with comprehension. Her grip tightened on the telescope, and she turned to look out the window, following its aim. It was pointed up into the sky over Cambridge, which had opened into a perfectly clear, crystalline blue day.

"In a way," Benton remarked, moving from the globe to stand near Sibyl at the window. He took her hands in his, rubbing his thumbs over her knuckles. "It gets back to the debate between Edwin and me. He thought that understanding death would give life its meaning. But I think that someone who spends all his time waiting to die might as well be dead already."

"Ben," she said. Fear ran cold in her veins, but she decided that she had to know the truth.

"Yes?"

"Why did you pick Lydia over me?"

There was a long pause, and the skin along the back of Sibyl's neck prickled, alive to his nearness.

His eyebrows furrowed, and he seemed at first not to know how to answer. "But I didn't," he said at length. "I suppose, after waiting for an assurance from you for so long, I—I thought you didn't want to have me."

She looked up into his gray eyes, soft with regret, about to argue with him, but before she could speak he took her in his arms and moved his mouth to hers, enfolding her in a tight embrace. Her eyes drifted closed as she surrendered to the feel of him, the warmth and taste of him in her mouth, his breath on her cheek, the certain hold of his hands at her waist.

"But, Ben," she murmured in his ear as his lips found the delicate spot below her ear, and then traced a lazy line down the side of her neck. "I did. I did want to have you."

He pulled away, his eyes leveled at hers, smiled, and growled, "Good." Then his arms were around her, and she laughed, his hands moved up her back, his mouth met her throat, her jaw, her mouth again, drinking her in with all the urgency of years wasted.

Sibyl heard her blood rushing in her ears, felt herself melting against his body, and as she sighed with pleasure and threaded her hands through his hair, reflected that she had never felt more alive.

WHEN THEY ARRIVED back at the Beacon Street house, Sibyl suggested, quietly, that they come in through the back door facing the river. She knew she was fooling herself if she thought that her absence from the house would escape notice, particularly given that she was still dressed in the same clothes she had been wearing the previous day, now rumpled, stained, and missing an overcoat. She tidied herself as best she could at Benton's apartment, repinning her hair and scrubbing the dirt from her face. But her eyes were bloodshot with fatigue and emotion, and her hands were shaking even worse than before.

They made it as far as the rear hallway before they were discovered, by Mrs. Doherty, of course, the usual first discoverer of anything that occurred in the Allston home. She waylaid them by the kitchen door and, passing a cursory if observing eye over Sibyl's obvious disarray, said, "I'm so sorry to bother, but I'm afraid we'll have to discuss the girl when you've got a minute, miss."

"Dovie?" Sibyl exclaimed. "Why, what's the matter?"

"No," Mrs. Doherty said, her eyes darting to the kitchen door. "Not Miss Whistler, miss. *The girl.* She's up and quit on us."

Sibyl had never been able to ascertain why Mrs. Doherty persisted in calling Betty Gallagher "the girl" rather than use her name. She didn't think she'd heard the housekeeper speak the cook's full name once in all the years of their joint employment. But apparently that would no longer be an issue below stairs in the Beacon Street house.

"Oh," Sibyl said, confused. "My word. But she didn't give any notice." She turned to Benton, perturbed. "Why, I only just spoke to her last night. Told her you were coming for breakfast."

"She didn't, at that," Mrs. Doherty said, managing to imply that she'd always expected this would happen. "And I wouldn't've said anything right off like this, you just coming in and all, only the kitchen help had to get the breakfast up themselves, and— Well, they did the best they could. I'm afraid it weren't quite up to snuff."

Sibyl thought back to the cook's angry, miserable face when she inquired about Harlan's leaving. She saw that Betty must have developed softer feelings for her brother than Sibyl had realized.

"That's all right, Mrs. Doherty, thank you. Is everyone up, then, I take it?"

"Oh, they're up, all right," the housekeeper said. Sibyl waited to hear if any further details might be forthcoming, but none were. The housekeeper only nodded with a knowing glare at Benton and disappeared into the kitchen. Sibyl and Benton exchanged a look, and then made their way into the front hall.

The first floor of the house was unusually bright, as someone had pushed back the heavy velvet curtains and left open both sets of pocket doors to the dining room and outer drawing room. Sibyl caught her breath, taken aback by how refreshing the carved biomorphic shapes of Helen's aesthetic imagination looked when illuminated by sunshine.

"But have you seen my gaiters?" she heard Harley call down the second-floor hallway. Footsteps and a thunk, as of a trunk being tipped over. "That's what I'll need, you know. They've given us a list."

"No, I haven't seen your cursed gaiters!" Dovie cried from the opposite side of the second-floor hall, a mixture of aggravation and misery. There was more pounding of feet, and a door slammed. Sibyl smiled gamely at Benton, and squeezed his hand.

"Why don't you go see if Papa's in the drawing room," she suggested. "I want to have a word with Harlan."

Benton stared hard down at her. "What are you going to say?"

She smiled, a sad, resigned smile. "I don't know yet," she confessed. "I just want to have a minute with him. I think I'll know when I get there."

He nodded. "All right," he said. "I'm just going to make a quick telephone call, if I may?"

She pointed him to the toadstool-shaped telephone nook under the stairs, and reflected, as he moved away, that silhouetted like that against the La Farge window, Benton looked like a Lapith in a Thessalonian glade, one of those mythical relatives of the centaurs, descended from Apollo. She smiled and made her way up the stairs.

"Harley?" she said, tapping softly on his door. It opened under the pressure of her knuckle.

She found her brother's room in a state of frantic disarray. Trunks stood open, and piles of shirts and woolen sweaters heaped in leaning towers.

"Did you find them?" he asked, his back to her as he rummaged through a drawer.

"No, I'm afraid not," Sibyl said, smiling. He glanced over his shoulder, tossing the stubborn lock of hair out of his eyes, and broke into a grin.

"Oh! Well, hi there," Harlan said, a glimmer of knowingness in his eyes. "Sure missed you at breakfast."

She arched her eyebrow at him and leaned against one of the posts of his bed, folding her arms.

"Looks like you're making an awful lot of progress," she said, surveying his packing.

"Well, I guess I'd better if I want to make my train," he said. "Got to go down to New York, you know, and change and catch another one to make the camp upstate. All the fellows are going."

"Even your friends from school?" she asked.

"Well, sure." Harley grinned, his eyes shining with excitement. "A lot of 'em are, anyway. We'll get in fighting shape, and then we'll join up with the Canadians. Can't sit around waiting all day for Wilson to get his head on straight. Fritz's got plenty of fight in him, looks like. I just hope it's not all over by the time I get there."

Sibyl smiled, surprised. "I never knew you to be such a follower of current events," she said.

He stuffed another few sweaters into the trunk on the floor, sat on it with his full weight, and lashed it closed.

"Well," he said, "I guess you're not far wrong. But for some reason—" He paused, staring into the middle distance. A shadow passed over his face, and he scratched under his chin as it went. "Oh, I don't know. I guess I just couldn't believe they'd torpedo that liner. *Lusitania.* I just couldn't believe they'd do it. All those people. None of them had anything to do with the war at all. They had no reason to die like that. Did they?"

She watched him, waiting.

He paused again, his hands hanging between his knees. "I mean, you read in the papers about everything that's going on over there, the Belgian orphans and the chlorine gas and everything, and it's so—remote. I guess for a long time it didn't seem like it was real. Or if it was, it didn't seem like it had anything to do with me. But then, that ship going down . . ." He trailed off, gazing out the window at the street below, and then met her gaze. "What kind of man would stand aside, idle, when something like that happens? I feel like I have to do something. I have to. I've sat aside long enough."

"Aren't you worried that it'll be dangerous?" she asked, as carefully as she was able.

He stood, shaking off his passing study, and bustled back to the pile of shirts on top of his highboy.

"Dangerous?" he echoed with a laugh. "Why, sure it'll be dangerous. It'd better be dangerous!"

"What makes you say that?" Sibyl asked, her eyes glimmering under a sheen of tears. She held very still, not blinking, to keep them in her eyes, where he couldn't see them.

He sighed, looking up at himself in the highboy mirror. Sibyl could see his face in the mirror, which looked older than when he came home from school those few short weeks ago. More like the man he dreamed of being.

"I guess," he said, gazing on his own reflection. "I guess there just comes a time, Sibsie, when a man has to distinguish himself. That's what it is. It's my time."

As he said this Sibyl wrapped her arms around her waist, cupping her elbows in her hands. She hesitated, then moved to stand next to him. He looked at her with some surprise, and she threw her arms around him, clasping him tightly to her. "Harley," she whispered in his ear. "Always my little lieutenant. I'm so proud of you."

He broke her embrace, laughing, embarrassed by her sudden show of emotion. "Oh, come now," he said with a grin, shaking her off.

But as Sibyl gazed on him, she thought she might never have seen her brother so determined. And, she realized, she might never have seen Harlan look so happy, either.

THE GAITERS, OF course, were never found, and when the taxicab arrived Harlan was still asking Mrs. Doherty if she could look just one more time in the laundry room, to see if they could have ended up there after a hunting expedition three months' earlier. While she insisted to him that they were not there, had in fact never been there, and while Lan Allston remarked to the hall stand that he felt certain gaiters could be obtained for a reasonable price even in the impenetrable wilderness of New York City, Benton Derby helped the cabbie load the trunks onto the rear of the taxi, lashing them one on top of the other as it idled at the curb. At last the trunks were secured, the gaiters were given up for lost, and Harlan stood with a rucksack over his shoulder on the front steps of the Beacon Street town house, facing his family.

"Harley," Dovie burst, unable to contain her objections any longer. "I wish you wouldn't go. What do you want to go for? It's nothing to do with you! Don't go. Don't."

He grinned, glanced at his father and sister with a twinkle in his eye, and then leaned down and kissed Dovie flush on the mouth. The kiss went on for a while, long enough for Benton to clear his throat.

"Come on, Doves. It'll be swell," Harlan said, gazing into her eyes with tenderness mixed with excitement. "I promise. And you won't even know I'm gone, I'll be back so fast."

The girl brought her hands up to her mouth, her eyebrows rising in the middle of her forehead into an inverted V of misery. The sound of sniveling could be heard behind her hands, and her eyes were two emerald pools of water. Harlan placed his hands on her shoulders and this time planted a kiss square on the top of her head. "You be a good girl, now. And you write me. Write me all you want. All right?"

She nodded, but the sniveling continued.

Harlan then turned to Lan Allston, whose chiseled face reflected a stoic impassivity that the Allston children had long taken as a substitute for emotion. Sibyl watched her father out of the corner of her eye. Deep beneath the false impassivity she could read the subtle signs of a man seized with grief. A man who had known this day would come, even before his son was born. She finally understood that the frozen features of her father's face were there to hide not how he felt about his children, but to hide what he knew from them. The stoic mask, one of the many faces Lan Allston showed the world, was worn at great cost to keep them free.

"Captain," Harley said, extending his hand. Their father took the young man's hand, shook it, and then he pulled his son to his breast and embraced him. His wrapped his arms tight around his son's shoulders, eyes squinted shut, jaw set in granite. He said nothing, their father. But Sibyl watched him hold his son, hold him tightly, and at the very corner of her father's closed eyes, she saw a glimmer of a tear. Lan Allston was not the sort of father to tell his children, in so many words, that he loved them. Sibyl knew it. Harlan knew it. And in that moment, he didn't need to.

Last, Harlan turned to Sibyl. "Well, Sibs," he said, with a grin. "I didn't go back to school. Think you'll ever forgive me?"

Sibyl smiled, and as she did so, she realized that she was wearing a stoic mask of her own. Deep inside her heart, where no one could hear, she screamed, *Harley, don't go! Stay here! Whatever you do, stay here, stay safe with us!* She felt two sets of eyes on her, belonging to her father and to Benton, watching, waiting. She swallowed, her fists taut at her sides.

"I guess you can always finish up when you get back," she said. Her cheek twitched, and she covered the twitch with a broader smile.

Her brother laughed a delighted laugh, threw his arms around her in a spontaneous embrace, and lifted her off her feet.

"Harley!" she cried, kicking her feet while the others laughed. "Come on! Put me down!" He put her down, grinned, and turned to Benton.

"Well, Derby?" he said. "You ready to go?"

"Just about," Benton said.

The bottom fell out of Sibyl's stomach.

"I beg your pardon?" she said, looking at him.

"He's on my same train," Harlan said, opening the back door of the taxi and tossing his rucksack inside. "Better run. Wouldn't want to miss it."

She stared at him, a strange buzzing in her ears. Benton looked down at her with a sad smile.

"What is he talking about?" Sibyl said, her eyes widening in panic. She reached out and took hold of his jacket sleeve. "Ben? What's Harlan talking about?"

"I'm going, too," he said, softly.

"But you can't."

"I can," he said, still smiling. "I must." He brought a hand up and laid it, softly, against her cheek.

"But," she protested, her eyes flushing with water. "But I don't want you to go. I want you to stay here."

He leaned down, not caring who saw, and kissed her. Sibyl lost herself in it, in the feel of his mouth on hers, in the gentle insistence of his lips and his hand cupping her cheek. He kissed her like he was sipping cool water, like it was the most natural and perfect thing in the world. Then he pulled away, and whispered, "I've had my things sent along to the station."

She held fast to his sleeve, her knuckles white. "Don't," she whispered, eyes looking up into his, pleading.

He leaned in, his mouth close to her ear, and said, "You didn't see me there, did you? Maybe I can look after him. Maybe we're freer than we know."

Then he turned, holding her steady in his gaze, and climbed into the taxicab next to Harlan. Twin streams of tears started snaking down Sibyl's face. Her father's hand slipped into hers and squeezed. On her other side, Dovie edged nearer, wrapping her arm around Sibyl's waist.

The taxi gunned and pulled away down Beacon Street. Sibyl couldn't stand it. Just when she finally found him again, Benton was leaving. Her lower lip trembled, and she bit down on it, hating him for going, hating herself for being unable to stop him. The taxi honked a merry *awoo-gah*, and Sibyl, Lan, and Dovie each raised a hand in farewell.

Before the cab had gone half a block, Harlan stuck his head out the rear window and called out, "Good-bye! Don't let old Baiji die on me, now!"

And then the taxi rounded the corner of Marlborough Street and was gone.

THE THREE OF them, Lan, Dovie, and Sibyl, stood in a knot on the front steps of the house for several minutes, as if waiting to see if the cab would come back. When it didn't, Lan finally let go of Sibyl's hand, and fumbled in his pocket for the chronometer.

"Hmmm," he said.

Sibyl turned to look at him, and said, "What is it, Papa?"

He smiled at her, and behind his ice blue eyes Sibyl saw the true, echoing depths of his sadness.

"Looks like they'll just make their train," he said, in a tone that Sibyl found impossible to read, and stepped back inside the house.

The door closed, and when it clicked shut Dovie's arm dropped from around Sibyl's waist.

"You," the girl hissed, turning miserable, accusing eyes on Sibyl. "You! Let! Him! Go!" With each word her voice rose in pitch, until on the last one it was nearly a scream.

"What do you mean?" Sibyl said, confused, so lost in her own grief that at first she didn't know what the girl was talking about.

"You said you'd talk to him!" Dovie shrieked. "You promised! How could you just let him go like that? How?"

Sibyl's heart quickened with mingled confusion and fear, and she remembered that Dovie was right. She had promised to speak with Harlan. And, of course, she had spoken with him. Just not the way Dovie had wanted her to.

"Dovie," she said, reaching a tentative hand toward the girl, who was shaking with sorrow and rage. Sibyl heard the sound of a window sash opening, somewhere down the street, and she swallowed, anxious to keep the girl from making a scene.

"No!" Dovie exclaimed, stamping her foot. "You promised! Now he's gone. Oh, he's gone, he's gone." With a moan the girl sank to the ground, her knees pulled up like a street urchin, burying her face in her hands, weeping. Surprised, Sibyl took a step back. Dovie wrapped her arms around her knees and sobbed into her skirts. "He's gone," she moaned. "What'll become of me now? What'll I do?"

Slowly, peering up and down the street to ensure that they were unobserved, Sibyl seated herself next to Dovie and wrapped an arm over her thin shoulders. "Dearest," she said gently. "You'll be fine. It'll be hard, having him gone, but you'll manage. You'll see."

"No, no, no," Dovie bawled, rocking back and forth. "You don't understand."

"Sure I do," Sibyl murmured, stroking the baby-fine hairs at the base of Dovie's neck. "You love Harlan. I know that. It's awful, saying goodbye to someone—" She paused, an uncomfortable realization dawning inside her. "To someone you love," she finished.

"No," she wailed. "I mean, yes, I do, of course I do, but that's not it."

"It's not?"

Dovie turned wet green eyes, black kohl puddling beneath them, onto Sibyl. Her nose bubbled, and her ruby lips were swollen from crying. Sibyl smoothed the hair away from her brow and kissed her forehead.

Dovie hiccuped and wiped her nose with the back of her wrist. She was still wearing one of Sibyl's shirts.

"Sibyl," she gasped. "I—I've got something I've got to tell you."

But deep within herself, Sibyl found she already knew what it was.

Interlude

THE EARLY LIGHT of dawn felt cool, drier, as though the miasma of night air had been swept away by the river and carried off to sea. Lannie inhaled, bringing the crisp, differently spiced air deep into his lungs. He felt in his pocket to reassure himself of his new chronometer and the last of his money. All was as it should be.

The scholar sighed with satisfaction. "Another day to be alive. We are fortunate, indeed." He stretched his hands overhead with a luxurious yawn, and smacked his lips. "I could do with some tea, and that's a fact."

They strolled at an easy pace, passing vegetable-laden wheelbarrows and a child driving pigs. They stopped at a window and procured two cups of tea from the woman within, paying her more than she asked.

"It's going to get hazy, later," Lannie remarked, squinting at the sky.

"It's not," Johnny said. "Too cool."

"Maybe it's cool now," Lannie said. "But you mark my words, John—those light clouds up there, like brushstrokes? There'll be haze by midday, and rain by nightfall. You see if there isn't."

Johnny shook his head, muttering about sailors thinking they knew everything God had planned, and it being worse for them when they were wrong.

"You've been robbed of your night's sleep," he remarked.

"That's true," Lannie agreed. Oddly, he didn't feel tired. He felt the tea warming his belly, felt the ease of his limbs in motion. He felt more alive in that instant of dawn than he had on any other day in his life.

"I'm thinking we'd best get you back to your crew."

Lannie looked down at his feet, watching his boots step through the dust. A sleeping cat, coiled in a ball, vanished with the vibrating of his steps.

"I guess so," he allowed without enthusiasm. Who knew what labor he'd be bent to during their time onshore, or what sort of mood he might find among the crew.

"Hm," the scholar mused, eyes on the heavens, as though reconsidering the weather. "I wonder where they might be?"

"Back at the whorehouse, I guess." Lannie was brought up short by Johnny's glare. "Sorry, my mistake," he said. "They're probably back at the"—he struggled, not knowing the right word—"back at the—"

"Yes," Johnny cut him off. "They probably are. That's where we'll go."

They walked for a while in silence, listening to the chirruping of birds. In the distance, a few peddlers were starting to shout their wares. The city was shaking off the last of its sleep. A new day was beginning.

They passed through the fortification wall that bounded the Old City and wound their way through narrow streets. At one point they loitered at an intersection, Johnny looking left and right.

"I think we came from that way," Lannie said, pointing left.

"Your ignorance is an embarrassment to us both," Johnny joked. "Anyway, the streets are about parallel. It won't matter much." They turned right, ambling under knotted plum trees weighed down with a colony of twittering songbirds.

After a few minutes' progress down a dim alley lined with hanging laundry, Lannie was certain they'd taken a wrong turn. He glanced at his companion. He thought Johnny might look nervous, but he spoke as though nothing were the matter.

"How long are you here for, then?" the scholar asked.

"Not sure," Lannie said. "A couple of weeks. However long it takes the captain to transact our business and refit."

"Long trip back."

"Uh-huh."

"Well, perhaps you'll come to dinner before you go," Johnny said, with studied carelessness. "My father will find your manners atrocious, and you'll find my mother's cooking inedible. However, you'll discover my sister to be beautiful, and when you insult her with your attention, I'll be forced to kill you. A perfect evening."

Lannie laughed aloud. "I don't see how I could possibly refuse. Thank you."

They walked for another few moments in silence, but Lannie could tell Johnny was smiling.

"I've got a sister, too," Lannie remarked. "She's not beautiful, though. She's thirteen, and a pest."

"I'm sure by the time I make it to Boston, she'll be beautiful."

"Oh, you won't find her in Boston," Lannie said. "She's a good Salem girl."

"She's a witch, then? A sorceress?" Johnny laughed.

"Johnny," Lan said, stopping to show that he was serious. "We don't discuss that."

The young man looked confused and bowed his head in contrition. "I apologize. I didn't know. Please forgive my mistake."

Lannie paused, long enough for Johnny to feel his faux pas, and said, "S'awright. I'd expect as much, from a barbarian."

The other boy laughed, and they shoved each other, playfully, before moving on.

The alley ended in a courtyard ringed by houses that had once been fine, but that had been subdivided into many smaller dwellings and allowed to slip into disrepair. Bony dogs poked in the dirt, and chickens roosted in a cluster of brambles at the center. One or two of the houses served as makeshift restaurants, with tables near their front doors. At one table lounged a band of rough-looking white men in sailors' dress. Lannie kept a weather eye on them. They were singing a chanty, beating time on the table with merriment that suggested they were still going from the previous night.

Johnny frowned, unsure which way to go. A withered woman shuffled out of the restaurant, carrying a tray with cups of tea and some rice buns, and one of the sailors reached over and pinched her on the behind. The woman screeched, which the sailor met with hearty laughter. Uneasiness circulated in Lannie's stomach.

"Johnny," he started to say.

"Shhh," the scholar shushed him. "I'm trying to figure out which way." He scratched under his hat. "I hardly ever come through this quarter. Too dirty."

"Hmmm," Lannie said, thrusting his hands into his pockets and trying to be inconspicuous.

"Less ask 'em, then," one of the sailors bellowed, standing up. "Hey, you there!"

Lannie pretended not to hear. Instead he looked at Johnny, willing him to hurry. Indifferent to the trouble brewing under the plum trees, Johnny thought, stroking his chin.

"I shed, you there!" the man shouted, his words slurring. Lannie kept his back to the group, deaf and invisible. Stumbling feet approached. "I'm talkina you!" Lannie was tapped, roughly, on the shoulder. Hot breath blasted the back of his neck. "We wanna know 'bout your sweetheart, there. His hair wants a cut, don't it? Hey! You!"

Lannie's stomach sank, and he turned to face the speaker.

His first impression was of the corrosive breath of rum and sour plum wine. Behind the putrid blast stood none other than Tom, black gap in his jaw leering with rot. On his shoulder, bizarrely, perched a bright blue bird, something Lannie had never seen before. Its intelligent eyes looked with curiosity at Lannie, and its iridescent tail swept down Tom's back.

"Well, lookee here, boys!" Tom slurred. "Why, if it ain't the little greenhorn his very own self! Still with that yellow bastard, I see."

Lan sensed Johnny move behind him, standing with his arms folded to make him look broader across the chest than he was.

"We were just looking for you fellows," Lan said easily. "It'll be time for us to get back aboard, won't it? See you've got a new pet, there. You fellows must've had quite a night."

Tom laughed. The cruel smile vanished from his face, and he said, "I have at that. Won 'im. Dice game." He stood, swaying, his eyes narrowed. "You inshulted me, Greenie. You'n that Chinkee bastard. Be wise not to return to the ship'a tall."

"Now, Tom," Lannie started to say, mollifying.

"*Tom*," the older sailor burst. "Just cause you're from some fancy family don't mean you're any better'n I. Not here. You'll call me Mister Morgan, til I tell you different." He shoved Lannie in the chest with the tips of his fingers, hard as the end of a shovel.

A sickening sense of déjà vu took hold of Lannie. He froze. He saw Tom, speaking insults that he couldn't hear behind the buzzing of his thoughts. He registered the circle of sailors closing in on them, drinking in the threat of violence. Himself, motionless at the center. And Johnny. It was subtly different. But unmistakable.

"Johnny," Lan said, struggling to keep calm. "You've got to leave. Right now."

The scholar was already rolling up the sleeve of his jacket, his eyes on the drunken sailor. "I think not, Yankee," he said, face grave. "I think it'd be best if I stayed."

"No." Lannie took Johnny by the shoulders and stared him in the face. "Listen to me. You've got to go. You've got to go right now!" He shook him, digging his fingers into the scholar's shoulders.

A titter rose from the group of sailors, and Tom emitted a brutal laugh. "That's it," he taunted. He rolled his shoulders, causing the blue parrot to take off with a squawk, alighting in one of the plum trees. "Send your handmaid away. Rather keep you to myself as it is."

At Tom's last word, Johnny cried out, "Duck!"

Without thinking Lannie did so, and the sailor's fist whooshed through the air over his head. From his crouch Lannie looked up in time to see Johnny's fist crunch into Tom's nose. Tom staggered back, hands on his face, as the other sailors clapped and laughed. Wads of money changed hands. Lannie stood, with Johnny next to him flexing the fingers on his right hand, and said, "Now, that's enough. Let's call it a day and go back to the ship."

A few yards away, Tom swayed, his back to them, a slick smear of blood spattering the dust at his feet. He leaned over, placing his hands on his knees, breathing heavily.

"All right?" Lannie called. "We'll all just go back. No harm, no foul." From Lannie's vantage point it looked as though Tom were nodding, his head down. Lannie felt his pulse throb in his neck. Then, without warning, Tom spun with a guttural scream, barreling toward Lan and Johnny with a chair brandished over his head.

"Johnny, get down!" Lan yelled, ducking against the blow. But it didn't come; instead Lan glanced under his arm and saw the chair in Tom's hands crash into the side of Johnny's skull. The scholar spun, his eyes rolled up to show their whites, and the boy collapsed in the dust, palms up, eyes open and glassy, jaw jutting at a strange angle. One leg twitched. An instant of silence seized the circle of sailors, who stepped backward in shock.

Lan scrambled on his hands and knees, blind with terror, over to Johnny. He pressed his fingers to the other boy's throat, digging in the flesh under the jaw for a pulse. The jaw felt loose, shattered into pieces. A rivulet of blood leaked from one of his nostrils. He wasn't breathing. Johnny's body felt void, a vessel emptied. The other sailors were quiet. Lan heard no sound apart from Tom's panting as he paced the courtyard, broken chair held at the ready.

A scream started somewhere deep inside Lan, rumbling in his breast until it exploded from his mouth, an anguished wail of horror. He got to his feet and rushed at the older sailor, unthinking, fists knotted at the ready. The other man pulled back the broken chair, as though winding up for a baseball pitch. He swung as Lannie came at him, whiffed within an inch of Lannie's ear, and then Lannie's shoulder collided into Tom's chest, the momentum bringing them both to the ground in a cloud of dust. The chair leg glanced off Lannie's skull, and then he was astride the older man, fists flying, pummeling Tom's face again and again and again.

The man's legs kicked in the dirt, beating their heels on the ground, and as he pummeled Tom's face, Lannie sensed the circle of sailors creep nearer. He felt hands on his shoulders. He landed one last blow and saw that Tom's hand had gone slack, the chair leg falling loose. His legs weren't moving. Lannie gasped, panting, gulping air, looking around, confused.

The hands at his shoulders eased him backward, helping him off the sailor sprawled on the ground.

"Lannie," said a voice. Lan looked around, eyes wild, coming to rest on the face of Richard Derby. His eyes looked worried. "Lannie," he said again. He held Lannie tightly by the shoulders, shaking him, as if to bring the boy back to himself. "That's enough."

"Dick, I—" Lannie stood, appalled. He stared at Tom's spread-eagled body, his face a blurry, barely human pulp. The gravity and reality of what he had done seized him, and Lannie's stomach rebelled. He doubled over, vomiting out tea and bile. Richard rested a hand on Lannie's back and glanced, on edge, at the rest of the crew.

"Come on," Richard said, a current of urgency in his voice. "It's time for us to go."

Lannie moaned in horror. "It happened, Dick," he gasped, eyes jumping between the two bodies lying motionless in the courtyard. "It happened. It was real."

"Yes," Richard said, keeping hold of the younger boy. "I'm afraid so. But now we've got to go."

"No, you don't understand," Lannie said, balling his fists in Richard's shirt and bringing his wild eyes close to his face. "I didn't stop it. It was real, and I didn't stop it."

Richard pried Lannie's grip from his clothes. "Listen," he muttered, voice barely audible. "We all saw what happened, all right? It was an accident." He raised his voice, addressing the rest of the group. "An accident, right? Couldn't be helped. You did everything you could to avoid it, didn't you, Lan? Didn't he, fellows?"

Murmurs of assent bubbled from the crowd of onlookers. Lannie's gaze darted from face to face, all tanned from weeks at sea, and he saw in the staring sailors' eyes a wall of total silence. They knew the truth. They would always know the truth. And as long as Lannie was loyal to them, as long as he backed them as they were backing him, he would be safe.

Richard dropped his voice to a whisper and said, "He weren't all that popular, Tom Morgan. I don't think anyone'll cause you trouble. In fact, you may have even made some friends. But, Lannie, we've got to *leave*. We've got to go right now, before the authorities start asking questions about the Chinese boy. All right?"

Richard held Lannie's gaze to underscore his seriousness. "All right?" he repeated.

Lannie let go of Richard's shirt and wailed, "I didn't stop it. Why couldn't I stop it?" His face cracked with despair, tears springing to his eyes. "Dick, I couldn't stop it." He covered his face with his hands, trembling.

"All right," Richard Derby answered for him, wrapping his arm around Lannie's shoulders. "Pay the woman and let's get going. Come on! Move!"

He barked the order, and the sailors leaped to action, someone tossing a wad of bills onto the table under the plums. They clustered around Lan and hustled him away, toward one of the alleys leading out of the courtyard. Lan glanced back over his shoulder at the lifeless form of his friend on the ground, its eyes open and unseeing. Johnny, with his weakness for women and opium, with the beautiful sister and the judgmental father, who would never know what had happened to his son. Lannie realized that he didn't even know Johnny's real name.

He hung his head, a sob escaping from his throat at the sin staining his soul, worsened by the sickening, horrifying fact that he had seen it coming.

"Hurry," Richard Derby hissed, and through his weeping Lannie managed to break into a trot.

Behind him was a squawking and a flurry of wings, and then sharp points, like talons, sank into the meat of Lannie's shoulder. He leaped aside with a surprised shout, but the talons held fast.

"Guess he's dead set on coming along," Richard said drily, referring to the shimmering bird on Lan's shoulder. "They're awful smart, you know. Parrots. He's like to have been on a ship to get here in the first place. From South America. Live for ages, too. He's probably even older'n you."

The sailors plunged into the maze of alleys in the International Settlement, rushing to make the ship in good time. Losing himself among them, Lan choked on his tears until they petered away. His jaw ached, his head throbbed, a crust of dried blood was stiffening in his hair, but he was surrounded by men in his confidence, men who would look death in the face for him. He set his mouth in a firm line, resolved to face down whatever punishments Providence would dole out to him. As he weighed the murder that would forever stain his soul, Lan felt himself being watched.

Out of the corner of his eye, sitting in an inscrutable ball on his shoulder, riding along as he trotted the back alleys of Shanghai, Lan spied the macaw. The animal returned his look with one black eye, shining with intelligence, a dispassionate observer to everything that Lan had done.

And everything that was to come.

TWENTY-EIGHT

The Back Bay
Boston, Massachusetts
October 17, 1917

Sibyl set her suitcase down on the stoop with a *thunk* and looked up into the welcoming face of the Beacon Street town house. It appeared much the same as always: a slumbering animal, covered in its fur of ivy. The season painted the ivy leaves bright crimson, and a passing autumn breeze ruffled them in soft, undulating waves. Sibyl sighed, pleased.

Home. She was ready to be home.

She stood on the stoop, surveying the expanse of Beacon Street, which also looked much the same, and inhaling the crisp aroma of cool earth and woodsmoke from the fireplaces up and down the block. Behind her, she heard the front door click open, and she turned to face it with a smile.

"Well," Mrs. Doherty said with a touch of impatience. "Come in, then, before you catch your death. And mind the carpet."

"Thank you, Mrs. Doherty," Sibyl said. As she stepped inside, Sibyl caught up the housekeeper with a quick embrace. The stolid Irishwoman stiffened, then relaxed, just enough to return the hug with an awkward pat on the back. Sibyl laughed and pulled off her hat.

The front hallway also looked the same, right down to the forgotten hats adorning the hall stand. Sibyl caught sight of herself in the hall stand mirror, and smiled at the reflection that she found there. Her cheeks were plumper, a healthy, rosy sort of plump, and her black eyes had more light in them than before. She'd been right, when she decided to go away. And just as right to come home.

"Where is he?" she asked the housekeeper, who was bending to address herself to Sibyl's suitcase.

The woman lifted it with a grunt and said, "Where'd'you think? In there." She gestured with her chin to indicate that he was in the inner drawing room, doubtless loitering over a newspaper, just where Sibyl had left him.

"Surprised he didn't go pick you up at the station," Mrs. Doherty remarked, delicate as always in her reproach. "You'd think he'd of wanted to pick you up with the car, the day you come home." Sibyl could tell that this oversight weighed heavily on the housekeeper, and wouldn't soon be forgiven.

"Oh, I asked him not to," Sibyl said in her father's defense, drawing off her gloves. "I wanted to come home on my own."

"Figures. No one ever could tell you a thing," the housekeeper said with equal parts gruffness and affection. She struggled away with the heavy luggage, dragging it in stages across the floor to the stairs. Sibyl noticed the struggle and realized with surprise that Mrs. Doherty was not, in fact, the ageless monolith that the Allstons had always assumed her to be. She was getting older. She would be getting tired. As her first act back in charge of the Beacon Street house, Sibyl resolved to employ some additional help within the next week, one or two girls whom Mrs. Doherty could pester and harangue to her heart's content.

Sibyl moved into the front drawing room, breathing deep the familiar smell of home, a specific alchemy of lemon oil soap and woolen carpet and polished wood. The curtains were all drawn back, and the late autumn sun passing through the ivy leaves sprinkled splashes of reddish light in dancing patterns across the Chinese rug. Sibyl looked up at the portrait of Helen, in its place of honor over the fireplace.

"Hello, Mother," Sibyl said. The painted likeness of Helen, frozen as though about to speak, didn't respond, of course, but Sibyl was glad to have greeted it, anyway. She strolled through the room, running her hand lightly over a chair back here, a credenza top there, reentering this strange place that was her home.

The sliding doors to the inner parlor were open, as though waiting. Sibyl caught her breath as she stepped into the cloistered drawing room, for she saw that the curtains were drawn back there as well. The inner parlor had always lain shrouded behind wooden shutters beneath a further layer of drapery. In some sense Sibyl had forgotten that the room had windows at all. She paused, surveying the glittering expanse of the Charles River arcing out below the vantage point of the town house. The sun was slipping lower, dappling the waves on the water with the rich reds and oranges of autumn. A small sailboat drifted leisurely along the path of the setting sun, its sail stained red in the evening light. Sibyl sighed with pleasure.

"It's nice, isn't it?" her father's voice asked, and she turned to find him standing behind her. With a delighted laugh she cried out, "Papa!" and threw her arms around his shoulders. He laughed as well, returning her embrace.

"It *is* nice," she agreed, turning back to the window with its sweeping river view. "I'd almost forgotten you could see the river from here. I don't know why we didn't keep the windows open all the time."

"Habit, I suppose," her father mused. They stood together, admiring the water, with the city of Cambridge beyond it dropping into the first darkness of evening.

"Well then," her father said. "You're home."

"I am," she confirmed, moving to take her customary seat across from her father's armchair.

He sat opposite her, one hand on his knee and the other over his mouth, appraising his daughter. "You look well," he pronounced after a short time.

"I feel well," she said with a little smile.

"So you're glad you went, then?" he asked. Behind the question she heard a flicker of concern. Never mind that they helped "all the best people" there. She knew there was a stigma. But if her father had seen some of the others, she wagered he would have been surprised. Certainly she herself had been. Like being part of Mrs. Dee's charmed *Titanic* séance circle, everyone locked together in mutual understanding of their basic human frailty. The stigma didn't trouble her. She knew with whom she shared it.

"Very," she said. With a wry smile she held her hands out at shoulder level for him to see. They hung there, in midair, without moving a muscle.

He chuckled, and then sighed. "Impressive," he said, his sad pale eyes lighting up for a passing moment. "Most impressive. Perhaps I should go, then."

"Perhaps you should," she said. In fact, she had planned to broach just that idea with him once she was settled in. Though for him, it would be much more difficult. Sixty-odd years of dependence wasn't going to be shed easily.

"Mmmmm," her father said, stroking his chin and looking at her. The sadness lingered behind his eyes, but Sibyl could tell that he was pleased she was home.

She leaned against the back of the armchair, stretching out her feet. "So," she said, wondering what they should talk about. "Have you had any word from Harley? His last letter to me was two months ago. He sounded in great spirits, though. Ready to tear the Hun apart with his own bare hands. He's a terribly overwrought letter writer, don't you find? Who knew he'd have such a taste for propaganda."

"Indeed," her father said. "Well, your brother always was on the impressionable side. It can be a virtue, in the proper context."

"I had one from Ben just a couple of weeks ago," she said. "But none from Harley. I assume any letters are all at the bottom of the sea now, what with the U-boats. Must be a trick getting any mail and supplies through at all."

"Hm," her father said. "U-boats."

He paused, hazarding a sidelong look at Sibyl, who noticed it, but said nothing. "No, I'm afraid I haven't had word of him in some time."

They sat for a while, not speaking, enjoying the silence of the house. In fact, the silence was deeper than Sibyl remembered. At first she couldn't decide what made it so. Something was missing. But what?

After a time she realized that the missing sound belonged to the mantel clock. She rose from her armchair and inspected it, tinking on the crystal with a fingernail. No ticking emanated from inside the case. The hands were frozen at 2:20.

"Oh," her father said, noticing her interest. "Yes. I stopped winding it. Too much bother. I always keep a watch with me, anyway, so what's the point? Just another thing to remember to do."

She rested her eyes on Lan Allston's face when he said this and noticed that under his feigned indifference was a sense, albeit subtle, of being freed of something. As if one of the many constricting binds holding him had loosened. The observation pleased her.

"Well," she said. "When's supper? I'm starved."

He stood and took her arm. "The usual time," he said. "But you'd best dress this evening, my dear. We have a guest."

"We do?" Sibyl said, her eyebrows rising. "Why, Papa. I specifically said for you not to make a fuss."

"Far be it from me to disobey a direct order," said the Captain. "I can assure you, no fuss will be made."

SIBYL ARRIVED BACK downstairs early, well before the appointed time for supper. Her dress was outmoded now, she knew, a pistachio satin with a round skirt and high waist, where all the newest fashions in the magazines and *Town Topics* featured these delicious long Grecian columns, figure skimming and narrow, in liquid patterns, topped with exotic headbands. So she would be frumpy for dinner at home this evening, and whoever their company was would just have to endure her lack of taste. Sibyl paused to regard herself in the hall stand mirror again, turning sideways to examine her profile. Well, the year would be over soon enough. Perhaps she would go to Filene's tomorrow, just for fun. Perhaps she'd even ride the elevated to get there. Such boldness!

She laughed at herself, for the timid person she knew herself to have briefly been, and then wandered into the front drawing room.

A man was seated there, his back nearly to her, in three-quarters view, with smooth combed hair, dressed in a simple dinner jacket. He was sitting in one of the stiff side chairs, angled toward the fireplace over which Helen presided, and he seemed to be gazing up at Helen's youthful portrait, lost in thought.

"Oh!" Sibyl exclaimed. "I'm terribly sorry to disturb you. I didn't know that anyone was—"

But she didn't finish her sentence, because while she spoke the man had gotten to his feet, and she saw that he was Benton Derby.

He crossed the room, quickly, and took her with his arms around her waist, clutching her to him. She gasped, and her arms slid up his back, her fingers knotting the material of his dinner jacket, holding on tight, as if to reassure herself that he was truly there.

"Ben," she breathed, her nose buried in his chest. She took a long breath, inhaling the smell of him, that spicy mixture of French shaving soap and his particular blend of tobacco, purchased from the bins at the tobacconist in Harvard Square.

"Hello," he whispered into her hair. His hand found the back of her head, then traced along her jaw. Benton tipped her chin up and pressed his mouth to hers. Sibyl felt her eyelids flutter and her knees loosen. His arm around her waist kept a sure grip on her, and she brought her hands to his waist, returning his kiss for a long, delicious minute.

When they finally broke apart Sibyl gazed up into his face, her eyes shining with happiness. But when she looked at him more closely, the smile froze. He had a jagged, angry scar zigzagging over his right eyebrow, down his cheek just under his eye, all the way to his chin. The skin of his cheek was puckered, as though the injury had sliced through the muscle underneath, and it had healed imperfectly. She struggled to conceal the recoil that she felt, but saw immediately that she had failed.

His eyes took on a wounded cast, seeing what she saw. She hurried to allay his fear, saying, "I'm sorry, I didn't know. Why didn't you tell me? Your letters never let on that anything had happened."

He looked down, pressing his forehead to hers. "I suppose I didn't want you to worry," he said. "It looks ugly, I know, but I was lucky. A few more inches in any direction and I could've been blind. I could've been dead. A lot of the others with me weren't so fortunate."

Sibyl swallowed, bringing a tentative hand up to brush her fingertip along the fresh scar. "I'm sorry," she whispered. "I'm just so glad to see you. I'm so glad you're home safe."

"Yes," he said with uncertainty. He paused, his arms still around her waist. "Sibyl, I . . ." he started, then looked away.

"What is it?" she asked. But as soon as she read the worry behind his gray eyes, she knew what he was preparing to tell her. She let her breath out slowly.

"It's Harley, isn't it," she said. Not asking, as a question, but stating it outright. A fact that she knew to be true.

Benton nodded, his lips pressed together, eyes blinking back whatever he might really feel about the information he had tasked himself with delivering to her.

She shuddered, and he held her more tightly.

"Was it," she asked slowly. "Was it the way that I—" She couldn't finish. Her heart seized with the sudden grip of guilt.

He nodded.

She leaned her cheek on his chest, gazing into nothing for a long minute. He held her, waiting.

"Did it hurt? Do you think?" she asked in a small voice.

"Honestly," he said, and she heard his voice from within his chest, "I think it was too fast for that. I'd be surprised if he felt anything at all."

She sniffed, blinking her eyes quickly. Still he held her.

"Poor Dovie," Sibyl said. "She'll take it so hard. We must tell her."

"I spoke with her," Benton said. "This afternoon. I called on her specifically. She took it better than I'd expected. I think, in some respects, she was expecting it."

"And Papa?" she asked.

Benton paused, and then said, "He knows."

Sibyl nodded, unsurprised. She pressed her cheek more firmly to his chest, feeling the rhythm of his heart beating deep beneath his jacket. The sound of his blood moving under his skin soothed her.

"Just tell me one thing," she said. "And then I won't ask any more." She pulled her head away and looked up into his eyes.

"One thing," Benton said.

"Right before," Sibyl said. "While he was there. In the middle of all of it."

"Yes?"

"Was he happy?" She searched Benton's face, probing for the answer that she wanted to find.

Benton's eyes softened, and a smile pulled at the corner of his mouth. "You know what? He was. He was in fine form. Healthy. Busy. Engaged. Even in the long hours we spent encamped, I never once saw him gamble. We'd just heard word about the Zimmermann telegram, that Germany'd tried to lure Mexico into the war, with the promise of returning Texas, New Mexico, and Arizona to them if Mexico helped their cause. Gracious, but you've never seen him so worked up. We all knew the States would enter soon, and everyone was feeling confident. We were stationed in Nord-Pas-de-Calais with the Canadian Expeditionary Force, preparing to retake Vimy Ridge. It was an important maneuver, Sibyl. It would make or break the Arras Offensive, if we could succeed."

"What happened?" she asked.

Sibyl had been following the war's progress in the papers as best she could during her time away, though she'd had to pay one of the kitchen girls at the sanitarium to smuggle the newspapers to her room. Too stirring for the nerves, the doctors had said. Sibyl didn't care. She no longer minded having her nerves stirred, particularly when it concerned people she loved.

"They were very keen on tactics for this one, because they knew the geography of the ridge would make it damned difficult for the Germans to defend with just a rigid trench line," Benton said, his eyes shining with excitement as he recalled the complexities of preparing for battle.

"So the Corps officers held some lectures to spread all the tactical knowledge the French had acquired at the Battle of Verdun. Well, I'll tell you, they had us rehearsing the maneuvers over and over again before the offensive. Harley, he was popular with the Canadian boys. After a while they were just itching to stop rehearsing and get on with it. He kept as cool a head as I've ever seen, and helped some of the younger fellows keep their concentration, too. You would've been proud of him, Sibyl."

She nodded, smiling. She tried to imagine Harley a leader of men, a wielder of influence, and found that she could picture it more easily than she expected.

"They split the campaign into four objectives, and the plan was for us to leap-frog our way to the ridge in stages, with enough speed that the Germans wouldn't have time to react. We were in an infantry group aimed at the third objective, a little town called Thelus in a small stand of woods outside of Vimy. For once we were going to have plenty of artillery, a lot more than the usual Corps allotment. In that part of the country there was an awful lot of fighting in tunnels underground, too, you know. We had to work hard to know not just the trench system, but also the tunnels underneath. Lots to prepare for, lots to get wrong."

Sibyl's eyes widened, imagining having to fight to the death in the darkness of a cave, like a mole against a weasel. The idea of such confinement made her panicky and ill.

"Well, in the months leading up to the offensive, we were intensifying our nighttime trench raids on Fritz. It got to be kind of a game, actually."

"A game?" Sibyl said, aghast.

Benton laughed and said, "Oh, sure. Companies would compete over how many prisoners we'd take, and what kinds of intelligence we could beat out of them." He saw the expression of horror on Sibyl's face at this casual allusion to violence, and tried to tamp down his enthusiasm to a level more appropriate for a drawing room.

"At any rate, Harlan had been made a company commander in February. Late one night, near the end of March, he led a raid on a German trench not far from Thelus. They put up a real fight, those fellows, and it got ugly. But we managed to take it. Eleven sniveling German kids taken prisoner, and Harlan had just cornered their commander. He'd torn a kind of document case off the man and just passed it to me when we saw the Kraut bastard was holding a grenade."

Benton paused, the muscle at his jaw twitching at the memory. Sibyl waited, gazing up into his face with its angry pink scar. Already she found she only saw it if she tried.

"Well," Benton said at length. "There wasn't any time. No time at all.

Without even thinking, Harley threw himself on the German commander. We all hit the ground and then it was over."

"Ben," she whispered, brushing her hand over his eyebrow and down his cheek. "Ben."

He smiled, disengaging from their embrace and leading her over to the bench in the bay window. "Well," he said, voice somber. "I'll spare you the details. But there's one more thing."

"What's that?" Sibyl asked, working to push the image of Harlan's last moments away from her mind.

He smiled out of one side of his mouth. "You don't know what was in the document case."

Her eyebrows rose in curiosity. "And what was in the case?" she asked.

"A map," he said, leaning his chin on his fist and smiling at her. "Of part of the German tunnel system under the trenches. It included a tunnel under the Thelus line. One we didn't even know about."

"Well," she said, a slow smile dawning across her face. "How about that."

He nodded, enjoying her smile. "How about that indeed. Having that map meant that when we finally launched the offensive we were in that much more command of the terrain. It was one less place they could surprise us. It was small, Sibyl, but it made a crucial difference." He paused. "We retook the ridge. The offensive worked."

He hesitated, looking at her. "He saved my life, Sibyl, and the lives of the men he was with. And he did it with honor. Selfless honor."

She sat, digesting what Benton had to say, her sadness mingling with pride, and also with something else—possibly relief. Relief that Harlan was able to become, however briefly, the best version of himself. Relief that his life could have a pinnacle like that, a moment when he would always be his best, and happiest, self.

A footfall shook her out of her thoughts, and she found her father emerging from the inner parlor, Baiji perched on his shoulder.

"I see you've been entertaining our guest. A bit early, aren't we, Professor Derby? A touch enthusiastic, perhaps?" Lan Allston smiled on them, and the smile broadened when he observed his daughter to be blushing.

"Surely you're not taking the macaw in to dinner with us, Papa," Sibyl protested, attempting to recover her decorum.

"Why not?" her father asked with a mock wounded cast. "He gets lonesome, sitting in the parlor all day long. Why can't he have a change of scene once in a while? He's very well traveled, you know. I picked him up in Shanghai."

"Yes," Sibyl said, rolling her eyes. "You've mentioned it. A time or two."

As though aware that he was a subject of discussion, the iridescent blue parrot stretched out his wings like a gargoyle, opened his mouth, and stuck out his tongue.

"Very expressive," Benton remarked, in the tone of a man who is being polite, but would prefer to keep his distance.

"He dotes on that bird," Sibyl said. "None of us have ever understood it."

"Not true," Lan said, moving to the mantel and gazing up at the painting. "Your mother was always very understanding about Baiji."

"She wanted to turn him into a hat," Sibyl remarked aside to Benton, who hid a smile.

Lan Allston sighed, gazing up at the painting of his wife. "I've always been rather partial to this painting," he remarked to himself. "She's frozen in time, almost. Just how I remember her. Always young. Always about to speak."

"Mother was always about to speak when she was alive, too," Sibyl said, half-joking, and half sad.

"Well, that's the real mystery of death, I think," her father remarked, eyes exploring the painting. The bird seemed to be gazing up at the portrait, too, his wings shimmering and settling along his back. "Think of that young fellow who was on the boat with them. The bookish one."

"Who?" Sibyl asked. She had taken Benton's hand in hers and was toying with his fingers.

"The Widener boy. Harry. Whose mother gave the library to Harvard."

"Such a generous gift," Benton remarked, tickling Sibyl's palm with his ring finger where her father couldn't see. She noticed that he wasn't wearing his wedding ring anymore. "I'm rather looking forward to seeing it when I get back to campus."

Lan Allston said a thoughtful "Hmmmm" and turned to gaze on Benton and Sibyl. His eyes, usually so clear and blue, were looking more watery than Sibyl remembered. Her father was getting older, too.

"A wealthy young man from a good family," Lan said. "Spent his time in leisured pursuits, collecting books, traveling the world. If he'd lived to be my age, that would've been the sum total of his life, you know. Family, of course, that's important. Civic duties. Philanthropic pursuits. I'm sure he was a fine young man, and would've made a fine old man, too, no doubt. He would live to be old and distinguished, and he would die, and there would be a respectful obituary in the paper, noting all his accomplishments, and omitting any allusion to his myriad personal faults, whatever they may have been. Then his children would've helped themselves to a few of the tomes he'd worked so hard to assemble, probably looking for value over content. The balance would be auctioned off. And that would be the end of it."

He paused, reaching up to scratch Baiji under the chin. The parrot seemed to smile, enjoying the scratch with lidded eyes. Sibyl and Benton exchanged a look.

"But consider this," her father continued. "Because that young man died on *Titanic*, his name is now synonymous with the finest university library in the world. His study is preserved, just as it was, for time immemorial. His collection stays whole. He has left a legacy. In a way, that damned boat going down was the greatest thing that could have happened to him. For what he wanted to be."

Her father smiled, his sad and stoic smile. Sibyl moved to stand next to him, threading her arm through his. There would be no need for Benton to tell him what had happened. He knew.

He had always known.

"Shall we go in to dinner?" she asked, rubbing her free hand on her father's upper arm. "We can bring Baiji if you like."

"Let's," the Captain said, moving toward the dining room at a stately pace. "Though we're still short a few people, by my count."

"I'm sure they'll be along," she said.

They made their way from the front parlor into the entry hall at the base of the stairs, Sibyl and Lan in the lead, Benton trailing behind. Then all at once there was a commotion from somewhere overhead, followed by a crash, and a whirring ball of activity came plunging down the front staircase at a run, skidding across the front hallway carpet and smacking right into Benton's legs. The ball of activity recoiled, rubbing its nose and blinking, and then after a long and pregnant pause, it opened its mouth and started to wail.

"Good heavens, who's this?" Benton exclaimed, surprised. He knelt next to the shrieking creature, who upon closer examination proved to be a little boy, about two years of age, with a fuzzy halo of blond hair, dressed in a navy sailor suit and small black boots.

"Oh, Professor Derby, I'm so sorry!" Dovie Whistler exclaimed, hurrying down the stairs and scooping the caterwauling boy up in her arms. Her hair was still cropped short, but her dress was a long, narrow column of buttercup yellow satin trimmed in lace, and her hair was held off her brow with a wide black band. "He's got so much energy, but he's so careless sometimes. Aren't you, Lannie?"

The boy confessed to his carelessness with a fresh shriek, which Dovie quieted with some jostling of him on her hip.

"My word," Benton breathed, peering at the little boy's face, and seeing that his assumption was absolutely true.

"Say hello to Professor Derby," Dovie prompted.

The ball of activity looked warily at Benton, red fist in mouth, and then buried his face in his mother's neck.

"He's shy," Dovie explained, patting the whimpering boy's back.

Benton's gaze met Sibyl's, his eyebrows shooting up. Slowly, Sibyl nodded, smiling out of one side of her mouth. Sibyl watched as Benton's eyes then moved to Lan Allston's face, and she saw that he found the old sailor so beaming with joy that whatever questions Benton might have thought to ask fell away as suddenly unimportant.

"I'm sure he's famished," Sibyl said. "And so am I. There's no reason to wait, is there?"

"No reason at all," her father said, taking her arm.

Epilogue

North Atlantic Ocean
Outward Bound
April 14/15, 1912

EULAH RAN UP laughing, Harry beside her, and collapsed in the chair next to her mother, out of breath, her cheeks pink from dancing. The two exchanged a quick electric look that Helen noticed with pleasure, and Harry seated himself beside his mother without a word.

"There you are!" Eleanor Widener exclaimed. "We lost sight of you. Must have been the crowd." She arched an eyebrow at her son.

"Must have been," Harry said, grinning.

Eulah reached a long arm over the table for her glass of water, gulping it down with abandon and an *aaaaaaaah* of audible pleasure.

"Gracious!" Helen exclaimed, watching her daughter fan herself with the dinner menu and noting her rosy cheeks and the droplets of dew on Eulah's upper lip. "Why, you'd think you were at a square dance. Eulah. Some restraint, please."

Her daughter turned merry, sparkling eyes on Helen, who felt herself soften as she always did when her youngest daughter smiled at her.

"Oh, come now, Mother," she said, twinkling. "There's nothing better than dancing! Perhaps you should dance, too."

Helen shook her head with a laugh. "Oh, I don't know about that," she demurred. "Dancing is for the young. But I don't even need to, so long as I can watch you. Are you enjoying yourself, my dear?"

"Oh, yes!" Eulah exclaimed. She picked up the vanilla eclair that waited on her dessert plate and took a delicate nibble from the end. "Mmmmm!" she moaned with pleasure, rolling her eyes heavenward. "Mother! Try it. Just a little."

"I couldn't," Helen said, brushing a wary hand over her stomach. "It was all too good. I mustn't."

She couldn't believe Eulah managed to eat at all, given that she'd spent all of dinner being led from one side of the dance floor to the other. Occasional young men attempted to cut in on her and Harry. Once, when the entree was served, he laughingly surrendered her to a rival so that he could sit down to eat. She'd foxtrotted by as Harry chewed, mouthing "Help!" in the direction of their table. Harry waved at her with his fork, grinning, pretending not to understand. By the time the foxtrot segued into a waltz, Harry was back on his feet.

"George, he's being terrible." Eleanor laughed with the indulgent smile of a mother who thinks her son isn't terrible at all. "You really must say something to him. Poor Miss Allston's not getting a moment's rest. She's already missed the asparagus."

"I don't think," her husband grunted, "there's much to miss about asparagus."

"Really, Helen," she whispered aside. "He's never like this. He's normally a very well-behaved boy."

Helen smiled beatifically, tapping her thumbs together in her lap. Her daughter spun by in the throng of dancers, hair falling loose over her shoulders, head tossed back, beaming.

When they finally regained the table, Helen looked over her daughter, noticing the falling down coiffure.

"Why, Eulah," she said. "What can have happened to your hat? With my butterfly brooch on it, thank you very much?"

"Oh!" she gasped over Harry's chuckling laughter. "My hat?" Eulah stared off into the distance, mouth twisted in a faux-serious smile. "My . . . hat?"

Helen shook her head, and nudged her daughter under the table with her toe. "Oh, for Pete's sake. You didn't lose it, did you?"

"Me? Never," Eulah whispered back. Then she added, "Maybe," and grinned.

The hour was growing late, and Helen noticed the crowd of diners beginning to thin. A few dancers still clustered at the end of the gallery, and men lingered over glasses of cognac while ladies in twos and threes picked their way back to the cabins. An eclair sat untouched on Eleanor Widener's plate as she sighed, taking another sip of her wine.

"I think I'd best be getting to bed," she mused to no one in particular.

"Are you all right, Mother?" Harry asked.

"Oh, yes. Just a slight headache, is all." She drew her evening cloak over her shoulders with a yawn. "George? Do you suppose you and Harry could . . . ?"

"Of course, my dear," George said. "As we all know, nothing will bring on a headache faster than an eclair in close proximity."

Harry and Eulah exchanged another high-frequency look, and Helen had to bite the inside of her cheek to conceal her excitement. Harry stood as George helped Eleanor get to her feet, fussing over her chair.

"Well," Eleanor Widener said, arranging her wrap and hunting about for her beaded pocketbook. "It's been a lovely evening. Mrs. Allston, a pleasure as always."

"Indeed," Helen said. "I do hope we'll see you in Boston one of these days."

"Well, Harry might be going up for his reunion," Eleanor ventured, with an eye on her son.

"Oh, I am," he assured her. He looked directly at Eulah and said, "I am."

"Why, that's just next month, isn't it?" Eulah exclaimed, and Helen kicked her under the table. She was as cunning in her dealings with men as poor Harley was at the card table. Really!

"I believe it is," Harry said, taking his mother's other elbow.

"We'd be so happy if you'd join us for supper while you're in town,

Mr. Widener," Helen said with perhaps too much majesty. Eulah grinned at him and nodded, a strand of hair drifting into her eyes.

"I'd love to," Harry said. George Widener made a show of rooting in his waistcoat pocket for his watch and consulting it with a weighty grunt.

"Ah," Harry said, observing his father's machinations. "Good night, then!"

"Good night," Eulah trilled. While she watched the Wideners make their way through the dining room, Helen watched her watch them.

When they were out of sight, Eulah plopped back in her chair with a gasp and immediately set to wolfing her eclair with unconcealed delight.

"Well, that Harry fellow certainly seemed nice, didn't he?" Helen said, launching a volley.

"Mmmhmmmm," Eulah said, giggling with a mouthful of pastry. She grabbed up a hasty napkin to save her bodice from crumbs of chocolate.

"He certainly seemed interested in *you*," Helen pressed. "Why, I don't suppose I've ever seen a boy so keen on dancing with a young lady. Were you nice to him, darling? Were you careful to ask him about himself? You didn't just talk his ear off, I hope."

"Of course," Eulah said, enjoying taunting her mother with the possibility that she could have been anything less than perfectly nice. "He told me ever so much about his book collection, you know. He was after a particular volume in Paris, he said. Something called *Le Sang de Morphée*."

"How very odd," Helen said before she could stop herself. "Well, at any rate, he certainly seemed keen to visit us for dinner next month, didn't he? So what do you think of that?"

Eulah leaned forward and took her mother's hand in hers with a smile.

"I think," she said, "that we should order some champagne."

As she spoke, Eulah raised one long, white arm and gestured for a waiter. He swanned over with a smile and Eulah mouthed the words *champagne, please*, gesturing at her mother and herself. The man cast the briefest glance at his pocket watch and then gave Eulah a wide beaming grin and disappeared.

"Champagne!" Helen exclaimed, shocked and pleased at once. "But we should be going to bed, my dear. It's late."

"Nonsense. We have nowhere to be," Eulah said, leaning one arm over the back of her chair, cocking her head to the side, and smiling with her eyes half closed. Her loosened pale brown hair drifted over her shoulder, and she tossed it back with a careless sweep of her hand. "Mother, it is quite possible that we are living at a magical moment. Have you ever considered that?"

"Why, whatever do you mean?" Helen simpered. The waiter appeared at their elbows, bending at the waist and presenting Eulah with the bottle, wrapped in a linen napkin and held so that she might view the label.

"Oh, dear. Do you know anything about champagne?" Eulah asked her mother. "I'm sure I don't." She looked left and right, possibly to see if there was some gentleman of their acquaintance whose opinion could be sought, but finding no one she turned to the waiter and said, "Oh, that will be lovely, thank you."

"Very good, mademoiselle," the man said with a nod. He turned away from them and released the cork with a festive pop. Some sweet froth spilled over the lip of the champagne bottle, and the waiter licked it from his thumb.

"I only mean," Eulah continued as the waiter poured two tiny widemouthed glasses of sparkling wine for the two Allston women, "that time seems to move faster, somehow, these days, I think. Why, just consider your life, Mother. When you were a girl you couldn't cross the ocean half as fast as we are right now. You couldn't send telegrams halfway round the world in a matter of moments."

Helen laughed. "But of course you could! Silly girl. I'm not as old as all that."

Eulah grinned and took a sip of her champagne to show that her loose grasp of the facts would do nothing to dissuade her from the larger point she was making.

"Mmmm. Perfect." She sighed. "Just perfect, thank you." She paused, savoring it with her eyes closed. Then she continued. "Electric light everywhere you go. Automobiles simple enough that even women can operate them. Cars make every place that much closer to every other place, you know, because they're so fast. The telephone. Why, you can talk to people across the city without even leaving the house. That brings people closer, too. In a little bit we'll get our suffrage, too, you mark my words. It's like the world is so eager to come into itself, that it's all we can do to keep up." She sighed, pleased. "I'm so fortunate to be young now," Eulah mused. "Don't you think so? I think about that all the time."

Helen sampled her own glass and found its sweetish fizz to be, as her daughter said, perfect. Cold and sharp and wonderful. She took another, longer sip, and closed her eyes, relishing the bright floral flavor. How did Eulah know just what was required to make a moment unforgettable? It was a real skill her little girl had. She had a way of seeing right into the heart of a situation, and knowing it for what it was.

Helen let her eyes come to rest on her child's face, full cheeked, blushing with life, a few rebellious strands of pale brownish hair sticking up comically into the air, like butterfly antennae. Before she could think what she was doing, Helen reached forward to cup her daughter's cheek in her hand, brushing her fingers over the girl's young skin.

"Oh, my dear," she said, sighing. "Have you had a lovely time? I only hope that you have."

"I have, Mother," Eulah said, turning her shining blue eyes on Helen's face. "In fact, I might be happier in this very moment than at any other time in my life. Happier than I could ever imagine being."

Helen dropped her hand to Eulah's shoulder and squeezed. Eulah poured a touch more wine for both of them, and they settled back in their chairs, the downward slope of their shoulders in repose marking them indelibly as mother and daughter. At the opposite end of the dining room the orchestra, looking a little sleepy around the edges, conducted a quick conference in which they seemed to debate whether enough people remained for them to play a few more songs. The consensus seemed to be that there was time for one or two more, but there was no particular rush. The plinking and plonking of instruments being retuned emanated from the end of the gallery.

Deep within the ship, under the hum of late-night conversation and the clinking of glasses, the clock, the one in the grand stair with sculptures of "Honor and Glory crowning Time," began to chime. Out of habit Helen listened, counting as she did with the mantel clock back home on Beacon Street, but as usual she lost track of the number of chimes. Must have been the wine, which, she had to admit, was going right to her head. Helen brought a hand to her temple and massaged it. Well, it couldn't be helped. She felt fine right now. Better than fine. She felt marvelous.

Tuning at the ready, the orchestra opened with the languid first few bars of the same song that was playing when Helen and Eulah arrived in the dining room for dinner. The tempo was slower now, sleepier, drawing the evening to a close.

"It's that song you like," Helen remarked, feeling herself lulled by the melody.

"Mmmmm." Eulah nodded. After listening for a bar or two, she started singing along with a husky alto. "Cuddle up, and don't be bluuuuue. All your fears are foolish fancy, mayyyyybe . . . you know, dear, that I'm in looooove with youuuuuu. . . ."

Helen smiled an indulgent smile at her daughter. "Singing at the dinner table," she said, shaking her head. "We just won't tell your father."

Eulah laughed, taking another sip of her champagne.

The orchestra continued to play, a few scattered couples swaying in each other's arms. The candlelight on each table flickered lower as the candles burned away, and the smell of burnt wax blended with the heady springtime scent of lilies in the air. Helen let her elbow come to rest on the dining table in a nest of cast-aside napkins, resting her cheek in her palm and letting her eyelids drift closed. She and Eulah sat together, listening to the languid music, not speaking.

Under her feet, Helen felt a subtle change. Her eyes opened. The vibrating of the ship's engines, so omnipresent and steady that she had stopped noticing it, had shifted in timbre, from a steady hum to a laboring *lug lug lug.* Helen moved her gaze to Eulah's face, to see if she noticed the change as well. A few of the remaining diners murmured among themselves, bending their heads together, speculating. Several men stood and strode to the windows of the dining room, looking out and down through the fog toward the water. But Eulah sat still, her head tipped back, eyes closed, long expanse of creamy neck exposed, lips curved in a tiny smile.

The orchestra gave no sign that they had noticed anything different, segueing into another slow-tempo popular tune, which Helen also couldn't identify. The dancing couples, after pausing to discuss among themselves the lurch they had felt, shook off their worries with a collective shrug and resumed dancing.

"Curious," Helen said to herself.

More alert, she straightened in her chair, surveying the dining room. Several of the gentlemen at the windows were locked in hushed conversation, hands moving, animated. A group of them hurried through the door to the deck together, while another group broke away to return to their tables, bending and whispering to their dining companions. Murmurs started to circulate among the dining tables. A few uniformed men rushed past the dining room windows, almost at a run.

Everyone else, however, carried on as usual. Full of vague disquiet, Helen waited. For a long few minutes, nothing happened.

Then, Helen heard a groaning, cracking sound, and the dining table shifted, scooting under her arm and sliding six inches down the floor, almost as though she were at one of Mrs. Dee's séances. It took a moment for Helen to figure out that the table had moved because the ship had listed to one side. Startled, she took hold of the table with both hands, eyes wide. A few women in the dining room let out surprised shrieks, but were soothed by the men sitting with them. The orchestra stopped playing, looking around themselves, uncertain. Outside the dining room, in the gallery below and along the walkways outside the windows, the thrum of running feet and shouts could be heard. Helen's heartbeat quickened.

Eulah opened her eyes and smiled at Helen. Her daughter looked so serene, so full of joy. Helen couldn't help but return the smile.

"Darling," Helen said. "Did you feel that?"

Eulah just smiled and shook her head. "Feel what?"

Helen stammered. "Why, I could have sworn—that is, it seems almost like—"

Eulah shook her head, smile widening. She leaned forward and took one of Helen's hands in both of hers. "Come, Mother," she said. "Let's go for a walk on the balcony."

"A walk?" Helen said, confused. "But . . ." She trailed off, looking around herself, uncertain. Outside, more shouts, and in the dining room the other passengers' voices were rising, and several of them were hurrying to the stairs.

"A walk," Eulah repeated, as smiling and serene as ever. She looked into her mother's eyes. Deep within them Helen read an absolute certainty that somehow caused all of Helen's anxiety to fall away. "Certainly. It's a beautiful night. And you only live once. This moment, Mother. This is all there is. I don't want to miss any of it."

Helen returned Eulah's smile, tentatively at first, and then with resolve. "Neither do I," she said, getting to her feet.

Eulah stood, smoothing her skirts with both hands, and folding Helen's hand under her arm. The two women exchanged a secret smile, and then moved arm in arm into the gathering darkness of the North Atlantic night.

Afterword

The Smoke Clears

ON MAY 27, 1917, a thirty-nine-year-old Bostonian dermatologist travel-ing by steamship across the Atlantic Ocean wrote a letter home to his wife. "The voyage has so far been very calm and pleasant," he said. "Since the *Titanic* hit the ice the steamers run south of where they used to go when you went over. . . . I like it better for though it takes longer there are more warm pleasant days. I assure you you would love this voyage. We've only sighted three vessels since we left N.Y. . . . The wireless posts base-ball scores, and I see that the Red Sox beat St. Louis. Life onboard is lazy but pleasant."

The reason that they had only sighted three vessels since leaving New York was that the dermatologist, a restless man who had spent his twen-ties assisting teams in Arctic exploration, and who had never reconciled himself to the tedium of day-to-day medical practice, was not on a plea-sure cruise. He was a first lieutenant medical officer with the Canadian Royal Fusiliers, traveling to the western front of the Great War. He was my great-great-uncle, and he would never see Boston again.

Reading his letters home in the Harvard University archives, a mod-ern scholar can't help but wonder what he's doing there. Why would a middle-aged man, married, established in his career, however tedious, leave the sedate safety of the Back Bay to volunteer in a war that does not seem to touch him directly? And what does his world look like? We have a very specific imagination of the United States in the twenties: flappers, jazz, bathtub gin, captured in films and quoted endlessly in popular culture ever since. But the decade leading up to the twenties isn't as firmly lodged in our imagination. What kind of world would our dermatologist have been turning away from?

Boston in the second decade of the twentieth century was a city in transition. In terms of technology and population, the city was beginning to resemble the Boston of 2011, but it was not entirely modern just yet. The country's first subway, the Tremont Street line, had been in operation since 1897, but horses still crowded the cobble and brick streets. Waves of immigration from Ireland and Italy had transformed the city's character, but its commercial life was still largely dominated by old English families. It was a city, and a time, in thrall to modernism, with its twin promises of technology and progress. But with change comes uncertainty.

Perhaps one of the largest, and most enduring, symbols of both the promise of modernism and its betrayal is the RMS *Titanic*. It haunts our culture even to this day, one hundred years after its abrupt and shocking loss. What was it about *Titanic's* sinking that, even five years later, put it so thoroughly at the center of the fears of a man heading into the theater of war?

For one thing, *Titanic's* loss was shocking because it revealed the real ramifications of a wealth disparity that is staggering even by today's standards. The fact is, as first-class women passengers, Eulah and Helen Allston would almost certainly have made it into a lifeboat. Only four first-class women passengers did not. By comparison, the mortality rate for all third-class passengers, including children, was nearly 75 percent. A first-class parlor suite ticket in 1912 cost $4,350, which some estimate to be the equivalent of over $90,000 in modern dollars—more akin to purchasing a ticket to outer space on Virgin Galactic than traveling across the Atlantic Ocean. The concentration of wealth and fame on that one ship, including the richest man in the world at the time, John Jacob Astor IV, together with the real Harry Widener and his parents, George and Eleanor, was confounding. As was the clear relationship between wealth and the odds of survival.

But of course, no one expected that the largest passenger steamship in the world would sink, certainly not on its maiden voyage. The passengers and engineers trusted its technological superiority to brave any treachery that the North Atlantic might throw its way. Americans wanted to trust technology and reason to solve all of our problems during this time period. We see the echo of this false confidence three short years later, when RMS *Lusitania*—another lavishly appointed steamship—sailed for Britain despite the public threat levied against it by the German consulate. *Lusitania* was thought to be able to outrun German torpedoes, but beyond that, the modern historian can't shake the sense that *Lusitania*, like *Titanic* before it, was considered too grand, too marvelous, too *modern* to be vulnerable to something as old-fashioned as horror and death. The shock of *Lusitania*'s weakness, coming so soon on the heels of *Titanic*'s sinking, helped to propel the United States from neutrality to engagement in the war that had convulsed Europe, much the way that the loss of the World Trade Center spurred our entry into war nearly a century later.

Death itself, and human consciousness more generally, was also subject to modernist inquiry. Professor Edwin Friend was a real Harvard psychologist, who perished on the *Lusitania* en route to a conference on psychical research in Britain. He was active in the American Society for Psychical Research, an organization of intellectuals founded in Boston in 1885, devoted to the scientific study of the possibilities of life after death and paranormal human ability. Spiritualism as a religion had been prevalent, particularly in New England and New York State, since the middle of the nineteenth century, and enjoyed a resurgence in the decades around the Great War. Helen and Sibyl would have found listings for séances and Spiritualist meetings in the Boston newspapers, right alongside listings for mainstream church services, temperance society meetings, and women's suffrage lectures. Occult inquiry was a part of mainstream thought; in fact, the most notable member of the American Society for Psychical Research was none other than psychologist, philosopher, and father of American Pragmatism, William James. Also a Harvard professor, and brother of the famous novelist Henry James, William was so convinced of the reality of the human spirit's persistence after death, so persuaded that such a fact was on the brink of being scientifically proven, that his widow Alice and brother Henry held several séances after his death in 1910, believing that the philosopher would do his utmost to contact them.

The first two decades of the twentieth century held out tantalizing promises of scientific advance in every avenue of human endeavor. While Benton Derby is a fictional character, his department at Harvard, the Department of Social Ethics, is not: it was the precursor to what we know today as sociology. "Social ethics" as a field sought to transform social ills like poverty and the care of the sick and the insane through rational principles of health and organization. Similarly, in 1909 Sigmund Freud gave his famous series of lectures at Clark University in Massachusetts, introducing the concept of psychoanalysis to the United States. The idea that social ills could be controlled by scientific principle applied not only to academia, however; this period also saw technocratic problem-solving at the government level, such as the passage of the Harrison Act in 1914, which brought opiates and cocaine under federal regulation for the first time, culminating in the better-known Volstead Act of 1919, which ushered in Prohibition. Before these interventions, opiates were a common ingredient in remedies for any ache or pain, from headache to nerves to infants' teething. To obtain a prescription for an opiate, one had merely to demonstrate evidence of addiction to a doctor, creating a vicious cycle of legitimate, but no less crippling, dependence.

Of course, the optimism embodied by such grandiose technological hopes was swiftly undermined by reality. The Great War is widely thought to have been such a bloodbath in part because the tactics of warfare had not yet caught up to the technology in use in the field. Men who set out to fight with honor discovered that the twentieth century had more in store for them than they could have ever imagined. Cavalry was no match for a tank. Anonymous, mechanized death carried little glory. The unsinkable *Titanic* sank. The world as it had been, both for good and for ill, would never be the same.

On September 27, 1917, the dermatologist wrote a letter home to his father. "It seems likely that we move forward tonight," he said. "There is a big attack on, as you doubtless know from the papers. So far we have gained ground and come out excellently for losses from all I can hear. Of course if you are not yourself in a show you know very little of what is going on, and even if you are you only know how it is near you. . . . We shall probably go in as holding troops and will probably get all that is coming to us. It will be my first chance at a real battle, and I must say I am rather looking forward to it."

On September 28, 1917, he was killed by an exploding shell. And, in some respect, the twentieth century began.

—KATHERINE HOWE
Marblehead, Massachusetts

Acknowledgments

I count myself singularly privileged to have such a fantastic community of friends, family, colleagues, and readers who have helped me bring this book to fruition. I am indebted first and foremost to my incredible literary agent, Suzanne Gluck, whose insight, guidance, and friendship never cease to amaze me; to my publisher, Ellen Archer at Hyperion, whose unflagging confidence, along with her wit, elegance, and good humor, provided crucial support; to my editor, Leslie Wells, who patiently and beautifully shepherded this book from abstract concept to completed manuscript; and to Matthew Pearl, who knows exactly what he did. Without these people, this book would not exist.

I am incredibly fortunate to be able to collaborate with people in the publishing world who are both fantastic at their work and a pleasure to know. At William Morris Endeavor, I am grateful to Eve Attermann, Raffaella De Angelis, Caroline Donofrio, Tracy Fisher, Erin Malone, Pauline Post, Cathryn Summerhayes, Becky Thomas, and Lauren Whitney for all the work they have done to support me and my writing. At Hyperion and Voice, I would like to thank Elisabeth Dyssegaard, Laura Klynstra, Kiki Koroshetz, Claire McKean, Cassandra Pappas, Shelly Perron, and Shubhani Sarkar for creating a gorgeous book. I am also honored to work with Mari Evans and her team at Penguin UK.

A tremendous number of friends, acquaintances, and colleagues have generously provided their support, expertise, critical commentary, and guidance as I have worked on this project, and I am grateful to all of them. In particular I would like to thank the following people: Satnam Anderson, Brunonia Barry, Kevin Birmingham, Deborah Blum, Jack Butterworth, Christopher Capozzola, Julia Chang, Amy Cole, Laura Dandaneau, Heather Folsom, Eli Friedman, Connie Goodwin, Bradley Hague, Will Heinrich, Peter Howe, Eric Idsvoog, John Johnston, Emily Kennedy, Shawn Klomparens, Kelley Kreitz, Brendan McConville, Ginger Myhaver, Peter Ogren, Tobey Pearl, Brian Pellinen, Bill Rankin, Rohit Shah, Shannon Shaper, Tara Smith, Weston Smith, Raphaelle Steinzig, Anne Sturtevant, Michelle Syba, Robert Wilson, and the illustrious Menagerie.

Historical fiction depends mightily on the accuracy of its research, and so I am indebted to several archives and archivists for materials and support. I would particularly like to thank Jean Marie Procious and the Salem Athenaeum for congenial writing space; the American Society for Psychical Research for insight into early-twentieth-century séances and the paranormal; the National Archives in Washington, D.C., for primary sources pertaining both to opium addiction in the early twentieth century and life at the Plattsburgh civilian training camp; Mugar Library at Boston University for work space and resources; the Harvard University Archives for details on the life of early-twentieth-century Harvard men; and the Smithsonian Institution for holding the original 1912 sheet music lyrics of "My Melancholy Baby." For those wishing to research further into questions of scrying, the Progressive era, Spiritualism, and other arcane matters of *The House of Velvet and Glass*, please visit my website at www.katherinehowe.com.

Lastly, I would like to express my gratitude to my family, particularly my parents, George and Katherine S. Howe, for their unflagging confidence, love, and support, and to Charles and Mouth, for being themselves. And finally, my deepest thanks go to my husband, Louis Hyman, whose book this is, for without him I could never find the plot.